Religion and Violence

Religion and Violence

Philosophical Perspectives
from Kant to Derrida

Hent de Vries

The Johns Hopkins University Press
Baltimore and London

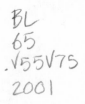

© 2002 The Johns Hopkins University Press
All rights reserved. Published 2001
Printed in the United States of America on acid-free paper
9 8 7 6 5 4 3 2 1

The Johns Hopkins University Press
2715 North Charles Street
Baltimore, Maryland 21218-4363
www.press.jhu.edu

Library of Congress Cataloging-in-Publication Data
Vries, Hent de.
Religion and violence : philosophical perspectives from Kant to Derrida /
Hent de Vries.
    p.   cm.
Includes bibliographical references and index.
ISBN 0-8018-6767-3 (alk. paper) — ISBN 0-8018-6768-1 (pbk. : alk. paper)
    1. Violence—Religious aspects.   2. Philosophy and religion.   I. Title.
BL65.V55 V75   2002
291.5′697—dc21   00-013055

A catalog record for this book is available from the British Library.

Publication was made possible in part by the support of the Netherlands
Organization for Scientific Research (NWO).

For Paola

One cannot weep over Abraham. One approaches him
with a horror religiosus, as Israel approached Mount Sinai.
KIERKEGAARD, *Fear and Trembling*
(trans. Howard V. Hong and Edna H. Hong)

Il y a de l'horreur dans le respect religieux.
And, in fact, there is a horror in religious respect.
ÉMILE DURKHEIM, *Les Formes élémentaires de la vie religieuse*
(trans. Joseph Ward Swain)

Contents

Preface and Acknowledgments

FAR FROM BEING OVER and done with, the religious tradition contains considerable semantic and symbolic potential, as well as systematic — that is to say, conceptual and analytical — resources that have yet to be mobilized to explore the most challenging theoretical issues in contemporary philosophy, social theory, and cultural analysis. No longer the property of the modern disciplines of dogmatic or biblical theology (based on affirmation of articles of faith and tradition), nor solely of concern to secular religious studies and anthropologically informed approaches to contemporary comparative religion, religion is crucial to the reassessment of recent debates concerning identity and self-determination, the modern nation-state and multiculturalism, liberal democracy and immigration, globalization and the emergence of new media, the virtualization of reality and the renegotiation of the very concept of the "lifeworld," to say nothing of the technologies of "life." These problems can scarcely be confined to disciplines whose explicit object of study is "religion."

Any analysis of contemporary society and culture calls out for an awareness of how the religious and theological are translated into the most mundane terms. The "chemistry of concepts" identified in Nietzsche's genealogy and the "secularization of theology in the concept" echoed by Adorno's dialectical use of the notion "natural history" may no longer adequately formulate this task. Alternative ways of exporting the theme of religion into received contexts of debate, discovery, and justification might yield conceptual innovations and empirically challenging new hypotheses. The categories and practices of religion are not the exclusive property of the scholarly discipline of theology in its traditional and modern guises and, perhaps, never were. This body of knowledge was always parasitic upon — and shot through with — notions that resonate with the larger culture. And the latter has always been bound up with incompletely secularized theologico-political elements, whose remaining — indeed, increasing — prominence takes ever new institutional and mediatized forms.

Once one transposes "religion" and "the theological" into new, un-
charted, and (halfway) secular territory, disciplinary approaches other
than those used in the study of religion "proper" may profit from being
exposed to an "archive" whose intellectual resources and renewed relevance we have hardly begun to comprehend. Any analysis of contemporary society and culture must come to terms with this "archive" (to draw
on Foucault's analysis of the term in *L'Archéologie du savoir* [*The Archeology of Knowledge*]), which is tied to the "positivity" of a "discourse"
whose "relative unity across time," "well beyond individual works, books
and texts," makes up a "historical a priori" of sorts.[1] The way in which this
"transcendental historicity," as Husserl and Derrida would say, is overdetermined by "religion," in all of its manifestations, forms the central
concern of this book; the insight that this inflection betrays a certain "violence" (to be defined) is its main thesis.

Questions that touch upon ethics and politics can especially benefit
from being rephrased in terms belonging to the arsenal of religious and
theological figures of thought and speech, all the more so when the association of such figures with a certain "violence" keeps moralism, whether
in the form of fideism or of humanism (the difference matters little), at
bay. Needless to say, such a turn or return to religion could not consist in naively invoking the religion of the Church Fathers or in perpetu-
ating some *theologia naturalis* or *metaphysica specialis* in a new guise.
Neither unreflecting faith—revealed theology of whatever nature—nor
onto-theology seems an option still available to "us," though the legacies
of the most orthodox and most heterodox manifestations of the theological are pertinent to my purpose, the positings of "positive religion" no
less than the negations of the *apophatic* way. The turn to religion I propose (in consonance with what one simply observes) attempts to articulate
an alternative, albeit no less engaged or systematic, view, not a fallback
theology or a quasi-religious bricolage.

I have sketched some reasons for a more fruitful engagement with religion and its *cultural memory in the present* in the predecessor to this book,
Philosophy and the Turn to Religion.[2] There I argued that this engagement

1. For the notion of an "archive," as well as the "archeology" that is its "analysis," see Michel
Foucault, *L'Archéologie du savoir* (Paris: Gallimard, 1969), 166–67 / *The Archeology of Knowledge and The Discourse on Language*, trans. A. M. Sheridan Smith (New York: Pantheon Books,
1972), 126–27.

2. (Baltimore: Johns Hopkins University Press, 1999). The expression "Cultural Memory

should be neither reactive, traditionalist, and thereby insensitive to the proper rigor of thought, nor overly modernist and anachronistic. Any plausible approach to religion should hesitate to transpose this topic to current debates in an unreflecting manner. The turn to religion, I suggested, consists in the attempt to situate oneself *at once* as closely as possible to *and* at the furthest thinkable remove from the tradition called the religious. That tradition includes the supposed historical revelations of the religions of the Book, theological attempts to systematize, canonize, and ontologize their implied doctrines, ecclesial forms imposed on their practices (hierarchical modes of transmitting learning, the calendar, baptism, the confession of faith, communion, the relation between the sexes, the culture of death), their rhetoric and visual imagery, and so on.

Clearly, such an approach shares certain premises with the rationalism and methodological atheism of the philosophy of religion in its phenomenological, hermeneutical, and analytical guises. Likewise, it shares the speculative and dialectical impetus of negative dialectics and (negative) political theology, just as it opens itself up to the wider empirical scope of contemporary comparative religious and anthropological studies. Moreover, it stands under the aegis of the historical phenomenon and existential possibility of post-theism — the proliferation and dissemination of the religious after and well beyond the most hegemonic of its manifestations. This phenomenon, precisely because of the challenge, the chances, and the perils with which it confronts us, must be engaged with extreme scruple — indeed, in *horror religiosus* alone. The present book focuses on the complex relationship between violence, philosophy, and testimony implied in this curious formula.

In *Philosophy and the Turn to Religion,* as well as in my comparative study of Theodor W. Adorno and Emmanuel Levinas, *Theology in Pianissimo,*[3] I argued, along different lines, that the engagement of twentieth-century philosophy and cultural analysis with questions of identity and difference, in the broadest possible sense, should be understood in light of an increasingly noticeable swerve into the twists and turns, the turns of phrase, of the religious heritage. Instead of posing these questions against the backdrop of age-old metaphysical distinctions and oppositions, I proposed rearticulating them in religious terms that seem at odds with their

---

in the Present" figures as the title and central focus of the book series I have been co-editing with Mieke Bal for Stanford University Press since 1995.

3. Forthcoming from Johns Hopkins University Press.

supposed modernity. Not that these metaphysical categories would be obsolete; on the contrary, they continue to inform and guide even the most radical conceptual transformations. But in so doing, I claimed, they are renegotiated in terms that are not originally—or necessarily—theirs. We seem to be dealing with a dialectics of Enlightenment all over again, but one in which religion—no longer mythology, as Adorno and Horkheimer thought—has taken the upper hand and will continue to do so for some time to come.

Nowhere is this more evident than in the recurrent and ever more insistent invocation of certain dominant but also heterodox theologemes—idioms, figurations, argumentative structures, and rhetorical devices—all of which may provide an interpretive key to the peculiar weight and often aporetic outcome of urgent theoretical and practical present-day debates. Their force extends to writings in the genre of political theology, whose influential legacy in modern philosophy dates back at least to Spinoza's *Tractatus Theologico-Politicus* and whose reverberations in the works of Kant, Carl Schmitt, Walter Benjamin, and others have received increasing attention in recent years.

Whereas the earlier book systematically reconstructed its problematic by returning to Kant's and Heidegger's philosophical engagement with religion, it took its inspiration from writings in the tradition of French phenomenology, notably Levinas, Jean-Luc Marion, and, especially, Derrida. Few thinkers, I suggested, have gone so far as Derrida in probing the limits of the modern discourse on religion, its metaphysical presuppositions, and its contemporary transformations in the linguistic, structuralist, narratological, pragmatist, and culturalist turns of twentieth-century thought. No author has more consistently foregrounded the unexpected and often uncanny alliances that have emerged between a radical interrogation of the history of Western philosophy and the religious inheritance from which it sought to set itself apart. In order to demonstrate this, I sought to push beyond formal analogies between the textual practices of deconstruction and the *via negativa* (apophatics, or negative theology) to address the necessity for a philosophical thinking that—like Derrida's work—situates itself at once close to and at the farthest remove from traditional manifestations of the religious and the theological. This paradox is captured in the phrase *adieu* (*à-dieu*), which signals at once a turn toward and leave-taking from God and is also a gesture toward and departure from the other of this other, namely, the demonic and the possibility of radical evil. Only by confronting such uncanny and difficult figures, I suggested, can one begin to think and act upon ethical and political imperatives in the contemporary world, characterized by trends toward globalization, multicultural citizenship, the influence of new media, as well as technologies that affect the very concept and delimitations of the private and the public including, more generally, "life" and the "lifeworld." A turn to religion, discernible in philosophy and cultural theory, anticipates and accompanies these developments.

In the present work I argue that the religious notions and theologemes whose theoretical and practical importance has become more and more evident in recent decades, in the wake of a certain Enlightenment,[4] must first be understood in their intrinsic relation to the concept of violence and its multiple analytical and pragmatic ramifications. I trust that this insight will enrich, complicate, and supplement the turn to religion that I propounded earlier. I suggest that the turn to religion can be studied in full force only if we are willing to rethink quite a few modern philosophical assumptions concerning ethical and political responsibility in light of what Kierkegaard, in *Fear and Trembling*'s surprising reading of the sacrifice of Isaac, calls a *horror religiosus*. This motif belongs to a chain of interrelated and at least partly or formally substitutable notions. These range from: Kant's discussion of radical evil (*das radikal Böse*) in *Religion innerhalb der Grenzen der blossen Vernunft* (*Religion within the Boundaries of Mere Reason*) (Chapter 1); to Éric Weil's understanding of the other of discourse in *Logique de la philosophie* (*Logics of Philosophy*) and Levinas's evocation of the sordid neutrality of the *il y a* in his early and later writings (Chapter 2); to Walter Benjamin's meditations on divine violence (*göttliche Gewalt*) toward the end of his "Zur Kritik der Gewalt" ("Critique of Violence"), which I will analyze with the help of Michel de Certeau's interpretations of divine anger in *La Fable mystique* (*The Mystic Fable*) (Chapter 3); all the way up to Derrida's sensitivity to the ever-looming possibility of monstrosity, the worst (*le pire*), of the resemblance and proximity of hospitality and hostility (Chapter 4). The list is far from complete.

This set of themes will enable us to articulate the intrinsic connection between religion and violence, a violence that is *virtually* everywhere and that thus lies at the source—and inhabits the very concept—of history and experience. It will not do to insist on a connection between violence and the sacred alone, as Levinas, in *Du sacré au saint* (*From the Sacred*

4. See John Gray, *Enlightenment's Wake: Politics and Culture at the Close of the Modern Age* (London: Routledge, 1995).

to the Holy) and René Girard, in *La Violence et le sacré* (*Violence and the Sacred*), would have us believe. Violence affects the heart of religion in its most elementary and its most general features. More specifically, already in *Philosophy and the Turn to Religion* I spoke of the idealizations that constitute the religious promise, in other words, of the *performativity* of its *à Dieu* in taking leave of (indeed, in its *adieu* to) existing ontologemes and theologemes, all dogma, every value, each image. I placed them against the backdrop of its always possible, even necessary, empirical slippage. This inevitable subreption, I argued, reveals a certain paradoxical conditionality of reason, of the philosophical, of language and experience in general. I concluded that idolatry, blasphemy, and hypocrisy are unavoidable in the pursuit of divine names and belong to the religious and the theological — and, by analogy, to reason — as such. They constitute a structural or essential "perverformativity," to cite a term Derrida introduces in *La Carte postale* (*The Post Card*). No apophatics, *via negativa*, or *via eminentiae*, whatever its integrity or success, could ever hope to escape this fate, this necessity, which, as Derrida reminds us, is a chance — our sole chance — as well. Without it, without the saying of the unsayable, without the negotiation with (and of) the absolute, nothing would be said or done at all. Nothing would be changed or saved; everything would be left up to the powers that be or their all too abstract negation. And these two possibilities come down to the same.

In the present work, I expand on this analysis by insisting on the fact — yet another *Faktum der Vernunft*, of sorts — that this "pervertibility," as Derrida calls it in other writings, brings us face to face with another side of the Other. Here we touch upon the *a-dieu*, as it were, another other, as absolute as the Other, to the point of being all too easily interchangeable with it.

IN ADDRESSING the figure of a *horror religiosus*, of a violence in the guise and the name of religion — and this means also against religion — the present work draws on insights enabled by two collective projects, whose results were published under the titles *Violence, Identity, and Self-Determination* and *Religion and Media*.[5] It further explores the premises of a third collective venue whose working title will be *Political Theologies*.

5. See Hent de Vries and Samuel Weber, eds., *Violence, Identity, and Self-Determination* (Stanford: Stanford University Press, 1997), and idem, eds., *Religion and Media* (Stanford: Stanford University Press, 2001).

The present work seeks to make good on several claims contained in my own conceptualization of—and contributions to—these three projects, which had to remain all too implicit in their respective contexts. These pertain to the turn to religion in philosophy and cultural analysis mentioned above, and take Kierkegaard's reference to a *horror religiosus* as more than a lurid metaphor. In doing so, the present analyses substantiate: first, why, in questions of ethics and politics, the religious, its intellectual systematization, and its practical instantiation, *must matter at all,* and second, why in this "permanence of the theologico-political" (to use an expression by Claude Lefort) the question of violence is inescapable and, as it were, omnipresent.

When considering this generalized, even universalized, violence, we must avoid trivializing the most blatant empirical occurrences of violence, whether psychological or sociopolitical, visible or invisible, recognized or attested to in silence. Yet a certain emphasis on the notion of violence—implying that violence, in a sense, is everywhere, even in the generalization presupposed by the critical use of the expression "everywhere" itself—entails not merely a *trivialization* of violence in its most obvious forms, but also an *intensification* of any analysis directed toward it. Insisting on the primacy of a certain violence—even in the heart of nonviolence as such—raises the stakes of every account that one would want to give of it: empirically, philosophically, testimonially. It signals the inevitable complicity—even or especially of the most distant, disinterested spectator—and thus subverts equally good conscience and bad faith.

Of course, this is not all there is to it. The turn to religion not only typifies and affects our understanding of the ethical and the political but also informs our analysis of "experience" at large, including the experience called the "aesthetic." In a series of studies on Philo of Alexandria, Schopenhauer, Ricoeur, Levinas, Blanchot, Lyotard, Celan, Nancy, Hölderlin, and Cavell, composed during the same period as the present work and collected under the title *Instances*,[6] I focus centrally on this question of the aesthetic—in literature and the arts—against the backdrop of the central hypothesis elaborated here and in my previous book. Indeed, like the ethico-political realm and its dilemmas, the content and structure of "aesthetic experience" (a pleonasm of sorts) takes on a peculiar poignancy and dynamic when placed against the horizon of a tradition that, especially in modernist and avant-garde artistic expressions, it had seemed to

6. Forthcoming from Stanford University Press.

subvert, namely that of the religious and the theological. One need not return to the extensive debates on the crisis of representation (unreadability, the sublime, etc.) in order to realize that, like ethics and politics, modern aesthetics and the experiences it theorizes are much less a matter of mimesis (an imitation of nature or, as Aristotle writes in the *Poetics,* of a praxis or action) or an expression of self than the belated effect and testimony of a far more complex and elusive—and, in many regards, traumatic—drama. This drama, a nonevent of sorts, points to a beyond of the aesthetic traditionally conceived. In its own way it necessitates a rethinking of all the things Kierkegaard has in mind when he speaks about the *horror religiosus,* but also of all the elements Levinas hints at when (for example, in "Dieu et la philosophie" ["God and Philosophy"]) he introduces the motif of the "divine comedy."

PORTIONS OF CHAPTER 2 appeared in Hent de Vries and Samuel Weber, eds., *Violence, Identity, and Self-Determination,* and in Adriaan T. Peperzak, ed., *Ethics as First Philosophy.* An earlier shorter version of Chapter 3 appeared in *Modern Language Notes,* and a short segment of Chapter 4 appears in Thomas Cohen, ed., *Jacques Derrida and the Future of the Humanities.* The introduction draws on some of the material included in my contribution to the co-edited volume *Posttheism: Reframing the Judaeo-Christian Tradition* (with Arie L. Molendijk and Henri A. Krop). All of these fragments, however, were considerably expanded and completely rewritten for the present publication.

In writing and revising the chapters of this book, I have once again incurred many debts. Without the hospitality, during 1997–98, of the Center for the Study of World Religions and the Minda de Gunzburg Center for European Studies, both at Harvard University, I would not have found the peace of mind to concentrate on rearranging the earlier drafts of this book and its predecessor. In this context, too, I found the inspiration for my contribution to the project *Religion and Media,* undertaken with Samuel Weber, as well as the resources to draft the proposals for another common project, *Political Theologies.* In preparing the final manuscript for publication, I have profited from the scrutiny of many friendly commentators. I have drawn many lessons from their criticism and helpful suggestions during numerous conversations and exchanges. I would like to thank here in particular Han Adriaanse, Seyla Benhabib, Rodolphe Gasché, Werner Hamacher, Burcht Pranger, Rafael Sanchez, Patricia Spyer, Martin Stokhof, Lawrence Sullivan, and Samuel Weber for their friendly encouragement and insightful comments at crucial moments of the writing of this book. I especially thank Helen Tartar for being a privileged and close reader of my texts throughout and am grateful to the staff at the Johns Hopkins University Press for the care with which they have guided this book through the different phases of its production. All mentioned have made this book a much better one than it would otherwise have been. I dedicate this book to Paola Marrati, whose love and lucidity gave me the force and the inspiration to finish it after all and to do so, not in *horror religiosus,* but in a joyful—and irreverent—mood.

Abbreviations

AL   Jacques Derrida. *Adieu à Emmanuel Levinas.* Paris: Galilée, 1997. Translated by Pascale-Anne Brault and Michael Naas under the title *Adieu to Emmanuel Levinas* (Stanford: Stanford University Press, 1999).

CF   Immanuel Kant. *Der Streit der Fakultäten.* Vol. 9 of *Werke in zehn Bänden,* ed. Wilhelm Weischedel (Darmstadt: Wissenschaftliche Buchgesellschaft, 1983), 267–393. Translated by Mary J. Gregor under the title *The Conflict of the Faculties* (Lincoln: University of Nebraska Press, 1992), and in *The Cambridge Edition of the Works of Immanuel Kant,* ed. Paul Guyer and Allen W. Wood (Cambridge: Cambridge University Press, 1996).

DP   Jacques Derrida. *Du droit à la philosophie.* Paris: Galilée, 1990.

DPC   Jacques Derrida. *Du droit à la philosophie du point de vue cosmopolitique.* Paris: Unesco, Verdier, 1997.

FK   Jacques Derrida. "Foi et savoir: Les Deux Sources de la 'religion' aux limites de la simple raison." In *La Religion,* ed. Jacques Derrida and Gianni Vattimo, 9–86. Paris: Éditions du Seuil, 1996. Translated by Samuel Weber under the title "Faith and Knowledge: The Two Sources of 'Religion' within the Limits of Mere Reason," in *Religion,* ed. Derrida and Vattimo (Stanford: Stanford University Press, 1998), 1–78.

FL   Jacques Derrida. *Force de loi: Le 'Fondement mystique de l'autorité.'* Paris: Galilée, 1994. Translated by Mary Quaintance under the title "Force of Law: The 'Mystical Foundation of Authority,'" *Cardozo Law Review* 11 (1990): 919–1045.

FT   Søren Kierkegaard. *Fear and Trembling: Dialectical Lyric, by Johannes de Silentio.* In vol. 6 of *Kierkegaard's Writings,* trans. and ed. Howard V. Hong and Edna H. Hong. Princeton: Princeton University Press, 1983.

GD   Jacques Derrida. *Donner la mort*. In *L'Éthique du don: Jacques Derrida et la pensée du don*, ed. Jean-Michel Rabaté and Michael Wetzel, 11–108. Paris: Métailié-Transition, 1992. Translated by David Wills under the title *The Gift of Death* (Chicago: University of Chicago Press, 1995).

GS   Walter Benjamin. *Gesammelte Schriften*. Ed. Rolf Tiedemann and Hermann Schweppenhäuser. Frankfurt a. M.: Suhrkamp, 1980. Translated in part under the title *Walter Benjamin: Selected Writings*, Michael W. Jennings, general editor. Vol. 1: *1913–1926*, ed. Marcus Bullock and Michael W. Jennings (Cambridge: Harvard University Press, 1996); Vol. 2: *1927–1934*, trans. Rodney Livingstone and others, ed. Michael W. Jennings, Howard Eiland, and Gary Smith (Cambridge: Harvard University Press, 1999).

ICT   Jean Wahl. Introduction to Søren Kierkegaard, *Crainte et tremblement, Lyrique-dialectique par Johannes de Silentio*, trans. P. H. Tisseau. Paris: Aubier Montaigne, 1984.

LP   Éric Weil. *Logique de la philosophie*. 2d ed. Paris: Vrin, 1967.

MF   Michel de Certeau. *La Fable mystique, 1: XVIe–XVIIe siècle*. Paris: Gallimard, 1982. Translated by M. B. Smith under the title *The Mystic Fable*, vol. 1: *The Sixteenth and Seventeenth Centuries* (Chicago: University of Chicago Press, 1992).

P   Jacques Derrida. *Psyché: Inventions de l'autre*. Paris: Galilée, 1987.

PF   Jacques Derrida. *Politiques de l'amitié*. Paris: Galilée, 1994. Translated by George Collins under the title *Politics of Friendship* (London: Verso, 1997).

PN   Emmanuel Levinas. *Noms Propres*. Montpellier: Fata Morgana, 1975. Translated by Michael B. Smith under the title *Proper Names* (Stanford: Stanford University Press, 1996).

RBR   Immanuel Kant. *Die Religion innerhalb der Grenzen der blossen Vernunft*. Vol. 7 of *Werke*, ed. Wilhelm Weischedel. Darmstadt: Wissenschaftliche Buchgesellschaft, 1983. Translated by George di Giovanni under the title *Religion within the Boundaries of Mere Reason, The Cambridge Edition of the Works of Immanuel Kant,* ed. Paul Guyer and Allen W. Wood (Cambridge: Cambridge University Press, 1996).

SD   Søren Kierkegaard. *The Sickness unto Death: A Christian Psychological Exposition for Upbuilding and Awakening.* Vol. 9 of *Kierkegaard's Writings,* trans. and ed. Howard V. Hong and Edna H. Hong. Princeton: Princeton University Press, 1980.

TI   Emmanuel Levinas. *Totalité et Infini.* The Hague: Martinus Nijhoff, 1961. Translated by Alphonso Lingis under the title *Totality and Infinity* (Pittsburgh: Duquesne University Press, 1969).

WD   Jacques Derrida. *L'Écriture et la différence.* Paris: Seuil, 1967. Translated by Alan Bass under the title *Writing and Difference.* Chicago: University of Chicago Press, 1978.

In all abbreviations and short-form citations where dual page numbers are given, the first page refers to the English translation, the second to the text in its original language.

Religion and Violence

Introduction: Horror Religiosus

THIS BOOK asks whether and to what extent the notion of violence inevitably illumines or shadows our ethico-political engagements and decisions, including, more broadly, our understandings of our identities, historical and in the present, collective and individual. The concept of violence is both empirical and, in ways I shall determine, transcendental or metaphysical, belonging to the realm traditionally ascribed to the a priori, to the intelligible or the noumenal (as Kant would say), in short, to ideality and idealization as such. Violence, in both the widest possible and the most elementary senses of the word, entails any cause, any justified or illegitimate force, that is exerted—physically or otherwise—by one thing (event or instance, group or person, and, perhaps, word and object) on another. Violence thus defined finds its prime model—its source, force, and counterforce—in key elements of the tradition called the religious. It can be seen as the very element of religion. No violence without (some) religion; no religion without (some) violence.

One way to put this is as follows: "religion" is the relation between the self (or some selves) and the other—some Other—a relation that, as Levinas has suggested, does not close itself off in a conceptual totality (or does so only arbitrarily, i.e., violently) and thus at least in part escapes human autonomy, voluntary decision, and so on. By the same token, "religion" also stands for the other—*the* Other—of violence. It evokes its counterimage, its opposite, redemption, and critique.[1] There is no contradiction here (or, if so, it is unavoidable), since this other (or Other) of violence is violence or violent still, in yet another meaning of the word.

To address violence in its relation to religion and in all the further complexity of its origins, mediations, and effects seems a topical project

1. That this formal characterization of religion, borrowed mainly from Levinas, is historically speaking a very limited one should be clear. See Jonathan Z. Smith, "Religion, Religious, Religions," in *Critical Terms for Religious Studies,* ed. Mark C. Taylor (Chicago: University of Chicago Press, 1998).

for many reasons. A cursory comparative philosophical analysis of the different conceptions of ethics and politics in recent debates concerning multiculturalism, citizenship, immigration, and democracy reveals the unspoken assumption that the modern genesis and contemporary transformation of the public sphere are related to—and signaled by— the changing sociopolitical and cultural role played by religion. Religion, these debates demonstrate, can no longer be—and perhaps never truly was—relegated to the sphere of privacy and individual conscience. Yet with few exceptions protagonists of the central positions in these debates—whether they place themselves in the traditions of critical theory, liberalism, communitarianism, neo-Aristotelianism, neopragmatism, or post-structuralism—seem unwilling to allow religion more than a marginal function in the constitution, definition, and redefinition of the public sphere.[2] All involved in these debates, however, agree that the public sphere articulates itself in modernity by engaging with the definition and practice of censorship and free speech, especially in view of the question of religious tolerance.

One of my main concerns will be to offer a philosophical analysis of the modern emergence and conceptualization of the public sphere as it is inaugurated in Kant's writings on religion (especially its relation to the sovereignty and the institutions of the modern state, notably the university). Not only is this the context in which Kant develops his thoughts on radical evil, but here, in the "General Observations" that conclude each of the four sections of *Religion innerhalb der Grenzen der blossen Vernunft* (*Religion within the Boundaries of Mere Reason*), one can find, as Stanley Cavell points out in *The Claim of Reason*, "a general theory of irrationality, a systematic account of what turn out, on this theory, to be a whole class of phenomena, each of them involving a particular distortion of human reason." Cavell continues: "Kant calls the four members of this class fanaticism, superstition, delusion, and sorcery. Not the least of the illuminations of his theory is its implied proposal that, as one may frame it, the cure for

2. For exceptions, see Ronald F. Thiemann, *Religion in Public Life: A Dilemma for Democracy* (Washington: Georgetown University Press, 1996); most of the contributions to Paul J. Weithman, ed., *Religion and Contemporary Liberalism* (Notre Dame: University of Notre Dame Press, 1997); and Veit Bader, "Religious Pluralism: Secularism or Priority for Democracy?," *Political Theory* 27, no. 5 (1999): 597–633. See also José Casanova, *Public Religions in the Modern World* (Chicago: University of Chicago Press, 1994), and the empirical studies included in Heiner Bielefeldt and Wilhelm Heitmeyer, eds., *Politisierte Religion: Ursachen und Erscheinungsformen des modernen Fundamentalismus* (Frankfurt a. M.: Suhrkamp, 1998).

Faustianism [in Cavell's words: "the wish to escape the human conditions of knowing"] and for skepticism are the same."[3]

Yet things are even more complicated. On the one hand, Kant's phenomenology of the elementary forms of religious life takes a decisive step beyond the parameters set by the earlier three *Critiques*. More skeptically, Kant now starts out from the problem of radical evil and successively demonstrates this evil to be ineradicable and increasingly capable of compromising not only each individual but all collective attempts to correct or contain it. The history of humankind is thus portrayed as a series of unsuccessful and ever more irrational sociopolitical means to further the good and establish the "kingdom of ends." The visible churches (the empirical forms of historical, revealed or positive, religion) and their opposing sects never come to reflect the invisible church (the form of forms, religion, and morality proper) without caricature. What is more, their exponential growth pushes the coming of this kingdom further and further away, into an ever more distant and insecure future. The more it approaches, the more it is deferred; the more it is obeyed, the more it is betrayed, as if the principle of intelligibility and that of empiricity were continuously and even progressively at odds and, indeed, at war.

On the other hand, for Kant religion does provide the critical correction (in a sense, the antidote) for the very distortion and intoxication that it might seem to bring into existence. Religion—more precisely, the pure and formal or transcendental concept of a moral religion as well as a rational theology—is pitted against a religiosity that in virtually all of its historical forms (including the ones determining Christianity) is tainted and infected by what Kant, in a remarkable formulation, calls an "admixture of paganism [*Beimischung von Heidentum*]." This expression captures what for Kant, at least in the writings that deal with religion and biblical and dogmatic theology explicitly, namely, *Religion within the Boundaries of Mere Reason* and *Der Streit der Fakultäten* (*The Conflict of the Faculties*), forms the limit, but also *the very element and the medium or mediation* of the philosophical, the rational, the general—indeed, of truth. Religion, not merely rational religion (or what comes down to the same, morality: a

3. Stanley Cavell, *The Claim of Reason: Wittgenstein, Skepticism, Morality, and Tragedy* (New York: Oxford University Press, 1979), 455. See also Arnold I. Davidson, "Religion and the Distortions of Human Reason: On Kant's *Religion within the Limits of Reason Alone*," in *Pursuits of Reason: Essays in Honor of Stanley Cavell*, ed. Ted Cohen, Paul Guyer, and Hilary Putnam (Lubbock: Texas Tech University Press, 1993), 67.

synonym for the philosophical and truly universal in the realm of human action), but religion in its historical, political, in short, empirical formation and, as Kant says, revelation both resists the "kingdom of ends" yet also, paradoxically, helps bring it into existence and into its own.

Thus Kant already sees that modernity does not, in a single stroke, render obsolete all religious categories (all figures of thought, rhetorical devices, concepts and forms of obligation, ritual practices, and so on). On the contrary, even where the "religious" can no longer be identified as an integral and compelling system of belief or, more indirectly, as a narratively constructed way of life, it provides critical terms, argumentative resources, and a bold imagery necessary for analyzing contemporary culture successfully. In other words, beyond its appeal to the latest findings of the empirical social sciences or to the most advanced conceptual tools provided by philosophical analysis and by literary and cultural studies, the comparative study of contemporary religion must recast these critical terms and the concrete phenomena to which they refer in light of the historical and lived tradition they seek to comprehend.

This double task becomes nowhere clearer than in attempts to understand the political and institutional arrangements with which modern liberal democratic societies regulate the interaction between their citizens, as well as between these citizens and "others" (legal aliens, citizens of other nations, immigrants, refugees, sans papiers, etc.). This variable practice of regulation extends to the relationship between living human beings and other others as well: the dead, the not yet living, the living of a nonhuman nature. Of course, artificial, virtual, or technologically construed others—or, for that matter, others that fit none of these categories—might someday pose a challenge to these demarcations, as they already have done in the imagination and thought experiments of philosophers, writers, and filmmakers. Here, Kant's thoughts on hospitality and cosmopolitanism could point the way. In principle, his philosophy of history and the endless emancipation from ineradicable evil it entails must involve all—thus also all nonhuman—moral agents: angels, automata, and the like. But why, then, does Kant hesitate to draw the full consequences from his observations?

IN AN ATTEMPT to further concretize and amplify the turn to religion, this book seeks to demarcate and rigorously circumscribe the motif of a certain horror religiosus. Kierkegaard introduces the term in Fear and Trembling, in a remarkable analysis of how the ethical and the political—modeled after their Kantian (and Hegelian) interpretations—are exposed to the figure of the religious. By this he means the sovereign, absolute, and (from our finite and human point of view) absolutely arbitrary act of divine will, of a figure and instance, that is, which—in the world of appearance—seem inseparable from their no less absolute defiguration. I suggest that it is this other Other, this other of the Other, of which Kierkegaard writes with so much vehemence when he addresses the demonic, in *Fear and Trembling*. The same motif also appears when, more generally, he speaks of anxiety and despair in *The Concept of Anxiety* and *The Sickness unto Death*, both of which will enable us to radicalize the Kantian perspective.

We are not far here, I argue, from the divine wrath of which Walter Benjamin and Michel de Certeau speak with so much force. Moreover, these motifs have found their way into Jacques Derrida's *Force de loi: Le "Fondement mystique de l'autorité"* ("Force of Law: 'The Mystical Foundation of Authority'"). As we will verify, they have also left their trace in his expositions of the relationship between hospitality and hostility (in the wake, once more, of Kant, Levinas, and Schmitt). Derrida—whose writings on the authors mentioned before will form my point of departure, even though I take elements of his analyses in directions he might not approve—speaks of the necessity and the imperative to be aware of "a history of radical evil, of its figures that are never simply figures and that—this is the whole evil—are always inventing a new evil" (FK 9/18). This passage comes from "Foi et savoir: Les Deux Sources de la 'religion' aux limites de la simple raison" ("Faith and Knowledge: The Two Sources of 'Religion' at the Limits of Mere Reason"), a text that contains Derrida's most explicit discussion of religion to date.

In a different context,[4] I have teased out some implications of Derrida's hypothesis, also introduced in this essay, that the "return of the religious" is intrinsically linked to the rise and the performative modalities perceived in and by the new teletechnologies. Here I want to circle back to this text once more to pick up its central motif of radical evil (*das radikal Böse*), whose conceptual and practical possibility, Derrida argues, is not unrelated to the abstraction or denaturalization often ascribed to religion (especially in its apophatic—i.e., negative theological—modes and expressions), as well as to the deterritorialization attributed to the new

---

4. Hent de Vries, "In Media Res," in *Religion and Media*, ed. Hent de Vries and Samuel Weber (Stanford: Stanford University Press, 2001). On Derrida's "Faith and Knowledge," see also my introductory chapter in *Philosophy and the Turn to Religion*.

media. The motif of radical evil necessitates beginning with a discussion of this topos in Kant's *Religion within the Boundaries of Mere Reason,* not least because of the explicit reference in the subtitle of Derrida's essay.

But what could a "history" of "radical" — meaning also nonempirical, transcendental, and even absolute — "evil" mean? How, exactly, does it relate to the history of religion, of divine wrath no less than its ultimate resolution, of theodicies and eschatologies, of apocalyptics and salvation? At one point in *Autrement qu'être ou au-delà l'essence* (*Otherwise Than Being or beyond Essence*), Levinas speaks of the task of construing a "history of the face." Times have changed, and there is no longer any real opposition between writing the history of the face (as Levinas more than anyone else attempted) and that of the worst violence (as Levinas did at one and the same stroke). Perhaps there never was. In fact, the apparent possibility, if not the empirical reality, of violence and its interruption go hand in hand. The modalities of its emergence and its containment are two sides of one and the same coin.

MY FIRST CHAPTER carefully retraces some of Derrida's steps in his monumental *Du droit à la philosophie* (*Of the Right to Philosophy,* or *From Right to Philosophy,* or *Right to Philosophy*), which concerns the theoretical and practical deconstructibility of the modern institution, especially the academic institution, the university as it defines itself as the expression of a philosophical or, more particularly, Kantian idea of reason. It seeks to illuminate the difficulties one encounters when posing the question of the institution, of institutionalization, of the common ground of institutions, of their foundation or founding, of their rationale and their telos. The central essays in Derrida's volume introduce his reading of *Religion within the Boundaries of Mere Reason* and *The Conflict of the Faculties,* works that have not received the same attention as the three *Critiques* in modern scholarship. While the *Critiques* are generally held to contain the most systematic and mature account of Kant's philosophical project, supplemented perhaps only by the set of smaller essays on history that some scholars have sought to interpret as a "fourth critique" of sorts, the writings on religion have not yet been granted their full theoretical weight.[5] These texts elaborate and refine the concept of moral religion in its *for-*

5. Hannah Arendt recalls — and dismisses — the expression "fourth critique" in the first of her *Lectures on Kant's Political Philosophy,* ed. Ronald Beiner (Chicago: University of Chicago Press, 1982), 7. The term is attributed to Kurt Borries, *Kant als Politiker: Zur Staats- und Gesellschaftslehre des Kritizismus* (Leipzig, 1928).

mality, as introduced by the critical writings and presupposed by the essays on the philosophy of history. They concentrate on its intricate, aporetic relation to the empirical *forms* of historically "revealed" religions, that is to say, to society, the political, the state, the church, the people, sects, movements, elites, and so on.

The Conflict of the Faculties engages this matter in discussing the inevitably conflictual relationship between the "lower" philosophical faculty in the modern university and the "higher" faculties (most significantly theology, but also law and medicine), which reflect the immediate interests of the national state. I argue that more than a defense of the independence or purity of the discipline of philosophy and hence of reason is at issue here: in fact, Kant elaborates a complex, and ultimately aporetic, theory of toleration and censorship under modern conditions. The conflict echoes and produces the instable balance between the dictates of sovereignty and of reason, the necessities of the political and freedoms of thought and of speech. It also allows us to conceptualize—and formalize—the space of their provisional and partial negotiation.

Religion within the Boundaries of Mere Reason—a text that is only broached in *Right to Philosophy* but centrally informs "Faith and Knowledge"—expands on the "conflict" by situating it in a larger context: that of the development of the moral principle and of moral religion in the history of humankind as a whole. Here the discussion of radical evil finds its place. I will argue that this notion can be interpreted with the help of Derrida's concept of absolute pervertibility, itself a retranslation of his earlier understanding of monstrosity, of the ever-looming possibility of the worst (*le pire*), the threat that shadows and, it would seem, conditions any promise. Since the structure of the promise underlies all events associated with human action—that is to say, the founding of states, the making and interpreting of laws, and every single decision made by individuals and groups—it similarly underlies contemporary theories of the speech act, performativity, and rule following, which incessantly refer to the legal realm and to juridical judgment. J. L. Austin, John Rawls, Stanley Cavell, and Judith Butler are just a few examples, who, to be sure, take these notions in very different directions indeed.[6] Derrida, I claim, adds a

6. See, e.g., J. L. Austin, *How to Do Things with Words,* 2d ed., J. O. Urmson and Marina Sbisà, eds. (Cambridge, Mass.: Harvard University Press, 1994; orig. pub. 1962); Stanley Cavell, *A Pitch of Philosophy: Autobiographical Exercises* (Cambridge, Mass.: Harvard University Press, 1994), chap. 2; Judith Butler, *Excitable Speech: A Politics of the Performative* (New York: Routledge, 1997).

fundamentally Kierkegaardian concern—in a word, the anxiety brought about by the *horror religiosus*—to this problematic.

Mutatis mutandis, this problematic had already been put forward in Derrida's "Déclarations d'Indépendance" ("Declarations of Independence").[7] I trace the development undergone by this first formalization of the law of reiterated institution qua foundation (of nations, states, and, indeed, institutions) and concentrate on its subsequent rearticulation in what seems a quasi-theological register in "Force of Law: The 'Mystical Foundation of Authority.'" What exactly, in this transition or transposition, if it is one (or just one), is gained or, for that matter, lost?

My opening chapter argues that, while Kant's *Religion within the Boundaries of Mere Reason* and *The Conflict of the Faculties* have often been read as further expositions and illustrations of his moral and transcendental theology, they have not received the attention they deserve as one of the first explicit—and still most powerful—philosophical conceptualizations of the relationships between religion, nation, community, and the public sphere. Although the Kantian heritage has often been reduced to an exploration of the nature of political legitimacy in light of a merely formal and procedural rationality, the philosophical relevance of these writings consists at least as much in interrogating arguments that seem to anticipate current debates over the implications of the concept and the practice of "multicultural citizenship" and the "law of peoples."[8] Moreover, while Kant's delimitations of the freedom of public speech form part and parcel of a critique of institutions—as is clear from his treatment of censorship, the idea of the university, and religious tolerance—his philosophical analysis of different types of statements and utterances has a direct bearing on the contemporary deployment of speech act theory in the analysis of cultural conflicts or the performativity of constructed cultural identities.

Kant's work helps spell out why there can be no ultimate neutrality, homogeneity—or, for that matter, secularism—of the public sphere and, more importantly, why this insight by no means implies that the formal critical task of reason has become obsolete. Where every other is totally

---

7. Jacques Derrida, "Déclarations d'Indépendance," in *Otobiographies: L'Enseignement de Nietzsche et la politique du nom propre* (Paris: Galilée, 1984); "Declarations of Independence," trans. Thomas Keenan and Thomas Pepper, *New Political Science* 15 (1986): 7–15.

8. These formulations I borrow from Will Kymlicka, *Multicultural Citizenship: A Liberal Theory of Minority Rights* (Oxford: Clarendon Press, 1995), and John Rawls, *The Law of Peoples* (Cambridge, Mass.: Harvard University Press, 1999). I will return to these authors in the following chapters.

other, following Derrida's puzzling and provocative phrase *tout autre est tout autre,* a genuine or responsible politics of difference comes into sight. Such a politics should not be confused with the politics of identity, nor with the communitarian discourses that have been pitted against the supposed formalism of modern liberal political theories. What is to count as different or other, let alone totally other, is by no means certain or given. No one could possibly identify with it or make it one's own.

Apart from exploring the concept of the public sphere with reference to Kant and his recent interpreters, notably Hannah Arendt and Jürgen Habermas, my first chapter therefore also indirectly addresses contemporary debates on political liberalism, communitarianism, and neopragmatism. Charles Taylor's essay "The Politics of Recognition," in particular, has inspired a new round of discussion concerning the philosophical dimensions of multiculturalism, its implied concept of citizenship, the consequences for liberal education, the academic curriculum, and so on.[9] The present project shares Taylor's concentration on the philosophical merit of concepts and issues whose discussion has too often been marred by political and academic controversy. My different angle lies in examining the multiple ways in which religion, censorship, and tolerance in their Kantian and post-Kantian determination not only shape our experience of the tensions between collective and personal cultural identities, but also affect our understanding of the conditions under which public dissension and cultural separatism can be resolved to a certain point.

In my second chapter, I explore an intricate logic of responsibility and irresponsibility that corresponds to the earlier — Kantian — considerations concerning radical evil and the tension between philosophical and biblical theology, as well as between moral and revealed (historical or positive) religion. Here my point of departure will be Kierkegaard's riposte

9. Charles Taylor, "The Politics of Recognition," in *Multiculturalism and "The Politics of Recognition,"* ed. Amy Gutmann (Princeton: Princeton University Press, 1992), and in Charles Taylor, *Philosophical Arguments* (Cambridge: Harvard University Press, 1995). See also, in the latter publication, "Liberal Politics and the Public Sphere." While Taylor's essays provide a context for discussing the philosophical stakes involved in the politics of recognition, one should in principle investigate fully the numerous critical responses to his position that have been made by a wide range of philosophers, social scientists, and cultural critics. I am thinking primarily of Kwame Anthony Appiah, Jürgen Habermas, and Amy Gutmann. But the rethinking of the public sphere and the challenge of multiculturalism and globalization for the modern project of political liberalism by Seyla Benhabib, Christine M. Korsgaard, Will Kymlicka, John Rawls, Richard Rorty, and Cornel West is also relevant in this context. See also Werner Hamacher, "One 2 Many Multiculturalisms," in *Violence, Identity, and Self-Determination,* ed. Hent de Vries and Samuel Weber (Stanford: Stanford University Press, 1997).

to the Kantian paradigm, as I have reconstructed it by elaborating—and extrapolating—some of Derrida's suggestions in *Right to Philosophy* and "Faith and Knowledge." My frame of reference in this chapter will be Derrida's reading of Kierkegaard's *Fear and Trembling*, which responds in part to earlier interpretations by Levinas and, often obliquely, by Eric Weil and Jean Wahl. In *Donner la mort* (*The Gift of Death*), Derrida, following these authors, reads the testimony of Abraham's sacrifice, the "instant of Abrahamic renunciation," and the violence that comes with it as the paradigm for what is at stake in every genuine ethico-political decision. I ask how we are to understand the disturbing fact—yet another "fact of reason," to use Kant's formulation—that only in the interruption of the ethical can responsibility, both practical and intellectual, be thought and exercised at all.

According to the paradoxical logic of responsibility and irresponsibility, the ethical becomes possible precisely in the disturbing possibility of its suspension—the possibility of violence and monstrosity, of the *revenant*, the specter, and the anonymous *il y a*—without, however, being able to affirm or assert itself with full force or as such, in its purity. Whatever force the ethical might have—a violence in its own right—is always tempered and countered, not only by the powers that be, but also by the structure of its own success. Its own excessiveness disrupts in advance all compliance—if not our respect for, then our conformity with the moral law, with justice. The ethical forbids, indeed precludes, all "good conscience."

This chapter takes its point of departure in a discussion of central concepts introduced by Eric Weil in *Logique de la philosophie* (*Logics of Philosophy*), concepts that have found their way into the texts of Levinas and into Derrida's reading of Levinas in "Violence et métaphysique" ("Violence and Metaphysics"). I begin by reviewing discussions by Derrida, Levinas, and Weil concerning whether violence is endemic to discourse and to the advent of being. If violence is in effect universal and universalizing is violent, I ask, does this not trivialize the concept of violence, vitiating the intensity of any ethico-political response to it? Through a reading of Derrida's account of the sacrifice of Abraham in *The Gift of Death*, I demonstrate that this is not necessarily so. Examining the figures of sacrifice and of obligation, one can show that the prerequisite of any genuine ethico-political act is a singular and secret decision, an act of testimony that passionately resists the traditional concepts of the ethical, the political, and even the "act." As such, it involves a relation that either touches upon violence or is touched by it: a *horror religiosus*. To be wakeful to this proximity of the best and the worst is to rediscover Mount Moriah, to which Abraham was called to sacrifice his son, as the everyday locus of our relation to everybody—and, indeed, to everything. To invoke this example and everything for which it stands is not to advocate a return to religion per se. Rather, it means embarking on an ongoing project that, as Derrida has convincingly argued, entails a "doubling" of God that is neither theistic nor atheistic, but lies at the source of all responsible discourse on responsibility.

I also raise an issue first broached in *Philosophy and the Turn to Religion,* the question of whether the concept and presupposition of the "possible"—of possibilization, of possibilism, and thereby of all inquiries into the conditions of possibility termed transcendental—is adequate to articulate this exposition and exposure of the ethical to its other. I argue that it is not. This chapter, though it starts out from a discussion of the concept of violence as developed by Levinas and Weil, revolves around Derrida's analysis of the "impossibility" of the ultimate "possibility" that Heidegger, in *Sein und Zeit (Being and Time),* equates with death—one's own death—alone. At this point I return to the conclusions of my earlier discussions of *Sauf le nom* and *Apories (Aporias).* Derrida introduces this motif also in the context of a discussion of Benjamin's "Zur Kritik der Gewalt" ("Critique of Violence") to which I will turn in Chapter 3: "The most rigorous deconstructions have never claimed to be . . . possible. And I would say that deconstruction loses nothing from admitting that it is impossible. . . . For a deconstructive operation *possibility* would rather be the danger, the danger of becoming an available set of rule-governed procedures, methods, accessible approaches. The interest of deconstruction . . . is a certain experience of the impossible" (FL 981).

What should, perhaps, also be maintained against all possibilism is what Kierkegaard, in *The Sickness unto Death*—a text that in other respects deeply influenced Heidegger's earliest thinking, in the 1920–21 lectures introducing the phenomenology of religion—calls "necessity." Kierkegaard writes: "Possibility and necessity are equally essential to becoming (and the self has the task of becoming itself in freedom). . . . A self that has no possibility is in despair, and likewise a self that has no necessity." [10]

10. S. Kierkegaard, *The Sickness unto Death: A Christian Psychological Exposition for Upbuilding and Awakening,* ed. and trans. Howard V. Hong and Edna H. Hong, *Kierkegaard's Writings,* vol. 9 (Princeton: Princeton University Press, 1980), 35. For an extensive discussion of Heidegger's lecture course *Einleitung in die Phänomenologie de Religion (Introduction into the Phenomenology of Religion),* see my *Philosophy and the Turn to Religion,* chap. 2.

Mutatis mutandis, the same could be said of the necessity of *Anankē*, of *la Nécessité*, of a certain phenomenality (in Kant's sense of the word), of mechanicity, of technicity, of a certain immanentism, naturalism, and so on. Perhaps repetition, *Wiederholung*, verification, and authentification should be located not only in the reaffirmation of the utmost possibility of the self (of freedom and autonomy, of self-determination, of one's own-most, nonsubstitutable, being toward one's own death), but also in the relation to the other and the Other, to cite the most relevant topoi that preoccupy Kant, Heidegger, and Levinas. Perhaps it consists at least as much — indeed, of necessity — in the weight of the already there, that is to say, of slippage, subreption, contamination, some admixture of pagan-ism, derailment, in short, of what is other than the other — or Other — and nonetheless belongs essentially (inevitably, necessarily) to it and forms part and parcel of the very experience, the experiment and the trial, of freedom. This double acquiescence — or double affirmation — is implicit in the texts of Kant, Heidegger, and Levinas; I take its consistent elucidation to be the main thread running through Derrida's entire oeuvre.

In the third chapter, I discuss the notion of mystic speech as concep-tualized by Michel de Certeau in *La Fable mystique* (*The Mystic Fable*), an interdisciplinary study of some major characteristics of sixteenth- and seventeenth-century mysticism. Only its first volume, published in 1982, was completed. I argue that this text should be read as a foil to Derrida's re-articulation of the mystical postulate in Montaigne, Pascal, and Benjamin. Doing so reveals the full force of Derrida's argument, but — in a sense to be determined — also highlights its unexpected reassessment of a certain interpretive and ethico-political violence, a *horror religiosus*, expressed, for example, in the citation from Joyce's *Finnegans Wake* on which Der-rida dwells extensively in *Ulysse gramophone* (*Ulysses Gramophone*): "He war." [11]

The interpretation of this motif of an ineluctable divine wrath against the backdrop of de Certeau's work on mysticism and the political con-firms the hidden correspondence between Derrida's writings on the insti-tution, the university, the media, and performativity, and the question of violence in all of its multiple ramifications. This impression is reinforced

11. Jacques Derrida, *Ulysse gramophone: Deux mots pour Joyce* (Paris: Galilée, 1987); "Two Words for Joyce," trans. Geoffrey Bennington, in *Post-Structuralist Joyce: Essays from the French*, ed. Derek Attridge and Daniel Ferrer (Cambridge: Cambridge University Press, 1984); "Ulysses Gramophone: Hear Say Yes in Joyce," trans. Tina Kendall, in *Acts of Literature*, ed. Derek At-tridge (London: Routledge, 1992).

by the in part posthumous publication of de Certeau's *La Culture au pluriel* (*Culture in the Plural*) and *La Prise de parole, et autres écrits politiques* (*The Capture of Speech and Other Political Writings*).[12] The former book contains "The Language of Violence," as well as essays on the university; the translator's afterword rightly characterizes it as "a founding charter for culture studies."[13] At the center of the latter collection stands a re-evaluation of the meaning and import of religion in transition from a specialized system of belief to a powerful — violently nonviolent — perfor-mance of speech, a "mystic speech" whose political and cultural implica-tions we are only now beginning to fathom. To call the model proposed by these writings a "heterology" captures only part of the movement at issue. Equally central to this performative and mystic speech is an almost tautological element. After establishing the unmistakable influence of de Certeau on Derrida's invocation of the mystical postulate, I bring Der-rida's phrase *tout autre est tout autre,* analyzed in the previous chapter, to bear upon the historical and systematic analyses of *The Mystic Fable.* In order to do so, however, we will need to backtrack for a detour through an author whose work is of great importance to our understanding of the theologico-political, in particular of the relationship between religion and violence.

Chapter 3, therefore, starts out by focusing on elements in the writ-ings of Carl Schmitt that are necessary for an understanding of the work of Benjamin. This excursus will help us to return briefly to Kant. After re-visiting Schmitt's conception of the political and the evil in human nature, of sovereignty and the miracle, I concentrate on two of Benjamin's major early essays, devoted to the problem of translation in relation to the sacred: "Über die Sprache überhaupt und über die Sprache des Menschen" ("On Language as Such and on the Language of Man") and "Die Aufgabe des Übersetzers" ("The Task of the Translator").

Translation, we shall see, forms the very act of interpretation, inven-tion, and negotiation — rather than, say, mediation or application, terms too dialectical and hermeneutic for Benjamin's and Derrida's taste — of the infinity and excessiveness of the law in the concrete contexts of the many,

12. Michel de Certeau, *La Culture au pluriel,* ed. Luce Giard (Paris: Seuil, 1994) / *Culture in the Plural,* trans. Tom Conley (Minneapolis: University of Minnesota Press, 1997); *La Prise de parole, et autres écrits politiques,* ed. Luce Giard (Paris: Éditions du Seuil, 1994) / *The Capture of Speech and Other Political Writings,* trans. Tom Conley (Minneapolis: University of Minnesota Press, 1997).

13. De Certeau, *Cultural in the Plural,* 149.

necessarily limited and limiting laws. Respect for cultural difference and the need (for lack of a better word) for integration meet here in a question of incarnation, instantiation, and hence translation.[14] The construction of the tower of Babel, discussed in Derrida's "Des tours de Babel" and elsewhere in his writings, would seem to form the most appropriate image of the perils involved in this undertaking.

My examination of these texts prepares for an interpretation of another curious religious motif adopted by Derrida: the mystical postulate as what paradoxically or, rather, aporetically founds and undermines or interrupts the authority of the juridical law. This notion is not unrelated to the emphatic notion of justice elaborated by Levinas. Drawing on de Certeau's pivotal work on the mystic fable, I argue that in its very structure this postulate is not so much an epistemological or axiological premise as something resembling an absolute performative, like the structure of address that marks all genuine prayer or like the promise, the attestation, or the gift. This gift, the gift of the gift—the giving of the gift as well as the gift's giving—exceeds and traverses all economic exchange in the broadest sense. Neither a merely theoretical construct nor a hypothesis, the notion of a mystical postulate thus touches upon central ethico-political questions, as Derrida makes clear in his hesitant rejoinder to Benjamin's "Critique of Violence" in "Force of Law," as well as in his interrogation of Marcel Mauss in *Donner le temps* (*Given Time*), a text that in its final pages circles back to the problem of radical evil in Kant.

The motifs of the mystical postulate and the gift underscore that Derrida's reassessment of the philosophical tradition—and his turn to religion in order to tease out this tradition's unthought or unsaid—rests on a singular practice or act of affirmation and reaffirmation. Any plausible analysis of the affinity between the thought of *différance* and the thought embarked upon by the traditional *via negativa* demands that we reconsider the interrogation of dialectical and nondialectical negativity throughout Derrida's texts. Such an analysis must discuss what, in his most recent writings, precedes, resituates, and renegotiates the negative in obliquely or, more often than not, explicitly religious terms. This is not the negation of the negative—that is to say, affirmation in the common, classical, and formal logical sense of the word. Instead, here we are dealing with a far more original or originary "af-firmation," that is to say, with a non-

14. See, e.g., Jacques Derrida, *Sur parole: Instantanées philosophiques* (Paris: L'Aube, 1999), 73–74.

thetic postulation that knows no fixity, firmness, or closure (all conno-tations that Derrida brings to bear upon the French *affirmation*, loosely associating it with the undoing of *fermeté* and *fermeture*).

Examples of this, Derrida suggests in "Comment ne pas parler" ("How to Avoid Speaking") and *De l'esprit* (*Of Spirit*), may be found in several heterodox forms of Judeo-Christian and Arabic mysticism, as well as in Heidegger's thought on the "nothing" in *Was ist Metaphysik?* (*What Is Metaphysics?*) and on the essence of language in *Unterwegs zur Sprache* (*On the Way towards Language*). In both these writings, Heidegger pre-pares a gesture of *Gelassenheit*, a letting go of (or release from) the tra-dition of representational thought, of metaphysics in its onto-theological constitution. This gesture, I argue in *Philosophy and the Turn to Religion*, already announces itself in Heidegger's early lectures on St. Paul and St. Augustine. But Heidegger almost immediately translates this motif and motivation into a "logic of presupposition" (to cite Derrida's *Aporias*) that fixates the original gesture's impetus and disruption and inscribes it into a fundamentally ontological—metaphysical—*possibilism* whose architec-tonics (that of classical and modern transcendental thought) can be de-constructed in more than one way.

In the final chapter of this book, I discuss Derrida's thoughts on hos-pitality and friendship in the writings of Levinas and, again, Kant. Draw-ing on the arguments presented in *Adieu à Emmanuel Levinas* (*Adieu to Emmanuel Levinas*) and in *Politiques de l'amitié* (*Politics of Friendship*), I suggest that both notions are nonsynonymous substitutions for openness to the other. In the present historical and political constellation—and, presumably, for some time still to come—religion, in the precise sense of this term sketched above, is, remains, or has once more become the privi-leged example of such openness, a welcoming that is inevitably an open-ness to the best and the worst. This actuality of religion does not express some metaphysical truth concerning the notions of hospitality and friend-ship, as if they were in essence—or even in their original and proper mean-ing—to be understood religiously or theologically. On the contrary, their association is above all pragmatic, based on a historical elective affinity and structural resemblance, one that may one day outlive itself (again).

This prominence of the religious will emerge once more in discuss-ing a few striking passages from Kant's work, here the *Metaphysik der Sit-ten* (*Metaphysics of Morals*) and *Anthropologie in pragmatischer Hinsicht* (*Anthropology from a Pragmatic Point of View*). Derrida takes up these two, in Kant's own words, "material" and "dogmatic" supplements to the

Critiques and gives them an important place in his discussions of friendship, in conjunction with the actual and as yet unexplored politics of cosmopolitanism and the democracy still—and forever—to come (*à venir*). These final motifs will permit us to circle back to central themes in Chapter 1: the question of the institution, not least the institution—or, rather, institutions—of philosophy, in the university and, happily, elsewhere.

Faithful to the question that guides us throughout, we will ask what it means that the theme and practice of hospitality (friendship, cosmopolitanism, democracy, and their functional equivalents), in Derrida's reading of these texts, goes hand in hand with the motif of and concern with *hostility*. In other words, the very idea and experience of friendship would seem to co-exist with a certain conceptual and factual violence that philosophy, freed from all moralism and idealism, should take pains not to obscure and gloss over.

Here the most important threads of Derrida's argument, I argue, are distilled from a renewed reading of Levinas's *Totalité et infini* (*Totality and Infinity*), of a structure of intentionality reoriented in the direction of religion—a formally indicated religion defined as the relation to the other that does not close itself off in a totality—and further explored in the analyses devoted to the logic of hospitality in *Adieu to Emmanuel Levinas*. Inherent in the structure of any welcome, Derrida demonstrates, is a second welcoming of what threatens the possibility of the first welcome. This perversion or, rather, "pervertibility"—since its actual, factual, or empirical occurrence is not what matters most here—is no mere accident, but belongs to the essence of the phenomenon and to the structure of phenomenality and its intelligibility as such. The possibility of the worst is once more the condition of the best.

Paradoxically, this is why there can be no such thing as experience or meaning as such or *kath'auto*. Levinas still attempts to maintain the contrary in *Totality and Infinity*, though later he severely revises his views, partly in response to Derrida's pressing questions in "Violence and Metaphysics."[15] Nor can there be a simple, nonaporetic, and unilinear process of the founding, conditioning, or possibilization of any such experience. The structure of possibilization (i.e., of revealability, *Offenbarkeit*, but also

15. Jacques Derrida, "Violence et metaphysique," in *L'Écriture et la différance* (Paris: Seuil, 1967) / "Violence and Metaphysics," in *Writing and Difference*, trans. Alan Bass (Chicago: University of Chicago Press, 1978). This essay has rightly become a classic. It is by far the most consequential and rigorous reading of the early Levinas, but the scope of its general argument reaches much further. It has set the standard for any future discussion of these matters.

of messianicity and Christianicity) remains contingent upon — and is thus somehow made possible by — the event (the revelation, *Offenbarung*, messianisms, the *kairos*, etc.) that it seemed to make possible in the first place. What supposedly came first, comes in fact and *de iure* later and vice versa.

Not only will the complex of questions discussed in this chapter allow us to circle back to a decisive influence on Benjamin introduced earlier — namely, Carl Schmitt's studies in *Political Theology* — it will also permit us to revisit some central moments passed over in silence in the first chapter's discussion of Kant. I will conclude by asking how, in particular, the Kantian theme of cosmopolitanism (and, at the societal micro-level, once again of friendship) takes shape in light of the premises and arguments from which I have taken my lead. What does cosmopolitanism mean against the backdrop of the proposed and observed turn to religion and its intrinsic relationship to (the problem of) violence, to the *horror religiosus* whose structure and pertinence forms our theme?

The concluding section of the book wraps up the argument and draws out some implications for the task of philosophy at the intersection of contemporary comparative religious studies, political theory, and cultural analysis. Addressing violence in relation to testimony requires nothing less than a sustained interrogation of the concepts, argumentative strategies, rhetorical devices, and central intuitions at the crossroads of the institutional disciplines that contribute to understanding these phenomena. The present work can aspire no more than to lay out some of the hypotheses and guiding assumptions that could direct and inspire such an inquiry. In that sense, the following exposition, in spite of its length and detail, remains programmatic in many respects and concludes nothing but the prolegomena inaugurating work still to be done.

Chapter One

State, Academy, Censorship

The Question of Religious Tolerance

THE CHAPTERS of this book all revolve around the question of how a certain cultural difference—that of religion and everything it implies (its functional equivalents as well as its partial negations and contestations)—manifests itself, especially in modern liberal-democratic and "pluralistic" societies. In these societies, an ability and commitment to recognize, respect, engage, and negotiate difference is held to be an integrative sociopolitical force, a necessary condition for relative social stability and a reservoir of potential imaginative response to the challenges of globalization, informationalism, and multiculturalism in the contemporary world. Cultural difference, "culture in the plural," to cite Michel de Certeau, entails divisive practices of cultural differentiation and dissemination. It also mandates a minimum societal synthesis, the quest for a certain communality and the provisional stabilization of shared ideas, values, and goods. Most existing empirical studies either take for granted the tension between these two opposite—centrifugal and centripetal—tendencies or view it as a problem to be resolved in merely pragmatic ways. For the most part, such studies do not view the problem of violence in its relation to cultural identity in the conceptual or imaginative and poetic (that is, narrative and rhetorical) terms about which philosophy and the testimony of religious traditions might have something to say.[1] By contrast, this book seeks to clarify the analytical and normative elements that determine the nature of cultural diversity in relation to the practices and imperatives of sociopolitical cohesion, its limits, and its internal contradictions, spell-

1. For an excellent overview of diverse conceptual and empirical approaches to violence, see Yves Michaud, *La Violence* (Paris: Presses Universitaires de France, 1998), and Daniel Dobbels, Francis Marmande, and Michel Surya, eds., *Violence et politique (Colloque de Cerisy, 1994)*, *Lignes*, no. 25 (Paris: Hazan, 1995), as well as Françoise Héritier, ed., *De la violence* (Paris: Éditions Odile Jacob, 1996), and *De la violence II* (Paris: Éditions Odile Jacob, 1999). See also Françoise Proust, *De la résistance* (Paris: Les Éditions du Cerf, 1997); Etienne Balibar, "Violence: Idéalité et cruauté," in *La Crainte des masses: Politique et philosophie avant et après Marx* (Paris: Galilée, 1997); and Beatrice Hanssen, *Critique of Violence: Between Poststructuralism and Critical Theory* (London: Routledge, 2000).

ing out the philosophical or, more broadly, theoretical underpinnings of the pivotal concepts of culture, identity, difference, and integration.

Religion—in relation to mediatization and the new technological media—enters into this complex field of questions as the backdrop for structural transitions from the supposed secularism of the Enlightenment (characterized by ideals of autonomy and self-determination) to the "information age," with its resurgent politics of identity and renewed hopes for universalism, as well as cosmopolitanism. In the process, the functions ascribed to modern subjectivity, to the political, the economy, the nation-state, the public sphere, privacy, and so on have been radically transformed. As Derrida has suggested in "Faith and Knowledge," such shifts are not unrelated to the geopolitical return of the religious, which has wide-ranging institutional effects and requires careful analysis. To what extent does this development necessitate a new comprehension of the ways in which cultural identity and diversity are constructed and diffused?

Instead of raising this question in terms either empirical or abstract, this chapter turns to central features of Kant's philosophy of religion in relation to the state and one of its defining—and fundamentally philosophical—institutions, the university. Kant's *Religion within the Boundaries of Mere Reason, The Conflict of the Faculties,* and some shorter essays on history, all of which deal with these matters in both a subtle and, I will argue, aporetic way, cast a remarkable light on the debates concerning the emergence of the modern public sphere and its present-day transformation in the challenges that globalization, multiculturalism, and the information age pose to the institutional arrangements that make up liberal democratic societies, their conceptions of citizenship, justice, tolerance, hospitality, and so on.

The Institution of Philosophy

For decades, the malaise of the modern academy has been a truism. In his elliptical reading of Kant in "Mochlos," Jacques Derrida suggests that the term *malaise* registers a dominant philosophical interpretation of the idea of the university that has contributed to ubiquitous discontent with its task and skepticism about its future.[2] In characterizing this sentiment

2. The English version of "Mochlos; or, The Conflict of the Faculties" was first published as the introductory chapter of a collection of essays presented in 1987 at the University of Alabama symposium "Our Academic Contract: The Conflict of Faculties in America" (*Logomachia: The Conflict of the Faculties,* ed. Richard Rand [Lincoln: University of Nebraska Press, 1992]). The essay was originally delivered as a lecture at Columbia University in 1980 on the occasion of the

as a profound malaise, even *mal-être*,[3] Derrida stresses that more than an intrainstitutional, regional, intramural, curricular, disciplinary, or inter-disciplinary crisis is at stake. This malaise cannot be reduced to current debates about the transformation of the humanities, the transformation of philosophy, or literary and cultural studies and their respective canons. It is situated elsewhere, if anywhere, provided there is a single localizable place for this *mal-être*, this sickness unto being, to use an expression that parodies Kierkegaard's *The Sickness unto Death*. Derrida locates it in the paradoxes and aporias that haunt the principle of reason and its articulation into separate domains: the theoretical and the practical, the constative and the performative, the quest for truth and the need to act, the scholarly and the public. In short, the malaise is produced by the tense and contorted relation between Enlightenment and politics that has defined the academy at least since Kant.

The lectures, reports, notes, and interview that comprise *Du droit à la philosophie*, the French volume in which "Mochlos" was published, all center, not on yet another recollection of the task assumed under (or in) the name of deconstruction, but on how the critical engagement of deconstruction "obliges" us to rethink the institution, notably the "institution of philosophy," "to the point of asking oneself what founds or, rather, *engages* the value of critical interrogation" (*DP* 108). This work asks what, precisely, constitutes or determines our present responsibility *in* and *for*, as well as *before*, that relatively new—and typically Occidental—institution called the university. This interrogation parallels Derrida's earlier discussion of that other modern institution called "literature" and goes hand in hand with the modern idea and practices of a democracy that for all its accomplishments remains forever to come. In his analysis the modern inventions of the university and of literature (and everything for which they stand) are two sides of the same coin, together demarcating the space—indeed, the staging or the scene—of contemporary utterance (i.e., of constatives, evaluatives, performatives, etc.).

The most obvious English translation of *Du droit à la philosophie*, namely, "Of the Right to Philosophy," focuses attention on existing socio-political and juridical systems of legitimation, as well as on the impossi-

---

centenary of the founding of its graduate school. It was later published in French in *Du droit à la philosophie* (*DP* 397–438). This book documents Derrida's most explicitly institutional and political work to date.

3. *DP*, 403. Jacques Derrida, *Du droit à la philosophie du point de vue cosmopolitique* (Paris: Éditions Unesco, Verdier, 1997).

bility of reason's auto-justification in purely epistemological or, for that matter, axiological, ethico-political terms. Yet reference to the *quaestio facti* and *quaestio iuris* covers only part of the title's semantic domain; it could also mean "Of the Straight and Shortest, Detourless Path to Philosophy" (see *DP* 42–43), with the silent hint that one cannot go straight to philosophy, talk straight, or, for that matter, be straight in philosophy, qua institution (i.e., the university) or qua discipline (i.e., the faculty). The exclamation "From Law (as *droit*) to Philosophy!" would also capture some positions taken in the book.

Derrida discusses at length the aporias in Kant's attempt, in *The Conflict of the Faculties,* to establish an "equivalence," a balance, compromise, or concordance, between the principles of pure reason adopted by the "lower" faculty of philosophy and a certain interpretation of "right" (*droit*) in light of the existing political formation represented by the "higher" faculties of theology, medicine, and law. The deconstruction of this "equivalence" makes clear that the task of how to do things, how to make them "right" in (or with) the institution forms part of the horizon in which to place the book's more technical studies. *Du droit à la philosophie* studies "the conditions under which arguments, categories, and values impose and maintain a certain authority, even where traditional authority itself is meant to be subverted."[4] All these associations encapsulated in the title *Du droit à la philosophie* indicate different angles from which the volume's central theme—institutional obligation, the institution of obligation as well as the obligation to institute—is addressed.[5] Yet the different historical, juridical, and philosophical angles employed in these analyses

---

4. Samuel Weber, *Institution and Interpretation* (Minneapolis: University of Minnesota Press, 1987), 19.

5. In *Institution and Interpretation* Samuel Weber notes that, by addressing the problematic of recasting the transcendental in conjunction with a plausible "politics," Derrida makes good in his writings on the academy his earlier claim in *La Vérité en peinture* (*Truth in Painting*) that deconstruction distinguishes itself from a purely formal analytical concern or from criticism and critique, strictly speaking, by touching on "material" institutions, and not merely on discourses or significant representations. *Du droit à la philosophie* could be read as an attempt to concretize this earlier general statement by making a difference instead of merely describing processes of signification or resignification in terms of the quasi-transcendental conditions of their possibility. In so doing, this work not only offers a "deconstructive pragmatics of institutions" (*DP* 20), a "programmatology," but marks a singular step (yet another *pas d'écriture*) that exemplifies what an institutional engagement—here, at this very moment, where we happen to find ourselves—must or should entail. See also François Châtelet, Jacques Derrida, Jean-Pierre Faye, and Dominique Lecourt, eds., *Le Rapport bleu: Les Sources historiques et théoriques du Collège international de philosophie* (Paris: Presses Universitaires de France, 1998).

ultimately only serve to prepare another "thought" (*pensée*), which puts these discursive strategies into perspective and reveals their essential, intrinsic limitation: "What, in fact, limits the declared universalism of philosophy? How does one decide that a thought or statement is acceptable as "philosophical"? Even when the arsenal of these questions does not distinguish itself from *philosophy* itself [*la* philosophie elle-même](if such a thing exists and claims a unity), one can still study in determinate contexts the modalities of the determination of the 'philosophical,' the divisions that this determination implies, the modes of access reserved for the exercise of philosophy" (*DP* 10–11).

From what standpoint, then, does Derrida raise the question (if it is one, if it still has the form of a question, and of just one) of the principle of reason and its implications for the university said to be built upon it? To pose the *quaestio iuris* of the foundation of this philosophical institution (and the reference *quaestio iuris* might in the end very well count as the dominant semantic effect of the title *Du droit à la philosophie;* see *DP* 12) is not in itself a juridical question. Nor can this act of institution be exhaustively described in terms either of a theoretical procedure aimed at producing arguable constatives or of a performative speech act that corresponds to certain determinable or describable contextual requirements. This conceptual opposition between the constative and the performative all too often takes for granted a certain determination of the principle of reason that is precisely "in question." Instead, the interrogation at stake precedes or exceeds the logical space opened by the demarcations within which, according to a widely accepted view, beginning with Kant, the university is supposed to function. Only thus can it illuminate how the foundation of the university—the act of its institution as well as the ground on which it is based—is not in itself "already strictly" (*DP* 435) philosophical (which is not to say that it is simply anti- or even unphilosophical).

The formal structure of this argument is familiar enough. It was already deployed in Derrida's "Declarations of Independence," where he argues that the act of founding an institution or a nation-state cannot be comprehended in terms of the laws or even the norms and values that it calls into being. *Du droit à la philosophie* reiterates this argument by recalling that the foundational gesture also determines the argumentative structure of the first preface to the *Kritik der reinen Vernunft* (*Critique of Pure Reason*). There, philosophy is called the guardian of a tribunal of reason that is to be instituted in response to an appeal (*Aufforderung*) that has apparently already preceded it. The critique of pure reason and the architectonics whose foundations it lays down are merely the repetition, or reiteration, of an age-old response to what is "in truth" or apparently— that is to say, phenomenologically—an immemorial call. That call derives its force from this precedence or anteriority, from its being before the law of reason (see *DP* 92–93). The responsible gesture of interrogating that law, in turn, could therefore no longer follow the method of a transcendental questioning, whether Kantian or fundamental-ontological (to use Heidegger's terminology in *Being and Time*). This is true for different reasons, not least because the quasi-transcendental structure of "implication"—or *reverse implication*[6]—uncovered here does not "fold itself back" to any "thetic" or "hypothetic" form of presupposition (*DP* 34). The Kantian critique consists in an "interpretative" *act* that refounds or invents. In so doing, it testifies to a responsibility responsive to an injunction or even obligation that, Derrida suggests, does not yet (*pas encore*) let itself be determined by the Kantian critique of pure practical reason. If the words *primacy* or *priority* are appropriate here, any moral law could be said to be based on—derived from, later than—this responsiveness rather than the reverse (*DP* 471; see also 472). Or so it seems. Without forcing the analogy, Derrida claims that at this point one could draw a certain parallel between this responsiveness and Heidegger's notion of the call or appeal (*Ruf, Anspruch*) that, according to *Der Satz vom Grund* (*The Principle of Reason*)—and like the promise or *Zusage,* which Derrida discusses in *Of Spirit*—provokes, evokes, and engages language, with a gesture (in Derrida's words, *l'engage de langage*) that "is," as it were, quasi-tautological and quasi-heterological at once.

Du droit à la philosophie interrogates this engagement and the "thought" or "practice" it inspires, haunts, enforces, or enacts by carefully rereading the most explicit philosophical legitimations of the task of philosophical learning in general (for example, Descartes's *Discours de la méthode* [*Discourse on Method*]), especially in the university, as analyzed by Kant, Hegel, and Heidegger, among others. Only through that laborious detour does responsibility—the response to the call for which instituting, the institution, is the prime example here—come into view, provoking a reconsideration that is no longer simply Kantian, Hegelian, or Heideggerian, though Derrida does not situate himself beyond the conceptual coordinates set by these authors' discourses. His text both repeats and re-

6. For the introduction of this concept and its relation to notions such as "transcendental historicity" and "formal indication," see my *Philosophy and the Turn to Religion,* chap. 3.

institutionalizes their most fundamental — indeed founding — operations. This rearticulation outwits the formal — indeed, formally irrefutable — insight that "an event of foundation cannot be simply understood in terms of the logic of what it founds" and that, consequently, the "origin of the principle of reason, which is also implicated in the origin of the University, is not rational" (DP 435). Everything depends on how exactly one rearticulates each of these "statements," which in themselves seem mere "truisms." Moreover, aside from their precise, idiomatic wording and the singular contexts that interest me here, one would have to pay special attention to their nonepistemological, nonphenomenological, and even nonontological status. As will become clear from my discussion, such "statements" should not be mistaken for constative, empirical, or apodictic propositions, or for axioms in disguise. Being quasi-transcendental instances, they must be thought along completely different lines, by invoking other modalities and by turning to rhythms and tones, oscillations and ellipses that are, perhaps, no longer even comprehensible via categories such as "modality." Neither hypothesis nor postulate, neither descriptive nor performative, strictly speaking, they force us to summon other credentials that will lead us back to the central thesis of this book. Indeed, we will have to look into such notions as Kant's *Creditiv*, which announces and offers yet another example of modern philosophy's paradoxical turn to religion, preparing the way for other testimonial modes of speaking to and away from the other — in Kant's own understanding, the absolute witness — while running the risk of facing the other of this other (again, in all the ambiguity of the *à dieu*): the worst or, as Kant puts it in the first part of *Religion within the Boundaries of Mere Reason,* radical evil.

IN SUM, discussions concerning the *philosophical* idea of the university — especially in its complex dealings with religion in its historical or positive forms — have a much wider relevance than it would seem at first sight. They stand for more than the modern transposition and, as Kant would seem to suggest, radical reversal of the medieval dicta *philosophia ancilla theologiae* (philosophy as the handmaid of theology) or *fides quaerens intellectum* (faith seeking understanding). The conflict of the faculties is revealing in other ways, as well. As I will argue, it stands for nothing less than the tension and dissension that characterizes the whole of modern culture, in particular multicultural societies. Its implications, especially those of the conflict between the philosophical and the theological faculties, and everything this registers — that is to say, the differences, differentiation, and *différends* of culture in its generality or even universality — thus reach far beyond the historical context that originally inspired Kant's conception. Though premised on the political and cultural interests of the emerging nation-state, might the Kantian idea of the university be rearticulated in a manner that passes the test of present-day challenges of transnationalism, religious nationalisms, globalization, the new media, the redefinition of tolerance and hospitality, the new cosmopolitanism, the related multicultural citizenship and curriculum debates, and the like?

These matters are bound up with recent discussions concerning the status of the public sphere in modern political liberalism (drawing on the writings of Hannah Arendt, Jürgen Habermas, John Rawls, and others), Kant's writings on history, and the bicentennial of the 1795 essay "Zum ewigen Frieden: Eine philosophische Abhandlung" ("Toward Perpetual Peace: A Philosophical Project").[7] Derrida's recent rethinking of the concept and politics of hospitality, of friendship, and of a democracy, republicanism, and cosmopolitanism still and forever to come indirectly addresses these debates, not least because this rethinking rests on a detailed rereading of Kant's postcritical writings, dismissed by some for their lack of rigor and their impressionistic and derivative character. I will argue that Kant's dated and seemingly obsolete considerations of the state and the academy, censorship and tolerance — with their particular bearing on the question of religion, historical revelations, and "ethnicities" — contain *in nuce* a challenging theory of cultural identity, difference, and integration.

Modernity and the Question of Religious Tolerance: Rereading Kant's *Conflict of the Faculties*

Derrida regards Kant's *The Conflict of the Faculties* (1798) as a watershed. It inaugurates and sets the tone for incessant reflection on a development that, at the end of the eighteenth century, made philosophy one of the faculties of a "constructum" or "artefact" (*DP* 406) of the state: namely, the modern university. In the process, the philosopher was given a social role unknown to thinkers like Descartes, Spinoza, Leibniz, and Hume: that of a university professor, an official of the state. He was no longer, as Derrida points out with reference to the concluding pages of the *Critique of Pure Reason*, an artist or technician (*Künstler*), but a public servant and teacher (*öffentlicher Lehrer; DP* 361).

7. See James Bohman and Matthias Lutz-Bachmann, eds., *Perpetual Peace: Essays on Kant's Cosmopolitan Ideal* (Cambridge: MIT Press, 1997).

In the late middle ages and the early modern period (in the universities, for instance, of Bologna, Paris, Cambridge, and Oxford), the relation between scholars, students, and the state was differently determined.[8]
The academy was still largely held to be a clerical institution and was not
yet seen as a major instrument in an emerging "public sphere," revolving
around the institution(s) of the modern—absolutist and national—state.
It was also, to be sure, not yet seen as a potentially (and relatively) free
space from which the abuse of absolute power could be, if not directly opposed, then at least indirectly or obliquely criticized. But from Kant's day
on, the scholar has above all been a functionary—a teacher, or *Dozent* (*DP*
359)—in an official institution for higher education in which the "entire
content of learning" as well as "the thinkers devoted to it" are treated in a
factorylike manner (Kant writes, "gleichsam fabrikenmässig"): that is to
say, according to the principles of a rationally founded "division of labor."
Each field of study (or *Fach*) was to be entrusted with its own functionaries or "trusties" (*Depositeure*).[9] A decade later, this process of academic
rationalization came to a head in the founding of the University of Berlin. Derrida describes it as an institutionalization of the very principle of
reason. Kant's *The Conflict of the Faculties* comes to represent the earliest
and most rigorous document of this "fate" (or *fatum; DP* 407) of intellectual, moral, and political responsibility in the guise of modern academic
discipline. Even though the immediate responses to Kant's text were few
and often negative, it deeply influenced the document Wilhelm von Humboldt drafted in 1809–10 as model for the University of Berlin, which was
eventually to bear his name.[10] That university was, later in the century,

8. See John W. Baldwin and Richard A. Goldthwaite, eds., *Universities in Politics: Case
Studies from the Late Middle Ages and Early Modern Period* (Baltimore: Johns Hopkins University Press, 1972), and also Hastings Rashdall, *The Universities of Europe in the Middle Ages*,
3 vols., ed. F. M. Powicke and A. B. Emden (Oxford: Oxford University Press, 1997; orig. pub.
1895, 1936).

9. See *CF*, Introduction.

10. On the first responses to Kant's *Conflict*, see Reinhard Brandt, "Zum 'Streit der Fakultäten,'" in *Kant Forschungen*, vol. 1, *Neue Autographen und Dokumente zu Kants Leben, Schriften
und Vorlesungen*, ed. R. Brandt and Werner Stark (Hamburg: Felix Meiner, 1987), 38–39, 66–71.
On Kant and Humboldt, see Timothy Bahti, "Histories of the University: Kant and Humboldt,"
Modern Language Notes 103, no. 2 (1987): 437–60. As Bahti notes, Humboldt's sketch or *Entwurf* was not so much a critical examination of the "idea" of the university, of the conditions for
its possibility, its systematicity, and its limits: "His incompletely retained and posthumously
published memorandum, 'Über die innere and äussere Organisation der höheren wissenschaftlichen Anstalten in Berlin' ["On the Spirit and the Organizational Framework of Intellectual
Institutions in Berlin"], projects—tosses out—an idea for a university" (ibid., 444). See Humboldt, *Gesammelte Schriften* (Berlin, 1903), 10:250–60, trans. in *Minerva* 8, no. 2 (1970): 242–50.

the intellectual blueprint for some of America's leading universities (Johns Hopkins and Columbia among them).[11]

In its task of teaching the totality of what is presently known, the university, according to Kant, can only be based upon fundamental belief in the possibility of a purely theoretical language guided by truth alone. That does not mean that the Kantian university would not recognize the distinction between fundamental and applied sciences, to use a somewhat anachronistic vocabulary. In fact, as Derrida sets out to demonstrate in "Mochlos," Kant's whole exposition is organized around the possibility of the internal division between two scholarly approaches that presuppose the institution of a frontier or a line of demarcation between descriptive, or constative, and prescriptive, or performative, language. That is to say, Kant's concept stands and falls with the possibility of upholding the distinction between being able to think and say, on the one hand, and being able merely to do, act, or obey, on the other.

According to Derrida, this confident assumption concerning the structure of language, thought, and speech — concerning the possibility of classifying and mastering its different acts — brings to light some of the most serious difficulties in Kant's analysis. Conflicts between the faculties and their respective speech acts are not merely empirical or accidental but can be said to constitute the Kantian academy and its philosophy *from within*. They belong to the institutional translation of the very discipline (*Disziplin*), canon (*Kanon*), architectonics (*Architektonik*), and finally history of

---

11. Bahti summarizes this by now familiar story: "Whether it is . . . the founding of Johns Hopkins, or the establishment of Ph.D. degrees and graduate schools at Yale, Harvard, and Columbia, the story, from roughly 1850 to 1880, is one of 'universitarization' (as opposed to the former 'collegialization') of American higher education, and the Germanicizing of the latter. The point of reference, for college presidents, professors, and graduate students, was the University of Berlin" (Bahti, "Histories of the University," 439). See also J. Pelikan, *The Idea of the University: A Reexamination* (New Haven: Yale University Press, 1992), 61: "The first section [of *The Conflict of the Faculties*] concludes with the admonition: 'And so the theologians have the duty, and thereby also the authorization [*Befugnis*], to uphold faith in the Bible. But they must do so without impairing the freedom of the philosophers to subject [this faith] continually to the critique of reason.' The admonitions of Kant's essay of 1798 will be even more pertinent in 1998, and well beyond, not only to the philosophical faculty and the theological faculty but to all the faculties of the university, to all the sister sciences, and to the community between teacher and teacher." As we shall see, it can hardly be maintained that Kant advocates a noninterventionist policy. A more complicated interaction is at work here.

For another assessment of Kant's writings against the backdrop of current debates over the university, in particular of the role played there by the study of the "literary," see Peggy Kamuf, *The Division of Literature; or, The University in Deconstruction* (Chicago: University of Chicago Press, 1997), notably 14 ff., 44 ff., 134 ff.

the formal conditions of the complete system of reason itself.[12] Although architectonics dictates the reconstruction of an ideal edifice (*Gebäude*) based on the critique of pure theoretical and practical reason, its very idea casts light only through "breaches" in this structure, in the absence of any secure, originary, or ultimate foundation. For all its enlightening fervor, the Kantian academy thus seems to lack an intelligible topography. It resembles a tower of Babel, which reaches vainly toward the heavens at a price Kant seems unwilling to pay: the confusion of tongues (*Sprachverwirrung*) and the global dissemination (*Zerstreuung*) of all workers of reason. This, Derrida suggests, might well be its essential vulnerability—the cause of its and, perhaps, our malaise—as much as, paradoxically, its unexpected strength.

This is not to say that the internal organization of the university as it existed in Kant's times rested on mere "chance" (*Zufall*). Kant rightly assumes a more complicated dynamic between historical and political contingencies, on the one hand, and the necessary invocation of reasonable grounds, on the other. These reasonable grounds may seem to be reflected by the institution's internal and external systematicity, but they also betray a certain elective affinity—here, of course, in Max Weber's sense of the term—with the political imperatives, maxims, and hegemonies of the day:

> Since all artificial organizations [*alle künstliche Einrichtungen*] are based on an idea of reason (such as that of a government) which is to prove itself practical in an object of experience (such as the entire field of learning at the time), we can take it for granted that it was made according to some principle contained in reason, even if only obscurely, and some plan based on it—not by merely contingent collections and arbitrary combinations of cases that have occurred. . . . Without attributing premature wisdom and learning to the government, we can say that by its own felt need (to influence the people by certain teachings) it managed to arrive a priori at a principle which seems otherwise to be of empirical origin, so that the a priori principle happily coincides with the one now in use. (*CF* 250 / 282–83, trans. modified)

Kant's analysis of the modern university is therefore neither a justification of its status quo nor the projection of a future, utopian institution that finds no halt or hint in experience as we know it. Nor does Kant attempt

---

12. Derrida speaks of the *arkhitektōn* in Aristotle's *Metaphysics* in *DP* 493. See also Kant, *Critique of Pure Reason*, B 735–36, A 707–8; B 860 ff., A 832 ff.

to revive the ancient Platonic and Aristotelian academy, with its ideal of a peripatetic, detached, and merely disinterested dialectics or *theoria*. If in "Von einem neuerdings erhoben vornehmen Ton in der Philosophie" ("On a Newly Arisen Superior Tone in Philosophy") Aristotle is praised for having established a prosaic concept of "work" in philosophy that should be opposed to the Platonic epistolary flirtation with enthusiasm, we should not forget that, for Kant, this classical "work" lacks the rigor of the decidedly modern transcendental critique. Furthermore, Kant hardly ventures in the direction of a traditional conception of the encyclopedia of learning. Neither the Greek ἐγκύκλιος παιδεία[13] nor the heritage of the *artes liberales* seems to have left any significant trace in *The Conflict of the Faculties*.

Instead, Kant's idea of the university, not unlike the tradition of natural law, functions as a model sufficiently like existing institutions of government to be recognizable or acceptable without losing its normative force and orienting purpose. His approach to the university, to its idea as much as to its internal institutional and external political pragmatics, is that of the *critical,* that is to say, transcendental philosopher. As one critic notes, the question he asks takes a form central to the three critiques: "How is a university possible — and how are the relations between its faculties, and between it and the state *conditioned — given that such a thing exists?*"[14]

This inquiry into the necessary and general conditions of possibility for a given, particular object of experience is the dominant, the most explicit feature of Kant's text. Yet his critical analysis of the rationale of the university and the principles that could regulate or moderate the inescapable conflict of its faculties as well as their respective relations to the state is more complex and paradoxical than it would seem at first sight. It takes the form of an unstable and structurally provisional "negotiation" between the rational necessity of an idea and the historical vicissitudes of its equally necessary limitation in the world of appearances or, as Kant will say, of historical forms (here, of so-called positive religion).

Such a negotiation would be in keeping with a certain confessional structure in the framing of this text, itself written in response to the official admonition of the sovereign to refrain from further publications on the

---

13. See Hent de Vries, "'Philosophia ancilla theologiae' bij Philo van Alexandrië, Over de verhouding van de propaedeutische disciplines, de filosofie en de wijsheid in Philo's traktaat, *De congressu eruditionis gratia,*" *Stoicheia* 3 (1987): 27–52.

14. Bahti, "Histories of the University," 444.

subject of religion. Justifying himself in a letter to the king that he pub-
lishes with obvious pleasure in the preface to *The Conflict of the Faculties,*
Kant concludes by confessing that in sincerity to others and, finally, to
God (*à Dieu*), he has always attempted to avoid "error that corrupts the
soul" and "careless expression that might give offense": "For which reason now, in my seventy-first year, when I can hardly help thinking that I
may well have to answer for this very soon to a judge of the world [*einem
Weltrichter*] who scrutinizes men's hearts, I can frankly [*freimütig*] present
this account of my teachings, which you [the King] demand of me, as
composed with the utmost conscientiousness [*mit völliger Gewissenhaftig-
keit*]" (*CF* 242 / 272).

The first and longest of the three essays comprising *The Conflict of the
Faculties* concerns the conflict between the "higher" faculty of theology
and the "lower" faculty of philosophy. Two years earlier, the subject matter and argumentation of this first part had been substantially set forth
in Kant's preface to the first edition of *Religion within the Boundaries of
Mere Reason,* the text that would trigger his conflict with the censor. In
preparation for the concrete issues discussed throughout the first part of
the *Conflict,* Kant deals with the irresolvable struggle for hegemony that
de facto and a priori governs the complicated relationship between the
faculty of philosophy and the faculty of theology (and that resembles in
many respects the relationship between phenomenology and theology,
fundamental ontology and ontic, positive belief, hence the problematic of
formal indication and transcendental historicity that, in *Philosophy and
the Turn to Religion,* I analyzed in Heidegger's early writings). Unsurprisingly, the text that was intended to follow up on this earlier exchange was
once again denied the imprimatur, for at the invitation of Staeudlin, a professor of theology who sympathized with Kant's cause and who had asked
him to restate his arguments, Kant seemed merely to reiterate the basic
premises of his understanding of the relation between biblical and rational—that is, philosophical—theology that had provoked the anger of the
censors.[15]

15. The translator of *The Conflict of the Faculties,* Mary M. Gregor, reminds us in her introduction that Kant's letter to Staeudlin of December 4, 1794, makes clear that "*The Conflict of
the Faculties* was the original title for the treatise that eventually became Part I of the work by
that name" (*CF* xxi). This part was subsequently titled "The Conflict of the Philosophical Faculty with the Theology Faculty" and was followed by two other parts, each written, as Kant
acknowledges in his preface, "for different purposes and at different times," even though, in
retrospect, they would seem to be "of such a nature as to form a systematic unity and combine

The second part, "The Conflict of the Philosophy Faculty with the Faculty of Law," did not escape the censor, either. Under the title "Erneute Frage: Ob das menschliche Geschlecht im beständigen Fortschreiten zum Besseren sei" ("A Renewed Question: Is the Human Race Constantly Progressing toward the Better"), it raises in no uncertain terms the moral, rather than the directly political significance, not of the French Revolution itself, but of the enthusiastic feelings it aroused in the hearts of bystanders. I will claim that this illustrates the modalities for significant change — if not in the terms of the debate, then at least in the position of the antagonists involved—that Kant envisions for the particular institution of the university and, filtered through it, for the process of history in general, of which the history of religion seems the exemplary instance.

By contrast, the third part, "The Conflict of the Philosophy Faculty with the Faculty of Medicine," appeared without problems in 1798, in the *Journal of Practical Pharmacology and Surgery*. It assumed the form of an open letter to a professor of medicine named C. F. Hufeland, the author of *Macrobiotics* (1796), and it was entitled "Von der Macht des Gemüths durch den blossen Vorsatz seiner krankhaften Gefühle Meister zu sein" ("On the Power of the Mind to Master Its Morbid Feelings by Sheer Resolution"). Though it does not provide the reader with a systematically compelling argument or a historically interesting hypothesis, as do the first and second parts of the book, it nonetheless provides analytical tools for interpreting the earlier sections, as Derrida has demonstrated in *La Vérité en peinture* (*Truth in Painting*) and "Mochlos."

Because of its centrality to the focus of my study—philosophy's engagement with the theological, in particular, its turn to religion, also the face to face with a certain horror, violence, or radical evil this entails— I will concentrate on the first part of Kant's *The Conflict of the Faculties* and make only brief excursions into the second and the third where this is inevitable or useful. We should begin, however, by recalling the central argument Kant lays out in the general introduction to *The Conflict of the Faculties*, written when he decided to bring the three independent parts together in a single volume. Here, he deduces the order of faculties from

---

in one work [*drei in verschiedener Absicht, auch zu verschiedenen Zeiten . . . abgefasste, gleichwohl aber doch zur systematischen Einheit ihrer Verbindung in einem Werk geeignete Abhandlungen*]" (*CF* 243 / 274). In the book's preface, these other sections are said to deal with the conflict between the philosophical faculty and the faculty of law or jurisprudence and with the faculty of medicine respectively. But they seem to do so only indirectly or obliquely.

the hierarchy dictated by reason. This hierarchical order corresponds to the three forms of order the government must give if it wants to be effective in exerting control over the people:

> According to reason (that is, objectively), the following order exists among the incentives [*Triebfedern*] that the government can use to achieve its end [*Zweck*] (of influencing the people): first comes the *eternal* well-being of each, then his *civil* well-being as a member of society, and finally his *physical* well-being (a long life and health). By public teachings about the *first* of these, the government can exercise very great influence to uncover the inmost thoughts and guide the most secret intentions of its subjects. By teachings regarding the *second,* it helps to keep their external conduct under the reins of public laws, and by its teachings regarding the *third,* to make sure that it will have a strong and numerous people to serve its purposes. So the ranks customarily assigned to the higher faculties — *theology* first, *law* second, and *medicine* third — are in accordance with reason. (*CF* 250 / 283)

This tripartition is structurally analogous to the dialectic of pure reason in the *Critique of Pure Reason,* which, following the classical division of the *metaphysica specialis,* operates with "I," the "world," and "God," respectively. These particular or regional domains, studied by the "higher" faculties, form the anthropologically fixed interests that make up the horizon of the dialectics (and thus the antinomy and paralogism) of pure reason; the pursuit of limitless, if not boundless, knowledge of the phenomenal world (and hence of the ontological) in general forms the prerogative of the "lower" faculty of philosophy and hence, technically speaking, of the analytic of pure reason, the modest progress of understanding, and so on.[16] More generally speaking, the antagonism between the two classes of faculties recalls the antithetics of the first *Critique* (A 426, B 454 ff.) and its contrast between the genuine practical interests of reason (formulated in the "thesis") and the relentless pursuit of theoretical truth (formulated in the "antithesis").[17] Thus we are dealing with a *Streit* that is internal to the architectonics of the university and the idea of reason upon which it is supposedly built. Yet, although reason is thus in conflict with itself, this conflict can only be disentangled and resolved by the self-discipline — and self-legislation — of reason itself: reason's auto-infection through empiri-

16. See Brandt, "Zum 'Streit der Fakultäten,'" 36.
17. Ibid.

cal surreption (and "admixtures of paganism") and its auto-immunization form two sides of the same coin.

WHENEVER AND WHEREVER the rational (objective) order of principles is left to itself, unprotected by reason and its critique, it will, according to Kant, be overruled and reversed by the power of custom based on natural and subjective inclinations. The rational order needs to be sustained, therefore, by a criticism that disposes of a certain limited — yet justified — force. This is the definition of *censorship:* a mitigated and controlled force that enters into a complex alliance with *sheer* force, here with monarchical power or sovereignty — a power on which censorship ultimately relies even though monarchy is also, in turn, dependent on that censorship to enforce its rule successfully, legitimately, and, if not democratically, then at least nontyrannically, nondespotically, and with genuine cosmopolitan intention. The ground, or reason, for this complex alliance can be found, Kant thinks, in human finitude, human nature, and, in particular, the human propensity not to freely choose the good, a propensity Kant describes at some length in terms of a "radical evil [*das radikal Böse*]" in the first part of *Religion within the Boundaries of Mere Reason.* In *The Conflict of the Faculties,* Kant elaborates this tendency to reverse the normative — that is to say, reasonable and moral — order of things: "According to *natural instinct,* . . . men consider the physician most important, because he prolongs their *life.* Next to him comes the jurist, who promises to secure their contingent *possessions.* And only last (almost at the point of death) do they send for the clergyman, though it is their salvation [*Seligkeit*] that is in question; for even the clergyman, no matter how highly he commends the happiness of the world to come, actually perceives nothing of it and hopes fervently that the doctor can keep him in this vale of tears a while longer" (*CF* 250–51 / 283–84).

Not the superior faculties of theology, law, and medicine but the inferior faculty of philosophy is charged with guarding against the return of the *status naturalis* in the very heart of the *status civilis.* Kant leaves no doubt that the higher faculties can never be completely trusted in this regard. Whereas they are commonly held to represent the most direct interests of the government (which is why they are called "higher" or "superior"), they are in the end perhaps not its most trustworthy allies or instruments. What, then, is their particular task? Do they guarantee the distinction, made by Kant in "Was ist Aufklärung?" ("What Is Enlightenment?") between the "private" and "public" use of one's own reason and freedom? Is *The Conflict of the Faculties* merely a blueprint for the institutional translation and transposition of that general formal distinction? If not, what concretizations, amendments, refinements, or displacements occur in the later essay?

The faculties of theology, law, and medicine, which represent governmental interests, are granted the right to order and to act in the public sphere, not directly, but only by letting themselves be represented. The higher faculties educate and train members of the "intelligentsia" — Kant speaks of *Litteraten,* that is, *Studirte* or "university graduates," who should be distinguished from scholars proper (*eigentlichen Gelehrten*). The latter category consists of scholars who are either part of the university or independent (*zunftfrei*), members of academies or scientific societies. The *Litteraten,* by contrast, serve as instruments of the government, as "practitioners" (*Geschäftsleute*) or "technicians" (*Werkkundige*) of higher learning: clergymen (*Geistliche*), magistrates (*Justizbeamte*), and physicians (*Ärzte*). As Derrida rightly notes in "Mochlos," this class would nowadays comprise virtually everyone who operates in the service — inside, outside, or at the fringes — of the modern institution called the university. Translated into the vocabulary of our time, he observes, this means that they represent "every responsible figure in the public or private administration of the university, every 'decision-maker' in matters of budgets and the allocation or distribution of resources (bureaucrats in a ministry, 'trustees,' etc.), every administrator of publications and archivization, every editor, journalist, etc."[18] As if he were echoing discussions of the modeling, for good and for ill, of institutions of higher learning on the imperatives of "performativity" (as suggested by Jean-François Lyotard's *La Condition postmoderne* [*The Postmodern Condition*]) or anticipating the recent depiction of the university's task in terms of "excellence" (as discussed by Bill Readings in *The University in Ruins*), Derrida goes a step further to ask, "Is it not, nowadays, for reasons involving the structure of knowledge, especially impossible to distinguish between scholars and technicians of science, just as it is to trace, between knowledge and power, the limit within whose shelter Kant sought to preserve the university edifice?"[19]

18. Derrida, "Mochlos," in *Logomachia,* ed. Rand, 16.
19. Ibid. See Jean-François Lyotard, *La Condition postmoderne: Rapport sur le savoir* (Paris: Minuit, 1979) / *The Postmodern Condition,* trans. Geoffrey Bennington and Brian Massumi

Kant insists that, as a class, civil servants—unlike the scholars at the university (Kant does not say much about the *zunftfrei* scholars at large) — are "not free to make public use of their learning as they see fit, but are subject to the censorship of the faculties [*nicht frei sind, aus eigener Weisheit, sondern nur unter der Censur der Facultäten von der Gelehrsamkeit öffentlichen Gebrauch zu machen*]." They "share in the executive, though certainly not legislative, power [*ausübende Gewalt*] in their field," and in this limited function, they deal directly with the people, a group Kant does not consider "incompetent," as the translation has it, but, Derrida reminds us, quite literally unenlightened, blind: a potentially disruptive group of *Idioten* (*CF* 248 / 280).

Amassed at the bottom of the social and political hierarchy, the people form a diffuse group. As the second part of the *Conflict* will argue, they are the passive material of an enlightenment of the populace (*Volksaufklärung*) that can take place, Kant is quick to point out, not from the bottom up, but only *from the top down*. That is to say, it can take place if, and only if, those at the top—the government, the ministers, and ultimately the monarch—let themselves be called upon by the voice of reason and are able to read the signs of its gradual but constant progress throughout the history of humankind. Here the faculty of philosophy comes into play, as the representative of the interest in (and of) truth rather than in (or of) any other human interest (with respect to salvation, personal property, the body, and the like). The "lower" faculty is, paradoxically, capable of taking a stand as well as being the stand-in for interest in the unmistakable disinterestedness that marks not only morality but, above all, the desire for truth and that somehow, for reasons that are far from clear or clearly stated, founds, enables, or promotes all other interests, those of the "higher" faculties included:

> It is absolutely essential that the learned community at the university also contain a faculty that is independent of the government's command with regard to its teachings; one that, having no commands to give, is free to evaluate everything, and concerns itself only with the interest of the sciences, that is, with truth: one in which reason is authorized to speak out publicly [*wo die Vernunft öffentlich zu sprechen berechtigt sein muss*]. For without a faculty of

---

(Minneapolis: University of Minnesota Press, 1984); Bill Readings, *The University in Ruins* (Cambridge: Harvard University Press, 1996); and J. Hillis Miller, "Literary Study in the Transnational University," in J. Hillis Miller / Manuel Asensi, *Black Holes / J. Hillis Miller; or Boustrophedonic Reading* (Stanford: Stanford University Press, 1999).

this kind, the truth would not come to light (and this would be to the government's own detriment); but reason is by its nature free and admits of no command to hold something as true (no imperative "Believe!" but only a free "I believe" [*kein crede, sondern nur ein freies credo*]). (*CF* 249 / 282)

According to Kant, *within* the university the lower faculty of philosophy has the absolute freedom to pass judgment on *whatever is* and thus to decide what is true and false. Yet no one can avoid asking this question, however implicitly. No one could willingly, consciously, sincerely, or responsibly — that is to say, without falling prey to a performative contradiction, without denying in fact what one holds dear as a matter of principle or *in thesi* — freely choose a life in untruth or in heteronomy: "We may well comply with a practical teaching out of obedience, but we can never accept it as true simply because we are ordered to (*de par le Roi*). This is not only objectively impossible (a judgement that *ought not* to be made), but also subjectively quite impossible (a judgement that no one *can* make)" (*CF* 255 / 290). Yet, interestingly, this very question, the question of truth, should not be asked by just anyone. Moreover, it should never be raised as such, explicitly, directly, *outside* the walls of the university, that is to say, beyond the confines of a paradoxically, indeed aporetically, limited or restricted public sphere. Thus, while all inquiry and all instruction presupposes the question of truth, only the faculty of philosophy is entrusted with the task of asking this question freely and autonomously, relying on the principles of thought in general and hence of reason alone: "The philosophy faculty can, therefore, lay claim to any teaching, in order to test its truth. The government cannot forbid it to do this without acting against its own proper and essential purpose; and the higher faculties must put up with the objections and doubts it brings forward in public, though they may well find this irksome [*lästig*], since, were it not for such critics [*Kritiker*], they could rest undisturbed in possession of what they have once occupied, by whatever title, and rule over it despotically [*despotisch*]" (*CF* 256 / 291).[20]

20. Further spelling out the role of the "lower" faculty, Kant writes: "Its function in relation to the three higher faculties is to control [*kontrollieren*] them and, in this way, be useful to them, since *truth* (the essential and first condition of learning in general) is the main thing, whereas the *utility* [*Nützlichkeit*] the higher faculties promise the government is of secondary importance. We can also grant the theology faculty's proud claim that the philosophy faculty is its handmaid [*Magd*] (though the question remains, whether the servant *carries her lady's torch before or her train behind*), provided it is not driven away or silenced. For the very *modesty* [of

Two restrictions, then, are imposed on this seemingly open or open-ended debate. They concern its participants and its addressees. The only class to be excluded, aside from "the people"—that is to say, most people—is the officials, who have been trained by the higher faculties and who, in their function as clergymen, civil servants, and medical doctors, can be forbidden to "contradict in public the teachings that the government has entrusted to them to expound in fulfilling their respective offices and from venturing to play the philosopher's role" (CF 256 / 291–92). Although he does not say so explicitly, Kant seems to rely on a certain strategic use of the well-known—and somewhat counterintuitive—distinction introduced in "What Is Enlightenment?" between the "private" and the "public" use of one's freedom. For officials to present their "objections or doubts about ecclesiastical and civil laws" in public, in their roles as functionaries, would be to confuse their "private" with their genuinely "public" use of freedom. In so doing, they "would be inciting the people to rebel against the government" (CF 256 / 292):

> The faculties, on the other hand, put their objections only to one another, as scholars, and the people pay no attention to such matters in a practical way, even if they should hear of them; for agreeing that these subtleties [Vernünfteln] are not their affair, they feel obliged to be content with what the government officials, appointed for this purpose, announce [verkündigt] to them. But the result of this freedom, which the lower faculty must enjoy unimpaired, is that the higher faculties (themselves better instructed [besser belehrt]) will lead these officials more and more on the right track of [or toward] truth [in das Gleis der Wahrheit]. And the officials, for their own part, also more enlightened about their duty, will not be repelled at changing their exposition, since it involves nothing more than a clearer insight into means for achieving the same end. (CF 256 / 292, trans. modified)

Let us leave for a moment this apparent instrumentalization, not only of all teachings, but also, more indirectly, of truth. It is hard to deny that here truth, notwithstanding its acknowledged fundamental character, is rendered secondary as a medium, even a vehicle, for the pursuit of another, outspoken political interest. The search for truth for its own sake

---

its claim]—merely to be free, as it leaves others free, to discover the truth for the benefit of all the sciences and to set it before the higher faculties to use as they will—must commend it to the government as above suspicion [unverdächtig] and, indeed, indispensable [unentbehrlich]" (CF 255–56 / 290–91).

is tolerated or even furthered, but not for its own sake.[21] Or is it, perhaps, the other way around? Does Kant only pay lip service to the interests of the government, presenting the philosopher's interest in truth as the government's best ally, while preparing quite a surprise? Whose interests are subjected to whom here? It would be easy to provide arguments for each of the possible, though contradictory, answers to this question. Only the tone of the text—Kant's decidedly ironic tone—betrays who is truly in charge. Might we even claim that, in Kant's view, the ultimate end of the political is disinterestedness par excellence? Why, then, does Kant continue to insist on the curious hierarchy between higher and lower? He gives a simple answer by pointing to what human nature and common sense tend to value or to privilege. But in so doing he also introduces a massive metaphysical presupposition—in essence, an empirical argument based on a generalization—that is ultimately not warranted by the practical philosophical principles that follow from (or that centrally inform and guide) his own critique: "A faculty is considered higher only if its teachings—both as to their content and the way they are expounded to the public—interest the government itself, while the faculty whose function is only to look after the interests of science [alone] is called lower" (CF 248 / 280-81), and can therefore be left to itself if and only if it does not overstep its limits.[22]

21. See Brandt, "Zum 'Streit der Fakultäten,'" 36-37: "What interest should the government take in a faculty that is not committed to articulating the respective interests of people themselves? In consequence, should the university not be reduced to the three faculties of public use [die drei Nutz-Fakultäten]? // The point of view on which Kant insists lies in the urge to truth [Wahrheitsdrang] in the three higher faculties themselves: without a separate [an independent, gesonderte] thematization of truth, the higher faculties cannot pursue the scholarly competence [Gelehrsamkeit] that the government wishes—philosophy, therefore, is halfway 'indispensable' [mittelbar 'unentbehrlich'] in a university that the government has instituted [or founded, errichteten]. . . . Only with the pursuit [or search, Suche] for truth and knowledge, free from all governmental supervision [or control, Regierungsbevormundung], initiated and kept vigilant by philosophy [durch die Philosophie in Gang gesetzten und wachgehaltenen] can the interest of the government, which does not aim at truth but at use [Nutzen] be realized" (my translation and my italics).
    22. A little later in the text, Kant further explains this curious hierarchy: "The reason why this faculty, despite its great prerogative (freedom), is called the lower faculty lies in human nature; for a man who can give commands, even though he is someone else's humble servant [as are the higher faculties with respect to the government], is considered more distinguished than a free man who [like the philosopher] had no one under his command" (CF 249 / 282). The respect here, of course, is a matter of fact or a sociohistorical given, not a matter of reason. Or is it? At times it seems that, according to Kant, no one can reasonably want there to be no answer—however provisional—to the question of sovereignty in the body politic.

These limits cannot be easily defined. For the philosophical faculty mimics or reiterates in itself—in its internal division between a department of historical knowledge and a department of pure rational knowledge—the dynamics the *Conflict of the Faculties* locates between this lower faculty and the three higher faculties, as well as between the university (the community of scholars) as a whole and the government or the public realm at large. On each side of the line taken to separate the university from its outside, one redrawn within its own walls, a similar tension resurfaces. In the philosophy faculty, the historical and systematical departments are not only respected and distinguished analytically, but also, more interestingly, studied "in their mutual relation to each other [*in ihrer wechselseitigen Beziehung auf einander*]." Kant can, therefore, conclude that the philosophy faculty rightfully "extends to all parts of human knowledge (including, from a historical viewpoint, the teachings of the higher faculties), though there are some parts (namely, the distinctive teachings and precepts of the higher faculties) which it does not treat as its own content, but as objects it will examine and criticize for the benefit of the sciences" (*CF* 256 / 291, trans. modified).

What, then, does it mean for the lower faculty to "overstep its limit" and what, moreover, does it imply for reason that it guarantees its generality, or universality, by affirming its own limitation? This aporia will bring us to the heart of the matter. It involves the complicated relationship, according to Kant, between the government and its university, as well as between the faculties and the demands of reason, as represented by the faculty that—again, so long as it does not "overstep its limit"—is at the furthest remove from the state's authority, namely, the faculty of philosophy.

In principle, the government prescribes or sanctions teachings regardless of their truth. This does not mean that the government should have no pragmatic or instrumental interest in truth—in the truth, that is, that forms the condition of possibility for all learning and that, in the long run, makes citizens more dependable than otherwise. But it cannot itself teach or establish the truth of what it prescribes. Were it to masquerade as a scholarly instance, it would risk undermining the unconditioned, unquestioned respect that is its due.

In an interesting footnote, Kant cites the example of the relationship between the constitutional power of the British monarch, his ministers, and Parliament as a model for the instable balance of power between the state and the faculties:

It is a principle in the British Parliament that the monarch's speech from the throne is to be considered the work of his ministers (since the House must be entitled to judge, examine, and attack the content of the speech and it would be beneath the monarch's dignity to let himself be charged with error, ignorance, or untruth). And this principle is quite accurate and correct. It is in the same way that the choice of certain teachings which the government expressly sanctions . . . must remain subject to scholarly criticism; for this choice must not be ascribed to the monarch but to a state official whom he appoints to do it — an official who, it is supposed, could have misunderstood or misrepresented his ruler's will. (*CF* 248 n. / 281 n.; see also 306 and 306 n. / 363 and 363 n.)

Note that Kant, in this example, compares the place of the lower faculty to that of Parliament tout court (instead of confining its position to Parliament's left side, that of the opposition party), whereas the higher faculties are identified with the ministers. Here, the lower faculty, as the faculty of unrestricted — theoretical — critique, could be said to represent the university as a whole: its idea, its reason, and indeed the very reason for its existence.

Note also that for Kant the king's authority (more precisely, his "speech from the throne," ex cathedra) resembles the empty signifier that some political philosophers — notably Claude Lefort and Ernesto Laclau — reserve for the place left open after the demise of theocracy and absolute monarchy.[23] That the monarch must be obeyed is beyond question, but what he dictates through his ministers and his guardians is or, rather,

---

23. To Lefort I will return below, in Chapter 3. For the present context, see Ernesto Laclau, "Why do Empty Signifiers Matter to Politics?" in *Emancipation(s)* (London: Verso, 1996), 36–46; see also his contributions to Judith Butler, Ernesto Laclau, and Slavoj Žižek, *Contingency, Hegemony, Universality: Contemporary Dialogues on the Left* (London, New York: Verso, 2000).

The historical dimensions of the dual structure of sovereignty analyzed by Kant are discussed by Ernst H. Kantorowicz, *The King's Two Bodies: A Study in Mediaeval Political Theology,* with a new preface by William Chester Jordan (Princeton: Princeton University Press, 1957, 1997), 20–21. Not just the freedom and sovereignty of the king with respect to his "own" decisions is thus guaranteed, but also the sovereignty of the body politic with respect to his finitude and personal limitations. Kantorowicz illustrates this "dual majesty," that is to say, the distinction between the *maiestas realis* and the *maiestas personalis,* by citing the Declaration of the Lords and Commons of May 27, 1642: "It is acknowledged . . . that the King is the Fountain of Justice and Protection, but the Acts of Justice and Protection are not exercised in his own Person, nor depend upon his pleasure, but by his Courts and his Ministers who must do their duty therein, *though the King in his own person should forbid them:* and therefore if Judgment should be given by them against the King's Will and Personal command, *yet are they the King's Judgments*" (21).

seems to be up for discussion. This distinction between the word of the king and that of his delegates opens up the "space" or the "interval" for political maneuvering, deception, or even "bribery." This flip side of the constitutional system should not receive too much publicity if it is to be effective, nor should it remain completely in the dark, lest the people forget. Instead, it must retain a certain visibility "under the highly transparent veil of secrecy [*Es bleibt . . . unter dem sehr durchsichtigen Schleier des Geheimnisses*]" (*CF* 306 n. / 363 n.; cf. *RBR* 165 n. / 806 n.).

As always, the limit here is the extreme situation that threatens to return the moral and legal order of the *status civilis* to the *status naturalis*, to the struggle of all against all, and that thus forms the exception to the rule, since "war is a situation in which *all* political power must be at the disposal of the sovereign" (*CF* 306 n. / 363 n.). As so often, here everything depends on the question of who can decide whether, where, and when a war is necessary. For Kant as for Carl Schmitt, sovereignty has to do with the question of who decides on the state of exception, on the everpresent possibility—the *ultima ratio* and, thereby, actuality—of war. In answer to this question, the distinction between an absolute or a limited (*eingeschränkter*) monarch becomes possible. Only the latter consults the people or, rather, their representatives, their parliament. The former, by contrast, claims absolute freedom to declare the ultimate act, that is to say, the act that imperils the possibility, purity, and integrity of all other acts, of the acts of all others.

THE PHILOSOPHER and the king, far from being ideally—let alone empirically—identical, thus take up similarly extreme positions in the spectrum of institutional possibilities that defines the modern state. Whereas the absolute monarch would have the absolute freedom to act, the philosopher would have the absolute freedom to know and speak the truth. Like the former, the latter is merely an extreme—and virtual—possibility, never given or realized as such if the state and its university are to exist or to function at all. Between the virtual possibilities of these two extremes, absolutes, or ab-solutes—since they withdraw themselves, in the final analysis, from all conceptual and any sociopolitical determination—the relations between state, academy, and censorship are defined. The pure performative (the command, as Kant has it, to "discuss as much as you want, but obey!") and the pure constative (the constatation of truth and falsity strictly speaking) are polar opposites that mark the force field within which an academic arrangement for the present—and, indeed, the whole order of the political and, as we will see, the religious—has to be negotiated and renegotiated, for as long as history has not come to its end.

The philosopher's acknowledged freedom, then, as Derrida rightly notes, is in principle *absolute,* but only insofar as it is a freedom of "judgment" exercised strictly within the confines of the academic parliament and the limited "public sphere" of its learned community. What is more, this intramural or intrainstitutional freedom concerns a judgment that remains within the limits of the "theoretical," the "judicative," the "predicative," and the "constative" (*DP* 426, 427). The faculty of philosophy does not prescribe. If, hypothetically, it were asked to prescribe the teachings of the other faculties, it could only resort to a simple but effective negative wisdom and counsel the government to treat the search for truth in a manner analogous to the economic principle of laissez-faire: "Just don't interfere with the progress of understanding and science" (*CF* 249 n. / 282 n.).[24]

What, then, brings this unwanted interference about? Kant sketches a complicated dynamic in order to explain why the government is dragged along in a conflict that is detrimental to its own purposes. It is a dynamic of seduction, of yielding, in which the people approach the practitioner of the higher faculties as if he were a prophet, miracle worker, or magician (*Wahrsager, Wundermann, Zauberer*), endowed "with knowledge of supernatural things" (or, rather, someone who "knows his way around with things supernatural [*mit übernatürlichen Dingen Bescheid weiss*]"; *CF* 258 / 294). Practitioners are always tempted to yield to this demand and will do so, Kant warns, "unless the philosophy faculty is allowed to counteract them publicly [*ihnen öffentlich entgegen zu arbeiten*]—not in order to overthrow their teachings but only to deny the magic power that the public superstitiously attributes to these teachings . . .—as if, by passively surrendering themselves to such skillful guides [*kunstreiche Führer*], the people would be excused from any activity of their own [*Selbstthun*] and led, in ease and comfort, to achieve the ends they desire" (*CF* 258 / 294).

24. Kant introduces this principle of noninterference with the following anecdote (*CF* 249 n. / 282 n.): "A minister of the French government summoned a few of the most eminent merchants and asked for suggestions on how to stimulate trade—as if he would know how to choose the best of these. After one had suggested this and another that, an old merchant who had kept quiet so far said: 'Build good roads, mint sound money, give us laws for exchanging money readily, etc.; but as for the rest, leave us alone!' If the government were to consult the Philosophy Faculty about what teachings to prescribe for scholars in general, it would get a similar reply."

If the higher faculties let themselves be enticed by the people — which, Kant insists, is inevitable — then they do not respect their destination (*Bestimmung*). In so doing, they will find themselves in an irresolvable conflict [*ein wesentlicher, nie beizulegender gesetzwidriger Streit*] with the lower faculty of philosophy. Moreover, as the people stake their claim to the officials supervised by the higher faculties, "the government, which can work on the people only through these practitioners, will itself be *led* [verleitet] to obtrude on the faculties a theory that arises, not from the pure insight of their scholars, but from the calculations of the influence their practitioners can exert on the people by it. For the people naturally adhere most to doctrines which demand the least self-exertion and the least use of their own reason, and which can best accommodate their duties to their inclinations [*Neigungen*]" (*CF* 258 / 295).

Kant calls this antagonism illegal (*gesetzwidrig*) because it is effectively self-destructive and the sure sign of a performative contradiction. Whenever and wherever the government gives in to these tendencies, it "authorizes anarchy" (Kant speaks of an *autorisirte Gesetzlosigkeit*) and commits an offense against reason. There can be no doubt that the imminence of reason's virtual death in the face of an overzealous interventionist policy of the government motivated Kant to elaborate the premises for a *regulated* conflict within and outside the university.[25] Yet, as Derrida rightly points out, the illegal conflict is not what interests Kant most. Overdetermined by subjective sentiments and subjected to a fatal outcome, this *Streit* remains in essence "pre-rational, quasi-natural, extra-institutional" (*DP* 432). In the section that deals with the legal or lawful (*gesetzmässig*) conflict of the higher faculties with the lower faculty, Kant therefore concentrates on a conflict that, while as inevitable as its illegal counterpart, leaves room for only a provisional truce or a negotiation, since it can never end the conflict nor prevent it from reemerging. Nonetheless, certain formal procedural principles can be provided that should guide any evaluation of the different positions involved.

The conflict should not be settled, for example, by means of peaceful compromise (*friedliche Übereinkunft*) alone. Like a legal process or lawsuit (*Prozess*), the conflict cannot be resolved except in the form of a sentence (*Sentenz*), the decision of a judge (indeed, a tribunal of reason), that carries the "force of law" (*des rechtskräftigen Spruchs eines Richters [der*

25. See Brandt, "Zum 'Streit der Fakultäten,'" 38.

Vernunft]) (*CF* 260 / 297). Anything less would result in a feigned consensus, one that necessarily ignores, or denies, the grounds on which the dispute is based (*denn es könnte nur durch Unlauterkeit, Verheimlichung der Ursachen des Zwistes und Beredung geschehen, dass er beigelegt würde*). It is not in the spirit of the faculty of philosophy to yield to such persuasion. That faculty is committed to the open presentation (*Darstellung*), not of just any doctrine, symbol, canon, or code, but of their truth content alone.

Philosophy, then, ought to investigate and judge with "cold reason" (*mit kalter Vernunft*) and remain "unintimidated" (*ungeschreckt*) by the alleged "sacredness" (*Heiligkeit*) of all things that cross its path. It should demonstrate resolve in rearticulating "alleged feeling" with the help of unambiguous concepts (*CF* 260 / 297):

> Regardless of their content, any teachings that the government may be entitled to sanction for public exposition [*öffentlichen Vortrag*] by the higher faculties can be accepted and respected [*angenommen und verehrt*] only as statutes proceeding from [the government's] choice [*Willkür*] and as human wisdom, which is not infallible [*unfehlbar*]. But the government cannot be completely indifferent to the truth of these teachings, and in this respect they must remain subject to reason (whose interests the philosophy faculty has to safeguard [*besorgen*]). Now this is possible only if complete freedom to examine these teachings in public is permitted [*durch Verstattung völliger Freiheit einer öffentlichen Prüfung*]. (*CF* 259 / 296) [26]

26. Kant continues: "So, since arbitrary [*willkürliche*] propositions, though sanctioned by the supreme authority [*höchsten Orts sanktionirte*], may not always harmonize with the teachings reason maintains as necessary, there will be a conflict between the higher and lower faculties which is, first, *inevitable*, but second, *legal* as well; for the lower faculty has not only the title [*Befugnis*] but also the duty [*Pflicht*], if not to state the *whole* truth in public, at least to see to it that *everything* put forward in public as a principle is *true*" (*CF* 259 / 296). The formulation recalls a remarkable passage in a note concerning the censorship of *Religion within the Boundaries of Mere Reason* found after Kant's death: "Recantation and denial of one's inner convictions is base, but silence in a case like the present is a subject's duty. And if all that one says must be true, it does not follow that it is one's duty to tell publicly everything which is true" (cited in the Introduction to *Religion within the Boundaries of Mere Reason*, xxxv). This principle of public conduct should not be taken as a sign of pragmatism or precaution, nor should it be overlooked that the categorical imperative rules out the possibility of lying. If asked a specific question, one should answer dutifully and not conceal the truth, even if it incriminates oneself or endangers others. This obligation, however, should not be confused with the pathological inclination to volunteer information. One does not have to speak what has not been solicited. See also the passage from a letter to Moses Mendelssohn written in April 1766: "It is indeed true that I think many things with the clearest conviction and to my great satisfaction which I never have the courage to say; but I never say anything which I do not think" (ibid., xxxvi n.).

Why, then, must the conflict return, in its legal form or otherwise? Kant explains this with the following formal and formally irrefutable argument, implying that, because the political mediates freedom via negotiation and compromise, the freedom it allows is ipso facto limited and channeled. Anticipating Hegel's *Phänomenologie des Geistes* (*Phenomenology of Spirit*), Kant knows that absolute freedom and terror resemble one another in their structure (or lack thereof) to the point of interchangeability. Unlimited freedom is the limit or, more precisely, the limit concept of the political. As such, it cannot be experienced in and for itself without running the risk of destroying the very condition of possibility for (its) experience: it can only be thought, postulated, as a *negative idea* of reason:

> There must always be statutory precepts [*Vorschriften*] of the government regarding teachings set forth in the public, since unlimited freedom to proclaim any sort of opinion [*die unbeschränkte Freiheit, alle seine Meinungen ins Publicum zu schreien*] is bound to be dangerous both to the government and to the public itself. But because all the government's statutes proceed from men, or are at least sanctioned by them, there is always the danger that they may be erroneous or unsuitable [*bleiben jederzeit der Gefahr des Irrthums oder der Zweckwidrigkeit unterworfen*]; and this applies also to the statutes that the government's sanction supplies to the higher faculties. (*CF* 260 / 297) [27]

This, then, explains why the lower faculty must be prepared for the reemergence of conflict and "never lay aside its arms" (*ihre Rüstung*). It must expand the scope of its investigations to include authoritative writings (*Schrift*) or statutes (*Statute*) that function as norms (such as the Bible), the code of law (*Gesetzbuch*) that constitutes the canon (*Kanon*) (such as the law of the land), and the symbolical books with which the higher faculties seek to capture and to excerpt the essence of their teachings and whose only function as an organon is to make the former more accessible to a more general public (*CF* 251 / 284).

All these teachings are, in a sense, what Arthur Schopenhauer, in an appendix to *Die Welt als Wille und Vorstellung* (*The World as Will and Representation*), defines as "truth in the garments of a lie," [28] that is, as an allegory valid for didactic purposes alone. Not that their function would be

27. Cf. *RBR* 160–61, 160–61 n. / 798–99, 799 n.; and, on freedom and the state, ibid., 204–5 n. / 862–63 n.
28. See Hent de Vries, "Zum Begriff der Allegorie in Schopenhauers Religionsphilosophie," in *Schopenhauer, Nietzsche und die Kunst*, ed. W. Schirmacher, *Schopenhauer-Studien* 4 (Vienna: Passagen, 1991).

merely strategic or political (which they also are), but their sedimentation in canonical and statutory teachings permits them to be necessary
(yet ultimately insufficient) markers along the infinite approximation of
the "kingdom of ends." In this way, the higher teachings provide themselves with a *form* that can make them visible and subject to *control*. There
is an "added arbitrariness" (*RBR* 180–81 / 828) in religion, in the historical contingency of its status, whose acknowledged danger the government
must allow not full but limited play. The higher faculties are under the
supervision of the government insofar as their practical instruction can
increase, stabilize, or impair the government's influence over civil society
as a communal being or essence (the *Publicum als bürgerliches gemeines
Wesen*). By contrast, and to the extent that their teachings are put forward in the name of theory, the higher faculties address themselves to the
learned community (*eine andere Art von Publicum, nämlich . . . das eines
gelehrten gemeinen Wesens, welches sich mit Wissenschaften beschäftigt; CF*
260 / 298). Here, there is no need for the government to intervene, since
the people "are resigned to understanding nothing about this" (*CF* 260 /
298).

Paradoxically, then, the interest and the role of the government in the
conflict of the faculties is to make sure that it has nothing to do with the
conflict and that it does not have to interfere. Its function is to ensure
that the conflict remains a *scholarly* debate, legal insofar as it does not
transgress the confines of the learned, academic community. Within these
limits, the faculty of philosophy has the right and the duty to evaluate
and, when necessary, to criticize, if not censure, the propositions set forth
by the higher faculties. In so doing—in doing without doing—it keeps
the government awake and vigilant: "Without its rigorous examinations
and objections, the government would not be adequately informed about
what could be to its own advantage or detriment" (*CF* 261 / 299). On the
other hand, Kant writes:

> If the businessmen of the faculties (in their role as practitioners [*Praktiker*])
> bring the conflict before the civil community (publicly—from the pulpits, for
> example), *as they are prone to do,* they drag it illegitimately before the judg-
> ment seat [*Richterstuhl*] of the people (who are not competent to judge in
> scholarly matters), and it ceases to be a scholarly debate. And then begins the
> state of illegal conflict mentioned above, in which doctrines in keeping with
> the people's inclinations are set forth, the seeds of insurrection and factions
> are sown, and the government is thereby endangered. These self-appointed

tribunes of the people, in doing this, renounce the learned professions, encroach on the rights of the civil constitution (stir up political struggles), and really deserve to be called neologists. (*CF* 261 n. / 298 n., emphasis mine)

Transforming the conflict into an illegal one, "handing over scholarly questions to the decision of the people," giving in to their desire to justify or remedy their transgression, as the higher faculties (or at least their pupils — practitioners, the clergy, civil servants, and medical doctors) will always be tempted to do, if only to protect or strengthen their position, jeopardizes not only the status quo in the state but the state's very existence and raison d'être. It imposes "a completely different form of government [*Regierungsform*]" or provokes a situation in which there is "a lack of any government [*eine Regierungslosigkeit (Anarchie)*]" (*CF* 261 n. / 298 n.). If the higher faculties or their practitioners were, on their own initiative, to start making changes in the decrees they are charged to expound, then the government must act upon its vigilance (*Aufsicht*) and censor them as irresponsible innovators (*Neuerer*). It should "not, however, pass judgment on them directly, but only in accordance with the most loyal verdict drawn from the higher faculties [*nach dem von der obern Fakultät eingezogenen allerunterthänigsten Gutachten*], since it is only *through the faculty* that the government can direct these businessmen to expound certain teachings" (*CF* 261 / 299).

Kant maintains that the conflict, always possible (if not perpetual or perpetually open), can co-exist (*zusammen bestehen*) with a consensus (*Eintracht*) between the learned and the civil communities in matters concerning "maxims" (*Maximen*) that, if followed, must "bring about a constant progress [*beständigen Fortschritt*] of both ranks [or, rather, classes, *Classen*] of the faculties toward greater perfection [*Vollkommenheit*]" (*CF* 261 / 299). Indirectly and gradually, this will also affect the civil community, the people. If such progress were to take place, it would, Kant predicts, eventually also "prepare the way for the government to remove all restrictions that its choice [*Willkür*] has put on freedom of public judgment" (*CF* 261 / 299). One day or another, it might very well reach the point where the last [*die Letzten*] would be the first [*die Ersten*], and the lower faculty would discover itself to be the higher, insofar as its relation to the government is concerned: "not, indeed, in [executive] authority [*nicht in der Machthabung*], but in counseling [*Berathung*] the authority [*des Machthabenden*] (the government [*Regierung*]). For the government may find the freedom of the philosophy faculty, and the increased insight gained from this freedom, a better means for achieving its ends [*Zwecke*] than its own absolute authority" (*CF* 261 / 299–300). While the lower faculty is, with regard to the higher faculties and the state that controls them, "powerless . . . except for its power to judge the truth," [29] from the ideal — transcendental — vantage point it can, paradoxically, orient itself toward an ulterior and, perhaps, ultimate reversal in the academic hierarchy. In a handwritten, unpublished note on one of the manuscripts of the introduction to the *Conflict*, Kant formulates this hope: "The lower faculty must one day become the highest, i.e., subject everything to the legislation of reason [*Die Unterste Facultät muss einmal die Oberste werden, d.i. alles der Gesetzgebung der Vernunft unterwerfen*]." [30]

Kant leaves no doubt that this reversal is not to be confused with a revolution in a strictly political sense. Nonetheless, the revolution of the scholarly way of thinking and judging — the *Revolution der Denkungsart* — would affect and displace relations of power in and of the university and the state. As one critic noted, this prospect is couched in formulations "replete with hedges and qualifications, ironic asides, and flirtations with despair." [31] Will it happen, then? And will it, if and when it happens, depend "entirely on chance"? What are we to make of the fact that Kant, generally careful in his choice of words, cites an explicitly messianic-apocalyptic passage — the expectation "and the last will be first" — in order to evoke this hope? Elsewhere, he takes great pains to avoid the connotations and peculiar tone this passage evokes in its original New Testament context. What is the relation between this "evangelical" rather than "Mosaic-messianic," as Kant would say,[32] anticipation of a reversal of academic hierarchy and Kant's equally intriguing answer to the question, raised in the second part of his book, of whether the human race is constantly progressing toward the better? Does Kant not in both cases rely on a hidden teleology or potentiality, signaled by certain events or occurrences in the realm of experience? If so, what is the difference between the scriptural revelation of these events and occurrences, studied by biblical theologians, and the historical revelation, to which, Kant believes and argues, the French Revolution testifies? Finally, how does this revolution affect Kant's concept of reason? To answer these questions, we must turn to the next section of the *Conflict*.

29. Timothy Bahti, "The Injured University," in *Logomachia*, ed. Rand, 59.
30. Cited in Brandt, "Zum 'Streit der Fakultäten,'" 31.
31. Bahti, "Histories of the University," 437.
32. See *CF* 282 / 331 and 288 n. / 340 n.: "not Messianic."

The Triple Sign: *Signum rememorativum, demonstrativum, prognostikon*

The second part of *The Conflict of the Faculties,* "A Renewed Question: Is the Human Race Constantly Progressing toward the Better?," [33] has drawn far more attention in recent debates than either the first or the third. Some of its most striking passages have been appropriated by Hannah Arendt in her posthumous *Lectures on Kant's Political Philosophy,* by Jean-François Lyotard in his *L'Enthousiasme (Enthusiasm),* the "Notices" on Kant in *Le Différend (The Differend),* and in *Leçons sur l'analytique du sublime (Lessons on the Analytic of the Sublime),* [34] and by Michel Foucault in his later work, notably three lectures and essays devoted to Kant's "What Is Enlightenment?"

For Foucault, these texts are less preoccupied with the question of history's origin, its internal finality, or its immanent teleology, end, or fulfillment, than with "the question of the present as the philosophical event to which the philosopher who speaks of it belongs." In discussing the progress of the human race, Kant asks himself, according to Foucault: "What is happening today? What is happening now? And what is this 'now' within which all of us find ourselves; and who defines the moment at which I am writing?" [35]

33. A "renewed question [*erneute Frage*]" since it had already been addressed in the third section of "Über den Gemeinspruch: Das mag in der Theorie richtig sein, taugt aber nicht für die Praxis" ("On the Common Saying: 'This May Be True in Theory, but It Does Not Apply in Practice'"), which appeared in the *Berlinische Monatschrift* in 1793. Brandt ("Zum 'Streit der Fakultäten,'" 46–47) and Klaus Reich in his edition of *Der Streit der Fakultäten* (Hamburg: Meiner, 1975) draw attention to the fact that Kant's essay is also a rebuttal of the critical response to "Zum ewigen Frieden" that Friedrich Schlegel had published in 1796. See Friedrich Schlegel, "Versuch über den Begriff des Republikanismus: Veranlasst durch die Kantische Schrift zum ewigen Frieden," in *Kritische und Theoretische Schriften,* ed. Andreas Huyssen (Stuttgart: Reclam, 1978). Schlegel's critique consisted in accusing Kant of effectively demonstrating that the idea of an eternal peace is not a merely empty notion, devoid of all politico-historical corroboration. Kant's riposte would seem to make good on this apparent lacuna.

34. On *The Differend,* see my "On Obligation: Lyotard and Levinas," *Graduate Faculty Philosophy Journal* 20.2/21.1 (1998): 83–112.

35. Michel Foucault, "Qu'est-ce que les Lumières?," in *Dits et écrits: 1954–1988,* vol. 4, *1980–1988,* ed. Daniel Defert and François Ewald (Paris: Gallimard, 1994), 679 / trans. A. Sheridan as "The Art of Telling the Truth," in *Critique and Power: Recasting the Foucault/Habermas Debate,* ed. Michael Kelly (Cambridge: MIT Press, 1994), 139. See also Foucault, "Qu'est-ce que les Lumières?," in *Dits et écrits,* 4:562–78 / "What Is Enlightenment?," in *The Foucault Reader,* ed. Paul Rabinow (New York: Pantheon, 1984), esp. pp. 33–34, 38 ff. These two lectures further elaborate a motif first addressed in a conference given at the Sorbonne in May 1978 and first published as "Qu'est-ce que la critique / Critique et *Aufklärung,*" *Bulletin de la Société française*

Kant's "What Is Enlightenment?" and the second part of *The Conflict of the Faculties* thematize — "for the first time," Foucault suggests — phi-

---

de Philosophie 84 (1990): 35–63 / "What Is Critique?," trans. Kevin Paul Geiman in *What Is Enlightenment?: Eighteenth-Century Answers and Twentieth-Century Questions*, ed. James Schmidt (Berkeley: University of California Press, 1996). James Miller, in *The Passion of Michel Foucault* (New York: Simon & Schuster, 1993), argues that these expositions on Kant only seem to inaugurate a turn in Foucault's thought, leading up to the three volumes of *Histoire de la sexualité* (*The History of Sexuality*) and focusing centrally on the question of the present and the ethos of critique. This preoccupation already informs Foucault's earliest work, culminating in the publication of *Les Mots et les choses* (*The Order of Things*). The influence of Kant on Foucault's thought predates that of Nietzsche and Blanchot, as is clear from his extensive work on Kant's *Anthropologie in pragmatischer Hinsicht* (*Anthropology from a Pragmatic Point of View*). Miller suggests that Foucault's interest in this particular text may have been provoked by a remark, made in passing, in Sartre's *Critique de la raison dialectique* (*Critique of Dialectical Reason*).

Only Foucault's "Notice historique" was, in effect, published, in I. Kant, *Anthropologie du point de vue pragmatique*, trans. M. Foucault (Paris: Vrin, 1964), and then again in *Dits et écrits*, vol. 1, ed. Daniel Defert and François Ewald (Paris: Gallimard, 1994). See also Mariapaola Fimani, *Foucault et Kant: Critique Clinique Éthique*, trans. Nadine Le Lirzin (Paris: L'Harmattan, 1998). In his introduction and notes to the translation of Kant's text, Foucault explores the specific temporality of the categorical and the a priori. This interpretation, which draws in part on his reading of Heidegger's *Kant und das Problem der Metaphysik* (*Kant and the Problem of Metaphysics*) forms the background for the discussion of the relationship between the empirical and the transcendental in the penultimate chapter of *The Order of Things*, where Foucault insists on the surreptitious confusion between the transcendental and the empirical, which Kant is at great pains to distinguish. In his earliest notes Foucault suggests, according to Miller, that Kant's *Anthropology* lays bare the "truly temporal dimension" of the a priori concepts analyzed in Kant's three *Critiques*: the *idées reçues* inventoried in the *Anthropology* repeat "in the same order and in the same language the a priori of the understanding and the imperatives of morality"; what is "given" in such precepts "mimics" the reasoning in the *Critiques*, and "seems to be able to function as an *a priori*" (*The Passion of Michel Foucault*, 140).

Here Foucault is at once close to and at a certain distance from Derrida's interpretation of the aporias of Kant's transcendental idealism, the parasitism of the transcendental upon the empirical and vice versa, the paradoxical architectural primacy of the *parergon*, etc. Being yet another "critique of impure reason," Derrida's argument with Kant finds its preparation in the early studies devoted to Husserl, to the logics of supplementarity, of transcendental historicity, and the like. Derrida remains much closer to the phenomenological project of the later Husserl and of Heidegger than does Foucault, whose explicit target, in *The Order of Things*, is the phenomenological solution to the question of the co-implication — and mutual exclusion — of the transcendental and the empirical. To be sure, Foucault directs his critique against Sartre and Merleau-Ponty, whose writings hardly form the main source of inspiration for Derrida. The unmistakable difference in point of departure and orientation between Foucault and Derrida is articulated most dramatically in their exchange concerning *Folie et déraison: Histoire de la folie à l'âge classique* (*Madness and Civilization: A History of Insanity in the Age of Reason*). I will briefly return to this debate at the end of Chapter 3. In interviews, Miller notes, Foucault presented *The Order of Things* as "a sequel and companion to *Madness and Civilization*, as a 'history of resemblance, sameness, and identity' that supplements the earlier work's history of difference, otherness, and dissociation. His new book thus offers a kind of post-Kantian 'Critique of Impure Reason' that (like Kant's *Anthropology*) deals 'with practices, institutions, and

losophy's own "discursive contemporaneity." It interrogates this contemporaneity as "an event whose meaning, value, and philosophical particularity it is the task of philosophy to ferret out and in which it has to find both its *raison d'être* and the grounds for what it says. Thus, when the philosopher asks how he belongs to this present, it is a quite different question from that of how one belongs to a particular doctrine or tradition. It is no longer simply the question of how one belongs to a human community in general, but rather that of how one belongs to a certain 'us,' an us that concerns a cultural totality characteristic of one's own time." [36] This interest, which takes the form of the questions "What is Enlightenment?" and "What is the Revolution?" in Kant and so many who followed in his footsteps, might well define philosophy in its modern moment and momentum, its paradoxical reflexivity, as the "discourse of modernity on modernity." [37] What is more, this interest in the present, in presentness, underscores anew that

> the *Aufklärung*, both as a singular event inaugurating European modernity and as permanent process manifested in the history of reason, in the development and establishment of forms of rationality and technology, autonomy and authority, is for us not just an episode in the history of ideas. It is a philosophical question, inscribed since the eighteenth century in our thoughts. Let us leave in their piety those who want to keep the *Aufklärung* living and intact. Such piety is of course the most touching of treasons. What we need to preserve is not what is left of the *Aufklärung*, in terms of fragments; it is the very question of that event and its meaning (the question of the historicity of thinking about the universal) that must now be kept present in our minds as what must be thought.[38]

---

theories on the same plane,' by looking for the 'isomorphisms,' or similarities in form, that organize (into a kind of historical *a priori*) the field of experience in any epoch" (*The Passion of Michel Foucault*, 149–50).

On the notion of the "today," see Derrida's preface to *The Other Heading*, entitled "Today," which introduces the republication of two newspaper articles, the second of which, "Call It a Day for Democracy" ("La Démocratie ajournée"), had appeared in the first of the supplements *Le Monde* published on the occasion of the bicentennial of the French Revolution (*Le Monde de la Révolution française*, January 1989). In this text Derrida returns to Kant and the question of publicity and censorship (Jacques Derrida, *L'Autre Cap* [Paris: Minuit, 1991], 113, 115–16 / *The Other Heading: Reflections on Today's Europe*, trans. Pascale-Anne Brault and Michael B. Naas [Bloomington: Indiana University Press, 1992], 99–100, 104–5).

36. Foucault, "The Art of Telling the Truth," 140–41 / 80.

37. Ibid., 141 / 681.

38. Ibid., 147 / 686–87.

According to this reading, Kant does not present the borderlines demarcating a specific historical period, but "the outline of what one might call the attitude of modernity."[39] This modernity can no longer be determined in terms of the *querelles des anciens et des modernes,* that is to say, in terms of a "comparative valuation" and a "longitudinal relation."[40] Rather, it must be understood in terms of a different mode, or modality, one that Foucault describes as a "'sagital' relation [from the Latin *sagittarius,* "archer," from *sagitta,* "arrow"] to one's own present."[41] As such it touches upon and is touched, as it were, tangentially or in passing by the historical and political experience of the French Revolution and, both Foucault and Lyotard imply, the revolutionary (and counterrevolutionary) events that have followed and will continue to follow in its wake. But the sagital relation is also a highly paradoxical, more precisely, an aporetic one, a relation without relation, as Derrida, following Blanchot and Levinas, would say, at least as elusive — some would say, ab-solute — as the rapport implied in or engaged by the transcendental historicity of conceptual and all other idealizations (according to the Husserl of the *Krisis der europäischen Wissenschaften und die transzendentale Phänomenologie* [*The Crisis of European Sciences and Transcendental Phenomenology*]) or the formal indication of fundamental ontological categories and existentials (according to the Heidegger of *Being and Time* and the early lecture courses). As a consequence, it forces us to rethink the very nature — the intelligibility and practical orientation — of the kingdom of ends.

In his philosophy of law, Kant describes the "endstate" as the standard in terms of which progress toward the better ought be judged. He portrays it as the civil and, at least in spirit (*der Idee nach*), republican constitution, which suits the people in their autonomy, abolishes despotism in the national state, and rests on principles that help to prevent the state from risking an offensive war (*Angriffskrieg*). Indeed, only by deterring this "source of all evil and corruption of morals" — in Kant's eyes the *summum malum* — can the human race be guaranteed, albeit "negatively," its "progress toward the better," in spite of all its infirmity [*Gebrechlichkeit*] and to the extent that it is "at least . . . undisturbed in its advance" (*CF* 304 / 362 and 301–3 / 358–59).

---

39. Foucault, "What Is Enlightenment?," 38 / 568.
40. Foucault, "The Art of Telling the Truth," 141 / 681. See also Hans Robert Jauss, "Literarische Tradition und gegenwärtiges Bewusstsein der Modernität," in *Literaturgeschichte als Provokation* (Frankfurt a. M.: Suhrkamp, 1970).
41. Foucault, "The Art of Telling the Truth," 141 / 681.

The Conflict of the Faculties poses a supplementary question by asking for a historical sign, for a supplement that in its very fragility and elusiveness *positively* signals, reflects, supports, or conditions and makes possible the critique of pure theoretical and practical reason and the latter's translation into principles of law and jurisprudence. In this attempt to read the signs of the times, Kant exposes the limits and paradoxes, even aporias, of his own critique by providing us with what Jürgen Habermas, reading Foucault reading Kant, calls an "instructive contradiction." Habermas points out that Kant explains "revolutionary enthusiasm as a historical sign that allowed an intelligible disposition in the human race to appear within the phenomenal world." [42]

In order to ascertain whether or not the human race continually progresses toward the better, one would not only have to determine the intelligible and free cause that makes this moral progress thinkable and possible in the first place, but also have to ask whether, where, and when such a possibility is in fact signaled, if not directly in or through experience, then at least with experience. [43] Since, however, we do not possess a God's eye point of view, we must content ourselves with a less spectacular vision. We require a sign or, more precisely, a sign of history (*Geschichtszeichen*) that "reflects" or "mirrors" *at once* the present, the past, and the future, with-

---

42. Jürgen Habermas, "Taking Aim at the Heart of the Present: On Foucault's Lecture on Kant's 'What Is Enlightenment?'" in *Critique and Power*, ed. Michael Kelly (Cambridge: MIT Press, 1994), 154, cf. 150–51. See also Jürgen Habermas, "Kants Idee des ewigen Friedens — aus dem historischen Abstand von 200 Jahren," in *Die Einbeziehung des Anderen: Studien zur politischen Theorie* (Frankfurt a. M.: Suhrkamp, 1996), and Reinhard Merkel and Roland Wittmann, eds., *"Zum ewigen Frieden": Grundlagen, Aktualität und Aussichten einer Idee von Immanuel Kant* (Frankfurt a. M.: Suhrkamp, 1996).

43. Everything here depends on the vantage point assumed by the critique: the difficulty consists in that the task of determining "progress" cannot be "resolved directly through experience" (*CF* 300 / 355). Though any understanding of the laws of nature presupposes that reason performs the Copernican turn, we are not so fortunate when we attempt to observe or predict the pattern of moral improvement or the lack thereof. "If the course of human affairs seems so senseless to us, perhaps it lies in a poor choice of position from which we regard it. Viewed from the earth, the planets sometimes move backwards, and sometimes not at all. But if the standpoint selected is the sun, an act which only reason can perform, according to the Copernican hypothesis they move constantly in their regular course" (*CF* 300 / 355). Without this change of perspective, one is forced to introduce an endless series of cycles and epicycles *ad absurdum* (*bis zur Ungereimtheit*). It is our misfortune (*Unglück*), Kant continues, that "we are not capable of placing ourselves in this [Copernican] position when it is a question of free actions. For that would be the standpoint of Providence [*Vorsehung*] which lies beyond all human wisdom, and which likewise extends to the free actions of man; these actions, of course, man can see, but not foresee with certitude (for the divine eye there is no distinction in this matter)" (*CF* 300–1 / 355–56, trans. modified).

out therefore constituting a living present, a retention and a protention of sorts. This sign is not simply the *kairos,* or *Augenblick,* that a long tradition, stretching from St. Paul through Luther and Kierkegaard all the way down to Heidegger, regards as the epitome of a temporality that is, if not fulfilled, then at least decisive and momentous. For the sign is not necessarily an instant *in* or *of* time. It "is" that which, while "being" *timely,* is at the same time time's other and thereby—if one pushes this interpretation beyond the letter and the spirit of Kant's text—not so much another time (that of, say, eternity or the *nunc stans*), but the very same time otherwise. It is the time of the other, the *contretemps, Unzeit,* all figures of an immediacy—or "im-mediacy," as Nancy writes—prominent in the writings of Levinas, Celan, and Derrida. (This peculiar temporality will form the subject of a separate study, entitled *Instances,* and I will not further discuss it here.) Neither past nor future, this signaled—indeed, attested—time, as discussed in the second essay of the *Conflict of the Faculties,* sustains a singular and singularizing relation to the present.[44]

Kant speaks of this sign as being marked by a threefold dimension that recalls and, it would seem, anticipates and prefigures the three co-originary structures of ecstatic temporality that Heidegger elaborates in the second division of *Being and Time.* Not unlike originary temporality (i.e., temporality properly speaking and assumed) or New Testament *kairos* and *parousia* (after which Heidegger models his conception, up to a certain point, as I have argued in *Philosophy and the Turn to Religion*), the Kantian motif of the "sign of history" is, at one and the same time, a *signum rememorativum,* a *signum demonstrativum,* and a *signum prognostikon.* In Foucault's words, this means "a sign that shows that it has always been like that (the rememorative sign), a sign that shows that things are also taking place now (the demonstrative), and a sign that shows that it will always happen like that (the prognostic sign)."[45]

What, then, is the nature of this "always" that signals itself in the present, as the present, enlightening the present, in the presence of the Revolution? And how should we distinguish its singular, yet highly complex and convoluted temporality from the *Gewesenheit,* the *Anwesenheit,* and the *Zukünftigkeit* that Heidegger seeks to differentiate with far more

---

44. See Kant's exclamation in *RBR,* 159 / 797: "If one now asks, what period in the entire known history up to now is the best? I have no scruple in answering, *the present.*" This preoccupation also informs Kant's assessment of the apocalypse (*RBR,* 161–63, 162–63 n. / 801–3, 803–4 n.).

45. Foucault, "The Art of Telling the Truth," 143 / 683.

analytical rigor than Kant does here? How, moreover, does the *Ereignis* of which Kant speaks in one version of this text when he indicates the *Begebenheit* of the *Geschichtszeichen* let itself be situated in relation to the *Ereignis* of which Heidegger makes so much in his later writings?[46] Finally, how does it compare to the *Jetztzeit* that Walter Benjamin, in a radically alternative register, seeks to articulate in his "Thesen über den Begriff der Geschichte" ("Theses on the Concept of History") when he seeks to articulate the *contretemps* that punctuate the rhythm of the proletarian revolution (but also, as the earlier "Theologisch-Politisches Fragment" ["Theological-Political Fragment"] reminds us, of the unannounced coming of the Messiah)?

Since Kant rejects prophecy as being based on a supernatural giving or communication (*Mittheilung*) and "widening" (*Erweiterung*) of insight beyond the range of possible experience—like any other intellectual intuition (*Anschauung*)—it is only on the basis of a natural divination or "premonitory sign" of the times (*nach den Aspecten und Vorzeichen unserer Tage*) (*CF* 304 / 391) that he can predict the progress of the human race toward the better. This process, he avers, can "from now on" no longer simply be rolled back, "provided that there does not, by some chance, occur a second epoch of natural revolution which will push aside the human race to clear the stage for other creatures, like the one which . . . submerged the plant and animal kingdoms before man existed. For in the face of the omnipotence [*Allgewalt*] of nature, or rather its supreme cause which is inaccessible to us, the human being is, in turn, but a trifle [*eine Kleinigkeit*]" (*CF* 305 / 362, trans. modified). The answer to the question at issue, namely, "Is the human race constantly progressing toward the better?" is not to be found, Kant stresses from the outset, in the "natural history of man," strictly speaking. That history is concerned with such questions as whether or not "new races [*Racen*, in the German text] may appear in the future." Rather, it concerns human "moral history" (*Sittengeschichte*) and, more importantly, human history "not as a species according to the generic notion (*singulorum*), but as the totality of men united socially [*gesellschaftlich*] on earth and apportioned into peoples (*universorum*)" (*CF* 297 / 351).

Historically and politically speaking, human beings are not a trifle. Setting aside the possibility of a natural catastrophe in which they would

46. See Jean-François Lyotard, *L'Enthousiasme: La Critique kantienne de l'histoire* (Paris: Galilée, 1986), 48 n. 1.

be overtaken by another species (or, for that matter, by machines, a possibility Kant does not consider), we have a "historical sign" on which to
rely, a sign that is neither noumenal nor simply natural. (Can the noumenal realm signal *stricto sensu*? Or, for that matter, inspire and affect us?)
Nonetheless, Kant says, in its very premonitory nature it is a phenomenon, not inasmuch as it belongs to the world of experience, which, being in
essence a world of cause and effect, can in principle be explained mecha-
nistically, but insofar as it leaves its indelible mark on (or in) something
of the phenomenal. Therein lies its sublimity, its immediacy, its being in
the world while not being of this world. This intermediary state, stance,
or instance is all the more impressive and, if we may say so, revelatory
and "effective" in its own right. Indeed, Kant stresses, "such a phenomenon in human history cannot be forgotten [or, rather, does not forget
itself, *ein solches Phänomen in der Menschengeschichte vergisst sich nicht
mehr*]" (*CF* 304 / 361, trans. modified). It reveals a disposition that could
not have been orchestrated by political calculation, but that can only
have been promised by human nature and freedom insofar as they can
be united by the principles of right; and it can do this, in its timing and
temporal structure, only as an indeterminate and contingent event ("was
die Zeit angeht, nur als unbestimmt und Begebenheit aus Zufall"; *CF*
304 / 361).

Even if, empirically and politically speaking, this revolution is in permanent danger of a relapse or derailment, even if, as Foucault rightly
notes, its very "content" seems almost irrelevant, its occurrence — more
precisely, the quasi-enthusiastic response in its disinterested spectators —
"*attests* to a *permanent potentiality* [or rather virtuality, *virtualité*] that
cannot be forgotten."[47] Again, this is not to suggest that the sign in question — the sign of history that Revolution, in a sense, in spite of the Revolution itself, allows to be read — refers to some ontological constancy. If it
can be said to signal the human moral disposition, then this propensity
is forever shadowed, haunted, and held in check by its flip side or mirror
image, of which Kant speaks in the opening chapter of *Religion within the
Boundaries of Mere Reason*: namely, radical evil and the *summum malum*.
The ever-looming possibility of the worst is here, once more, the condition of the best yet to come. Mutatis mutandis, the same could be said of
the reasonable hope — which is neither certainty nor even anticipation, let

47. Foucault, "The Art of Telling the Truth," 146 / 686, emphasis mine.

alone prophecy, the mouthpiece of Providence—that one day the lower faculty will turn out to be the higher or the highest.[48]

In the present context, however, before the end of all things, Kant lays claim to no other "right" for the faculty of philosophy than that of the freedom of speech, albeit a freedom of speech that is neither public nor private in any strict sense. It may be a freedom to speak the truth and describe "what is," but it must nonetheless fail to say "what is to be done."[49] So long as this right—a right to question rights, the very form of the question *de iure*—remains respected and protected, the conflict of faculties can be a legal one. It can be described in terms of an antagonism (*Antagonism*), as a conflict of faculties united in view of a common telos (*Endzweck*). Only then can it prevent itself from relapsing or degenerating into a state of war or anarchy, the inevitable consequence of the illegal, self-destructive form of the conflict. There, Kant explains, the conflict degenerates into a dissension (*Zwietracht*) stemming from opposed ultimate purposes regarding the "*Mine* and *Thine* of learning." Like their political counterparts, these matters pertain not only to "property [*Eigenthum*]"—whether intellectual, symbolic, or economic—but also to the right of freedom. The latter, like truth, is the "necessary condition [*Bedingung*]" of the former. And if freedom—as a postulate or a fact (in all the overdetermination of the Kantian *Faktum der Vernunft*), rather than an empirical practice or experience—comes before property, then, Kant infers, the "outcome [*Resultat*]" of this analysis can only be that "any right granted to the higher faculty entails permission for the lower faculty to bring its scruples [*Bedenklichkeit*] about this right before the learned public" (*CF* 261–62 / 300). Before the community of scholars, that is; not before the public in the broader sense of the people or the *Idioten*.

The Voice from Nowhere: Philosophy and the Paradoxical Topography of the University

The demarcation of the rights and competencies of the different faculties thus conceived stands and falls with the existence or, rather, the insti-

48. Again, it should be noted that this analysis provides only a minimal "negative wisdom," not the certainty ascribed to Providence. This is not to deny, as Foucault rightly observes, that there is nonetheless a strong "positive" account of the "stakes" of this modern ethos marked by Kant's text. Foucault mentions several of them: "generality," "systematicity," "homogeneity." See Foucault, "What Is Enlightenment?," 49–50 / 576–77.

49. In this it differs from what Derrida, in *The Other Heading*, calls a "right of response" or "reply" (*droit de réponse*) (*The Other Heading*, 105 ff. / 121 ff.).

tution of a "frontier," an indivisible "line" or decidable "limit" (*DP* 357) that is held to separate descriptive and prescriptive, constative and performative, intrainstitutional and public utterances. Derrida calls our attention to this drawing of the line — thereby to *the delimitation of an inner free space for the university to speak out* — as well as to the paradoxes and aporias that result. On the one hand, philosophy is assigned the role of overseeing and supervising the principle of reason and is thus cast as the guardian of its tribunal. On the other hand, it cannot really enforce its rule. Caught in a peculiar double bind, it must simultaneously affirm and deny its autonomy. To preserve its integrity, it must speak the truth but not act upon it; it must speak *for all*, but not *to all*. In order to preserve its character as a formal and transcendental discourse, it must ultimately restrict its own diffusion, popularization, or even publication in the realm of the empirical. In order to serve the *res publica*, it must, so to speak, not go public and enter the diffuse, ambiguous realm of public opinion. *Paradoxically, aporetically, it protects its universality only to the degree that it excludes or ignores its outside.*

This ambiguity revolves around a curious interpretation of the "public space," a dimension that, as Derrida recounts in *L'Autre Cap* (*The Other Heading*), "reaches its philosophical modernity with the Enlightenment, with the French and American Revolutions, or with discourses like Kant's that link the *Aufklärung* — the progress of Enlightenment and of the day — to the freedom of making *public* use of reason in all domains (even though reason is not reducible to the [public] 'opinion' that it must also submit to critique)."[50] In *The Conflict of the Faculties* and elsewhere, Kant attempts to exorcize this dimension of public opinion — of an opinion that is "de jure neither the general will nor the nation, neither ideology nor the sum total of private opinions," neither a "subject" nor an "object," but rather the "god of a negative politology,"[51] ubiquitous and disturbing like a specter. He vainly attempts to reconcile his appreciation of this emerging public sphere with a traditionalist interpretation of its constitutive members, their opinions, lack of autonomy, responsibility, resolution, and so on. From a merely formal perspective — but a formal account is precisely what is being given here — there is not much difference between this reluctant Kantian appreciation of the public sphere and its subsequent depreciation in authors such as Kierkegaard and Heidegger. Indeed, Arendt,

50. Ibid., 96 / 113.
51. Ibid., 87–88 / 105–6.

Habermas, Foucault, and Lyotard vehemently protest this ultimately limited view of the public—as, precisely, limited, restricted, finite, natural, all too human, in short, the state of fallenness par excellence. Derrida's remarks about the public domain—about journalism, the "democracy to come," the new international, cosmopolitanism, and a politics of virtual inclusion that extends toward past and future generations, the nonhuman, and so on, as elaborated in *The Other Heading, Spectres de Marx* (*Specters of Marx*), and *Politics of Friendship*—could be read as a contribution to that ongoing debate. This line of thought takes hold in a rereading that revises some of Kant's most basic assumptions, such as the horizon of infinite approximation that limits the radicality of the "regulative idea," the teleological interpretation of history as a progress in the direction of the kingdom of ends, and so on.

Derrida reminds us in *Du droit à la philosophie* that the preface to Kant's *Metaphysics of Morals* leaves no doubt that the system of pure intelligible principles of law can *as such* never become "popular" because, following a classical hierarchy, the people are situated on the side of the empirical and contingent. Only the results or conclusions of the metaphysics of morals, its application to particular cases (as discussed in the supplementary remarks), not the premises on which they are based, are accessible to common sense (*gesunde Vernunft*). Whenever a philosopher wants to communicate his findings, he must resort to a sensible (re)presentation or *Versinnlichung* of his concepts. The pedagogy involved in this indispensable transmission consists in the paradoxical task of relating freedom to human nature as available to us in spatiotemporal experience and studied—"from a pragmatic perspective [*in pragmatischer Hinsicht*]"—by anthropology. However, this movement, which takes place "*between* the pure and the impure" (*DP* 534), no longer belongs to the gamut of tasks the faculty of philosophy can set itself, if it does not transgress its boundaries and allow its concepts and propositions to become dogmatic and material, *schwärmerisch* and premised on an unwarranted intellectual intuition, mystagogic presentiment (*Ahnung*), or divination. In the formal labor of philosophy proper, no ontico-empirical slippage is permitted. The task of the philosopher is a strictly prosaic, not a poetic or more broadly aesthetic endeavor. The aesthetic comes into play, however, wherever philosophical scholarship—in spite of or, rather, because of its universalistic intent and import—leaves the confines (and hence, in a sense, the particularism) of the academic discipline, the state apparatus, called the university.

It is publication, the distribution and dissemination of knowledge and scholarship, that is sanctioned or censored, not its truth or truth content. The latter remains untouchable and, in a sense, inexpressible or at least unpublishable. Philosophy, then, being the guardian of truth, the principle of reason, and the idea of the university, *must and must not mediate between itself and its other, between its freedom and its limitation.* Precisely this aporia, Derrida argues, demonstrates that the institutional place of philosophy, the cornerstone—the very meaning and truth—of Kantian architectonics, is in the final analysis no longer localizable and therefore unjustifiable. Caught in this aporia, the critique of philosophy and everything for which it stands can, strictly speaking, no longer be said to take place as such, that is to say, here and now, in the present, as an intelligible discipline. (See *DP* 361.) Nor has it thereby become a discipline that can be termed empirical or historical and that would be based on documents, revelations (or accounts thereof), testimonies, statutory precepts, and so on. If what is specifically philosophical can nonetheless be thought to come to pass somehow, somewhere, swirling (rather than circling, concentrically, as Kant seems to believe) around its "ideal," it cannot approach this telos in a regulated—teleological—process or within a horizon of infinite, yet asymptotic approximation.

In consequence, Derrida shows that the coming into its own of the university—of philosophy (*its* philosophy), as well as of the democracy or, as Kant would be more likely to say, the republican government it both presupposes and demands—remains forever to come (*à venir*). It remains to come, as Derrida notes, "not like a future reality but as what will always keep the essential structure of a promise and doesn't happen [*arrive*] as such [*comme telle*]." [52] The philosophical faculty is thus inscribed in a paradoxical topography that allots it no proper place. Derrida speaks of a "mobile non-place" (*DP* 509). Yet only by playing its impossible role, by living its unlikely, inapparent existence, by taking, occupying, or as-

---

52. Ibid., 41 / 60. That this promise cannot come "as such [*comme telle*]" is another way of saying that all *Versprechen* is also always *sich Versprechen*. Derrida stresses this theme in *Mémoires—pour Paul de Man* (Paris: Galilée, 1988) / *Mémoires for Paul de Man*, trans. Cecile Lindsay, Jonathan Culler, and Eduardo Cadava (New York: Columbia University Press, 1986); *De l'esprit: Heidegger et la question* (Paris: Galilée, 1987); *Of Spirit: Heidegger and the Question*, trans. G. Bennington and R. Bowlby (Chicago: University of Chicago Press, 1989); and elsewhere. Referring to Paul de Man's reading of Rousseau in *Allegories of Reading: Figural Language in Rousseau, Nietzsche, Rilke, and Proust* (New Haven: Yale University Press, 1979), Derrida recalls that the "illocutionary mode" of making the law is that of the "promise." The law is *proleptic, to-come* (*Mémoires*, 127 / 125).

suming its virtual place without place, properly speaking, can philosophy—paradoxically, aporetically—impose an order that protects against
the permanent danger of despotism, tyranny, demagogy, or sectarianism
outside the university, as well as against the dogmatism inside it. Its critical
power is its factual impotence.

Can, must, or should it then censor? The preface to the first edition
of *Religion within the Boundaries of Mere Reason* defines censorship as "a
criticism which has coercive power" (*RBR* 60 / 653). The force of this definition is clear: a power that could be said to be pure and without critical
guidance would be indiscriminate and would thus have to remain silent or
inarticulate when asked to judge particular issues and texts. Strictly speaking, it would not be able to censor. (See *DP* 350 and 347.) Pure power would
be a specimen of the *total war* that casts its shadow from behind every
unenlightened *absolute monarch* and remains a possibility—an inevitable
(and necessary?) threat—and, indeed, the antipode and flip side of even
the most enlightened, progressivist, and democratic form that political
power—the rule of law—can assume. And the latter, in Kant's eyes, is
epitomized by the king, the symbolic instance but also the empirical instantiation of sovereignty.

Conversely, the criticism that could said to be pure and without empirical or performative force would have no discriminatory power either.
Strictly speaking, it would not be able to censor. It would be merely the
inaudible whisper of an eternal peace, which is betrayed at the very moment it is declared and which is therefore forced to remain imminent and
distant, regardless of history's infinite or asymptotic approximation of its
"idea" or "ideal."

In order to deal with this aporia, Derrida notes, one would have to engage the question of "the best censorship [*la meilleure censure*]." If these
extremes are taken for what they are—namely, the limit of reasonable discourse and possible experience, or the limits of sheer force and pure critique that *as such* can never take hold in the finite world of appearance
or in the moral history of humankind—then censorship is de facto never
lifted. There is, in a sense, nothing but censorship, and thought and history are faced with the infinite task of invoking "censorship against censorship." [53]

---

53. *DP* 370. Indeed, the very instant of decision in these matters is illustrated, in the essay
on the principle of reason in its relation to the *pupilles* of the university, by reference to Aristotle's *De anima*. Derrida draws on the figure of the "diaphragma" to exemplify the necessary

Could the "strategic calculation" this perennial censorship demands still be understood in terms of Kant's critique of pure practical reason — as its consequence, its effect, if not its imperative? Or is it merely a skill, an art, or a craft? What if Kant had not insisted on distinguishing between philosophy's task as a *Gesetzgeberin,* on the one hand, and the practices of a mere *Vernunftkünstler,* on the other? Surely, Kant's critique oscillates between the extremes of all thought, all Enlightenment, every institution, every politics. Derrida interprets Kant's politics as an attempt to "take notice" and to "make up the balance [*prendre acte*]" between the state as a censoring power and the philosophical endeavor to delimit this power. This difficult negotiation of and with power — but also of and with violence, force, and the ever-looming possibility of the worst — takes place by opposing it not with a "counter-power [*un contre- pouvoir*]," but with "a kind of non-power [*une sorte de non-pouvoir*]," that is, a reason "heterogeneous" to the state's power to censor, a reason that may not be censored and that must, in return, not itself censor. As the forceless "force of the better argument" (to cite Habermas's formulation), it would be unable to give orders and, consequently, devoid of executive authority. (See *DP* 351–52.)

STRICTLY SPEAKING, then, Kant distinguishes between two ways of speaking in public. On the one hand, there is a speaking to the public *in general* that, by its very nature, threatens its truth content, makes it ambiguous (the object of curiosity rather than of resolute interrogation), and turns it into an action: into a pragmatic and often merely occasional or even opportunistic stance, based on subjectivist or hypothetical maxims rather than responding to a categorical imperative defining what all should want for all, under all circumstances and for all times. On the other hand, there is a speaking to the *particular,* selected public of the scholarly community, which, even if it utters the truth and stirs up conflict, does not constitute an action.

Against the backdrop of this aporetics, Derrida suggests that Kant's conception could justify or at least tolerate two conflicting, even contradictory, conclusions. Kant's *Conflict of the Faculties* defines both the con-

---

moderation and modesty of the gaze of the scholar, the student, the pupils of the university. The alternative to the panoptic view of the regime of reason no less than the mystagogic vision of self-styled illuminati is neither the blindness of all insight nor a God's eye point of view, but the incessant and restless oscillation of the *Augenblick* that knows how and when to open and close (*DP* 466).

ditions under which a university can sanction "the most totalitarian forms of society" and the premise for the constitution of a "place of the most intractable liberal resistance against all abuse of power" (*DP* 417). This resistance, Derrida writes, could be considered in turn (*tour à tour*) "the most rigorous" and "the most powerless" (*DP* 417). If the university resembles this idea, if it is indeed centered on the pursuit of truth for its own sake—the only thing, Kant says, that cannot and should not be censored—it could very well be the vehicle of both the worst and the best of all possible worlds.

Is this still our situation? What might the apparent aporia of Kant's text be able to teach us about the present-day academy's chances of restating the cause of Enlightenment? To be sure, other oppositions have come to replace, if not radically displace, the ones on which Kant's academy and its conflicts relied. No doubt the tasks and interests that Kant ascribes to the two different classes of faculties run through each individual scholar as well as through each individual academic discipline worthy of the name. The same could be said of the ever more complex relations between the university as a whole and the state, its functionaries, and the people. This complexity has transformed the university from within and without. Thus, the Kantian tripartition of the former higher faculties has given way to an increasingly specialized field of empirical, theoretical, and applied disciplines. For good reason, these no longer limit their inquiries to the traditional definition of human interests in terms of salvation, property, and physical well-being. Moreover, they are quite capable of examining the truth content of their respective statements without the help of philosophers. Most importantly, censorship, wherever and to the degree that it exists, no longer obeys the regulated, limited, legal, and public role Kant ascribes for its concept and practice.

In this proliferation of interests and changing roles, the malaise and the *mal-être* of which Derrida speaks has been diversified rather than mitigated. It has become both generalized and intensified. If the aporias that destabilize the Kantian academy are increasingly difficult to localize or to comprehend in the context of the present-day university, they are even more difficult to master. In a passage that rehearses the central argument of "Mochlos," Derrida summarizes the most salient challenges of the present constellation in terms that bring out the continuity no less than the difference between our situation and that of Kant. Something has changed dramatically, escaping the premises and the paradoxical logic upon which the modern academy remains based, such as the institution and archiving of memory, the appropriation of what has been forgotten, the salvaging of what has been lost to oblivion. For all these premises still exclude the possibility of a more radical destruction whose idea forms the limit and, perhaps, the condition of all genuine understanding, of all scholarship and all critique:

> Why and how do the university, the editorial process, and memory in general practise their hierarchies in terms of a body, a corpus, a problematic, a thematization, a language or an author? . . . Why is such hegemony annihilated now and then without a remainder? . . . The figure of an eclipse is still governed by teleological optimism. . . . It assumes that any text, once occulted, minorized, abandoned, repressed or censored . . . ought to reappear, if possible like a star! Justice has to be done! This optimism [which, Derrida adds, he has "never shared"] also inspires a politico-psychoanalytic concept of repression: what was repressed is stored in the unconscious of a culture whose memory never loses a thing. There is a political unconscious, no doubt, and also a politico-academic unconscious — we should take them into account, so as to analyze, so as to act — but there are ashes also: of oblivion, of total destruction, whose "remains" in any case do not stay with us forever.
>
> Not even an eclipse, then! The body in question is not even deprived for a while of light — it is simply burned. This incineration, this finitude of memory corresponds to a possibility so radical that the very concept of finitude (already theological) is in danger of being irrelevant. Without it, perhaps, the violences of censorship and repression would not even be imaginable. So too, for the violence marking every procedure of legitimation or canonization. Sometimes this violence is overtly political, and one could undoubtedly give examples, other than those now canonical or academic in turn, of literatures, languages and discourses belonging to oppressed (or colonized) nations or classes, to women or blacks. To these massive and very obvious examples, we ought to add examples less visible, less direct, more paradoxical, more perverse, more overdetermined.[54]

The present malaise, then, if any malaise there be, demands a new, more "enlightened," that is to say, more "vigilant" thought of the concept of reason, of its principle as well as its institution. No longer simply Kantian, Marxist, or Freudian, this critique implies not that one replace, but that one infinitely displace and rearticulate the "ontologico-encyclo-

---

54. Jacques Derrida, "Canons and Metonymies: An Interview with Jacques Derrida," in *Logomachia: The Conflict of the Faculties,* ed. Rand, 198.

pedic" paradigm (*DP* 586) according to which the fundamentally philosophical concept of the university—the concept of reason "as an institution" (*DP* 428)—has been modeled during the last two centuries. If Kant
is the single most important philosopher to inaugurate this paradigm and
its model, then he is also the first, in spite of himself, to lay bare its structural limitations and its aporetics. This is nowhere more evident than in
his analysis of the ways in which the philosophical question becomes en-
tangled in the problem of the theological and, more importantly, of religion. In what follows, we will be reading Kant's exposition as allegory,
as the example par excellence, of a compelling stance on responsibility in
relation to the political, the theological, the theologico-political, and religion in the strictest and broadest sense of the word, whether taken as rational religion (*Vernunftreligion*) or as historical, positive, ontic, and presumably revealed religion (*Offenbarungsreligion*). This allegory extends well
beyond the letter of Derrida's analyses in, for example, *Du droit à la philosophie,* "Mochlos" and "Faith and Knowledge." Nonetheless, it confirms
their basic tenets: the quasi-phenomenological, quasi-transcendental reduction of *Aufklärung* to a vigilance that, within the confines of possible
experience and given the very structure of phenomenality, remains forever shadowed by its double, counterbalanced or thrown off balance by
the neither physical nor psychological but, Kant says, *natural* disposition
(*Anlage*) of *radical evil,* the temptation that must be risked at the price of
losing one's freedom and, indeed, one's responsibility.

IF THE DOUBLE BIND of the Kantian academy in general and of its faculty
of philosophy in particular consists in being troubled—and enabled—by
the aporia of having to restrict or prohibit the publication of a discourse
in order to safeguard its intellectual and moral rigor (or, as Derrida puts
it, "un discours rigoureux en science et en conscience"), that is to say, its
rationality and universality, then this "postulation" is, when taken strictly,
"contradictory in itself, intrinsically in conflict with itself, as if it were already no longer translatable *in* Kant's text, from one end to another / from
itself into itself [*de lui-même à lui-même*]" (*DP* 419–20). Within the university, philosophy may give itself the law and speak the universal truth
in all matters, particularly as regards the propositions of the "superior"
faculties of theology, law, and medicine. So long as it speaks the truth and
nothing but the truth, it has the right and the duty to censor the inevitable
obscurantism of the other faculties, which, in their desire to dominate,
bend their ear toward the voice of the people. So long as it speaks without

doing, so long as it addresses every truth *formally,* in terms of the condition for its possibility, it is exempt from the need for external legitimation.

In its general, external effects, however, it must be controlled, censored. It must be counted, calculated, and held accountable by another tribunal. (See *DP* 352.) It must be subjected to a critique that, unlike any critique of pure reason, operates, to all appearances, as a legal and executive force, more often than not, as might dictating right. *To speak universally, it must be limited, curtailed, and abridged.* In speaking freely about truth while allowing the censor to prevent this speech from truly becoming an act, the faculty of philosophy guards itself against immodest claims. Kant writes that this very *Anspruchslosigkeit* of being "merely free, as it leaves others free, to discover the truth for the benefit of all the sciences and to set it before the higher faculties to use as they will . . . must commend [it] to the government as above suspicion and, indeed, indispensable." In all this, however, the place of the philosopher remains a very modest one. Like his faculty, he will be at best a stand-in for the general interest, which is the true disinterestedness of the pursuit of truth. But this disinterested interest is only expressed before a restricted, learned audience and is not allowed to enter the arena of grand politics.[55] In the final analysis, the government, the central authority, must be relied upon where truth is at stake.

Then again, only by paradoxically restricting itself — a disciplined restraint equivalent to the self-control of the lower, philosophical faculty — can genuine sovereignty exert legitimate power. This much is clear from the following passage, which sums up the dynamic Kant sees at work in the relationship between the university and political authority, between the philosopher and the king: "The theologians . . . have the duty incumbent on them, and consequently the title, to uphold biblical faith; but this does not impair the freedom of the philosophers to subject it always to the critique of reason. And should a dictatorship [*Dictatur*] be granted to the

---

55. Kant seems to make an exception to this rule when he mentions the role of philosophers of law who, in the *Volksaufklärung,* the "public instruction of the people in its duties and rights vis-à-vis the state to which they belong" (*CF* 305 / 362), are decried as "enlighteners." Kant comes to their defense by arguing that "their voice is not addressed confidentially to the people (as the people take scarcely any or no notice of their writings) but is addressed respectfully to the state" (*CF* 305 / 363). What they do, then, it is to "implore the state to take to heart that need which is felt to be legitimate" (*CF* 305 / 363). This, however, they can do "by no other means than that of publicity in the event that an entire people cares to bring forward its grievances (*gravamen*). Thus the prohibition of publicity impedes the progress of a people toward improvement" (*CF* 305 / 363).

higher faculty for a short time (by a religious edict [as, in fact, had happened in Kant's day]), this freedom can best be secured by the solemn
formula: *Provideant consules, ne quid respublica detrimenti capiat* [Let the
consuls see to it that no harm befalls the republic]" (*CF* 287 / 338).

   To explain further the implications of the internal contradiction within
the lower faculty's discourse of truth, which is that of the university overall, given that the university's higher faculties also speak to the people
only indirectly, through the mediation of their practitioners, let me recapitulate the tension between philosophy and theology, a central concern of *The Conflict of the Faculties*. The first examples Kant gives of this
conflict, Derrida reminds us in "Mochlos," "pertain to the sacred, to faith
and revelation."[56] These are not just any examples. Not only do they indicate the specific point where the transcendental—the purity and purely
formal character of the intelligible, the rational, and reason, as well as the
categoricity of its single, general, and universal imperative—touches upon
(some would say, slips into) the empirical, thereby demonstrating the inevitability, indeed the necessity, of subreption and, as Kant says, *Idolatrie*,
but, revealingly, they are drawn from the tradition called the religious.
Why does it provide exemplarity par excellence? And why is the relationship between the philosophical and the theological—between transcendental or rational and biblical, dogmatic, and supranatural theology—
indicative of more wide-ranging structures of language, experience, and
history in general? In what sense, exactly, is the debate concerning the
religious the shortest route toward a full, formal, and concrete explication
of the nature of the ethical and the political as it progresses, or so Kant
seems to think, over time? Why, finally, do Kant's ideas concerning universal cosmopolitanism, perpetual peace, and the kingdom of ends find
their prime model in—and, as it were, amalgamate with—the concept of
history as salvation and eschatology, however asymptotic or a matter of
infinite approximation, rather than history as revolutionary, apocalyptic,
or abrupt?

Paganism, Religion Proper, and the Politics of Theology: Kant's *Religion within the Boundaries of Mere Reason*

In the preface to the second edition of *Religion within the Boundaries
of Mere Reason*, Kant distinguishes three different approaches to theology.
The first, the task of the clergy, is the "welfare of souls." The second, in

56. Derrida, "Mochlos," 27 / *DP* 432.

addition to this previous responsibility, is a scholarly task within the university as a public institution. To the extent that both approaches can claim to be involved in biblical theology, the second, scholarly approach is entitled to resist the intrusion — that is, the censorship — of the first, clerical approach. Yet over and against both the biblical theologians within the academy and the clergy outside it, Kant places a third category: the philosophical theologians, who are members of the lower faculty. Between biblical and philosophical theologians — the most interesting and complex opposition here (but again, why exactly? On what grounds is this exemplary relationship based?) — Kant draws the line, stating that, in the last resort, philosophical theology "must have complete freedom to expand as far as its science reaches, provided that it stays within the boundaries of mere reason and makes indeed use of history, languages, the books of all peoples, even the Bible, in order to confirm and explain its propositions, but only for itself, without carrying these propositions over into biblical theology or wishing to modify its public doctrines" (*RBR* 61 / 655–56). If a trespass has taken place, the functionaries of the church can rightly protest and censor. Wherever there is doubt, however (that is to say, in most cases), the responsibility of judgment falls to the higher faculty.

As Karl Vorländer notes, Kant does not protest the existence of censorship as such but demands that the censorship of clerical writings, which touch upon biblical theology, be submitted to the judgment of the theological faculty alone.[57] It can be entrusted with this task because, like the lower faculty, though perhaps more indirectly and less wholeheartedly, it remains committed to the prosperity of the sciences:

> Indeed, in a case like this the primary censorship is the prerogative of this faculty [of theology] and not of the faculty of philosophy; for with respect to certain doctrines the former alone holds privilege, whereas the latter deals with its own openly and freely; only the former, therefore, can make complaints that

57. Karl Vorländer, Introduction to Immanuel Kant, *Die Religion innerhalb der Grenzen der blossen Vernunft,* ed. Karl Vorländer (Leipzig: Meiner, 1937), xlii n. 1, cf. lxxix–lxxx. See also Josef Bohatec, *Die Religionsphilosophie Kants in der "Religion innerhalb der Grenzen der blossen Vernunft"* (Hildesheim: Georg Olms Verlagsbuchhandlung, 1966; orig. pub. Hamburg: Hoffmann und Campe,1938); and M. Naar, "Introduction" to Emmanuel Kant, *La Religion dans les limites de la simple raison,* trans. J. Gibelin (Paris: Vrin, 1996). After completing an earlier version of this chapter, I found my interpretation confirmed in the Tanner lectures "Kant on Reason, Morality, and Religion," presented by Onora O'Neill at Harvard University in February 1996. I am grateful to Professor Christine M. Korsgaard for providing me with a copy of these lectures, as well as her own comments on them, entitled "Religious Faith, Teleological History, and the Concept of Agency."

its exclusive right has been impinged upon. However, in spite of the verging of the two bodies of doctrine in one another and the anxiety about a transgression of boundaries by philosophical theology, doubt about an encroachment can easily be averted if it is only borne in mind that any such mischief does not occur because the philosopher *borrows* something from biblical theology to use for his own purpose, for biblical theology itself will not want to deny that it contains much in common with the doctrines of mere reason and, in addition, much that belongs to the science of history or linguistic scholarship and is subject to the censorship of these [disciplines]; rather, even granted that the philosopher uses whatever he borrows from biblical theology in a meaning suited to mere reason but perhaps not pleasing to this theology, [the mischief occurs] only because the philosopher *brings* something *into* biblical theology itself and thereby seeks to fit it for other ends than it is fitted for. (*RBR* 62 / 656)

But can one borrow without importing something into oneself? Can one borrow without taking away from the other? And can one do this without giving in return? Can what has been borrowed be returned as the same? In other words, could this exchange between two bodies take place without their both being somehow affected internally and essentially? If the mutual instrumentalization of these bodies does not touch deep inside, but leaves them external to each other — as Kant writes, "like oil and water" — why, then, was this mixture necessary in the first place? What is the necessity of this appearance?

Details aside, *The Conflict of the Faculties* reaffirms the basic tenets of this analysis. Here, too, Kant maintains that in conflicts (*Streitigkeiten*) that deal with pure practical reason the philosophical faculty can rightfully assert "the prerogative to state the case without objection and to instruct the process, in so far as its formal aspects are concerned" (*CF* 281–82 / 330, trans. modified). With respect to its material aspects, the faculty of theology can rightfully assert its role as *prima inter pares* (*CF* 282 / 330).

Theologians — both clergymen and scholarly biblical theologians — rely on the historical events the Bible "reveals" for their purported knowledge of the existence and the essence of God. They do not rationally prove God's existence. Only philosophy could, if at all, settle this issue: theoretically, rather than practically or ethico-theologically, *quod non*. Throughout his critical writings, Kant leaves little doubt that the classical onto-, cosmo-, and teleological proofs for the existence of God are inconclusive, inconsistent, or based on untenable premises.

The biblical theologian, then, cannot but base his knowledge of the existence and essence of God on what Kant, not without irony, calls "a certain (indemonstrable and inexplicable) *feeling* [Gefühl]" (*CF* 252 / 285). This feeling is not founded in "nature" but is a supernatural gift, a matter of grace. It consists in a change of heart and is thus—indirectly, by way of a detour through sensible and symbolical representations—also a "moral influence [*moralische Einwirkung*]" (*CF* 252 / 386).[58] But this is only half the story: "As far as our will and its fulfillment of God's commands is concerned, the biblical theologian must not rely on nature—that is, on man's own moral power (virtue)—but on grace (a supernatural but, at the same time, moral influence), which man can obtain only by an ardent faith that transforms his heart—a faith that itself, in turn, he can expect only through grace" (*CF* 252 / 286).

Even though the theologian testifies to faith and the revelations on which it is said to be based, this does not entitle him to make his belief in the divine origin of the Bible an issue of public debate. Just as attempts at rational proof of the existence of God should be confined to scholars, so the open evaluation of revelatory signs, miracles, and prophecies would lure the *Idioten* into "impertinent speculations and doubts" and undermine their "trust [*Zutrauen*]" in their instructors. The people are not the only ones easily lost when confronted with such matters. Should the biblical theologian cease to rely merely on his faith and its grounding in incomprehensible feelings and authoritative documents and instead venture into the realm of allegory, that is to say, of a purely rational, moral, or spiritual meaning behind the letter of the texts, he would overstep the boundaries of his competency. In so doing, Kant writes, he "leaps . . . over the wall of ecclesiastical faith . . . and strays into the free and open field of private judgment and philosophy. And there, having run away from spiritual government [*geistlichen Regierung*], he is exposed to all the dangers of anarchy [*Anarchie*]" (*CF* 252 / 286, trans. modified).

Kant acknowledges that, in this delineation of the limit and scope of biblical theology, he is speaking of this discipline only in its purity, insofar as it is not "contaminated by the ill-reputed spirit of freedom that belongs to reason and philosophy [*von dem verschrieenen Freiheitsgeist der Vernunft und Philosophie noch nicht angesteckt ist*]" (*CF* 252 / 286). In the world of appearances, however, this ideal type cannot exist as such. The pure biblical theologian is always already a hybrid figure who neither

58. Cf. *RBR* 179 ff. / 865 ff.

simply studies the Bible nor operates within the limits of reason alone, but does a little of each. What are the consequences of this interpenetration of two ideal characters and the respective orders for which they stand? Kant writes: "As soon as we allow two different callings [*Geschäfte von verschiedener Art*] to combine and run into each other [*in einander laufen lassen*], we can form no clear notion [*keinen bestimmten Begriff*] of the characteristic [*Eigentümlichkeit*] that distinguishes each by itself" (*CF* 252 / 286, trans. modified). Whoever concerns himself with religion — and thereby, "subjectively considered," with "the recognition of all our duties as divine commands" (*RBR* 177 / 822)[59] — must operate on both sides of the line thought to separate the intelligible and the empirical. Being a citizen of two realms, one *must* combine and inscribe into one another what one *ought* to keep apart. Or so it seems.[60]

Yet the distinction between the biblical and the philosophical, or rational, theologian can and should be upheld, if only as a point of departure, method, perspective, and orientation, if not aim or telos. The former is a scholar of Scripture (*Schriftgelehrte*) and a servant of the faith of the church (*Kirchenglaube*), based on statutory laws that are said to have originated in or emanated from another's (divine) will (*d.i. auf Gesetzen beruht, die aus der Willkür eines andern ausfliessen*). The latter, by contrast, is a scholar of reason and a servant (if one can still speak of servitude where autonomy is at issue) of religious faith proper. He is a scholar and servant of a *Religionsglaube*, grounded in interior laws (*innern Gesetzen*) deducible from pure practical reason. Here Kant draws, then immediately effaces, a clear distinction between two forms of religion, more precisely between religion proper and its form, its modes and modalities of appearance. He writes:

> That religion [religion proper] cannot be founded [*gegründet*] on decrees [*Satzungen*] (no matter how high their origin) is clear [*erhellt*] from its very concept. Religion is not the sum [*Inbegriff*] of certain teachings regarded as

59. Cf. also *RBR* 142 n. / 822 n.
60. At times, Kant appears to be stressing that the necessity of the phenomenal order outweighs the freedom of the noumenal, in other words, of the intelligible character. Indeed, he writes that, in its pursuit of the "highest good" — the *höchstes Gut, summum bonum*, or the constellation in which nature and the freedom, happiness and the worthiness to be happy, can ultimately or fundamentally harmonize — reason itself demands to be inscribed and translated into "the real." This convergence is reason's reasonable expectation as much as its desire or need (*Bedürfnis*). Kant sees no betrayal or contradiction here but follows the scholastic doctrine according to which *ens et bonum convertuntur*. I will return to this motif below.

divine revelations [*Offenbarungen*] (for that is theology), but the sum of all
our duties regarded as divine *commands* as such [*der aller unserer Pflichten
überhaupt als göttlicher* Gebote] (and subjectively the maxim to fulfill them
as such). As far as its matter or object is concerned, religion does not differ
in any part from morality, for it is concerned with duties as such. Its distinction from morality is a merely formal one, that is to say, a legislation of reason
in order to give morality through the idea of God, which it itself has gener-
ated, influence on man's will to fulfill all his duties [*Religion unterscheidet sich
nicht der Materie, d.i. dem Object, nach in irgend einem Stücke von der Moral,
denn sie geht auf Pflichten überhaupt, sondern ihr Unterschied von dieser ist
bloss formal, d.i. eine Gesetzgebung der Vernunft, um der Moral durch die aus
dieser selbst erzeugte Idee von Gott auf den menschlichen Willen zu Erfüllung
aller seiner Pflichten Einfluss zu geben*]. (*CF* 262 / 300–301, trans. modified)

Religion as well as ecclesiastical faith, philosophical as well as biblical theology are all, to a greater or lesser extent, pedagogic or epagogic means
to the same end. In their own incomparable and incommensurable ways,
they all revolve around a center that justifies, controls, and purifies, if not
censors (for it is a critique without force), their truth-value, to wit: pure
practical reason, the moral law, and its categorical imperative. Precisely
in light of this central concern, Kant notes that the distinction between
these forms—between the "content" of the one pure form, on the one
hand, and its innumerable concrete forms, on the other—while necessary
or essential, is paradoxically also provisional and contingent, not to say
arbitrary.

Whereas the sum (the *Inbegriff*) of revelations comprises the faith of
the church and the sum of morality contains what is rational in the faith
of religion, this division, Kant writes, is neither "precise" nor "in keeping
with ordinary usage; but it may stand for the time being [*einstweilen*]" (*CF*
273 n. / 316 n.). The division in question is a means to an end and can help
orient our thinking for the time being, that is to say, for as long as history
has not come to its end, an end that, for Kant, might be an eternal "to
come," a *Nimmertag* (*CF* 275 n. / 320 n.). Its distinction, then, is not based
on ontology, on the critical separation of the intelligible and the empirical.
Rather, it is inspired by the need for *orientation*, a need one should distinguish from mere pragmatism, prudence, and heuristics, let alone oppor-
tunism. In the final analysis, the *positioning* of thought vis-à-vis a religion
is neither reducible to "positive" religions nor somehow present or valid
elsewhere. Kant writes: "There is only one religion. Although there are

indeed different varieties of belief in divine revelation and its statutory teachings, which cannot spring from reason — that is, different forms in which the divine will is represented sensibly so as to give it influence on our minds — there are not different religions. Of these forms Christianity, as far as we know, is the most adequate [*die schicklichste Form*]" (*CF* 262 / 301).

This is not to say that Christianity, being the most apt form religion has assumed, is a coherent whole with an indivisible meaning. In Christianity, notably in its founding and statutory document, the Bible, we can distinguish two seemingly incommensurable yet somehow interwoven parts ("Dies findet sich nun in der Bibel aus zwei ungleichartigen Stücken zusammengesetzt"; *CF* 262 / 301): first, a rational canon of religious faith based on pure reason alone and, second, an organon, or vehicle of ecclesiastical faith. The latter, Kant clarifies, is "based entirely on statutes that would need to be revealed in order to be able to pass for sacred doctrine and precepts for how to live [*die einer Offenbarung bedurften, wenn sie für heilige Lehre und Lebensvorschriften gelten sollten*]" (*CF* 262–63 / 301, trans. modified).

Once again, the difference between properly religious and merely ecclesiastical faith is identified with that between necessary, or categorical, moral principles given to us a priori by the law that reason gives itself and contingent or hypothetical statutory doctrines given to us a posteriori through the experience of purported historical revelations and the incomprehensible "feelings" they produce. Yet this essential distinction, decisive for the conception of any transcendental thought (indeed for any differentiation between the originary and the derived, norm and example, critique and empiricism) is also immediately blurred. Kant suggests that the porosity of the dividing line between religion proper and its mere forms explains why the very term *religion* is necessarily ambiguous. With respect to rational and ecclesiastical religion, he writes: "Since we also have a duty to use this latter didactic material [*Leitzeug*] with regard to the former end, provided it can be taken as divine revelation [which can never be known for certain, but only believed on the basis of our own incomprehensible feelings as well as the testimony of others], we can thereby explain why the name of religious faith [i.e., religion proper] commonly also comprises the ecclesiastical faith that is based on Scripture" (*CF* 263 / 301, trans. modified). How, then, does Kant determine the relation between the canon and its organon, between faith and its vehicles? How, moreover, can the latter, as the inessential or secondary, be of some relevance to the former, as the essential and primary? How, in other words, can the conditioned be somehow conditioning, not so much *constitutive of* it but *necessary for* and *necessarily before* it? If Kant's whole text can be read as a dynamic mapping or topography of a changing of institutional places (of the last and the lower becoming the first and the higher), then how does this affect the specific context that concerns us here?

At first sight, Kant's demarcations seem to leave little confusion about which comes first (logically, ontologically, morally, and chronologically speaking). He writes: "The Scriptures contain even more than what is in itself required for eternal life; part of their content is a matter of historical belief [*Geschichtsglauben*], and while this can indeed be useful [*zuträglich*] to religious faith as its mere sensible vehicle [*blosses sinnliches Vehikel*] (for this or that person and for certain eras), it is not an essential part of religious faith" (*CF* 263 / 302, trans. modified). The apparent reversal of that order seems the result of a dogmatic confusion by the higher faculty, whose members "insist on this historical content as divine revelation as strongly as if belief in it belonged to religion" (*CF* 263 / 302). This confusion (*Vermengung*) must be opposed by the lower faculty, which concentrates instead on what exactly in biblical revelation is true of religion properly speaking (*die eigentliche Religion*). Yet Kant goes on to argue that the vehicle is not an organon or an instrument pure and simple. It also contains, or conveys, *some truth*, if not entirely and not at all properly, then analogically, symbolically, allegorically. In so doing, it is itself, in turn, carried and mediated by a method of instruction (*Lehrmethode*). More precisely, this method forms part of the vehicle that it transports. Unlike that vehicle, however, it is not based on revelation. Kant defines it as a pedagogy and rhetoric of apostolic "discretion." As such, it belongs to an essential and essentially harmless negotiation with the cultural practices and the hegemonic ideas of the day. These ideas can be anthropomorphic (*kath'anthrōpon*) and are, if not outrightly idolatrous, at least not based on truth (*kath'aletheian*): "A *method of teaching* [*Lehrmethode*] too, is connected with this vehicle (that is, with what is added on to the teachings of religion [*Religionslehre*]). This method is not to be taken as divine revelation but as something left to the apostles' discretion [*die man als den Aposteln selbst überlassen und nicht als göttliche Offenbarung betrachten darf*]. However, we can accept it as valid in relation to the way of thinking in the apostles' times (κατ᾽ ἄνθρωπον [*kath'anthrōpon*]), not as part

of doctrine [*Lehrstücke an sich selbst*] (κατ᾽ ἀλήθειαν [*kath' aletheian*])"
(*CF* 263 / 302).

Kant gives two examples, one negative and one positive. The first example of a vehicle an apostle might silently permit is the belief of the possessed in their delusion (the *Wahn* of the *Besessenen*). Even though it can be harmful, especially if it stiffens into the *Schwärmerei* of enthusiasm, it is, in the forms narrated by the Bible, relatively innocent and, moreover, obsolete. The second vehicle the apostle might actually endorse is more telling. It is, Kant writes, "the interpretation of the history of the old covenant as a prototype [or example, *Vorbilder*] for that which happened in the new, which [Kant adds with an unmistakably anti-Semitic twist], if they are mistakenly included, as Judaism, as part of the doctrine of faith [*Glaubenslehre*], can well make us moan: *nunc istae reliquias nos exercent* ["those remnants now weary us"], Cicero" (*CF* 263 / 302, trans. modified).

In the tradition of German Idealism, Judaism had often been reduced to the merely abstract or negative presentation of the formality of the pure moral law and thereby, ironically, to Kantianism. Notwithstanding the famous passage in the *Kritik der Urteilskraft* (*Critique of Judgment*) invoking the prohibition on images, Kant will have no part in that equation here. An even more disturbing example (of the "euthanasia" of Judaism) will make this painfully clear.

The convoluted nature of the Scriptures — being, containing, or conveying at once religion's canon and its organon — ignites hermeneutical struggles and even wars, inside and outside the academy. In this conflict the higher faculty suspects the lower of evacuating the Bible's content, whereas the lower accuses the higher of reifying its form. Both are correct. In Kant's words:

> For this reason scriptural erudition [*Schriftgelehrsamkeit*] in Christianity is subject to many difficulties in the art of exegesis [*Auslegungskunst*], and the higher faculty (of biblical theologians) is bound to come into conflict with the lower faculty over it and its principle. For the higher faculty, being concerned primarily for theoretical biblical knowledge, suspects the lower faculty of philosophizing away [*wegzuphilosophieren*] all the teachings that must be considered real revelation and so taken literally, and of ascribing to them whatever sense suits it. On the other hand, the lower faculty, looking more to the practical — that is, more to religion than to dogma — accuses the higher of so concentrating on the means, dogma, that it completely loses sight of the final end, inner religion, which must be moral and based on reason. And so,

when conflict arises about the sense of a scriptural text, philosophy—that is, the lower faculty, which has truth as its end—*claims the prerogative of deciding its meaning.* (*CF* 263–64 / 302–3, emphasis mine)

Kant reminds us of the irony that the members of the higher faculty of theology, the biblical theologians, will often find themselves caught in a performative contradiction. Uncomfortable with biblical passages concerning the concepts of God's will and nature that seem at odds with what are generally held to be the true principles of religion, they inadvertently tend to follow the dictates of their own reason. In so doing, they implicitly admit that what is presented in all too human or literal terms must be understood in a rational or spiritual manner more "worthy of God" (*CF* 266 / 306). Here, the role of the philosophical theologian would be to unmask the discrepancy between a superior tone and an unacknowledged rational, hermeneutic practice. The critique of the philosophical faculty is to be the critique, not so much of the idol and idolatry (*RBR* 202 / 859), as of religious ideology and its fetishism. It is a critique of the inflation of the value of the text despite its often limited, moral use: a fetishism, Kant implies, that is inherent in every form of religion as we know it.[61]

As a general rule, the faculty of philosophy goes one step further and takes a position that the higher faculty can never fully adopt, if and so long as it remains faithful to itself. It takes to task not only the reification of form, but also the presupposition that the belief attached to this form matters or is constitutive at all:

61. Cf. Vorländer, Introduction, *Die Religion innerhalb der Grenzen der blossen Vernunft*, xlvii: "*Principally* speaking, there exists no difference between the different religious cults; from 'sublimated' Puritan belief to the most banal fetishism: it is all fetish — and feudal service. [*Prinzipiell existiert zwischen den verschiedenen Kultusreligionen kein Unterschied, vom 'sublimierten' Puritanertum bis zum gröbsten Fetischismus: es ist alles Fetisch — und Frondienst.*]" Kant himself writes: "*Priestcraft* . . . is the constitution of a church to the extent that a *fetish-service* is the rule; and this always obtains wherever statutory commands, rules of faith and observances, rather than principles of morality, make up the groundwork and the essence of the church. Now there are indeed many ecclesiastical forms in which the fetishism is so manifold and mechanical that it appears to drive out nearly all of morality, hence also religion, and to usurp their place, and thus borders very closely on paganism. Here, however, where worth or the lack thereof rests on the nature of one principle which binds above all others, there is no question of a more or less. If that principle imposes humble submission to a constitution as compulsory service and not rather the free homage due to the moral law *in general*, then however few the imposed observances, let them but be declared as unconditionally necessary and it is enough for a fetish-faith through obedience to a church (not a religion). The constitution of this church (hierarchy) can be monarchical or aristocratic or democratic: this is merely a matter of organization; its constitution still is and remains under any of these forms always despotic" (*RBR* 198 / 852–53).

With regard to scriptural teachings that we can know only by revelation, faith is not in itself *meritorious* [*hat an sich kein* Verdienst], and lack of such faith, and even doubt opposed to it, in itself involves no *guilt* [Verschuldung]. The only thing that matters in religion is *deeds* [*alles kommt in der Religion aufs* Thun *an*], and this ultimate aim and, accordingly, a meaning appropriate to it, must be attributed to every biblical dogma [*Glaubenslehren*].

Dogma [*Glaubenssätzen*] is not what we ought to believe . . . , but what we find it possible and useful to admit for practical (moral) purposes, although we cannot demonstrate it and so only believe it. If we ignore this moral consideration and admit as a principle faith merely in the sense of theoretical assent — assent, for example, to what is based historically on the testimony [*Zeugnis*] of others . . . — such faith is no part of religion because it neither makes nor gives proof of a better man; and if such belief is feigned [*erkünstelt*] in the soul, thrust upon it only by fear [*Furcht*] and hope, then it is opposed to sincerity [*Aufrichtigkeit*] and so to religion as well. (*CF* 267 / 307- 8) [62]

True, for Kant all testimony must inevitably pass as merely empirical, contingent, apparent, and arbitrary.[63] While it induces certain moral "feelings," its significance falls short of the "historical sign [*Geschichtszeichen*]" that Kant attributes to the French Revolution, especially to the effect imposed on its spectators. The temporality and singularity of testimony — for example, the biblical and early Christian accounts of miracles, to which we shall return below (see Chapter 3) — is apparently not granted the (dialectical, analytical, existential, or phenomenological) weight that it will obtain in later writers, Kierkegaard, Levinas, and Derrida among them. Yet Kant's position has a certain complexity of its own.

62. Cf. *CF* 270–72 / 312: "We cannot have religious faith unless we are *convinced* of its truth, and its truth cannot be certified by statutes (declaring themselves divine pronouncements); for, again, only history could be used to prove that these statutes are divine, and history is not entitled to pass *itself* off as divine revelation. And so for religious faith, which is directed solely to the morality of conduct, to deeds, acceptance of historical — even biblical — teachings has in itself no positive or negative moral value and comes under the heading of what is indifferent." Yet the *adiaphora* play their decisive role as necessary, provisional, and discriminatory markers that cannot and should not be avoided.

63. "The assent of a testimonial is always something empirical; and the person whom I am supposed to believe on the basis of his testimony must be an object of experience." Immanuel Kant, "Von einem neuerdings erhobenen vornehmen Ton in der Philosophie," in *Werke*, ed. Wilhelm Weischedel, (Darmstadt: Wissenschaftliche Buchgesellschaft, 1983), 5:386 / "On a Newly Arisen Superior Tone in Philosophy," trans. Peter Fenves, in *Raising the Tone of Philosophy: Late Essays by Immanuel Kant, Transformative Critique by Jacques Derrida*, ed. Peter Fenves (Baltimore: Johns Hopkins University Press, 1993), 61.

The dogmatic, literal interpretation of the Scriptures could certainly serve its purpose in the public presentation (*Vortrag*) of the faith of a church. But Kant hastens to add that since "ecclesiastical faith, as the mere vehicle [*Vehikel*] of religious faith, is mutable and must remain open to gradual purification until it coincides [*Reinigung bis zur Kongruenz*] with religious faith, it cannot be made an article of faith itself. This does not mean that it may be attacked publicly in the churches or even passed over dry-shod [*mit trockenem Fuss*]; for it comes under the protection of the government, which watches over public unity [*Eintracht*] and peace [*Frieden*]. However, the teacher should warn [the people] not to ascribe holiness to dogma itself but to pass over, without delay [*ohne Verzug*], to the religious faith it has introduced" (*CF* 267 / 308).

On the one hand, Kant insists that the means are not yet the end, but that the organon, in a long process of constant approximation and cathartic removal of empirical remainders, can and will become congruent with the canon. *The vehicle would thus become what up until then it has only transported.* On the other hand, Kant leaves no doubt that the believer should not be delayed by the detour the vehicle represents, and makes both possible and inevitable. What, then, inspires the delay? Why does this ecclesiastical faith, being a detour on the way to the morality the government wants for its subjects, fall explicitly under the government's protection? The answer to these questions lies in the nature of the vehicle. When Kant introduces the testimony or attestation (*Zeugnis*) of the Scriptures, he cites it neither as epistemological, empirical proof nor as aesthetic ornamentation. He neither reduces the actual testimony to conveying the text's moral spirit nor locates it in the Scriptures' worldly and literal meaning, which is marked by an element of arbitrariness or historical overdetermination. The interpretation and effect of Scripture can be measured by mere allegorization no better than by obstinate orthodoxy. Testimony gives witness to the passage, if not the intersection or mediation, between the intelligible and the sensible, the noumenal and the phenomenal. It attests to the possibility or, rather, the example of an application that can edify the hearts of all people:

> A sermon directed to edification as its final end (as any sermon should be) must develop its lesson from the *hearts* of the listeners, namely, from the natural moral predisposition that is present in even the most unlearned human being; for only then will the attitude of will it brings forth be pure. The *testimonies of* Scripture connected with these teachings should also not be treated

as historical arguments confirming their truth (for morally active reason needs no such argument, and besides, empirical cognition could not yield anything of the sort), but merely as examples in which the truth of reason's practical principles is made more perceptible through their application to facts of sacred history. But this too, is a very valuable gain for peoples and states throughout the whole world [auf der ganzen Erde]. (CF 288 / 339–40, trans. modified)

The testimony of the Scriptures can speak to the heart only if it appeals to a preexisting rational and moral predisposition in man that makes this testimony—this "example" of an "application"—possible in the first place. Thus, Kant writes that Christ has given us an "example conforming to the prototype of a humanity well-pleasing to God" (RBR 157 / 794), an archetype that, in its turn, is exemplary for Christ. Indeed, if for Kant Christianity is the name of true religion—of the positive religion that comes closest to religion as such—then this Christianity (or, as Heidegger, following Overbeck, would say, this "Christianicity") predates the coming (both the first and the second) of Christ. This said, we seem to be dealing here with what Hannah Arendt, in Lectures on Kant's Political Philosophy, calls the "exemplary validity" and the tertium comparationis of aesthetic or reflective (as opposed to determinant) judgment. Rather than thinking the particular as contained under a given universal, as determinant judgment does, reflective judgment, Kant explains in the introductions to the Critique of Judgment, ascends from a given particular for which it seeks a universal. This exemplarity, Arendt argues, is analogous to, yet different from, the transcendental schema of which Kant speaks in the Critique of Pure Reason, which is oriented toward cognition and leads into the very heart of the synthesis a priori that enables true knowledge.[64]

64. An "exemplar"—and Arendt reminds us that the word example comes from the Latin eximere, "to single out some particular"—is a singular instance, object, or occurrence that "is and remains a particular that in its very particularity reveals the generality that otherwise could not be defined" (Arendt, Lectures on Kant's Political Philosophy, 77, cf. 84). Arendt thereby construes a certain analogy between the example and the schema. The latter, as Theodore M. Green and Hoyt H. Hudson note in their translation Religion within the Limits of Reason Alone (New York: Harper & Row, 1934), 181 n., is a "spatio-temporal or sensuous form of what, in its essence, does not possess this character." See Immanuel Kant, Kritik der reinen Vernunft, vols. 3 and 4 of Werke, ed. Wilhelm Weischedel / Critique of Pure Reason, trans. and ed. Paul Guyer and Allen W. Wood, The Cambridge Edition of the Works of Immanuel Kant (Cambridge: Cambridge University Press, 1998), B 176 ff. In his interpretative essay, Ronald Beiner explains that Arendt "quotes Kant to the effect that what the schemata do for cognition, examples do for judgement)" (Arendt, Lectures on Kant's Political Philosophy, 79; see Immanuel Kant, Kritik der Urteilskraft,

This circularity should also serve as a principle of scriptural interpretation. For if all genuine action, following a basic premise of the *Kritik der praktischen Vernunft* (*Critique of Practical Reason*) and the *Grundlegung zur Metaphysik der Sitten* (*Foundations for a Metaphysics of Morals*), all doing (*Thun*) should be represented (*vorgestellt*) as originating (*entspringend*) from man's autonomous deployment of his moral forces (*Kräfte*), rather than as an effect imposed upon him from without, through the influence of some higher cause, "with respect to whose working man could behave only passively [*leidend*]" (*CF* 267 / 308, trans. modified), then this principle of interpretation conflicts with the apparent meaning of at least some biblical stories. Scriptural passages that seem to imply "a mere passive submission [*eine bloss passive Ergebung*]" to a power that is said to cause "holiness [*Heiligkeit*]" in us if only we surrender and believe must be read against the grain. This *lectio difficilior* does not stretch the principle of autonomy beyond its limit, but, paradoxically, allows it to hint at a source it can no longer explain on its own but accepts as a gift of "grace": "It has to be made clear . . . that *we ourselves must work at developing that moral predisposition* [*wir müssen an der Entwicklung jener moralischen Anlage in uns selbst arbeiten*], although this predisposition does point to a divine source that reason can never reach (in its theoretical search for causes), so that our possession of it is not meritorious, but rather the work of grace" (*CF* 268 / 309). Everything depends on a problem of presentation that in turn depends on how we define (or present) human nature.[65] While we should always start out from what we

---

vol. 8 of *Werke*, ed. Weischedel / *Critique of Judgment*, trans. J. H. Bernard [New York: Hafner, 1951], par. 59). For Kant, however, there is a difference between the "schematism of analogy" and the "schematism of objective determination." The latter entails an extension of our knowledge and leads up to anthropomorphism. Kant writes: "We must always resort to some analogy to natural existences to render supersensible qualities intelligible to ourselves. . . . The Scriptures too accommodate themselves to this mode of representation when, in order to make us comprehend the degree of God's love for the human race, they ascribe to Him the very highest sacrifice which a loving being can make . . . although through reason we cannot form any concept of how a self-sufficient being could sacrifice something that belongs to his blessedness" (*RBR* 107 n. / 718 n.). The consequence of limited analogy, to be distinguished from the Scholastic doctrine of the *analogia entis*, is that "between the relation of a schema to its concept and the relationship of this very schema of the concept to the thing itself there is no analogy, but a formidable leap (*metabasis eis allo genos*) which leads straight into anthropomorphism" (*RBR* 107 n. / 719 n.).

65. "If by nature we mean the principle that impels us to promote our happiness [*Glückseligkeit*], and by grace [*Gnade*] the incomprehensible moral disposition [*Anlage*] in us—that is, the principle of pure morality—then nature and grace not only differ from each other but often come into conflict. But if by nature (in the practical sense) we mean our ability to achieve

ourselves are obliged and able to do, this obligation would not exclude the possibility, indeed the necessity, of a "supernatural supplement." Indeed, that is a "demand" or "need" (*Bedürfnis*) of reason:

> If man's own deeds are not sufficient to justify him before his conscience (as it judges him strictly), reason is entitled to adopt on faith a supernatural supplement [*eine übernatürliche Ergänzung*] to his insufficient justice (though not to specify in what this consists). That reason has this title is self-evident. For man must be able to become what his vocation [*Bestimmung*] requires him to be (adequate to the holy law); and if he cannot do this naturally by his own powers, he may hope to achieve it by God's cooperation from without (whatever form this may take). We can add, further, that faith in this supplement for his deficiency is sanctifying, for only by it can man cease to doubt that he reach his final end . . . and so lay hold of the courage and firmness of attitude he needs to lead a life pleasing to God (the sole condition of his hope for eternal life). But we need not be able to understand and state exactly what this replenishment is (for in the final analysis this is transcendent and, despite all God Himself might tell us about it, inconceivable to us). (*CF* 268 / 309–10, trans. modified)

Here and elsewhere, Kant seems to side with Johann Georg Hamann. Philological, historical, empirical, and dogmatic method is incapable of capturing the moral basis and significance of religion. In passing, Kant paraphrases Hamann as saying that only the "descent into the hell of self-knowledge paves the way to deification [*Nichts als die Höllenfahrt der Selbsterkenntnis bahnt uns der Weg zu Vergöttung*]." [66] Kant writes: "Only

---

certain ends by our own powers in general, then grace is none other than the nature of man in so far as he is determined [*bestimmt*] to actions by a principle which is intrinsic to his own being, but supersensible (the representation of his duty) [*sein eigenes inneres, aber übersinnliches Prinzip (die Vorstellung seiner Pflicht)*]. Since we want to explain this principle, although we know no further ground for it, we represent it as a stimulus [*Antrieb*] to good produced in us by God, the predisposition to which we did not establish in ourselves, and so, as grace. For sin (evil in human nature) has made penal law necessary (as if for servants); grace, however, is the hope that good will develop in us — a hope which becomes alive by the belief in our original moral predisposition to good and by the example of humanity as pleasing to God in His Son. And grace can and should become more powerful in us (as free beings), if only we let it act in us, that is to say, if we let the mindsets [*Gesinnungen*] of the conduct of life that resemble such a holy example become active" (*CF* 268 / 308–9, trans. modified).

66. Cited in Immanuel Kant, *Der Streit der Fakultäten*, ed. Klaus Reich (Hamburg: Meiner, 1959), xii. For another reading, see Brandt in "Zum 'Streit der Fakultäten,'" 78 n. 60. On Kant and Hamann, see Frederick C. Beiser, *The Fate of Reason: German Philosophy from Kant to Fichte* (Cambridge: Harvard University Press, 1987), chap. 1; on Hamann generally, see Isaiah

a moral interpretation . . . is really an authentic one—that is, given by the God within us: for since we cannot understand anyone unless he speaks to us through our own understanding and reason, it is only by concepts of our reason, in so far as they are pure moral concepts and hence infallible, that we can recognize the divinity of a teaching promulgated to us" (*CF* 271–72 / 314–15). Kant hastens to add, however, that the critical potential of these words should be distinguished from their possible *mystical* misunderstanding, which is one of the intellectual sources of the excessive censorship in Prussia under Frederick William II. In fact, Kant's insistence that the government deny mysticism the protection of a public ecclesiastical religion is directed at least as much against the immediate advisers of the king as it is against pietist and revolutionary sects.

True, in the appendix to the first part of *The Conflict of the Faculties,* Kant includes a meditation on the resemblance between the critique of pure (practical) reason, on the one hand, and a certain interpretation of mysticism, on the other. This similarity is neither completely denied nor fully granted, if only because here Kant lets another speak. The appendix takes the form of a letter written by Carol Arnold Wilmans, the author of a dissertation entitled "De similitudine inter Mysticismum purum et Kantianam religionis doctrinam" ("On the Similarity between Pure Mysticism and the Kantian Religious Doctrine"; 1797). By including it, Kant writes in a footnote, he does not intend to suggest that his views entirely harmonize with those expressed in the letter. Although he asserts that no resemblance (*Ähnlichkeit*) between the two should be admitted without restriction (that is to say, *unbedingt*),[67] he does not present a radical disclaimer either. Here Kant lets the reader—first of all, this promising "young man"—judge for himself if and in what sense the comparison might be useful.[68]

Berlin, *The Magus of the North: J. G. Hamann and the Origins of Modern Irrationalism,* ed. Henry Hardy (London: John Murray, 1993).

67. Cf. *CF* 288 n. / 340 n.

68. The translators of Kant's introduction to Reinhold Bernhard Jachmann's *Examination of the Kantian Philosophy of Religion in Respect of the Similarity to Pure Mysticism Which Has Been Attributed to It* (Königsberg, 1800) note all too confidently: "It is evidently out of kindness that Kant left it to Jachmann [his student, friend, amanuensis, and early biographer] to respond to Wilman's (absurd) suggestion that there might be an affinity to Kantian moral religion and any form of religious mysticism" (Immanuel Kant, *Religion and Rational Theology,* trans. and ed. Allan W. Wood and George di Giovanni, *The Cambridge Edition of the Works of Immanuel Kant* [Cambridge: Cambridge University Press, 1996], 331). In his preface to Jachmann's work, Kant sees his friend's book as aiming to refute a more emphatic notion of mysticism than the one

Kant does not feel compelled to defend his rules for a rational interpretation of Scripture against the objection that it results in an allegorical
and mystical reading that would undercut the essence of both the Bible
and philosophy because he fears the charge of being unbiblical or irrational. Instead, he demonstrates the virtual impossibility of both the orthodox and, more indirectly, the allegorico-mystical position by a reductio
ad absurdum:

> If the biblical theologian mistakes the husk [*Hülle*] of religion for religion
> itself, he must explain the entire Old Testament, for example, as a continuous
> *allegory* (of prototypes and symbolic representations [*Vorbildern und symbo-
> lischen Vorstellungen*]) of the religious state still to come — or else admit that
> true religion (which cannot be truer than true [*wahrer als wahr*]) had already
> appeared then, making the New Testament superfluous. As for the charge
> that the rational interpretation of the Scriptures is mystical, the sole means
> of avoiding mysticism (such as Swedenborg's) is for philosophy to be on the
> lookout for a moral meaning in scriptural texts and even to impose it on them.
> For unless the supersensible (the thought of which is essential to anything
> called religion) is anchored to determinate concepts of reason, such as those
> of morality, fantasy [*die Phantasie*] inevitably gets lost in the transcendent,
> where religious matters are concerned, and leads to an Illuminism in which
> everyone has his private, inner revelations, and there is no longer any pub-
> lic touchstone of truth [*öffentlicher Probirstein der Wahrheit*]. (CF 270 / 312,
> trans. modified)

If thought or, for that matter, the thought police (*die Polizei im Reiche der
Wissenschaften*) — that is to say, the censor — is to get any grip on people's
innermost feelings and beliefs, as it must, it should first isolate the forms
of their representation. To judge these forms critically requires, not reify-

---

alluded to in *The Conflict of the Faculties* (and in Wilman's dissertation): "Now the question is
whether wisdom is *infused* into a person from above (by inspiration) or its height is *scaled* from
below through the inner power of his practical reason. // He who asserts the former, as a passive means of cognition, is thinking of a chimaera [*Unding*] — the possibility of a *supersensible
experience* which is a direct self-contradiction (representing the transcendent as immanent) —
and bases himself on a certain mysterious doctrine called 'mysticism'; this is the opposite of
all philosophy and just because of this it (like the alchemist) puts the greatest stock in being
superior to the labor of all those rational but troublesome investigations of nature, dreaming
the while of being blessed with the sweet state of enjoyment" (*Religion and Rational Theology*,
333). The translator's note bases its judgment in part on Kant's replies to Wilman's letters (published in the second, correspondence, section of *Immanuel Kants Gesammelte Schriften*, ed. the
Prussian Academy of Sciences, 12:202, 207, 230, 259, 277, 279).

ing them as if they had any truth-value in themselves, but measuring the distance between them and the center (the inner circle) around which they revolve.

Religion properly speaking—which is essentially moral, rational, and, in that sense, natural—must be conceived as "one, universal, and necessary, it cannot vary" (*CF* 272 / 315). Its differentiation into forms or sects, each of which has its own dogmas, rites, and idiosyncrasies, based on the Bible or on tradition, takes on ever more divisive features "*to the extent* [*so fern*] that belief in what is merely the vehicle of religion is taken as an article of religion" (*CF* 272 / 315, emphasis mine). But can this substitution, this quid pro quo, ever be avoided (as it clearly must and should)? If every form of faith deviates from the purely moral, natural, or rational core of religion, if religion, moreover, is not a pure content but a form, albeit the ultimate and unconditional form, the purified and purifying form as such—what could possibly escape being defined as a dogma or a sect? Might not every empirical or positive religion—that is to say, religion historically, anthropologically, sociologically, and psychologically speaking—be described, in Kant's own terms, as "pagan"? Christianity would be no exception. Even if this were not true of Christianity as such, if such a "thing" there be, it would apply to every concrete, phenomenal, statutory, symbolic, or institutional form Christianity has assumed throughout history or that it will be able to take on in the future. If the visible church—in Augustine's words, the *ecclesia militans*—can be said to be sectarian in this respect, would not the "invisible church," its purest form, also suffer the same fate as soon as its peace announces itself as the end of history, indeed of all things?

Kant identifies Christianity with the very "idea" of religion. In response to the objection of biblical theologians that the philosophical interpretation of Christianity reduces revelation to "natural religion," he exploits the ambiguity of the adjective *natural* and claims to distinguish natural from *naturalistic* religion:

> Christianity is the Idea of religion, which must as such be based on reason and to this extent be natural. But it contains a means for introducing this religion to human beings, the Bible, which is thought to have a supernatural source; and in so far as the Bible (whatever its source may be) promotes moral precepts of reason by propagating them publicly and strengthening them within men's souls, we can consider it the vehicle of religion and accept it, in this respect, as supernatural revelation. Now only a religion that makes it a principle

not to admit supernatural revelation [in this sense] can be called *naturalistic*.
(*CF* 269 / 310–11)

Christianity is not a naturalistic religion because it allows for the possibility, if not the necessity, of supplementary means of revelation — that is to say, supernatural revelations — which may serve as a vehicle for the "introduction" (Kant speaks of "ein übernatürliches Mittel der Introduction") of religion into the hearts of men as well as a vehicle for the foundation (*Stiftung*) of a community, the church, that teaches, professes, and confesses it publicly. What, then, does it mean that Christianity, as a natural, rational, moral religion, *allows for the possibility* of a supernatural supplement? What does it mean that it allows for the possibility of a supplement that can be helpful or necessary to some at one time or another, depending not so much on human finitude (which is of all times), as on historical contingency (to be determined by "apostolic discretion" alone)? Kant's critiques give more than one example of the paradox that reason itself provides reasons for its own supplementation. Moreover, in our context Kant states that "the kind of characteristics that experience provides can never show that a revelation is divine: the mark of its divinity (at least as the *conditio sine qua non*) is its harmony with what reason pronounces worthy of [*anständig für*] God" (*CF* 270 / 312–13).

Furthermore, the fact that harmony with reason is the *conditio sine qua non* of the divine character of revelation does not imply that the mark of divinity is identical with what reason dictates. Harmony is not sameness; it is a resemblance, consonance, or attunement. It means that reason allows for a minimal space or interval in which divinity is supplementary — that is to say, other, more, and later or a posteriori — with respect to the a priori principle by which it is somehow conditioned, justified, recognized, or deduced as universal. Mutatis mutandis, one could maintain for Kant's notion of a rational, natural, moral, pure, or genuine religion what Derrida, in *The Other Heading,* ascribes to the modern phenomenon of public opinion. Like its apparent counterpart, religion "does not *express itself,* if one understands by this that it exists somewhere deep down, *before* manifesting itself in broad daylight, as such, in its phenomenality. It *is* phenomenal. It is no more *produced* or *formed,* indeed *influenced* or *inflected,* than simply *reflected* or *represented,*" [69] and this not only by the press and the media. First and foremost, it is reflected and represented by

69. Derrida, *The Other Heading,* 95 / 112.

the endless series of individual and collective *forms* of testimony and re-articulation, which, with Kant, we might be tempted to call "sectarian" as much as "ecclesiastical," "idolatrous" as much as "pagan."

But what does it mean to be "pagan"? Kant introduces this term in a passage that deserves careful analysis. It strikingly anticipates contemporary debates, if only because it corrects the widespread interpretation of his work as an exposition of the principles of political liberalism, the neutrality of the public sphere, while keeping its distance from the much-decried politics of identity, recognition, and the like. Indeed, in *The Conflict of the Faculties* Kant's position is neither unrestrainedly progressive nor downright conservative; his views comply with those of present-day multiculturalists as little as with their monoculturalist counterparts. Kant's writings on religion and history — teasing out his wrestling with what might be called, with the later Husserl and the early Derrida, the transcendental historicity of religion in its very ideality, in the very formality of its form and innermost center — might help to address the issue common to the construction of the notion of modernity and the public sphere as it articulates itself through the definition and the practice of censorship, free speech, and religious tolerance, including recent debates over liberalism, communitarianism, critical theory, neopragmatism, philosophy, and multiculturalism.[70] Kant can help us understand why no

---

70. Contrast Talal Asad, *Genealogies of Religion: Discipline and Reason in Christianity and Islam* (Baltimore: Johns Hopkins University Press, 1993), 202: "Kant's ideas of public, publicity, and critical reason have become part of a Habermasian story of the progressively liberating aspect of secular, bourgeois society." For Asad, Kant's texts document the emergence of a conceptual distinction in the genesis of the modern liberal tradition: "one in which unquestioned obedience to authority prevails (the juridical definitions upheld by the state); the other consisting of rational argument and exchange, in which authority has no place (the omnipresence of criticism)" (ibid., 204). This distinction, Asad goes on to suggest, must be viewed against the backdrop of seventeenth- and eighteenth-century Europe, torn by "sectarian" wars in the wake of the Reformation (ibid., 206). That context conditioned attempts to establish a strong, centralized modern state and to redefine religion in terms of personal "belief" by relegating it to the "newly emerging space of private (as opposed to public) life" (ibid., 205). From that point on, Asad claims, religion was seen as "the source of uncontrollable passions within the individual and of dangerous strife with the commonwealth. It could not, for this reason, provide an institutional basis for a common morality — still less a public language of rational criticism" (ibid.). Asad bases his argument on a "commonplace" among historians of this period, namely, that religion was "gradually compelled to concede the domain of public power to the constitutional state" (ibid., 207). In this view, religious toleration was primarily a "political means to the formation of strong state power" rather than "the gift of a benign intention to defend pluralism. . . . [T]he locus of intolerance had shifted. . . . Not only were religious beliefs now constitutionally subordinated to the state, but the principles of morality were henceforth to be theorized separately from the domain of politics" (ibid., 206). This historical construction

consensus between these positions is likely to announce itself any time soon, if ever.

Multiculturalism Reconsidered

In *Religion within the Boundaries of Mere Reason,* as well as in the first part of *The Conflict of the Faculties,* Kant presents religion as the "middle ground" on which power and reason meet, penetrate, and permeate each other, then keep each other in balance. The various forms of religion compromise what are in fact two *formalist* extremes—absolute sovereignty and pure critique—neither of which can account for the sociality, the commonality as well as the dissensus, that marks modern and ancient states. Religious tolerance is not only, or not primarily, a ruse of power, based on cynicism or hypocrisy alone. It manifests an ontological pluralism that is the essence of the political.[71]

I have examined how, in their Kantian determination, religion, tolerance, and censorship not only structure our experience of the historical and the political but also affect our understanding of the conditions under which cultural difference can be *addressed* rather than *worked through,* as dialectical or psychoanalytic approaches to these issues suggest. What is at issue is neither some unreflected immediacy nor the repression of what has so far remained unconscious.[72] Kant's work helps to clarify why the

---

(and reconstruction) of religion "ensures that it is part of what is *inessential* to our common politics, economy, science, and morality. More strongly put: religion is what actually or potentially divides us, and if followed with passionate conviction, may set us intolerantly against one another" (ibid., 207). Whatever the merits of this historical—indeed, genealogical—reading, my own emphasis in the preceding pages has been a slightly different one. See also Talal Asad, "Religion, Nation-State, Secularism," in *Nation and Religion: Perspectives on Europe and Asia,* ed. Peter van der Veer and Hartmut Lehmann (Princeton: Princeton University Press, 1999).

71. See also Thierry Wanegffelen, *L'Édit de Nantes: Une histoire européenne de la tolérance du XVIe au XXe siècle* (Paris: Librairie Générale Française, 1998); Marc Shell, *Children of the Earth: Literature, Politics, and Nationhood* (New York: Oxford University Press, 1993), chap. 2; David A. J. Richards, *Toleration and the Constitution* (New York: Oxford University Press, 1986), 67–162; and Michael J. Sandel, *Democracy's Discontent: America in Search of a Public Philosophy* (Cambridge: Harvard University Press, 1996), chap. 3.

72. The analysis of this turn to religion—beyond morality—should not be confused with what Charles Taylor, in his *Sources of the Self: The Making of the Modern Identity* (Cambridge: Harvard University Press, 1989), 63, calls the need for a "higher-order good" or "hypergood." Nor does the introduction of religion fall under the critique of the modern and postmodern reduction of morality to obligation, since I am concerned with what in "obligation" points beyond obligation or responds to something preceding it. While this beyond entails a "cross-cultural" claim (cf. ibid., 67–68), that claim cannot be validated or substantiated by anybody, not at any point in time, no matter what the universalism and decenteredness of his or her culture. "Religion"—or what is thought of as religion here—is of a totally different order. Yet—

public sphere can never be neutral or homogeneous and, more importantly, why this insight by no means implies that the formal, critical task of reason has become obsolete.

Kant's definition of paganism contains the key to his complex, yet extremely subtle, position. He writes:

> According to the *accepted* view, the principle of division in matters of faith is either *religion* or *paganism* [Heidentum] (which are opposed to each other as A to non-A [*die einander wie A und non A entgegen sind*]). Those who profess religion are commonly called *believers* [Gläubige]; those who profess paganism, *infidels* [Ungläubige]. Religion is the kind of faith that locates the *essence* [das Wesentliche] of all divine worship [*Verehrung*] in man's morality; paganism is the kind that does not, either because it lacks the concept of a supernatural and moral being [*eines übernatürlichen und moralischen Wesens*] [in which case, Kant adds in parentheses, it is an "*Ethnicismus brutus*"], or because it makes something other than the attitude [*Gesinnung*] of a morally well-conducted walk of life [*eines sittlich wohlgeführten Lebenswandels*], hence the non-essential [*das Nichtwesentliche*] of religion, a part of religion [*Religionsstück*] [in which case, Kant adds in parentheses, it is an "*Ethnicismus speciosus*"]. (CF 272–73 / 316, trans. modified)

Formally speaking, the difference between religion and paganism is merely the difference between true philosophical universalism and a disingenuous particularism, which can have many forms and which, as the quotation suggests, will either negate or displace the moral content of religion proper. The first position, "brute ethnicity," seems (to relapse into) the prerational or amoral *status naturalis*—the limit situation, the *summum malum* of the war of all against all, the antiparadise of humans propelled into history.

The second position, "specific ethnicity," marks, if not the cosmopolitan *status civilis*, then at least history's slow but steady progress toward the better. Here, humans are guided by the ideal of the *summum bonum*, which, like the other extreme, the *status naturalis*, is not part of finite history. It is the highest good, the correspondence, if not the identity, of the intelligible and the empirical, whose realization is guaranteed by God alone. Human cultures can only approximate this infinitely removed

---

and here lies the paradox or, rather, aporia that I retrace—it would be equally misguided to take this order in a purely heterological sense (assuming such a heterology would be thinkable at all, as anything other than a *flatus vocis*).

ideal, in comparison with which they are all not only imperfect but, strictly speaking, *false*. Indeed, any hierarchy of particular values would reveal its falsity in light of a rational truth value that is not only given a priori but that can also be hoped for, that may well become part of our experience and thus be given a posteriori—if not in our times, then at least for the future to come; if not in this life, then at least for the life hereafter:

> To claim *universality* [or generality, Allgemeinheit] for a dogma [*Kirchen-glauben*] (*catholicismus hierarchicus*) involves a contradiction [*Widerspruch*], for unconditioned universality presupposes necessity, and since this occurs only where reason itself provides sufficient grounds for the tenets of faith, no mere statute can be universally valid. Pure religious faith, on the other hand, can justly claim universal validity (*catholicismus rationalis*). So a division into sects [*Sectirerei*] can never occur in matters of pure religious belief. Wherever sectarianism is to be found, it arises from a mistake on the part of ecclesias-tical faith: the mistake of regarding its statutes (even divine revelations) for essential parts of religion, and so substituting [*unterzuschieben*] empiricism [*Empirism*] in matters of faith for rationalism and passing off what is merely contingent as necessary in itself. Now since, in contingent doctrines, there can be all sorts of conflicting articles [*Satzungen*] or interpretation [*Auslegung*] of articles, we can readily see that mere dogma [*der blosse Kirchenglaube*] will be a prolific source [*eine reiche Quelle*] of innumerable sects in matters of faith, unless it is purified [*geläutert*] by pure religious faith. (CF 273 / 316–17, trans. modified.)

In order to determine this purification (*Läuterung*) (CF 273 / 317) or "rectification" (CF 274 / 318) in more detail and to provide it with the best touchstone practicable (*zum Gebrauch schicklichste Probirstein*), Kant introduces an interesting notion of *hybridity,* not of two cultural givens or belongings, but of an allegedly non- or meta-cultural, that is to say, necessary and essential teaching, on the one hand, and its merely contin-gent and local or historical cultural inscription, on the other. To the extent that the latter is taken for the former, the essence of religion is distorted by what Kant almost describes as an *infection* by paganism. Paradoxically speaking, this contamination can become total, an idolatry without reli-gion proper, which destroys not only morality or Christianity, but also the life of the body politic: "To the extent that any dogma gives out merely statutory teachings of faith as essential religious teachings, it contains a certain *admixture of paganism* [*eine gewisse* Beimischung von Heiden-tum]; for paganism consists in passing off the externals (non-essentials) [*das Äusserliche (Ausserwesentliche)*] of religion as essential. This admixture can gradually advance [*gradweise so weit gehen*] to such a level that it turns the entire religion into mere dogma, which presents common practices [*Gebräuche*] as if they were laws, and so becomes sheer paganism" (*CF* 273 / 317, trans. modified). What for Kant looms behind this characterization "sheer paganism [*baares Heidentum*]" is clear enough. It is the generalization of idiosyncrasies and, thereby, the danger of a disintegration of the public sphere, of civilization, and a relapse into the *status naturalis* that confronts us ultimately with the *summum malum,* to wit: the omnipresence of total war, the hither side of despotism. Then again, this is only the virtual limit case of a much broader spectrum of intermediate possibilities:

> *Paganism* [Heidentum (Paganismus)] [is], according to its etymology, the religious superstition of people in the woods [*der religiöse Aberglaube des Volks in Wäldern (Heiden)*] — that is, of a group whose religious belief has no ecclesiastical system of government [*Verfassung*] and hence no public law [*öffentliches Gesetz*]. The Jews, Mohammedans, and Hindus, however, refuse to recognize as law anything that differs from theirs, and designate other peoples, who do not have exactly the same ecclesiastical rites [*Observanzen*], with the title of rejection [*Verwerfung*] (Goj, Dshauer, etc.) — that is, of infidels. (*CF* 273 n. / 317 n., trans. modified)

With a seemingly anti-Roman Catholic twist, Kant associates any practice that attributes absolute value to what in the end (and compared to that end) can only be a relative and contingent vehicle — one, moreover, that in its very phenomenality remains at an infinite distance from the noumenal and only as such intelligible core of religion proper — with the common pejorative denominator "clericalism," *Pfaffentum.* As mere historical faith, Kant writes elsewhere (with a reference to the New Testament, *James* 2:17), it "is dead, being alone" (*RBR* 143 / 773),[73] that is, if it is not followed by works or, more precisely, by the sole disposition — the good will (a "cause through freedom") — that counts as morally effective: "Ecclesiastical authority to pronounce salvation or damnation according to this sort of faith [c]ould be called clericalism [*Pfaffentum*]. And self-styled Protestants should not be deprived of this honorific title if they insist on making the essence of their creed belief in tenets and rites which reason says noth-

---

73. Kant continues: "of itself, considered as declaration, contains nothing, nor does it lead to anything that would have a moral value for us" (*RBR* 143 / 102).

ing about, and which the most evil and worthless man can profess and observe as well as the best" (*CF* 274 / 318).[74]

Unlike the practical, rational faith of religion, which works on the human soul in the very consciousness of its freedom (*Bewusstsein der Freiheit*), ecclesiastical belief imposes itself forcibly, even violently, on human conscience (*dass der Kirchenglaube über Gewissen Gewalt ausübt*). Such belief takes different forms and produces different reactions, creating particular social dynamics that are of direct relevance to the government. Again, though rational and historical or ecclesiastical religion must be radically and unmistakably distinguished, the former, paradoxically, "cannot be indifferent to the character of its vehicle which we adopt in our dogma" (*CF* 274 / 319). Conversely, the latter is dead or merely a dead letter without — unless, as Heidegger might have said, it is *corrected* by — the former. Not unlike the relation without relation between right (*le droit*) and justice (*la justice*), their dynamics is one of mutual exclusion and inclusion at once. Together they make up the drama of social movement, of history, and, for Kant, of finitude.

Kant distinguishes three different historical movements: *separatists*, who withdraw themselves from the visible community of the church; *schismatics*, who split the church in view of its public form, but agree on the content (*die Materie*) of its creed; and, finally, *sectarians*, in the more strict or limited sense of the word, who are dissidents (*Dissidenten*) with respect to certain doctrines and gather in small societies that are not necessarily secret but are unacknowledged by the state (*vom Staat nicht sanctionierte Gesellschaften*). Some of them — whom Kant calls pious clique members (*Klubbisten der Frömmigkeit*) — indulge in secret teachings that are not destined for the general public (*nicht fürs grosse Publicum gehörende, geheime Lehren*). Amidst all these isolationists and dissenters, Kant distinguishes yet another group. This group can be said to react, not only to the established, visible, and acknowledged church, but also to all of the aforementioned deviant forms. This group of *syncretists* or, as Kant puts it, "false peacemakers," are, despite all appearances, in fact

worse than sectarians, because they are basically indifferent to religion as such and take the attitude that, if there should be an ecclesiastical faith of the people at all [*wenn einmal doch ein Kirchenglaube im Volk sein müsse*], one is as good as another so long as it lends itself readily to the government's aims. This prin-

74. Cf. *RBR* 194 n. / 847 n. on the term *Pfaffentum*.

ciple is quite correct and even wise when the ruler states it in his capacity as ruler [*im Munde des Regenten, als eines solchen*]. But as the judgement of the subject [*im Urtheil des Unterthanen*] himself, who must ponder this matter in his own — and indeed his moral — interest [*Interesse*], it would betray the utmost contempt for religion; so that the very question of the quality of the vehicle of religion, which someone adopts in his dogma, cannot be indifferent to religion. (*CF* 274 / 319, trans. modified)

Worse than sectarians, the syncretists are as dangerous as their counterparts, the representatives of "sheer paganism." Here, once again, the extremes — which are also extreme abstractions — seem to meet, because the indifference to all *adiaphora* has the same effect as their total fetishization. If each extreme were possible as such, rather than being virtual possibilities of an utmost limit, then they would threaten the civil and the moral order in roughly the same way. *Extreme syncretism* and *sheer paganism* would undercut the possibility that religion could serve as a provisional and differential medium of discriminatory markers enabling the government to influence people's innermost thoughts. What is more, paganism and syncretism, being the opposite poles of lack of civilization and *over*civilization, both endanger the gradual but, Kant believes, constant human historical progress toward the better.

On the one hand, the division into sects — which in Protestantism takes the form of a multiplication of churches — can be taken as a sign (*Zeichen*) that the government leaves it to the people to choose in freedom among the many forms of faith. More broadly speaking, Kant invokes the topos of Babel by stating that, like the division between religions, the mere "difference of tongues" may well be a "design of Providence" that guards against human hubris and facile universalisms.[75]

On the other hand, this pluralist situation cannot be regarded as good in itself. It is based, not on the principle of general agreement and unity apropos the essential maxims of faith (*wesentliche Glaubensmaximen*), as would be required by any rational concept of religion, but rather on an ever-increasing disagreement arising from what is idiomatic, idiosyncratic, and inessential (*Ausserwesentlichen*). The last, however, should ultimately be subordinated to what Kant regards as religion's essence or final

---

75. See *RBR* 153 n. / 787 n.: "If we are allowed to assume a design of providence here, the premature and hence dangerous (since it would come before human beings have become morally better) fusion of states into one is averted chiefly through two mightily effective causes, namely the difference of languages and the difference of religions."

aim: namely, the moral perfection of man. Kant leaves no doubt that in this final sense religion proper has only an indirect—im-mediate and non-phenomenologizable—role to play in the universal history of humankind that it affects from afar or, what comes down to the same thing, from within the interiority of reason and the human heart.[76] Strictly speaking, this ideal, symbolized by the figure of Christ—who matters not as a historical character but as the moral example par excellence and the personification of the principle of good—can only be realized by and in the context of the invisible church.[77] Still, Kant expresses the hope that "with the government's favor [Begünstigung], time will gradually [nach und nach] bring the formalities [Förmlichkeiten] of faith . . . closer to the dignity of their end, religion itself" (CF 275 / 320). This purified, de-formalized religion—religion qua religion, as it were—is neither abstract (a mere general, universal, let alone empty idea) nor concrete (in the etymological sense of the Latin concrescere, of which Hegel made so much); ab-solute, it expresses itself solely in the conviction that one can please God only through a purely moral attitude of will (Gesinnung). Thus, while one form of religion would come closer to the core of religion than others, its end—its telos and cessation—implies the annihilation or sacrifice of all form, of all formalities, in favor of a contentless, absolute, or pure form: one, moreover, that no longer allows for any further extension and is, therefore, quite literally the very point—the concentration, contraction, centripetal force, implosion, or entropy—of religion. In this end—the pure form of the moral law expressed by the categorical imperative—all religion as we

---

76. Cf. RBR 153 / 788: "We can expect to draw a universal history of the human race from religion on earth (in the strictest meaning of the word); for, inasmuch as it is based on pure moral faith, religion is not a public condition; each human being can become conscious of the advances which he has made in this faith only for himself. Hence we can expect a universal historical account only of ecclesiastical faith, by comparing it, in its manifold and mutable forms, with the one, immutable, and pure religious faith." (Cf. also RBR 177–79 / 142–45.) One major difference between Kant and Derrida remains the rigor with which the latter, in the footsteps of Husserl even more than of Heidegger, develops the consequences of a historicity that is transcendental and thus affects not only classical and modern determinations but, perhaps, any possible concept of the "transcendental" and the "possible." In Kant's writings on religion, we merely find an assertion of the co-implication of two sources that taken together constitute the historical and the universal, indeed, the theologico-cosmo-political.

77. This is not to forget that Christ must be seen, Kant stresses, as the founder, not of religion proper or even of the invisible church, but of the visible church that in history comes nearest to these two and is therefore called "true." Christ, Kant writes, is "the person who can be revered, not indeed as the founder of the religion which, free from every dogma, is inscribed in the heart of all human beings (for there is nothing arbitrary in the origin of this religion), but as the founder of the first true church" (RBR 181 / 828).

know it finds its destination and, if not its sublimation, then at least its sublimity and elevation. But also, as the rational kernel and vigil of moral progress, as its quasi-providential guardian, it empties out the order of phenomenality, thus amassing its very force of appeal: *the black hole of Enlightenment.* The more it is religion properly speaking, the less it is religion as we know it or in any other plausible — conceptually or empirically determinable — sense of the term. *Plus d'une religion.*

Uncannily, Kant speaks explicitly of one particular ending in this context. He begins by mentioning the "euthanasia of Judaism [*Die Euthanasie des Judentums*]," which, he insists, does not consist so much in the Christian dream and illusion (*Träumerei*) of a general conversion of the Jews to Christianity — to Christianity, that is, insofar as it is a "messianic" faith — but in a very different sort of erasure. This erasure is in tune with Kant's claim, in the second book of *Religion within the Boundaries of Mere Reason*, that the institution of Jewish "theocracy" was essentially unable to overcome the "realm of darkness." That, Kant believes, becomes possible only through the "revolution" of interiority — the "change of heart" — for which the Greek sages provided a useful yet insufficient preparation (*RBR* 119 / 735). What in Judaism prepares for the sudden arrival of Christianity, Kant alleges, has a Greek provenance. In itself, if one can say so, Judaism is nothing but the "outer observance" or "mechanical worship" that defines the political constitution of theocracy.[78] Where it seems more, it is either infused with and enlightened by Greek wisdom or, paradoxically, the first beginnings of the Christian revolution — not so much political but interior or rather spiritual — in which it itself cannot take part:

> The euthanasia of Judaism is pure moral religion, freed from all the ancient statutory teachings, some of which will have to be retained in Christianity (as [and as long as it will be] a messianic faith). Now this difference in sects must finally also disappear and this in such a way that what is called the conclusion of the great drama of the change of religion on earth [*des Religionswechsels auf Erden*] (the restoration [or restitution?] of all things [*die Wiederbringung aller Dinge*]), brings about at least in spirit that there will be only one shep-

---

78. Cf. *RBR* 156 / 792, 119 / 735, and, notably, 155 / 790: "All its commands are of the kind which even a political state can uphold and lay down as coercive laws, since they deal only with external actions. And although the Ten Commandments would have ethical validity for reason even when they had not been publicly given, yet in that legislation [theocracy] they are given with no claim at all on the *moral disposition* in following them (whereas Christianity later placed the chief work in this) but were rather directed simply and solely to external observance."

herd and one flock [*da nur ein Hirt und eine Herde Statt findet*]. (*CF* 276 / 321, trans. modified)[79]

Until the end of all things, until the curtain falls, until all garments are lifted and thus cease to be veils, until the emergence of the unified community under a single guidance — a moment, a *Nimmertag*, that might never come as such — the government must negotiate and differentiate in order to evade extremes. The state must mediate between the naturalisms, orthodoxies, and mysticisms that characterize sects, dissenters, schismatics, and the indifferent. It must keep the positions for which they stand (or refuse to stand) *in* or, rather, *off* balance. In other words, it must censor, deploying the weapons of its critique and supplementing them, if need be, with a critique of its weapons.[80]

All the divergent forms of ecclesiastical or pagan faith, whatever the nature of their retreat from the hegemonic forms of community, have social and political implications of their own, and none of them, Kant claims, can provide a general or generally acceptable model for civil society at large. Speaking of particular mystical, pietist sects, Kant notes:

If it were possible for a whole people to be brought up in one of these sects, what sort of national physiognomy [*Nationalphysiognomie*] would this people be likely to have? For there is no doubt that such a physiognomy would emerge, since frequently repeated mental impressions, especially if they are contrary to nature, express themselves in one's appearance and tone of voice, and facial expressions eventually become permanent features. *Sanctified* [Beate] or ... *divinely blessed* [gebenedeiete] faces would distinguish such a people from other civilized and enlightened peoples (not exactly to its advantage); for this is a sign of piety in caricature [*Zeichen der Frömmigkeit in Caricatur*]. (*CF* 279 n. / 325–26 n., trans. modified)

---

79. In his subtle and in the end sympathetic discussion of Kant's moral philosophy, Theodor W. Adorno has pointed to an equally disconcerting passage from Kant's pen. See Theodor W. Adorno, *Negative Dialektik*, in *Gesammelte Schriften*, vol. 6, ed. Rolf Tiedemann in cooperation with Gretel Adorno, Susan Buck-Morss, and Klaus Schultz (Frankfurt a. M.: Suhrkamp, 1997), 291 and 292 and 292 remark / *Negative Dialectics*, trans. E. B. Ashton (New York: Continuum, 1973), 296, 296–97 n. For a detailed discussion of Adorno's interpretation of Kant, see my *Theologie im pianissimo: Die Aktualität der Denkfiguren Adornos und Levinas'* (Kampen: J. H. Kok, 1989) / *Theology in Pianissimo: Theodor W. Adorno and Emmanuel Levinas*, trans. Geoffrey Hale (Forthcoming from Johns Hopkins University Press).

80. More often than not, however, as Kant's own example makes clear, the censor has more subtle means at his disposal.

By contrast, the statutory precepts of the Bible provide religion with a form resembling that of government and make it thus more able to sustain and survive civil society. In this sense, Kant suggests that the ecclesiastical faith of the Bible can function as a vehicle that renders religion visible and subject to control. This consideration introduces the pragmatic question with which Kant concludes his general remark "On Sects": when should the government grant a sect the status of a church instead of merely tolerating its existence, and when must it censor and prohibit its public appearance? There must be some vehicle, some ecclesiastical or pagan form of faith, if the government is to have a purchase on the aspirations of its subjects. This, again, is why Kant's most solemn reservations involve the extremest: the mystics and sheer pagans who refuse or ignore all "protocols"[81] and the syncretists who accept — identify, confuse, or conflate — everything. By the same token, the reduction of the forms of religion to a vehicle or a veil for another end entails, as we have seen, a radical critique of the forms of Christian orthodoxy that aver that belief in their dogma alone can guarantee salvation. In their zealous pursuit of *adiaphora*, they forget the primacy of principles of morals.

Thus Kant says of the "General Observations" concluding each of the four books of *Religion within the Boundaries of Mere Reason* that, in their dealings with "works of grace," "miracles," "mysteries," and "means of grace," they are *parerga*, essential nonessentials, as it were:

> These are, as it were, *parerga* to religion within the boundaries of pure reason; they do not belong within it yet border on it. Reason, conscious of its impotence to satisfy its moral need, extends itself to extravagant [*überschwenglich*] ideas, which might make up for this lack, though it is not suited to this enlarged domain. Reason does not contest the possibility or the actuality of the objects of these ideas; it just cannot incorporate them into its maxims of thought and action. And if in the inscrutable field of the supernatural there is something more than it can bring to its understanding, which may however be necessary to make up for its moral impotence, reason even counts on this something being made available to its good will even if uncognized, with a faith which (with respect to the possibility of this something) we might call *reflective*, since the *dogmatic* faith which announces itself to be a *knowledge*, ap-

---

81. "Least of all can the government raise mysticism, as the people's view that they themselves can share in supernatural inspiration, to the rank of a public ecclesiastical faith, because mysticism has nothing public about it and so escapes entirely the government's influence" (*CF* 281 / 329–30).

pears to reason dishonest or impudent; for to remove difficulties that obstruct what stands firm for its own (practically), when these difficulties touch upon transcendent questions, is only a secondary occupation (*parergon*). (*RBR* 96 / 704 n.)[82]

Transporting dogma into religion — as all positive, historical, revealed religion will always have done — is dangerous because it creates the delusion of inner experiences ascribed to enlightenment and magical operations or sorcery and thereby unavoidably promotes "fanaticism," "superstition," "illumination," and "thaumaturgy."[83] The desire to keep religion pure and to itself can fare no better, however. It would mean abandoning history and finitude to opt for indifference — syncretism and mysticism (and the distinction matters little here) — and hence to choose the worse of two evils.

The only acceptable position, then, holds the dogma, the statutory and ecclesiastical form of faith, to be an insufficient yet inevitable and provisional vehicle of religion proper, an index of the necessary contingency — and, indeed, transcendental historicity — of morality, regardless of its equally necessary universal or categorical intent. Its aprioricity is shot through with and transported by something of the empirical. Whatever its alleged orthodoxy and authority, this vehicle is not only potentially fetishistic or idolatrous. It will always already be tainted by an "admixture of paganism." So long as history has not come to its end, this "error" must be accepted as yet another transcendental illusion, whose appearance — whose unwarranted and surreptitious semblance — can be unveiled but not simply done away with.

SEEN AGAINST THIS BACKDROP, Kant's strategies for dealing with the reinstatement or reinforcement of censorship by the state do not stem from his desire to avoid, or his anxiety about, the "unpleasant consequences" of a "political martyrdom," however mitigated. Nor can they be understood in terms of mere pragmatism and prudence. Rather, they should be interpreted as following immediately from the premises and the logic of this text, notably, from the postulation that future change will come,

82. On the concept of the *parergon*, see Ulrike Dünkelsbühler, *Kritik der Rahmen-Vernunft: Parergon-Versionen nach Kant und Derrida* (Munich: Wilhelm Fink, 1991), and, of course, Jacques Derrida, *La Vérité en peinture* (Paris: Flammarion, 1978) / *The Truth in Painting*, trans. Geoff Bennington and Ian McLeod (Chicago: University of Chicago Press, 1987).

83. See Cavell, *The Claim of Reason*, 455, and Davidson, "Religion and the Distortions of Human Reason."

not from the bottom up, but from the top down.[84] Yet in demanding that all improvement toward the better be channeled through the government and its institutions, Kant's text is organized according to the same *political metaphysics* that regulates the distinction between high and low, right and left in the academy and in the division of the seats in its "parliament." Since these distinctions are oriented, not only by a traditional hierarchy of classes, but also by the cosmological givens of heaven and earth, as well as by the subjective experience of the body,[85] the metaphysics in question is no less vulnerable, even in terms of Kant's own critical thought.

Kant's solution presupposes something like the scholastic dictum *ens et bonum convertuntur,* that the good and the order of being must somehow be convergent, analogous, translatable into one another.[86] In a sense, this presupposition had already secretly motivated the postulates of pure practical reason and the concept of the "highest good" (the *summum bonum*). It reappears here to redeem the same project. Nothing, however, justifies or guarantees this identity or analogy of, or even resemblance between the intelligible and the empirical, ought and is. Kant would argue that reason and morality are entitled to seek — indeed, demand and desire — some translation or application, however indirect and in whatever near or distant future.[87] But this *Bedürfnis* of pure reason is its first — inevitable or necessary — betrayal.

84. Cf. *CF* 307 and 307 n. / 366 and 366 n. Not only the philosopher, the rational theologian who is at odds with his biblical colleagues, but also the government needs the vehicle of sensible representation, of dogma, and, in a sense, idolatry and superstition. This need should not be confused with the *Bedürfnis* that demands that morality, although independent and autonomous, can nonetheless be said to extend to religion, more importantly, to "the idea of a mighty moral lawgiver, outside the human being" (*RBR* 59–60 / 652). This supplement does not imply that morality requires a more than merely formal and, therefore, material determining ground for the will to be able to know, or conform to, its duty. Reason is not indifferent to the outcome of any such free choice: "Although on its own behalf morality does not need the representation of an end which would have to precede the determination of the will, it may well be that it has a necessary reference to such an end, not as the ground of its maxims but as necessary consequence accepted in conformity to them" (*RBR* 58 / 650).

85. Cf. Brandt, "Zum 'Streit der Fakultäten,'" 37.

86. See Hendrik Johan Adriaanse, "Het morele godsbewijs, in het bijzonder bij Kant," *Wijsgerig Perspectief* 5 (1983/1984): 173–80.

87. Vorländer cautions his readers that Kant has not succeeded in providing a philosophical justification for religion proper as a relatively independent orientation of "feeling." Kant would have betrayed his own premises had he introduced theologemes that lead in the final analysis to unwarranted subreptions: "What we get, therefore, is a morality applied to religion [or, religiously applied morality, *religiös angewandte Moral*]: Religion — as a matter of fact, the Christian, New Testament, religion — *insofar as* it has moral content. Isn't the purity of morality

Here lies one of the more compelling reasons for Kant's compliance with the institution of censorship. It is as if his feigned gesture of sub-mission — at once sincere and cunning — signaled yet another "fact of rea-son," namely, that there can, strictly speaking, be no pure or purely formal morality or moral religion "within the limits of reason alone," *if* the human race is considered to be "constantly progressing toward the better," and *if* this progress relies — however minimally or provisionally — on a force that is not merely individual and spiritual, or of "the better argument," but descends from the top down, depending on the state's authority and its *ultima ratio,* its power to censor. Along the way — within the "prospect of an immeasurable time" (*CF* 304-5 / 362) — a preparatory, didactic, and even epagogic role needs to be assigned to the government. In this sense, Kant's text can be read as *an affirmation, not of this or that politics but of politics "as such,"* of its necessity in history, for as long as it lasts. Only this affirmation can provide reasonable ground for the hope that "gradually" "violence on the part of the powerful will diminish and obedience to the laws will increase" (*CF* 307 / 365, trans. modified).[88]

---

thereby jeopardized in a certain way? We believe: when morality in itself does not need the idea of God, then it does not "inevitably" lead to religion. . . . Already in the *Critique of Practical Reason* the supplement [or addition, *Hinzufügung*] of the "highest Good" and the "postulates" represented a deviation from the strong criteria for a pure ethics that rests on nothing but itself [*auf sich selbst ruhenden Ethik*]. Even stronger this highest Good as telos [*Endzweck*] makes its appearance in the preface of our text [i.e., *Religion within the Boundaries of Mere Reason,* нdv]. But this telos, in spite of all provisos [*Verklausulierungen*], is no longer a purely moral one, since it is based on a "natural property" and a "need" of human beings. Thus, the belief in a future life rests on the "general moral disposition in human nature" even though, on the other hand, the "potentiality of the human being"[*Menschenvermögen*] does not suffice in helping it to bring about. As a consequence, God appears in the first place as a distributor [*Austeiler*] of happiness [*Glückseligkeit*] that is commensurate with the worthiness for happiness [*Glückswürdigkeit*] — and this will hardly be sufficient in the eyes of a religious person."

88. One of the most concise and precise formulations of this complex position — and im-position — of philosophy and morality can be found in the preface to *Religion within the Bound-aries of Mere Reason:* "If morality recognizes in the holiness of its law an object worthy of the highest respect, at the level of religion it represents an object of *worship* in the highest cause that brings this law to fruition and thus morality appears in its majesty [as the highest good, the *summum bonum*]. Everything, however, even the most sublime object, is diminished under the hands of human beings whenever they apply its idea to their use. That which can be ven-erated truthfully only so far as respect for it is free, is forced to accommodate itself to those forms which can be given authority only through coercive laws; and that which of itself exposes itself to the public criticism of all, must submit to a criticism which has coercive power, i.e., to a censorship. // However, since the command, Obey authority! is also a moral one and its ob-servance, like that of any duty, can be extended to religion, it is fitting that a treatise dedicated to the definition of the concept of religion should itself offer an example of this obedience —

Concentricity and Monocentrism

What, in sum, is the relation between rational religion (*Vernunft-religion*) and revealed religion (*Offenbarungsreligion*)? Kant compares them, not to strictly separated spheres, but to concentric circles. In the preface to the second edition of *Religion within the Boundaries of Mere Reason*, he writes: "Regarding the title of this work (since doubts have been expressed also regarding the intention hidden behind it) I note: Since, after all, revelation can at least comprise also the pure *religion of reason*, whereas, conversely, the latter cannot do the same for what is historical in revelation, I shall be able to consider the first as the wider sphere of faith that includes the other, a narrower one, within itself (not as two circles external to one another but as concentric circles)" (*RBR* 64 / 569). Derrida's reading helps us to single out the centrist or monocentrist presupposition of Kant's philosophical theology.[89] Somewhere, for Kant, there must be a center — *one* center — and only one or the other, *either* revealed *or* rational religion (according to Kant the latter, the smaller of the two circles), lies closest to it. Not that one could easily measure the distance between the two circles, or between either one and their purportedly common center. More importantly, Kant asserts that these fundamentally incommensurable circles can still somehow be said to revolve around a common measure: the highest good, the ideal of reason, and, ultimately, God. Although they are abstractions (from one another), one circle would nonetheless somehow lead or point toward the other.

Derrida points out that we can never hope to determine with either epistemological or moral certainty which of the circles (if *circles* they are) is more central or closer to the center (if there is one, just one). Reason alone cannot decide whether it is historical revelation (*Offenbarung*) or, on the contrary, pure moral religion (*die reine Vernunftreligion*). The problem of which comes first or is primary — a particular, positive revelation captured by dogma or a rational religion (a problem inspired by the "logic of presupposition" that Derrida discusses in *Aporias* and that I have re-

which, however, cannot be demonstrated merely by attending to the law in a single state regulation while [remaining] blind to all others, but concomitantly only through coherent respect for all regulations" (*RBR* 60–61 / 652–53).

89. In his text, Derrida gets it the wrong way round, however, confusing the letter if not the spirit of Kant's text, and stating that rational religion encompasses revealed religion ("Autour du même centre, le cercle intérieur est celui de la religion révélée ou historique, le cercle extérieur celui de la religion rationelle"; *DP* 357–58).

constructed at some length in *Philosophy and the Turn to Religion*) — is irresolvable in any rigorous, decidable way. Philosophically speaking, we are dealing here with an undecidability that is neither accidental nor the result of a lack of reasoning, but reveals a general and universal structure of revealability (*Offenbarkeit*) itself. It can only be solved through resolve, through conscientious resolution, that is to say, through decision, affirmation, confession, and testimony. Everything thus comes down to the question of orientation, of how to orient oneself in thinking, a question that in 1786 Kant raises explicitly in a polemic with Jacobi, in "Was heisst sich im Denken orientieren?" ("What Does It Mean to Orient Oneself in Thinking?").[90] This problem, in turn, Derrida writes, entails that of the "lever" of thought and action: "When one asks how to be oriented in history, morality or politics, the most serious discords have to do less often with ends . . . than with levers."[91]

Yet the distinction between the intelligible and the empirical, between the noumenal and the phenomenal, between pure, rational, moral faith and the historical forms of ecclesiastical dogmatics or paganism — and hence between reflective faith and orientation, testimony and the choice of levers — can no longer be upheld where the "example" of religion is at issue. This "truth" of religion and the conflicts of interpretation it generates, I have argued, might well reveal a central feature of thought and action in general. More and other than just any example, religion is exemplary for the experience of deconstruction that affects all institutions from within, no less than in relation to the political and thus from without.

The Stoic motif of the circles (I will return to this in my final chapter), betrays a central impetus that Kant's analysis shares with the hermeneutic tradition and that I have contrasted (in the final chapter of *Philosophy and the Turn to Religion*) with the deployment of the rhetorical and mathematical figure of the ellipse/ellipsis. To structure thought, experience, and history around a principle of *concentricity* — of no more than two circles that revolve around each other and that interpenetrate as time goes by — is no more convincing than to premise them on, say, a metaphysical sphere that gives everything its proper place from the outset, irrespective of tem-

90. Immanuel Kant, "Was heisst: sich im Denken orientieren?," in *Werke,* ed. Wilhelm Weischedel (Darmstadt: Wissenschaftliche Buchgesellschaft, 1983) / "What Does It Mean to Orient Oneself in Thinking?," trans. Allen W. Wood, in *Religion and Rational Theology, The Cambridge Edition of the Works of Immanuel Kant,* trans. and ed. Allen W. Wood and George Di Giovanni (Cambridge: Cambridge University Press, 1996).

91. Derrida, "Mochlos," 31 / *DP* 436.

poral progress, or on a unilinear and teleological movement of spirit that will inevitably bring history to a close, that is to say, full circle. Philosophical thought offers no such guarantee.

Kant's figure of the ever expanding and narrowing innermost of two concentric circles—of a rational theology that will continue to purge ecclesiastical forms of their historical contingencies until the end of all things, while simultaneously being drawn in an opposite, spiraling movement toward a heart, origin, ground, and center that reason alone cannot penetrate—does not match well the aporetics that mark philosophy's institutionalization. Its paradoxical logic explains why one cannot predict when, where, and how the reversal of the academic order will take place, if it takes place at all. If one chooses to read the phrase "the last will be first" as evoking a "regulative idea" or "ideal" that can only be approached asymptotically, one should be aware that this interpretation is complicated by the letter and spirit of *The Conflict of the Faculties* and, though less directly, *Religion within the Boundaries of Mere Reason*. Kant's Christological reflections provide the key to understanding this reversal. The "change of heart" for which the paradigmatic figure of the humiliated and incarnated God stands conjures up the "possibility" and the modality the "revolution" Kant discusses in the second part of *The Conflict of the Faculties*. Already in *Religion within the Boundaries of Mere Reason*, we find that this revolution can only be affirmed by the spectator, in this case through the absolute witness that is the omniscient and omnipresent God.

Ineradicable Evil

The permanent danger of despotism, dogmatism, sectarianism, fanaticism, superstition, esotericism, and thaumaturgy (in short, *Schwärmerei*) is given with the fallibility of man, which, in the first part of *Religion within the Boundaries of Mere Reason*, is closely linked to his originary—in Kant's words, *radical*—evil.[92] If Kant postulates the necessity of a certain, limited

92. For an interpretation of the first part of Kant's book, see also Paul Ricoeur, "Une herméneutique philosophique de la religion: Kant," in *Lectures 3: Aux frontières de la philosophie* (Paris: Seuil, 1994) / "A Philosophical Hermeneutics of Religion: Kant," trans. David Pellauer, in *Figuring the Sacred: Religion, Narrative, and Imagination*, ed. Mark I. Wallace (Minneapolis: Fortress Press, 1995); idem, "Le Mal: Un défi à la philosophie et à la théologie," in *Lectures 3*; the lemma "evil" in Howard Caygill, *A Kant Dictionary* (Oxford: Blackwell, 1995, 1999), 179–82; Myriam Revault d'Allonnes, "Kant et l'idée mal radical," in *Ce que l'homme fait à l'homme: Essai sur le mal politique* (Paris: Flammarion, 1995); Jacob Rogozinski, "Ça nous donne tort (Kant et le mal radical)," in *Kanten: Esquisses kantiennes* (Paris: Kimé, 1996) / "It Makes Us Wrong: Kant and Radical Evil," in *Radical Evil*, ed. Joan Copjec (London: Verso, 1996); Jacob Rogozinski,

censorship, then this necessity is, in the final analysis, based on affirming the "fact" of human finitude, a fact grounded in the inextirpable "propensity to evil" that he discerns in human "nature."

Kant begins *Religion within the Boundaries of Mere Reason* by invoking a bleak picture of the human moral state, past and present. He sketches future prospects in light of different historical views of Paradise, the Fall, human progress, possible redemption, and so on. Judging from experience, we can only conclude that none of these historical representations can answer the question of how to understand the origin and the pervasive nature of evil. In fact, the ineradicable propensity to evil in human nature should be understood in a way that escapes all empirical and dogmatic explanations. Evil is innate, but in a sense that circumvents biological, ontogenetic, and phylogenetic determinations:

> Since the first ground of the adoption of our maxims, which must itself again lie in free power of choice, cannot be any fact possibly given in experience, the good or the evil in the human being is said to be innate (as the subjective first ground of the adoption of this or that maxim with respect to the moral law) only *in the sense* that it is posited as the ground antecedent to every use of freedom given in experience (from the earliest youth as far back as birth) and is thus represented as present in the human being at the moment of birth — not that itself is the cause. (*RBR* 71 / 668)

Human evil would thus seem to be grounded in *natality,* in the ontological determination given in and with birth, an existential characteristic about which Heidegger seems to remain largely silent. If one wished to parody the famous line from *Der Ackermann aus Böhmen* (*The Farmer from Bohemia*) Heidegger quotes and interprets in *Being and Time*—"As soon as a man comes to life, he is at once old enough to die [*Sobald ein Mensch zum Leben kommt, sogleich ist er alt genug zu sterben*]" [93]—one could say that as soon as man is born, he is old enough to be evil. This is not to suggest that biological birth is to be taken as the empirical cause, or givenness, of "sin." The human propensity to sin must instead be thought of as an

---

Le Don de la Loi: Kant et l'énigme de l'éthique (Paris: Presses Universitaires de France, 1999), esp. 266 ff.; and Eric Weil, "Le Mal radical, la religion, la morale," in *Problèmes kantiens,* 2d ed. (Paris: Vrin, 1998).

93. Quoted after Martin Heidegger, *Sein und Zeit* (Tübingen: Max Niemeyer, 1979), 245 / *Being and Time,* trans. John Macquarrie and Edward Robinson (New York: Harper & Row, 1962), 289. For a discussion and further references, see my *Philosophy and the Turn to Religion,* 260 ff.

always pending and apparently compelling *possibility* inherent to all (well-intended) action and never as a simply avoidable corruption that time can redeem, if not eradicate. Radical evil, Kant holds, does not consist in merely neglecting to combat inclination, as Stoics of all ages would have it. The "cause" of the "transgression" of moral duty is a "special, positive principle (evil in itself)" (*RBR* 102 / 711).[94]

Kant's whole moral philosophy is built upon this contrast between a positive principle of negativity (i.e., radical evil) and a negative principle of positivity (i.e., the moral law), each of which counterbalances—and, to a certain extent, conditions—the other. Yet all these terms ("positive," "negative," "principle") are in need of further qualification. The positive principle of negativity, of "wickedness" (*Bosheit*), is neither empirical nor intelligible but *invisible*—"an invisible enemy, one who hides behind reason and hence is all the more dangerous" (*RBR* 101 / 709)—and spiritual or, rather, spectral.[95] Its uncanny sublimity is so central to its function that Kant illustrates it with an infernal as opposed to a heavenly logic:

94. Kant reasons as follows. The Stoic conception of evil in terms of a "*neglect* to combat" one's inclination (inclinations that are in themselves innocent) is caught in an irresolvable paradox and must, therefore, give way to a philosophically more sound understanding of the lack of fulfilling one's duty: "Since this omission [of which the Stoic speaks as if evil were merely a *privatio boni*] is itself contrary to duty (a transgression) and not just a natural error, and its cause cannot in turn be sought (without arguing in a circle) in the inclinations but, on the contrary, only in that which determines the power of choice as free power of choice (in the first and inmost ground of the maxims which are in agreement with the inclinations), we can well understand how philosophers—to whom the basis of an explanation remains forever shrouded in darkness and, though absolutely necessary, is nonetheless unwelcome—could mistake the real opponent of goodness" (*RBR* 102–3 / 711). By contrast, Kant points out that the very first sign or "act" of goodness can only consist in forsaking the "perversion" that may inhere in a maxim—and thereby in freedom—itself. Whereas inclinations merely obstruct the "*execution*" (*RBR* 102 n. / 711 n.) of good maxims, the disposition of the will decides whether these universalizable maxims are willed at all and for their own sake. Not to will them is genuine evil.

95. Kant writes: "We should not therefore be disconcerted if an apostle represents this *invisible* enemy—this corrupter of basic principles recognizable only through his effects upon us—as being outside us, indeed as an evil *spirit*: 'We have to wrestle not against flesh and blood (the natural inclinations) but against principalities and powers—against evil spirits'" (*RBR* 103 / 711). The citation is (a misquotation) from Ephesians 6:12. Conversely, we may think of the good principle—the "good and pure principle of which we are conscious"—in terms of a "good spirit that presides over us" (*RBR* 111 / 724). The latter, Kant muses, "carries confidence in its own perseverance and stability, though indirectly, and is our Comforter (Paraclete) whenever our lapses make us anxious about its perseverance" (*RBR* 111–12 / 724). This confidence is not built on any empirical progress, spiritual exercises, or introspective soul-searching. The stability and constancy with which we are comforted is never given as such. Kant observes: "Certainty with respect to the latter is neither possible to the human being, nor, so far we can see, morally beneficial" (*RBR* 112 / 724).

It is a peculiarity of Christian morality to represent the moral good as differ-
ing from the moral evil, not as heaven from *earth,* but as heaven from *hell.*
This is indeed a figurative representation, and, as such, a stirring one, yet not
any the less philosophically correct in meaning — For it serves to prevent us
from thinking of good and evil, the realm of light and the realm of darkness,
as bordering on each other and losing themselves into one another by gradual
steps (of greater and lesser brightness); but rather to represent them as separated by an immeasurable gap. The total dissimilarity of the basic principles
by which one can be subject to either one or the other of these two realms, and
also the danger associated with the illusion of a close relationship between the
characteristics that qualify somebody for one or the other, justify this form of
representation which, though containing an element of horror, is nonetheless
sublime. (*RBR* 103 n. / 712 n.)

Postulating the possibility of the worst at the very root of the possibility of the best does not prevent Kant from entertaining yet another
possibility, that of a sudden revolution, a "change of heart." This change
does not announce itself as the result of a moral progress in time, but is
its precondition, commencement, or promise. Rather, its revolution — in
an ambiguity of meaning reminiscent of the comparison, in the second
preface to the *Critique of Pure Reason,* of the *Revolution der Denkungsart*
to Copernicus's *De Revolutionibus,* as well as to the French Revolution —
has a specific, circular, or elliptical temporality of its own.[96] It is at once
timeless — *plus d'un temps,* no more time and more than one time or more
of one time — and the heartbeat or the inner clock of reason's unseen yet,
Kant believes, providential movement throughout the universal history of
humankind.[97]

96. For the different scientific and sociopolitical connotations of the concept of revolution,
see I. Bernard Cohen, *Revolution in Science* (Cambridge: Harvard University Press, 1985).

97. Mutatis mutandis, Derrida subscribes to the same temporal logic of repetition, iterability, serialization, nonsynonymous substitution, and so on. In a contribution to *Le Monde,*
written on the occasion of the bicentennial of the French Revolution and republished in *The
Other Heading,* he writes: "Given that good will (which is indispensable) will not be enough to
change things, that no longer fall under logic of simple 'consciousness' and of a juridical — that
is, inadequate — concept of responsibility, given that technical procedures and formal legality
(which are indispensable and can always be improved) will never reach the end of this im-
measurability, given that whenever it is a question of response and responsibility, of address
and destination, etc., the philosophical concepts that we have inherited have never sufficed;
given all this, one will recall the French Revolution only by appealing to other revolutions. The
memory of a promise, such an appeal or call seeks a new tone. It no doubt, will no longer
be 'revolutionary,' and it must take this time — beyond the 'revolutionary day'" (Derrida, *The
Other Heading,* 107–8 / 123).

The restoration of the original position, the genuine human predisposition toward the good that forms the hidden telos of history, must and must not take place in time if it is to take place at all. Thus, on the one hand, Kant can write that "the moral subjective principle of the *disposition* by which our life is to be judged is (as transcending the senses) not of the kind that its existence can be thought as divisible into temporal segments but rather only as an absolute unity" (*RBR* 111 n. / 725 n.). On the other hand, however, he hastens to add that only in the relative stability of the path taken following the change of heart can a person become worthy of luck and hope to prove his godliness. Only *over time* can the revolution — the rebirth or new creation — progress toward the good and discharge the original debt incurred close to the equally original disposition toward the good. For God the absolute witness, however, these contradictory aspects of human progress from wickedness to holiness — aspects reducible only in part to the fact that man has both an intelligible character and an empirical nature, since the contradiction between temporality outside of time and the reiteration of this timeless time over time runs through the realm of the intelligible as well — form a unity, and not just the two sides of a chance toss of the coin (the human *coup de dés,* as it were). Once more, the revolution, this time of a single individual's decision, can be perceived by the spectator — here, the Spectator par excellence — alone. To observe morality, its progress and perils, demands nothing less than the viewpoint of God:

> For him who penetrates to the intelligible ground of the heart (the ground of all the maxims of the power of choice), for him to whom this endless progress is a unity, i.e., for God, this is the same as actually being a good human being (pleasing to him); and, to this extent, the change can be considered as a revolution. For the judgment of human beings, however, who can assess themselves and the strength of their maxims only by the upper hand they gain over the senses in time, the change is to be regarded only as an ever-continuing striving for the better, hence as a gradual reformation of the propensity to evil, of the perverted attitude of mind. (*RBR* 92 / 698)[98]

And yet even for the divine witness — especially for the absolute witness — the human revolution can only be a failure, doomed in advance by a gap or distance that no infinite approximation can be certain (or rea-

---

98. Cf. *RBR* 113–14 / 728: "Satisfaction must be rendered to Supreme Justice, in whose sight no one deserving of punishment can go unpunished."

sonably hope?) to bridge. Here we stumble upon the genuine secret—in Kant's words, the *mysterium*—of morality and of faith. While Kant is adamant that "duty demands nothing but what we can do" (*RBR* 92 / 698),[99] he leaves no doubt that what we can—and thus, by implication, must— do is here and now never enough. Hence, the severest judgments must be passed on the best of our resolutions and efforts: "The distance between the goodness which we ought to effect in ourselves and the evil from which we start is, however, infinite, and, so far as the deed is concerned—i.e., the conformity of the conduct of one's life to the holiness of the law—it is not exhaustible in any time. Nevertheless, the human being's moral constitution ought to agree with this holiness. . . . And this . . . change of heart . . . must . . . be possible because it is a duty" (*RBR* 108 / 720). At this point Kant introduces a double solution: he postulates an infinite time after the time given us in this life, which allows an in principle infinite range of possibilities for pleasing God (*RBR* 108–9 / 720–21), and he speculates about the possibility—apparently at once reasonable and incomprehensible— of divine assistance: "Only with respect to that which God alone can do, for which to do anything ourselves would exceed our capacity and hence also our duty, there we can have a genuine, i.e., a holy, mystery of religion (*mysterium*). And it might perhaps be useful only to know and to understand that there is such a mystery rather than to have insight into it" (*RBR* 165 n. / 806 n.).

As Derrida reminds us, the law of pure practical reason ought to be obeyed out of respect. But from the very moment that this "sublimity" becomes tainted by human hands, "respect" must be summoned from elsewhere. Which of the faculties can interrogate and comprehend this evil at the root of human nature and thus understand the necessity of censorship? (See *DP* 350, 523.) Derrida recalls the first note to the fourth part of the first book of *Religion within the Boundaries of Mere Reason*, in which Kant provides the missing link between the analysis of evil and the thematics of *The Conflict of the Faculties*. This note is added to the following passage:

> Whatever the nature, however, of the origin of moral evil in the human being, of all the ways of representing its spread and propagation through the members of our species and in all generations, the most inappropriate is surely to imagine it as having come to us by way of an inheritance from our first par-

99. Cf. also *RBR* 94 / 702: "For if the moral law commands that we *ought* to be better human beings now, it inescapably follows that we must be *capable* of being better human beings."

ents; for then we could say of moral evil exactly what the poet says of the good: *genus et proavos, et quae non fecimus ipsi, vix ea nostra puto* ["Race and ancestors, and those things which we did not make ourselves, I scarcely consider as our own"]. (*RBR* 86 / 689)

To this citation from Ovid's *Metamorphoses*,[100] Kant adds a note to the effect that the higher faculties in the university tend to "explain this transmission of evil each in terms of its own speciality, as *inherited disease, inherited guilt,* or *inherited sin*" (*RBR* 86 n. / 689 n.). In so doing, they are, according to Kant, to be faulted not only for inadequately interpreting the origin, the *radix,* of evil, thus neglecting its intimate link with freedom — that freedom is premised on its necessary possibility and vice versa.[101] Kant also takes them to task for not being radical enough, for reducing their explanation of the origin of evil to the mere forms of its transmission, spread, and propagation. The theological faculty, once again, provides us with the most interesting — and most problematic — hypothesis. It regards evil as "the personal participation by our first parents in the *fall* of a condemned rebel; either we were at the time ourselves accomplices (though not now conscious of it); or even now, born under the rebel's dominion (as Prince of this World), we prefer his goods to the supreme command of the heavenly master, and lack sufficient faith to break loose from him, hence we shall eventually have to share in his doom" (*RBR* 86 n. / 690 n.).

Why Kant is forced to distance himself from this view should be clear from what we have argued thus far. But in what sense can philosophy, more precisely, the "lower faculty," explain the radicality of evil as well as the modes of its transmission? In other words, in what sense can philosophy establish the rational ground of the principle and the practice of censorship in general?[102] The answer lies in that its origin, not unlike the "causality through freedom" that constitutes morality in its very possibility, is essentially *inscrutable.* Like the free decision to observe what is moral, the propensity to evil must be situated beyond or, rather, on this side of experience and knowledge.

That humans are neither angels nor beasts — as Pascal knew — that the radical evil in human nature must be thought of as an intermediate possibility lingering between the extremes of mere animality and the diabolic,

---

100. Ovid, *Metamorphoses,* 13:140–41.
101. Cf. *DP* 356.
102. Cf. ibid.: "La vérité de la censure n'est accessible qu'au philosophe, à la Faculté de Philosophie."

is the subject of an intriguing analysis toward the end of Derrida's *Given Time*. Here, in a reading of the final words of Baudelaire's "La Faux Monnaie" ("Counterfeit Money"), a reading prepared for many years earlier in *Parages*, Derrida draws attention to the remarkable differences between Baudelaire's and Kant's interpretation of the nature of evil (differences, incidentally, that help us situate Derrida's own approach to this problem):

> Man's natural tendency toward evil is "radical" since it corrupts maxims at their very foundation and therefore prevents an eradication of that evil by means of other maxims. The order of the senses alone cannot explain this evil since sensibility deprives man of freedom and forbids one to speak of evil in this regard. By itself, sensibility would make of man an animal. But for all that, man cannot make of transgression a principle or a moral motive: he would be, in that case, a diabolical being. Now, so Kant thinks or asserts, it is a *fact* that he is not such a being. Kant's whole argumentation seems to proceed from the *credit* granted to this supposed *fact*. Since freedom remains the condition of evil, since it distinguishes here man from animal, let us not forget, in the context that is ours here, the terms in which Kant defines such a freedom. Because speculative philosophy must leave interdeterminate the law of a causality called freedom, the law of causality "by freedom" (*durch Freiheit*), the determination of freedom by the moral law can never be shown or demonstrated; it remains, from the theoretical point of view, negative. It remains the correlate of a belief, a credit, even, Kant says, of a "letter of credit [*créance*]" (*Creditiv*).[103]

This brings us back, once again, to the concept and the practice of confession, of the "circumfession [*circonfession*]," and all of its implications for the structure of the testimonial, the attestation — matters I have discussed at length in *Philosophy and the Turn to Religion*. The reference to the *Creditiv* is derived from an expression in *Critique of Practical Reason:* "This kind of letter of credential [*diese Art von Creditiv*] of the moral law — that it is itself laid down as a principle of the deduction of freedom as a causality of pure reason — is fully sufficient in place of any a priori justification, since theoretical reason was forced *to assume* at least the possibility of freedom in order to fill a need of its own." [104] Derrida points out that Kant's critique

103. Jacques Derrida, *Donner le temps, 1: La fausse monnaie* (Paris: Galilée, 1991), 209 n. / trans. by Peggy Kamuf as *Given Time* (Chicago: University of Chicago Press, 1994), 165 n. 31.

104. Immanuel Kant, *Kritik der praktischen Vernunft*, vol. 6 of *Werke*, ed. Wilhelm Weischedel (Darmstadt: Wissenschaftliche Buchgesellschaft, 1983), 162 / *Critique of Practical Reason*, in *Practical Philosophy, The Cambridge Edition of the Works of Immanuel Kant*, trans. and

of pure practical reason is associated with a general economy of infinity. In "Faith and Knowledge," he adds that not by accident is *Religion within the Boundaries of Mere Reason* also a book about radical evil. If the turn to religion as well as the "return of the religious" are, as Derrida suggests, intrinsically bound up with "at least certain phenomena of radical evil," then the following question should also be asked: "Does radical evil destroy or institute the possibility of religion," as well as that of ethics and politics?[105] Does it both sublate and inaugurate, or do neither of the two? Or does it, perhaps, do both at once or one thing after the other, in the circularity of an endless repetition, of testimony and of violence? Could it not be argued that the possibility of religion is also the possibility of radical evil, if it is true, *concesso non dato,* that religion and radical evil are "possible" or "possibilities" at all?[106]

The Academic Contract: Old and New

The texts collected in *Du droit à la philosophie* suggest that, at least since the eighteenth century, "the transformation of the university" has required the permanent reformulation of its "charter," the "founding, somehow, of a different, even if unwritten, constitution."[107] Yet this promise remained unfulfilled. In our days, Derrida writes, the promise of a "new academic *Aufklärung*" seems to be "demanding far more of us than did the eighteenth century's or the one they recently talked about in Frankfurt."[108] This gesture, although it analyzes and perhaps reinforces a specifically modern predicament, is in itself neither modern nor, to use an all too facile terminology, "postmodern." Rather, it attempts to "reawaken [*réveiller*]" and "resituate" a much older or even immemorial obligation that precedes, exceeds, and traverses every existing as well as every pos-

---

ed. Mary J. Gregor (Cambridge: Cambridge University Press, 1996), 178. See also Derrida, *Given Time,* 165, n. 31 / 209 n. 1.

105. Jacques Derrida, "Foi et savoir: Les Deux Sources de la 'religion' aux limites de la simple raison," in *La Religion,* ed. Jacques Derrida and Gianni Vattimo (Paris: Seuil, 1996) 55, cf. 62 / "Faith and Knowledge: The Two Sources of 'Religion' within the Limits of Mere Reason," trans. Samuel Weber, in *Religion,* ed. Derrida and Vattimo (Stanford: Stanford University Press, 1998) 41, cf. 42.

106. That "religion" should be understood as "possible" or a "possibility" is, in fact, far from certain, since these notions are premised on a metaphysics of potentiality, *dunamis, entelecheia,* and hence metaphysical possibilism, whose presuppositions, I have suggested in *Philosophy and the Turn to Religion,* can be deconstructed at their very core. We can now see why the same holds true for its silent companion, namely, violence or, in Kantian parlance, "radical evil."

107. Derrida, "Canons and Metonymies," 210.

108. Ibid., 211.

sible future philosophical and institutional determination (*DP* 486). From its very inception, thought would have been linked up with a responsibility that would escape the generality of laws and the stability of existing forms. *Du droit à la philosophie* seeks to think and to practice this responsibility without reducing it — once more — to a metaphysical principle, to a formal law or even to an ethico-political norm or criterion. To the extent that no institution can exist without deconstructable — and always already deconstructed or self-deconstructing — distinctions, the very concept of the institution thus remains problematic.[109] This does not mean that deconstruction discredits the Kantian notion of critique, nor that it envisages a practice that would situate itself beyond any institution. What is at stake is the necessity (or, what is the same, the responsibility) of reinscribing these two philosophical concepts — critique and institution — in a logic (in Derrida's words, a "graphic of iterability"; *DP* 88) capable of explaining the necessary interplay of their inevitable repetition and equally inevitable change.

In consequence, deconstruction could never "limit itself to a reassuring methodological reform within the confines of a given organization," nor could it "reduce itself to an irresponsible destructive parade . . . that would have the even more certain effect of leaving everything as it is and consolidating the most immobile forces in the university" (*DP* 424). To be sure, the displacements deconstruction brings about could not easily be captured by the traditional programs, parades, and banners (of, say, right and left) in which and with which "the political" is often framed and staged (*DP* 424). For this reason, Derrida suspects, deconstruction is regarded as being too partisan by some and too quietistic by others. Its discourse can be situated neither on the right nor on the left side of the Kantian academic parliament, nor according to the principle of any parliamentary distribution. Rather, it operates as a mobile "parasite" that moves back and forth and leaves its detractors in doubt as to whether it mediates a concordat between the two parties or classes of faculties involved and thereby advances the quest for "eternal peace," or whether it seeks to "reignite" the eschatologico-apocalyptic fires that have endangered the university from its earliest beginnings. But all these possibilities still move within the confines of Kant's text and are restricted by it.[110]

109. Cf. *DP* 88: "La déconstruction est une pratique institutionelle pour laquelle le concept d'institution reste un problème."

110. Cf. Derrida, "Mochlos," 29, and *DP* 434.

At stake here is a more complex—a double and elliptical—movement. In interrogating the ultimate ground of institutions, in particular the philosophical institution (the university) that Kant studies in *The Conflict of the Faculties,* deconstruction does not simply resort to a superior tone. Rather, this interrogation reaffirms its allegiance to a new Enlightenment—Derrida writes: "Je suis résolument pour les Lumières d'une nouvelle *Aufklärung* universitaire" (*DP* 466)—in which a certain reiteration of the Kantian project will be unavoidable and even, to a certain extent, desirable and responsible. Although this analysis demonstrates that the rigor of Kantian architectonics is visible only through the breaches in an edifice that has become inhabitable like a ruin or that, more likely, was never more than a phantasm,[111] it remains conscious that the very question of whether or under what conditions a new institutional, academic responsibility would be possible retains, in its generality, a modern transcendental and critical, or Kantian, form. What is more, the ruin and the phantasm are not merely "negative" or illusory.[112]

Kant, we found, justifies the political *factum brutum* of a given institution by analyzing the conditions of its possibility in ideal (or pure) rational and juridical terms. For love of the ruin that already in its foundation it resembles, recalls, and invokes, Derrida, by contrast, endeavors to transform this factual structure while going beyond what is given, or *possible,* on the basis of it or any other structure. Could there be any institutional form appropriate to the new responsibility, a "community of thought" that would not leave the principle of reason "unquestioned," a "community" that, therefore, would be irreducible to the scientific community, but that—with an unavoidable performative contradiction—would interrogate the foundation of the institution itself (*DP* 488–89)? Derrida leaves the question open. However, the detailed documentation on the preparation and the establishment of the Collège International de Philosophie

111. Cf. *DP* 409.

112. In "Force of Law" Derrida admits that one day he would like to write, following Walter Benjamin and, he adds, "maybe against Benjamin, a short treatise on the love of ruins": "What else is there to love, anyway? One cannot love a monument, a work of architecture, an institution as such except in an experience itself precarious in its fragility: it hasn't always been there; it will not always be there; it is finite. And for this very reason I love it as mortal, through its birth and its death, through the ghost or the silhouette of its ruin, of my own—which it already is or prefigures. How can we love except in this finitude? Where else would the right to love, indeed the love of right, come from [*D'où viendrait autrement le droit d'aimer, voire l'amour du droit*]?" See Jacques Derrida, *Force de loi: Le "Fondement mystique de l'autorité"* (Paris: Galilée, 1994), 105 / "Force of Law: The 'Mystical Foundation of Authority,'" trans. Mary Quaintance, *Cardozo Law Review* 11 (1990): 1009.

could be read as naming an institution that would move beyond the existing forms of institution.[113] Indeed, Derrida writes, every interpretation of theorems, philosophemes, or theologemes—for example, in *Du droit à la philosophie,* the concepts and figures that together somehow constitute the "idea" of the Western university—would imply or, rather, call forth or invent a new institutional "model" (*DP* 422).

Every interpretation, therefore, would be characterized by a distinctive responsibility even though it is impossible to say "for what and for whom" (*DP* 422–23). Would this responsibility be for the past, for those who have passed away, or for those who are still—and, perhaps, forever—to come? In any institution, the responsibilities of interpretation will have "the form and the content of a *contract*" (*DP* 423). This contract does not precede the act of interpretation. It is written and signed in a process of negotiation with, and transformation of, the preexisting hegemonic patterns of interpretation that overdetermine both the institution and society at large. Whether or not we can find and define it in its purity, academic responsibility, Derrida writes, would at the very least consist in spelling out the political implications and aporias of research and teaching at the institution we call the university, whose boundaries are less certain than ever. Yet, he suggests, in every "reading" and in any "construction of a theoretical model," in the "rhetoric of an argumentation," in "mathematical formalization" no less than in the presentation of "historical material," an institution is at work, "a type of contract signed, an image of an ideal seminar constructed, a *socius* implied, repeated, displaced, invented, transformed, threatened or destroyed": "The institution does not only consist of walls and external structure that surround, protect, guarantee or limit the freedom of our work; it is also and already the structure of our interpretation" (*DP* 424). Mutatis mutandis, the same could be said of the interpretation of a poem or of poetological studies.[114] This is one reason why the practice of deconstruction is not just, or not even primarily, a hermeneutical method or technique that reinvents our ways of dealing with archives and contemporary forms of knowledge and language within the context of a given institution, which is itself taken for granted. Rather, it should be understood as taking a stand—as a *prise de position* (*DP* 424)—with regard to that institution. The deconstructive readings in *Du droit à la philosophie* not only displace the conceptual oppositions that govern Kant's

---

113. Cf. *DP* 551 ff. See also Châtelet, Derrida, Faye, and Lecourt, eds., *Le Rapport bleu.*

114. Cf. *DP* 422 and 486–87, respectively. For an analysis of the relationship between responsibility and poetics, see my *Instances.*

text, but also affect the integrity of the sociopolitical structures that rely upon these presuppositions, that sanction and reinforce them. But the attempt to found a new institution and to reverse or displace the order of its hierarchy, however radical the intention, could never force a radical rupture with the edifice—whether ruined or phantasmatic—that precedes it. In order to take a step forward or beyond, it would have to "negotiate a compromise" with the traditional order that it seeks to displace and that offers in itself or that offers itself as the stepping stone from which the leap to another place could be made, if such a leap is possible and desirable. Where this is so, everything would come down to finding and using "the best [or right] lever" for change (*DP* 435–46).

It is no accident that the Greek word for "lever," *Mochlos,* figures as the title for Derrida's reflections on the aporias of Kant's *The Conflict of the Faculties* and the task of a new academic responsibility. Aside from recalling a term Kant himself cites in a footnote—*hypomochlium* (*CF* 320 n. / 382 n.)—the Greek word *mochlos* stands for the necessary and impossible task of "negotiating" the old and the new, the past, the present, and the future. Derrida chooses it deliberately: "At a time when this text ["Mochlos"] could wrongly be considered hostile to a traditional concept of the university, even dangerous for the 'humanities' and their canons, [this text intended,] through the choice of this somewhat learned word, to reaffirm a taste for the classics, the desire and the necessity of a certain memory. So *Mochlos* also signifies Mnemosyne, Clio, Mneme, Anamnesis."[115]

Instead of allowing oneself to be taken over by a certain ("popular" or "academic") pathos of "activism," one should recall Derrida's permanent *laudatio* of historical, philological, and even discursive knowledge.[116] The title "Mochlos" thus also counters the claim that deconstruction stands for a new barbarism intent upon obliterating the "canons and norms of classical culture." Even though the word *Mochlos* could easily function as the proper name of a monster and thus ironize the fear of deconstruction's

115. Derrida, "Canons and Metonymies," 204.

116. See Jacques Derrida, *Positions* (Paris: Minuit, 1972) / trans. Alan Bass (Chicago: University of Chicago Press, 1981): "It is true that I am very interested in the history of philosophy in its 'relative autonomy.' This is what appears indispensable to me: the theoretical critique is also a 'discourse' (which is its specific form), and if it is to be articulated rigorously along with a more general practice, it has to take into account the most powerful *discursive* formation, the powerful, extended, durable, and systematic formation of our 'culture.' It is on this condition that one will be able to avoid empiricist improvisation, false discoveries, etc., and that one will give a systematic character to deconstruction" (*Positions,* 102 n. 21 / 68 n. 13, trans. modified).

alleged iconoclasm, its main semantic allusion remains the "trampoline" or "strategic lever." Responsibility with respect to the institution should adhere to a paradoxical rhythm of at once adopting the most traditional and rigorous standards of academic competence and going as far as possible in the direction of thinking the groundless ground of the principle of reason. Such a questioning would have to operate on both sides of the line that is said to demarcate and divide the university internally and externally. Just as the paradoxical or aporetic position of the lower faculty is said to promise the reversal and displacement of the existing academic and nonacademic hierarchical order, so this thought would be all the more effective or promising when it acquiesces in its marginality and affirms its aporetics:

> In the university, as elsewhere, one must always deal with contradictory injunctions in the form of the "double bind." Since we always have to assume responsibilities quickly, lest the action be endlessly delayed, the question of "What to do?" or "How to do it?" is always a strategic question, the question of ... a "negotiation" between two contradictory imperatives, both of which exclude negotiation, and at least one of which presents itself as "categorical" or "unconditional." Is there, in the face of such antinomies, a good stratagem? Is strategy not impossible? Does the concept of strategy hold when the question of the better outcome is the very thing that gives rise to the antinomy? The Western university ... is still, for a while at least, the place where questions of this kind can be posed.... At any rate the question is not excluded, any more than the person who poses it or tries to draw certain consequences from it. But let us not indulge in too many illusions: this tolerance can be explained by the fact that the question has not yet been posed truly, effectively, noisily enough, or because the effective consequences are not yet visible, understood, measured. But as soon as they become suspect or obscurely glimpsed, then of course signs of nervousness appear.[117]

No responsible institutional politics could ever escape this "double gesture" or "double postulation" (*DP* 491), which is also a double science and a doubling of science: both more of this science and no more of this science (*plus d'une science*), both an intensification and its ironization, at once the last and best science can offer and that which is least of all science, at the furthest remove from science (as we know it, strictly speaking). At stake here, as *Positions* puts it, is the attempt to "avoid both simply *neutraliz-*

117. Derrida, "Canons and Metonymies," 205.

ing the binary oppositions of metaphysics and simply *residing* within the closed field of its operations, thereby confirming it."[118] Without leaving the demands of critical reason behind, it thus pushes a multiplied and divided responsibility to its utmost limit and beyond. It stretches it beyond the theoretical, the practical, the categorical, and the possible, each of which retains a formal or minimal limitation. The very notion of the limitation of responsibility — of its being assigned to a particular time and space, a particular sphere, whether public or private, whether imagined or real, whether a priori or a posteriori — would again transform it into a complacent *"good conscience"* (*DP* 108). Against this background, Derrida suggests, "if responsibility must always be excessive, incalculable, forever carrying beyond the measurable norms and the units of measurement of law and morality; if responsibility is something that responds only to the other within us, and can therefore never be reappropriated, resubjectivized or reconstituted autonomously — a heteronomy of this kind needs to keep some quality of the *an-human*."[119]

However, it would be equally wrong — and, indeed, no less unjust — to exaggerate the excessiveness of this deconstructive displacement of academic (and more than simply academic) responsibility in view of the "anhuman." Insistence on excess alone would reduce this responsibility to sheer moralism, just as would downright legalism or acting merely "in conformity with duty." If it were not betrayed, if some economy did not come to restrict its measureless demand, if, finally, mitigation and limitation did not haunt emphatic responsibility and "resist" its "gentle but *intractable* [*intraitable*] imperative,"[120] responsibility would, for all its dynamism, stiffen into the complacency of a good conscience. Only in being interrupted, restricted, and censored by what it is not — that is to say, com-

---

118. Derrida, *Positions*, 41 / 56, trans. modified.

119. Derrida, "Canons and Metonymies," 204–5. Derrida explicitly distinguishes the term *anhuman* from *inhuman* (ibid.). This is one of many points where Derrida distances himself from Jean-François Lyotard, whose *L'Inhumain: Causeries sur le temps* (Paris: Galilée, 1988) / *The Inhuman: Reflections on Time*, trans. Geoffrey Bennington and Rachel Bowlby (Stanford: Stanford University Press, 1991) strikes a different tone from the one adopted (or "raised"?) here. On the question of the "human," the "an-" and "anti-human," see Beatrice Hanssen, "'The correct/just point of departure': Deconstruction, Humanism, and the Call to Responsibility," in *Enlightenments: Encounters between Critical Theory and Recent French Thought*, ed. Harry Kunneman and Hent de Vries (Kampen: Kok Pharos, 1993); on Lyotard's *inhumain*, see my article "On Obligation: Lyotard and Levinas," *Graduate Faculty Philosophy Journal* 20, no. 2; 21, no. 1 (1998): 83–112.

120. Jacques Derrida, *Passions* (Paris: Galilée, 1993), 76 n. 3 / trans. David Wood in *On the Name*, ed. Thomas Dutoit (Stanford: Stanford University Press, 1993), 133 n. 3.

parison and distribution — can absolute responsibility be prevented from turning into its virtual opposite. Here, as always, the best resembles the worst.

In "Les Pupilles de l'Université: Le Principe de raison et l'idée de l'Université" ("The Principle of Reason: The University in the Eyes of Its Pupils"),[121] Derrida broaches a model for pursuing the ellipticity of *Aufklärung* or "thought" without getting caught in a vicious circle of pure repetition or becoming paralyzed before an inescapable abyss. There he sketches a rhythm of alternation in which both the archaeological and the anarchic extremes of all discourse keep each other in (or, rather, off) balance. The formal structure of the ellipse, the interplay of two foci that are mutually exclusive and yet always already point to one another, indicates the paradoxical structure of these polar constellations. Here, the blindness of one pole is the insight of the other (and vice versa). Both these constitutive "moments" oscillate in a permanent, open dialectic in which neither of the two foci implied in all utterance is ever fully able to determine the (act of) institution and organize the dialectic around one center, not even that of vigilance. Like the ellipse, which decenters the circle, the apparent repetition of the "levers" would draw a circle only in a very peculiar, inflected, or even contorted way.[122]

"Thought," Derrida argues, requires both the principle of reason and what lies beyond (or before) it. It requires a double gesture, an alternating movement of archeology and anarchy, of tradition and openness, of memory and chance. Between these two poles, only the difference, only the suspension and inversion of the "breath," "accent," or "enactment" (*mise en oeuvre*) of this "thought" (*DP* 495–96) — its *Atempause* and *Atemwende*, to cite Celan — could decide. To emphasize one of the poles would be a nonformalizable and nonphenomenologizable gesture, depending on singular testimony alone. This "decision of thought," Derrida continues, is "always risky, it always risks the worst," but this is the price one has to pay

121. Jacques Derrida, "Les Pupilles de l'Université: Le Principe de raison et l'idée de l'Université," *DP* 461–98 / trans. Catherine Porter and Edward P. Morris as "The Principle of Reason: The University in the Eyes of Its Pupils," *diacritics* 13, no. 3 (1983): 3–20.

122. This figure of the "ellipse with two focal points" occurs in more than one context: for example, in Jacques Derrida, *Moscou aller-retour* (La Tour d'Aigues: L'Aube, 1995) / "Back from Moscow, in the USSR," in *Politics, Theory, and Contemporary Culture*, ed. Mark Poster (New York: Columbia University Press, 1993), where it invokes "Moscow and Jerusalem" and, Derrida writes, "does not fail to cross another ellipse, if that is possible, the one that stretches between a para-Oedipal Greek mythology and a revelation of the Mosaic or messianic type" (ibid., 200 / 21).

if one does not wish to "barricade" oneself and others against the future
that is (the) to come (*DP* 496). And yet, one step too many in the direction of a more radical principle or archē, one step too far beyond it, in
the hope of some quasi-mystic divination of an originary an-archy, could
produce a new, more subtle, and more powerful hierarchy than the one
deconstructed (*DP* 495). Indeed, at any given point a step in either direction—or even the refusal to step—would be vulnerable to appropriation
by the very forces it seeks to contest.

The ellipse of alternation or polarization is always in danger of being
disrupted by omission or even obliteration (by ellipsis, that is). Again,
this possibility is a necessary possibility and no mere accident. Any genuine attempt to submit the demands of formal reason to those of vigilance
would be excessive to the point of bringing about its own virtual eclipse.
In precisely this sense, Enlightenment is divided in and against itself. Only
an uneasy—incalculable—balance could protect all thinking and institutional practice against the apocalypse or eschatology (or, what comes
down to the same thing, the reification or petrifaction) that constantly
threatens it.[123] In order to counterbalance this ineradicable danger, the
university must "walk on two feet," supporting itself on one while lifting
the other in anticipation of the next step or leap.[124] Elliptical movement
keeps the archaeological and the anarchic extremes of discourse in and off
balance. As it walks on two feet—or, simply, if it walks—the university
respects the rhythm of alternation.

A FEW OF THE NOTES to the concluding third part of *The Conflict of the
Faculties* seem to confirm this analysis of the importance of alternation, of
the conflict (*Streit* or *différend*) of academic thought, and its ineradicable
exposure to the possibility of war and worse. In one note Kant writes: "The
purpose of walking in the open air is precisely to keep one's attention moving from one object to another and so *to keep it from becoming fixed* on any
one object" (*CF* 322 n. / 385 n.). Of course, for Kant this distraction and
relaxation only serves as preparation for more adequately fixing the object
of thought. For him, walking, despite its association with the peripatetic
ideal of the ancients, does not describe the nature of thinking as such. Yet

123. Cf. *DP* 434. For a further analysis, see the introduction to Harry Kunneman and Hent
de Vries, eds., *Enlightenments: Encounters between Critical Theory and Recent French Thought*
(Kampen: Kok Pharos, 1993), and *Philosophy and the Turn to Religion*, chap. 6.
124. Cf. *DP* 437.

a little earlier in this curious text Kant proposes a way to counterbalance the pathological states of mind known as hypochondria and melancholia, which are affections, not of the intelligible character, but of the psyche and, most importantly, of the *scholarly* psyche. Here, we find a possible Kantian response to Derrida's diagnosis of academic malaise or *mal-être:* "The exact opposite of the mind's power to master its pathological feelings is *hypochondria,* the weakness of abandoning oneself despondently to general morbid feelings that have no definite object (and so making no attempt to master them by reason). Since this sort of melancholia (*hypochondria vaga*) has no definite seat in the body and is the creature of imagination, it could also be called a *fictitious* disease" (*CF* 318 / 378).[125] Kant also identifies it as a "fainthearted brooding," a "kind of insanity," and "self-torment," and goes on to propose, if not a definitive cure, then at least the possibility of alleviating its more disturbing symptoms: "A reasonable human being does not permit himself any such hypochondria; if uneasiness comes over him and threatens to develop into melancholia — that is, self-devised illness — he asks himself whether his anxiety has an object. If he finds nothing that could furnish a valid reason for his anxiety [*Beängstigung*], or if he sees that, were there really such a reason, nothing could be done to prevent its effect, he goes on, despite this claim of his inner feeling, to his agenda for the day" (*CF* 318 / 379).

This remedy is only possible, of course, on the condition that the mind master its self-generated problems and ignore all others. The same possibility enables Kant to distinguish between, on the one hand, a purely rational, philosophical medical science that relies on the power of human reason and self-imposed regimens alone, and a merely "empirical" or "mechanical" version of this discipline, which seeks the help of "external physical means" such as "drugs" and "surgery," [126] on the other. The limits of this distinction stand and fall with the same conceptual opposition between the pure and the impure, the noumenal and the phenomenal that we have discussed above and have found wanting. This does not mean that Kant overestimates what medical science can do. On the contrary, if there is any conflict in this third and final part of *The Conflict of the Faculties,*

125. On Kant's hypochondria, see Susan Meld Shell, *The Embodiment of Reason: Kant on Spirit, Generation, and Community* (Chicago: University of Chicago Press, 1996), 264–305. On melancholia, see Raymond Klibansky, Erwin Panowsky, and Fritz Saxl, *Saturn und Melancholie: Studien zur Geschichte der Naturphilosophie und Medizin, der Religion und der Kunst,* trans. Christa Buschendorf (Frankfurt a. M.: Suhrkamp, 1990).

126. Cf. *CF* 316 / 375.

it is that philosophical medical science should distance itself from the denial of death. It should neither deny the patient's perpetual exposure to
death nor attempt to stave it off at all costs. Death is not a disease and,
therefore, not pathological, even though medical science is hard pressed
to adopt this irrational view of man's nature because of popular demand.

Speaking of another note in which Kant addresses the difference between the left and right feet of Prussian soldiers as they march, Derrida
recalls how this *foot*note evokes the "'lowest' level," at the bottom of the
page in a text by an official of the "lower" faculty, thereby reminding us
once more of "the problems of evaluation, hierarchization and canon-
ization."[127] Appended to a strikingly autobiographical passage, which expresses worry about insomnia, old age, and the relative weakness of the
body's left side compared to the right, the note concludes: "The advantage of the right side over the left can also be seen from the fact that, if
we want to cross a deep ditch, we put our weight on the left foot and step
over with the right; otherwise we run the risk of falling into the ditch. The
fact that Prussian infantrymen are trained to *start out* with the left foot
confirms, rather than refutes, this assertion; for they put this foot in front,
as on a fulcrum [*hypomochlium*], in order to use the right side for the impetus of the attack, which they execute with the right foot against the left"
(*CF* 320 n. / 382 n.).

Derrida puts his finger on the neuralgic spot of this philosophical pamphlet: "What happens when a philosopher (and moreover a professor of
philosophy, a state functionary) says 'I,' and talks about his health? And
when he associates the 'risk of falling' with a military question as posed
for the foot-soldiers of his country?"[128] Kant explicitly addresses the first
problem in discussing the different status of the third part of *The Conflict of the Faculties,* where the note is located (*CF* 314 and 314 n. / 372 and
372 n.). The second question is more difficult. Does this association reveal
a certain conjunction between *logos* and *polemos,* not unlike the one Derrida explores in Heidegger, Schmitt, and others, notably in *The Politics of
Friendship*? We will return to this question in our final chapter.

What seems clear is that the concept of war functions in Kant's text
as an indication, not so much of the extreme case — the *casus belli* — that
can be decided upon by (absolute) sovereignty alone, but of the permanent danger or even imminence of the *status naturalis* that, as we have

127. Derrida, "Canons and Metonymies," 206.
128. Ibid.

seen, is given with the division of tongues and religions as such: "So too the so-called religious struggles, which have so often shaken the world and bespattered it with blood, have never been anything but squabbles over ecclesiastical faiths. And the oppressed have never really complained for being hindered from adhering to their religion (for no external power can do this), but for not being allowed to practice their ecclesiastical faith publicly" (*RBR* 141 / 769). War or religious war, for Kant, is apparently not imaginable in the *status civilis* in which reason—rational religion— has full reign. It erupts only in the difference between the *status civilis* and the *status naturalis,* given with history and human finitude, over which looms the shadow of the *summum malum.*

Not least, the footnote, Derrida suggests in this same context, invokes the left-right distinction that has haunted—and continues to trauma- tize—all Western European *theopolitologies.* Lest we miss the reference to the likely fatal consequences of this spatial abstraction, which directs so much of our orientation in the world, Derrida brings the reference to feet and shoes down to earth, down to what annuls and forbids all abstraction, even though it lets itself be addressed only as a "phantom" subject: "It is tied in particular to a scene which both is and is not very academic, be- tween two Jewish professors who fled the Nazis; and it involves Heidegger as well, his peasant ideology, the question of the subject and a crowd of ghosts, some of whom came back from the death camps in their shoes, represented, I mean, insofar as phantoms, as shoes without bodies." [129]

In the context of a discussion of the perilous task of the university, these shoes could stand not only for a theoretical debate between, say, an art historian (Meyer Shapiro) and a philosopher (Heidegger) [130] concern- ing the at bottom undecidable character of the attribution of a meaning to the pictoral sign or mark, in this case, Van Gogh's painting of shoes. (To whom do these shoes belong? To a peasant woman, to a city-dweller, to the painter? What, precisely, is or was their function? Do they belong together, that is to say, form a pair?) The still life of the shoes also recalls the ever present danger of a certain political engagement, already present in the "pathos of the 'call of the earth'" or even in the "peasant ideology [*idéologie terrienne*]" [131] that dominates the Heideggerian appropriation or restitution of their meaning. It is no accident that in the reading of this

129. Derrida, "Canons and Metonymies," 207.

130. On the problem of right and the left in relation to Kant's "What Does It Mean to Orient Oneself in Thinking?," see Heidegger, *Being and Time,* 142–44 / 108–9.

131. Jacques Derrida, *The Truth in Painting,* 272 and 273 / 311 and 312, respectively.

discussion Derrida emphasizes all the elements we have been analyzing up to now: the question of institution, of how and where to place one's feet, of how to orient one's thinking while continuing to ask whether *ça marche* ("Who is walking?" "With whom?" "With what?" "On whose feet?").[132]

Rather than forming a pair of two symmetrical objects, to be carried away as and by an identifiable subject, Van Gogh's painted shoes create an uncanny, menacing, and even diabolical atmosphere. That, Derrida suggests, explains the overhasty gesture of so many interpreters in reassuring themselves by explaining this indetermination away. Indeed, Meyer Shapiro's attempt to criticize Heidegger's reading of this painting in *Der Urspung der Kunstwerks* (*The Origin of the Work of Art*) by proposing a cosmopolitan rather than a pastoral interpretation could be viewed as another attempt to reduce the shoes' uncanny suggestive force. Yet precisely this abyssal monstrosity remains to be thought and acted upon. It is a motif that leads us back to the heart of the ethical, of the political, and of their relation to the religious.

132. Ibid., 263 / 300. Here, Derrida notes, one would have to raise the most serious questions about Heidegger's politics, notably in the inaugural lecture of 1929, "Was ist Metaphysik? ("What Is Metaphysics?"), and the rectoral address of 1933, "Die Selbstbehauptung der deutschen Universität" ("The Self-Assertion of the German University"). These texts cast their shadow on the inquiry into the principle of reason some twenty years later in *Der Satz vom Grund* (*DP* 492). Even if Heidegger later shifted ground and displaced the classical schematics adopted in these lectures (see *DP* 404–5), the line drawn between science and philosophy, on the one hand, and "thought," on the other, still assumes, in Derrida's account, a radically different "form and function" (*DP* 29, 38). It is, in sum, a dividing line, divided in itself, that does not allow "thought" to come into its own. Cf. Derrida, "Canons and Metonymies," 208–9.

Chapter Two

Violence and Testimony

Kierkegaardian Meditations

IN "VIOLENCE AND METAPHYSICS," Derrida discusses questions raised by Emmanuel Levinas and Eric Weil: Should violence be ascribed to the philosophical logos, to the identity and totality aspired to in its very concept? Or should it be seen as a violation of this order by some singular and anarchic "other" whose alterity has not been appropriated and domesticated by rational and coherent discourse? Should one think of violence as a transcendental category—the very introduction of a category or concept of violence being the first act or declaration of war—or should one restrict this term to the ruptures that mark the contingent historical, political, psychological, and symbolic instances of all empirical conflict? Does this distinction constitute a genuine alternative? Could the meaning of violence, as Levinas argues with increasing intensity, be expanded to whatever takes place in the realm of beings: to ontology or, more precisely, to whatever "lets beings be"—namely, Being, as Heidegger has it, or *Seyn,* whether put under erasure or not? Or should it be reserved, as Weil claimed no less emphatically, for occurrences that disturb the coherence of philosophical discourse, less in abstract acts of negation than in the most enigmatic yet persistent ways? Is violence philosophy's other?

In 1963, the year before Derrida published his essay, Levinas paid tribute in *Difficile liberté: Essais sur le judaïsme* (*Difficult Freedom: Essays on Judaism*) to Weil's magnum opus, the 1951 *Logic of Philosophy.* He writes: "We owe to Eric Weil's great thesis—whose philosophical importance and tenacity of logic will impose themselves—the systematic and vigorous use of the term 'violence' in its opposition to discourse. . . . We, however, give it a different meaning."[1]

1. Emmanuel Levinas, *Difficile liberté: Essais sur le judaïsme* (Paris: Albin Michel, 1976), 18 n. 1 / *Difficult Freedom: Essays on Judaism,* trans. Seán Hand (Baltimore: Johns Hopkins University Press, 1990), 296 n. 4, trans. modified. On Weil, see also Emmanuel Levinas, *En découvrant l'existence avec Husserl et Heidegger* (Paris: Vrin, 1977), 189, and "Violence du visage," in *Altérité et transcendance* (Montpellier: Fata Morgana, 1995) 177–78.

What is this other meaning of "violence"? How is it to be distinguished from and opposed to "discourse"? In determining "violence" as the other of "discourse," Levinas gives the former an extremely wide-ranging meaning, whereas the latter is taken in a much stricter ethico-religious sense.[2] Indeed, Levinas allows the semantic field of the possible connotations of "violence" to expand until it includes virtually every situation and concept not comprised in the intersubjective relation to the other. This relation to the other, to the other (*l'autre* or *l'Autre*) as neighbor (*autrui*) as well as to God, the *illeité* that leaves His trace in the other's face, is described as "discourse" (as *le Discours* and as *le Dire*, respectively). Discourse is thought to be somehow without (or beyond and before) violence: "The Other, Exteriority, do not necessarily imply tyranny and violence. *An exteriority without violence is the exteriority of discourse.*"[3] It comes to interrupt violence, brings it to a halt, if not empirically, then at least ethically, through an appeal that is a judgment, a judgment over history, independent of its purported end(s).

Violence, by contrast, is said to take place whenever the other is not welcomed or addressed as such. This is so, Levinas claims, wherever discourse attempts to subtract itself from the realm of interlocution and interpellation — whether to achieve a rational coherence or an irrational chaos — or where the terms of this relation are exposed to each other, not as totally other, as they should be, but as alter egos, as each other's mirror images, each other's negations or, what amounts to the same thing, each other's (rational or irrational, diffuse or anonymous and neutral) totality. Wherever the self relates the other to the sameness of its own horizon, the other's singularity will be effaced. But conversely, wherever the self is overtaken or absorbed by the other — by an otherness, that is, or by an obscure, diffuse, anonymous, neutral totality — violence has taken place. Levinas claims that only between these two poles — which are extremes bound to collapse into each other — can one envision the drama of a genuine "spiritual life."

What is meant by this expression? How do the life and the spirit it promises succeed in distancing or demarcating themselves from violence,

---

2. The very possibility, that is to say, the postulation and phenomenological description or rhetorical evocation of the absolute difference between *la signification* and *le sens* is the central axiom or, rather, credential of Levinas's project.

3. Emmanuel Levinas, *Entre nous: Essais sur le penser-à-l'autre* (Paris: Grasset, 1991), 34 / *Entre nous: Thinking-of-the-Other*, trans. Michael B. Smith and Barbara Harshav (New York: Columbia University Press, 1998), 22.

from death, from the "absolute violence" to which I am "exposed" in death, to "murder in the night"?[4] Levinas writes:

> Nothing is more ambiguous than the term "spiritual life." Could we not make it more precise by excluding it from any relation to violence? But violence is not to be found only in the collision of one billiard ball with another, or the storm that destroys a harvest, or the master who mistreats his slave, or a totalitarian State that vilifies its citizens, or the conquest and subjection of men in war. Violence is to be found in any action in which one acts as if one were alone to act; as if the rest of the universe were there only to *receive* the action; violence is consequently also any action which we endure without at every point collaborating in it.[5]

Levinas seems to determine "violence" as any force or power that characterizes natural phenomena, as well as forms of human interaction in which the self, the other, or all others are not treated as free or as ends in themselves, but rather as objects subjected to an end outside themselves, to which they have not consented. Levinas stretches the definition even further by stating that almost "every causality is in this sense violent: the fabrication of a thing, the satisfaction of a need, the desire and even the knowledge of an object. Struggle and war are also violent." As if this list were not already inclusive enough, he concludes by observing that, last but not least, there is also violence "in the poetical delirium and enthusiasm displayed when we merely offer our mouths to the muse who speaks through us; in *the fear and trembling through which the Sacred carries us away;* there is violence in passion, be it the passion of a love, that wounds our side with a perfidious arrow."[6]

Thus, violence can be found in whatever narcissistic strategy the self adopts to capture, thematize, reduce, use, and thus annul or annihilate the other. Violence can likewise be found wherever some otherness engulfs or seizes upon the self and forces it to participate in what it — in and of itself and, precisely, as other — is not. Transcendental and other (mythical and sacred, empirical and ontic) violence, secretly correspond, if only because the former — while expressing itself through the power of argument and the force of the concept — could be said to neutralize, elevate, displace, and guard the latter. Here one totality or identity comes to substitute for

4. Cf. *TI* 233 / 259.
5. Levinas, *Difficult Freedom,* 6 / 18.
6. Ibid., 6–7 / 18, trans. modified, my italics.

another, sublating the frenzy and anxiety that stigmatize the first into the tranquil serenity that is the trademark of the second. This is the logic of our tradition, of philosophy in its relation to myth and religion. Nonetheless, the latter still cast their shadow across the former, haunting it with possibilities that cold reason declares obsolete or would prefer simply to forget. In consequence, the philosopher's "second violence" resembles or even repeats the "first violence"[7] that precedes it and that, in a sense, calls it into being. More precisely, the philosopher uses a mitigated (not a pure) violence against an already mitigated or transformed violence in order to prevent the latter from becoming pure (again).

As the only exception to this rule, Levinas seems to present the absolute relation to the absolute, the one that withdraws, by its very definition (or rather infinition) from every totality, from all identity, and, ultimately, from all being, from all *Sein,* from all *Seyn,* from its gift, its time, its *Ereignis,* and so on. Other or otherwise than Being, the intrigue or emplotment of the *In*-finite in the finite charges the latter with a sense at once of inspiration, prophecy, election, or holiness and of obsession, persecution, and trauma. But is this extreme possibility not somehow haunted and haunting—and, in that sense, violent—in turn? Does it not draw on a prephilosophical experience of a "fear and trembling" that it seeks to flee?

Levinas obliquely refers, of course, to the rearticulation, in Kierkegaard's *Fear and Trembling,* of what is arguably the most painful example in the history of religion of the violence of the other as it announces itself in the breaches of a sacred and sacrificial order. Out of a virtually endless series of possible connotations of violence, the uncanny scene of the "binding" (*Akedah*) of Isaac, as related in Genesis 22, will serve as a guiding thread throughout my discussion of violence in relation to notions of testimony, death, and sacrifice, as articulated by Levinas and Derrida. This context will help analyze what it means to define the concept of violence through a process of *generalization* or even *universalization* that both *intensifies* and *trivializes* the scope and the limits of its meaning. Although theoretically and philosophically impossible to decide, the distinction between these two alternatives marks all that matters ethically, politically, and otherwise.

7. For this terminology, see *LP* 59. The important third part of the introduction to this work is entitled "Philosophie et violence," and its first section carries the title "La Violence et le discours" (54–86). Cf. Jean Greisch, "L'Analyse de l'acte de croire entre histoire et épistémologie," *Recherches de science religieuse* 77, no. 1 (1989): 13–44, esp. 21 ff.

Unlike Weil, who establishes a connection between the coherence of discourse and nonviolence, Levinas regards "coherence in ontology," in whatever form it assumes, to be "violence itself."[8] Not even the concept of relationship—whether dialectical, dialogical, or religious—not even the appeal to alterity in general or as such can help. What escapes coherence is the singularity of a certain gesture, in the beginning that of language, of the saying that precedes and enables all that is said. As if anticipating his own later analyses of the gift in its irreducibility to any economy of restitution, Derrida reconstitutes this thrust of Levinas's argument: "The ego and the other do not permit themselves to be dominated or made into totalities by a concept of relationship. And first of all because the concept, . . . which is always *given to the other,* cannot encompass the other, cannot include the other. The dative and vocative dimension, which opens the original direction of language, cannot lend itself to inclusion in and modification by the accusative or attributive dimension of the object without violence" (*WD* 95 / 141). Yet are the dative and vocative not also dimensions of language? Are not all performative gestures—the language that conveys theories and philosophies as well as the violence of all ontological coherence by giving, addressing, or exposing them to the other—violent in some respect as well? Can one give without violence, without the possibility, risk, or danger of violence? What would it mean to think of violence as an inescapable horizon or inherent potentiality of any act, of any passivity?

As the central thesis of *Totality and Infinity,* Levinas recalls that the violence of the concept, like that of coherence in ontology, is not just a contingent human defect. Rather, this transcendental violence should be seen as the condition of possibility for all other—empirical, historical, psychological, or physical—real violences and, equally, for their opposite. It is the condition of possibility, not for eternal peace, but for the perennial and intermittent suspension of the hostilities of war. Against the background of this ambiguity—that violence is at once transcendental ideality and empirical reality, at once fatal and enticing, necessary and haphazard, a threat as well as a promise and chance—Levinas notes: "I refer myself to works . . . of Kojève, Hyppolyte, and Eric Weil, as well as to a much older wisdom that has never ignored the necessity of the State. But it is the fundamental contradiction of our situation (and perhaps of our condition),

8. *WD* 315 n. 42 / 171 n. 1. For a different view, see Patrice Canivez, *Weil* (Paris: Les Belles Lettres, 1999), 13 n. 7 and passim.

called Hypocrisy in my book, that we simultaneously need the hierarchy taught by Athens and the *abstract* and somewhat *anarchic* ethical individualism taught by Jerusalem as both are necessary to suppress violence. Each of those principles, left to itself, only accelerates the opposite of what it wishes to guarantee."[9]

The historical articulation of this antinomy does not lead toward some dialectical mediation or reconciliation, whether distant or imminent. On the contrary, the force of this opposition—being bound by two conflicting, contradictory, or even incommensurable orders—does not allow for any future ontological coherence. Yet, paradoxically, precisely this dispiriting unity of its differences and differends constitutes the drama of finitude and of history.

Levinas endorses Weil's insistence on the contrast between violence and discourse. Yet he interprets quite differently the meaning of these terms and the possibilities and realities for which they stand. Even if the predominance of violence in the work of both thinkers may be marked by their similar historical experiences in the Second World War, their different interpretations of violence and discourse reveal different appreciations of central categories in the tradition of Western philosophy that culminated in the speculative dialectics and the absolute idealism of Hegel.

Weil's position is not simply Hegelian, with Levinas assuming the role, so often ascribed to his work, of the anti-Hegelian. Things are more complicated, if only because for Weil the pursuit of reason is only *one* human possibility, what is more, *only a possibility*, never a necessity. In this respect, as in many others, this pupil of Ernst Cassirer is closer to Kant than to Hegel: a post-Hegelian Kantian.[10] For him, the concept of necessity applies only to the domain of hypothetico-deductive reasoning, not to the reality that concerns philosophy: "Philosophy *obliges itself*, in a free and primary decision, to coherence."[11] Yet, though philosophy may pursue the "idea" of absolute knowledge and thereby postulate an intelligible struc-

9. This remark was made during the discussion that followed the presentation of "Transcendance et hauteur," *Cahier de l'Herne*, ed. Catherine Chalier and Miguel Abensour (Paris: L'Herne, 1991), 50–74, 64; see also 72. See *TI* 24 / xii and *WD* 153 / 228.

10. See Eric Weil, *Philosophie et réalité: Derniers essais et conférences* (Paris: Beauchesne, 1982), 23 ff., esp. 50, and 95 ff. Cf. Paul Ricoeur, *Du texte à l'action: Essais d'herméneutique* (Paris: Seuil, 1986), 2:393 ff. See also Paul Ricoeur, "La 'philosophie politique' d'Eric Weil," in *Lectures 1: Autour du politique* (Paris: Seuil, 1991); "De l'Absolu à la Sagesse par l'Action," ibid.; "Violence et langage," ibid.

11. Weil, *Philosophie et réalité*, 24.

ture of reality, it should not forget the indelible difference between this structure and what it structures. To neglect this was Hegel's mistake.[12]

According to Weil, at least one other, ineradicable possibility exists. That is violence, the refusal of discourse—the discourse of the other, the infinite striving for its infinite coherence—in favor of a merely individual or personal discourse, which is deemed unique and whose purported unicity is superimposed on all other discourses (*LP* 57). Only "free choice" can decide between the two possibilities of reason and "nonreason" or violence (in Weil's universe, the alternative to "truth"). From the viewpoint of discourse and its intended or implied coherence, this choice can only appear "absurd" (*LP* 56). Weil stresses that no coherent or discursive reason can be given for being coherent or for entering discourse. The decision to be just is, in the final analysis, unjustifiable and a priori incomprehensible. For Weil, the choice for either violence or discourse is neither violent nor discursive, but free. The choice of reason instead of violence cannot be deduced by reason or reconstructed on the basis of empirical, that is, psychologistic or anthropological, phylo- or ontogenetic generalizations. Although in his *Problèmes kantiens* (*Kantian Problems*) Weil compares the possibility of violence to the Kantian understanding of "radical evil" as an ineradicable propensity to evil, he does not consider the choice of discourse to affirm (or reaffirm) a *Faktum* of reason. On the contrary, being a free choice, it is a possibility to be realized. For Weil, discourse is "good" because it allows one to arrive at the *désintéressement* that is the "silence of the gaze [*regard*]" (*LP* 10). Discourse and reason are the highest human aspiration, the "expression of the last desire," which is the paradoxical "desire to be free, not of need [*besoin*], but of desire" (*LP* 11). To realize and relinquish this desire marks the transition from *homo faber* to *homo theoreticus*. The latter, the "being" that "sees," has a regard for the "presence" that lies beyond "becoming" and "destruction," for the *nunc stans*, the "true eternity," which is to be distinguished from "infinite duration." His gaze "grasps the totality [*le tout*] in its unity" and is ineffable, not because of its ephemeral character, but thanks to its "transcendent force," which makes it escape the inherent "negativity" of language, not by one stroke, but through the ironic deployment of this negativity against itself (*LP* 11).

Here, one must ultimately rely upon the theological category of a God given in "sentiment" alone: on a Truth that rejuvenates and "purifies" in a

12. Ibid., 49–50.

"beyond of existence" that is "not necessarily an existence in the beyond"; on a Truth, moreover, that does not "appear," that "*is* not," strictly speaking, but of which it can only be said that "there is," *il y a,* that it gives and "creates" (*LP* 188). Toward this Truth, this God, the most appropriate attitude would be calm confidence, obedience, comprehension, and love, which, as Weil explains, should be seen as more than a mere "*means* of salvation," since whoever possesses it has found a "resting place [*repos*]" in which he is freed from his "solitude" and faces an Other whose "absolute existence" is able to give him absolute recognition (*LP* 179).

Once coherence is chosen, it can at any moment be interrupted and thus destroyed by the violence of "silence," "incoherent language," an "act of negation," the deployment of a mere "'technical' discourse" that loses sight of its end, or, finally, the sheer idiosyncrasy of "personal sentiment," which expresses and seeks itself as such (*LP* 65). The affirmation that this violence is irreducible, that its possible recurrence cannot be excluded, marks the difference between philosophy and, say, theology and metaphysics or between absolute idealism and the most dogmatic forms of dialectical materialism. Yet we should not forget, Weil suggests, that nonviolence (or truth) is not only the "point of departure" but also "the final end [*le but final*] of philosophy" (*LP* 59). Whenever discursive coherence is chosen—and, in the absence of pure immorality, it has always already been chosen—it demands nothing less than the reiteration of the (essentially incomplete) totality of the history of thought (cf. *LP* 68). In any concrete history, this choice between violence and coherence already lies behind us: "The fact even of the possibility of pure violence appears only at the end." Even the slightest form of organizational life already presupposes a choice of coherence, more or less. And yet, though the diabolical seems a limit-idea, the total absence of moral sense is not unimaginable. Throughout the history of ideas it has loomed behind most distinctions, and not only those between good and evil, God and the devil. Weil affirms that the very structure of discourse, its coherence and its telos, can only be understood "on the basis [*sur le fond*] of what is radically opposed to discourse."[13] Interestingly enough, he compares this logical presupposition with the structure of Aristotelian metaphysics, which affirms that one can comprehend form only on the basis of matter, of a matter, moreover, that in itself cannot be thought positively without referring to what is radically opposed to it, namely, form.

13. Ibid., 56.

By contrast, as Derrida reminds us, for Levinas the "end" of finite history, in all the ambiguity of a telos and a cessation or sublation, is not "the absolute coherence of the Logos with itself in itself" or "harmony in the Absolute System" but, on the contrary (if an oppositional logic is at all pertinent here), "peace in separation, the diaspora of absolutes" (*WD* 315 n. 42 / 172 n. 1). In this "peace" or "diaspora," is not the violence of the concept, of the "hierarchy taught by Athens" that had domesticated and appropriated the violence—in Levinas's words, the anarchy—of the world of appearance, of myth and the sacred, itself, in turn, violated and overcome, displaced and held at a distance, in the relation called "ethical"? Does the truth of monotheism, wherever it reveals itself as a "religion of adults," as a relation to the totally other that removes itself from all idolatry, from all superstition and imagery, from all rites and all incarnation, force and enforce a separation between this peace of absolutes and the reign of empirical and transcendental violence that Levinas ascribes to mythology and ontology? Could the immediacy or the enigma of the relation to the absolute ever put an end to violence and, moreover, do so nonviolently?

Levinas chooses this question as his point of departure, both in the opening pages of *Totality and Infinity* and elsewhere. As the first article in *Difficult Freedom* formulates it:

> But is a cause without violence possible? Who welcomes without being shocked? Let mystics be reassured: nothing can shock reason. It collaborates with what it hears. Language acts without being subdued, even when it is the vehicle for an order. Reason and language are external to violence. They *are* the spiritual order. If morality must truly exclude violence, a profound link must join reason, language and morality. If religion is to coincide with spiritual life, it must be essentially ethical. Inevitably, a spiritualism of the Irrational is a contradiction. Adhering to the Sacred is infinitely more materialist than proclaiming the incontestable value of bread and meat in the lives of ordinary people.... The intervention of the unconscious and, consequently, the horrors and ecstasies which it feeds . . . all this is linked ultimately to violence.[14]

But is the relation to the other not violent in its own right? Levinas leaves no doubt that the absolute other (or Other) affects me without absorbing or effacing me and without becoming integrated into me. The relation of self to other, he writes, "while remaining one of the more in the less, is

14. Levinas, *Difficult Freedom*, 7 / 18–19.

not transformed into the relationship in which, according to the mystics, the moth drawn by the fire is consumed in the fire." [15] In other words, the relation does "not sink into participation, against which the philosophy of the same will have the immortal merit to have protested." [16] Nor can the other be reduced to an intentional object or an alter ego, to a being among beings that is part of my world and thus enters my horizon.

What, then, remains? Is there a thinkable, livable, practicable, or even desirable relation that could respect the other as independent, separate, indeed ab-solute, in the etymological sense of the Latin verb *absolvere*? Could the Other withdraw from all the violent determinations that tie or bind "Him" to the order of beings, to the present and the present-at-hand, but also to history, historicity, and ultimately to logos and Being as such? Could He ever do so without some, however minimal or sublime, divine violence? Would this absolute relation to the absolute not be the end of all reason, of all *logon didonai*, of all discussion?

For Weil, violence starts precisely here, in the presupposition or invocation of the radical or total other and its absolution from everything else. Derrida summarizes his position: "The discourse Weil acknowledges as nonviolent is ontology, the project of ontology, . . . 'Harmony between men will be established by itself if men are not concerned with themselves, but with what is'; its polarity is infinite coherence, and its style, at least, is Hegelian" (*WD* 315 n. 42 / 171 n. 1). [17] Violence, by contrast, pertains to "alterity" or "the will to alterity" much more than to the discourse of totality, which is not, as Levinas would have us believe, essentially finite, but truly infinite. According to Weil, the coherence of this infinite totality would be nonviolent insofar as it no longer assumes or encounters an "irreducible finitude" (*WD* 315 n. 42 / 172 n. 1) of whatever arbitrary otherness would endanger and thus violate the order of reason and the harmony between people it makes possible.

Levinas is not unaware of this objection, of course. His condemnation of the violence of the sacred, of its diffuse, anonymous, and neutral heteronomy (its invocation of forces and gods, of powers and raptures) endeavors to demarcate *two heterogeneous experiences of the heterogeneous,* one violent and one marked by the "peace of absolutes." Yet this attempt is not without some violence of its own. Even without succumbing to the

15. Emmanuel Levinas, *Collected Philosophical Papers,* trans. Alphonso Lingis (Dordrecht: Martinus Nijhoff, 1987), 54, trans. modified.

16. Ibid.

17. Derrida is referring to *LP* 28 ff., "La Naissance de l'ontologie, le discours."

temptation to erase this difference, one might surmise that violence would not let itself be banned to one side of the line held to separate the ethical relation without relation to the other (as absolute) from the nonrelation that immerses the self in the other as the Same or, conversely, reduces this other to the self-same. A certain possibility of violence and violation remains inscribed on the very face of the face, of the *vis-à-vis* that characterizes the encounter with the other as other, as the *tout autre* and the *autrui* irreducible to any form of the Same or the Selfsame. This possibility is acknowledged by Levinas and described or, rather, evoked in vivid and lurid details, especially in his later works.

One of the most challenging features of Levinas's writing, one that keeps his work at an infinite distance from all forms of complacent moralism, is that, regardless of his incessant emphasis on the "peace of absolutes," he does not shy away from the "shock" with which "the revelation of the infinite conquers my consciousness,"[18] gives it conscience, and makes it responsible, as violence. Here, of course, violence is attributed — paradoxically — to the "welcoming of a being to which [consciousness] is inadequate" (*TI* 25 / xiii). This violence, therefore, is not of the same order as the violence that it comes to judge or bring to a halt. The violence with and as which the good appears is not identical with the violations of identity attributed to terror and war, yet in its very structure it seems to resemble "the worst."

Levinas invites us to consider an unsentimental and unsettling account of the intrigue and drama of responsibility and the testimony it provokes. At its most disturbing, violence does not just aim at the face of another, at a face that is human; it also, as Jean-Luc Nancy stresses, "originates from a face, on which wickedness can, occasionally, be read as the devastation of this same face."[19] Even beyond this distinction between good and evil, another violence — the violence of another other — lurks.

By articulating this possibility, Levinas seems to prepare an answer to one of the many pertinent questions raised by Derrida in "Violence and Metaphysics," in a reading that haunted Levinas's writing from "The Trace of the Other" to *Otherwise Than Being* and beyond. Derrida formulates this question indirectly by remarking that both Levinas and Weil, in their common preoccupation with violence — whether that of the concept, the

18. Adriaan Peperzak, *To the Other* (West Lafayette, Ind.: Purdue University Press, 1993), 129.

19. Jean-Luc Nancy, *L'Expérience de la liberté* (Paris: Galilée, 1988), 184 n. 1 / *The Experience of Freedom*, trans. Bridget McDonald (Stanford: Stanford University Press, 1994), 204 n. 2.

finite totality, or the totally other who comes to unsettle the concept, the totality, and their coherence—point to the discourse of the infinite and the absolute as what either escapes, substitutes, sublates, defers, or interrupts the reign of violence. Against the backdrop of their common presupposition, Derrida doubts whether this dilemma, in which violence is identified either with the order of the finite or with the realm of its other (whether with the finite order's negation or otherwise), constitutes a true alternative.

Notwithstanding their differences, Levinas and Weil share sufficient premises to be counted among the philosophers of a certain metaphysical epoch whose end is not yet in sight—whose end may, perhaps, never come—but whose delimitations and limitations are becoming increasingly clear, especially in light of the question of violence. Derrida writes: "One should examine the common presuppositions of this convergence and divergence. One should ask whether the predetermination, common to these two systems, of violation and pure logos, and, above all, the predetermination of their incompatibility, refers to an absolute truth, or perhaps to an epoch of the history of thought, the history of Being" (*WD* 315 n. 42 / 172 n. 1).

Derrida suggests that violence cannot be restricted to any single metaphysical predetermination, whether as an essential property of the self or as the prerogative of the other, as totality or as alterity, coherence or its absence. Nor can nonviolence be said to be the privilege of the infinite or Infinite and the peace it is believed to inspire. To the extent that these determinations could be seen as belonging to the history of thought *as* ontology—of "Being thinking itself" (*LP* 61)—and of metaphysics, neither the finite nor the infinite could aspire to remove itself from the differential notion called "violence." They are carried and traversed by a history whose worst memories continue to haunt their very best moments. No break with this intermittent interruption of the tradition of violence, whether by the In-finite (Levinas) or by the infinite coherence of discourse (Weil), could ever hope to be total. What is other than violent remains somehow violent, or is unable to express (Levinas) or realize (Weil) itself without resorting to the order it seeks to escape or invoking some violence of its own. Discourse, whether infinite or not, whether ethical or not, demands some negotiation with its other—namely, violence—if it is to minimize the risk of allowing the worst violence to come to pass.

In oblique reference to Levinas's definition of religion as the relation to the other that does not close itself off in a totality, Derrida explains this risk as follows: "If one calls this experience of the infinitely other Judaism [which, Derrida hastens to add, is "only a hypothesis for us"], one must reflect upon the necessity in which this experience finds itself, the injunction by which it is ordered to occur as logos, and to reawaken the Greek in the autistic syntax of his own dream. The necessity to avoid the worst violence, which threatens when one silently delivers oneself into the hands of the other in the night" (*WD* 152 / 226).

Thus "Violence *and* Metaphysics" — as in Levinas's title *Totality and Infinity*, the conjunction is not trivial or simply enumerative — leaves no doubt that "*within history* . . . every philosophy of nonviolence can only choose the lesser violence within an *economy of violence*"(*WD* 313 n. 21 / 136 n. 1). Consequently, *within history* — and, strictly speaking, Derrida notes, no critique of violence could ever be meaningful, effective, or relevant and responsible elsewhere — nonviolence is somehow violent: "Like pure violence, pure nonviolence is a contradictory concept. . . . Pure violence, a relationship between beings without face, is not yet violence, is pure nonviolence. And inversely: pure nonviolence, the nonrelation of the same to the other (in the sense understood by Levinas) is pure violence. Only a face can arrest violence, but can do so, in the first place, only because a face can provoke it" (*WD* 146–47 / 218).

But, Derrida continues, if one accepts this Levinasian proposition, one should take it one step further by showing that this provocation and interruption of violence — *in* and *by* the face — can never take place beyond or outside of, or before a certain metaphysically overdetermined history of Being, which *lets* beings be and, in that sense, can also be said to open or free or allow the face to face. Without this history, without the thought of Being, there would only be the impossible experience of a pure nonviolence, which is indeterminate to the point of being interchangeable or confused with its alleged counterpart of pure violence. By contrast, the history and the thought of Being, while never without a certain relation to violence — nothing is without a certain relation to violence — would come "as close as possible to nonviolence": "A Being without violence would be a Being which would occur outside the existent: nothing; nonhistory; nonoccurrence; nonphenomenality. A speech produced without the least violence would determine nothing, would say nothing, would offer nothing to the other; it would not be *history*, and it would *show* nothing; in every sense of the word, and first of all in the Greek sense, it would be speech without *phrase*" (*WD* 147 / 218).

Since speech is what, according to *Totality and Infinity*, singles out the relation to the other—the face does not just glance at us, but first it speaks—since, moreover, there can be no speech without phrasing, the denunciation of violence must engage in an intricate negotiation with violence. Can it do so without using it in return or without mobilizing a violence of its own that, incomparable or incommensurable with the first, can only counter it by, paradoxically, measuring itself against it? Can it do justice without doing violence to this justice? Derrida does not think so: "There is no phrase which is indeterminate, that is, which does not pass through the violence of the concept. Violence appears with *articulation*. And the latter is opened only by the . . . circulation of Being. The very elocution of nonviolent metaphysics is its first disavowal" (*WD* 147-48 / 219).

Since one cannot avoid speaking, since there can be no denunciation of violence without the act or gesture of a certain *phrazein,* one must oppose violence, if not in the name, then at least with the help of another—less violent or otherwise violent—violence. To invoke violence against violence would mean to enter an "economy" of violence, to wage war on war, and thus to be truly responsible, historically speaking that is, *in* and *for* history, indeed *in* and *for* the history of Being: "Hence, only in its silent origin, before Being, would language be nonviolent. But why history? Why does the phrase impose itself? Because if one does not uproot the silent origin from itself violently, if one decides not to speak, then the worst violence will silently cohabit the *idea* of peace?" (*WD* 148 / 219-20).

What necessity, what imperative might summon this nonviolent origin to betray itself violently (in and through the media of the concept and of history) to avoid being confused with the "worst violence"? Whence comes the force, the need, or the injunction to escape the cohabitation with *le pire,* with absolute, pure, or divine violence and to enter the mediated, mitigated, relative, differential, deferred, and deferring violence of history? What is the systematic, ontological, or deontological necessity or force by which the "silent origin" of language is "called outside itself by itself"? Derrida suggests the following answer:

> If light is the element of violence, one must combat light with a certain other light, in order to avoid the worst violence, the violence of the night, which precedes or represses discourse. This *vigilance* is a violence chosen as the least violence by a philosophy which takes history, that is finitude, seriously; a philosophy aware of itself as *historical* in each of its aspects (in a sense which tolerates neither finite totality, nor positive infinity), and aware of itself . . . as

economy. . . . Speech is doubtless the first defeat of violence, but paradoxically, violence did not exist before the possibility of speech. The philosopher (man) *must* speak and write within this war of light, a war in which he always already knows himself engaged; a war which he knows is inescapable, except by denying discourse, that is, by risking the worst violence. This is why the avowal of this war within discourse, an avowal which is not yet peace, signifies the opposite of bellicosity; the bellicosity—and who has shown this better than Hegel?—whose best accomplice *within history* is irenics. *Within history* which the philosopher cannot escape, because it is not history in the sense given to it by Levinas (totality), but is the history of the departures from totality, history as the very movement of transcendence, of the excess over the totality without which no totality would appear as such. . . . It is difficult to think the origin of history in a perfectly finite totality (the Same), as well as, moreover, in a perfectly positive infinity. If, in this sense, the movement of metaphysical transcendence is history, it is still violent, for—and this is the legitimate truism from which Levinas always draws inspiration—history is violence. (*WD* 117 / 173)

Do we know, then, precisely where violence comes from, where it begins, resides, or ends, and what (or whom), exactly, it is directed at? Is it a fact, or *Faktum,* of reason in Kant's sense, as much as, say, a "fact of life," even of "spiritual life"? If violence seems to lose its specificity as physical, psychological, political, colonial, structural, domestic, sexual, or verbal violence, do we have a clear idea of what would bring violence to a halt and mark its cessation? Is the silent individual or collective gesture or is the utopian end-state of nonviolence the absolute opposite of violence: its annihilation, mitigation, repression, negation, or sublation? Is nonviolence nonviolent, in the strict sense of the word? If it is not, how would its violence differ from violence's more brutal and manifest empirical (physical, psychological, social, personal, or symbolic) effects, to say nothing of "the worst violence"? Could one retrace the most elusive or remote aspects of violence—for example, the violence in and of nonviolence—without turning them into metaphysical, ontological, or theological categories? Without doing them violence in turn? And, finally, could any such question ever be answered theoretically, once and for all, independent of all context?

Critiques of violence are not without violence, of course. They are successful only if they turn violence inside out, if they are somehow violent in turn, turning good violence against bad or the worst violence. No one has analyzed this complementary, supplementary complicity—and its intrinsic dangers—at greater length and with more consequence than Derrida. Not only does this insight preoccupy such earlier writings as "Violence and Metaphysics," it persists into more recent texts such as *Of Spirit*, "Force of Law," and *Politics of Friendship*. It is articulated, above all, in *The Gift of Death*, where the earlier analysis of a generalizable, that is to say, no longer limitable or strict economy of violence is systematically linked to the topos that I introduced in *Philosophy and the Turn to Religion*, namely, the recurring citation of the figure of the *à dieu* or *adieu*. That text will enable us to relate the question of violence to that of *divine* violence and, indeed, of Kierkegaard's motif of a *horror religiosus*.

This *à dieu* or *adieu*, spelled as one word or not, signaling an address, a speaking toward "God" (*à dieu*) no less than a gesture of leave-taking—an *adieu*, that is, to "God" at the very moment one directs oneself to "Him," an *adieu*, moreover, to the "God" thematized and addressed by others, here and now, in the past and the future—this singular and singularly divided *à dieu / adieu* does not have the form of an epistemological or axiological a priori, a presupposition or postulate, either of which would retain an element, a reminiscence, of constative or prescriptive language. And yet the *à dieu / adieu* reveals a similar structure, namely, that of a condition and uncondition (*incondition*) of possibility for authority, responsibility, and decision. In its quality of a peculiar, a singular and absolute, performative, its evocation, pronunciation, and translation testify to the very structure of testimony.

In retracing the figure of the *à dieu / adieu*, one can only be struck by the uncanny resemblance of this motif to some of the most disturbing motifs in Benjamin's "Critique of Violence," which, as Derrida has pointed out in "Force of Law," risk resembling, if not mimicking or mirroring, the worst. We will return to them at some length in the next chapter. In speaking of the *à dieu / adieu*, are we dealing with another figure of divine violence? In an unsettling way, the testimony of this unconditioned condition (which, paradoxically, is also a conditioning *un*conditionality) is bound, both structurally and quite literally, to a scene of *sacrifice*—rather, to a *sacrificing of sacrifice*, one Derrida reads as the paradigm of every genuine decision.[20] Moreover, this sacrifice—as the sacrifice of the self's identity

20. Jacques Derrida, *Points de suspension*, ed. Elisabeth Weber (Paris: Galilée, 1992), 157–58 / *Points . . . : Interviews, 1974–1994*, ed. Elisabeth Weber, trans. Peggy Kamuf and others (Stanford: Stanford University Press, 1995), 148–49.

and thus as *self*-sacrifice — becomes the sacrifice of any self-sacrifice transformed into a norm, an ideology, or a religious demand.

To prepare the ground for this discussion, let us return to a text that, more than any other, challenges the Levinasian perspective without taking Weil's position: Kierkegaard's *Fear and Trembling*. In the reception of this text, Levinas and Derrida part company. Or so it seems.

Rereading *Fear and Trembling*

At first glance, Levinas's intransigent critique of Kierkegaard's distinction of the ethical from the religious dimension seems to pose no major obstacle to retracing what is at stake in *Totality and Infinity* or interpreting the later works. What bothers Levinas in Kierkegaard ("What disturbs me in Kierkegaard," he writes in one of two pieces on this author reprinted in *Noms propres [Proper Names]*),[21] is that his notion of a subjective existence that in its irreducible interiority or secrecy retreats from the order of the general and universal and thereby "rejects all form" is, paradoxically, also in danger of adopting an "exhibitionistic" and "violent" pathos (*PN 76 / 112*). It is, Levinas claims, perhaps since Kierkegaard and not since Nietzsche that we have learned what it means to philosophize with a hammer and thus to become sensitive to a "new tone in philosophy" (*PN 72 / 106*). This new tone exalts in "a permanent scandal," in an "opposition to everything," and is in some regards the prelude or overture to the worst violence yet to come. There is a certain resonance here, Levinas suggests, with all the tremors brought about by National Socialism and its intellectual and cultural allies (*PN 76 / 112*).

This violence and "harshness [*dureté*]" of Kierkegaard's writing manifests itself at the moment in the dialectical lyric at which personal existence, in "moving beyond [*dépassant*]" the aesthetic stage (*PN 72 / 106*), also "transcends [*dépasse*] ethics" (*PN 76 / 112*) in order to enter the religious realm of a faith that no longer lets itself be justified on external grounds. This transgression not only turns faith into an absolutely singular event in which sublime communication and utter solitude coincide; it also reduces the ethical to the general, to the rule of law applicable to

---

21. *PN 76 / 112*. On the multifaceted history of interpretation of the sacrifice of Isaac before and beyond Kierkegaard's *Fear and Trembling*, see Robert L. Perkins, ed., *Kierkegaard's 'Fear and Trembling': Critical Appraisals* (Alabama: University of Alabama Press, 1981), and Jill Robbins, *Prodigal Son / Elder Brother: Interpretation and Alterity in Augustine, Petrarch, Kafka, Levinas* (Chicago: University of Chicago Press, 1991), 74 ff.

all, in which the very secret of the self as well as of its innermost secret decisions will always be betrayed (*PN* 72 / 106).

But, Levinas asks, does the ethical really reside where Kierkegaard thinks it does, namely, in some generality? Does it not consist in a responsibility toward another person (to *autrui*) that, instead of absorbing me in the universal, "singularizes" me by putting me in a "unique" and irreplaceable position (*PN* 76 / 113)? Does Kierkegaard's association of the ethical with the general not prejudge the interpretation, given in *Fear and Trembling*, of the story of how God tempted Abraham by demanding that he offer his son Isaac as a burnt offering on Mount Moriah? Is it an accident that Kierkegaard chooses to ignore another story, in which Abraham intervenes on behalf of the few just who might still be found in the idolatrous cities of Sodom and Gomorrah, destined for destruction (Genesis 18:23–32)? Is it not precisely here, in Abraham's ethical gesture, that the very "precondition [*le préalable*]" for "any possible triumph of life over death" is formulated as a "bestowal of meaning [*donation de sens*] . . . despite death" (*PN* 77 / 113)? Is it not here, finally, in the relation to the Infinite that emerges only in and as this responsibility for (other) mortals, that Abraham becomes aware of his own finitude or mortality? The exclamation "I am but dust and ashes," Levinas reminds us, "practically opens the dialogue, and the annihilating flame of divine ire burns before Abraham's eyes each time he intervenes" (*PN* 74 / 109).[22]

Kierkegaard is wrong, Levinas insists, to identify the ethical that Abraham leaves behind, in raising the knife, with an abstract universal distinguished from the religious realm. The most remarkable moment in the narrative is not when, through an encounter with the infinite God, the finite subject is said to "elevate itself to the religious level" — as if God were to be found outside, above, beyond, and external to the ethical order — but rather the instant in which Abraham hears the voice that calls him back to the ethical order: "That he obeyed the first voice is astonishing: that he had sufficient distance with respect to that obedience to hear the second voice — that is the essential" (*PN* 77 / 113).

Are the two voices that Levinas sets apart in his reading of Genesis 22 not in fact different intonations or modulations of one and the same voice, that of the one Other, the Other as the One? Does God speak in different

---

22. Cf. Emmanuel Levinas, *La Mort et le temps* (Paris: L'Herne, 1991), 135.

tongues here? Are his dictates contradictory, since He first promises that in Abraham's seed—beginning with Isaac, given to him in old age—all the generations of the earth will be blessed (*FT* 17),[23] and then seems to make the fulfillment of this promise impossible by demanding that Isaac be sacrificed? Is the voice that calls Abraham to order, interrupts his sacrifice, and recalls him to the ethical God's genuine voice, whereas the first (the one that brings him to the point of committing the crime) is only a simulacrum, a *flatus vocis* open to misinterpretation? Is it the ruse of a demonic impostor, or the—perhaps, necessary—temptation of the ethical?[24] Is the One haunted by its other, by a double, by a violent doubling that it—of necessity—inflicts upon itself? And is this why the One becomes violent in turn?

In *Mal d'archive: Une impression freudienne* (*Archive Fever: A Freudian Impression*), Derrida seems to suggest as much: "As soon as there is the One, there is murder, wounding, traumatism. *L'Un se garde de l'autre.* The One guards against / keeps some of the other. . . . *L'Un se fait violence.* The One makes itself violence. It violates and does violence to itself, but it also institutes itself as violence."[25] Moreover, Derrida continues, this violent self-doubling reiterates and commemorates "Necessity itself, *Ananke*," ad infinitum: "The One, as self-repetition, can only repeat and recall this instituting violence."[26] That Necessity is a chance or, rather, a mixed blessing as well. For where the One becomes the One plus at least one or perhaps the One less than one, One minus One—the One being no longer one or One but Other, other, its own other—where the One collapses in on itself or is shattered and disseminated as the more than One as well as no more One, there, Derrida writes, "religion" cannot but begin

23. Cf. Genesis 17:15–19, 18:10–15, 21:1–12.

24. Speaking of a similar doubling, Derrida's *Specters of Marx* seems to unfold the same intrigue in its reading of *Hamlet:* "The one who says 'I am thy Father's Spirit' can only be taken at his word. An essentially blind submission to this secret, to the secret of his origin: this is a first obedience to the injunction. It will condition all the others. It may always be a case of still someone else. Another can always lie, he can disguise himself as a ghost, another ghost may also be passing himself off for this one. It's always possible" (Jacques Derrida, *Spectres de Marx: L'État de la dette, le travail du deuil et la nouvelle Internationale* [Paris: Galilée, 1994], 27 / *Specters of Marx: The State of the Debt, the Work of Mourning, and the New International,* trans. Peggy Kamuf [New York: Routledge, 1994], 7–8).

25. Jacques Derrida, *Mal d'Archive: Une impression freudienne* (Paris: Galilée, 1995), 124–25 / *Archive Fever: A Freudian Impression,* trans. Eric Prenowitz (Chicago: University of Chicago Press, 1996), 51.

26. Ibid., 51 / 135–26.

and resurface, time and again.[27] For better and for worse, there is "division and iterability of the source."[28]

These assertions are based, of course, on some of Derrida's earliest insights into the supplement — or the prosthesis — of the origin and confirm the analyses, put forward in "Force of Law" and *Politics of Friendship*, concerning the quasi-mystical violence at the foundation and the very heart of states, of the law, of collective identities, even of the self. These motifs should not be identified with Levinas's central claim that being "human" or "spiritual" consists in *être à deux*, even though for Levinas, who distances himself explicitly from the tradition of dialogical philosophy to the extent that it is presupposes an element of fusion or reciprocity, this apparent duality is also already complicated by a logic of the third that, if ignored, leads one to the worst of all violences. In Derrida this insight is even more pronounced and is articulated with reference to Carl Schmitt's *Politische Theologie* (*Political Theology*). Schmitt, in turn, draws heavily on the Church Fathers, notably Gregory of Nazianzus, and their dogmatic preparation of "political Christology" (see Chapter 4).

The Modality of Persecuted Truth

Abraham was the greatest of all, great by that power whose strength is powerlessness, great by that wisdom whose secret is foolishness, great by that hope whose form is madness, great by the love that is hatred to oneself.

(*FT* 16–17)

What is new in Kierkegaard's phenomenology of the paradox of Abraham's (and all genuine) faith, Levinas explains, is his discovery, not of some drama of salvation and consolation, overdetermined by a Christian tradition, but of the formal description of the different — of the differential and more or other than differential — modality of a "persecuted truth," as distinguished from the presentation of all-triumphant truth. This original design of transcendence is, Levinas writes "the knot of an intrigue which separates itself from the adventure of being that runs through the phenomenon and immanence, a new modality which expresses itself in the 'if one wishes' [*si l'on veut*] and 'perhaps' [*peut-être*] and that one must not reduce to [*ramener à*] the possibility, to the reality and the necessity of formal logics, to which even skepticism refers itself."[29] Persecuted truth

27. See FK 19 / 29.
28. Ibid., 65 / 85.
29. Levinas, *En découvrant l'existence avec Husserl et Heidegger*, 209.

is not a privation or limitation of the manifestation of all things for all eyes—although it is, indeed, not of this world.[30] Nor does it reduce itself to or reveal itself in (and as) the "clearing" of Being in and through which everything that is presents itself as what it is. The proper modality of persecuted truth withdraws itself from the very play of revealing and concealing "in which immanence always wins out over transcendence" (*PN* 78 / 115). Its truth does not present itself as Truth or as Being, nor does it take the form of a "Mystery" (*PN* 78 / 114-15). Its mode is, rather, that of a "humility" (*PN* 78 / 114) and a "total *incognito*" (*PN* 69 / 103) that gives itself without giving *acte de présence*. Incognito, it speaks only as long as and to the extent that it does not betray its "origin" or "name." Persecuted, it speaks on the condition of anonymity or pseudonymity, not unlike the author of *Fear and Trembling*, who hides behind the name Johannes de Silentio. It speaks, finally, while creating the transcendental illusion that nothing—at least nothing determinate, nothing about it—is said. Thus, Levinas writes, "its presentation is equivocal: it is there as if it were not there. . . . Someone began to say something—but no! He said nothing. Truth is played out on a double register: at the same time the essential has been said, and, if you like, nothing has been said. . . . Revelation—then looking back on it [*après coup*], nothing" (*PN* 78 / 115).

In *En découvrant l'existence avec Husserl et Heidegger* (*Discovering Existence with Husserl and Heidegger*), Levinas illustrates the enigma of the trace by invoking the ambiguity of both seduction by a lover and diplomacy.[31] These examples, taken from the realm of eros and enmity, politics and war, would seem to be at the furthest remove from the ethical relation to the other. By contrast, in *Le Temps et l'autre* (*Time and the Other*) and *Totality and Infinity* eroticism is described as a structure that resembles the transcendence of metaphysical desire, whereas the realm of politics is relegated to the order of the same and of violence. The later work, notably *Otherwise Than Being*, reverses this schematics by defining politics as the realm of the mediation of the other (of justice, that is), while relegating eros to the order of the same, as contrasted with agape.

Levinas stresses that the "new modality of truth" exemplified in the story of Genesis 22 as read by Kierkegaard is hardly an idiosyncratic invention. It is the "translation of an epoch" which has come to learn the

30. Levinas concludes the essay "Herméneutique et au-delà" (*Entre nous*, 74 / 91) by suggesting that Kierkegaard was in fact the first philosopher who no longer thinks God in mundane terms: "C'est le premier philosophe qui pense Dieu sans le penser à partir du monde."
31. Levinas, *En découvrant l'existence avec Husserl et Heidegger*, 208.

historical contingencies that make up the Scriptures of the positive religions, the religions of the Book, yet remains susceptible to the voice that echoes or resonates within them (*PN* 78–79 / 115).

Levinas claims, however, that Kierkegaard's attempt to subtract the secret interiority of the subject both from the aesthetic stage of "sensible dispersion" (*PN* 67 / 100) and despair, and from the ethical generality of the legal order, the social institution, and intersubjective communication is bound to fail. According to Kierkegaard, only the continuously reiterated *salto-mortale* of faith, a leap into the "solitary tête-à-tête" with God (*PN* 70 / 103), would in its very silence constitute true communication. But the *ipse* that Kierkegaard seems to adopt here and to oppose to the Hegelian dialectic remains, Levinas claims, a constitutive moment of the order of the Same, an *idem* that ultimately cannot escape the speculative logic of Absolute Idealism. In its very incommunicability—in the *brûlure* of its sin and in the thirst for salvation, which can be neither expressed nor mitigated by any objective order—it retains the structure, if not of self-reflection, then at least of a self-centeredness, of a *"tensing on oneself [tension sur soi]"* (*PN* 67 / 100). The Kierkegaardian self betrays here both its Christian and its pagan sources.

The first seems the least difficult to determine, since the very title of Kierkegaard's book superimposes the injunction, in Philippians 2:12, to "work out your own salvation with fear and trembling; for God is at work in you" onto the Genesis narrative. The reference to Paul hints that the believer (the disciple, Abraham) must work at his faith while remaining in suspense about its outcome, in the certainty that God alone will ultimately decide. For Derrida, this can be inferred not only from the content but also from the form of Paul's epistles: "If Paul says 'adieu' and absents himself as he asks them to obey . . . , it is because God is himself absent, hidden and silent, separate, secret, at the moment he has to be obeyed. God doesn't give his reasons. . . . Otherwise he wouldn't be God, we wouldn't be dealing with the Other as God or with God as *wholly other* [tout autre]" (*GD* 57 / 59).

The second, pagan source of the Kierkegaardian self, the one with which Levinas most takes issue, is identified in its modern existentialist form as the idée fixe of self-identification, not so much according to a formal tautological scheme—"the repetition of A is A"—as in harmony with concrete phenomenological structures that describe the "identification of A as A" as "the anxiety of A for A" (*PN* 68 / 101). The quest of existence for its own redemption and pardon thus resembles the Hegelian struggle for recognition (*Anerkennung*), as well as Heidegger's notion of care (*Sorge*),[32] both of which, Levinas maintains, are nothing but schematizations and translations of the sixth proposition of the third part of Spinoza's *Ethics*, the *conatus essendi*. This premise, the presupposition that *Unaquaeque res, quantum in se est, in suo esse perseverare conatur* ("Every being makes every effort insofar as it is in it to persevere in its being") is what Levinas puts into question: "The human *esse* is not *conatus* but disinterestedness and adieu."[33] It does not emerge as a superstructure to Being (*un étage au-dessus de l'être*), but marks a "for-nothingness" (*gratuité*) in which the perseverance of (and in) Being "undoes itself [*se dé-fait*]."[34] Otherwise, and more paradoxically than the anthropology of the West can fathom, "humanity [*humanité*]" can only be thought responsibly as "the fact of suffering for the other, even up to the point of, within one's own suffering, suffering for the suffering that my suffering imposes upon the other."[35] The irreducibility of a responsible subjectivity, then, of the responsibility of the self as well as of the risks it has to run, should be understood in terms different from those of a philosophy of identity and/or speculative totality, along very different lines from those sketched by Kierkegaardian, existentialist "nonphilosophy" (*PN* 69 / 102). The ethical moment cannot be identified with the usurpation of a purported, pure, and silent interior by an exterior order of objectivity (*PN* 68–69 / 102).

The Infinite is an inassimilable alterity, a difference and absolute past with respect to everything that shows itself, that signals itself, symbolizes itself, announces itself, remembers itself [*se rémémore*], and, thereby, makes itself

32. Of course, Heidegger's relation to Kierkegaard is more complicated than is suggested here. According to Heidegger, Kierkegaard's notion of existence lacks the ontological formalization that characterizes the existential structure of *Sorge* or care. As Heidegger formulates it in *Being and Time*: "In the nineteenth century, Søren Kierkegaard explicitly seized upon the problem of existence as an existentiell problem, and thought it through in a penetrating fashion. But the existential problematic was so alien to him that, as regards his ontology, he remained completely dominated by Hegel and by ancient philosophy as Hegel saw it. Thus there is more to be learned philosophically from his 'edifying' writings than from his theoretical ones — with the exception of his treatise on the concept of anxiety" (Heidegger, *Being and Time*, 494 n. vi, cf. 492 n. iv / 235 n. 1, cf. 190 n. 1).

33. Levinas, "La Mort et le temps," cited in *GD* 47 / 71.

34. Levinas, "La Mort et le temps," 32.

35. Emmanuel Levinas, "Les Dommages causés par le feu," in *Du sacré au saint: Cinq Nouvelles Lectures talmudiques* (Paris: Minuit, 1977), 167 / "Damages Due to Fire," in *Nine Talmudic Readings*, trans. Annette Aronowicz (Bloomington: Indiana University Press, 1990), 188, trans. modified.

"contemporaneous" [se "contemporise"] with what it comprehends. Absolution, anachoresis—to which realm [séjour]? . . . Retreat like an adieu which does not signify itself by opening itself to the gaze in order to overflow it by light, but by extinguishing itself to the point of the incognito in the visage that faces one. It is necessary and imperative . . . that there be someone who is no longer glued to being and who, whatever the risks and the dangers, responds to the enigma and seizes the allusion: the subjectivity, that is alone, unique, secret, and that Kierkegaard has glimpsed.[36]

Kierkegaard would have seen that the dialectical transition from the egocentric self to discourse, described by Hegel as the "possibility of speaking," is only thinkable as covering over "a distant impossibility of discourse" (PN 68 / 101). The very notion of persecuted truth would come to stand for the insight (although there is nothing to be seen here) that, dialectically or speculatively speaking, the very moment and momentum of the subject's decision is an inexplicable instant of "madness," a "moment of crisis," which is never given without passion.[37]

Levinas doubts whether the irreducibility of this passionate decision should be ascribed to the subject's interiority. In the final analysis, not the secret of the individual ego but, Levinas claims, only the Other (l'Autre) disrupts the totality and the political totalitarianism of the Hegelian system (TI 40 / 10). This other does not have the objectivity of a political or symbolic order, nor does it attain the generality and relative stability of a logical category—of, say, alterity as such. Rather, this Other, whether as autrui or as the Infinite that leaves its trace in the other's face or visage, is always singular, indeed, always contested, persecuted, haunted, mirrored, and mimicked by the worst.

In Levinas's account of the ethical, the ethicity of ethics is not kept at a safe distance from its other, as if it could calculate or wager without being haunted by the specter of the immoral or amoral. On the contrary, the premoral anonymity of the "there is," the il y a, the chaotic tohu v'vohu that is said to precede the divine act of creation but that at any time can come to unsettle the world of beings, forms and deforms the condition of possibility for every ethical intrigue. The para-experiences of the exotism

36. Levinas, En découvrant l'existence avec Husserl et Heidegger, 214–15.
37. "Every movement of infinity is carried out through passion, and no reflection can produce a movement. This is the continual leap in existence that explains the movement, whereas mediation is a chimera, which in Hegel is supposed to explain everything and which is also the only thing he never has tried to explain" (FT 42 n.).

of modern art, of the phenomenological thought experiment of world destruction, of fatigue and sleeplessness remind us of this (conceptually and experientially) impossible possibility of the possible as well as of the possible impossibility of all possibilities.

The interminable passage from absolute obligation to the ethical order, mediated by reason and the state, then back to the an-archy of responsibility and "down" into the depths of a trauma,[38] an absurdity of suffering for the other, for nothing—this alternation constitutes the drama of an ethics that is neither that of neo-Aristotelian virtue nor that of Kantian pure duty, but takes place in the space opened up by Nietzsche without being confined to it. The *au-delà* (or the *en deça*) of Levinasian transcendence is beyond the "beyond" of "beyond good and evil."

Levinas never forgets to inscribe the other, oblique face of the Other into his description of the ethical situation: there is no ethical transcendence without trans-descendence, we read in *Totality and Infinity*. (Cf. *TI* 93 / 66.) And, as *Otherwise Than Being* demonstrates, the indifferent, yet radically different and "horrifying [*horrifiant*]" *il y a* to which this descent into—and beyond—the elements of or the elemental in our experience leads us is, finally, a "modality" of the otherwise than being that disrupts the *conatus essendi*, the perseverance of each being in its own being, particularly in the face of its own death.[39] Only this "*il-y-a*-tic" modality of the relation to the ab-solute breaks away from the "Eleatic" God who, since Parmenides, has been "contaminated" by Being.[40] Moreover, the recurrence of—and the return into—the *il y a* protects this ab-solute relation to the ab-solute from being misunderstood and perverted in a moralistic sense.

In Levinas's later work only violent figures, figures that make one speechless—a catastrophic fire, an ignition, burning, flame, holocaust, and cinders[41]—suffice to evoke the passion of this responsibility, in which the subject is not simply eclipsed but literally burns up, like a candle or a

---

38. That the concept of trauma has become something like an organizing, yet deeply unstable, category in the humanities and behavioral sciences is shown by Ruth Leys in *Trauma: A Genealogy* (Chicago: University of Chicago Press, 2000).

39. Emmanuel Levinas, *Autrement qu'être ou au-delà de l'essence* (The Hague: Martinus Nijhoff, 1974), 208–9 / *Otherwise Than Being or Beyond Essence*, trans. Alphonso Lingis (Dordrecht: Kluwer, 1991), 163–64.

40. Ibid., xlviii / x.

41. See Emmanuel Levinas, *De dieu qui vient à l'idée* (Paris: Vrin, 1982), 110, 119 / *Of God Who Comes to Mind*, trans. Bettina Bergo (Stanford: Stanford University Press, 1998), 66–67, 72.

torch. Levinas speaks of *"gnawing away at oneself* [se ronger]," [42] thereby giving yet another meaning to the notion of "incarnation," [43] that of a carnage in the flesh: that the infinite leaves this intrigue in the finite is another way of saying that responsibility eats its way in and through the flesh, infinitely. Solely by hollowing itself out—only by turning itself inside out—is the self capable of giving. Responsibility is the consummation—the self-consummation—of the self. And yet, self-consummation *is* not, properly speaking: it signals an otherwise than being, an otherwise than whatever is.

The intrigue of inspiration entails an experience that is nothing less than *catastrophic,* that disturbs and disrupts the paradoxical logic of desire, the very modality of responsibility. Not only does the apparent negativity of the infinite (the *In* in *l'Infini*), in the very drama of its "divine comedy," characterize the structure of a desire that deepens and exalts to the measure that it approaches the desirable, which is more than more, immeasurable,[44] not only does the desirable call forth the immeasurable, seemingly by a perverse, parabolic arithmetic that allows no calculation, no distributive justice, and no restitution, but "the more just I am, the more guilty I am. I am 'in myself' through the others [*plus je suis juste— plus je suis coupable. Je suis 'en soi' par les autres*]." [45] Here, responsibility turns out to be a nonevent, inexplicable in terms of natural inclinations, social constructs, or cultural phantasms, which in its very taking place resembles a "devouring fire that devastates the place in the etymological sense of the term 'catastrophe' [*catastrophant le lieu, au sens étymologique du terme*]." [46] In an ironic, even violent displacement of Heideggerian topology or *Erörterung,* Levinas writes that the infinite "affects thought by devastating it and at the same time calls upon it; in a 'putting it back in its place' it puts thought in place. It awakens it." [47] There will be no magic fire of purification or of purifying suffering: "This element of a 'pure burning,' for nothing, in suffering, is the passivity of suffering which prevents its reverting into suffering [freely, willingly, consciously, or unconsciously] assumed, in which the for-the-other of sensibility, that is, its very sense, would be annulled. This moment of the 'for nothing' in suffering is the

42. Levinas, *Otherwise Than Being,* 121 /155 (emphasis by Levinas).
43. Ibid., 121 / 156.
44. Levinas, *Of God Who Comes to Mind,* 67 / 111.
45. Levinas, *Otherwise Than Being,* 112 / 143.
46. Levinas, *Of God Who Comes to Mind,* 66–67 / 110; trans. modified.
47. Levinas, *Collected Philosophical Papers,* 176.

surplus of non-sense over sense by which the sense of suffering is possible."[48]

IN THE PASSAGE from the self to the other is a passing away in which the
self becomes its own other in an endless, infinite incineration as the "pure
burning," a *"pure brûlure," pour rien.* Instead of being a simple eclipse of
the subject, desire infinitely prolongs the passion. Desire, being without
end—without telos and without any possible resolution, being unable to
end—is an eternal *passage*, a constant *passing away*, a *passivité à mort*[49]
that is at once an *arrêt de mort*, to use Blanchot's expression, and an *au
delà de ma mort*.[50]

Mutatis mutandis, the same would hold for the phenomenology that
testifies to this intrigue of the In-finite in the finite. At times, the consummation seems to affect the subject of Levinas's text in another sense: as
a devastation of subject matter. Its subject matter presents itself without
truly entering the present, without occupying any presence, since it gives
itself only to be seen, heard, or read, in an act of self-destruction that prevents it forever from entering or offering a generalizable form or content
of meaning that a philosophical hermeneutic could recuperate. Nor could
any juridical application or aesthetic expression capture or concretize the
singular signifyingness evoked, for the radicality—or, to avoid any reference to a *radix*, the an-archy—that pervades the circular discourse of
Otherwise Than Being presses the very structure of its text to the point of
self-destruction.

In addressing the substitution of the subject, Levinas makes clear that,
strictly speaking, he can speak only of *his* substitution for the other: "*My*
substitution—it is as *my own* that substitution for the neighbor is produced."[51] It is only "in me," he continues, "and not in another, in me and
not in any individuation of the concept Me," that the self offers and opens
itself to the other: "To say that the other has to sacrifice himself to the
others would be to preach human sacrifice!"[52] and thereby the epitome
of immorality. Ethics never prescribes what the other should or should
not do. Strictly speaking, the secret and the testimony of responsibility

48. Levinas, *Otherwise Than Being*, 196 n. 21 / 150 n. 21; trans. modified.
49. Ibid., 124 / 159.
50. See my "Lapsus absolu: Some Remarks on Maurice Blanchot's *L'Instant de ma mort*,"
Yale French Studies 93 (1998): 30–59.
51. Levinas, *Otherwise Than Being*, 126 / 161.
52. Ibid., 126 / 161 and 162.

are not generalizable. The substitution for the other is marked by an irreducible *mineness*. Self-sacrifice is not universalizable. Its fundamental contradiction is that the demand that the other substitute himself/herself *for me* destroys the ethical situation by inscribing in it my own interest — my own *conatus essendi:*

> To the idea of the infinite there corresponds only an extravagant response. What is imperative here is a "thought" that hears/understands more than it hears/understands, more than its capacity and with which it cannot be contemporaneous, a "thought" which, in that sense, can go beyond its death.... To go beyond one's death, that is to sacrifice oneself. The response to the *assignation* of the sacrifice of the Enigma is the generosity of the sacrifice outside the known and the unknown, without calculation, since it goes toward the Infinite.... I approach the Infinite by sacrificing myself. The sacrifice is the norm and the criterion of the approach. And the truth of the transcendence consists in establishing a harmony [*la mise en accord*] between one's discourses and one's acts.[53]

The ambiguity in "the sacrifice is the norm and the criterion of the approach" implies, not that Levinas subscribes to a religion of sacrifice (what kind of sacrifice would that be?), but that in the absolute relation to the absolute — which for him, unlike Kierkegaard, is the ethical relation — every norm and criterion, in the strict and common sense of these terms (as *ethos* as much as abstract forms of morality), is sacrificed. The need for some accord between words and deeds does not contradict this paradox. And the tonal metaphorics that describes or evokes its performativity or, rather, performance is no accident.

The "pure burning" stands for a "surplus of non-sense over sense," indeed, a "suffering for nothing," for an other who withdraws himself from the relation to the point of not even showing his face. This withdrawal or *ab-solvere* of the ab-solute other — an absolute relation with the absolute, as *Fear and Trembling* has it — prohibits responsibility from ever being assumed in freedom or in good conscience. An entry from Kierkegaard's *Journals and Papers* makes this clear: "Fear and Trembling (see *Philippians* 2:12) is not the *primus motor* in the Christian life, for it is love; but it is what the oscillating balance wheel is to the clock — it is the oscillating balance wheel of the Christian life" (*FT* 239).

How, then, should we understand the relationship between Kierke-

---

53. Levinas, *En découvrant l'existence avec Husserl et Heidegger,* 215.

gaard's displacement of ethics and that other ethics, that other ethics of
the other, the ethics of that other other, for which the names of Levinas
and Derrida stand? Why their common obsession with the worst, with
a certain suspension of the ethical, whether through the sacrifice of the
ethical or through the haunting non-sense of the *il y a*? How are we to
read the uncanny circumstance in which the binding (*Akedah*) of Isaac
on the altar of a holocaust entails a double or even triple bind, in which
the moral community, God, and the demonic are inextricably bound up
together? "We read in sacred scripture: 'And God tempted and said: Abraham, Abraham, where are you? But Abraham answered: Here am I'" (*FT*
21). Throughout Levinas's writings, the utterance "Here am I!" (*me voici,
hinneni*) epitomizes the first and last word of responsibility, of its wakefulness and vigil. Is it any accident that he takes it from this biblical passage,
whence it derives an almost paradigmatic stature?

Derrida's reading of Kierkegaard in *The Gift of Death* can help answer
that question by shedding light on the suspension of the ethical in the
face of the totally other or the other than other (the totally other than
totally other). It further demarcates the movement and implications of the
à dieu, whose semantics — and more than simply semantic potential — is
only partly rendered by the translations "to-God" or "toward God." Like
Kierkegaard and Levinas, Derrida reads the story of the sacrifice of Isaac
as the narrative ellipsis of the paradoxical logic of obligation, absolute
responsibility, duty, and decision that marks the ethical — and, perhaps,
more than simply ethical — relation with the absolute Other, for which
"God" is the singular and most proper name. "Violence and Metaphysics"
and "En ce moment, dans cette ouvrage, me voici" ("At this very moment
in this work here I am"), at the heart of *Writing and Difference* and *Psyché:
Inventions de l'autre* (*Psyche: Inventions of the Other*), mark the first two
major instances of Derrida's encounter with the work of the (early and
later) Levinas. Lest we be tempted to interpret Derrida's exegesis of Genesis (of this genesis of morals, mediated by a reading of *Fear and Trembling,*
though Nietzsche's *Genealogy of Morals* is not entirely absent) as a supplement to these early readings, we should remember that, as always, this
supplement was already there, setting the tone for the very first text. Already in "Violence and Metaphysics" Derrida draws attention to a certain
injustice and an unresolved debate in Levinas's reading of Kierkegaard:
"Let us add, in order to do him *justice,* that Kierkegaard had a sense of the
relationship to the irreducibility of the totally-other [*Tout-Autre*], not in
the egoistic and esthetic here and now, but in the religious beyond of the

concept, in the direction of a certain Abraham." Not unlike Levinas, Derrida continues, Kierkegaard sees "in Ethics, as a moment of Category and Law, the forgetting, in anonymity, of the subjectivity of religion." Against this backdrop, finally, for Kierkegaard "the ethical moment is Hegelianism itself, and he says so explicitly. Which does not prevent him from reaffirming ethics in repetition, and from reproaching Hegel for not having constituted a morality" (*WD* 111 / 164).

In juxtaposing the names and thought of Kierkegaard and Levinas, despite the latter's repeated admonition against confusing the Christian thirst for personal salvation with the genuine desire for the other, we should not forget, Derrida continues, that "as concerns the essential in its initial inspiration Levinas's protest against Hegelianism is foreign to Kierkegaard's protest" (*WD* 111 / 164). This is not because Levinasian ethics is "an Ethics without law and without concept, which maintains its non-violent purity only before being determined as concepts and laws" (*WD* 111 / 164). As we have seen, the ethical in Levinas's sense is not without some violence of its own. Rather, Derrida reminds us, Levinas "warns us against confusing — as one is so tempted to do — his anti-Hegelianism with a subjectivism, or with a Kierkegaardian type of existentialism, both of which would remain . . . violent . . . egoisms" (*WD* 110 / 162).

According to Kierkegaard, as Derrida elaborates in *The Gift of Death,* the testimony of obligation entails an anxiety in the face of a given death or of a giving of death, of a *donner la mort,* which is also a monstrosity: the necessity of choosing between one's love and the sacrifice of this love. Abraham transgresses the order of the ethical, in Kierkegaard's eyes the validity of and respect for a universal law or generality, Kantian morality (*Moralität*), Hegelian ethical life (*Sittlichkeit*), and even simple common sense: in short, what ties us not only to formal or abstract rules but also to family, neighbors, friends, and nation. By obeying what he takes to be God's command to sacrifice his beloved son, and by keeping his intentions secret, by speaking, of necessity, to no one, Abraham violates — indeed, sacrifices — the basic principles that govern every human community. Ethically speaking, Kierkegaard insists, Abraham commits a criminal act, and his sacrifice is nothing but murder. From a religious perspective, however, a perspective that can only be ascribed to God and the "knight of faith," Abraham's decision represents "the movement to infinity," at once a movement of renunciation, of "infinite resignation," and a "grasping everything again by virtue of the absurd" (*FT* 40). As Kierkegaard explains somewhat later in the text: "Is he justified? Again, his justification is the paradoxical, for if he is, then he is justified not by virtue of being something universal but by virtue of his being the single individual" (*FT* 62).

In what sense, then, could what is here called the religious relation — that is, the sacrifice of what one loves in a movement of infinite resignation — be understood as the condition, more precisely, the uncondition, of possibility for the ethical? As Derrida notes, Kierkegaard employs a hetero-theonomical figure to speak of absolute obligation, in a formal parallel to the Kantian autonomy of pure practical reason, which is also attained through a certain sacrifice — through the *Aufopferung* of the senses and the pathological passions that haunt the concept of duty. This resemblance is the topic of Derrida's *Passions,* but is also addressed in *The Gift of Death.* In Kant it takes the following form: "The good principle is present, therefore, just as much in the abandonment of the evil as in the adoption of the good disposition, and the pain that by rights accompanies the first derives entirely from the second. The emergence from the corrupted disposition into the good is in itself already sacrifice (as "the death of the old man," "the crucifying of the flesh") and entrance into a long train of life's ills which the new human being undertakes in the disposition of the Son of God" (*RBR* 114 / 729). Kant refers, of course, to Romans 6:2, 6 and Galatians 5:24, whose Christological perspective he reaffirms, generalizes, and, inevitably, trivializes as the figure for each single instance of responsibility, for all giving oneself death. One paradigmatic example casts its light over all others and is, in a sense, nothing outside them: "The suffering which the new human being must endure while dying to the *old* human being throughout life is depicted in the representative of the human kind as a death suffered once and for all" (*RBR* 115 / 729–30).

Yet in *Religion within the Boundaries of Mere Reason* and *The Conflict of the Faculties* Kant repeatedly condemns Abraham for not having respected the voice of duty, which allows "no special duties to God."[54] That God would have uttered a "terrible injunction" like the one in the biblical narrative could be maintained only on the basis of "historical docu-

---

54. See Ronald M. Green, *The Hidden Debt: Kierkegaard and Kant* (Albany: State University of New York Press, 1992), 89, 202–3. Cf. Sylviane Agacinski, *Aparté: Conceptions et morts de Søren Kierkegaard* (Paris: Aubier Flammarion, 1977) / *Aparté: Conceptions and Deaths of Søren Kierkegaard,* trans. Kevin Newmark (Tallahassee: Florida State University Press, 1988), 79 ff.; J. Rogozinski, "Vers une éthique du différend," in *Enlightenments: Encounters between Critical Theory and Recent French Thought,* ed. Harry Kunneman and Hent de Vries (Kampen: Kok Pharos Publishers, 1993); Peter Fenves, *"Chatter": Language and History in Kierkegaard* (Stanford: Stanford University Press, 1993), 145 ff.

mentation," which, by its very nature, by having been transmitted and interpreted by finite beings or mortals, will always contain a possibility of "error" and which, therefore, does not allow for any "apodictical certainty."[55] In *The Conflict of the Faculties* Kant explains this as follows:

> A code of God's *statutory* (and so revealed) will, not derived from human reason but harmonizing perfectly with morally practical reason toward the final end—in other words, the Bible—would be the most effective organ for guiding men and citizens to their temporal and eternal well-being, if only it could be accredited as the word of God and its authenticity could be proved by documents. But there are many difficulties in the way of validating it.
>
> For if God should really speak to man, man could still never *know* that it was God speaking. It is quite impossible for man to apprehend the infinite by his senses, distinguish it from sensible beings, and *recognize* it as such. But in some cases man can be sure that the voice he hears is *not* God's; for if the voice commands him to do something contrary to moral law, then no matter how majestic the apparition [*Erscheinung*] may be, and no matter how it may seem to surpass the whole of nature, he must consider it an illusion [*Täuschung*].

In a important note that summarizes the essential dilemma or aporia that concerns us here, in this series of readings of Genesis 22 (reading Derrida reading Levinas reading Kierkegaard), Kant adds that we could "use as an example" the "myth of the sacrifice that Abraham was going to make by butchering and burning his only son at God's command (the poor child, without knowing it, even brought the wood for the fire). Abraham should have replied to this supposedly divine voice: 'That I ought not to kill my good son is quite certain. But that you, this apparition [*du, der du mir erscheinst*] are God—of that I am not certain, and never can be, not even if this voice rings down [*herabschallte*] to me from (visible) heaven.'"[56]

---

55. *RBR* 203–4 / 861–62. The context of these formulations is very peculiar. Kant cites the example of Abraham while speaking of a zealous "inquisitor [*Ketzerrichter*]" who "clings fast to the exclusiveness of his statutory faith even to the point, if need be, of martyrdom [*bis allenfalls zum Märtyrertume*]" (*RBR* 203 / 860): "That to take a human being's life because of his religious faith is wrong is certain, unless (to allow for the most extreme possibility) a divine will, made known to the inquisitor in extraordinary way, has decreed otherwise. But that God has ever manifested this awful will is a matter of historical documentation and never apodictically certain" (*RBR* 203 / 861).

56. *CF* 283 remark / 333 remark. Later in the text, Kant once more returns to the "myth" of the sacrifice in a note on "superstition." Here he recalls the "subtle Jewish art of exegesis" of one of the disciples gathered at Pentecost, who succeeds in reading this sacrifice as "the symbol of the world-saviour's own sacrifice." On the sacrifice of Isaac, cf. *RBR* 124 / 744. This reference is made in the context of a discussion of miracles to which we will return in Chapter 3.

Here one sacrifice—the *Aufopferung* of one's having succumbed to an "aesthetic" apparition—ought to overcome, indeed sacrifice, another: namely, the "butchering and burning" of a living child. Here a certain ambiguity characterizes the relation between the structure of Kantian morality and that of sacrifice. Although Kant's condemnation of Abraham is unequivocal, indeed categorical, the concept of duty and thus of the moral law remains unthinkable without invoking some notion of sacrifice. Kant does so quite literally, by speaking of *Aufopferung*, albeit self-sacrifice, a sacrifice of the natural self. The *formal structure* of this giving away, this leave taking, or this death of the self qua nature unwittingly mimicks the repudiated blood sacrifice of the other (of the natural offspring, that is, of Isaac). But is an analogy, even the most formal, ever innocent? [57] According to Kierkegaard, the absolute command to which Abraham responds extricates itself from the form of generality and universality that, in the intelligible realm of pure duty—in acting "out of duty" rather than merely "conforming to duty"—characterizes Kant's conception of the moral law, the categorical imperative.[58] This conception lacks the qualities of and qualifications for an absolute command. Absolute duty—in Derrida's words, a duty "toward God and in the singularity of faith," substituting for the other without being able to expect or demand any substitution or restitution in turn—"implies a sort of gift or sacrifice that functions beyond both debt and duty, beyond duty as a form of debt. This is the dimension that provides for a 'gift of death' [*donner la*

---

57. The Kantian sublime (*das Erhabene*) reiterates the same figure. As Jean-Luc Nancy reminds us, it "produces itself in a 'sacrifice' of imagination, which turns out to be abyssal in itself [*s'abîme en elle-même*]" (*Une pensée finie* [Paris: Galilée, 1990], 87). Nancy draws on the analysis provided by the *Allgemeine Anmerkung zur Exposition der ästhetischen reflektierenden Urteile*, as well as on par. 26 of the *Critique of Judgment*. Is it accidental that in this context Kant also evokes the biblical prohibition of the image of God? And is the formal, structural analogy between all these forms of sacrifice philosophically irrelevant? Or morally indifferent?

58. Though Kierkegaard's discussion is a critique less of Kant than of Hegel, responding more to the section on "the good and conscience" in the *Philosophy of Right* than to the texts just mentioned, we should not forget that for Hegel also the moment of ethical decision comes to pass in a transition from mere violence to legitimate force, in particular, in the sublation of subjective violence by objective *Gewalt*. One is reminded of the trajectory that finds its telos in the paragraphs devoted to the state, notably in the staggering affirmation that for modern subjects "sacrifice [is] for the individuality of the state . . . the substantial relation of everyone and therefore a *universal duty* [*die Aufopferung für die Individualität des Staates das substantielle Verhältnis aller und hiermit allgemeine Pflicht ist*]" (Georg Wilhelm Friedrich Hegel, *Grundlinien der Philosophie des Rechts*, ed. J. Hoffmeister [Hamburg: Meiner, 1955], 281 / *Elements of the Philosophy of Right*, ed. Allen W. Wood, trans. H. B. Nisbet [Cambridge: Cambridge University Press, 1991], 363).

mort] which, beyond human responsibility, beyond the universal concept of duty, is a response to absolute duty" (*GD* 63 / 64).

Conversely, Kant's reservation about a Kierkegaardian position *avant la lettre* is no less outspoken. That we would have to "work out our own salvation *with fear and trembling*" is, as he parenthetically notes in *Religion within the Boundaries of Mere Reason*, "a hard saying, which, if misunderstood, is capable of driving one into the darkest enthusiasm [*finstersten Schwärmerei*]" (*RBR* 109 / 722). If understood well, however, the saying from Philippians 2:12 may discourage or mitigate good conscience.

Let us return to the structure of the sacrifice or the gift, to the giving of death said to figure this structure of the excess of a beyond of duty, an "*over-duty.*" [59] Abraham, Kierkegaard writes, "had faith that God would not demand Isaac of him, and yet he was willing to sacrifice him if it was demanded. He had faith by virtue of the absurd, for human calculation was out of the question; it was certainly absurd that God, who required it of him, should in the next moment rescind the requirement. He climbed the mountain, and even in the moment when the knife gleamed he had faith—that God would not require Isaac" (*FT* 35–36). Abraham has faith "by virtue of the absurd, by virtue of the fact that for God all things are possible" (*FT* 46). This absurdity, this "possible," Kierkegaard clarifies, "does not belong to the differences that lie within the proper domain of the understanding. It is not identical with the improbable, the unexpected, the unforeseen" (*FT* 46). Nonetheless, understanding reflects ceaselessly on the impossible, the unthinkable, in the realm of the finite and temporal. The "testimony" (*FT* 47) of faith is only authentic, that is to say, only a testimony properly speaking, insofar as it acknowledges—at the very same instant—the necessity of this visible order, the legitimacy of its ethical claims, as well as the absolute command to transgress, to go beyond them, to leave them behind.

> The two duties must contradict one another, one must subordinate (incorporate, repress) the other. Abraham must assume absolute responsibility for sacrificing his son by sacrificing ethics, but in order for there to be a sacrifice, the ethical must retain all its value; the love for his son must remain intact, and the order of human duty must continue to insist on its rights [*à faire valoir ses droits*].
>
> The account [*récit*] of Isaac's sacrifice can be read as a narrative develop-

59. Jacques Derrida, *Apories* (Paris: Galilée, 1996), 38–39 / *Aporias*, trans. Thomas Dutoit (Stanford: Stanford University Press, 1993), 16–17.

ment [*portée*] of the paradox constituting the concept of duty and absolute responsibility. This concept puts us into relation (but without relating to it, in a double secret) with the absolute other, with the absolute singularity of the other, whose name here is God. (*GD* 66 / 66)

If the first recognition of this double affirmation or doubled binding were not as pertinent as the second, we could hardly speak of "resignation," let alone of "infinite resignation." Only where resignation forms the "antecedent," Kierkegaard writes, is faith more than a merely "esthetic emotion," that is to say, "not the spontaneous inclination of the heart but the paradox of existence" (*FT* 47).

In order for faith to be what it is, it would thus have to "look the impossibility in the eye" (*FT* 47), risk the worst, and face the chance that in committing the crime—in the willingness to sacrifice, to give death— nothing would be given in return, everything would be taken away, and the whole episode would be less an "ordeal" (*FT* 52) than just a murder. According to Kierkegaard, only the "paradox of faith" turns this possible murder into a possibly "holy and God-pleasing act"; only the paradox of faith, then, could give "Isaac back to Abraham again" (*FT* 53).

This paradox confirms a confessional logic.[60] Just as Derrida portrays himself in "Circumfession" as the last of the Jews and the last of the eschatologists—"last" taken each time in all the ambiguity of *the latest* (i.e., most actual and advanced), and *the least,* in other words, the ultimate, most at risk and perverse—so also Abraham is found to be "at the same time the most moral and the most immoral, the most responsible and the most irresponsible of men, absolutely irresponsible because he is absolutely responsible" (*GD* 72 / 72).

Abraham, Derrida comments, is responsible "to God and before God [*à Dieu et devant Dieu*]" (*GD* 72 / 72), face to face with a God who withdraws himself from this relation and shows, if anything, his nether, ugly side. The face of the other is a Janus face. The bind (and *Akedah* means, literally, binding) is double in that it ties Abraham and Isaac to the apparition of a God who at least appears to have at least two faces. This doubling of the good God who gives and his seemingly evil genius who takes away accounts for the unsettling tension of this story, as well as of every act. Abraham, Kierkegaard writes, was "the first to feel and to bear witness to that prodigious passion that disdains the terrifying battle with the raging elements and the forces of creation in order to contend with God. . . . The

60. See my *Philosophy and the Turn to Religion,* 347 ff.

first to know that supreme passion, the holy, pure, and humble expression for the divine madness that was admired by the pagans" (*FT* 23).[61]

In suspending the ethical in favor of a purportedly religious obligation, Abraham demonstrates what it takes to assume responsibility for an absolute command. His passion when faced with the sacrifice of his son, his anxiety at having to sacrifice his love, is the example set for every decision—once and for all. It is the example of all exemplarity. Every ethical decision that deserves the name takes place as the similar pronunciation of a singular shibboleth and thus retains a certain idiosyncrasy or secrecy. As soon as it enters language and becomes part of discourse or even the subject of discussion, not to mention a *Diskurs,* an ethical decision loses its distinctive character, its significance or, rather, *signifiance,* to use the formulation Levinas employs to indicate how the ab-solute relation with the ab-solute manifests itself without appearing, presenting, revealing, or even being "itself."

Abraham shows that in every genuine decision the ethical *must* be sacrificed. Morality *ought* to be suspended "in the name of" an ab-solute duty or obligation that is always "singular" and for which the name—the proper and most proper name—would be "God." Strictly speaking, this name is neither common nor proper. As the unpronounceable Tetragrammaton, *JHWH,* it names the unnamable and therefore forces a rupture in the typical grammatical function of the name, that of capturing the multiple senses of Being. The trace that it leaves in the face, in the face of the Other, facing his or her death, is also—always already—*effaced.*[62] Under this regime, "God," in Derrida's reading, serves as the index or "figure" not only of the *wholly other*—the *tout autre*—but also of every other, of every other that is every bit other, that is, of *tout autre.* Derrida's text plays here with "the distinction between two homonyms *tout* and *tout,* an indefinite pronominal adjective (some, someone, someone other) [*quelque, quelconque, un quelconque autre*] and an adverb of quantity (totally, absolutely, radically, infinitely other)" (*GD* 82 / 80).

In this reading, "God" is other than Himself; He is His own other. As the radically other, God is everywhere, that is, wherever there is the other, whenever there are others. And all that can be said about the anxious silence of Abraham in his relation to God (*à Dieu*) could be applied to—or, rather, reiterates itself in—our relation to everybody and perhaps,

61. Cf. Plato, *Phaedrus,* 244–45 c, 265 b.
62. Levinas, *La Mort et le temps,* 26.

Derrida adds, to everything else (*GD* 78 / 77). The extraordinary, scandalous story of the sacrifice of Isaac, as read by Kierkegaard, concludes Derrida, thus shows us "the very structure of what occurs every day [*du quotidien*]" (*GD* 78 / 77), that is, of everydayness itself, without allowing any inference of a proper or authentic dimension implied by this ordinariness (as Heidegger would have it). Each gesture of the other toward me obligates me to respond by sacrificing the other of the other, his or her (or its) other gesture, or the absence thereof, but also the other other and, finally, all the other others. The relation to the other demands that I sacrifice the ethical, that is to say, "whatever obligates me also to respond, in the same way, in the same instant, to all the others" (*GD* 68 / 68). Unlike Heidegger in *Being and Time,* Derrida suggests that every action takes place by ignoring—and thus (though Heidegger does not say this) by violating—others. Every action is not so much indifferent to conscience but "unconscientious" (*gewissenlos*).[63]

To say adieu, if only for an instant, to the ethical order of universal laws and human rights by responding to a singular responsibility toward an ab-solute other—for example, the other par excellence, God—implies sacrificing the virtual totality of all innumerable others. Yet this singular dramatization and intensification of responsibility by no means lessens my equally absolute responsibility toward all other others, toward all that concerns them, directly and indirectly, whether they know it or not. Without ever being able to master *their* situation, I alone will have been obligated to substitute for these others, and to be their hostage: "Ipseity, in its passivity without the *archē* of identity, is hostage. The word *I* means here *I am,* answering for everything and everybody [*me voici, répondant de tout et de tous*]."[64]

The "third person"—*le tiers*—would therefore not mitigate my absolute obligation, but rather broaden and deepen it. This circumstance, precluding every stasis or stance, gives new meaning to the phrase that in (the) face of the other I am haunted by others. In the open-ended, permanent alternation of the *Saying* and the *Said,* of substitution and justice, of

---

63. Cf. "Factically, however, any taking-action is necessarily 'conscienceless [*gewissenlos*],' not only because it may fail to avoid some factical moral indebtedness, but because, on the null [*nichtigen*] basis of its null [*nichtigen*] projection, it has, in Being with Others, already become guilty towards them. Thus one's wanting-to-have-a-conscience becomes the taking-over of that essential consciencelessness within which alone the existentiell possibility of *being* 'good' subsists" (Heidegger, *Being and Time,* 334 / 288).

64. Levinas, *Otherwise Than Being,* 114 / 145, trans. modified.

anarchy and economy, of the non-negotiable and of negotiation, the *différend* of conflicting responsibilities finds neither resolution nor rest. This is not to say that testimony is primarily a social or sociological category, nor is its violent extreme, called "martyrdom." Martyrdom is based on a form of recognition by an Other that is not an other shaped by public opinion (*l'opinion publique* or society, in Durkheim's terminology) but an absolute instance followed by an equally absolute act of instantiation in need of being repeated ad infinitum. It entails a "recognition" — if that is the right word[65] — that, Kierkegaard thinks, is above all "psychological" (some would say metaphysical), since it is characterized by a fundamental rethinking of our common understanding of the premises and concept of sociality and individual consciousness, intersubjectivity and subjectivity, externality and inwardness, immanence and transcendence. To follow this line of thought means to pay homage, once more, to the basic tenets of the writings of Kierkegaard, arguably the most radical thinker on the philosophical, theological, and psychological significance of martyrdom, of its conceptual structure, its existential dimension, and its practical implications.

The "Possibility of the Offense": Kierkegaard on Martyrdom

The influence of no person's life is as great as a martyr's, it takes effect only after they have put him to death.

For between God and man there is a struggle and it's a matter of life and death — wasn't the God-man put to death?[66]

If, with Kierkegaard, we take martyrdom to stand for a nonsocial form of *absolute* recognition — of a "recognition" in which at least one of the

65. As we shall see, the logic of responsibility and irresponsibility, the ethical and the religious, testimony and martyrdom that interests us here should be distinguished from powerful alternative articulations that seek to reconstruct, analyze, or deconstruct the relation of self to other, often in opposition to Heidegger's fundamental ontology of *Dasein* and *Mitsein*. See Axel Honneth, *Kampf um Anerkennung: Zur moralischen Grammatik sozialer Konflikte* (Frankfurt a. M.: Suhrkamp, 1992) and *Die zerrissene Welt des Sozialen: Sozialphilosophische Aufsätze*, 2d ed. (Frankfurt a. M.: Suhrkamp, 1999); Simon Glendinning, *On Being with Others: Heidegger, Derrida, Wittgenstein* (London: Routledge, 1998); and, perhaps, Jean-Luc Nancy, *Être singulier pluriel* (Paris: Galilée, 1996). Needless to say, I cannot hope to spell out these distinctions in sufficient detail here.

66. Søren Kierkegaard, *Papers and Journals: A Selection*, trans. Alistair Hannay (London: Penguin, 1996), 312 and 353.

terms *absolves* itself from the relation, to the extent that this relation (indeed, without relation) can no longer be seen as taking place *between* them, according to some *inter*subjective model (leaving the poles, here the subjects, unaffected or intact) — some caution is in order. Any identification of the constitution of this nonautonomous self by a nonpublic Other with "psychology" (Kierkegaard's word) risks doing injustice to the elusive and obscure — the paradoxical and aporetic — character of the logic of martyrdom. According to Kierkegaard, the construction and inner constitution of the martyr entails a process of individualization and singularization that transcends the boundaries, not only of the societal, the public, and the private, but also of the ego-psychological and psychopathological as they are normally and normatively defined. What Kierkegaard has in mind cannot be reconstituted according to the premises of empirical psychology or psychoanalysis in its various guises. Why this is so can easily be grasped from the fact that, according to Kierkegaard, "next to God there is nothing as eternal as a self," or that "a self is indeed infinitely distinct from an externality" (*SD* 53).

The misrecognition, the ill-constituted relation that for Kierkegaard forms anxiety, despair, and the sickness unto death is the flip side or mirror image of faith, properly speaking. It can propel faith into existence or at least form a condition of its "possibility" and therefore "necessity." This misrecognition does not play itself out at the psychosomatic or group-psychological level, but pertains to the fact that human beings are above all *spirit*. The drama of religion, the *horror religiosus* to which testimony testifies at its extreme, is pneumatological. No doubt this category may make anthropologists, social scientists, historians, and philosophers skeptical and, perhaps, nervous. The structure of spirituality is neither a state of affairs that can be described nor a relation between ideas or persons (subjects, groups, etc.) that can be reconstructed and interpreted, but a paradoxical performative act whose success and contextual requirements remain forever in the dark. Extrapolating a motif Derrida introduces in *La Carte postale* (*The Post Card*), we touch here upon a "perverformativity" whose genesis, structure, and effect remain implied in whatever (descriptive, normative, evocative, or edifying) account one might give of it; its perfection or perfectibility goes hand in hand with *pervertibility*.[67] In

---

67. This emphasis on perfectibility in light of pervertibility casts an interesting light on the discourse of "perfectionism" and "moral perfectionism," introduced, for example, in John Rawls, *A Theory of Justice*, and discussed extensively in the writings of Stanley Cavell. Cavell

a sense, the "spiritual" and the "demonic" occupy the same "space"; they resemble each other in their very structure. Or so, of necessity, it seems. That "deconstruction" helps us to understand this analogy, not between beings and Being or between the created and the Divine, but between the best and the worst—an analogy that has gained a particular poignancy during the human catastrophes of the last century—explains why one can "recognize in it the last testimony—not to say the martyrdom—of faith in the present *fin de siècle*. This reading will always be possible."[68]

Kierkegaard views martyrdom and self-sacrifice in terms that relate in radically new ways to modern definitions of "publicness" and "privacy" to be found in Kant's essays on Enlightenment (as interpreted by Foucault), *Religion within the Boundaries of Mere Reason,* and *The Conflict of the Faculties.* The theologico-political, ecclesial, and more broadly institutional order Kant diagnoses at the moment of its modern constitution, the dawn of its "transformation" (or *Strukturwandel,* as Habermas calls it) is experienced and chastised by Kierkegaard, in his diary, as "the age of disintegration." Roughly speaking—and Kierkegaard, philosophizing with a hammer, as Levinas remarks, speaks in rough terms—this age is typified by a dissolution of "the System," of the Hegelian system, which "signified not—as the systematicians themselves comfortably supposed—that completion had now been achieved, but that like an over-ripe fruit it indicated ruin."[69] The age of dissolution is an epoch in which nationalities, the public, and the crowd have gained unwarranted prominence, though a crisis of this historical constellation in turn announces itself.

Kierkegaard addresses the category of the single individual in relation to social recognition (or the lack thereof), to the body politic (or the lack thereof), to the church (or the lack thereof, as it substitutes a petrified and all too manifest Christendom for original Christianity's invisible community of saints) within the context of this analysis. Yet the single individual, he observes, is a dialectical category rather than a historical product—not static or simply ahistorical, but dialectical in that its concrete form (and it

---

traces the notion back to the tradition of American transcendentalism as exemplified by Thoreau and Emerson.

68. Jacques Derrida, "Comment ne pas parler: Dénégations," in *Psyché: Inventions de l'autre* (Paris: Galilée, 1987), 539 / "How to Avoid Speaking: Denials," in *Languages of the Unsayable: The Play of Negativity in Literature and Literary Theory,* ed. Sanford Budick and Wolfgang Iser (New York: Columbia University Press, 1987), 7.

69. Kierkegaard, *Papers and Journals,* 350.

is a *form*, a relation) *varies according to empirical context.* What does that
mean? Kierkegaard notes, with an imagery at once subtle and violent:

> "The single individual" is a category that lends itself to being used in two
> ways: in times where all is security and life and though held in indolent trance,
> "the single individual" is the category of awakening; when everything is tot-
> tering it is the category of conciliation. He who understands how to use this
> category will in times of peace appear quite otherwise than in times of agi-
> tation, yet it will be the same weapon he uses. The difference is like using
> a sharp and pointed instrument as a goad, to hurt, and then the very same
> instrument to clean a wound. But never will this category "the single indi-
> vidual," if properly used, hurt the maintenance of religious truth. In time of
> peace its role will be, without altering anything externally, to awaken inward-
> ness to a heightened life in the established; in time of rebellion its role will
> be savingly to draw attention away from the external, to guide the individual
> towards an indifference to external change and to strengthen the individual in
> inwardness. The category of the single individual is always related to inward-
> izing. Earthly reward, power, honour, etc., are not bound up with its proper
> use, for what are rewarded in the world are of course only changes, or work
> for change, in externals — inwardness is of no interest to the world, which is
> indeed externality.[70]

The sole incarnation of this single individual is the martyr. Although according to Christianity[71] there is only one incarnation — only Christ was
martyred and died for the sins of all — in Kierkegaard as in Kant, the incarnation of Christ, along with the *kenosis* and martyrdom it entails, forms a
paradigm for all subsequent belief, for all ethico-religious decisions, and
thus for all decisions properly speaking. The figure of incarnation extends
still further: retrospectively, all acts of testimony that precede its singular
occurrence are illuminated and justified by this singular example of singularity. In this sense, Kierkegaard writes in *Fear and Trembling*, Abraham
was the first martyr.

Kierkegaard implies that this paradigm will be copied even better in
the future than was possible in the past. On the one hand, the uncanny
images in the passage cited above, in *Fear and Trembling* and elsewhere,

70. Ibid., 351.
71. Lest we forget, Kierkegaard does not deem himself worthy to communicate Christianity
directly (hence the pseudonyms, aesthetic devices intended to "deceive the readers [the author
included] into the truth"). See Michael Theunissen, *Der Begriff der Verzweiflung: Korrekturen
an Kierkegaard* (Frankfurt a. M.: Suhrkamp, 1993), 13 n. 1.

portray martyrdom as the emblematic figure for the drama of witness-ing and of existential authenticity as such, although for Kierkegaard this term means something very different from what Heidegger understands as *Eigentlichkeit*, Sartre as *authenticité*, or Charles Taylor and, more re-cently, Alessandro Ferrara as "authenticity." Being the purest form of sub-jectivity—the relation of self to self and self to other—it is of all ages. On the other hand, however, Kierkegaard indicates that the structural and figural resemblance between witnesses at all times and the martyrs par ex-cellence (Abraham, Christ) is becoming ever more prominent and relevant to understanding the spirit of *our* times.

The martyr of the future, Kierkegaard suggests, conveys a message that is publicly staged, but whose theatricality—yet another aesthetic device—is more indirect than is suggested by the current, more anthropologically oriented interpretations of "martyrdom."[72]

> "[T]he martyr," this "martyr of the future" ("the missionary" who uses the category "the single individual" educationally), will have in him and in re-sponse to the age ("the age of reflection") a superior reflection, and faith and courage besides to venture, will need an infinite task (or preparation) in re-flection *in* becoming or *in order* to become a martyr. In this he will differ from any previous (i.e., immediacy's) martyr who needed only faith and courage to stake his life. Unlike all previous martyrs, the martyr of the future will have a superior reflection to serve him in determining (of course in unconditional obedience to God)—in freely determining—what kind of maltreatment and persecution he is to suffer, whether he is to fall or not, and if so where, so that he manages to fall at dialectically the right spot, so that his death wounds in the right place, wounds the survivors. It will not be "the others," as it was pre-viously, who fall upon the martyr, who then simply has to suffer—no, it will be "the martyr" who determines the suffering.[73]

Martyrdom, as Kierkegaard presents it, may take the form of pseudo-nymity, but also that of "hiding for the time being in the cautious in-

---

72. Any empirical discipline should hesitate simply to adopt historically and systematically overdetermined concepts and categories such as the theologeme of the *martyrium*. Yet the same reticence should prevail when, guarded by strict methodological atheism and sound skepticism about this Christian paradigm, such empirical approaches prefer to interpret cultural conflict via non-Christian topoi such as Greek tragedy, as in the "tragic conflict" or "stoic resolve" so often invoked both in the current interest in Hellenist ethics, from the later Foucault and Pierre Hadot to Martha Nussbaum, and in theories and models of "rational choice."

73. Kierkegaard, *Papers and Journals*, 351–52.

cognito of a *flâneur.*[74] In all these strategic, variable forms, an ethico-religious impetus or intention is at work, one devoid of any particular content and independent of all determinate context, both of which impose a different form on the singular — in Kierkegaard's monocentrist view, the *one* — drama of human existence. This intention — or intentionality — resembles what in modern speech act theory is known as a performative (in this case, an *absolute* performative). According to Kierkegaard, this gesture or gesticulating consists in a peculiar discipline of the martyr "precisely *not to teach* the ethical but to mark out the ethical ethically, to put the qualitative force of the ethical into play, and by the same token in some measure — again in qualitative contrast to the System, teaching, and all that — give it support personally in existence itself."[75] Not many persons, Kierkegaard is convinced, will ever come close to this life of and in the spirit: most will lack this "courage to be" (to cite Paul Tillich's formulation); most will not have "learned to fear, have not learned 'to have to' without any dependence, none at all, upon whatever else happens" (*SD* 57). Indeed, seen from the outside, to live in faith, to be up to it, comes down to a "defiant madness that insanely fills out time with nothing" (*SD* 57). Here we are dealing with an incomprehensibility that, *pace* Kant, we cannot even understand as incomprehensible, but that can only be revealed and believed. Christian teaching is Socratic and ironic in that it guards faith against speculation, "keeping watch so that the gulf of qualitative difference between God and man may be maintained as it is in the paradox and faith, so that God and man do not, even more dreadfully than ever in paganism, do not merge in some way, *philosophice, poetice* [philosophically, poetically], etc., into one — in the system" (*SD* 99).[76] The reservation, therefore, pertains to literary fiction, tragedy, and comedy, no less than to metaphysical reflection: "Even Shakespeare seems to have recoiled from essentially religious collisions. Indeed, perhaps these can be expressed only in the language of the gods. And no human being can speak this language" (*SD* 127).

Kierkegaard's logic, a *sacrificium intellectus,* is one of martyrdom and death, of giving oneself (a certain) death. Similarly, despair, testimony,

---

74. Ibid., 353 and 351.

75. Ibid., 350–51.

76. "To comprehend is the range of man's relation to the human, but to believe is man's relation to the divine. How then does Christianity explain this incomprehensibility? Very consistently, in a way just as incomprehensible: by revealing it" (*SD* 95, see also 129 n.).

and martyrdom are dialectically related to death, to the sickness unto death and its remedy in (or through) faith alone. This remedy is highly paradoxical; the inner tension between its two contradictory sides makes up the drama of human existence.

On the one hand, faith is despair's opposite, a sort of constancy or stasis: "The formula that describes the state of the self when despair is completely rooted out is this: in relating itself to itself and in willing to be itself, the self rests transparently in the power that established it" (SD 14).[77] This motif would seem to run counter to the interpretation of *Fear and Trembling* ventured above. The fact that for Kierkegaard faith consists in a certain "consistency" in life or rather existence echoes the Augustinian insistence on *continentia* (rather than, say, the Emersonian image of being true to one's self, developed in the essay "Self-Reliance," that would shun "a foolish consistency").[78] Moreover, constancy holds the middle ground between the two false extremes that polarize bourgeois society and the established church. Hannay describes them as follows:

> In a spiritless society whose institutions have nominally taken over spirit's functions, no real basis for spirit, or true selfhood, remains in the established forms of life. Spiritual possibilities then tend to find their outlets outside such forms in madness, religious intoxication, the cult of the aesthetic, or in utopian politics. This, from the individual's perspective, is one way of failing to maintain the synthesis. The other is for the individual to duck below the level of its own spiritual possibilities and lead a spiritually emasculated life of worldliness. The solution which *The Sickness unto Death* prescribes for despair is faith, or willing acceptance of the task of becoming a self posited not by itself but by a transcendent power.[79]

On the other hand, however, the consistency of faith stands in permanent need of being reaffirmed (that is to say, repeated) and is thus in permanent danger of being contested and hence not repeated (exposed to further — repeated — sin). Faith, therefore, is anything but a quietist state of mind; its constancy is constantly tested. Even the most tranquil or tran-

---

77. See also the final sentence of the book: "In relating itself to itself and in willing to be itself, the self rests transparently in the power that established it. This formula . . . is the definition of faith" (SD 131).

78. Ralph Waldo Emerson, "Self-Reliance," in *Selections from Ralph Waldo Emerson*, ed. Stephen. E. Whicher (Boston: Houghton Mifflin, 1957), 153.

79. Kierkegaard, *Papers and Journals*, 285–86.

sitory state may conceal the greatest despair.[80] The difference is difficult to tell and requires an act of faith alone.

Likewise, in the very act of its decision lurks the danger of indecision. What is more, *in risking anything at all, it risks all at once.*[81] This potential — and necessary — instability of the constancy of faith is developed nowhere clearer than in Kierkegaard's *The Sickness unto Death,*[82] which, together with "Repetition," spells out the "psychological" dynamics — more precisely, the dialectics — of forms of despair as instantiations of sin and possibilities for existence and faith: "Precisely because the sickness of despair is totally dialectical, it is the worst misfortune never to have had that sickness: it is a true godsend to get it, even if it is the most dangerous of illnesses, if one does not want to be cured of it" (*SD* 26).[83]

Martyrdom, according to Kierkegaard, is *testimony at its logical — and "psychological" — extreme.* It announces the moment at which the finite world and the restlessness of its of seemingly infinite possibilities finds its end; a person dies to the world, and a balance or "synthesis" with necessity is (re)established. But this utmost possibility — the limit and limitation of the possible — is no longer a possibility in a strict (that is, humanly possible) sense of the word: "The critical decision does not come until a

80. Kierkegaard writes: "The superficial view is very easily deceived in determining whether or not despair is present. Not to be in despair can in fact signify precisely to be in despair, and it can signify having been rescued from being in despair. A sense of security and tranquillity can be the despair, and yet it can signify having conquered despair and having won peace." And a little earlier: "Despair can be affected, and as a qualification of the spirit it may also be mistaken for and confused with all sorts of transitory states, such as dejection, inner conflict, which pass without developing into despair. But the physician of the soul properly regards these also as forms of despair; he sees very well that they are affectation. Yet this very affectation is despair: he sees very well that this dejection etc. are not of great significance, but precisely this — that it has and acquires no great significance — is despair" (*SD* 24).

81. Kierkegaard gives the following bleak depiction of the "religion for adults," to cite Levinas's *Difficult Freedom*: "The believer, one who rests in and has his life in the consistency of the good, has an infinite fear of even the slightest sin, for he faces an infinite loss. Immediate individuals, the childlike or childless, have no totality to lose; they always win and lose only something particular or something in particular" (*SD* 107–8).

82. Further helpful introductions and commentaries can be found in the translation by Alastair Hannay (London: Penguin, 1989), 1–32, and that by Hans Rochol (Hamburg: Felix Meiner, 1995), ix–lxxii.

83. Cf. "The common view that despair is a rarity is entirely wrong; on the contrary, it is universal. The common view, which assumes that everyone who does not think or feel he is in despair is not or that only he who says he is in despair is, is totally false. On the contrary, the person who without affectation says that he is in despair is still a little closer, is dialectically closer, to being cured than all those who are not regarded as such and who do not regard themselves as such" (*SD* 26).

person is brought to his extremity, when, humanly speaking, there is no possibility" (*SD* 38). Testimony is necessity refound and, in Kierkegaard's view, the divine *ultima ratio* of human existence. By counterbalancing the possible with necessity, Kierkegaard would thus—*pace* Heidegger and in anticipation of Derrida's invocation of the Greek (and Freudian) *Anankē* —correct the *possibilism* that keeps philosophy from the essential and the self from taking hold in existence: for "if possibility outruns necessity so that the self runs away from itself into possibility, it has no necessity to which it is to return; this is possibility's despair. The self becomes an ab-stract possibility; it flounders in possibility until exhausted but neither moves from the place where it is nor arrives anywhere, for necessity is literally that place" (*SD* 35–36). But, of course, the reverse, possibilizing movement of abstraction, the rupture with immediacy and externality in the direction of transcendence, is no less essential. Here an even greater risk is run.[84]

Testimony implies some martyrdom to begin with. In any testimony, martyrdom—and, in Kierkegaard's view, some martyr—still (or already) casts its shadow. To say this is to strip martyrdom of its historical, an-thropological, and empirical determinants, at once to generalize and to trivialize its meaning as a *factum brutum* of the history of religions and to transform it into a figure of the structure of religious and nonreligious testimony as such.[85] This means that the possibility of martyrdom, of a certain death, lies at the root of any genuine testimony. (Hence one should take issue with the distinction between "heroic" martyrs, on the one hand, and accidental martyrs, on the other. Indeed, one should question the very distinction between martyrdom and testimony; it seems gradual rather than categorical.) Kierkegaard evokes this double meaning of death: "In Christian terminology death is indeed the expression for the state of deep-est spiritual wretchedness, and yet the cure is simply to die, to die to the

---

84. Kierkegaard speaks of the need for a "self that is won by infinite abstraction from every externality, this naked abstract self, which, compared with immediacy's fully dressed self, is the first form of the infinite self and the advancing impetus in the whole process in which a self becomes responsible for its actual self with all its difficulties and advantages" (*SD* 55).

85. This seems Kierkegaard's strategy as well: "No human being ever lived and no one lives outside of Christendom who has not despaired, and no one in Christendom if he is not a true Christian, and insofar as he is not wholly that, he still is to some extent in despair. No doubt this observation will strike many people as a paradox, an overstatement, and also a somber and depressing point of view. But it is none of these things. It is not somber, for, on the contrary, it tries to shed light on what generally is elevating, inasmuch as it views every human being under the destiny of the highest claim upon him, to be spirit" (*SD* 22).

world" (*SD* 6). This dying to the world, Kierkegaard elaborates, is exemplified by the testimony of the single individual whose indifference — a being *in* the world without being part of it — ultimately entails the suffering of martyrdom, in one way or another, whether physically or spiritually, knowingly or not. Kierkegaard sees this suffering as a category of human existence with a particular poignancy in modernity. As we have seen, it takes the form of an existential structure of resistance or acquiescence; the difference matters little, but depends on context alone.

Whereas in Kant absolute power and infinite powerlessness, sovereignty and pure reason, the king and the philosopher form each other's opposite extremes and mirror images — two possibilities of, precisely, necessity and possibility that should not be collapsed into each other but confronted, balanced, and negotiated in view of an ultimate reversal (the higher becoming the lower, the last becoming the first, etc.) — in Kierkegaard a constitutive polarity and polarization make up the drama of history:

> The first form of rulers in the world were "the tyrants," the last will be "the martyrs." In the world's evolution this is the movement . . . from worldliness to religiousness. No doubt there is an infinite difference between a tyrant and martyr, yet they have one thing in common: compulsion. The tyrant, himself with a craving for power, compels by force; the martyr, in himself unconditionally obedient to God, compels through his own sufferings. So the tyrant dies and his rule is over; the martyr dies and his rule begins.[86]

Universal worldliness or (virtually) total secularism forms the foil against which the martyr — the last and the first witness — can emerge. According to a curious political theology, Kierkegaard holds that, not feudalism or aristocratic oligarchies, but modern democracies and mass cultures form the context in which the martyr may, once again, appear. In the margin of the passage cited, Kierkegaard notes: "Worldliness will be at its maximum, must have reached its most frightful ascendancy, when only martyrs can be the rulers. When one person is the tyrant, the mass is not completely secularized; but when 'the crowd' wants to be the tyrant, then worldliness has been made completely universal and then only the martyr can be ruler."[87]

The martyr has the future. If there is faith ("But I wonder," Kierke-

86. Kierkegaard, *Papers and Journals*, 352.
87. Ibid.

gaard writes, "whether faith is to be found on earth"; *SD* 129), then it will
be contested according to its authenticity, and there will be an exact correspondence between its sincerity qua *pure or absolute performative* and
the risk and danger to which it is exposed from without *and* within. Here
too the possibility of the worst is the condition for the best. The threat,
a certain apocalyptics, is, in other words, the flip side of the promise, of
eschatology. Again, this is no accident. It is intrinsic to—it belongs to
the very structure of—testimony and is intimately related to what Kierkegaard calls *sin* and *despair,* both of which constitute the failure to bear
witness, that is to say, to witness the drama of revelation and salvation.[88]
Yet sin and despair are, paradoxically, also the condition of this drama.
Sin also singularizes to the point where no dialectical relation between
the particular (*das Besondere*) and the general (*das Allgemeine*), in Hegel's
sense of the word, can put it into perspective, let alone get an adequate
grip on it. Thus Kierkegaard writes, as if he were speaking of faith, sin's
opposite: "The category of sin is the category of individuality. Sin cannot
be thought speculatively at all" (*SD* 119). But sin is not evil, not demonic.
Nor is despair.

> Is despair an excellence or a defect? Purely dialectically, it is both. If only
> the abstract idea of despair is considered, without any thought of someone
> in despair, it must be regarded as a surpassing excellence. The possibility of
> this sickness is man's superiority over the animal, and this superiority dis-
> tinguishes him in quite another way than does his erect walk, for it indicates
> infinite erectness or sublimity, that he is spirit. The possibility of this sick-
> ness is man's superiority over the animal; to be aware of this sickness is the
> Christian's superiority over the natural man; to be cured of this sickness is the
> Christian's blessedness.
>
> Consequently, to be able to despair is an infinite advantage, and yet to be
> in despair is not only the worst misfortune and misery—no, it is ruination.[89]

Or again:

> Despair over sin is dialectically understood as pointing towards faith. The
> existence of this dialectic must never be forgotten . . . ; in fact, it is implied

88. To miss its mark is perhaps what at the most fundamental level constitutes sin (in Greek:
hamartia, as in the Greek *hamartanō,* "I miss the mark"). The Greek word *martus,* the eye- or
ear-witness, lies at the origin of the classical, New Testament, and modern understanding of
martyr. I am indebted to Peter Dreyer for having reminded me of this parallel.
89. *SD* 15.

in despair's also being the first element of faith. . . . In the life of the spirit, everything is dialectical. Indeed, offense as annulled possibility is an element of faith, but offense directed away from faith is sin. That a person never once is capable of being offended by Christianity can be held against him. (*SD* 116 n.)

In all of this, Kierkegaard is at once close to and at a certain remove from Kant's doctrine of radical evil, which may form a subtext for all of his meditation on martyrdom, on the relationship between morality and religion.[90] Radical evil is, Kant writes, the acquired propensity of the human soul toward evil, toward the worst. As such, it is the sure sign of human freedom, for humans are neither beasts nor angels. Yet, Kierkegaard insists in a note made in passing in *Papers and Journals:*

> Kant's theory of radical evil has just one fault: he does not make it quite clear that the inexplicable is a category, that the paradox is a category. Everything really turns on this. What people have always said is this: To say that we cannot understand this or that does not satisfy science, which insists on comprehending. Here lies the error. We must say the very opposite, that if *human* science refuses to acknowledge that there is something it cannot understand, or, more accurately still, something such that it clearly understands that it cannot understand it, then everything is confused. For it is a task for human understanding to understand that there is something, and what it is, that it cannot understand. Human cognition is generally busily concerned to understand and understand, but if it would also take the trouble to understand itself it must straightaway posit the paradox. The paradox is not a concession but a category, an ontological qualification which expresses the relation between an existing cognitive spirit and the eternal truth.[91]

90. Green notes that there are some "seventeen explicit references to Kant found in the works published by Kierkegaard during his lifetime" and "thirty-one entries mentioning Kant (excluding references in reading or lecture notes) found in Kierkegaard's posthumously published *Papers*" (*The Hidden Debt*, xiv). According to Green, we can find a "major, and largely unacknowledged, intellectual borrowing" by Kierkegaard, who nonetheless, whether deliberately or unconsciously, sought to "obscure the degree of his indebtedness" (ibid., xv–xvi, cf. xviii). In sum, Green claims, Kierkegaard was "not only one of the best of Kant's nineteenth-century readers but also the genuine heir to the legacy of Kant's developed religious and ethical thought" (ibid., xvi). A hint toward the end of *The Sickness unto Death* may corroborate this view. Kierkegaard writes: "On the whole, it is unbelievable what confusion has entered the sphere of religion since the time when "thou shalt" was abolished as the sole regulative aspect of man's relationship to God. This "thou shalt" must be present in any determination of the religious" (*SD* 115).

91. Kierkegaard, *Papers and Journals,* 255.

Unlike radical evil, the sickness unto death of which Kierkegaard speaks is a category or, as Heidegger would say, an existential of sorts. Its central features, sketched out in *The Sickness unto Death,* describe a human condition that is universal, irrevocable (and, in that sense, radical), and identifiable throughout all ages. An entry in the *Papers and Journals* formulates apodictically how the expression "the sickness unto death" should be taken. Central to its meaning are:

1. Its hiddenness.
   Not just that that person who has it, or one who has it, may wish to hide it. No, the awful fact that it is so hidden that one can have it without knowing it.
2. Its generality.
   Every other sickness is limited in one way or other, by climate, age, etc.
3. Its continuation.
   Through all ages — in eternity.
4. Where is the seat?
   In the self.[92]

Though we are dealing with a category located (as are all categories, in Kant's view) in the self, Kierkegaard leaves no doubt that the psychological, dialectical, rhetorical, and lyrical exposition of this theme remains tainted by the individuality, indeed, the radical singularity of its author. The author can neither speak for himself or on behalf of others, since this would be pretentious, nor not speak, since such "silence" is a "shamelessness, a fraud, a cunning insurrection against God, who does not want ideality's demands to be suppressed at all."[93] Kierkegaard operates under the guise of a pseudonymous author, but as some entries in the *Papers and Journals* demonstrate, he was only too painfully aware of the extent to which this mode of presentation involved and exposed him as a witness and a martyr before God:

> If a better qualified person will not do it and it still has to be done, then a less qualified person must venture it and thereby involve him in a contradiction that is, humanly speaking, a kind of treason against himself — namely, to apply himself diligently, and to concentrate totally on ideality's demands, unto his own humiliation. If he succeeds, his own imperfection will show itself to be

92. Ibid., 299–300.
93. *SD* 158 (a note from 1849 to be found in the *Papirer* X B 16).

proportionately greater and greater . . . I am quite prepared for that: indeed, I do all I can to make myself the one who is incriminated, as if I were the only one. (*SD* 158)[94]

While the martyr justifies himself publicly, even or precisely by writing pseudonymous works, clearly doing so entails a double insecurity. First, his testimony may not claim any truth for itself in a strict sense of the word. Thus, Hannay notes, "Although Kierkegaard wished to indicate that the intention behind the whole pseudonymous authorship had been religious from the start, resolved as he now was to depict for people the high spiritual standards which religious faith and observance required, he nevertheless felt unable to present himself in his own person as someone able to exemplify those standards and to judge others. So this could not be the way in which *he* 'spoke' to his contemporaries."[95] In all of this, the question of the generic status of Kierkegaard's text remains: is it philosophical argument, psychological analysis, theological exegesis, pastoral edification, or something else again?

Second, as an expression and discourse of faith, such writing — like this very faith — remains haunted by the "possibility of the offense." Although the structure of faith is one of rest and transparency, that possibility lies at its base: "Christian doctrine is the teaching of the God-man, about the kinship between God and man, but of such a nature, please note, that the possibility of the offense is, if I may say so, the guarantee whereby God

---

94. A little later, Kierkegaard writes: "Really and truly, I judge no one. Even if I myself am striving after perfection — for it would indeed be blasphemous to praise the ideal and not strive after it oneself — I nevertheless judge no one; and even if I may have a psychologist's eye — I nevertheless see people in such universality that I truly can be said to see no one — yet I judge no one. . . . I myself am the only one dealt with negatively and personally in the book" (*SD* 158-59, *Papirer* X B 18). Hannay comments on the *Papers and Journals* of the period between 1850 and 1853: "During this time he became ever more preoccupied with understanding what in a journal entry from 1851 he refers to as his 'task.' The terms in which he tries to grasp his task in life include (1) his own 'heterogeneity,' which was precisely what prevented him [from] 'realizing the universal' . . . , a fact which he constantly traces back to his childhood; and (2) the prevalence of 'Christendom,' a naturalization and therefore gross distortion of the true Christian message which (3) he now sees it as his task to champion in the face of Christendom; and finally, (4) the problem of how to champion Christianity when what Christianity requires is not teachers or writers but witnesses. The thought of his own death becomes ever more insistent as a possible player in his life's operation, and the topic of martyrdom, which had its origin in his treatment by the 'rabble' during the *Corsair* affair, constantly recurs" (ibid., 454-55). For testimonies concerning Kierkegaard's role as a witness/martyr, see *Encounters with Kierkegaard: A Life as Seen by His Contemporaries*, ed. Bruce H. Kirmmse, trans. Bruce H. Kirmmse and Virginia R. Laursen (Princeton: Princeton University Press, 1996).

95. Kierkegaard, *Papers and Journals*, 286; see also 348-49, 459-60.

protects himself against man's coming too close. The possibility of offense is the dialectical element in everything essentially Christian" (*SD* 125). The offense not only lies in the offense taken—the refusal of faith, without whose possibility there can be no faith at all—it also lurks as a possibility behind or beyond faith at its most authentic moments: "Not to be in despair must signify the destroyed possibility of being able to be in despair; if a person is truly not to be in despair, he must at every moment destroy the possibility" (*SD* 15). Forsakenness and abandonment—the logical extremes of despair in all of its conscious or unconscious, heightened or latent manifestations—form the inherent risk of the very gift of faith: "What a rare act of love, what unfathomable grief of love, that even God cannot remove the possibility that this act of love reverses itself for a person and becomes the most extreme misery—something that in another sense God does not want to do, cannot want to do" (*SD* 126).

Thus, while the opposite—and, in a sense, the dialectical cessation, sublation, and elevation—of despair, as Kierkegaard suggests in the opening pages of *The Sickness unto Death*, is a sensibility that Augustine would have called *continentia*, one that resists and subtracts itself from the deconcentration (or *defluxus*) that haunts public life, curiosity, and so on, this stability and consistency is nonetheless of an instantaneous nature, in need of permanent repetition. That reaffirmation is necessary in order "to be maintained in existence—and God does want that, for he is not a God of confusion" (*SD* 117).

Repetition—"faith" or "spontaneity after reflection," all being synonyms for a religious category sui generis, that is, beyond or before all categorization of a more metaphysical or empirical nature—is all in all not so much a matter of public display, the staging of a beautiful or horrific death. On the contrary, at the heart of faith, Kierkegaard suggests, lies a reiterated destruction of the "possibility of the offense" which can be found in the *forum internum* of inwardness alone. That such a destruction must take place is not in doubt, despite virtual interchangeability with its opposite, despair. The latter must be overcome, to be sure, but without its always latent or actual presence, there could be no faith, no knowledge of, or, rather, no fear of God: "the impression that there is a God [is] an infinite benefaction that is never gained except through despair" (*SD* 27). Yet despair itself is not this "benefaction." As a matter of fact, it is at the furthest remove from it; more precisely, at once infinitely close to and infinitely distant from it.

Any social recognition *comes later,* premised on a sublime—and horrific—indifference vis-à-vis others that constitutes our freedom and that alone can explain why, paradoxically, these others can matter to us at all. But the genuine testimony of martyrdom therefore also still lies ahead of us. Only where tyranny, whether that of the single tyrant or that of the crowd and the public, has exhausted itself "like an overripe fruit," indicating ruination, will the proper contours of martyrdom as it (perhaps for the first time) engages the single individual finally come into view.

Tautology and Heterology: *Tout autre est tout autre*

In *The Gift of Death,* the thematization and problematization of the sacrificial structure takes a form resembling the double bind that haunts so many of Derrida's earlier writings. It could be formalized as follows: *in being responsive and responsible one must, at the same time, also be irresponsive and irresponsible* (*GD* 61 / 61), sacrificing one while respecting the other. Being responsible demands a double response or allegiance to the general and the singular, to repetition and to the unique, to the public sphere and to the secret, to discourse and silence, to giving reasons as well as to madness, each of which tempts the other. Indeed, Derrida writes, one does not have to raise a knife in order to slaughter one's own son to be caught in this logic of a given death which prescribes that one "can respond only to one (or to the One), that is, to the other, by sacrificing that one to the other" (*GD* 70 / 70). That sacrifice, that preference for one other over another, Derrida insists, is always *unjustifiable,* for "every other is totally other [*Tout autre est tout autre;* in David Wills's translation, "Every other (one) is every (bit) other, every one else is completely or wholly other]" (*GD* 68 / 68). Every other (that is to say everybody, everything) is other than every other other (i.e., other than everybody and everything else); put otherwise, every other (everybody, everything, e.g., God) is *totally* other, an other in an absolute sense of the word, another absolute. Of this, "God" would be both the "figure" and the "name": "What can be said about Abraham's relation to God [*à Dieu*] can be said about my relation without relation to *every other (one) as every (bit) other* [tout autre comme tout autre]" (*GD* 78 / 76).

But are not some others more other than others, more other than just ab-solutely other? Are not some others other otherwise? Is not God, as the tradition suggests, other—*the* Other—par excellence? Perhaps. Who knows? Precisely this uncertainty constitutes the other as other and—a fortiori—defines the Other, not in his, her, or its otherness, but as a singular Other. Otherwise, the other—for example, God—would be an apodictic notion, not demanding to be believed but self-evident and ready at hand, in the open for everyone to see. "God" is only given—indeed, only gives—in secret. His very name is a cryptogram, his very manifestation encrypted (and, according to at least one tradition, tied to a crypt). The same could be said of the gesture with which one gives oneself to God or to every totally other that takes his place. For if the response cannot measure up to the demand, if the former and the latter are inversely proportional to each other or, rather, are disproportionate, one can never know or calculate whether one has given enough or at all: "A gift that could be recognized as such in the light of day, a gift destined for recognition, would immediately annul itself. The gift is the secret itself, if the secret *itself* can be told. Secrecy is the last word of the gift which is the last word of the secret" (*GD* 29–30 / 36).

Derrida acknowledges that this reading pushes the analysis of *Fear and Trembling* beyond commentary, let alone an interpretation *e mente auctoris*.[96] If one claims there can be no ethical generality that is not always already subject to the Abrahamic paradox; if one infers, moreover, that "at the instant of every decision and through the relation to *every other (one) as every bit other* [à tout autre comme tout autre], every one else asks us at every moment to behave ourselves as knights of faith," then this analysis, Derrida concedes, "displaces a certain emphasis [*portée*] of Kierkegaard's discourse: the absolute uniqueness of Jahweh doesn't tolerate analogy; we are not all Abrahams, Isaacs, or Sarahs either. We are not Jahweh" (*GD* 79 / 77).[97]

96. See also the section "La Littérature au secret: Une filiation impossible," which was added to the new French edition of *Donner la mort* (Paris: Galilée, 1999), 161–209.

97. Along different lines, Levinas continues to insist on a difference between the Other as God and the Other as *autrui*, as neighbor (the difference between "us" and God seems to be beyond question here): "I cannot describe the relation to God without speaking of my concern for the other. When I speak to a Christian, I always quote Matthew 25: the relation to God is presented there as a relation to another person. It is not a metaphor: in the other, there is a real presence of God. In my relation to the other, I hear the Word of God. . . . [I]t is literally true. I'm not saying that the other is God" (*Entre nous*, 109–10 / 128). The circumstance that the Other as God leaves only his trace in the face of the other Other, in the visage of *autrui*, gives rise to a paradox. On the one hand, the difference in the analogy between the in-finite Other as God and the ab-solute as *autrui* explains why there can be no strict or absolute distinction between the ethical in general (or, for that matter, the ethical as the general) and the religious, as *Fear and Trembling* suggests. On the other hand, Derrida observes that since Levinas wishes to uphold a certain indelible difference between the two Others—God, the Infinite, the Illeity is neither a Thou nor a grand *Autrui*—he cannot say or write something that is completely different from what Kierkegaard intends (*GD* 83–84 / 83–84). Accordingly, the relation to the Other can no longer be seen as simply or exclusively ethical. As long as one holds God and

As with violence, the generalization, universalization, or infinite substitution of "God," of the infinitely other that is everywhere or everyone
or everything (else) — *tout autre est tout autre* — promises to trivialize the
burden of this notion as much as to intensify it. It begs the question of
God, of the other, of their relation, of their relation to the same, and so
on and so forth. It evades this question no less than it takes it for granted,
as the *petitio principii* or, indeed, the tautology of all thought, all action,
all judgment. Yet the impossibility of ascribing or assigning an identifiable
and responsible agent (God, Abraham, and those who follow their trace
without ever being able to claim to follow *in* their trace) is precisely what
is in question here. It is in this sense of a heterology, of sorts, that "we"
could be said to "share" with Abraham

> what cannot be shared, a secret we know nothing about, neither him nor us.
> . . . Such is the secret truth of faith as absolute responsibility and as absolute
> passion, the "highest passion," as Kierkegaard will say; it is a passion that,
> sworn to secrecy, cannot be transmitted from generation to generation. In this
> sense, it has no history. This untransmissibility of the highest passion, the nor-
> mal condition of a faith which is thus bound to secrecy, nevertheless dictates
> to us the following: we must [*il faut*] always start over [begin anew, *recom-
> mencer*]. A secret can be transmitted, but in transmitting a secret as a secret
> that remains secret, has one transmitted at all? Does it amount to history, to
> a story? Yes and no. (*GD* 80 / 78)

Therefore, Derrida reminds us, *Fear and Trembling* concludes by invoking the "nonhistory of absolute beginnings which are repeated, and
the very historicity that presupposes a tradition to be reinvented each step
[*pas*] of the way, in this incessant repetition of the absolute beginning"
(*GD* 80 / 78). In its very structure, the history of religion is thus nothing
but the sequence, the *sériature*, or the incessant *re-instantiation* of the "instant" of decision: of a "performance" marked by the "stigma of its punctuality," indeed, by a "no-time-lapse" (*GD* 77, 95 / 76, 90) and that, because
of its elusiveness and almost virtual character, matters all the more.

---

the Other, *autrui,* at a distance from each other, ethics and religion, as relations to the totally
other, cannot entirely coincide. Nor, for that matter, can they be entirely separated. Of the transcendence toward God (*à Dieu*), it is said that it is "neither linear, like the intentional aim, nor
teleological, tending toward an end in the punctuality of a pole and thus stopping at entities
and substantives, nor even initially dialogical, naming a *thou*. . . . The fact that transcendence
is produced from the (horizontal?) relationship with the other person means neither that the
other person is God nor that God is a great Other Person" (*Entre nous,* 73–74 / 90).

À dieu, adieu, a-dieu

Paraphrased and varied, mimicked and parodied, affirmed and displaced, the à dieu still retains something of its untranslatability. If "God," the invocation of "God" — speaking on the subject of or addressing oneself to God — is exemplary, does this exemplarity necessarily imply that "God" is the sole, or even the best, example, as if the name or term "God" stood for the highest or most elevated Being among beings? It means, rather, that "God" is the example par excellence, privileged not because of any quality that this name or entity can claim to possess in and of itself, but because of the (intentional, spoken, or silent) act of our attribution. This act stands in relation to a powerful, inspiring, and terrifying history, which cannot be interpreted in terms of a metaphysical, onto-theological epoch of *Seinsgeschichte* and *Seinsgeschick,* or reduced to a mere enumeration of data.

Not only does every decision condemn itself to remain secret — in the final analysis, there is nothing more to say about it (*il n'y a rien plus à en dire*) — ultimately, every genuine, that is, absolutely singular, responsibility condemns itself to silence and demands a *sacrificium intellectus,* if not more, and if only for an instant.[98] But the more responsible (and, if one might say so, the more singular) it is, the more guilty, the more responsible for others, it becomes (*"plus je suis juste—plus je suis coupable"*).[99] The mere facticity of my existence already incites (or should incite) bad conscience with respect to, vis-à-vis, the Other, and thus the genuine fear of God given with the "risk of occupying — beginning with the very *Da* of my *Dasein* — the place of an Other and, thus, in the concrete, of exiling him, dooming him to a miserable condition in some 'third' or 'fourth' world, bringing him death."[100] This fear of God does not have the modality of the *Befindlichkeit* described in *Being and Time,* where "fear [*Furcht*]" comes to "double the intentionality of a feeling affected by a being in the world."[101] Nor does it correspond to *Angst* of some sort. The fear and trembling re-

98. Cf. Levinas, *Otherwise Than Being,* 107 / 136: "Indicible et, par là même, injustifiable."
99. Ibid., 112 / 143. Cf. Levinas, *Of God Who Comes to Mind:* "The fission of the subject is a growth of obligation in proportion to my obligation to it; it is the augmentation of culpability with the augmentation of holiness, an increase of distance in proportion to my approach" (73–74 / 120).
100. Emmanuel Levinas, "Diachrony and Representation," in *Time and the Other,* trans. Richard A. Cohen (Pittsburgh: Duquesne University Press, 1987), 110 (trans. modified). The French text was republished in *Entre nous,* 177–97, cf. 188.
101. Emmanuel Levinas, *Transcendance et intelligibilité* (Geneva: Labor et Fides, 1984), 26.

vealed by the intrigue of Genesis 22 has, Levinas suggests, an entirely different structure.[102]

The suspension of all naturalistic, rational, or communicational ethics makes clear that to speak in or of obligation amounts to speaking of and to "God." It is to speak of and to the *tout autre,* in the sense of the totally other, but also in the sense of every other. In short, it is to speak of and to every other totally other, in a gesture in which the address and a certain suspension — an *à dieu* and an *adieu,* a going toward God and a leave-taking — enigmatically coincide. The *a* — in all the ambiguity of *à* and *a,* with and without *accent grave,* separated from and linked to *dieu* — stands as much for a turning toward as for a turning away from, and only thus would it, according to Levinas, constitute the enigma, "duration," "inspiration," and "prophecy" of time. The turn of phrase introduced into language by the *adieu* marks the distance from any linear movement stretched out in the direction of a goal, telos, or vision.[103] The address would thus be marked by a farewell to the omnipotent, omniscient, and benevolent God of onto-theology and, in the same gesture, face the oblique, nether, flip side of God, the other — un- or a-godly — face of the Other, the faceless face of no god, *pas de dieu, Niemand,* or a "transcendence to the point of absence."[104]

Adieu, then — to say nothing of the *Aha-Erlebnis* (Ah . . . , yes God), which might be the latest form of Aquinas's dictum "and this is what all call God" — would also mean that, in the end, every decision is *at least as much up to the other, to the totally other,* as it is made by the singular instance called "me." A *dieu* might also mean: here, everything is ultimately "up to God" (*c'est à Dieu,* as it were, *pas à moi, pas à nous ou à vous,* but, in the final analysis, up to God). Up to God, strictly speaking, *or* — provided there is a real alternative or opposition here — up to the singular singularity that, for a long time now, we have come to call "difference," the "trace," the "other," and so on, and which "is," if we can still say so, "in" and "for" "itself" neither one nor indivisible, but multiple, fractured, other than itself, other than other, other than difference and, consequently, God, in yet another sense. But, if it is up to the other (up to, say, "God" or to the "self as other"), is the other also up to it (i.e., ready

102. In *Being and Time,* Heidegger refers to *The Concept of Anxiety* and notes: "The man who has gone farthest in analyzing the phenomenon of anxiety — and again in the theological context of a 'psychological' exposition of the problem of original sin — is Søren Kierkegaard " (*Being and Time,* 492 n. iv / 190 n. 1).

103. Cf. Levinas, *Transcendance et intelligibilité,* 36.

104. Levinas, *Of God Who Comes to Mind,* 69 / 115. *Niemand* is from Celan.

for it, willing and able to take it on)? What, in other words, could this singular singularity do, if anything? What does it make possible, if anything? Is this what it does: make *possible*? Is it certain that it is itself *possible*? Could an *im*possibility make something *possible*? Could it, while being impossible and perhaps even because of its impossibility, still somehow — paradoxically — become the possibility of a possibility? Of more than one possibility? Of a possibility that is more than one, more than itself, more than possible, and, therefore, strictly speaking, other than itself, that is to say, *im*possible? Is this what the formula *tout autre est tout autre* seeks to convey, if anything?[105]

There is a final meaning of the adieu, of another given salutation or benediction. Derrida describes it as follows: "Before all constative language 'adieu' can just as well signify 'hello,' 'I can see you,' 'I see that you are there,' I speak to you before telling you anything else — and in certain circumstances in French it happens that one says *adieu* at the moment of meeting rather than separation" (*GD* 47 / 50).

By the same token, every given death could be said to open as much as close a future, a to come (*à venir*), for better and for worse. Could one imagine a death allowing *nothing* beyond itself, a last negation and a final step without all the ambiguities of the *pas au-delà* analyzed by Blanchot and, in his wake, by Derrida? Could one think or experience an end that is truly the end, in the strict — or limited — sense of the word, an end of all things (*Das Ende aller Dinge*)? This question refers us back to the apocalyptical and eschatological structure I discussed in the final chapter of *Philosophy and the Turn to Religion*. Suffice it to note that *The Gift of Death* accentuates that a certain exposure to death forms the condition no less than the uncondition of decisions, of testimony, of all experience and, in that sense, of "all things." If what I have suggested so far is true, then at this point Derrida follows and radicalizes a Levinasian figure of thought.

Granted, neither Levinas nor Derrida mentions the possible privative interpretation of the *a-dieu* that, perhaps somewhat violently, can be distinguished from the *à dieu* as address and the *adieu* as a gesture of leave-

105. According to Wittgenstein, neither a tautology, an aporia, nor a logical contradiction is capable of conveying or depicting any truth or empirical content: "Tautologies and contradictions are not pictures of reality. They do not represent any possible situations. For the former admit *all* possible situations, and the latter *none*" (Ludwig Wittgenstein, *Logisch-philosophische Abhandlung / Tractatus Logico-Philosophicus*, vol. 1 of *Werkausgabe* [Frankfurt a. M.: Suhrkamp, 1984], 43, 4.462 / *Tractatus Logico-Philosophicus*, trans. David F. Pears and Brian F. McGuinness [London: Routledge, 1995], 35, 4.462).

taking or departure. Only Kierkegaard seems explicitly to thematize the fact that, in Abraham's silent agony, both the divine and the demonic cast their shadows or, more uncannily still, shadow or haunt, if not mirror, each other. While the "tragic hero," "the favorite of ethics," stands for the "purely human," the one who can "understand," whose "undertakings are out in the open," the knight of faith belongs to a different category, to a category beyond all categories. And "if I go further" here, Kierkegaard writes, "I always run up against the paradox, the divine and the demonic, for silence is both. Silence is the demon's trap, and the more that is silenced, the more terrible the demon, but silence is also divinity's mutual understanding with the single individual" (*FT* 88).

To my knowledge, no better interpretation of this uncanny resemblance has been given than the one proposed by Jean Wahl, one of the first commentators on Kierkegaard in France and the author of *Études Kierkegaardiennes* (*Studies on Kierkegaard*), who, in his introduction to the French translation of *Fear and Trembling*, points out that all its portraits of Abraham, Isaac, and Sarah are "haunted by the demon." Kierkegaard's writing incessantly borders upon and flirts with (*côtoie*) "the abysses of the demonic" (*ICT* viii).[106]

Judging this "flirtation," Wahl explains the inevitability or necessity of this resemblance and haunting:

> Like the religious, the demonic is outside the general, above the general, in an absolute relation with the absolute; just like religious natures, demonic natures have "their root in the paradox." Here Kierkegaard indicates that vast and somber region. In general, people seldom talk about the demonic, even though in our days that domain above all demands to be explored. But he insists on the idea that one can only escape the demonic paradox by means of [or through, *par*] the divine paradox. Whoever has sinned has placed himself outside the general, but in a negative manner; he will no longer be able to save himself unless, having lost all rapport with the general, he places himself in a positive rapport with the absolute. Ethics is insufficient truly to make one leave one's sin behind. (*ICT* ix)

Later in the text, Wahl reminds us that at one point Kierkegaard had considered explaining the sacrifice demanded of Abraham on the basis of

---

106. Cf. Jean Wahl, *Études Kierkegaardiennes* (Paris: Fernand Aubier, 1938). See also Jill Robbins, *Altered Reading: Levinas and Literature* (Chicago: University of Chicago Press, 1999), 101 ff.

some fault or prior sin. The reason he renounces this idea, Wahl notes, following Geismar's 1929 study *Søren Kierkegaard*, is that the *mysterium tremendum* that forms the "element" of all fear and trembling is here taken to reveal God's *grandeur* rather than our limitation. Sin will be the subject of *The Concept of Anxiety* and *The Sickness unto Death*. *Fear and Trembling*, Wahl concludes, suggests that to locate the terrible flip side of our condition — and, indeed, of all faith — in an original sin is too "facile" (*ICT* xviii n. 1). Kierkegaard's reasoning at this point demonstrates at least a formal resemblance to the Kantian doctrine of radical evil, whose nature is also incommensurable with any previous trespass. Yet for Kant the *tremendum* is neither a quality nor an aspect of God's grandeur. It is not so much the other side of God, but God's other, albeit a counterpart that is at least equally inscrutable.

In the hour of despair, Wahl notes, according to Kierkegaard, the knight of faith can only close his eyes: "Man says *adieu* to all understanding; he gives himself over to God [*à Dieu*] in all his weakness. At the same moment he recognizes the impossible and believes in the possibility; for everything is possible for God [*à Dieu*]" (*ICT* xiv). The first gesture — that of the suspension of the ethical, infinite resignation — is a movement by which our exposure to the absolute separates us "violently [*violemment*]" from the "real [*du réel*]." The second gesture — that of the movement of faith — "violently [*violemment*]" leads us away again from this refuge and returns us to the real so as to "conquer and to transfigure" it. These two violences, however, do not occur after one another, as consecutive moments "in" time, but at one and the same time, that is to say, "with one breath [*d'un seul souffle*]" (*ICT* xvii–xviii). More precisely, the movements of faith are indelibly temporal and historical, yet at the same time not of this world, eternal. As Wahl notes, faith both demands and suppresses time: for faith to be what it is, that is to say, to escape "immanence," it must be clear that "there has not always been faith" (*ICT* xii). At the same time, faith annuls time or at least "transforms" its ordinary concept. It evokes a certain "contemporaneity," which allows us to be more than mere spectators of the "Christian drama" (*ICT* xii), and in which we are no longer "spared" its anxieties. Faith marks the instant in which time, after having gone through a painful preparation, touches upon eternity, "consecrates time," and "begins a new time" (*ICT* xii).[107] Derrida says as much when he

---

107. Cf. "L'instant qui commence l'éternité prend place dans un processus long et douloureux. Durée et instant éternels sont intimement mêlés l'un à l'autre" (*ICT* xvi–xvii).

writes, in *The Gift of Death*, that the giving of death entails a temporality of its own: a temporality of the "instant," which, paradoxically, belongs to an "atemporal temporality," to an ungraspable "durée" (*GD* 65 / 66) that is incomprehensible to any work of negation or mourning, but can only be affirmed.

These two gestures correspond to two divine contradictions. By asking Abraham to sacrifice his son, God contradicts his promise that Isaac will be the first of innumerable offspring. In a second instance, however, God allows Isaac to live, thereby contradicting the first contradiction. According to Wahl, Kierkegaard's text betrays the marks of a double will (*double volonté*): a will to transgression and a will to return and integrate. Like the Nietzschean idea of perpetual trespass and eternal recurrence, Kierkegaard's doubling of the direction of the will constitutes a break with the more static "classical idea of the ideal" (*ICT* xxiv). Both Nietzsche and Kierkegaard seek to substitute for this notion, not so much some dialectical dynamism, guided by the mediation of the concept and its other and with a view to their ulterior and ultimate sublation, but rather the simultaneous affirmation of an irreducible "destruction" and "construction" (*ICT* xxv). In the latter moment of reaffirmation—the repetition given only to one who has survived the test—the knight of faith not only rediscovers the commonality of the finite world, of morality and its generality, but also finds a "new heaven and a new earth" (*ICT* xix–xx).

Following a similar paradox, Levinas, who is an avid reader of Wahl and cites him on more than one occasion, describes how the ungenerous sonority of "the impersonal being: *il*"[108] at the basis of the *il y a* is *as ab-solute as its equally incommensurable counterpart,* the infinite or the *illéité.* Indirectly—perhaps without intending to do so—the *il y a* in Levinas's analysis seems thus to form and de-form the very condition for and possibility of the trace of the *illéité.* Disturbingly, the *illéité* (the "third person: He at the root of the You [*Tu*]")[109] together with the *il y a*— which is yet another excluded third, neither present nor absent, beyond Being and not-Being, without common measure with the Heideggerian *es gibt*—thus constitute the two poles of the same elliptical experience. In this experience, God withdraws Himself from the order of representation and cannot be identified as either a subject, an object, or an interlocutor, strictly speaking. Levinas admits as much: "God is not simply the 'first

108. Emmanuel Levinas, *Éthique et Infini* (Paris: Fayard, 1982), 37.
109. Levinas, *Of God Who Comes to Mind,* 69 / 114.

other [*autrui*]' or the 'other [*autrui*] par excellence,' or the 'absolutely other [*autrui*],' but other than the other [*autrui*], other otherwise, and other with an alterity prior to the alterity of the other [*autrui*], . . . and different from every neighbor [*tout prochain*], transcendent to the point of absence, to the point of [*jusqu'à*] his possible confusion with the agitation [*remue-ménage*] of the *there is* [il y a]."[110] The *il y a* and the *illéité*, therefore, alternate, change places, resemble, or substitute for each other to the point of becoming almost interchangeable. Referring to Dante, Levinas speaks of a divine comedy "taking place in the ambiguity between temple and theater, but wherein the laughter sticks in your throat at the approach of the neighbor."[111]

To face the Other, then, implies at the same time to face the other than the Other, the absolutely other of the Other, the *il y a* rather than the *illéité*, and this *to the point of sacrilege*. Again, Levinas's critical reading of *Fear and Trembling* seems to provide sufficient reasons for this conclusion: even if Abraham embarks upon his mission at the break of dawn, the nocturnal element cannot be left behind but filters through the daylight; night casts its shadow *en plein jour*.[112]

The Gift of Death devotes much attention to the motif of light and darkness, seeing and not seeing. Both Jan Patočka's *Essais hérétiques sur la philosophie de l'histoire* (*Heretical Essays on the Philosophy of History*), with their radical inversion of Platonism and the New Testament (notably Matthew, to which Kierkegaard obliquely refers), revolve around two forms of the secret: the radiance of dark light and the seeing that is, in turn, not seen. While the last aspect is taken to reveal the very structure of divinity, of the absolute and absolutely interior witnessing that we have encountered above, the former — the invocation of darkness — adds a new element to the analysis. Derrida inscribes Patočka's essays in the tradition of reflections on the originary *polemos* in and of Being that leads from Heraclitus to Heidegger and Schmitt. The secret genealogy of European responsibility is also a *polemo-ontology*, as is apparent from the essay Patočka entitles "The Wars of the Twentieth Century and the Twentieth Century as War."[113] It is based, Derrida points out, on a "paradoxical phe-

110. Ibid., 69 /115.

111. Ibid.

112. Cf. Emmanuel Levinas, "Les Dommages causés par le feu," in *Du sacré au saint: Cinq Nouvelles Lectures talmudiques* (Paris: Minuit, 1977), 168 / "Damages Due to Fire," in *Nine Talmudic Readings*, trans. Annette Aronowicz (Bloomington: Indiana University Press, 1990), 189–91.

113. Paul Ricoeur, in his preface to the French translation of this work, terms it "strange

nomenology of darkness" and implies a "secret alliance between night and day" (*GD* 17 / 24).

In sum, Abraham's decision, like any other genuine ethico-political act, gives *testimony* where it passionately resists the concepts of the ethical, the political, and the common notion of "act." Abraham's decision does not testify in the sense of giving a demonstration, a lesson, or an illustration for all to see. Not unlike *Bezeugung*, which, according to *Being and Time*, reveals death to be "*Dasein's* most proper possibility," his *attestation* is "not a simple characteristic to be noted or described." [114] In the final analysis, a certain paradoxical attestation comes to determine any reading that — rightly or wrongly — claims to describe the conditions of possibility, the co-originary structures, of all modes of existence, of decisions, of giving (oneself) death, and so on. The same holds for any philosophical or literary interpretation of concrete — historical and contemporary — examples of this attestation.

In *Aporias*, Derrida evokes the inherent performativity of this attestation, insisting that the "constant imminence" of which — and from which — it speaks "must be *assumed*." [115] This is not to say that it is taken for granted, intuitively grasped, or posited in some thetic or hypothetical mode of reasoning. On the contrary, here, as in *Of Spirit*, Derrida stresses the fact — yet another fact of reason, one that precedes the Kantian *Faktum der Vernunft* — that this absolute performativity must be affirmed.

Thus, Derrida writes, if there is a "moral" to be found in the biblical text of Genesis 22 as read by Kierkegaard and Levinas, we should not too easily conclude that the narration (*récit*) is simply a *fable* of responsibility. To take it as a fable would already (or still) mean that it loses the "quality of a historic event [*événementialité*]" (*GD* 66 / 66–67). By the same token, the very act of interpreting the sacrifice of Isaac belongs, Derrida notes, to the same bloody scene that it seeks to depict, to translate, or to transcribe, if only by emphasizing some singular threads in its fabulous texture, while leaving out — that is, *sacrificing* — others (*GD* 70 / 70). The history of the bloody conflicts between the "religions of the Book" — Judaism, Christianity, and Islam — can be interpreted as the history of as many attempts to appropriate the secret font of this narration of the *à dieu* /

---

and in many respects frightening" (cited in *GD* 16–17 / 24). This particular analysis, with its reference to Ernst Jünger's *Der Kampf als inneres Erlebnis*, determines the contours of Patočka's rethinking of the historical and the political as a whole.

114. Derrida, *Aporias*, 64 / 115.

115. Ibid.

adieu, of the *unto-death,* of the *zum Tode* read as *à dieu / adieu,* and vice versa.

Yet this history of sacrifice forbids reading "death"—or "God"—in terms of some ontological constancy, as a perennial figure or disfiguration operating from within a self-same identity. *Aporias* analyzes the "indeterminacy" of "death," reminding us of a fact that is "overwhelming, well known, and immensely documented," namely, that "there are cultures of death," or that "in crossing a border, one changes death . . . ; one no longer speaks the same death where one no longer speaks the same language,"[116] an insight that Heidegger's fundamental ontology, perhaps, too easily disregards as being of merely derivative historical, anthropological, or cultural—that is, ontic—interest.[117] Toward the end of *Aporias,* Derrida also

116. Ibid., 24 / 51.

117. Yet, Heidegger observes that death is always inscribed in some ritual of mourning: "The 'deceased' [*Der "Verstorbene"*], as distinct from the dead person [*dem Gestorbenen*] has been torn away from those who have 'remained behind' [*den "Hinterbliebenen"*], and is an object of 'concern' in the ways of funeral rites, interment, and the cult of graves. And that is so because the deceased, in his kind of Being, is 'still more' than just an item of equipment, environmentally ready-to-hand, about which one can be concerned. In tarrying alongside him in their mourning and commemoration, those who have remained behind *are with him,* in a mode of respectful solicitude. Thus the relationship-of-Being which one has towards the dead is not to be taken as a *concernful* Being-alongside something ready-to-hand. // In such Being-with the dead [*dem Toten*] the deceased *himself* is no longer factically 'there.' However, when we speak of 'Being-with,' we always have in view Being with one another in the same world. The deceased has abandoned our *'world'* and left it behind. But *in terms of that world* [Aus ihr her] those who remain can still *be with him.* // The greater the phenomenal appropriateness with which we take the no-longer-Dasein of the deceased, the more plainly is it shown that in such Being-with the dead, the authentic Being-come-to-an-end [*Zuendegekommensein*] of the deceased is precisely the sort of thing which we do *not* experience. Death does indeed reveal itself as a loss, but a loss such as is experienced by those who remain. In suffering this loss, however, we have no way of access to the loss-of-Being as such which the dying man 'suffers.' The dying of Others is not something which we experience in a genuine sense; at most we are always just 'there alongside.' // . . . We are asking about the ontological meaning of the dying of the person who dies, as a possibility-of-Being which belong to *his* Being. We are not asking about the way in which the deceased has Dasein-with or is still-a-Dasein [*Nochdaseins*] with those who are left behind" (*Being and Time,* 282–83 / 238–39).

Moreover, he leaves no doubt that the very difficulty, indeed paradox, is that the fundamental ontological analysis has to move beyond its own methodological formality while affirming the latter as the key to articulating the understanding it unfolds: "Within the framework of this investigation, our ontological characterization of the end and totality can be only provisional. To perform this task adequately, we must not only set forth the *formal* structure of end in general and of totality in general; we must likewise disentangle the structural variations which are possible for them in different realms—that is to say, deformalized variations which have been put into relationship respectively with definite kinds of entities as 'subject-matter,' and which have had their character Determined in terms of the Being of these entities. This task, in turn,

describes the proliferation of this singular structure in terms that delimit a *politics of death,* that is to say, a politics that — for once, from here on, or as a rule? — holds its breath at *the death of the other,* a politics that is prepared to stand face to face with *death as the other,* with *the other as death as well as dead, as not yet dead, that is, mortal, and, as no longer dead, as specter.* Derrida concludes, foreshadowing the central thematics of *Specters of Marx* and *Politics of Friendship:* "There is no politics without an organization of the time and space of mourning, without a topolitology of the sepulcher, without an amnesic and thematic relation to the spirit as ghost [*revenant*], without an open hospitality to the guest as *ghost . . . ,* whom one holds, just as he holds us, hostage."[118] Such a hospitality would welcome "the absolute *arrivant*" — what or who is, strictly speaking, "not even a guest."[119] It extends into cosmopolitan dimensions with pragmatic proportions that are equally messianic and universal. While reinscribing and rearticulating the most salient figures from the tradition called the religious, this politics of death — welcomed or, rather, demanded by a genuinely hospitable thought and welcoming, of necessity (*Anankē,* once more), the real possibility of both the best and the worst — requires the most rigorous and down-to-earth elaboration of institutional and juridical minutiae.

Doubling "God" and God's Double

There were countless generations who knew the story of Abraham by heart, word for word, but how many did it render sleepless?

(*FT* 28)

The intricate logic of responsibility and irresponsibility described as "the gift of death" (as the giving of death, of *donner la mort*) could be regarded, Derrida suggests, as the common ground on which such different discourses as those of Kierkegaard, Heidegger, Patočka, Levinas, Marion, and "perhaps" Ricoeur stand (*GD* 49 / 53). The list could easily be ex-

---

presupposes that a sufficiently unequivocal and positive interpretation shall have been given for the kinds of Being which require that the aggregate of entities be divided into such realms. But if we are to understand these ways of Being, we need a clarified idea of Being in general. The task of carrying out in an appropriate way the ontological analysis of end and totality breaks down not only because the theme is so far-reaching, but because there is a difficulty in principle: to master this task successfully, we must presuppose that precisely what we are seeking in this investigation — the meaning of Being in general — is something which we have found already and with which we are quite familiar" (*Being and Time,* 285 / 241).

118. Derrida, *Aporias,* 61–62 / 112.
119. Ibid., 34 / 67.

panded. In different ways, these authors all convey the insight that "the sense of responsibility is in all cases defined as a mode of a 'giving one-self death'" (GD 43 / 47). Their common feature is that this logic does not begin by invoking "*the event of a revelation or the revelation of an event*" (GD 49 / 52) to explain the paradox or, rather, the aporia of the ethical re-lation, its secret and its *mysterium tremendum,* its relation to the ab-solute other as well as the other of this other. The logic in question first proposes theorizing "the possibility of such an event" (GD 49 / 52). While unable to immunize itself against its *re*inscription into the religious idiom or into theology, it offers first of all a "nondogmatic doublet of dogma, a philo-sophical and metaphysical doublet, in any case a *thinking* that "repeats" the possibility of religion without religion" (GD 49 / 53).

Along these lines, it could be argued that Levinas's *à dieu* — the to-God no less than the leave-taking, the *adieu,* of every *à dieu,* inevitably haunted by the specter of no-god or no-one's-god, *a-dieu* or *pas de dieu* — inter-sects with the ongoing project of a *neither theistic nor atheistic "doubling" of God* that lies at the source of all (responsible discourse on) responsibility and that does not allow itself to be reduced to the source or the resources of any one positive religion or worldview.

Saying or writing *mon Dieu,* "my God," addressing oneself to the other, time and again, would come down to saying or writing the very same thing, yet differently. The logic of the *a* of adieu / à dieu, whether taken as a nondialectical negation or privation, or as address, as a pure *pro Deo,* would thus help us begin to spell out the alphabet and the grammar of religion, of positive religion and all its functional equivalents, as well as what they may have made possible or revealed, if not of religion *as such.* There is no reason why, in thus retracing the steps of this discourse — trac-ing it again and tracing it *otherwise* — we should stop here, at an incidental reading of the *a* of the *à dieu,* the *adieu,* or the *a-dieu,* and not link onto it an endless seriature, moving on to analyze its *b* and *c,* inventing, if need be, yet another alphabet. Indeed, as Levinas writes in "Dieu et la philoso-phie" ("God and Philosophy"), "God," in all the ambiguity of the *à dieu /* *adieu* (and, perhaps, *a-dieu*) signifies, not "as the theme of the religious discourse which names God," but, rather, "as the discourse which, at least to begin with, does not name him, but says him with another form of address than denomination or evocation."[120]

What, then, is the neither theistic nor atheistic doubling of the secret

120. Levinas, *Of God Who Comes to Mind,* 62 / 104.

source or resource of which Derrida speaks in *The Gift of Death*? The very aporia of all decision can be read, Derrida argues, as the mutual exclusion and implication of theoretical and practical consciousness, of the universal and the singular, as an irresolvable tension between Platonic and Christian paradigms that unfolds throughout the history of Western moral and political thought. This doubling not only mimics the doubling that already constitutes onto-theology, continues to unsettle it from within, and thus affects—indeed, divides—the borderline between Platonism and Jewish philosophy, Platonism and Christianity, Platonism and Islamic thought; it also characterizes the oppositional, heretical, and antinomian movements that have and will come to haunt those paradigms again and again.

Seeking to uphold the distinction between phenomenology and theology, between "revelation as possibility" and "revelation as historicity," Jean-Luc Marion, in response, writes that his "only disagreement has to do with the identification of this 'doublet' [i.e., of the "nondogmatic doublet of dogma"] indifferently as 'philosophical, metaphysical'; when it is a matter of thinking the possibility, and especially the radical possibility, of the impossible itself, phenomenology alone is suitable—and not at all metaphysics, which is a thought of actuality par excellence." [121]

Derrida, however, suggests something somewhat different. When he introduces the "nondogmatic double [*doublet*] of dogma, a philosophical and metaphysical double, in any case a *thinking* that 'repeats' the possibility of religion without religion," he recalls a decidedly nonphenomenological mode of thinking that might be more adequate—or, in any case, more responsive—to the attempt to address the "concept of responsibility" and the series of notions that come with it (justice, decision, testimony, etc.):

> The concept of responsibility is one of those strange concepts that give food for thought without giving themselves over to thematization. It presents itself neither as a theme nor as a thesis, it gives itself without giving itself to be seen, without presenting itself in some "giving itself to be seen" of phenomenological intuition. This paradoxical concept also has the structure of a certain secret—of what one calls, in the code of certain religious cultures, mystery. The practice [*exercise*] of responsibility does not seem to leave any other choice but this one . . . , that of paradox, heresy, and secrecy. More serious still,

121. Jean-Luc Marion, "Metaphysics and Phenomenology: A Relief for Theology," *Critical Inquiry* 20 (1994): 572–91, 590 n. 35.

it must always run the risk of conversion and apostasy: there is no responsibility without a dissident and inventive rupture with tradition, authority,
orthodoxy, rule, or doctrine. (*GD* 27 / 33–34, trans. modified)

Nor could it be thought or lived as a radical, abstract break with tradition.
Here the relation between discontinuity and continuity should be thought
completely otherwise. And here the logic of the specter and of spectrality
reveals its pertinence.

No phenomenology, to say nothing of metaphysics or philosophy,
could ever hope to intuit, construe, or reconstruct analytically the givenness or the gift of this concept without concept. No thought — not even
the thought proposed here — could ever undo this indeterminacy and the
praxis for which it stands or that it calls into being and inspires.[122] Only its
modality can be circumscribed, with the help of the figure of the secret or
mystery as it pervades the religions of the Book, and not them alone. Precisely the question of attribution, of construing genealogies, of assigning
a place of origination for responsibility, is at issue here. It would therefore be difficult, perhaps even impossible, to decide whether the "knight
of faith" — the figure of Abraham as he has been presented since the Genesis story was written down, including how he has been read by Kierkegaard and others — is, properly speaking, "Jewish, Christian, or Judeo-
Christian-Islamic" (*GD* 64 / 65). The sacrifice that he was prepared to risk
should, rather, be seen as belonging to what might be called "the common
treasure, the terrifying secret of the *mysterium tremendum* that is a property of all the three so-called religions of the Book as the religions of the
races of Abraham"(*GD* 64 / 65) and, one might add, that haunts others
whether they know it or not. In Kierkegaard's decidedly Christian reading, the sacrifice of Isaac — of a son sacrificed by his father and ultimately
saved by God — is seen as the foreshadowing and "analogy" (*GD* 80 / 78)
of the Passion of the Son of Man.

There is structural resemblance, then, between the history of conversion and heresy, of interiorization and repression, which continues somehow to affirm what it denies, and the sacrifice of love that is the essence

122. Cf. "We must continually remind ourselves that some part of irresponsibility insinu-
ates itself wherever one demands responsibility without sufficiently conceptualizing and the-
matizing what 'responsibility' means; *that is to say everywhere*. One can say *everywhere* a priori
and nonempirically, for if the complex linkage between the theoretical and practical . . . is, quite
clearly, irreducible, then the heterogeneity between the two linked orders is just as irreducible"
(*GD* 25–26 / 32).

or, rather, the secret of absolute responsibility, of responsibility beyond the very distinction between "in accordance with duty" and "out of pure duty" that informs the Kantian and, perhaps, every philosophical project:

> The absoluteness of duty, of responsibility, and of obligation certainly demands that one transgress ethical duty, although in betraying it one belongs to it and at the same time recognizes it. The contradiction and the paradox must be endured *in the instant itself.* The two duties must contradict one another, one must subordinate (incorporate, repress) the other. Abraham must assume absolute responsibility for sacrificing his son by sacrificing ethics, but in order for there to be a sacrifice, the ethical must retain all its value; the love for his son must remain intact, and the order of human duty must continue to insist on its rights. (*GD* 66 / 66)

But the history and genealogy of European responsibility of which Patočka speaks is also a history of sacrifice. And only the reiterated instantiation of this sacrificial structure (rather than, say, its ritual or actual practice) explains why, as the epilogue to *Fear and Trembling* puts it: "Each generation begins all over again" (*FT* 122).[123] This citation returns us to the consideration from which we set out: the paradoxical fact that the very concept and instant of responsibility at once resists — or should we say sacrifices? — and calls for a history, a genealogy, or a story. On the one hand, the "passion" of Abraham's faith is untransmittable and without history, without story, precedent, and effect. As Kierkegaard writes, no "worldly wisdom" (*FT* 37) can result from the paradox. On the other hand, its very structure turns out to be a secret, which is transmitted from one instant to the next. Kierkegaard is perhaps not alone in acknowledging that in the end Abraham's conduct remains as inscrutable as the moral law against whose majesty it rebels. Not even the structure of the secret, then, is ever comprehended or transmitted *as such.* Much more or much less than a logical or existential paradox of faith is risked here. *The Gift of Death* demonstrates that the religious figure of sacrifice and the violence it entails is the key to understanding what is at stake in responsibility, in situations both extreme and quotidian. The same could be said of the thought of "incineration," of the "holocaust," of "cinders" that runs through almost all

---

123. This emphasis on the now or, rather, on the instant or *Augenblick* is mirrored in the fact that faith does not allow any anticipation, whether of the best or of the worst: "He who always prepares for the best grows old and is deceived by life, and he who is always prepared for the worst grows old prematurely, but he who has faith — he preserves an eternal youth" (*FT* 18).

of Derrida's texts, "well before *Of Spirit* which speaks exclusively of this, and . . . well before *Shibboleth* . . . whose sole theme it is."[124] One should not think here only of *Glas* and *Feu la cendre* (*Cinders*), which address explicitly the "all-burning" — the *brûle-tout*, the holocaust, the sacrifice in which all (*holos*) is burned (*caustos*) — for the quasi-psychoanalytic figuration of *dissemination* in terms of "that which does not return to the father" is also circumscribed in *Positions*, only in order to be rearticulated, in *The Gift of Death*, as "the instant of Abrahamic renunciation."[125]

More than any other work, *Glas* remains the *locus classicus* that initiates this analysis of the figureless figure of the *brûle-tout* in a patient reading of Hegel's philosophy of religion, notably, the no longer simply dialectical transition between natural religion, aesthetic religion, and absolute religion. *Glas* situates this analysis in the larger context of Hegel's portrayal of Abraham, the sacrifice of Isaac, the essence of Judaism, and the spirit of Christianity in his early theological writings.[126] The genealogy and idealistic teleology of religion is shown for what it is: a remarkable reconstruction of religion as a limited, figural representation of God that in its very trajectory is held out between the abysses of two extremes, both of which evoke a destruction of figural presence — of the presence, that is, of all figure — at the very beginning as well as the very end of religion. Between these poles, then, religion constitutes itself as a *pas de dieu*, as a step on the way to the absolute that, however, never attains the absoluteness of divine knowledge. The latter is reserved for philosophy alone:

> Natural religion, the first moment of religion (immediate consciousness and sense-certainty) counts three moments whose first (the first moment of the first moment) is also, like *Sa* [*Savoir absolu*, Absolute Knowledge], at the other end, absence of figure, irrepresentable moment. The figure withdraws at the origin and the end of religion, before and after religion: whose becoming literally describes a consuming destruction of the figure, between two suns. Another jealousy of the Hegelian god who begins and ends by making disappear — in fire — its own proper figural representation. The jealousy, this *zelos* does not boil down to the passion of the Jewish God that never shows himself.

124. Derrida, "Canons and Metonymies," 211.

125. *GD* 96 / 91. Cf. "Lapidarily: dissemination figures that which *cannot be* the father's [*la dissémination figure ce qui ne revient pas au père*]" (*Positions*, 86 / 120).

126. Derrida lists the references: *Glas* (Paris: Galilée, 1974), 40, 51 ff., 80 ff., 111, 124, 136, 141, 158, 160, 175 ff., 233, 262, 268 ff., 271, 281 ff., 288 ff.; *Glas*, trans. John P. Leavey Jr. and Richard Rand (Lincoln: University of Nebraska Press, 1986), 32–33, 41 ff., 68 ff., 96, 108, 119, 123, 139–41, 155 ff., 207–8, 235, 240–43, 253 ff., 259 ff.

Here God shows himself neither at the beginning nor at the end of times, but that is in order to show himself the whole time through his figures and in an absolute light.[127]

Yet the absolute light, the blaze of the all-burning, must also call for its own cessation. It cannot *not* give rise to the system, its determinations, its concept, for which it is nonetheless the essential preparation.[128] Against this background, Derrida writes that the all-burning, of which sacrifice is the most striking figure, annuls or sacrifices itself. On this performative contradiction, this aporia, rests the system of absolute idealism and the totality of its historical and conceptual articulations. What opens its circular, spiraling movement lies forever behind it: "an offer by which the all-burning annuls itself, opens the annulus. . . . This sacrifice belongs, as its negative, to the *logic* of the all-burning. . . . If you want to burn all, you must also consume the blaze, avoid keeping it alive as a precious presence. You must therefore extinguish it." [129]

This aporetic figure of disfigurement, a topos of devastation, also haunts Derrida's more recent writings. Let me cite another example, again dealing with death: here, the death of a friend. As *Politics of Friendship* reminds us, in the very concept of friendship a host of questions announces itself, not the least of which is the aporia, the possible impossibility, of mourning. In *Memoires for Paul de Man*, Derrida writes:

What do we mean by "in memory of" or, as we also say, "to the memory of"? For example, we reaffirm our fidelity to the departed friend by acting in a certain manner *in memory of* him, or by dedicating a speech *to his memory*. Each time, we know our friend to be gone forever, irremediably absent, annulled to the point of knowing or receiving nothing himself of what takes place in his memory. In this terrifying lucidity, in the light of this incinerating blaze where nothingness appears, we remain in *disbelief* itself. For never will we believe either in death or immortality; and we sustain the blaze of this terrible light through devotion, for it would be unfaithful to delude oneself into believing that the other living *in us* is living *in himself*: because he lives *in us* and because we live this or that in his memory, in memory of him.

This being "in us," the being "in us" of the other, in bereaved memory, can be neither the so-called resurrection of the other *himself* (the other is dead

127. Ibid., 237 / 264.
128. Cf. Rodolphe Gasché, *Inventions of Difference: On Jacques Derrida* (Cambridge: Harvard University Press, 1994), 192 ff.
129. Derrida, *Glas*, 240–41 / 268–69.

and nothing can save him from this death, nor can anyone save us from it), nor the simple inclusion of a narcissistic fantasy in a subjectivity that is closed upon itself or even identical to itself. If it were indeed a question of narcissism, its structure would remain too complex to allow the other, dead or living, to be reduced to this same structure. Already installed in the narcissistic structure, the other so marks the self of the relationship to self, so conditions it that the being "in us" of bereaved memory becomes the *coming* of the other. . . . And even, however terrifying this thought may be, the first coming of the other.[130]

Finally, it is no accident that *The Gift of Death* addresses this motif in topological terms, as being raised by a certain place, Mount Moriah, which comes to stand for the site that situates and stages the real and symbolical sacrifices that mark history. Moriah is seen as another, as the nether side of Jerusalem, the place to which one does *not* turn one's face when one prays or otherwise contemplates one's next step. This place recalls the bloody primal scene—the *Urszene*—which founds, grounds, and (if remembered) uproots not only societies and religions, but also the most trivial decisions of our daily existence: Moriah, Derrida writes, is "our habitat every second of every day" (*GD* 69 / 69), in a nonfigural and nonrhetorical sense. It is not only the situation of everydayness but also a name for and the theater of an undeniable historico-political specificity.

According to the second book of Chronicles (chapters 3 and 8), Derrida recalls, this "so-called place of sacrifice [*le lieu-dit du sacrifice*]" is the site where God appeared to David and where Solomon decided to build the temple. It is also the place where the Islamic holy places of the Dome of the Rock and El Aksa are located, where we find, close by the wall of lamentation, the road Christ is said to have followed carrying the cross. Indeed, Derrida concludes, all the monotheisms, that is to say, all the religions of the Book, "make war with fire and blood, have always done so and all the more fiercely today, each claiming its particular perspective on this place and claiming an original historical and political interpretation of Messianism and of the sacrifice of Isaac. The reading, the interpretation, and the tradition of the sacrifice of Isaac are themselves sites of bloody, holocaustic sacrifice. Isaac's sacrifice continues every day" (*GD* 70 / 70).

The same should be said, mutatis mutandis, of all other messianisms, humanisms, atheisms, agnosticisms, and so on. The structure of *giving*

130. Jacques Derrida, *Memoires for Paul de Man*, 21–22 / 43–44.

death, and thus of sacrifice, literally or figuratively, would pertain to the essence and aporia of existence. Here, again, one would have to return to the analyses of death by Heidegger, Levinas, Freud, and Marx, to discourses that are at once unsurpassable and ultimately inadequate. Derrida says as much in *Specters of Marx:* "The war for the 'appropriation of Jerusalem' is today the world war. It is happening everywhere, it is the world, it is today the singular figure of its being 'out of joint.' . . . [L]et us say that in order to determine in its radical premises Middle-Eastern violence as an unleashing of messianic eschatologies and as an infinite combinatory of possibilities of holy alliances . . . , Marxism remains at once indispensable and structurally insufficient."[131]

To retrace the figure of *à dieu* as the silent echo of the holocaust of Genesis 22, as well as of all utter burnings, all sacrifices in which all (*holos*) is burned (*caustos*), is not an attempt to revive the Stoic doctrine of the *ekpurosis,* a universal conflagration in which the whole world returns to the primeval fire. Nor is it a tasteless theodicy of whatever divine or metaphysical agency allowed "Auschwitz" to happen: the murder in the camps cannot and ought not be thought in terms of a logic of sacrifice pure and simple — and who could even imagine it in terms of self-sacrifice?[132]

Rather, the *à dieu / adieu* names a "given death" — *la mort donnée* — given wherever and whenever responsibility comes to pass. That is to say, *everywhere* and *always.*[133] It comes as no surprise, therefore, that Derrida admits a certain resemblance or, rather, co-implication of this abyss (chaos, aporia, and antinomy) that opens up (in) every genuine decision and the "open mouth [*bouche ouverte*]" signaling speech (or the lack thereof) and hunger (*GD* 84, 86 / 81, 82).

Needless to say, it is tempting to shy away from so many "lurid figures."[134] What are we to think of these uncanny expressions, especially that of sacrifice? Are they really necessary, inevitable, helpful, responsible, traces of mourning that cannot be removed without affirming the worst,

131. Derrida, *Specters of Marx,* 58 / 101.
132. Cf. Nancy, *Une pensée finie,* 94 ff.
133. *Being and Time* makes that very clear: "Dasein, as thrown Being-in-the-world, has in every case already been delivered over to its death. In being towards its death, Dasein is dying factically and indeed constantly, as long as it has not yet come to its demise. When we say that Dasein is factically dying, we are saying at the same time that in its Being-towards-death Dasein has always decided itself in one way or another" (303 / 259).
134. I cite the formulation Neil Hertz uses in his reading of the more disturbing turns of phrase in the writings of Paul de Man (Neil Hertz, "Lurid Figures," in *Reading De Man Reading,* ed. Lindsay Waters and Wlad Godzich [Minneapolis: University of Minnesota Press, 1989]).

the worst of the worst (*le pire du pire*), rather than its mere possibility? And in what sense, finally, could these motifs help us to come to terms with the question of the terminal, with what, in *Aporias,* is called a "politics of death"? Is it not more productive to de-transcendentalize and to de-figure the figure of death as and through sacrifice, whether symbolic or not, and to link it in a more concrete, but also less challenging, manner to the givens of the history of religion, anthropology, psychoanalysis, and the like?

Perhaps. But in so doing, one would lose sight—indeed, would sacrifice—what enables Derrida's reading to unsettle confident assessments of this as socio-historical material, as well as the premises and methodologies that guide its reconstruction as data. Speaking of responsibility and of testimony in the violent language of sacrifice adds something decisive to analyses of these phenomena that would not have been possible in another—supposedly less violent and seemingly more responsible—language. Speaking of sacrifice, of the giving of death as an *à dieu / adieu* to be assumed or affirmed, reminds us of the quasi-theological overdeterminations of every genuine ethico-political decision, which are its inevitable risk. *The possibility of the worst is the condition—the limit and the de-limitation—of the best. The possibility of the suspension of the ethical is what makes the ethical possible.* One does not have to speak, as Kierkegaard does in *Fear and Trembling,* of a teleological suspension of the ethical: it suffices to acknowledge that without the possibility or the risk of the worst, of derailment and perversion, no call to action and no call of conscience could ever claim to be unconditional. Instead of imposing itself categorically or, more precisely, forgoing all general form, with an absolute (and absolutely singular) urgency, its manifestation would, like that of the Austinian performative, be guaranteed or stabilized by past or present contexts of origination and by future horizons of expectation. Only the structural similarity between the diabolical and evil genius of the *il y a,* on the one hand, and ethical transcendence, on the other, between *horror* and the *sublime,* in Levinas's words, guarantees that the very moment and momentum of the ethical response is that of "a deficit, a wasting away and a foolishness in being,"[135] an entering of the "divine comedy" in which there is no place for tragic heroes, but only for the silent testimony of the saint, the wordless gesture of the knight of faith.

Against this backdrop, Derrida writes in *The Other Heading:* "Hope,

135. Levinas, *Of God Who Comes to Mind,* 69 / 114.

fear and trembling are commensurate with the signs that are coming to
us from everywhere in Europe, where, precisely, in the name of identity,
be it cultural or not, the worst violences, those that we recognize all too
well without yet having thought them through, the crimes of xenopho-
bia, racism, anti-Semitism, religious or national fanaticism, are being un-
leashed, mixed up, mixed up with each other, but also, and there is nothing fortuitous in this, mixed in with the breath, with the respiration, with
the very 'spirit' of the promise." [136] To take our lead from the figure of the
giving of death and the sacrifice it entails, to insist on its systematicity as
much as on its historical singularity, serves to remind us of the "necessary
passage through the transcendental" that problematizes any overly hasty
or confident ascriptions of (divine) violence or nonviolence to empirical
(psychological, sociological, historical, or, for that matter, linguistic and
symbolic) constellations.

Politics, being the struggle for a lesser evil, for a mitigation, reduction,
or even abolition of violence, the violence of the self as much as that of the
other, should be considered an obligation no less than a necessity. Yet its
pursuit of the better is always shadowed and haunted by what — in itself
or as politics' other — resembles or measures itself against the apparitions
and specters of the worst. In the final pages of *Specters of Marx,* Derrida
supplements this view:

> Present existence or essence has never been the condition, object, or the *thing*
> [chose] of justice. One must constantly remember that the impossible ("to let
> the dead bury their dead") is, alas, always possible. One must constantly re-
> member that this absolute evil (which is, is it not, absolute life, fully present
> life, the one that does not know death and does not want to hear about it) can
> take place. One must constantly remember that it is even on the basis of the
> terrible possibility of this impossible that justice is desirable: *through* but also
> *beyond* right and law.[137]

The "terrible possibility" invoked is not a possibility in the sense in which
Heidegger and the tradition speak of the possible. It is neither *dunamis,*
potentia, nor *Vermögen.* Worse, the "always possible" future amnesia con-
jured up — a self-sufficiency and indulgence in the fullness of life here and
now — might very well have to rely on *much less* or *much more* than a
potential or reservoir of evil. Radical evil consists in nothing that "we"

136. Derrida, *The Other Heading,* 6 / 12–13.
137. Derrida, *Specters of Marx,* 175 / 278.

might do, but rather in the unimaginable phantom of a full presence or total absence, neither of which can ever be faced directly or as such. Even though precisely this unimaginable phantom provokes, rather than inspires, ethics and responsibility—the fear of justice *"through* but also *beyond* law"—this call is dealt with in various mitigated ways, not least the "cultures of death" of which Derrida speaks in *Aporias*.

All this is not to invoke an awakening (*éveil*) that would be the "somber flip side [*revers*] of a logics of sacrifice. . . . This logic states: only extreme horror keeps reason in a state of wakefulness [*en éveil*]. The logic of sacrifice said: the only wakefulness is the wakefulness with respect to the horror."[138] Indeed, evil may no longer be thinkable as the absence of the good, as a mere *privatio boni*. If that is so, evil must be circumscribed, if not as a presence, then at least as a certain "positivity." The word is Jean-Luc Nancy's. In *L'Expérience de la liberté* (*The Experience of Freedom*), Nancy relates the "modern *fascination* with evil" to the experience that there is "a proper 'positivity' of evil, not in the sense that it would come to contribute in one way or another to some *conversio in bonum* (which always rests on its negativity and on the negation of this negativity), but in the sense that evil, in its very negativity, without dialectical sublation, forms a positive possibility of existence."[139] This given of evil—indeed, this giving of death—by no means justifies death or legitimates violence, let alone evil.

In a fascinating but troubling Talmudic reading, "Les Dommages causés par le feu" ("Damages Due to Fire"), Levinas writes that the exposition of my always already being exposed to sacrifice or to Evil (*le Mal*) does not necessarily lead to an unintended justification of the unjustifiable, of violence and ultimately war.[140] Even though sacrifice is everywhere, there remains a striking difference between risking the worst, suspending the ethical for the sake of an absolute obligation in which the *il y a* resonates as a "modality of transcendence," and committing a crime against humanity, deciding for the worst of the worst. In *Fear and Trembling*, Kierkegaard says as much: "It is only by faith that one achieves any resemblance to Abraham, not by murder" (*FT* 31). War is everywhere, even in the heart of peace, even in peace of the heart.[141] There is no way out,

138. Nancy, *Une pensée finie*, 93.

139. Nancy, *The Experience of Freedom*, 123 / 160; cf. "Evil [the fury of evil] does not exist as a dialectical moment; it is an absolute possibility of freedom" (155 / 199).

140. Cf. "The priority of the just would be due to its laying itself open to sacrifice" (Levinas, "Damages Due to Fire," 186 / 163, trans. modified).

141. Nancy recalls Pascal's words in the *Pensées:* "Circumcision of the heart, true fasting,

no interior refuge, no safe haven, here or elsewhere, which would be without terror or suffering. "Damages Due to Fire" pushes this analysis to an insupportable extreme. Commenting upon a Talmudic passage, Levinas writes:

> Here you have the ubiquity and the omnitemporality of the violence which exterminates: there is no radical difference between peace and war, between war and holocaust. The extermination has already begun during peace-time. . . . Everywhere war and murder lie concealed, assassination lurks in every corner. . . . There would be no radical difference between peace and Auschwitz. I do not think that pessimism can go much beyond this. Evil surpasses [dépasse] human responsibility and leaves not a corner intact where reason could collect itself [se recueillir].
>
> Unless, that is, this thesis is precisely a call to man's infinite responsibility, to an untiring wakefulness [éveil], to an absolute [absolue] insomnia.[142]

We live in an age and a world that has lost its very "worldliness" ("mondanité" même) and become a place where there is "no way out" (le sans-issue), no localizable exterior, and which, therefore, no longer allows any proper space or dwelling where one could be (or be there): a sans-lieu and non-lieu of which the exile and the diaspora of Israel would be the universal example. And yet there will always be (and there will always have been) a chance to invent or institute a limit to limitless violence. There will always be (and there will always have been) a chance for innumerable and limitless responsibilities that would attest to the limitation of unlimited, illegitimate, or illicit violence. The claim, then, that violence is everywhere can never legitimate the failure to act.

Levinas exemplifies this paradox as follows: "Yes, war criminals do exist!"[143] They can and should be held accountable for their deeds and be prevented from having free reign. For this justice to be possible or carried out, however, the fires of destruction, consummation, and revenge must be "transfigured" into a "protective" fire, into "a defensive barrier."[144] Here, the question of ethics in its necessary ex-position to the beyond-of-ethics — that is to say, to the infra-, super-, hyper-, and, in the precise sense, meta-ethical suspension of the sacrifice — transforms itself into a question

---

true sacrifice, true temple: the prophets showed that all this was necessarily spiritual. — Not the flesh that perishes, but the one that does not perish" (Une pensée finie, 77).

142. Levinas, "Damages Due to Fire," 192–93 / 174, trans. modified.

143. Ibid. 196 / 179.

144. Ibid., 196 / 180.

of politics. The theologico-political consideration gives way to what—in the quotidian and down-to-earth realm of practical life and politics, even at its most utopian and experimental moments—will, in the end, have the greatest urgency. That is the answer to the question "What to do?," and it is an always singular decision.

Beyond Sacrifice

At first glance, Derrida's discussions in *The Gift of Death* do not seem to allow for the possibility, even the moral necessity, of a "beyond of sacrifice." He makes no reference to the *unsacrificeable*, which Jean-Luc Nancy defines as the very finitude and eventhood (or *Ereignis*) of existence. Nancy takes Heidegger's formulation that, properly speaking, Being *is* not ("Zeit und Sein"), not in a privative sense—as if Being's relation to being were that of a dialectical negativity—but as an "ontological affirmation," a circumscription of what "freedom," the "experience of freedom," means. If the essence of *Dasein*, as *Being and Time* has it, can be found only in its very existence, its finitude, then this existence cannot be sacrificed because it has already been "offered to the world"—by no one, to no one.[145] It can only be destroyed, or shared.

What is undeconstructable, for Derrida, is not finitude, the ontological difference between beings and Being—even though this distinction has (had) its limited analytical and strategic use—but the fact that the historicity of finite existence remains tainted by a certain religiosity (theologemes and the rites of "positive" religion), of which "sacrifice" is a salient example. This "fact" is not merely empirical, but has a structural necessity.

145. Likewise Heidegger's formula *Sein zum Tode* should not be translated as *être pour la mort*, as if it obeyed the "finality" of some "sacrificial logic," but as *être à la mort* (Nancy, *Une pensée finie*, 21 and 21 n. 1). See Nancy, "L'Insacrifiable" (*Une pensée finie*, 101 / "The Unsacrificeable," trans. Richard Stamp, in *Finite Thinking*, ed. Simon Sparks [forthcoming from Stanford University Press]): "Finitude is not a 'moment' within a process or an economy. . . . [W]hen it is thought through rigorously and in accordance with its *Ereignis*, 'finitude' signifies that existence cannot be sacrificed. // It cannot be sacrificed because it is already, in itself, not sacrificed, but offered to the world. There is a resemblance here, and the difference is hard to tell. Yet nothing could be more dissimilar. . . . // To say that existence is offered is, certainly, to use a word from the vocabulary of sacrifice. . . . But this is in order to underscore that, if we must say that existence is sacrificed, it is sacrificed by no one, to nothing." See also ibid., 102: "*It is not even offered or sacrificed to a Nothingness, to a Nothing or an Other, in whose abyss it would still impossibly enjoy its own impossibility of being*. On this point Bataille and Heidegger must relentlessly be corrected. Corrected, which is to say: withdrawn still further from the slightest drive toward sacrifice." Lacan's invocation of *le Dieu obscur* (*Le Seminaire*, 11 [Paris: Seuil, 1973], 247; cited by Nancy, ibid., 100, cf. 103) should similarly be corrected. On the notion of "sacrifice," see also Nancy, *The Experience of Freedom*, 52 / 74.

As a "fact of reason," however, it may someday outlive itself and whither away, for reason is far from timeless, being constituted from within by a transcendental historicity whose central features, as we have seen, interested Derrida from early on.

For Nancy, the multifaceted Western appropriation of the sacrifice, from Socrates and St. Paul through St. Augustine and Pascal up to Nietzsche and Bataille, Heidegger and Jünger, has mimicked — metamorphosed, transfigured — the same hypothetical (postulated, or, rather fabricated) original structure. The foundation from which the West departs is merely hypothetical because there is no empirical or analytical means of establishing what ancient sacrifice once meant for its early spectators, participants, perpetrators, and victims. Apart from the traditional Christian interpretation that reduces sacrifice to self-sacrifice — in the final analysis, of God by God, as in the doctrine of *kenosis* that, retrospectively and proleptically, is the measure of all other acts of faith (including responsibility) [146] — the meaning of ancient sacrifice has been, in anthropological and ethnological writings, reduced to a diffuse "communion" or "participation" (Lévy-Bruehl); its logic is portrayed as that of a simple exchange, a primitive gift, a *do ut des*. Nancy writes: "In fact, economics [*l'économisme*] forms the general framework of representation in which the West takes over a priori all sacrifice, with the intention of proceeding to a general 'sublation' of this economics." [147]

This imagined concept of community qua communion and its practice was increasingly subjected to a movement of spiritual sublation and interiorization, in which the most sacrificial (cultic, ritual, and corporeal) moment of sacrifice was itself relentlessly "sacrificed." The procedure was no restricted economical exchange but an elevation of (and into) a different order, which received its distinctive profile by contrast with the bloody simulacrum. The history of Western onto-theology was thus read as the unfolding of a process of generalized transubstantiation of broken bodies and spilled blood.[148]

146. Jill Robbins's helpful overview of the biblical references to, as well as the anthropological and philosophical theories concerning sacrifice recalls the allegorical appropriations of the story of Genesis 22, studied, for example, in Erich Auerbach, *Mimesis:* "The sacrifice of Isaac prefigures the Golgotha event . . . in the symbolism of the three days, in Isaac's carrying the wood of his sacrifice (as Christ carried his own cross), and most prominently, in the free consent of the sacrificial victim" (Jill Robbins, "Sacrifice," in *Critical Terms for Religious Studies,* ed. Mark C. Taylor [Chicago: University of Chicago Press, 1998], 293).

147. Nancy, *Une pensée finie,* 82.

148. Nancy refers to Hegel's *Vorlesungen über die Philosophie der Religion* (in Georg Wil-

Yet the displacement of sacrifice through reconceptualization and figuration, precisely as a structure of repetition, retains elements of what it seeks to overcome: an ineradicable fascination with violence and cruelty.[149] While it operates through "mimetic rupture" and establishes a schema — a "formal indication," the early Heidegger would have said — in comparison with which all previous instantiations are (retrospectively) revealed as ontico-empirical or primitive and pagan variations (or deviations), a certain historical lineage and systematic congruity nonetheless prevails. No revolution or parricide could escape being implied in what it seeks to overcome, as if a gigantic tautology reigned over all attempts at a genuine heterological thought, as if one could not but devote oneself once more to sacrifice (and thus sacrifice oneself), even in the act of sacrificing the concept and practice of sacrifice once and for all (as Nancy writes: "Sacrifice to sacrifice by sacrificing sacrifice").[150]

helm Friedrich Hegel, *Vorlesungen: Ausgewählte Nachschriften und Manuskripte*, vols. 3–5, ed. Walter Jaeschke [Hamburg: Felix Meiner, 1983, 1984, 1985] / *Lectures on the Philosophy of Religion*, trans. R. F. Brown, P. C. Hodgson, and J. M. Stewart with the assistance of H. S. Harris [Berkeley: University of California Press, 1984, 1985, 1987]) as the most extended reflection on this spiritualization brought about by dialectical logic. Hegel claimed that in a truly spiritual religion there is no more sacrifice (or only sacrifice in a figural sense of the word).

149. Nancy, *Une pensée finie*, 79. Nancy points out that already in "La Pharmacie de Platon" (in *La Dissémination* [Paris: Seuil, 1972], 152–53 / "Plato's Pharmacy," in *Dissemination*, trans. Barbara Johnson [Chicago: University of Chicago Press, 1981], 132–34), Derrida establishes a relationship between mimesis and sacrifice. Yet another relationship could be established between sacrifice and confession. One example might suffice here. Nancy (*Une pensée finie*, 87) recalls the opening words of book 5 of Augustine's *Confessions*: "Accept the sacrifice of my confessions from the ministry of my tongue, which Thou hast formed and stirred up to confess unto Thy name."

150. *Une pensée finie*, 72. True, this would be a formulation in which "the value of the word displaces itself, dialectically, at each instant" (ibid.). Nothing but the word — *sauf le nom*, as Derrida puts it in a different context — would thus seem to remain in place in this at bottom nonsynonymous substitution of words (concepts and verbs). Yet it is also clear that this referral raises the stakes of the analysis. First, by invoking a certain complicity with a larger tradition, which takes a hyperbolic, superlative form: "Sacrifice is left behind *only for a higher, truer mode of sacrificial logic*" (ibid., 78). Second, by undoing its weight through a subtle but effective trivialization (*repetitio ad absurdum*). Supposedly, the (infinite and interiorized) truth of (finite and exterior) sacrifice is no longer sacrifice in any strict, that is to say, determinable sense: "In a sense, there is no more sacrifice" (ibid.). More precisely: "The finite functions and exteriority of sacrifice are sublated, but a fascinated gaze stays fixed upon the *cruel* moment of sacrifice as such . . . the same Hegel who abandons religious sacrifice reclaims the full value of warlike sacrifice for the State. (And what does Marx say of the proletariat — those who 'possess a character of universality because of the universality of their sufferings'? While sublating sacrifice, the West *sets up* a fascination with and for the cruel moment of its economy" (ibid., 79). Of course, one would still need to differentiate between the spiritualized and dialecticized figure of sacrifice at the intermediate level of representation (or *Vorstellung*) in Hegel's philosophy of

This is not to say that Nancy claims that sacrifice—its practice, concept, or figure—is philosophy's (or, at least, speculative dialectic's) final word on its relationship to whatever other or otherness. On the contrary, "The Unsacrificeable" revolves around the possible—and, indeed, necessary or imperative—horizon of a beyond of Western sacrifice, the end (*fin*) of its practice and the closure (*clôture*) of its phantasm.[151] This is evident from the way in which serious reflection on the worst—the camps—imposes a subtle but dramatic inversion in the logic of the sacrifice. Nancy describes it as follows:

> Extreme horror alone keeps reason awake. The logic of sacrifice said: the only awakening is an awakening to horror, in which the moment of truth shines through. The two statements are far from being confused. But the latter can always conceal the truth of the former. . . . [T]he horror of sacrifice here topples silently outside sacrificial *meaning*, outside all possibility of meaning. . . .
>
> Sacrifice would topple here, silently, into an opposite that is also its culmination: a revelation of horror with no means of access, no appropriation, save that of this infinite, or rather indefinite, revelation itself.
>
> A sacrificial interpretation of the camps is thus undoubtedly possible, even necessary, but only on the paradoxical condition of being overturned into its opposite (from Holocaust into Shoah): this sacrifice leads nowhere, it does not provide any means of access.[152]

There could be a revelation of the sacrifice, then, but one without positivity and without result.[153] What remains of sacrifice as a historical and theologico-political trope and, perhaps, philosopheme is, paradoxically, the "unsacrificeable": bare(ly) existence, that is to say, infinite—indeed, indefinite—finitude.[154]

---

religion and its even more consequent sublation—and hence, disappearance—at the highest level of the concept (or *Begriff*) of absolute knowledge. And here, too, the (invisible?) contours of sacrifice remain decipherable. In order to establish this translatability of the logic of the sacrifice into the logic of Hegelian *Logik*—and one reading solicits the other—we would need to retraverse the whole argument Derrida develops in *Glas*.

151. Nancy, *Une pensée finie*, 70–71.

152. Ibid., 93–94.

153. It is here that Nancy's analyses resonate with those of Agamben. See Giorgio Agamben's *Homo Sacer: Il potere sovrano e la nuda vita* (Turin: Einaudi, 1995) / *Homo Sacer: Sovereign Power and Bare Life*, trans. Daniel Heller-Roazen (Stanford: Stanford University Press, 1998), and *Quel che resta di Auschwitz* (Turin: Bollati Boringhieri, 1998) / *Remnants of Auschwitz: The Witness and the Archive*, trans. Daniel Heller-Roazen (New York: Zone Books, 1999).

154. See also the central chapter, entitled "The Result," of Jean-François Lyotard's *Le Diffé-*

The closure of the phantasm of sacrifice—the reversal (as we have seen, the "sacrifice") of sacrificial logic—might finally enable us to liberate known forms and concepts of "community" from their association with imagined fusion, communion, and all of its familiar (indeed, *familial*) equivalents. We touch here upon the problematics Derrida addresses in *Glas* as well as in *Politics of Friendship*, both of which interrogate and deconstruct the metaphysical and biological underpinnings of traditional and modern conceptions of belonging (the holy family, brotherhood, consanguinity, etc.). Such a perspective, Nancy claims, makes "community" independent of religion traditionally conceived, but also of the supposed "revelations" of "nonsacrificial religion" advocated by such radically opposed authors as Levinas and Girard.[155] Neither Levinas's "religion of adults" nor Girard's claim that the Christian tradition is an exception to the sacrificial logic determining the history of myth and rites is tenable.[156]

---

rend (Paris: Minuit, 1983) / *The Differend: Phrases in Dispute*, trans. Georges Van Den Abbeele (Minneapolis: University of Minnesota Press, 1988).

155. Other heterological thinkers who could be mentioned are: Jean-Luc Marion, whose work I discussed in the first two chapters of *Philosophy and the Turn to Religion*, and Michel de Certeau, whose writings will occupy us in the following chapter. See also Roberto Esposito, *Communitas: Origine et destin de la communauté*, trans. from the Italian by Nadine Le Lirzin, with a preface, "Conloquium," by Jean-Luc Nancy (Paris: PUF, 2000), 3–10.

156. Levinas's position is set out in *Difficult Freedom* and his "confessional" Talmudic writings. Girard's Christian alternative to sacrifice is developed in René Girard, *Des choses cachées depuis la fondation du monde: Recherches avec Jean-Michel Oughourlian et Guy Lefort* (Paris: Grasset & Fasquelle, 1978) / *Things Hidden since the Foundation of the World*, trans. Stephen Bann and Michael Metteer (Stanford: Stanford University Press, 1987). Nancy steers clear of either position and writes: "If *mimesis* is an appropriation of the other by alteration or suppression of the proper, does it not have a structure equivalent to that of sacrifice? . . . So, should one found sacrifice upon mimesis—for example, found it upon an anthropology of mimetic violence and rivalry (in the manner of Girard), which turns sacrifice into a symbolization after the fact, and which appeals to a 'revelation' to suspend its violence? (In that case I must admit that, however subtle the analyses, the 'positive' character of such an anthropological 'knowledge' is as alien to me as the other kind of 'positivity' associated with the motif of a 'revelation'" (*Une pensée finie*, 83 n. 1). Although Girard's theory of mimetic desire is first developed in the context of a reading of literary texts, in *Mensonge romantique et vérité romanesque* (Paris: Bernard Grasset, 1961) / *Deceit, Desire, and the Novel: Self and Other in Literary Structure*, trans. Yvonne Freccero (Baltimore: Johns Hopkins University Press, 1965), this model is expanded, with the help of ethnological material, in *La Violence et le sacré* (Paris: Bernard Grasset, 1972) / *Violence and the Sacred*, trans. Patrick Gregory (Baltimore: Johns Hopkins University Press, 1977), and *Things Hidden since the Foundation of the World*. The "fundamental ontology" that results aims to explain how religions—that is to say, processes of ritualization, sacralization, and scapegoating—enable society to deal with the originary violence that the rivalry of mimetic desire entails. In *Things Hidden*, especially, Girard presents a possible exception to—and way out of—mimetic rivalry, its violence, and the no less violent sacrificial logic it calls forth: Judeo-Christian revelation. Nancy and Derrida, respectively, question the anthropological given and its possible

Even more than Nancy, Derrida insists on the persistent and per-
nicious character of sacrifice, its legacy, and its logic. In his work, the
notion of sacrifice retains distinctive features, by contrast to episodic mentions of the term (*Opfer, Aufopferung*) in Kant's practical philosophy and
its more fundamentally ontological, anthropological, and psychoanalyti-
cal uses in the early and later Heidegger, in the *Homo Sacer* trilogy by
Giorgio Agamben, and in Girard's *La Violence et le* sacré (*Violence and
the Sacred*). He does not invoke any "unsacrificeable" meaning and function of "existence," its "decision," the "experience" of its "freedom" —
in its neither negative nor positive "revelation." This reflects a difference
in philosophical and theologico-political temperament between him and
Nancy. Derrida's *Le toucher, Jean-Luc Nancy* consists in a long meditation on these differences, which not only concern nuances in vocabulary,
tonality, and so on, but reveal a more substantial disagreement, first, about
the deconstructibility of concepts such as freedom and community or
being-with (terms on which Nancy—with and against Heidegger—continues to insist) and, second, about the possibility of "the deconstruction of Christianity"[157] (about which Derrida is downright skeptical:
"De-Christianization will be a Christian victory").[158] We are dealing,
therefore, with "two irreducibly different 'deconstructive' gestures," whose
"analogy" or "affinity" remains to be determined.[159] To speak of "the"
deconstruction of "Christianity" in general remains a gesture *still* too
Heideggerian—that is to say, too "epochal" and, perhaps, too "eschatological"—for Derrida's taste. There will be no simple beyond of "Christianity"—and hence no beyond of sacrifice—any time soon. This is not
because Christianity and the sacrifice are ontological categories or anthropological constants, but through a complex process of *reverse implication*
they continue to shed their light (and cast their shadow) on all attempts
to think and move beyond them.

Yet in *The Gift of Death* the antisacrificial stance is not completely
absent, either. Moreover, in conversation with Nancy, Derrida observes

---

cure, taken as fundamental (an anthropological constant, of sorts) and posited in historical
revelation. For a critical discussion of Girard, see also Philippe Lacoue-Labarthe, "Typographie," in Sylviane Agacinski et al., *Mimesis: Des articulations* (Paris: Aubier-Flammarion, 1975),
233 ff. / "Typography," in *Typography: Mimesis, Philosophy, Politics*, trans. Christopher Fynsk
(Cambridge: Harvard University Press, 1989), 43–138, 102 ff.

157. Jean-Luc Nancy, "La Déconstruction du christianisme," *Les Études philosophiques* 4
(1998): 503–19 / "The Deconstruction of Christianity," trans. S. Sparks, in de Vries and Weber,
eds., *Religion and Media*.

158. Jacques Derrida, *Le toucher, Jean-Luc Nancy* (Paris: Galilée, 2000), 68 and 68 n. 2.

159. Ibid., 323–24.

that Heidegger and Levinas "do not sacrifice sacrifice," [160] thereby suggesting indirectly that a certain "sacrificial structure" — in other words, certain
forms of "eating the other," whether symbolically or otherwise — needs to
be treated with the utmost reservation.[161] In *Glas*, Derrida earlier writes
that the sacrifice, both as "gift" and as an "all-burning," ultimately "sacrifices itself." [162] *Given Time* expands on this argument by commenting on
Marcel Mauss's *Essai sur le don* (*The Gift*): "Sacrifice will always be distinguished from the pure gift (if there is any [*s'il y en a*]). The sacrifice
proposes an offering but only in the form of a destruction against which
it exchanges, hopes for, or counts on a benefit, namely a surplus-value or
at least an amortization, a protection, and a security." [163] And "Faith and
Knowledge," finally, speaks of a "process of *sacrificial indemnification*" as
well as of the "ellipsis" of sacrifice, indicating that "sacrificing sacrifice," an
inevitably sacrificial sacrifice of the theme and practice of sacrifice, constitutes the "ellipsis or originary duplicity" of religion, the fact that its respect for the "sacrosanct" — paradoxically or aporetically — "*both requires
and excludes*" sacrifice. Hence the essential ambiguity of the expression
"sacrificing sacrifice": "The latter always represents the same movement,
the price to pay for not injuring or wronging the absolute other. **Violence**
of sacrifice in the name of non-violence" (FK 28, 52 / 41, 69).

While it remains an essential possibility (if we continue to use this
metaphysical language), the sacrifice is thus not everything, not even the
utmost or most essential possibility with which Heidegger identifies the
"being toward death" (*Sein zum Tode, être à la mort*), but merely the hypo-

---

160. Jacques Derrida, " 'Il faut bien manger': ou Le Calcul du sujet," in *Points de suspension*
(Paris: Galilée, 1992), 292–94 / " 'Eating Well,' or the Calculation of the Subject: An Interview
with Jacques Derrida," in *Who Comes after the Subject?* ed. Eduardo Cadava, Peter Connor, and
Jean-Luc Nancy (New York: Routledge, 1991), 112–13; reprinted in *Points . . .* , 278–80.

161. In the writings of these authors, Derrida suggests, we are confronted with "a place
left open, in the very structure of these discourses (which are also 'cultures') for a noncrimi-
nal putting to death [*une mise à mort*]. Such are the executions of ingestion, incorporation, or
introjection of the corpse. An operation as real as it is symbolic when the corpse is 'animal' . . . ,
a symbolic operation when the corpse is 'human.' But the 'symbolic' is very difficult, truly impossible to delimit in this case, hence the enormity of the task, its essential excessiveness, a
certain unclassifiability or the monstrosity of that *for which* we have to answer here, or *before*
which . . . we have to answer" (ibid., 112). One should carefully determine when and where
sacrifice fails to "sacrifice sacrifice" and thereby resembles a "justification of putting to death,
putting to death as denegation of murder" (ibid., 115).

162. Derrida, *Glas*, 244 / 271.

163. Derrida, *Given Time*, 137 / 174. On the expression "s'il y en a," which accompanies
all of Derrida's recent discussions of "the event, the invention, the gift, the pardon, testimony,
hospitality, etc.," see *Le toucher, Jean-Luc Nancy*, 323–24.

thetical—postulated or fabricated?—foil against which all decisions of human existence receive their distinctive profile.[164] What is more, language concerning the sacrifice is neither constative (a description of matters of fact) nor simply performative (a contextually guaranteed act that brings this peculiar referent into existence). Its mode is that of a "fable," as we shall see in the next chapter, a "mystical postulate," consisting in a variation upon the theme and mode of testimony, confession, and the apophatic that I have discussed earlier.[165]

DERRIDA'S REPEATED REFERENCE to Heidegger's essay "Die onto-theologische Grundverfassung der Metaphysik" ("The Onto-Theological Constitution of Metaphysics") in *Identität und Differenz* (*Identity and Difference*) is crucial to understanding the complex affinity and dual origin of history and structure that has interested us here. Heidegger concludes this exposition by insisting that one cannot pray or sacrifice to (or before) the god of metaphysics, the highest being or *causa sui*. Since he refuses to postulate a concept or idea of God before or independent of the constitution of metaphysics as onto-theology—since a God uncontaminated by beings and Being literally makes no sense—one must assume

164. This might explain why, referring to Heidegger's *The Origin of the Work of Art*, where truth is said to articulate itself as "an originary struggle" or *Urstreit*, Derrida stresses the relationship between two distinct modalities of being: the act that founds the state and what Heidegger calls the "essential sacrifice" (*das wesentliche Opfer*). (See the final section of Derrida's "L'Oreille de Heidegger: Philopolémologie (*Geschlecht* IV)," in *Politiques de l'amitié* [Paris: Galilée, 1994], 415 / "Heidegger's Ear: Philopolemology (*Geschlecht* V)," trans. John P. Leavey Jr., in *Reading Heidegger: Commemorations*, ed. John Sallis [Bloomington: Indiana University Press, 1993], 213). Heidegger writes: "One essential way in which truth establishes itself in the beings it has opened up is truth setting itself into work. Another way in which truth occurs is the act that founds a political state. Still another way in which truth comes to shine forth is the nearness of that which is not simply a being, but the being that is most of all. Still another way in which truth grounds itself is the essential sacrifice. Still another way in which truth becomes is the thinker's questioning, which as the thinking of Being, names Being in its question-worthiness. By contrast, science is not an original happening of truth, but always the cultivation of a domain of truth already opened" (Martin Heidegger, *Ursprung des Kunstwerks*, in *Holzwege* [Frankfurt a. M.: Vittorio Klostermann, 1972], 49- 50 / "The Origin of the Work of Art," in *Poetry, Language, Thought*, trans. Albert Hofstadter [New York: Harper & Row, 1971], 61–62; cited also in Derrida, *Points . . .* , 306 / 315-16). He implies that sacrifice—including, paradoxically, the essential sacrifice—is not all there is (or is not all there is to being). Not only is this sacrifice framed between other modes of being (or Being) and its history; the general structure of sacrifice, being based on one particular (Western, more precisely, Christian) concept, practice, or event of "sacrifice" reveals itself in singular instances of decision alone. The thinking of sacrifice as such gives way to—is, in a sense, sacrificed in favor of—a logic of the event and the instant.

165. See *Philosophy and the Turn to Religion*, chaps. 2 and 5.

that, for Heidegger, the God to whom one offers oneself (or another, or some thing) in truth, in sacrifice, and in prayer, can only announce Himself after the tradition of onto-theology has unfolded and exhausted itself completely.[166] What, then, is the relation between prayer and sacrifice? Are these words synonyms or comparable figures that evoke or provoke one and the same experience? Are they just names for the co-originary and thus inseparable or co-temporaneous modes or modifications of what — in its very essence — must be thought of as an atheological or areligious structure? Why are these particular names more prominent than others? What do they have to do with each other? What do they do to each other? Does prayer sacrifice? Is sacrifice the ritual practice that accompanies an ultimately silent prayer? Can one conceive of any religion without the concept and the ritual practice of prayer and sacrifice?

These questions could easily give rise to the concern Derrida raises toward the preliminary conclusion of his analysis of the figure of sacrifice in Heidegger. Referring to Heidegger's insistence that Germans have been deaf to the voice of Hölderlin, turning the poet's poet into an "exemplary sacrifice"[167] — who, as Heidegger implies in 1933-35, will be followed by the thinker who articulates his fate and who thus becomes yet another sacrificial victim — Derrida doubts whether Heidegger himself is sufficiently sensitive to the historical constellations and appropriations that condition any discourse on sacrifice.[168] The pertinent question is "the choice [la choix]" between different "qualities" and "events" of the sacrifice.[169] Although Heidegger distances himself from the ultranationalist and biologistic or racist appropriations of both Hölderlin and Nietzsche, he uses the logic of the sacrifice to place individual ethico-political acts in a more fundamental historical light, said to make them possible and to "invest every kind of accident with a destinal meaning."[170] This primacy of the Seinsgeschick is articulated most explicitly in the Hölderlin and Nietzsche lectures (as well as in the later essays devoted to the question of technology), but its foundations are already laid in the analyses of being toward death in Being and Time, where Heidegger's possibilism finds its most powerful formulation.[171]

166. Derrida, Points . . . , 306-7 / 316-17, and idem, "Heidegger's Ear," 215 / 417-18.
167. Derrida, "Heidegger's Ear," 215 / 418; cf. Points . . . , 306-7 / 316-17.
168. Derrida, "Heidegger's Ear," 211 / 413.
169. Ibid., 215 / 418.
170. Derrida, Points . . . , 308 / 318.
171. Yet another context would be the "Brief über den Humanismus" ("Letter on Humanism"), included in the discussion of "possibilism" in Philosophy and the Turn to Religion.

However, Heidegger's later work thematizes sacrifice in a more re-markable way, "the stakes of which have yet to be measured."[172] Hugo Ott cites a formulation from 1933: "We contemporaries stand in the struggle for the new reality. We are only a transition, only a sacrifice [*Wir Heutigen stehen in der Erkämpfung der neuen Wirklichkeit. Wir sind nur ein Übergang, nur ein Opfer*]."[173] Several other instances throughout Heidegger's more important writings justify the conclusion that sacrifice plays more than a merely marginal role. Thus *Being and Time* cites "sacrifice" in its analysis of the being toward death. The "Postface" to "What Is Metaphysics?" locates sacrifice at the very heart of "freedom." The Hölderlin lectures on *Germanien* and *Der Rhein*, as well as *Einführung in die Metaphysik* (*Introduction to Metaphysics*) emphasize especially the sacrifice of poets, thinkers, and founders of states (*Dichter, Denker, Staatsmann*) who, as Derrida notes, "hear what is unheard-of in the originary *polemos*"[174] and whose voice is therefore destined to be overheard by the people. Derrida notes that, in Heidegger's account, this *Überhören* is a sacrifice of "truth" through which truth both manifests and reveals itself. Following this *non-negative negation of truth through sacrifice* — a nondialectical logic of sacrificing truth that is also the truth of this sacrifice — the founders must be slain and forgotten or "overheard."[175] Derrida adds that Heidegger is scarcely the first or the only one to indicate the structural "necessity of a sacrificial exclusion" for any political or symbolical order. Sacrifice could well be another economical yet strategic figure, which at once formalizes and concretizes an insight imposed on all philosophy (from at least Rousseau, say, to transcendental pragmatics and beyond) by reinscribing it into the history of religions, their mythologies, and cultural practices. This insight, rephrased in a different idiom (and "in another

172. Derrida, *Points . . .* , 306 / 316.

173. Hugo Ott, *Martin Heidegger: Unterwegs zu seiner Biographie* (Frankfurt a. M.: Campus, 1988), 231.

174. Derrida, *Points . . .* , 306 / 316.

175. Cited in Derrida, "Heidegger's Ear," 213 / 415. In this context Derrida writes: "The brief remark of the *Einführung . . .* on intolerance is supported by a thought of *sacrifice*, a more radical, harder and more gripping [*saisissante*] thought that had been developed in the earlier seminar of the same year on *Germanien*, the first seminar on Hölderlin, in particular in section 10 that inscribes that poem and Hölderlin in the horizon of a thought of Heraclitus, even if Heidegger does not neglect the difference of times between the two. The fact of not hearing . . . the poet that announces the future being of a people is defined as a sacrifice. *Überhören* is in truth a sacrifice. It is even the sacrifice of truth. . . . In truth, this sacrifice of truth is the very movement of truth. The initiators or the first-born *must* be sacrificed (*müssen die Erstlinge geopfert werden*)" (ibid., 212–13 / 414–15, trans. modified).

tone," Derrida writes),[176] is that founders or founding acts necessarily retain an eccentric position with respect to the order that they have helped
to inaugurate: "The founder is excluded from the founded, by the founded
itself, which cannot tolerate the abyssal void and thus the violence on
which foundations stand or rather are suspended."[177] Derrida seeks to
clarify this paradoxical logic—of institution, of the theologico-political,
and of the (ultra-, quasi-, or simili-) transcendental—in his engagement
with Carl Schmitt, Walter Benjamin, and Michel de Certeau, whose writings will form the subject of Chapter 3.

Sacrifice, Derrida writes in "Force of Law," also belongs to the very
founding and structure of the intentional subject; it unfolds, *Adieu* will
add, as fundamental openness and hostility toward its intentional object,
that is to say, its other(s). This will form the theme of our chapter 4. Indeed, there seems to be an "affinity between carnivorous sacrifice, at the
basis of our culture and our law, and all the cannibalisms, symbolic or
not, that structure intersubjectivity in nursing, love, mourning and, in
truth, in all symbolic or linguistic appropriations."[178]As we will see in the
next chapters, not only the founding and the structures of subjectivity
and intersubjectivity are tainted by the practice or mimicry of sacrifice.
According to Benjamin's "Critique of Violence," one should also ascribe
the very foundation of all sociopolitical or juridical authority to a violently mythical, mystical, and, indeed, "sacrificial" moment.[179] This is not
to say that this moment stands on its own. In the generalized and restricted
economy of violence that we have analyzed, the sacrifice and the "beyond
sacrifice" must keep each other in balance. Only thus does "sacrifice" form
the element of responsibility.

176. Ibid., 213 / 415.

177. Derrida, *Points . . .* , 306 / 316. Cf. idem, "Heidegger's Ear," 213 / 415: "This necessity for
sacrificial exclusion can be interpreted in Heidegger's tone. . . . But the necessity of sacrificial
foreclosure can also be formalized abstractly and in another tone, like that of Rousseau, for example, when he explains that the founders or the legislators must not belong to the very thing
they found or institute; they must be strangers to it or taken for strangers, a priori excluded.
Ostracism and sacrifice, suppression, repression, foreclosure, the impossibility of tolerating the
founding instance and authority, are structurally part of what is founded. The institution or the
foundation cannot itself be founded; it inaugurates above an inaudible abyss, and this knowledge is intolerable. Which, by definition, moreover, is not knowledge. It is the experience of
the foundation as the experience of *Abgrund*. What founds or justifies cannot be founded or
justified."

178. FL 953.

179. Ibid., 1041.

Chapter 3
Anti-Babel

The Theologico-Political at Cross Purposes

IN THE PRECEDING CHAPTERS, I have discussed what relationship might exist between *positive* religion, based on historical revelations or testimonies thereto, and the discipline—the concepts and arguments—of philosophy. It has occurred to me (and I am certainly not the first to have noticed) that the opposition between the two is not as obvious or irrevocable as has often been assumed. On the contrary, there seems *reason* to *believe* that the philosophical discourse of modernity (and not of modernity alone), despite its self-declared enlightenment and autonomy, continues to respect the boundaries and limits once imposed by the tradition called the religious. "Philosophy within the Boundaries of Mere Religion" might well have been the title of an interesting book on this subject. Philosophy, its argument might go, never really emancipated itself from the systematic limits—semantic and figural, rhetorical and imaginative—imposed upon it by religion. In fact, these restraints were enabling conditions. Historical religion, including the natural religion or onto-theology implied within (or based upon) it was the transcendental condition of possibility for the philosophical, that is to say, for all the categories and conceptual structures that are supposed to inform (and form themselves in) the empirically or *positively* given.

True, a book with this particular title—"Philosophy within the Boundaries of Mere Religion," or "Within the Limits of Religion Alone," that is to say, "Religion Pure and Simple"—would run the risk of falling back into an age-old and even obsolete position. Turning to religion by simply returning to it, without turning against religion, without turning religion around and against itself, the book could well be merely traditionalist, presenting more of the same or the same all over again. Grounding philosophy in religion rather than the other way around, insisting, if not on their identity, then at least on the dependency of the one on the other rather than on a possibilization that would be reciprocal and therefore, strictly speaking, no transcendental conditioning at all—all this would hardly be interesting. It has been done before. Indeed, we haven't been able to do anything else.

But what would this position entail? What could it mean to turn to *positive* religion with a *philosophical* purpose, concept, or argument in mind? What exactly is being posited and presupposed here? Was philosophy not always intent on being free, on having no presuppositions (no prejudices or prejudgments) at all and hence, in a way, on being its own presupposition alone? Was the principal of all philosophical principles not the *Prinzip der Voraussetzungslosigkeit*?

Any plausible answer to such questions needs to come to terms with the concept of *Setzung, Voraussetzung,* and its analogues. In addition to drawing on a long rhetorical, aesthetic, and political tradition, might this notion continue an even older and more pervasive heritage? The concept of *Setzung,* it seems, receives at least part of its historical weight and intellectual force from a religious and theological archive whose semantic, analytical, and figural potential has not yet exhausted itself and whose persisting and renewed relevance we have not even begun to fathom.

At the opening of this chapter, the notion of *Setzung* will return us to the question of the religious, followed by the central preoccupation of "political theology." Turning to an example taken from Kant's writings concerning religion and the positivity of historical religion, I will then concentrate on the status of the miracle, a notion that, in Kant's paradigmatic yet extremely paradoxical — some would say aporetic — exposition of the autonomy of reason and morality in relation to the historical, remains conditioned by an indelible theological tradition. This example will prepare the ground for extensive discussion of two Kierkegaardian thinkers who increasingly have centered their writings on the concept of the theological as it pervades the problem of foundational, counterrevolutionary, and revolutionary violence. The views of Carl Schmitt and Walter Benjamin articulate two extreme theoretical and practical possibilities that the *horror religiosus* holds in store, wherever it touches upon the question of the theologico-political. Like Kant, Kierkegaard, Weil, Levinas, Girard, Lacoue-Labarthe, Derrida, and Nancy, their respective positions form a foil against which to present my argument — my hypothesis, rather — that: first, the turn to religion discernible in modern and contemporary philosophy goes hand in hand with a reassessment of the ethical and the political; and second, this reassessment of the good, the just, and the best, their conditions and their promise, ultimately takes place in light of a concern with the possibility, the reality, or the risk and threat of "the worst." Hence, the preoccupation with violence: empirical and transcendental, human or divine. In order to clarify these issues, I will draw on the insights of Jakob Taubes and Michel de Certeau, two interpreters whose work will help situate the positions of Schmitt and Benjamin, shifting the balance away from the Kantian-Kierkegaardian analysis whose limits we have been exploring.

Positive Theology

Setzung, Voraussetzung, and their analogues[1] — the "positive," the "positing," and the *positum* — all are philosophical compounds whose meaning has been influenced either by Greek *tithenai, tithesthai,* "to place," "to affirm," "to assume," or, in the translation "to posit," by the past participle *positus,* which comes from Latin *ponere,* meaning "to put" or "to put down." To posit would indicate to "suppose a proposition (*Satz*)" and the "postulation of the existence of an entity." Yet positing has a performative aspect as well: "What is posited is not simply affirmed to be real, but is thereby made real."[2]

Thus defined, the concept figures prominently in both the modern philosophy of law (in the formulation "positive law" as opposed to "natural law") and in eighteenth-century discussions concerning the status of "positive" historical or revealed religions as distinguished from natural or, as Kant puts it, rational and moral religion. Yet what is the exact relation between *Setzung* as a rhetorical, political, and aesthetic concept, on the one hand, and the positing or *positum* ascribed to law and religion in their concrete manifestations, that is to say, in their empiricity and phenomenality, on the other? What is the positive or the *positum* in these different domains, if that is what they are?[3]

---

1. In what follows I have made use of the lemma on "positing and presupposition" in Michael Inwood, *A Hegel Dictionary* (Oxford: Blackwell, 1992), 224–26. The suggested link between "positing," the "positive," and *positum* (as in positive law and positive theology) is mine. See also Werner Hamacher, "Der ausgesetzte Satz: Friedrich Schlegels poetologische Umsetzung von Fichtes absolutem Grundsatz," in *Entferntes Verstehen: Studien zu Philosophie und Literatur von Kant bis Celan* (Frankfurt a. M.: Suhrkamp, 1998) / "Position Exposed: Friedrich Schlegel's Poetological Transposition of Fichte's Absolute Proposition," in *Premises: Essays on Philosophy and Literature from Kant to Celan,* trans. Peter Fenves (Cambridge: Harvard University Press, 1996).

2. Inwood, *A Hegel Dictionary,* 224.

3. In his 1927 lecture "Phänomenologie und Theologie," Heidegger defines the *positum* in the following formal terms. A science, for example, theology, is "positive" when it is based upon — and strictly limits itself to — "the founding disclosure of a being that is given and in some way already disclosed." In Christian theology, this is not so much "Christianity as something

That any full discussion of the concept of *Setzung* as act and action should sooner or later turn to religion already seems clear from Fichte's dictum, formulated in the *Grundlage der gesamten Wissenschaftslehre* (*The Science of Knowledge*) of 1794–95, according to which the "I" *posits* itself: "Das Ich setzt sich selbst" or, more specifically, "Das Ich setzt ursprünglich schlechthin sein eigenes Sein [The I originally posits its own being as such]."[4] Fichte's phrase signals not only the unprecedented audacity of the autonomy and self-constitution of the subject—here according to a subjective idealism that borders upon solipsism, that is to say, a transcendental egotism of sorts—it also echoes the monotheistic biblical thesis of the "I am I," "I am that I am," "I am who I will be": namely, the self-proclamation of the God of Israel in Exodus 3:13–15.[5]

Positing itself as a self, giving itself the law—which is what *auto-nomy* means—the I, in its ownmost being (*sein eigenes Sein*), at the same time *subjects* itself to what is arguably the most heteronomous of all the hypotheses and all institutions that have punctuated the history of humankind, namely, the Law of the Other, of the Being called the highest, the absolute and sole autonomous I, the One who goes by the name of God, by the "I am that I am."

More than a biblical reference—"the echo of a name," as Hendrik Birus, following Jean Paul, Jorge Luis Borges, and others, calls it—is at stake here. Indeed, should we choose to remain deaf to this "echo"—or lack faith in its reference—a remarkable analogy still should give us pause. Fichte's dictum signals a trans*position* of the central metaphysical definition of God as *causa sui* onto the self-description of the thinking—in this

that has come about historically, witnessed by the history of religion and spirit and presently visible through its institutions, cults, communities, and groups" (Martin Heidegger, "Phänomenologie und Theologie," in *Wegmarken* [Frankfurt a. M.: Vittorio Klostermann, 1976], 51 / "Phenomenology and Theology," in *Pathmarks*, ed. William McNeill, trans. James G. Hart and John C. Maraldo [Cambridge: Cambridge University Press, 1998], 43). The *positum* makes this history possible: "Theology does not belong to Christianity merely because, as something historical, the latter has a place in the general manifestations of culture. Rather, theology is a knowledge of that which initially makes possible something like Christianity as an event in world history. Theology is a conceptual knowing of that which first of all allows Christianity to become an originarily historical event, a knowing of that which we call Christianness [*Christlichkeit*] pure and simple" (ibid., 43 / 52). For a discussion, see my *Philosophy and the Turn to Religion*, chap. 3.

4. Johann Gottlieb Fichte, *Grundlage der gesamten Wissenschaftslehre: als Handschrift für seine Zuhörer*, intro. Wilhelm G. Jacobs (Hamburg: Felix Meiner, 1997; orig. pub. 1794), 16, 18.

5. Hendrik Birus, "'Ich bin, der ich bin': Über die Echos eines Namens (Ex. 3, 13–15)," in *Juden in der deutschen Literatur: Ein deutsch-israelisches Symposium*, ed. Stéphane Mosès and Albrecht Schöne (Frankfurt a. M.: Suhrkamp, 1986).

case, acting and self-governing—subject. It is by now commonplace to re-call that the subjectivist and then Copernican turn, upon which Descartes, Kant, Fichte, Hegel, and, mutatis mutandis, Husserl and Heidegger built their ontologies and phenomenologies is an "onto-theo-anthropological" variation upon a much older metaphysical theme. Jean-Luc Marion, for example, has reinscribed the phenomenological project into the older tra-dition without denying any of its most radical aspirations and innovations.

The I that posits itself as its own cause and that thereby posits and assumes its freedom to choose itself as *causa sui* liberates itself by sub-jecting itself to that most rigid (and most unquestioned) of all meta-physical presuppositions. On closer scrutiny, its freedom is conditioned and its condition of possibility is metaphysical dogma. The religious and onto-theological reverberations of the Fichtean dictum—the nontempo-ral positing of the absolute and supra-individual "I"—expand into the realm of the political, as well. Derrida makes that very clear in his essay "Onto-Theology of National-Humanism (Prolegomena to a Hypothesis)," which presents a reading of Fichte's *Reden an die deutsche Nation (Dis-courses to the German Nation*, 1808), stressing that the "self-positing of self-identification of the nation always has the form of a *philosophy* which, although better represented by such and such a nation, is none the less a certain relation to the universality of the philosophical."[6] As a key to understanding the constitution of the "I" and the collectivity of selves, the concept of *Setzung* forms part of the theologico-political repertoire.

Political Theology Revisited

To discuss these matters in more precise terms, we should turn to the project of political theology, as outlined and critically assessed by thinkers as diverse as Carl Schmitt, Walter Benjamin, Jakob Taubes, Michel de Cer-teau, Claude Lefort, and Jean-François Courtine. Schmitt believes that the

6. Jacques Derrida, "Onto-Theology of National-Humanism (Prolegomena to a Hypothe-sis)," *Oxford Literary Review* 14, no. 1–2 (1992): 10. A little earlier Derrida states: "Even before any elaboration of the concept of nation and of philosophical nationality, of idiom as national philosophical idiom, we know at least this much—it's a minimal but indubitable predicate—namely, that the affirmation of a nationality or even the claim of nationalism does not happen to philosophy by chance or from the outside, it is essentially and thoroughly philosophical, *it is a philosopheme*. What does this mean? It means at least that a national identity is never posited as an empirical, natural character" (ibid.). In the context of this complex set of questions, see also Derrida's reading of Hermann Cohen (and Franz Rosenzweig) in "Interpretations at War: Kant, le juif, l'Allemand," in *Phénoménologie et politique: Mélanges offerts à Jacques Taminiaux* (Brussels: Ousia, 1990) / "Interpretations at War: Kant, the Jew, the German," *New Literary History* 22, no. 1 (1991): 39–95.

concept of the theologico-political enables a "sociology of legal concepts" to do its analytical and discriminatory work. For Benjamin and Taubes, the concept signals an almost apocalyptic sensibility to the timelessness and achronicity of the revolution, a sensibility whose mirror image they both discern in the counterrevolutionary pathos and impetus of Schmitt's early writings. Lefort and others provide a more ascetic exposition of the formal similarities between the theological and the political, whose value is, above all, heuristic.

Many thinkers, therefore, have noted that the political draws on the resources and the vicissitudes of the religious. Schmitt remains the most notorious and intriguing, especially in the opening lines of the third chapter of *Political Theology*, where he claims that all decisive concepts of the modern doctrine of the state are "secularized theological concepts." By this he not only suggests a *historical* teleology or developmental process, implying that the theological concepts were transposed onto political doctrine—for example, the concept of the almighty God onto that of the omnipotent lawgiver—but announces an interest in the *systematic* and *structural* resemblance between the two. The latter is essential, Schmitt believes, for a "sociological consideration" of these concepts:

> All significant concepts of the modern theory of the state are secularized theological concepts not only because of their historical development—in which they were transferred [*übertragen*] from theology to the theory of the state, whereby, for example, the omnipotent God became the omnipotent lawgiver—but also because of their systematic structure, the recognition of which is necessary for a sociological consideration of these concepts. The exception in jurisprudence is analogous to the miracle in theology. Only by being aware of this analogy can we appreciate the manner in which the philosophical ideas of the state developed in the last centuries.[7]

What, then, is the relevance of the miracle for the discipline of theology, for biblical and historical theology, or for natural and rational theology, for disciplines that Schmitt—with one exception—fails to distinguish? How does this significance shed light on the practice of jurisprudence, seen from what Schmitt calls a "sociological" point of view? And how, finally, does the turn to religion—to the theologico-political— allow a more powerful interpretation of the genealogy of modern states,

7. Carl Schmitt, *Politische Theologie: Vier Kapitel zur Lehre von der Souveränität* (Berlin: Duncker & Humblot, 1990; orig. pub. 1934), 49 / *Political Theology: Four Chapters on the Concept of Sovereignty,* trans. George Schwab (Cambridge: MIT Press, 1988), 36.

the legality of their institutions, and their rule of law? Before turning to Kant, we should answer these questions at least tentatively.

Schmitt leaves no doubt that the demise of a certain theism caused the theologico-political impetus to be forgotten and replaced with another, supposedly less dangerous, assumption. Drawing on a positivist topos common to Auguste Comte no less than to Max Weber and members of the Vienna Circle and the early Frankfurt School, Schmitt attributes the development that was responsible for this forgetting to the "secularization process [*Säkularisierungsprozess*]," which he conceives, quite naively, to be the historical and intellectual transition through different stages (*Stufen*) running from theology through metaphysics up to the moral-human and the economical.[8]

Schmitt thus takes the institution and self-understanding of the modern state and its parliamentary democracy to task in the name of a return to theism or some functional equivalent—the translation (*Übertragung*), transformation, reinscription, and displacement of the theological: "The idea of the modern constitutional state triumphed together with deism [*setzt sich mit dem Deismus durch*], a theology and metaphysics that banished the miracle from the world. This theology and metaphysics rejected not only the transgression of the laws of nature through an exception brought about by direct intervention [*durch einen unmittelbaren Eingriff eine Ausnahme statuierende Durchbrechung der Naturgesetze*], as is found in the idea of a miracle, but also the sovereign's direct intervention in a valid legal order [*geltende Rechtsordnung*]."[9]

That the miracle thus becomes a figure for political decision—in particular, for the decision that defines the political as such: the sovereign's declaration of the state of exception—is fully in tune with Schmitt's interpretation and appreciation of the deliberative process of liberal parliamentary democracies. Modern states, he suggests, tend to forget or ignore what made and makes them possible: an act of foundation and institution, sovereignty and decision, whose legitimation is impossible, both in terms of the juridico-political order that precedes it *and* on the basis of the order, the principles and the rule of law, it establishes and *posits* itself.[10]

8. Carl Schmitt, "Das Zeitalter der Neutralisierungen," in *Der Begriff des Politischen* (Berlin: Duncker & Humblot, 1991) / *The Concept of the Political,* trans. Stracy B. Strong (Chicago: University of Chicago Press, 1996).

9. Schmitt, *Political Theology,* 36–37 / 49.

10. That this view allowed or enabled Schmitt's radically antidemocratic, authoritarian, and eventually national-socialist and anti-Semitic political stance seems evident. The interesting

218 Religion and Violence

Schmitt suggests that, although all political concepts are secularized theological ones, there is, in stricter terms, an analogy between the realm of the political or juridical, on the one hand, and the theological, on the other. Yet the precise relation between these two terms of comparison is anything but clear. Courtine has argued that Schmitt hesitates between stating two positions: first, that the political finds its origin in the theological that it has tended to suppress and sought to forget (to its own detriment and partly in vain) and, second, that there is merely a structural resemblance—albeit an illuminating one—between the two.

The difference could be attributed to a certain shift in Schmitt's position between the publication of *Political Theology* in 1922 and its sequel, *Politische Theologie II*, which appeared in 1970. He seems to have corrected himself in response to criticism, notably from Hans Blumenberg. Whereas, Courtine notes, in *Political Theology* Schmitt implies a relation of "derivation" and "foundation"—and nothing else enables one to speak of "secularization" or even "neutralization"—his position in *Political Theology II* seems more careful. There he emphasizes a proximity in structure between the political and the theological: in other words, a simple "homology," which is less vulnerable than the stronger assumption of a "genealogy," according to which one conditions and informs the other, while allowing one to think the "transposition," "translation," or "redistribution [*Umbesetzung*] of concepts, schemas, and doctrines from one domain to the other." [11]

Yet the ambiguity plays itself out at the level of the early text, where Schmitt oscillates between a Weberian invocation of an elective affinity between the theological and the political (the more modest view) and a historicist—or sociologistic—reduction of the one to the other (the more metaphysical view). The latter can take at least two different forms: that of a theory of "secularization" and "neutralization" (the reduction

question is whether this stance was an *inevitable* consequence of his rethinking of the political—that is to say, the essence and the very structure of politics—in light of the theologico-political, invoking the miracle as the privileged figure for all genuine juridical decisions, acts of sovereignty, and the like. Would the figure of the miracle and the theologico-political presupposition on which it relies be—in principle—immune to any such fatal appropriation if its premises and implications were spelled out in full rigor? There is no simple answer to this question. Yet most of the authors who interest us here have insisted on strikingly similar characteristics and overdeterminations of the political in its formal structure. How, then, could a possible association of their work with the most disastrous elements in Schmitt's legacy be avoided? The cautious answer to this question should be: *not on philosophical grounds alone*.

11. Jean-François Courtine, "Problèmes théologico-politiques," in *Nature et empire de la loi: Études suaréziennes* (Paris: Vrin, 1999), 167–68.

of the theological to the political) or that of "strategic re-theologization" (reminding the political of its supposed theological origin, in what, in Schmitt's case, comes down to a truly counterrevolutionary gesture).

The theologico-political, like the concept of *Setzung,* "positing," the *positum,* or the "positive," is an index of the principle of interpretive (for example legal) indeterminacy and the violence that of necessity looms within it. We touch here upon a paradox in the philosophy of law or in the appearance of any *positum,* one Schmitt was not the first to point out.[12] What seems new is that Schmitt explicitly recognizes that this indeterminacy everywhere borders upon the theological and does not hesitate to describe its modality with the help of some of that tradition's most remarkable tropes: not only does he invoke *creatio ex nihilo* and the miracle, but he also draws a remarkable analogy between the juridical and the theological notions of *scriptura:*

> The clearest philosophical expression of that analogy is found in Leibniz's *Nova Methodus* (par. 4, 5). Emphasizing the systematic relationship between jurisprudence and theology, he rejected a comparison of jurisprudence with medicine and mathematics: "We have deservedly transferred the model of our division from theology to jurisprudence because the similarity of these two disciplines is astonishing. [*Merito partitionis nostrae exemplum a Theologia ad Jurisprudentiam transtulimus, quia mira est utriusque Facultatis similitudo.*]"
> Both have a double principle [*duplex principium*], reason [*ratio*] (hence there

12. Hegel, albeit in more sober terms, formulates a similar insight in his *Grundlinien der Philosophie des Rechts* (*Elements of the Philosophy of Right*): "Determination by the concept imposes only a general limit [*Grenze*] within which variations are also possible. But such variations must be eliminated if anything is to be actualized, at which point a contingent and arbitrary decision is arrived at within the limit referred to. // It is in this *focusing* of the universal . . . — i.e. in its *immediate application* — that the *purely positive* aspect of the law [*das rein Positive der Gesetze*] chiefly lies. It is impossible to determine by *reason,* or to decide by applying a determination derived from the concept. . . . It is reason itself which recognizes that contingency, contradiction, and semblance have their (*albeit limited*) sphere and right, and it does not attempt to reduce such contradictions to a just equivalence" (G. W. F. Hegel, *Grundlinien der Philosophie des Rechts,* ed. J. Hoffmeister [Hamburg: Meiner, 1955], par. 214 / *Elements of the Philosophy of Right,* ed. Allen W. Wood, trans. H. B. Nisbet [Cambridge: Cambridge University Press, 1991], 245). Hegel's portrayal of this indeterminacy and the decision it requires seems less dramatic than that of Schmitt, yet the indeterminacy internal to the system and rule of law — an indeterminacy that in Schmitt's reading finds its measure in the extreme case of the state of exception, the decision between life and death, friend and foe — is also in Hegel ultimately based on a quasi-theological premise. The moment of indeterminacy is not only internal to the system; externally, a certain decision lies at the origin of the law as well. The positing and the state of law itself, Hegel writes, finds its source and authority in a absolutely free act of divine will. Schmitt recognizes Hegel as an ally in *The Concept of the Political,* 62–63 / 62–63.

is a natural theology and a natural jurisprudence) and scripture [*scriptura*], which means a book with positive revelations and directives.[13]

There is a dual source of authority, then. Indeed, the reference to "two sources" of the theologico-political reveals a profound ambiguity in Schmitt's texts.

Schmitt must invoke some theological transcendence (and, as we shall see, some theory of original—if not, in Kant's sense, radical—evil) because of the conceptual insufficiency of all secularist, contractualist, and utilitarian accounts of the possibility of political authority and the rule of law, sovereignty, and decision. More recent game- and systems-theoretical or communitarian and multiculturalist counterparts to the classical modern paradigms are no exception. According to Schmitt, the political order is systematically—inevitably, necessarily—referred to its structural incompletion, which cannot be understood in immanent (historical, empirical, or, more broadly, intelligible) terms alone. Hence the conceptual need to refer to the theologico-political. Schmitt writes:

> It should be of interest to the rationalist that the legal order itself can anticipate the exception [*Ausnahmefall*] and can "suspend itself [*sich selber suspendieren*]." That a norm or an order ... "posits itself [*sich selber setzt*]" appears plausible to the exponents of this kind of juristic rationalism. But how the systematic unity and order can suspend itself in a very concrete case is difficult to construe, and yet it remains a juristic problem as long as the exception [*Ausnahmezustand*] distinguishes itself from juristic chaos, from some random anarchy. ... From where does the law obtain this force [*Kraft*], and how is it logically possible that a norm is valid except for one concrete case that it cannot factually determine in any definitive manner [*den sie nicht restlos tatbestandmässig erfassen kann*]?[14]

In the first place, the theologico-political does not "posit itself as what it is in itself" (as does, for example, the idea, according to Hegel's *Enzyklopädie der philosophischen Wissenschaften im Grundrisse* [*Encyclopaedia of the Philosophical Sciences in Outline*], par. 251).[15] It gives itself only (to be seen, understood, or felt—the difference matters little) in the transition from one realm to the next, from, say, the noumenal to the phenomenal, none of which has existence as such. As such, I would even claim,

13. Schmitt, *Political Theology*, 37–38 / 50.
14. Ibid. 14 / 21, trans. modified.
15. Cf. Inwood, *A Hegel Dictionary*, 224.

the theologico-political reveals the nonexistence of these realms in and of themselves.

That the indeterminacy of the law touches upon the theological finds a second expression as well. The problem of the political is formulated in response to the possibility of evil — radical and apocalyptic violence — which needs to be contained. (Reference to the figure of the *katēchon,* the instance that holds off the violence of the Anti-Christ until the Second Coming of Christ, in the second letter of Paul to the Thessalonians, 2:6, is hardly fortuitous here.) More generally, Schmitt bases the concept of the political upon an anthropological and theological hypothesis concerning the corrupted nature and original belligerency of human being. There is, he believes, an "intrinsic relationship" between plausible political theories and the theological dogma concerning the Fall. By contrast, for Kant the concept of radical evil neither ties man's propensity toward the immoral and unlawful to a doctrine of original sin nor prejudges the equally ineradicable possibility of doing what is good.

Third, according to Schmitt, sovereign decisions can in themselves — in their very structure — be described in terms of miracles and their paradigm, that is to say, as *creatio ex nihilo.* God's divine action creates the world, but he sustains and renews it in its continued existence as well.

There is a structural similarity between the very definition of the political and the theological, therefore, not only in *the disruptive moment of its origin or foundation,* but also in the *continuation and sustained renewal of the order it is thus believed to ground.* Both moments — and not just the first, founding one — belong to the theologico-political and exemplify its paradoxical, indeed aporetic, structure. Roughly, these two moments would seem to resemble — or "echo" — the *creatio ex nihilo* and the *creatio continua* of which Christian doctrine speaks in its most orthodox and heterodox formulations. What is more, as the most significant "prefigurations" of the political and the juridical, these theological motifs would seem to find a common structure and repeated exemplification in the event — the eventfulness and eventuality — of the *miracle.*

Schmitt attributed this idea to the seventeenth-century *occasionalists* (Malebranche among them), whose critical reaction to Descartes's meditations on metaphysics signaled the very locus and modality of the "transformation of the divine into the civic."[16] Schmitt, therefore, is not only

16. Patrick Riley uses this formulation in *The General Will before Rousseau: The Transformation of the Divine into the Civic* (Princeton: Princeton University Press, 1986).

indebted to the thinkers of the counterrevolution but also—and, perhaps, first of all—to *occasionalism* in the tradition of Catholic theology, to which a central chapter of *Politische Romantik* (*Political Romanticism*) is devoted.[17]

Mutatis mutandis, the same holds true for the influence of the Protestant thinker Kierkegaard. The "either-or" punctuates the pages of *Political Theology*, evoking the absoluteness of the nondialectizable opposition that decision must resolve.[18] Moreover, the ominous expression *Ausnahmezustand* finds one of the most telling of its historical references in a quote from Kierkegaard that concludes the first chapter of that text:

> Precisely a philosophy of concrete life must not withdraw itself from the exception and the extreme case, but must be interested in it to the highest degree. The exception can be more important to it than the rule, not because of a romantic irony for the paradox [*aus einer romantischen Ironie für das Paradoxe*], but because the seriousness of an insight goes deeper than the clear generalizations [*Generalisationen*] inferred from what ordinarily repeats itself. The exception is more interesting than the rule [*Normalfall*]. The rule [*Das Normale*] proves nothing; the exception proves everything: It confirms not only the rule [*Regel*] but also its existence, which derives only from the exception. In the exception the power [*Kraft*] of real life breaks through the crust of a mechanism that has become torpid by repetition. A Protestant theologian who demonstrated the vital intensity possible in theological reflection, also in the nineteenth century stated: "The exception explains the general and itself. And if one wants to study the general correctly, one only needs to look around for a true exception. It reveals everything more clearly than does the general. Endless talk about the general becomes boring; there are exceptions. If they cannot be explained, then the general also cannot be explained. The difficulty is usually not noticed because the general is not even thought about with passion [*Leidenschaft*] but with a comfortable superficiality. The exception, on the other hand, thinks the general with intense passion."[19]

Perhaps not accidentally, the quote is from Kierkegaard's *Repetition*.[20] But the formal principle—a certain logic of supplementarity, iterability,

---

17. Carl Schmitt, *Politische Romantik* (Berlin: Duncker & Humblot, 1991; orig. pub. 1919).

18. See Schmitt, *Political Theology*, 8, 53, 55 / 14, 69, 71.

19. Ibid., 15 / 22, trans. modified.

20. Cf. Kierkegaard, *Repetition: A Venture in Experimenting Psychology by Constantin Constantius*, vol. 6 of *Kierkegaard's Writings*, ed. and trans. Howard V. Hong and Edna H. Hong (Princeton: Princeton University Press, 1983), 227. In contrast with Kierkegaard (and Schmitt),

"transformation [*Transformation*]," and, as Schmitt notes, "*auctoritatis interpositio*"[21] — that lies at the heart of ideality seems clear when analyzed in its own terms. The principle of legal indeterminacy is thus merely *redescribed* in particular theological terms and thereby, paradoxically, widened and deepened — indeed, generalized and intensified — into a category of "existentiality"[22] and history as such. What for Kierkegaard is the drama of decision at the level of each single individual, repeated in every generation, is for Schmitt the "destiny" or "fate [*Schicksal*]"[23] of the political at the level of the collective (ominously, of the *Volk* as opposed to the liberal-democratic, and at bottom Kantian, "public [*Publikum*]" and the Marxist concept of the proletarian "mass").[24] And yet, the adoption of Kierkegaardian testimony, of its structure and pathos, amounts to a trivialization as well. Not only is a theological figure invoked to describe what could be analyzed in its own terms — leaving us with the question, Why make the reference at all? — but if the moment of decision is virtually everything and everywhere, then it is at the same time a nothingness and nowhere to be found as such.

Of Miracles: Kant's Political Theology

If the "permanence of the theologico-political" has been forgotten and repressed, if not overcome, in the philosophical discourses of modernity, the religious has become an increasingly explicit concern in contemporary debates concerning the political (*le politique*), as well as politics (*la politique*) in its more down-to-earth commitments. This political turn to religion, we have seen, takes many forms. One of its most powerful formulations can be found in writings that define the constitution and the transformation of the public sphere in terms of its mediation by and negotiation of religion. Religion — historical and positive or revealed religion, and everything for which it stands — is portrayed as a vehicle that supports

---

Heidegger does not think of authentic existing in terms of an *Ausnahmezustand*. See *Being and Time*, 168 / 130: "*Authentic Being-one's-Self* does not rest upon an exceptional condition [*Ausnahmezustand*] of the subject, a condition that has been detached from the 'they' [*das Man*]; it is rather an *existentiell modification of the 'they'* — of the 'they' as an essential existentiale [*eine existenzielle Modifikation des Man als eines wesenhaften Existenzials*]."

21. Schmitt, *Political Theology*, 31 / 42.

22. Schmitt, *The Concept of the Political*, 59 and 65 (where the translation erroneously has "possibility") / 60 and 65.

23. Ibid., 78 / 77.

24. Ibid., 72 / 71.

or translates reason (that is to say, moral or rational religion) as much as obstructing or even betraying it.

Here Kant's account of rational religion in relation to historical religion (*Geschichtsglaube*) — that is to say, the political — once more demonstrates its unsurpassed relevance. The theologico-political is nothing but the tension between two spheres, the intelligible or noumenal and the empirical or phenomenal: between two concentric circles that interpenetrate each other, or so Kant believes and hopes, as history progresses. As we have seen in Chapter 1, in Kant's writings on religion, notably *Religion within the Boundaries of Mere Reason* and *The Conflict of the Faculties*, political sovereignty retreats behind the manifest formations — in Kant's words, the *Satzungen* and *Observanzen* — that make up the history of religion and that stand between an abstract principle of absolute power, on the one hand, and the idea of reason and rational religion or pure morality, on the other. Between the absolute position or positing (*Setzung*) of the political or moral law and the dis-position (the *Entsetzung*, as it were) of radical evil lies the realm of the empirical, historical, and political, in which humankind is equally enabled and obstructed in its progress toward the better.

In this history made up of religion in its manifest formations, the miracle, like most theologemes, plays an ambiguous role. On the one hand, its theoretical and practical relevance is dismissed. The moral law and the moral agent must stand on their own: autonomous, self-sufficient, and self-determining. On the other hand, the miracle is given a more central or decisive role than its designation as a *parergon* (Kant's word) seems to suggest. Let me explain this ambiguity or, rather, contradiction in Kant's thought.

At first glance, Kant seems to follow the phenomenalist skepticism of David Hume, who, in *Dialogues Concerning Natural Religion, The Natural History of Religion,* and *An Enquiry Concerning Human Understanding,* had already destructed the argument traditionally used to justify authentication by miracles.[25] The argument ran as follows: "Granted both that

25. From a different perspective, Karl Barth and Emmanuel Levinas condemn belief in miracles as religion qua unbelief (*Unglaube*) and as a religion of infants, respectively. This does not prevent Barth from describing faith itself in terms of a miracle: the fourth chapter of his *Der Römerbrief: Zweite Fassung (1922),* "Die Stimme der Geschichte," opens with a section entitled "Glaube ist Wunder." See Karl Barth, *Der Römerbrief: Zweite Fassung (1922)* (Zürich: Theologischer Verlag Zürich, 1989), 98 ff. Levinas does not tire of describing the enigma of the trace in terms of a miraculous event that exceeds the very order of phenomenality. Not unlike the

the power of performing miracles (i.e., bringing about events impossible within the natural order) could only be conferred upon a man by God, and that God would not confer such a power upon those misrepresenting him, then any man who performed miracles gave evidence in so doing that he had authority from God to deliver a revelation, and hence that the revelation was true."[26] Hume's riposte, in section X of the *Enquiry* (entitled "Of Miracles") consists simply in raising the suspicion that "it is more probable that the historical records are in some way inaccurate than that the miracles they relate actually took place."[27] This argument—like the one propounded by Spinoza, in Chapter 6 of the *Tractatus Theologico-Politicus* (likewise entitled "De miraculis")—anticipated the textual criticism that, from the nineteenth century onward, would treat the Bible as a historical document like any other. In consequence, the prophecies of the Old Testament and the miracles of the New Testament, as a commentator claimed in 1776, would have to "depend for much of their credibility on the truth of that religion whose credibility they were first intended to support."[28]

Superficially, Kant seems to side with the relentless sarcasm of the lemma on miracles in Voltaire's *Dictionnaire philosophique* (*Philosophical Dictionary*), as well as with the deist Hermann Samuel Reimarus, whose unfinished *Apologie oder Schutzschrift für die vernünftigen Verehrer Gottes* (*Apology or Defense for the Rational Worshippers of God*)—written in 1743 and published posthumously from 1774 to 1778 by Lessing as *Wolffenbütler Fragmente*—served as one of the pretexts for the "pantheism controversy" of 1785–86. Reimarus, to whose work Kant refers explicitly in *Religion within the Boundaries of Mere Reason*, "rejected all supernatural revelation, denied both the existence and religious significance of miraculous events, and attacked the biblical histories themselves as contradictory, fraudulent, and generally unreliable"[29]—all claims that Lessing, but not Kant, sought to refute.

---

allegorical readings of all ages, and in partial agreement with Rudolf Bultmann, both Barth and Levinas could be said to demythologize the miracle and to strip it of all its supernatural and historical content. That is not to say that they simply spiritualize its meaning. Neither a literal truth nor a mere metaphor, the miracle is treated, not as a by-work of grace, as a *parergon*, of sorts, but as an approximative redescription of the formal structure of experience, more precisely, of experience par excellence.

26. J. C. A. Gaskin, Introduction to David Hume, *Dialogues Concerning Natural Religion and The Natural History of Religion* (Oxford: Oxford University Press, 1993), xii.

27. Ibid.

28. Ibid.

29. *RBR* xvi. The reference to Reimarus can be found in *RBR* 120 n. / 737 n.

Yet, as I indicated, skeptical reservation is only part of the story, merely the first step in Kant's complex strategy. On a closer look, reference to miracles has a regulative or even constitutive function in the architectonics of Kant's argument.[30] Not only are miracles, like all the teachings and statutes of positive religion, instrumental in overcoming the religion of mere cult — and with it the merely immanentist polity characteristic of the most obsolete of its social forms, namely, for Kant, Judaism — they reveal *an inescapable and irreducible phenomenality and hence transient modality of the intelligible* as well. Here is Kant's paradoxical interpretation:

> If a moral religion (to be cast [*setzen*] not in dogmas [*Satzungen*] and observances but in the heart's disposition to observe all human duties as divine commands) must be established, eventually all the *miracles* which history connects with its inception must themselves render faith in general [i.e., historical, positive religion] dispensable. . . . Yet, when a religion of mere cult and observances has run its course and one based on the spirit and the truth (on moral disposition) is to be introduced in its place, it is entirely conformable to the ordinary human way of thinking, though not required by the [new] religion, if the introduction of the latter be accompanied and as it were adorned by miracles, to announce the end of the previous one which without miracles would not have had any authority at all. (*RBR* 122 / 740–41)

There are at least two miracles, then, two types of miraculous events, and Kant seems eager to keep them apart. There are miracles that take themselves for what they seem and those whose performers are fully aware that they are merely aesthetic and didactic modes of presentation. The wonders they work are *parerga*. They are historical signs — modes of signification — that know their ultimate moral indifference *and that efface themselves.*

But there are also miracles that complicate this seemingly simple distinction. Hence the importance of a more subtle differentiation.

> If we however ask: What is to be understood by the word *miracles* [*Wunder*]? they can then be defined (since what really matters to us is to only know what they are *for us*, i.e., for our practical employment of reason) as events in the world, the causes and *effects* of which are absolutely unknown to us and so must remain. And we can think of either *theistic* or *demonic* miracles—the

30. Notably in the section at the end of the second part of *Religion within the Boundaries of Mere Reason* that has Karl Vorländer's heading "Von den 'Wundern'" — with the word *miracles* in quotation marks.

latter being divided into *angelic* miracles (miracles of good spirits [*agatho-dämonische*]) and *satanic* spirits (miracles of evil spirits [*kakodämonische*]), though of the demonic miracles only the satanic really come into question, for the *good* angels (I know not why) give us little or nothing at all to say about them. (*RBR* 124 / 743)

This explanation does not yet make the word *miracle* into a meaningful concept, for two reasons: a *formal* one, regarding the structure of the event supposedly indicated by this word; and one pertaining to the miracle's *content*, which, Kant insists, is at least in part undecidable:

> Regarding *theistic* miracles, we can of course form a concept of the laws governing the actions of their cause (as an omnipotent etc. and hence moral being), but only a *general* concept, so far as we can think of him as the creator and ruler of the world, according to the order of nature as well as the moral order, for we can obtain immediate and independent cognition of the laws of these orders, and reason can then employ them for its own use. Should we, however, accept that from time to time, and in special cases, God allows nature to deviate from such laws, then we do not have the least conception, nor can we ever hope to attain one, of the law according to which God promotes any such occurrence (apart from the *general moral* law that whatever God does will all be good, in virtue of which, however, nothing precise is established with respect to the particular event). Here reason is paralyzed, for it is held back in its affairs according to recognized laws while not being instructed into a new one; and it can never hope to be thus instructed in the world. (*RBR* 124 / 743–44)

The second reason why the word *miracle* does not provide us with a coherent concept that could in any meaningful way contribute to our knowledge, experience, or moral character, pertains to the undecidability, not of its formal structure (or "law"), but of its content, its substance. Here, we arrive at best at a negative stipulation, allowing us to dismiss all supposed miracles that are in conflict with the dictates of moral reason. We would know, therefore, what occurrence cannot possibly constitute an example of a good, angelic miracle; but it must remain undecided whether, in all other — apparently positive — events a good spirit was at work.

We know what a miracle is not, but not whether a miracle has in fact taken place. We cannot and should not count on miracles, therefore. And yet, when everything in one's own power has been said and done — to the impossible, Kant says, nobody is obligated — one may nonetheless hope or believe on subjective, practical grounds that supplementary measures will be effected by God himself:

> Since God can lend a human being no power to produce effects supernaturally (since that is a contradiction); since, on his part, according to the concepts that he forms for himself of the good ends possible in this world, a human being cannot determine how divine wisdom judges in these matters and hence cannot, by means of the wish that he nurtures in and by himself, make use of the divine powers for his purposes, it follows that a gift of miracles, specifically one which is up to the human being himself whether he has it or not . . . , is not, taken literally, in any way to be thought of. Such a faith, therefore, if it has to have any meaning at all, is simply an idea of the preponderance that the moral constitution of the human being, if a human being were to possess it in the full perfection pleasing to God (which he however never reaches), would have over all other moving causes which God in his supreme wisdom might have; hence a ground for being confident that, if we were ever to become *all* that we should be and (in continued approximation) can be, nature would have to obey our wishes which, however, would in this case never be unwise. (*RBR* 211 / 872–73 remark)

We cannot wager, however, that this supplementary effect—yet another miracle of sorts—will come about. To do so would mean falling victim to "fetishism," the superstition of being able to master or influence supernatural effects. Kant condemns these practices indiscriminately, wherever they occur:

> Between a *shaman* of the Tunguses and the European prelate who rules over both church and state, or . . . between the wholly sensuous *Wogulite,* who in the morning lays the paw of a bear skin over his head with the short prayer "Strike me not dead!" and the sublimated *Puritan* and Independent of Connecticut, there certainly is a tremendous distance in the *style* of faith, but not in the *principle;* for as regards the latter, they all equally belong to one and the same class, namely of those who place their service of God in something . . . which cannot by itself constitute a better human being. (*RBR* 195 / 848)

We should not count on miracles, therefore, even though in every individual change of heart (every conversion), as well as all collective progress of the human race in historical time, events are produced whose modality—signaled by the "sign of history [*Geschichtszeichen*]"—is *almost* as miraculous as the miracle. Foucault, Lyotard, and, from another perspective, Hannah Arendt make much of this "sign of history," which occupies an intermediary place between the "voice of reason" and the "gift of the law," on the one hand, and the *Satzungen* that are miracles, on the other.[31] Neither strictly noumenal nor purely phenomenal, its intelligibility resides in a peculiar *transient* moment whose proper mode of temporality and performativity is precisely in question. The miracle, by contrast, would seem to reside on the side of the phenomenal and could hence never signal the intelligible as such.

Yet the analytical or categorical distinctions between the different modalities of the ethico-religious view Kant propounds — the moral law, historical and moral religion, the enthusiasm inspired by the French Revolution in its spectators, signaling moral progress in humankind — are far from convincing. Like any separation and then hierarchization of the rational and the empirical, the noumenal and the phenomenal, they inevitably deconstruct themselves at the very moment of their — equally necessary — constitution. Their place in the architectonics of Kant's critique and "material writings" is a foundationless positing, an imposition and deposition. It never quite coincides with itself. Like the "I" that Fichte proclaimed and the God after which it supposedly modeled itself, it annuls itself in the very moment of its emergence.

Yet without it no political order could come into being and no history could take its course. Likewise, the miracle is a condition of action, even though we should, Kant suggests, act as if it were no factor at all. Unlike Schmitt, Kant *acknowledges* this circumstance. *What was once impossible without the miracle must now be seen as having been possible — indeed, necessary or imperative — without it.*[32] In other words, Kant does

31. Another parallel is "special effects." A special effect is an effect without (immediately or empirically determinable) cause. Moreover, it is an event whose intrinsic technicity — or fabrication — belongs to its very essence. The opposite to a special effect would be a natural phenomenon. Special effects have all the characteristics of the signs that Gilles Deleuze — for example, in his reading of Proust's *À la recherche du temps perdu,* in *Proust et les signes* (Paris: Presses Universitaires de France, 1964) — discusses as *rencontre,* as an irreducibly violent encounter that, he writes (citing Proust and not Ricoeur, who would say the same of symbols), "gives one to think [*donne à penser*]." The formulation "the gift of the law" is taken from Rogozinski, *Le Don de la loi.*

32. A perverse reading of Kant with the help of Benjamin would be possible here, especially with reference to the latter's short narrative "Rastelli erzählt . . ." (*GS* vol. 4, pt. 1.2, pp. 777–80 / "Rastelli Narrates," trans. Carol Jacobs, in *The Dissimulating Harmony: The Image of Interpretation in Nietzsche, Rilke, Artaud, and Benjamin* [Baltimore: Johns Hopkins University Press, 1978], 117–19).

Benjamin recounts the story of a juggler whose artful performance with a magic ball was — seemingly — dependant on the active support of an unseen helper, a dwarf inside the ball who

not deny the occurrence and the special effect of the miracle, only that
it should be granted an ontological (read: physical or causal) and axio-

---

made it move in miraculous ways. The juggler's career culminates when, in the final, most important performance of his life at the court of the Sultan of Constantinople, he unwittingly
accomplishes these unusual acrobatics without his invisible assistant, who has fallen ill but
was able to notify his master only after the "fact." The special effect of the dancing ball, made
possible, quite literally, by a manipulation and thus a certain craftsmanship, artificiality, and
technicity, takes on here a miraculous quality of its own, and not just in the eyes of the unin-
formed spectators. Whether the magician operates with or without his invisible helper, there is
no observable difference between the fabricated and the genuinely or autonomously performed
act. It would seem as though the magician's creative force had unwittingly absorbed and internalized his assistant's technique to the point of no longer needing it. Or did the dwarf merely
mimic his master's telekinetic gestures all along? The story leaves the question open. It suggests
that the miraculous presupposes a certain technicity, even when the latter actually withholds
its support. Moreover, whether the dwarf is present or absent, technicity in turn relies on a
certain structure of belief, namely, the perception of the spectators.

It is impossible not to be reminded here of another unseen helper, the dwarf in the automaton of historical materialism that Benjamin evokes in the first of his "Theses on the Concept
of History." It opens with a similar narrative: "The story is told of an automaton constructed
in such a way that it could play a winning game of chess, answering each move of an opponent
with a countermove. A puppet in Turkish attire and with a hookah in its mouth sat before a
chessboard placed on a large table. A system of mirrors created the illusion that this table was
transparent from all sides. Actually, a little hunchback who was an expert chess player sat inside
and guided the puppet's hand by means of strings. One can imagine a philosophical counterpart to this device. The puppet called 'historical materialism' is to win all the time. It can easily
be a match for anyone if it enlists the services of theology, which today, as we know, is wizened
[klein] and has to keep out of sight" (Benjamin, Gesammelte Schriften, vol. 1, pt. 2, p. 693 / Illuminations, trans. Harry Zohn, ed. and intro. Hannah Arendt [London: Fontana Press, 1992],
245). The machine, which is "transparent" from all sides, must function as if it does without any
further manipulation, that is to say, without the invisible efficacy of the invincible dwarf (the
almost supranatural and oblique support of the theological, operating as a silent and magical force). Yet it is far from certain that, if it were to do without the support (of the dwarf, of
the theological), it would not continue to make the same moves and follow the same schemes.
The fully operative automaton, like the fully internalized technicity of the magician's act, is no
less mysterious and no less miraculous than the dual structure of the cooperation — in fact, the
sagital relationship (as Foucault might have said) — between their two sources (natures, bodies,
etc.). In a sense, it is its culmination: its demise and fulfillment. Impossible to tell which is
which.

By the same token, Derrida states that "any testimony testifies in essence to the miraculous
and the extraordinary from the moment it must, by definition, appeal to an act of faith beyond
any proof. When one testifies, even on the subject of the most ordinary and the most 'normal'
event, one asks the other to believe one at one's word as if it were a matter of a miracle. Where
it shares its condition with literary fiction, testimoniality belongs a priori to the order of the
miraculous. This is why reflection on testimony has always historically privileged the example
of miracles. The miracle is the essential line of union between testimony and fiction." Derrida
associates the miraculous with "the fantastic, the phantasmatic, the spectral, vision, apparition,
the touch of the untouchable, the experience of the extraordinary, history without nature, the
anomalous" (Maurice Blanchot, The Instant of My Death / Jacques Derrida, Demeure: Fiction

logical (read: moral) role. Reason and philosophical theology move away from the miracle; obscurantism and dogmatic theology, enthusiasm and illuminatism move toward it.

Although Schmitt does not deny that the miracle, due to a supposed process of secularization, has become virtually obsolete, he deplores this as the loss of the political, its *ex nihilo,* its decision, indeed, its sovereignty. Schmitt's procedure consists in reducing political theories to what he takes to be their essential structure — not their daily function but their *ultima ratio.*[33] This revolt against the "age of neutralizations" — more fundamentally, this unwillingness to grant any role to the intermediary *potestas indirecta* of all ages — is absent from Kant's text. The Protestant Kant is here more "Catholic" than the Catholic Schmitt, who, as one commentator remarks, behaves "more 'like a Protestant' neither respectful of the intermediate instances nor relying on representation, referring solely to his own faith or the sovereign authority."[34] But in 1923 Schmitt had already, in *Römischer Katholizismus und politische Form* (*Roman Catholicism and Political Form*), expressed the view that the Church represents a *complexio oppositorum,* an ideal (and hierarchical) order in which political and intellectual contradictions are — authoritatively, dictatorially — resolved.

Kant also expresses the desire for an ultimate — an absolute and total — community, but this desire is for an "ideal [*Ideal*]" of reason, a regulative idea whose telos can only be approximated asymptotically, never as such or only in the *Nimmertag,* the "end of all things," which presupposes a

---

and Testimony, trans. Elizabeth Rottenberg [Stanford: Stanford University Press, 2000], 75 / "Demeure: Fiction et témoignage," in Michel Lisse, ed., *Passions de la littérature: Avec Jacques Derrida* [Paris: Galilée, 1996], 54. Yet another author to be considered in this context would Kleist (see Françoise Proust, *L'Histoire à contretemps: Le Temps historique chez Walter Benjamin* [Paris: Éditions du Cerf, 1994], 120 ff.)

33. In a discussion of Joseph de Maistre, Schmitt observes a "reduction of the state to the moment [*Moment*] of the decision, consequently to a pure decision not based on reason and discussion and not justifying itself, that is, to an absolute decision created out of nothingness [*eine reine, nicht räsonnierende und nicht diskutierende, sich nicht rechtfertigende, also aus dem Nichts geschaffene absolute Entscheidung*]. That essentially is dictatorship, not legitimacy" (*Political Theology,* 66 / 83, trans. modified).

34. Heinrich Meier, *Die Lehre Carl Schmitts: Vier Kapitel zur Unterscheidung politischer Theologie und politischer Philosophie* (Stuttgart: Metzlerische Verlagsbuchhandlung and Carl Ernst Poeschel, 1994) / *The Lesson of Carl Schmitt: Four Chapters on the Distinction between Political Theology and Political Philosophy,* trans. Marcus Brainard (Chicago: University of Chicago Press, 1998), xii–xiii; idem, *Carl Schmitt, Leo Strauss, und "Der Begriff des Politischen": Zu einem Dialog unter Abwesenden* (Stuttgart: Metzlerische Verlagsbuchhandlung, 1988) / *Carl Schmitt and Leo Strauss: The Hidden Dialogue,* trans. J. Harvey Lomax (Chicago: University of Chicago Press, 1995).

genuine conversion of heart and the eradication of radical evil (something impossible under finite conditions, that is to say, so long as we are not united with God). Until that day, we have *almost* nothing but statutes and observances to go by. They form the vehicle that transports—and inevitably distorts—the substance of morality by making the intelligible visible and the noumenal subject to control. Religion, in its historical formation, pragmatically realizes the almost ideal.

Some miracle, something of the miraculous, seems (to have been) required for morality to take hold—that is, to become political—in the history of humankind. And yet, the very reference to and invocation of the miracle obstructs the formulation of the moral point of view and its progressive—albeit necessarily approximative, that is to say, incomplete—realization *in* (or *as*) history. This ambiguity (paradox, aporia) is only reinforced by the double relativization that the miracle undergoes with respect to its past and present role in the establishment, first of revealed, then of moral—that is to say, natural, rational, and pure—religion.

As Kant notes in passing, not only are there no Roman accounts of the miracles of which the New Testament speaks; we have no means of knowing whether the supposed miracles produced moral effects in the original Christian community (*RBR* 158 / 795). He seems even more cautious about the present: "The present situation of human insight being what it is, some new revelation ushered in through new miracles can hardly be expected" (*RBR* 160 / 798).

The positings and presuppositions of historical faith, therefore, its articles of faith and central dogmas as well as the more peculiar extensions of natural religion that Kant treats in his "General Observations" in *Religion within the Boundaries of Mere Reason*, are nothing but *parerga*, literally "by-works." Yet they belong to what needs to be posited—*presupposed* and *postulated*—somehow, at some time or another.[35]

---

35. Somewhat cynically, Kant notes that there is an intrinsic need (*Bedürfnis*) of finite beings to resort to tradition and to the written word: "A holy book commands the greatest respect even among those (indeed, among these most of all) who do not read it, or are at least unable to form any coherent conception of religion from it; and neither the highest respect [*die höchste Achtung*] nor subtle argument [*Vernünfteln*] can stand up to the knockdown pronouncement *thus it is written* [*niederschlagenden Machtsspruch: da steht's geschrieben*] . . . ; and history proves that never could a faith based on scripture be eradicated [*vertilgt*] by even the most devastating political revolutions [*Staatsrevolutionen*], whereas a faith based on tradition and ancient public observances meets its downfall as soon as the state breaks down [*Zerrütung des Staates*]. How fortunate [*Glücklich!*], when one such book, fallen into human hands, contains complete, besides its statutes legislating faith [*Glaubensgesetzen*], also the purest moral

Kant seems to argue that even if, unlike Hume,[36] one grants the empirical and metaphysical possibility of the miracle, one must still acknowledge that it can serve no practical purpose (anymore). From the moment moral religion is established in the hearts of men, even from the moment it is seen (and realized) as an existential possibility that coexists with an ineradicable evil with which it is in competition as long as history has not come to a close, the miracle (or reports thereof) will turn out to be *morally indifferent.* Its invocation, therefore, is of limited *political* use. It cannot enter into the maxims of practical reason. And yet Kant leaves no doubt that practical reason could not have taken its course—or moved toward its fulfillment in the finite order of phenomenality, that is to say, of history and the political—were it not for the introductory means (and mediation) of statutes and observances to which the miracle gives rise.

Some divine action (*creatio ex nihilo, creatio continua,* supernatural revelation, and, indeed, miracles) has (or had) at some point to be assumed, postulated, posited, affirmed as a *positum* of sorts, for morality—reason, pure religion—to come into its own, that is to say, to become public, universal, all in all, as its very concept demands. That is the paradox (or is it an aporia?) upon which Kant's thought is based. The tension that it reveals can only be mitigated, negotiated, by a pragmatic engagement—indeed, a politics—of sorts. This is not to deny that Kant's view tends toward a certain agnosticism, a suspending of all definitive judgment concerning the supposed relevance of the miracle for human knowledge and individual morality: a reasonable person "does not incorporate faith in

---

doctrine of religion, and this doctrine can be brought into the strictest harmony with those statutes (which [in turn] contribute to its introduction [(*als Vehikeln*) *ihrer Introduktion*]). In this event, both because of the end to be attained thereby and the difficulty of explaining by natural laws the origin of the illumination [*Erleuchtung*] of the human race proceeding from it, the book can command an authority equal to that of a revelation" (*RBR* 140 / 767-68, trans. modified). What is this happy coincidence, this stroke of luck, that alone warrants the harmony between historical and moral or pure religion, between the outer and the inner circle? The expression *Glücklich!,* Kant explains in a note, is "an expression for everything wished for, or worthy of being wished for, but which we can neither foresee nor bring about through our effort according to the laws of experience; for which, therefore, if we want to name a ground, can adduce no other than a generous providence [*eine gütige Vorsehung*]" (*RBR* 140 remark / 768 remark).

36. As recent discussions in the analytical philosophy of religion have shown, Hume's argument in "Of Miracles" is not as invincible as it has always seemed. See David Johnson, *Hume, Holism, and Miracles* (Ithaca: Cornell University Press, 1999), and, from a different perspective, C. A. J. Coady, *Testimony: A Philosophical Study* (Oxford: Oxford University Press, 1992), chap. 10, "Astonishing Reports."

miracles in his maxims (either of theoretical or practical reason), without contesting their possibility or actuality" (*RBR* 125 n. / 745 n.). They are, to parody a famous expression of Richard Rorty, "what it is better for us *not* to believe," especially in the long run, as history comes to a close, moves toward eternal peace, and perfects itself well beyond what is politically possible.

I tend to disagree, therefore, with the common interpretation — reiterated by the editors of the *Cambridge Edition of the Works of Immanuel Kant* — according to which Kant "had no patience at all for the mystical or the miraculous" and was "deeply skeptical of popular religious culture, severely disapproving of religious ceremonies, and downright hostile to the whole idea of ecclesial authority." [37] True, Kant's "religious temper was enlightened rather than conservative or enthusiastic," but, I believe, only when we interpret his position with attention to *echoes* of the religious can we understand why his "principles, as applied to religion, were quite radical in their implications," even though "his views and practices concerning their application to thought and culture were those not of a radical but of a moderate and a mediator." [38]

Indeed, as the authors just quoted continue, Kant believed that "the human race could no more fulfill its moral vocation apart from organized religion than it could achieve justice through anarchy. Kant accepted the church as the necessary vehicle of genuine religious faith and hence our best hope for the moral progress of the human race. If it was an imperfect (in some respects even an unsuitable) vehicle, it was nevertheless indispensable." [39] But if the ontological and axiological differentiation between the intelligible and the empirical — and hence between pure and historical or ecclesial religion — is the central premise upon which Kant's analyses are based, then the "defect" of moral religion's imperfect realization in the visible church is not merely its being "in some respects . . . unsuitable" — or simply "in need of gradual reform through persistent effort constantly guided by rational inquiry" [40] — for then the abyss between the two concentric circles remains unbridgeable. Only a leap of faith, only a miracle, an empirically and intellectually fundamentally unwarranted sign

37. General Introduction to Immanuel Kant, *Religion and Rational Theology*, trans. and ed. Allen W. Wood and George Di Giovanni, *The Cambridge Edition of the Works of Immanuel Kant* (Cambridge: Cambridge University Press, 1996), xxiii.
38. Ibid.
39. Ibid., xxiv.
40. Ibid.

could establish faith in reason's consistency with itself, that is to say, in its progress through the history of humankind.

Far from being a mere *parergon*, then, the short exposé "Of Miracles" might offer the key to deciphering Kant's political theology. The Kantians in modern political theory may not have seized upon the enormous analytical possibilities that Kant's writings on religion hold in store for us. There we might find a possibility of being Kantian once again, without subscribing to the formalism and abstract universalism with which his transcendental philosophy is so often identified. In spite of its very title, Kant's *Religion within the Boundaries of Mere Reason* could provide all the necessary elements for a critique of *impure reason*. Should we not wonder, then, that these elements are introduced in an engagement with "religion"?

Finally, Kant's project, thus reconstructed, would allow us to give new meaning to the concept of a "political theology," well beyond the premises and pitfalls of the Schmittean universe and quite independent of the "theologies of liberation" that, in the 1960s, defined themselves in radical confessional and ecclesial terms. Far from being a mere historically interesting or relevant "sociology" of juridical ideas and procedures, of sovereignty and decision, Kant's political theology enables us to recast the terms of many actual debates concerning the transformations of the public sphere, the modalities and effects of its newest mediatizations, and so on.

For Kant, "religion" is not only the realm that allows one to address radical evil as well as the whole historical spectrum of distortions of reason (fanaticism, superstition, delusion, sorcery), but also its remedy. The dual source of religion — the duality yet concentricity of its circles — opens up the possibility of a critical correction to the very intoxication that it might seem to have brought into existence. Religion — more precisely, the pure and formal or transcendental concept of a moral religion and of rational theology — is pitted here against a religiosity that in virtually all of its historical forms is tainted and infected by what Kant, in his remarkable formulation, calls the "admixture of paganism." This expression captures what, for Kant — at least in the writings that deal explicitly with religion and biblical and dogmatic theology, that is, in *Religion within the Boundaries of Mere Reason* and *The Conflict of the Faculties* — forms both the limit and the very element of the philosophical, the rational, the general, and, indeed, truth. Religion, not merely rational religion (or morality: a synonym for the philosophical and truly universal in the realm of human action), but religion in its historical, political, and empirical formation, both resists the "kingdom of ends" and, paradoxically, helps bring it into existence and into its own.

Kant thus already sees that modernity does not imply that all religious categories (figures of thought, rhetorical devices, concepts and forms of obligation, or ritual practices) have become obsolete in a single stroke. On the contrary, even where the "religious" can no longer be identified as an integral and compelling system of belief—or, more indirectly, as a narratively constructed way of life—it provides us with the critical terms, argumentative resources, and bold imaginary that is necessary for a successful analysis of contemporary culture. In other words, the study of religion must not only base itself on the latest findings of the empirical social sciences or on the most advanced conceptual tools provided by philosophical, literary, and cultural analysis. The critical terms of these disciplines must also be recast in light of the tradition they seek to comprehend. If in actual political discussion this reference will not immediately work miracles, it may very well have another—and no less salutary—effect.

"Les extrèmes se touchent"

In *Political Theology*, the reference to the analogical function of the miracle disappears as abruptly as it is introduced. Schmitt mentions it only in passing, announcing that he will treat it at length in another context (he does so in *Political Romanticism*). In the earlier text, he seems more interested in the congruent—and rather strict—formal schema of the theological and the political. Thus, after recalling that the "fundamental systematic and methodological significance" of such "analogies" had been a major insight in his writings all along, he continues:

> What is relevant here is only the extent to which this connection is appropriate for a sociology of juristic concepts. The most interesting political application of such analogies is found in the Catholic philosophers of the counterrevolution, in Bonald, de Maistre, and Donoso Cortes. What we immediately recognize in them is a conceptually clear and systematic analogy, and not merely that kind of playing around [*Spielereien*] with ideas, whether mystical, natural-philosophical, or even romantic, which, as with anything else, so also with state and society, yields colorful symbols and images.[41]

In what sense could the miracle, in its systematic analogy with the juridical—and more broadly political—acts of sovereignty, provide a concep-

41. Schmitt, *Political Theology*, 37 / 50, trans. modified.

tual clarity to be distinguished from the suggestive ornamental symbols and images that festoon the traditions of mysticism, natural philosophy, and Romanticism? What, in other words, does the "sociology of juridical concepts" that Schmitt proposes imply? And what, finally, does he mean when he writes, in his *Glossarium*, that he considers himself to be "a theologian of jurisprudence"? How, in sum, should we understand Schmitt's interpretation of the theological, the political, the theologico-political? What should we think of the limits—not to mention the perils—of his early treatise, to say nothing of its notorious subsequent elaborations and appropriations (the engagement with authoritarianism, dictatorship, anti-Semitism, and Nazism)? What meaning should we attribute to the invocation of figures and theologemes such as *creatio ex nihilo*, the miracle, revelation, the *katēchon*, or the "political Christology" in which they find their ultimate expression (according to *Political Theology II*)? Are these figures merely metaphors (aesthetic devices, *parerga*) that serve a didactic or strategic purpose alone and with whose help Schmitt is "theologizing the exception"[42] he had formulated before (and would again formulate later), without and seemingly independent of any specific reference to the theological? Why, then, do these figures occur at all?

Drawing on his conversations with Schmitt, Jakob Taubes explains the scope of Schmitt's *Political Theology* by comparing it to a "historiography in nuce, compressed in the mythical image."[43] What could it mean to attribute to mythical images such a decisive and, more importantly, *systematic* role? For one thing, the miracle, in its formal structure—or in its messianic logic (as Taubes, in close proximity to yet quite remarkable distance from Schmitt, says)—reveals the most general and fundamental trait of the political event. Speculatively speaking, the miracle reflects the political "in and for itself"; phenomenologically speaking, it shows it "as such." By way of a negative characterization, we could begin by observing that this structure is ignored or distorted by the three positions that, according to Schmitt, carry the day in political thought and that he charac-

---

42. See John P. McCormick, *Carl Schmitt's Critique of Liberalism: Against Politics as Technology* (Cambridge: Cambridge University Press, 1997), 133 ff.

43. Jakob Taubes, *Ad Carl Schmitt: Gegenstrebige Fügung* (Berlin: Merve, 1987), 25. Taubes continues: "It is the advantage of the guild [*Zunft*], that mythical images or mystic terms are vague oracles, flexible and submissive to any will, whereas the scientific language of positivism has a prerogative with respect to truth. Nothing can be further from the real situations than this historicist prejudice. In the struggle with historicism [*Historismus*], Carl Schmitt found himself in agreement with Walter Benjamin or, more precisely, Walter Benjamin found himself in agreement with Carl Schmitt" (ibid., 25–26).

terizes in an at once subtle and deeply problematical—because historically tainted—way:

> Whereas the pure normativist thinks in terms of impersonal rules, and the decisionist implements [or pushes through, *durchsetzt*] the good law of the correctly recognized political situation by means of a personal decision, institutional legal thinking unfolds in instances and forms [*Einrichtungen und Gestaltungen*] that transcend the personal sphere. And whereas the normativist in his degeneration [*Entartung*] makes of law the mere functional mode of a state bureaucracy, and the decisionist is always in danger—because of the punctuality of the moment [*Punktualität des Augenblicks*]—of missing the abiding being [*ruhende Sein*] that is contained in every great political movement, so an isolated institutional thinking leads to the pluralism [*Pluralismus*] characteristic of a feudal-corporate growth that is devoid of sovereignty. The three spheres and elements of the political unity—state, movement, people—thus may be joined to the three juristic types of thinking, both in their healthy [or wholesome, *gesunden*] and degenerate [*entarteten*] manifestations.[44]

The present-day equivalents to these positions could easily be reconstructed, and so could the pitfalls of analyses that too eagerly follow Schmitt's hierarchical categorization of this complex field in terms of soundness and degeneration (albeit in different terms). Nor would anyone wish to follow Schmitt in reducing the constitutive elements of the political or the body political to terms of state, movement, and people. Yet this dense little paragraph reveals something of interest. First, it implicitly condemns decisionism pure and simple. The miracle hardly finds an analogy in the *Punktualität des Augenblicks*, which supposedly separated itself from the *ruhende Sein* at the bottom of the political movement (and, we may assume, of the state and the people as well). On the contrary, the decision is seen as interrupting a certain pattern of regularity—for example, of parliamentary deliberation—without which such deliberation lacks weight and force. It allows the juridical process to make the law and to enforce it. Schmitt would have seen, Taubes insists

> that man, whatever he does or says, does so in time. . . . At the latest at the end of days, at one time or another it is all over. One cannot always discuss and discuss, endlessly, at one time or another the moment will come that one acts. That is to say, the problem of time is a moral problem, and decision-

---

44. Schmitt, *Political Theology*, 3 / 8, trans. modified.

ism [*Dezisionismus*] means that things cannot go on endlessly. At one time or another this process in parliament . . . , regardless whether the king convenes with his secret councils or whether the parliament meets, they will do so in time, and at one point or another they must act. Whoever denies this is unmoral, since he doesn't understand the human condition, which is finite and, because finite, must separate, that is to say, must decide.[45]

The decision that underlies juridical practice and the very idea of law is based, not on a mystery, but on an aporia. Schmitt explains:

> Every legal thought brings the legal idea, which in its purity can never become reality, into another aggregate condition and supplements it with an element that cannot be derived either from the content of the legal idea or from the content of a general positive legal norm that is applied. Every concrete juristic decision contains a moment of indifference regarding its content, because the juristic conclusion cannot be deduced in full rigor [*bis zum letzten Rest*] from its premises, and the circumstance that a decision is necessary remains an autonomous determining moment. This has nothing to do with the causal or psychological genesis of such a decision, even though the abstract decision as such is also of significance, but with the determination of the legal value [*des rechtlichen Wertes*]. . . . [W]hat is inherent in the idea of decision is that there can never be absolutely declaratory [*deklaratorischen*] decisions. That constitutive, specific element of a decision is, from the perspective of the content of the underlying norm, something new and alien [or strange, *Fremdes*]. Looked at normatively, the decision is *born out of nothing* [aus einem Nichts geboren]. The legal force [*Kraft*] of the decision is different from the result of justification [*Begründung*]. Ascription is not achieved with the aid of a norm but, inversely, only from such a point of ascription [*Zurechnungspunkt*] is it determined what a norm and what normative adequacy [or rightness and correctness, *Richtigkeit*] is. A point of ascription cannot be derived from a norm, only the quality of a content.[46]

Interestingly, Schmitt points out that the abstractness of this decision becomes "sociologically" speaking more and more telling and urgent in an age whose internal "economy" is increasingly regulated by modern media. Schmitt speaks of an "age of intense commercial activity [*Zeitalter einer intensiven Verkehrswirtschaft*]."[47] For all his opposition to "politics

45. Taubes, *Ad Carl Schmitt*, 62.
46. Schmitt, *Political Theology*, 30 and 31–32 / 41 and 42–43, trans. modified (my emphasis).
47. Ibid., 30 / 41.

as technology,"[48] there seems to be a structural affinity and even reversibility between the two. One could just as well be taken for the other and neither has ontological primacy per se.

What is more, Schmitt seems well aware that the concept of sovereignty — of the state of exception, the essence of the political — is anything but a neutral historical description or representation of empirical fact. Nor is it a formal structure a priori. Yet its essential transcendentality and irreducible transcendence is not simply to be found elsewhere, in some metaphysical realm or *Hinterwelt*, either. Instead, it is constituted by a singular act, a *Tathandlung,* a *freie Tat,* and, in terms reminiscent of Fichte, a *Sich-selber-Setzen,*[49] of sorts. The decision upon which the state of exception is based does not produce itself on the basis of an empirical generalization or by way of rational deduction. As the central category and the primal form of law (*Rechtsform*), it is neither synthetic nor analytic; it reveals itself in the free act of decision alone. It is its own warrant; indeed, it posits itself. In its essence, therefore — and as the upsurge and sedimentation of the political — the law is not positive in a conventionalist sense but radically posited. It is a positioning and imposition of sorts. More precisely, the form of the law is not this law, or at least not the many forms this law inevitably takes. Part metaphysical essence, part regulative idea, the form Schmitt evokes is that of irreducible and unjustifiable — that is to say, pure — power.

> Sovereignty is the highest, legally independent, underived power. Such a definition can be applied to the most different political-sociological configurations and can be enlisted to serve the most varied political interests. It is not the adequate expression of a reality but a formula, a sign, a signal. It is infinitely pliable [*unendlich vieldeutig*], and therefore in practice, depending on the situation, either extremely useful or completely useless. It utilizes the superlative, "the highest power," to characterize a true quantity [*realen Grösse*], even though from the standpoint of reality, which is governed by the law of causality, no single factor can be picked out and accorded such a superlative. In political reality there is no irresistible highest, that is to say, greatest power [*Macht*] that operates according the certainty of natural law.[50]

As a singular instance of — and stand-in for — absolute power, an open place and an empty signifier of sorts, sovereignty absolves itself from all

---

48. See McCormick, *Carl Schmitt's Critique of Liberalism.*
49. See Schmitt, *Political Theology,* 29 and 40 / 39 and 53.
50. Ibid., 17 / 26.

empirical relations, from causality and content. Hence the analogy with the theological, which is a formal similarity, a structural resemblance, an elective affinity, relevant in that it highlights, generalizes, and intensifies — that is to say, raises the stakes of — the indeterminacy at the heart of the political, of sovereignty and the law.

The editors of Jakob Taubes's *Die politische Theologie des Paulus* (*The Political Theology of Paul*) note that the lesson of Schmitt's conception of political theology — at least for Taubes, in his lifelong critical engagement with Schmitt — can be seen in the observation that there are "no 'immanent' categories on the basis of which a political order can legitimate itself. On this issue Schmitt and Taubes (as well as the Paul that Taubes has in mind) seem in agreement.[51] Whereas Taubes (and Paul) draw from this the conclusion that there cannot be legitimate political orders at all, but only legal ones — a position that understands itself as 'negative political theology' — Schmitt retains the postulate of a representative political order that takes its legitimacy from the divine reign of God that it makes apparent. Only the truth that has been revealed as the will of God can found an authority that lays claim to obedience."[52]

However, neither position — neither Taubes's consequent negativism nor Schmitt's absolute "positivism" — seems defensible on philosophical grounds alone. In a sense, they come down to the same. Schmitt notes that the counterrevolutionary and revolutionary — the archaic and anarchical — positions resemble each other in their very structure. Speaking of Donoso Cortes in the concluding paragraph of *Political Theology*, he notes:

> Donoso was convinced that the moment [*Augenblick*] of the last battle had arrived; in the face of radical evil [*des radikalen Bösen*] there is only dictatorship,

---

51. Others, notably Heinrich Meier, have also argued that Schmitt resorts to the theological in the more emphatic sense of the word. For a redefinition and an intellectual history of the concept of political theology with reference to Schmitt, see the introduction to Jan Assmann, *Herrschaft und Heil: Politische Theologie in Altägypten, Israel und Europa* (Vienna: Carl Hanser, 2000), 15–31, and, of course, albeit without any mention of Schmitt, Ernst H. Kantorowicz, *The King's Two Bodies: A Study in Mediaeval Political Theology* (Princeton: Princeton University Press, 1997; orig. pub. 1957).

52. Wolf-Daniel Hartwich, Aleida Assmann, and Jan Assmann, Afterword, in Jakob Taubes, *Die politische Theologie des Paulus*, ed. Aleida and Jan Assmann et al. (Munich: Wilhelm Fink, 1993), 176. On Schmitt and Taubes, see also Marin Terpstra and Theo de Wit, "'No Spiritual Investment in the World As It Is': Jacob Taubes's Negative Political Theology," in *Flight of the Gods: Philosophical Perspectives on Negative Theology*, ed. Ilse N. Bulfhof and Laurens ten Kate (New York: Fordham University Press, 2000).

and the legitimist principle of succession becomes at such a moment empty dogmatism. Authority and anarchy could thus confront each other in absolute decisiveness [*in absoluter Entschiedenheit*] and form the clear antithesis mentioned above: when De Maistre says that every government is necessarily absolute, an anarchist says literally [*wörtlich*] the same; only, with the help of his axiom of the goodness of man [*Axioms vom guten Menschen*] as well as of the corrupt government, he draws the opposite practical conclusion, namely, that every government should be opposed [or struggled against, *bekämpft*], because all government is dictatorship [*weil jede Regierung Diktatur ist*]. Every pretension of a decision must be evil for the anarchist, because the right [*das Richtige*] emerges by itself [*sich von selbst ergibt*] if the immanence of life is not hampered by such pretensions. Yet this radical antithesis forces him to decide himself resolutely against the decision [*sich selbst entschieden gegen die Dezision zu entscheiden*]; and this results in the odd [or rare, *seltsame*] paradox whereby Bakunin, the greatest anarchist of the nineteenth century, had to become in theory the theologian of the anti-theological [*Theologe des Anti-Theologischen*] and in praxis the dictator of an antidictatorship.[53]

As so often, extremes meet. Unwittingly, the anarchist reiterates the presupposition on which the reactionary bases his rejection of the modern state. Unintentionally, the latter provides the theoretical arsenal for the assaults of the former. Likewise, Derrida observes, one might wonder

> how does the most uncompromisingly conservative discourse, that of Schmitt, manage to affirm, in certain respects, so many affinities with what are apparently, from Lenin to Mao, the most revolutionary movements of our time? Who would have been their common enemy? And how can one explain the interest in Schmitt shown by certain extreme-left-wing movements, in more than one country? . . . There is more to be learned from these equivocations than from many right-minded [*bien-pensantes*] denunciations. . . . Those who are satisfied with mere denunciation too often conceal their apathy and misapprehension — indeed, their denial of the very thing that Schmitt at least, in his own way, through his reactive panic, apprehended. Which way was that? (PF 107–8 n. 4 / 102–3 n. 1).

Any reassessment of the theologico-political, in the wake of Schmitt's small treatise, must steer clear of two schematic interpretations that block

---

53. Schmitt, *Political Theology*, 66 / 83–84, trans. modified. On the notions of good and evil human nature and the differences and parallels between authoritarianism and anarchism, see also *The Concept of the Political*, 58–61 / 59–61.

a more challenging use of this concept. I think in particular of two observations that Jürgen Habermas makes in his review of the English translation of *Der Begriff des Politischen* (*The Concept of the Political*). Comparing Schmitt's reference to the theological with the one found in European
political theologies of the sixties (for example, in the writings of Johann
Baptist Metz, Jürgen Moltmann, and others), as well as in the liberation
theologies of Latin America, Habermas notes a striking difference: "As a
matter of fact, ... the morphological resemblances between the theological
and political philosophical figures of thought, presented in Spenglerian
fashion, were for him [Schmitt] not an end in themselves. The comparison, for example, between the role of the miracle in theology and that of
the state of exception in political philosophy was intended to give a dimension of depth [*Tiefendimension*] to his doctrine of sovereignty."[54]

Whether Schmitt's invocation of the analogy between the theological
and the political is based on a Spenglerian morphology remains to be seen.
Clearly, however, the theological is not simply used as a metaphor or a
trope to give excessive weight — indeed, a *Tiefendimension* — to the analysis of the political and its states of exception. Schmitt tirelessly dismisses
the ornamentalist view: political theology is not an aesthetic mode of presentation, a *parergon*. As a concept, it serves an analytical purpose: the
formal indication of a systematic parallel and structural intertwinement.

Of course, the transposition of theological concepts into the realm
of the political (and vice versa), their association with the aesthetic and
the technological, and, finally, their inscription into a discourse with a
supposedly more general philosophical ambition should be treated with
some caution. Schmitt himself seems aware of that danger: "Legal form
[*Rechtsform*], technical form, aesthetic form, and finally the concept of
form of transcendental philosophy denote essentially different things."[55]
A little later, he continues: "In the contrast [*Gegensatz*] between subject
and content of the decision and in the proper meaning of the subject lies
the problem of the juristic form. It does not have the a priori emptiness
of the transcendental form because it arises precisely from the juristically
concrete. The juristic form is also not the form of technical precision because the latter has an essentially teleological interest [*Zweckinteresse*] that
is essentially material [*sachliches*] and impersonal. Finally, it is also not

54. Jürgen Habermas, "Die Schrecken der Autonomie: Carl Schmitt auf englisch," in *Eine Art Schadensabwicklung* (Frankfurt a. M.: Suhrkamp, 1987), 110 / translated under the title "Sovereignty and the Führerdemokratie," *Times Literary Supplement*, September 26, 1986.
55. Schmitt, *Political Theology*, 27 / 37.

the form of aesthetic production [*Gestaltung*], because the latter knows no decision."[56]

The precision with which this passage states Schmitt's systematic purposes enables us to address the second of Habermas's characterizations. Habermas states:

> Carl Schmitt's polemical discussion of political romanticism obfuscates . . . the aestheticizing oscillations of his own political thought. . . . What interests him most is . . . the aesthetic of violence. The sovereignty that is interpreted after the model of creation out of nothing, acquires through the relation to the violent destruction of the normative as such an aura [*Strahlenkranz*] with surrealist meanings. This calls forth the comparison with Georges Bataille's concept of sovereignty and explains why Carl Schmitt felt himself at one time forced to congratulate the young Walter Benjamin for his essay on G. Sorel ["Critique of Violence"].[57]

Yet the claim that the theologico-political must be viewed, in Kantian parlance, as an aesthetic mode of presentation or, in formal-pragmatic terms, as a dramatization and exaggeration surely misses the essential point. Might one not express a genuine philosophical interest in the theological forms of argumentation that make up the theologico-political—even or especially in those that articulate the apocalyptic flip side of the messianic logic sketched out by Taubes—while giving a more complicated picture of liberal society as well as the inevitable (risk of) violence it entails? Such an approach would neither long for a "new dispensation" nor practice the "politics of theological despair,"[58] but resignify those designations beyond a limited and pejorative use.

Like Habermas's work, Schmitt's considerations inscribe themselves in a tradition of discourses concerning Western modernization and rational-

---

56. Ibid., 34–35 / 46.

57. Habermas, "Die Schrecken der Autonomie," 111–12. Habermas gives a far more differentiated and compelling analysis of Schmitt's work in other writings, such as *Faktizität und Geltung: Beiträge zur Diskurstheorie des Rechts und des demokratischen Rechtsstaats* (Frankfurt a. M.: Suhrkamp, 1992) and *Die Einbeziehung des Anderen: Studien zur politischen Theorie* (Frankfurt a. M.: Suhrkamp, 1996), where he discusses it in terms of its juridical arguments, while abstracting as much as possible from its theological or supposedly aesthetic frame of thought. The main text of reference there is Schmitt's influential *Verfassungslehre* (Berlin: Duncker & Humblot, 1993; orig. pub. 1928). The reference to Sorel is, of course, to Georges Sorel's 1908 classic *Réflexions sur la violence*, ed. Michel Prat (Paris: Seuil, 1990).

58. I borrow these formulations from Mark Lilla's article on Schmitt in the *New York Review of Books*, May 15, 1997, p. 44.

ization. As Taubes has pointed out, the first three chapters of *Political Theology* were published under the title "Soziologie des Souveränitätsbegriffs
und Politische Theologie" ("Sociology of the Concept of Sovereignty and
Political Theology"), in a volume of writings in honor of Max Weber.[59]
Taubes cites a passage from Schmitt's *Ex Captivitate Salus* (*Redemption
from Captivity*) that confirms this link to Weber: "We are aware that the
scholarly discipline of law [*Rechtswissenschaft*] is a specifically European
phenomenon. It is not just practical wisdom [*Klugheit*] and not just a matter of craftsmanship [*Handwerk*]. The discipline of law is deeply caught
up [*verstrickt*] in the adventure of Western rationalism."[60] The linkage,
Schmitt continues, is to the tradition of Roman law and the Catholic
Church, to a double ancestry from which it seemed able to liberate itself
only during and after the confessional civil wars and thanks to its more
than strategic alliance with the modern state.

Taubes, who appreciated the book not as a juridical essay but as a
"theologico-political treatise,"[61] leaves no doubt that the law has never
been completely emancipated from religion (or the theological). What
is more, secularization comes at an enormous price: obfuscation of the
essence of the political, which for Schmitt always remains related to a
certain *horror religiosus,* though not in Kierkegaard's sense of the term.[62]
Speaking of the fourth chapter of *Political Theology,* which deals with
the conservative, counterrevolutionary philosophies of de Maistre and
Donoso Cortés, among others, Taubes notes that here the political is seen
as inherently linked to the dark side of the religious imaginary. This determines Schmitt as an "apocalypticist of counterrevolution":

59. Melchior Palyi, ed., *Hauptprobleme der Soziologie: Erinnerungsgabe für Max Weber* (Munich, 1922); see Taubes, *Ad Carl Schmitt,* 11. Taubes was the editor of the series "Religionstheorie
und Politische Theologie" and of its first volume, entitled *Der Fürst dieser Welt: Carl Schmitt
und die Folgen* (Munich, 1983).

60. Taubes, *Ad Carl Schmitt,* 12–13. See, for an overview, Harold J. Berman, *Law and Revolution: The Formation of the Western Legal Tradition* (Cambridge: Harvard University Press,
1983).

61. Taubes, *Ad Carl Schmitt,* 14.

62. Taubes writes: "Already from early on, I had suspected in Carl Schmitt an incarnation of the Dostoevskian 'Great Inquisitor.' Indeed, in a stormy conversation in Plettenberg in
1980, Carl Schmitt told me that whoever does not recognize that the 'Great Inquisitor' is simply
right against all the enthusiastic traits of a Jesus-inspired piety [*jesuanischen Frömmigkeit*] has
neither understood what [to be a] Church means nor what Dostoevsky—against his own conviction—and 'forced by the force [violence, *Gewalt*] of the formulation of the problem has in
fact signaled'" (ibid., 15).

Carl Schmitt's reference to the "Satanism" of that time remains unforgettable. "Satanism" does not represent a secondary literary metaphor, full of paradox, but a strong intellectual principle.

He recalls Satan's elevation to the throne in the unforgettable lines of Baudelaire, which condense [or express poetically, *verdichten*] the concern [or intention, *das Anliegen*] of a generation:

"Race de Cain, au ciel monte

Et sur la terre jette Dieu!

[Descendants of Cain, ascend to heaven

And throw God down to earth]"[63]

Taubes is interested in quite different, even opposed, consequences of the historical "coincidence of the political and theological symbolic," whose semantic and systematic potential articulates, for him, an "apocalyptics of revolution."[64] This, he hastens to add, should be distinguished from the "illusions" of "messianic Marxists" such as Ernst Bloch and Walter Benjamin — "Their mystical tonality [*mystische Tonart*] in Marxism didn't please me, since I have too much respect for the Marxist system of coordinates [*Koordinatensystem*], in which, it seems to me, there is simply no place free for religious experience" — as well as the "trivialized"[65] versions of their intellectual impetus in the "political theologies" of the Catholic and Protestant left in Europe (Taubes mentions Johann Baptist Metz and Jürgen Moltmann, who, in turn, draw on the work of Ernst Bloch) and in Latin America. For Taubes, something else is at stake in the tradition reawakened by Schmitt:

> What concerned me at that time and concerns me still today is a new conception of time and a new experience of history, an experience that opens with Christianity as eschatology (itself, in turn, the anxiety and consequence of the apocalyptics of the first pre-Christian century).
>
> Carl Schmitt intuited something of this when in his antiapocalyptic affect and in his love for the Roman form of the church he spoke "of the Christian empire as guardian (*Kat-echon*) of the Antichrist."
>
> Empire means here the historical power [*Macht*] that can hold off the ap-

63. Ibid., 9. See Schmitt, *Political Theology*, 64 / 81.
64. Taubes, *Ad Carl Schmitt*, 20.
65. Ibid., 21. Taubes continues: "The critique of ideology eats away and devours every religious substance. . . . In spite of the energetic spiritual efforts on behalf of the concept and the image in Ernst Bloch and Walter Benjamin, there remains a hiatus that cannot be mastered for Marxist purposes" (ibid.).

pearance of the Antichrist and the end of the present era [*Äon*], a force [*Kraft*],
qui tenet, according to the words of the apostle Paul in the second letter to
the Thessalonians (chapter 2). This conception of empire lets itself be documented by many statements of Germanic monks [*Mönche*] from the Frankish
and Ottonian time . . . up to the end of the Middle Ages. One even sees here
the signature [or mark, *Kennzeichen*] of a historical epoch. The empire of the
Christian Middle Ages lasts as long as the thought of the *Kat-echon* is alive.

For an originary Christian faith, I believe that no historical image [*Ge-
schichtsbild*] other than that of the *Kat-echon* is possible. The faith that a
keeper [*Aufhalter*] holds back the end of the world establishes the only bridge
that leads from an eschatological paralysis of all human actions [or history,
Geschehens] to a wonderful historical power [*grossartigen Geschichtsmächtig-
keit*], like that of the Christian empire of the German kings.[66]

Nonetheless, a crucial difference between Schmitt and Taubes remains,
regardless of a more general or formal agreement with regard to the structural features of historicity and the relationship between the political and
the theological. In *The Political Theology of Paul,* Taubes speaks of the
questions of *Political Theology* as "the formulations of problems that led
Schmitt astray — or made him err [*in die Irre führten*] — but that are at least
formulations of [genuine] problems."[67] He also refers to his own earliest critique of Schmitt's project, according to which "the mystical phase,
that is to say, the democratic phase, was skipped by Schmitt, and there is
in him, in *Political Theology I,* a pure hierarchical floodgate [or cataract,
Katarakt]." He writes: "Carl Schmitt thinks apocalyptically, but from the
top, from the authorities [*Gewalten*] down; I think from the bottom up.
What we have in common is an experience of time and history as interval [*Frist*], as a stay of execution [*Galgenfrist*]. That is originarily also a
Christian experience of history. . . . True, history as interval can be interpreted in many ways and lose its edge [*an Schärfe verlieren*]. . . . But only
through the experience of the end of history has history come to be the
'one way street [*Einbahnstrasse*],' in which Western history, at least for us,
presents itself."[68] Taubes goes on to note that Walter Benjamin, author of
a collection of aphorisms published as *Einbahnstrasse,* first perceived this
problematic actuality of Schmitt's thought, provided one could turn it,

---

66. Schmitt, *Der Nomos der Erde im Völkerrecht des Jus Publicum Europaeum,* cited after
Taubes, *Ad Carl Schmitt,* 21–22.
67. Taubes, *Die politische Theologie des Paulus,* 142.
68. Taubes, *Ad Carl Schmitt,* 22–23.

so to speak, upside down. Taubes cites one of Benjamin's "Theses on the Concept of History": "The tradition of the oppressed teaches us that the 'state of emergency [*Ausnahmezustand*]' in which we live is not the exception but the rule. We must attain to a conception of history that is in keeping with this insight. Then we shall clearly realize that it is our task to bring about the real state of emergency [*die Herbeiführung des wirklichen Ausnahmezustandes*], and this will improve our position in the struggle against Fascism."[69] He comments:

> Here Walter Benjamin introduces the founding words of Carl Schmitt, borrowed and turned upside down. The "state of exception," jeopardized [*verhängt*] by Carl Schmitt in a dictatorial manner, dictated from the top down, becomes in Walter Benjamin a doctrine of a tradition of the repressed. The "now-time [*Jetztzeit*]," an uncanny abbreviation [*ungeheure Abbreviatur*] of messianic time, determines both Walter Benjamin's and Carl Schmitt's experience of history. Both are characterized by a mystic conception of history, whose essential dogma [*Lehrstück*] concerns the relationship of the holy order to that of the profane. The order of the profane, however, cannot be constructed with the help of the idea of the kingdom of God. That is why theocracy has for them . . . not a political but only a religious meaning. . . .
>
> [W]hat seen from the outside unrolls as a process of secularization, desacralization [*Entsakralisierung*] and de-divinization [*Entgöttlichung*] of public life, and what understands itself as a process through stages of neutralization all the way up to the "neutrality [*Wertfreiheit*]" of science as an index for the technical-industrial form of life, has also an interior face, which testifies to the children of God in the Pauline sense, and hence is the expression of a reformation that fulfills itself.[70]

As in his other writings,[71] Taubes insists on a certain systematic and analytical relevance of the theological that informs — and forms itself in —

---

69. Walter Benjamin, "Über den Begriff der Geschichte," *GS* 1.2:697 / "Theses on the Philosophy of History," in *Illuminations*, ed. Hannah Arendt, trans. Harry Zohn (New York: Schocken Books, 1969), 257, trans. modified.

70. Taubes, *Ad Carl Schmitt*, 28–29.

71. Taubes develops his position in more detail in *Die politische Theologie des Paulus*. See my discussion of this text in *Philosophy and the Turn to Religion*, 187–88 n. 28. The collection of essays published under the title *Vom Kult zur Kultur: Bausteine zu einer Kritik der historischen Vernunft*, ed. Aleida and Jan Assmann, Wolf-Daniel Hartwich, and Winfried Menninghaus (Munich: Wilhelm Fink, 1996) offers further intellectual and historical background against which this philosophical testament — unique in its blending of exegesis, critical theory, and autobiography — should be read. The latter volume covers a wide spectrum of issues in the

the political, that is to say, in its institutions, its conception of sovereignty and exception, event and decision. The category of the theological shows

intellectual history of this century, German-Jewish relations, the encounter between a radical philosophical hermeneutics and the most challenging—and, more often than not, heterodox—insights from the tradition called the religious. As the subtitle, chosen by the editors, indicates, these essays, lectures, and protocols, taken together, constitute the elements of a remarkable "critique of historical reason." Whereas *Die politische Theologie des Paulus* develops a logic of the messianic that draws on St. Paul's letter to the Romans, its reception in New Testament scholarship (Bultmann, Barth, and others), and its philosophical counterparts (Heidegger, Benjamin, Schmitt), *Vom Kult zur Kultur* sketches an even more outspoken hermeneutics of apocalypticism, gnosticism, and manicheism. As such, the book traces the trajectory of a lifetime of research that spans from Taubes's early publication, in 1947, of *Abendländische Eschatologie* (Munich: Matthes & Seitz, 1991) to his lectures on St. Paul, published posthumously. It does so in closely related studies that take, on the one hand, the form of sharp and often polemical intellectual portraits (as in the chapter devoted to Franz Overbeck, Martin Buber, Paul Tillich, and Karl Barth) and, on the other, that of systematically oriented discussions of themes and topoi (as in the discussions of messianism, surrealism, polytheism, ideology, etc.). At times Taubes situates himself uneasily between these two approaches; I think of his interesting reading of Heidegger's inaugural lecture "Was ist Metaphysik?" (1929)—of the transition from "nothing" qua adverb to "the Nothing" qua substantive—and its ridicule by the logical positivist Rudolph Carnap, in his 1931 "Überwindung der Metaphysik durch logische Analyse der Sprache." Taubes also offers more theoretical expositions on the relationships between Judaism and Christianity, analogy and dialectics, psychoanalysis and philosophy, or psychoanalysis and religion.

These essays constitute what the editors call Taubes's "Gesammelte Aufsätze zur Religions- und Geistesgeschichte," but they are important not only because of their descriptive and interpretative force (i.e., as intellectual portraits or sharp characterizations of trends in philosophy, theology, and critical theory). Many of the essays are highly programmatic, concerning the agenda for work that remains to be done. Taubes identifies two main lines of inquiry as tasks for the immediate future: first, he is preoccupied with the resources and the potential dangers of "myth" (a theme that links him to the first generation of the Frankfurt School, notably Theodor W. Adorno, Max Horkheimer, and especially Walter Benjamin); second, he insists on relating the argumentative and analytical potential of theology to political theory and vice versa (an obsession he shares with Carl Schmitt). In both cases, as the editors note, we are dealing with a strand of thought that rethinks the theological "from the standpoint of philosophy, especially from the philosophy of history." Put otherwise, theology is conceptualized here "after the Copernican turn." Theology is taken to be a commentary on the segments of meaning that remain in situations of crisis, after the disintegration of all symbolism; theology, moreover, is not viewed here as a positive—dogmatic—doctrine, but as a negativistic heuristic in view of the totally Other.

Taubes's essays offer an interesting and challenging compendium of a host of religious categories that have had—and still have—wide circulation in "critical theory," psychoanalysis, and more radical forms of theology. He approaches these categories with philosophical acuity and great historical erudition. But he frames them in a more general theoretical perspective—indeed, a "critique of historical reason" and of cultural memory—whose originality is beyond dispute. In a sense, Taubes could be said to bridge the gap between the tradition of hermeneutics that runs from Hegel, Schleiermacher, and Dilthey through Gadamer via Odo Marquard, on the one hand, and that of critical theory (Benjamin, Adorno), on the other. In so doing,

its pertinence everywhere and does not let itself be restricted to the confines of some interiority, whether that of the heart, conscience, or the private:

And who determines the separation of domains: theology, jurisprudence, etc.
. . .? The curriculum of universities, the commerce [Betrieb] of liberal society?
What today is not "theology" (except theological chatter [Geschwätz])? Is
E[rnst] Jünger less "theology" than Bultmann or Brunner? Kafka less so than
Karl Barth? And surely the question of law must today be formulated "theologically": that is to say, it should be asked: What does a system of law [ein
Recht] look like, given that atheism is our fate [Schicksal]? Without divine
right, must the Western world suffocate in blood and madness, or can we separate right and injustice "out of the terrestrial-mortal situation of man"? The
contemporary situation is much more difficult than the situation around the
turn of the century [die Zeitwende] because, decisively, we live post Christ,
regardless of the momentary hausse of religious markets (restorative business
[Restaurationsgetue], nothing more!). . . . The problem of political theology is
that it takes aim in the dark [ein Treffen ins Schwarze] (does the term stem from
C. S.?). It is far from being exhausted [or used up, ausgenutzt]. Political theology is perhaps "the" cross of all theology. Will the latter ever come to terms
with the former? Christianity (Augustine) refused the problem (like all chili-
astic movements, antinomianism—is it thus present indirectly in Christian
consciousness after all, albeit with a bad conscience?). Judaism "is" political
theology—that is its "cross," since theology does not let itself be reduced to
its division [Division] by: "political," since the law is after all not the first nor
the last, because "even" between human beings there are relationships that
"transcend," "transgress upon" the law—love, compassion, forgiving (not at
all "sentimental," but "real").[72]

Schmitt, who claims to have originated the term *political theology*,
would agree. In a letter that responds indirectly to Taubes's letter just
quoted, he noted: "Taubes is right: today everything is theology, except
what the theologians declare to be such [Heute is alles Theologie, mit Ausnahme dessen, was die Theologen von sich geben]."[73]

---

he covers new ground, as well. Taubes's critique of historical reason stands out by its uncanny
ability to draw on the most heterodox and idiosyncratic elements of the religious tradition, its
political theologies, and the semantic, argumentative, and figurative potential they continue to
have for the present.
72. Taubes, *Ad Carl Schmitt*, 34–35.
73. Cited after ibid., 37.

What might the broader conception of the theological thus *reclaimed* entail? What relation, for example, does it entertain with the mythical and the mystical, with the language of paradise—in other words, with divine speech, the language of angels—and with the language of humans after the Fall, with the dissemination of tongues and the end of all things? To these questions, the writings of Walter Benjamin propose a remarkable answer that casts yet a different light on the theses that we have investigated so far. Indeed, they confirm our earlier intuitions, especially when read, not just on their own terms and in their proper historical context (as they clearly should be), but in light of a theoretical vocabulary and systematic perspective first formulated by Michel de Certeau, then elaborated and radicalized by Jacques Derrida. Derrida's discussion of the mystical postulate, as informed by de Certeau and deployed in a rereading of Benjamin, permits him to rearticulate "divine" violence according to the logic of sacrificing sacrifice, discussed in the previous chapter and summed up in *Aporias:* "Perhaps nothing ever comes to pass except on the line of a transgression, the death [*trépas*] of some 'trespassing.'"[74] Here, again, the issue is that of transgressing the limits of the philosophical and the ethical in the direction of the religious and, more precisely, the theologico-political.

Rereading Walter Benjamin

In May 1916 Walter Benjamin wrote to Martin Buber, who had asked him to contribute to the journal *Der Jude* (*The Jew*), that the spirit of Jewish tradition was "one of the most important and persistent objects of [his] thinking."[75] Benjamin had met Buber in 1914, when Buber had invited him to give a lecture for the *Freie Studentenschaft* in Berlin. His relation to Buber had from the start been marked by a certain intellectual reservation, which became more evident after the outbreak of the war. Unsurprisingly, he declined Buber's 1916 invitation. In a letter of July 1916, Benjamin denounced in clear terms the political orientation of Buber's

---

74. Derrida, *Aporias,* 33 / 66.

75. Walter Benjamin, *Briefe* (Frankfurt a. M.: Suhrkamp, 1966), 1:125 / *The Correspondence of Walter Benjamin: 1910–1940,* ed. Gershom Scholem and Theodor W. Adorno, trans. Manfred R. Jacobson and Evelyn M. Jacobson (Chicago: University of Chicago Press, 1994), 79.

    This and the remaining sections of this chapter draw on material that I first presented in an early article entitled "Theologie als allegorie: Over de status van de joodse gedachtenmotieven in het werk van Walter Benjamin," in H. J. Heering, ed., *Vier joodse denkers in de twintigste eeuw: Rosenzweig, Benjamin, Fackenheim, Levinas* (Kok: Kampen, 1987), and then in a more elaborated version in "Antibabel: The 'mystical postulate' in Benjamin, de Certeau, and Derrida," *Modern Language Notes* 107 (1992): 441–77.

Der Jude, most importantly because of the enthusiasm so many of its con-
tributors expressed for the experience (*Erlebnis*) of the war and, more indirectly, because of its interpretation of Zionism.[76] Moreover, the letter
marks the end of his earlier interest and engagement in the movement
of Gustav Wyneken and inaugurates the unmistakable skepticism about
mainstream German social democracy that characterizes so many of his
later texts, notably "Critique of Violence" and the final "Theses on the
Concept of History."

In one of the early letters to Buber, Benjamin formulated his critique
in terms that indicate the main preoccupation and major premises of his
first independent views on language and contain *in nuce* his views on the
relationship between this conception of language and the question of politics, as well as of these two and the theological. One passage stands out as a
paradoxical formulation of the intricate connection or even unity between
word and effective action. With this paradoxical formulation Benjamin —
by postulating an immediate, magical, secret, and yet salutary power of
the mute, "mystical" foundation of language — seeks to explain why the
word cannot be reduced to an instrumental means for action:

> My concept of objective and, at the same time, highly political style and writ-
> ing is this: to awaken interest in what was denied to the word; only where
> this sphere of speechlessness [*Sphäre des Wortlosen*] reveals itself in unutter-
> ably pure power [or force, violence, *in unsagbarer reiner Macht*] can the magic
> spark leap between word and moving deed [*bewegender Tat*], where the unity
> of these two equally real entities resides. Only the intensive aiming of words
> into the core of intrinsic silence is truly effective [*Nur die intensive Richtung
> der Worte in den Kern des innersten Verstummens hinein gelangt zur wahren
> Wirkung*].[77]

Buber did not respond to the letter, and no further cooperation developed.
In retrospect, however, these sentences can be read as the programmatic statement of a lifelong concentration on the "essence" of language, an
"essence" in which knowledge, right (as well as morality), and art, following the Kantian tripartition of the faculties of human reason, are curi-
ously "founded." The program that began, Benjamin explained in a letter

76. Cf. Gershom Scholem, *Walter Benjamin—Die Geschichte einer Freundschaft* (Frankfurt
a. M.: Suhrkamp, 1975), 41. See also Paul Mendes-Flohr, *From Mysticism to Dialogue: Martin
Buber's Transformation of German Social Thought* (Detroit: Wayne State University Press, 1989),
chap. 3.

77. Benjamin, *Correspondence,* 80 / 127.

to Ernst Schoen in December 1917, as a "desperate inquiry into the linguistic conditions of the categorical imperative [*verzweifeltes Nachdenken über die sprachlichen Grundlagen des kategorischen Imperativs*]," [78] distinguishes itself by the peculiar form of its "linguistic turn," not only from the modern critical project but also from any objective or absolute idealism. Hamann shows the way here, rather than Kant, Hegel, or Schelling. Moreover, Benjamin's early reflections betray a fascination with language in which the early German Romantic writings, the modern French lyric, and, more indirectly (that is to say, mediated through the studies of Gershom Scholem), the tradition of Jewish mysticism or Kabbalah enter into a singular configuration. [79] Here, I will focus on just one aspect of this configuration, one that seems to determine or found all others: the "mystical" element.

It has often been noted that this "mystical" moment in Benjamin's writing reveals a religious or theological desire to restore a lost or broken totality and identity. [80] In what follows, I ask what remains of this critique in light of alternative — and, I believe, more plausible — readings of this quasi-theological figure. This requires a detour through discussions of the "mystical postulate," principally by Michel de Certeau and Jacques Derrida, whose dealings with the mystical shed yet another light on the "turn to religion" that we have observed — and advocated — throughout. Moreover, their hypotheses offer themselves to further systematization, formalization, and analytical confirmation in a host of contemporary philosophical discourses, whether phenomenological or hermeneutical, dialectical or analytic. They also allow for the reformulation and eventual corroboration of more empirical inquiries into the relationship between language and the political, the political and politics in its everyday sense.

78. Ibid., 118 / 165.

79. See Beatrice Hanssen, *Walter Benjamin's Other History: Of Stones, Animals, Human Beings, and Angels* (Berkeley: University of California Press, 1998), and idem, "Philosophy at Its Origin: Walter Benjamin's Prologue to the *Ursprung des deutschen Trauerspiels*," *Modern Language Notes* 110 (1995): 809–33.

80. Cf. Bernd Witte, *Walter Benjamin — Der Intellektuelle als Kritiker: Untersuchungen zu seinem Frühwerk* (Stuttgart: J. B. Metzlerische Verlagsbuchhandlung, 1976), 123; and Werner Fuld, *Walter Benjamin, Zwischen den Stuhlen: Eine Biographie* (Munich: Carl Hanser, 1979), 75: "Die Rückerkenntnis des Ursprungs, die erneute verinnerlichte Versenkung in den Kern der Identität, das ist, was Benjamin unter 'Philosophie' verstand." On the notion of the "Urphänomen," see Hannah Arendt, "Walter Benjamin," in *Men in Dark Times* (San Diego: Harcourt Brace Jovanovich, 1968); idem, *Walter Benjamin, Bertolt Brecht: Zwei Essays* (Munich: Piper, 1971), 7–62.

In Derrida's writings of the 1980s,[81] the early work of Walter Benjamin plays an increasingly important role. In a text entitled "Des tours de Babel," as well as in several scattered remarks throughout the conversations in *The Ear of the Other*, Derrida engages in a detailed discussion of Benjamin's conceptions of language as formulated in the 1916 "On Language as Such and on the Language of Man," as well as in the 1923 "The Task of the Translator." In his lecture "Force of Law: The 'Mystical Foundation of Authority,'" Derrida pursues the same line of investigation further in an analysis of Benjamin's thoughts in the 1921 essay "Critique of Violence." Other relevant excursions into Benjamin can be found in *Specters of Marx* and *Politics of Friendship*.

Beyond exploring a remarkable resemblance or affinity between Benjamin's earliest program and the task of deconstruction, in these readings Derrida voices a profound uneasiness that is expressed with increasing candor in the itinerary he follows from "Des tours de Babel" to "Force of Law." Despite certain striking similarities with respect to the problem of linguistic representation in general and juridico-political representation in particular, the two authors differ on at least two counts. Benjamin's "metaphysical" assumption of a "divine" and "pure" origin of language before its "fall," as well as his appeal to an ultimate, quasi-eschatological overcoming of this finite language's ambiguities by a "divine violence," causes Derrida to distance himself from this thought and the politics it would seem to imply. First, not only is Benjamin's critique of a "bourgeois" conception of language as representation, as well as of the parliamentarism (of democracy qua representation, legality qua procedure) characteristic of the Weimar republic, "revolutionary" in the sense of being "Marxist" and "messianic," but the desire for a past origin and for immediate forms of noncommunicative—that is, no longer mediated— "communication" (or *Verständigung*), modalities that for Benjamin mark the forms of cooperation prefigured by the "general proletarian strike," seems outright "reactionary." Second, Benjamin's positions on the theological presuppositions or origin of language and the political, plus his fascination with a liberating violence, entertain relations with Schmitt and Georges Sorel (to mention only two of the most important sources) that, for Derrida, seem too close for comfort. In contradistinction to this

---

81. I will not comment here on Derrida's remarks on Benjamin in "+ R (par dessus le marché)," in *La Vérité en peinture* / "+ R (Into the Bargain)," in *The Truth in Painting*, 148–82, nor on Derrida, *Moscou aller-retour* / "Back from Moscow, in the USSR."

revolutionary-reactionary ambivalence, Derrida's deconstruction of the axioms of Benjamin's essays prepares a radically different—more differentiated or more *differential*—account of the functioning of the "mystical postulate" at the intersection of language and politics.

Yet things are more complicated. The risk that worries Derrida in Benjamin's texts haunts their deconstructive reading (which, increasingly, bases itself on them) as well. The difference between the two thinkers' texts—two programs of a coming philosophy (compare Benjamin's "Über das Programm der kommenden Philosophie" ["On the Program of the Coming Philosophy"]) or a philosophy to come, that is to say, still and forever to come (and the difference between these formulations and their corresponding intellectual dispositions may be all there is to say)—is therefore a difference within the limits of a certain inevitable, necessary repetition and betrayal. It takes shape only within the displacement of an ineluctable relation (without relation) to an "abyss" that, in metaphysical parlance, is the condition of all language, politics, and law. There are at least two ways of thinking and acting upon this mystical abyss, in which "God," "divine force," and "the worst" are never far away, whether from the reader or actor, or from each other.

Before discussing Derrida's reading of Benjamin, I will first retrace some of the steps taken by Michel de Certeau to circumscribe the elusive subject of "mysticism."[82] Second, I will briefly examine Derrida's quasi-transcendental analysis of de Certeau's discussion of the "mystical postulate." This will bring us, once again and from a different perspective, to a critical reassessment of the theory of "speech acts."[83] Both excursuses will shed light on the premises of Derrida's approach as well as, more in-

82. For an earlier discussion of "mysticism," this time in the context of "apophatic theology," see my *Philosophy and the Turn to Religion*, chap. 2. On the motif of Babel in relation to that of "hospitality," see ibid., 322–24. In the present chapter I extend this interpretation in the direction of the theologico-political and the conception of language it entails. That there are other possible approaches to the question of mysticism goes without saying. In addition to the ones that appear in my earlier book, see, for a radically different approach, with special emphasis on Indian traditions, Frits Staal, *Exploring Mysticism: A Methodological Essay* (Berkeley: University of California Press, 1975). For a comprehensive and subtle discussion of the mystical in the context that interests us in the following, see Peter Tracey Connor, *Georges Bataille and the Mysticism of Sin* (Baltimore: Johns Hopkins University Press, 2000). On the historical relationship between mysticism, monasticism, and violence, see further Burcht Pranger, "Monastic Violence," in de Vries and Weber, eds., *Violence, Identity, and Self-Determination*, 44–57, and idem, *Broken Dreams: Bernard of Clairvaux and the Shape of Monastic Thought* (Leiden: E. J. Brill, 1994).

83. See *Philosophy and the Turn to Religion*, 404 ff.

directly, on the implications of Benjamin's early reflections on language, history, politics, and the law.

The Originary Affirmation of Mysticism

"Mysticism," Michel de Certeau writes, "is the anti-Babel. It is the search for a common language, after language has been shattered. It is the invention of a 'language of the angels' because that of man has been disseminated."[84] With these words, de Certeau describes mystical discourse as a "historical trope" for "loss,"[85] as a response to the disintegration of a culture in which objects of meaning and even God himself seemed to have vanished. Yet, de Certeau continues, mysticism does not respond to this loss by substituting for it new doctrines or institutions. Instead, it discovers a new mode of handling the disintegrated tradition of theological, scriptural, and patristic knowledge; that is, it uses or experiences the same language *otherwise*. De Certeau relates the procedure to that of negative or apophatic theology: "It is as though the function of mysticism were to bring a religious *episteme* to a closure and erase itself at the same time."[86] The interplay of this closure and erasure can easily be explained. In the fragmented, "Babel-like," and virtually eclipsed language of tradition, the common ground or the very preliminaries for communicating its contents, which had been taken for granted, need to be established and re-established, and this operation needs to be repeated ad infinitum: "Mystic discourse itself had to produce the conditions of its functioning as language that could be spoken to others and to oneself" (*MF* 164 / 225–26), as well as its continuation or conservation.

Mysticism, de Certeau claims, begins with a singular original and reiterated affirmation, a singular "act" — an original positing or *Setzung,* as Fichte would have said — an "I will," a *volo,* in which or through which an empty space is created, invented, or instituted, a space hospitable to the new *modus loquendi* or *modus agendi.*[87] In the mystic text, this *volo* func-

84. Michel de Certeau, *Heterologies: Discourse on the Other,* trans. B. Massumi (Minneapolis: University of Minnesota Press, 1986), 88; see also *MF* 155 / 216. Cf. also Michel de Certeau, *La Faiblesse de croire,* ed. Luce Giard (Paris: Seuil, 1987), chap. 7, "La Rupture instauratrice"; Luce Giard, "Biobibliographie," in "Michel de Certeau," in *Cahiers pour un temps* (Paris: Centre Georges Pompideau, 1987), 245 ff.; Luce Giard et al., *Le Voyage mystique: Michel de Certeau* (Paris: Cerf, 1988), and the contributions to *À partir de Michel de Certeau: De nouvelles frontières,* in *Rue Descartes* 25 (Paris: Presses Universitaires de France, 1999).

85. De Certeau, *Heterologies,* 80.

86. Ibid., 37.

87. One difficult question is how this analysis of the mystical postulate carries over into or

tions as the linguistic and practical a priori formerly constituted by the abstract corpus of theological learning and its institutional base. Without the *volo,* no new speech is possible. Mysticism thus defined can no longer be explained in terms of an apologetics that seeks to reorient the will of its addressees to accept certain assertions or predicates about the divine being, the literal and figural meaning of the Scriptures, the sacraments, the hierarchical order of the church, the first and last things, the afterlife, punishment and retribution, and so on. Instead of being part of the content of faith—let alone its ideological effect or epiphenomenon—the mystic *volo* is the silent ground of such a doctrine. Indeed, mysticism is its secret point of departure, the force that makes it possible at all.

At the same time, this mystical ground presupposed by all utterance makes all new discourse impossible. Not only does it haunt the rupture initiated by an ethical demand that no language or practice can ever hope to satisfy (*MF* 167 / 229-30), but its force—the very "act" of its invention—is betrayed from the very moment it is pronounced, reflected, or narrated in all the futile attempts to justify, preserve, or renew it.

To a degree, de Certeau stresses, the mystic discourse of the sixteenth and seventeenth centuries, by introducing the motif of the *volo,* anticipates the pragmatic modality of what, since Austin's *How to Do Things with Words,* has come to be known as the performative speech act. It is a doing of sorts, not a description, affirmation, or negation of a state of affairs or of mind. Instead of reaffirming a historically transmitted doctrinal corpus of constatives pertaining to the existence and the essential attributes of a divine reality, its created order, and its sanctioned hierarchies, the mystic authors expressed a radically new way of experiencing and redirecting language in general.

More specifically, mystic speech, instead of postulating a reality or knowledge that precedes the utterance (as with "constatives"), resembles the performative classified by speech act theory as a *promise* (*MF* 173 / 237). Its primary function is illocutionary or, rather, *allocutionary,* driven by an absolute address to the absolute. Yet de Certeau leaves no doubt that

---

resonates with de Certeau's other historiographical, cultural, and political writings. See Michel de Certeau, *L'Écriture de l'histoire* (Paris: Gallimard, 1975) / *The Writing of History,* trans. Tom Conley (New York: Columbia University Press, 1992); idem, *L'Invention du quotidien I: Arts de faire,* ed. Luce Giard (Paris: Gallimard, 1990); idem, Luce Giard, and Pierre Mayol, *L'Invention du quotidien II: Habiter, cuisiner,* ed. Luce Giard (Paris: Gallimard, 1994). See further Michel de Certeau, *La Prise de parole, et autres écrits politiques* / *The Capture of Speech and Other Political Writings,* and, finally, idem, *La Culture au pluriel* / *Culture in the Plural.*

the *volo* is not a performative or a promise in the sense most speech act theorists, including Austin and Searle, have in mind. The mystic *volo* is not a constative, but it lacks the social or conventional context that renders the performative speech act "successful." On the contrary, the *volo* presupposes and entails the bracketing or even destruction of all such circumstances. It thereby reveals the limit of all performatives, indeed, of the very concept of the performative. The mystic *volo* no longer allows, let alone guarantees, the translation or "metamorphosis" of linguistic utterance into social contract.[88] The *volo* is less a *vouloir dire*, to re-cite the well-known formula from Derrida's *La Voix et le phénomène* (*Speech and Phenomenon*), which de Certeau reiterates at this point, but "a volition out of which speech is born, or may be born" (*MF* 175 / 240). The *volo* is thus ab-solute in the etymological sense of the word: it absolves itself from all objects, all means, and all ends. This circumstance does not entitle us to associate the *volo* with an act of pure—or, as Hegel would say, abstract—negation. Rather, the *volo* is an irreducible and infinite gesture of unconditional *affirmation*. With oblique reference to Spinoza's phrase *omnis determinatio est negatio*, de Certeau explains why this must be so: "Whereas knowledge delimits its contents through a procedure that is essentially that of the 'no,' a labor of distinction ('this is not that'), the mystic postulate poses the unlimited [*l'illimité*] of a 'yes'" (*MF* 174 / 239, trans. modified). Such a "yes" must be presupposed—and thereby posited or postulated—in every distinct "yes" and "no," in their opposition as much as by the dialectical sublation of their posited positivity and negativity. This pre-positional "yes," de Certeau suggests, manifests itself in the modality of the future anterior. The "yes" has, in a way, always already taken place. It has always already been given, although it never gives "itself" as such, that is to say, "in all purity." We can never hope to grasp it in and for itself, because every constative utterance with which we could circumscribe its nature already presupposes or engages its purported object or subject, before even a word has been spoken. Moreover, the "yes" is irreducible to an occurrence or phrase that a definite article (*the*) might stabilize in a certain unity or number: *the "yes" is everywhere and nowhere, one and multiple.* Consequently, no transcendental or linguistic meta-discourse is ever able to distance itself from it, turn its back on it, return to it, let alone reflect and speculate on its intent or meaning (*P* 640). Because the *volo* is

---

88. *MF* 173 / 238. De Certeau comes close here to the analysis of the social contract that Stanley Cavell gives in the opening pages of *The Claim of Reason*.

the affirmation of a beginning or opening rather than of anything determinate, mystic speech implies a certain *non-vouloir*. The *volo* pertains to everything and nothing, to everyone and nobody. It constructs the space in which what is either positively given or negative could be experienced or said at all (i.e., posited, negated, or even denegated).

In de Certeau's analysis, the *volo* is no longer thinkable as the fulfillable intention of a subject constituted and identifiable prior to it. The *volo* is no longer the willing or saying of something determinate. In its very ab-soluteness, it is a *nihil volo*, emptied out to the point of becoming almost interchangeable with Heidegger's interpretation of the *non-vouloir* of Meister Eckart's *Gelâzenheit* as a release or "letting-be" (*MF* 166–67, 169–70 / 228–29, 232). Not unlike Wittgenstein's *Tractatus Logico-Philosophicus*, which claims that it is precisely not "*how* things are in the world that is mystical, but *that* it exists [*Nicht* wie *die Welt ist, ist das Mystische, sondern* dass *sie ist*]," [89] the mystic writings could thus be said to "display a passion for what *is*" rather than for *what* it is that is.

Mysticism, in de Certeau's sense, entails an originary opening up of all language. At the same time, it implies the "circumcision" (*MF* 136 ff. / 185 ff.) of this language. Like the infinite detours of negative theology, it paradoxically only signifies through the fact that it removes (and withdraws itself from) language's signifyingness (*MF* 137 / 189). Mystic speech disappears in what it discloses: accordingly, it only says by unsaying, writes by unwriting. And the alterity that, in so doing, it reveals and conceals has no identity or name independent of this movement. In de Certeau's words:

> The other that organizes the [mystic] text is not the (t)exterior [*un hors-texte*]. It is not an (imaginary) object distinguishable from the movement by which it (*Es*) is traced. To set it apart, in isolation from the texts that exhaust themselves in the effort to say it, would be to . . . identify it with the residue of alterity of already constituted systems of rationality, or to equate the question

89. Proposition 6.44, in Ludwig Wittgenstein, *Tractatus Logico-Philosophicus*, 73 / 84. In proposition 6.432 Wittgenstein states: "*How* things are in the world is a matter of complete indifference for what is higher. God does not reveal himself *in* the world. [Wie *die Welt ist, is für das Höhere vollkommen gleichgültig. Gott offenbart sich nicht in der Welt*]" (ibid.). Yet another discussion opens here, concerning the relationship between Benjamin and the earlier and later Wittgenstein, as Stanley Cavell observes in "Benjamin and Wittgenstein: Signals and Affinities," in *Philosophie in synthetischer Absicht / Synthesis in Mind*, ed. Marcelo Stamm (Stuttgart: Klett-Cotta, 1998), and, earlier, in *A Pitch of Philosophy: Autobiographical Exercises* (Cambridge: Harvard University Press, 1994).

asked under the figure of the limit with a particular religious representation.
... It would be tantamount to positing, behind the documents, the presence
of a what-ever, an ineffability that could be twisted to any end.[90]

Instead of attempting to define a purported "object," understanding mysticism therefore means formalizing the different aspects of its writing, of its style or tracing, of an infinitely reiterated (i.e., repeated, altered, and even annihilated) invisible step (pas).[91] All mystic speech is centered on this essential indeterminacy and from it receives a peculiar force: a force, de Certeau claims, that is the echo in language of the divine anger and violence that Jacob Böhme and others postulate at the origin of everything that exists, at the very beginning of history (MF 169 / 231; cf. P 205). This mutual implication of an originary violence and the functioning of language (as well as law and politics) is what interests Derrida in his analysis of the "mystical postulate" in de Certeau and Benjamin.

In "Nombre de oui" ("A Number of Yes"), Derrida follows out the peculiar logic that governs de Certeau's reconstruction, set forth in The Mystic Fable, of the originary affirmation in (and of) the mystic text, asking both what it presupposes and what it seeks to exclude. Such an analysis, Derrida advances, could be termed "quasi-transcendental" or "quasi-ontological" (P 641), formulations that do not signal any lack of rigor but, on the contrary, expose the narrative, fictional, or, more precisely, fabulous features of the mystical postulate and thereby attempt to subtract it from the metaphysics of the modern, subjective will that still haunts de Certeau's analysis, notably in his identification of the originary affirmation with an "I" that has enough determination to say of itself, in the first person singular: "I will [volo]" (P 645).

As de Certeau's own descriptions suggest, the silent presupposition of all utterance, the affirmation of mystic speech that engages even the most negative predication, is, strictly speaking, neither an act of speech nor an act at all, pronounceable in the present by a conscious "I" that would have enough self-presence to express, to put into words, what it intends. Rather, the general direction of de Certeau's analyses seems to imply that the volo only resembles an "absolute performative" (P 647), given that it is neither "performative" nor "absolute" in any generally accepted or intelligible sense of these terms. More precisely, one would have to admit that the

90. De Certeau, Heterologies, 81–82.
91. Ibid., 82.

originary affirmation "is" not at all. Although it opens the "happening" of any event (and in that sense, perhaps, even precedes the very *Ereignis* of Being), it is as such—in itself—neither an event nor any other determinable presence (or coming into presence). No fundamental ontology, no transcendental inquiry into the subjective, theoretical, and practical conditions of this affirmation, let alone any ontic, empirical discourse, could ever adequately describe its singular occurrence. And since the "yes" can never become a theme or subject of any possible (hypo)thesis, the very introduction of this figure can therefore, strictly speaking, never have the epistemic qualities of a "postulate." The modality of its manifestation as well as its philosophical articulation could only be that of a *quasiment:* its logos is that of a "fable" (*P* 648).

In the context of this analysis, published in 1987, four years before his discussion of the "mystical postulate" in "Critique of Violence," Derrida recalls a revealing passage in Franz Rosenzweig's *Der Stern der Erlösung* (*The Star of Redemption*):

> Yea [*Das Ja*] is the beginning. Nay [*Das Nein*] cannot be the beginning; for it could only be a Nay of the Nought [*Nichts*]. . . . This non-Nought [*Nicht-nichts*] is, however, not independently given, for nothing at all is given except for the Nought. Therefore the affirmation of the non-Nought circumscribes as inner limit the infinity of all that is non Nought. An infinity is affirmed: God's infinite essence, his infinite actuality, his Physis [*Physis*]. Such is the power [*Kraft*] of Yea that it adheres everywhere. . . . It is the arche-word [*Urwort*] of language, one of those which first makes possible, not sentences, but any kind of sentence-forming words at all, words of parts of the sentence. Yea is not part of a sentence [*Satzteil*], but neither is it a shorthand symbol for a sentence, although it can be employed as such. Rather it is the silent accompanist of all parts of a sentence, the confirmation, the "sic!" the "Amen" behind every word. It gives every word in the sentence the right to exist, it supplies the seat on which it may take its place, it "posits." The first Yea in God establishes the divine essence for all infinity. And the first Yea is "in the beginning."[92]

92. Franz Rosenzweig, *Der Stern der Erlösung*, vol. 2 of *Gesammelte Schriften* (The Hague: Martinus Nijhoff, 1976; orig. pub. 1921), 28–29 / *The Star of Redemption*, trans. W. W. Hallo (New York: Holt, Rinehart &Winston, 1971), 26–27. Cf. *P* 643–44; "A Number of Yes," trans. B. Holmes, *Qui parle* 2, no. 2 (1988): 125.

Rosenzweig is by now generally regarded as an important source of Benjamin's early thought. See Stéphane Mosès, "Walter Benjamin und Franz Rosenzweig," in *Deutsche Vierteljahrschrift für Literaturwissenschaft und Geistesgeschichte* 4 (1982): 622–40, as well as the studies collected in his *L'Ange de l'histoire: Rosenzweig, Benjamin, Scholem* (Paris: Seuil, 1992). See also

Derrida comments only on those elements of this passage that are illustrative of de Certeau's remarks on the "mystical postulate." According to Rosenzweig, he notes, the originary "yes" is both a word and something apparently beyond or, rather, before every determinate language, before even the pronunciation of any particular "yes." As the inaudible companion of all speech (as well as all writing), the "yes" thus has a transcendental status similar to that of the "I think" (*Ich denke*) that, as Kant posited, accompanies (*begleitet*) all our representations (*Vorstellungen*). As the hidden ground or source of all language, the "yes" both belongs and does not belong to what it makes possible or calls into being.[93] The quotation from Rosenzweig obliquely points to this singular postulation.

In the remainder of his analysis, Derrida spells out its far-reaching implications. The "yes," Derrida continues, is not only a quasi-transcendental or quasi-ontological notion in the sense that can be drawn from Rosenzweig and de Certeau, it is also a *quasi-analytical* notion: that is, it cannot be reduced to one simple element, structure, or event. It is marked in advance by the "fatality" of a doubling or repetition that implies the inevitable — necessary — possibility of its betrayal and perversion. Not only is the "yes" strictly speaking never first — as if it were just another *primum intelligibile* or *principium* — it also calls for another "yes." Being a promise, no affirmation can stand alone: at least one more "yes" must come to remember and reconfirm it. This reiteration brings with it an inescapable menace or risk. In consequence, the fabulous "yes" is contaminated a priori by the possibility of a forgetting that could also be signaled by its mere mechanical repetition or parody (*P* 649). Nothing — no good conscience, no sincere engagement, no effective political strategy — could ever claim to be able to prevent this. That disturbing circumstance ensures that no originary affirmation allows a distinction between a "space" in which

---

Ulrich Hortian, "Zeit und Geschichte bei Franz Rosenzweig und Walter Benjamin," in *Der Philosoph Franz Rosenzweig (1886–1929)*, ed. Wolfdietrich Schmied-Kowarzik (Freiburg: Karl Alber, 1988), 2:815–27.

93. See Derrida, "A Number of Yes," 130; *P* 648. Another reference to the "originary word [*Urwort*]" in Rosenzweig and the cited passage from the *Star of Redemption* can be found in Derrida, *Ulysse gramophone*, 122 n.: "A wordless *yes* could thus not be an 'originary word,' an arche-word (*Urwort*). Nonetheless, it resembles it, and that is the whole enigma, as one can resemble God [*comme on peut ressembler à Dieu*]. And it is true that the *yes* of which, for example, Rosenzweig speaks has the originarity of an *Urwort* only to the extent that it is a silent word, mute, a sort of transcendental of language [*une sorte de transcendental du langage*], before and beyond every affirmative proposition. It is the *yes* of God [*de Dieu*], the *yes* in God [*en Dieu*]" (my translation). This added note is missing from the translation "Hear Say Yes in Joyce," in *Acts of Literature*, ed. Derek Attridge, 256–309, cf. 296.

the "yes, yes" echoes a *divine* voice or force, and a *Nietzschean* one in which this "yes" is parodied (*MF* 176 / 241).

Does de Certeau suggest anything otherwise when he asks: "Is that space divine or Nietzschean?" (*MF* 175 / 240). Is it not revealing that he leaves this question unanswered? He insists that all mystic speech has, for essential reasons, to remain a celebration of "madness": "a spiritual practice of 'the diabolical'" (*MF* 176 / 242). Not unlike Derrida, in his analysis of the concept (and the condition of the possibility) of "prayer" in "How to Avoid Speaking," de Certeau makes clear that the *volo*, even though it inaugurates an "ethical" moment and thus opposes language's inevitable insincerity, cannot and indeed must not once and for all undo its capacity to lie. On the contrary:

> "Angelic" intervention does not win out over lies. It does not succeed in forcing them to retreat. Paradoxically, the intervention generalizes lying, as if, from an accidental illness, the lie were to become a structure of language. The *volo* does not, like the Cartesian *cogito*, initiate a field for clear and distinct propositions to which a truth value might be assigned. Far from making up a field of its own, it brings about a general metaphorization of language in the name of something that does not arise from language and that leaves its mark there. Instead of supposing that *there are lies somewhere*, and that by tracking them down and dislodging them a truth (and an innocence?) of language can be restored, the mystic preliminary [*préalable*] posits an act that leads to the use of *all language as fallacious*. Taking the *volo* as one's point of departure, all statements "lie" in relation to what is said in saying [*le dire*]. If there is understanding between speakers, it is not, then, based on an accepted truth but on a way of acting or speaking that uses language as an endless betrayal of the intention. (*MF* 176 / 241)

The distinction between the Nietzschean and the divine spaces must therefore remain uncertain or undecidable. For similar reasons Derrida may ask whether Rosenzweig "still speaks as a Jew, or as the already over-Christianized Jew he has been accused of being, when he calls upon us to heed the originary *yes* in certain texts whose status remains by nature uncertain, texts which waver—like everything saying (the) *yes*—the theological, the philosophical (transcendental or ontological) and the song of praise or the hymn."[94] This indecision may be less an accidental—that is, biographical or psychological—trait than a structural uncertainty. In

94. Derrida, "A Number of Yes," 124–25; *P* 643.

order for any alliance, engagement, or faith to become what it is, it is necessary for the first "yes" to be erased and reiterated in a second "yes" that is more than a merely natural, logical, or programmed effect of the first. This forgetfulness and betrayal are "the condition itself of fidelity," for only thanks to this "danger" (*P* 649) can the second "yes" claim to have made a genuine step beyond the first and thereby, in its turn, be a new, unique, and, in that sense, "first" affirmation.

Could the reading of this singular logic of affirmation, which is also a logic of iterability, be of help in understanding some of Benjamin's most enigmatic phrases, for example, the intriguing passage in which "God" is identified as both the origin and the addressee of the essence of human language as it reveals itself in the name? Is this what Benjamin "intended" or "had in mind"? Is it how we should read him in order to "make sense" of his often puzzling formulations? Can these two questions ever be rigorously separated? Can the quasi-transcendental interpretation of de Certeau and Rosenzweig shed light on the dilemma that from the very beginning has paralyzed the reception of Benjamin's work: the question of whether his thought should be regarded as an exercise in Jewish philosophy—as the reinterpretation of traditional religious notions in light of a distinctively modern experience—or, on the contrary, as a progressive evolution toward a historical materialism in which the messianic motifs are transfigured into mere tropes of a disruptive moment?[95] Nowhere has

95. At one point de Certeau mentions Benjamin and refers, in the context of an excursion on angels, to the short text entitled "Agesilaus Santander" (written in 1933; in *GS* 2:712–15 / 6:20–23; see *MF* 230 / 315). But the parallel remains to be calculated.

Theodor W. Adorno, one of the first and most perceptive readers of Benjamin, would have denied the parallel between Benjamin's notion of "theology" and the *Urja* in Rosenzweig. In an unpublished letter of March 8, 1955, to Dr. Achim von Borries (at that time a student in Zürich), Adorno, asked to support a reedition of the *Der Stern der Erlösung* and provoked to comment on the possible resonances between Rosenzweig's work and Benjamin's *Ursprung des deutschen Trauerspiels*, responded as follows (I cite the crucial passage from the letter, which Dr. von Borries was kind enough to send me in 1986): "R. belongs at the other side and remained his whole life something of a Jewish consistorial deacon. Between the climate of his book and that of Benjamin's lies, therefore, the abyss which separates conformity from a genuinely radical thought, and this is by no means just a matter of political temperament but relates to the heart of metaphysics itself. [*R. gehört auf die andere Seite und hat sein ganzes Leben lang etwas vom jüdischen Konsistorialrat behalten. Zwischen dem Klima seines Buches und dem Benjamins liegt eben doch der Abgrund, der den Konformismus von einem wirklich radikalen Denken trennt, und das ist keineswegs eine Sache der blossen politischen Gesinnung, sondern bezieht sich auf das Innerste der Metaphysik selber.*]" With this lapidary characterization, presented in his familiar apodictic manner, Adorno, far from denying the obvious metaphysical and "theological" or Jewish moments in Benjamin's work, confidently restores the line of demarcation between what would seem to be two distinct uses of tradition: its appropriation and prolonga-

this debate in Benjamin scholarship adequately registered that the very distinction between a "serious" adoption of a theological vocabulary and its "mere citation" or "allegorization" cannot be sustained. Here Derrida's analysis of the mystical postulate in de Certeau, as well as his demonstration of the impossibility of establishing a rigorous distinction between the theological and the non- (or a-) theological might enable us to find a way out of this last, and most persistent, binary opposition.[96]

---

tion in conformity to preexisting codes of interpretation versus its radical rethinking, reversal, or inversion—i.e., profanation—in light of new, incommensurable constellations of modern experience. Benjamin's work, Adorno notes elsewhere, would save theology by radically secularizing it (Theodor W. Adorno, "Säkularisierung der Theologie um ihrer Rettung willen," in *Über Walter Benjamin*, ed. R. Tiedemann [Frankfurt a. M.: Suhrkamp, 1970], 41). This transformation would primarily serve a critical objective: "His essayism is the treatment of profane texts as if they were holy. By no means has he clung to theological relicts or, like the religious socialists, linked up the profane realm [*Profanität*] with a religious meaning [*Sinn*]. Rather, he expected only from the radical, unprotected [*schutzlosen*] profanation [*Profanisierung*] a chance for the theological legacy that disappears [and wastes itself, *sich verschwendet*] in it." Benjamin's work thus places theological figures in a new configuration, in which their semantic intent or content is suspended or bracketed. In the same vein, Scholem associates Benjamin's (later) work with "a materialist theory of revelation . . . whose object no longer forms part of the theory" (Scholem, *Judaica* [Frankfurt a. M.: Suhrkamp, 1963], 2:222; see idem, *On Jews and Judaism in Crisis: Selected Essays*, ed. Werner J. Dannhauser [New York: Schocken Books, 1976], 172–97). Adorno implies that Rosenzweig's "new thought" ("Das neue Denken" is the title of one of Rosenzweig's most important essays) is nothing but a "clerical" attempt to reconcile an ideal—supposedly ahistorical—paradigm (Judaism) with its imperfect, empirical realization (in the history of the missionary Christian church). A more careful reading of the *Stern*, which cannot be attempted here, would find that things are more complicated. Rosenzweig considered his book less a Jewish or religious book than a "system of philosophy," which should be distinguished from what was understood under the term "philosophy of religion [*Religionsphilosophie*]." For the most detailed account of these questions to date, see Stéphane Mosès, *Système et Révélation: La Philosophie de Franz Rosenzweig*, with a preface by Emmanuel Levinas (Paris: Seuil, 1982).

96. Not only are different conceptions of Enlightenment ultimately dependent upon an irreducibly finite structural *infinity*, which manifests itself in incomparable, perhaps incommensurable, ways, but at times the discourse on formal (or procedural) rationality seems to be brought back to, or at least confronted with, a pure attentiveness irreducible to any of its categories, precisely because the latter are always already traversed and unsettled by *Aufmerksamkeit*. Rainer Nägele analyses this logic of disturbance by recalling Walter Benjamin's citation from Malebranche, according to whom this attentiveness would be the "natural prayer of the soul." This citation and the context in which it occurs—a reading of Kafka's "dialectical *Aufklärung*"—subvert, Nägele suggests, the demarcations ascribed to modern Enlightenment, such as the *Gattungsunterschied* between philosophy and literature, the borderlines drawn between the West and the East, and the demarcation of the latter two, on the one hand, and the tradition of Haggadah and Halacha, on the other. The result of this subversion is not postmodern anarchy, but the exploration of another *Aufmerksamkeit*, one no longer intimidated by the modern opposition of seriousness to play (or *Witz*), of the profane (or the natural) to the theological. This *Aufmerksamkeit* is intimately connected with a turn to writing, more precisely, to the

To further explore this possibility, I will turn to two mystic "fables" that Derrida discusses, in an attempt to exemplify the singular performativity of the postulate of originary affirmation via his reading of Benjamin's early thoughts on language in "Des tours de Babel" and of Benjamin's "Critique of Violence" in "Force of Law: the 'Mystical Foundation of Authority.'" These texts reveal just how questionable is the basic assumption underlying the dilemma of distinguishing the theological from the nontheological, as well as the debate it has provoked.

"In the Beginning—No Beginning": The Originary Catastrophe and the Gift of Language

In "On Language as Such and on the Language of Man," written in 1916, two years before Rosenzweig's *Star of Redemption* and in response to his discussions with Scholem, Benjamin develops his ideas via an exegesis—"with intrinsic reference to Judaism [*in immanenter Beziehung auf das Judentum*]"[97]—of the first chapters of Genesis. It is here in particular, he suggests, that we find an expression of the essence of language, the idea of a prelapsarian divine language, with its human reflex in the proper name, and the paradigm of the "fall" from this originary language into a conventional means of "communication," as narrated by the story about the original sin and the expulsion from Paradise, which is amplified by the episode concerning the failed project of building the tower of Babel and the confusion of tongues that ensued (in Paradise, of course, there was only one language) (*GS* 70–71 / II.1, 152). His reading is less a contribution to Bible scholarship in any linguistic or historicist sense than an attempt to formulate the prolegomena to any future metaphysics that aspires to capture the "essence" of language, and he leaves no doubt that such a metaphysics could only be established in close cooperation (or connection, *innigste Verbindung*) with inquiries commonly attributed to the philosophy of religion (*Religionsphilosophie; GS* 66 / II.1, 146).

Benjamin focuses on a second strain in the biblical creation story (Genesis 2:19–20) where attention is centered, not on the creation ex nihilo of all things through the divine Word (as in Genesis 1), but on the

reading or decipherment of a convoluted *Schrift*. See Rainer Nägele, "Die Aufmerksamkeit des Lesers: Aufklärung und Moderne," in *Enlightenments: Encounters between Critical Theory and Contemporary French Thought*, ed. Harry Kunneman and Hent de Vries (Kampen: Kok Pharos, 1993); and idem, *Theater, Theory, Speculation: Walter Benjamin and the Scenes of Modernity* (Baltimore: Johns Hopkins University Press, 1991), notably chap. 8, "Tropes of Theology."

97. Benjamin, *Correspondence*, 81 / 128.

origin of human history in a paradisiacal situation. Here it is related that all living creatures were made from the material of the earth and that the gift (*Gabe, GS* 68 / II.1, 148) of language elevated man over the rest of (a mute) nature. In Adam's giving of names, the divine creation completes (*vollendet, GS* 65 / II.1, 144), supplements, and redeems itself.[98] This passage in Genesis, Benjamin infers, demonstrates that every genuine "metaphysics" of language must begin by postulating that language is ultimately an inexplicable and mystical reality, a reality that cannot be seen or described in and for itself but only in (or through) the detours of its unfolding (*GS* 67 / II.1, 147). In the giving of names and in the necessary translation of one language into others (*GS* 69-70 / II.1, 15), language comes into its own. The essence of language has no human addressee, no object, and no means. In it, in the name, the spiritual essence of man addresses itself to God, thereby dividing and diffusing itself and its indeterminate referent, God (*"in the name, the spiritual being of man communicates itself to God* [im Namen teilt das geistige Wesen des Menschen sich Gott mit]"; *GS* 65 / II.1, 144, trans. modified).

Benjamin sets this metaphysics apart from two alternative theories of language. He is quick to criticize a naive "mystical" (*GS* 69 / II.1, 150) theory of language, according to which the word is identical with the essence of the thing. Originally, the thing has neither word nor name. Its mute, nameless language is at best a "residue" (*Residuum; GS* 74 / II.1, 157) of the divine word through which it has been created. It has to wait for the "higher" human language to be named and redeemed, not in one "spontaneous" act, but in an infinitely differentiated process of translation and elevation whose movement finds its ultimate destination as well as its "unity" (*Einheit;* ibid.) and "objective guarantee" (cf. *GS* 70 / II.1, 151) in God himself. Benjamin indirectly concedes that this translation hardly takes place in a homogeneous and continuous space. If, as he notes, the things of nature "have no proper names, except in God" (*GS* 73 / I.1, 155),

---

98. *GS* 72 / II.1, 155: "Speechlessness: that is the great sorrow of nature (and for the sake of her redemption the life and language of *man* . . . are in nature)." It is no accident that the "Erkenntniskritische Vorrede" ("Epistemo-Critical Prologue") to the *Ursprung des deutschen Trauerspiels* published in 1928, calls Adam, not Plato, the father of philosophy (*GS* I.1, 217; *The Origin of the German Tragic Drama,* trans. John Osborne [London: Verso, 1994], 37). On Benjamin's philosophy of language, see Michael W. Jennings, *Dialectical Images: Walter Benjamin's Theory of Literary Criticism* (Ithaca: Cornell University Press, 1987), 92 ff.; Michael Bröcker, "Sprache," in *Benjamins Begriffe,* ed. Michael Opitz and Erdmut Wizisla (Frankfurt a. M.: Suhrkamp, 2000), 2:740-73; and Astrid Deuber-Mankowsky, *Der frühe Walter Benjamin und Hermann Cohen: Jüdische Werte, Kritische Philosophie, vergängliche Erfahrung* (Berlin: Vorwerk 8, 2000).

then in the language of man it is difficult to see how a genuine restitution of the relationship between word, name, and thing can be more than a regulative idea. This ultimate discrepancy between the divine word and human language is there from the very beginning, when the latter is said to be a reflection (*Reflex; GS* 68 / II.1, 149) of the former. The diversification or multiplication of human languages is characterized by an infinity that, in comparison to the absolute and creative force of the divine word, remains always "limited" and divisible or "analytic" (ibid.). At the point where human language, in its deepest image (*tiefste Abbild*), participates most intensely in the infinity of the divine word—to wit, in the (human) proper name—it allows no knowledge.

Although the discrepancy between the divine and the human word is thus given with the event of appellative language as such, Benjamin seeks to illustrate this difference by relating it to a postulated, fictive, or fabulous turning point in the genesis of all things: to the moment of original sin, which he identifies with the emergence and fall of the human word ("the Fall [*Sündenfall*] marks the time of birth [*Geburtsstunde*] of the *human word*"; *GS* 71 / II.1, 153, trans. modified), that is, with a seemingly irreversible process in which language becomes a mere means (*Mittel*) and in which the word and the name thus degenerate into mediatory signs (*Zeichen*). Here, in the original catastrophe of language, we find the roots of the second, "bourgeois" theory of language, which Benjamin explicitly condemns: the theory that language communicates a semantic content separable or even distinguishable from the communicability of language as such. This decisive event is the mythical origin of law and right, including all judgment (*Urteil*), together with conceptual "abstraction [*Abstraktion*]" (*GS* 71–72 / II.1, 153–54). From here, Benjamin infers, it will be just a step (*nur noch ein Schritt; GS* 72 / II.1, 154) to the plurality of tongues. As the linguistic and collective repetition of the first, moral and individual Fall, which inaugurated an originary and universal debt, the episode of Babel—the postlapsarian lapsus into a plurality of tongues—further amplifies the ruin of the Adamic language that marks the fall *into* history (rather than any catastrophe *in* history).[99]

99. Stéphane Mosès argues that the idea of a mythic fall of language does not have a parallel in Rosenzweig's *Stern*. Unlike Benjamin, Rosenzweig would not identify the notion of revelation (*Offenbarung*) with the originary language before its perversion into a means of communication. On the contrary, for Rosenzweig communication and dialogue would be the actual form of the revelation, i.e., the opening up of the pagan self (Moses, "Benjamin und Rosenzweig," 629, 634). For a further discussion, see Martin Jay, "Politics of Translation: Siegfried

This fall of human language into history is a departure from the "pure" and "immanent" "magic" (*GS* 71 / II.1, 153) of the name: it is the emergence of a general use of language in which the name can no longer live without being affected or hurt. This occurs when language begins to communicate something (*etwas*) outside of itself. That is the moment prefigured by the Fall. The original dispersion within (as well as between) language(s) thus touches upon a moral paradox, for, Benjamin stresses, the knowledge of good and evil promised by the snake is "nameless [*namenlos*]" and thereby null and vain (*nichtig; GS* 71 / II.1, 152). In a sense, this knowledge is the only evil that existed in Paradise. Not illegitimate usurpation of a divine prerogative — the knowledge of good and evil — causes Adam's fall, but rather the quest(ion) of this knowledge itself. Unlike the purity and adequacy of the immanent "magic" that characterizes the language of names in Paradise, the knowledge attributed to the tree of life is *external*. It is not the creative prolongation of creation enacted in the pure giving of names, but the mere imitation (*Nachahmung; GS* 71 / II.1, 153) of the "actuality" (*Aktualität; GS* 68 / II.1, 149) of the divine word. The language of names thus loses itself in a necessary repetition — and translation — of a divine force in which it finds its origin and to which it aspires.

In "The Task of the Translator," Benjamin starts out from the premises of this early metaphysics of language. There he stresses that language's invisible unity or ground can be restored only because each language intends a pure essence that none of them is capable of expressing all by itself (that "this one thing is achievable not by any single language but only by the totality of their intentions supplementing one another: the pure language"; *GS* 257 / IV.1, 13). Paradoxically, then, this translation demanded by and aspiring to the "pure language," insofar as it is a process of redemptive integration and return to the origin, can only be a movement of self-effacement: "In this pure language — which no longer means or expresses anything but is, as expressionless and creative Word, that which is meant in all languages — all information [*Mitteilung*], all sense [*Sinn*], and all intention [*Intention*] finally encounter a stratum in which they are destined to be extinguished [*erlöschen*]" (*GS* 261, cf. 258–60 / IV.1, 19, cf. 15–16).

More than merely contrasting the promised "pure speech" (see Zephaniah 3:9) or the "gift of tongues" (Acts 2:4) or diabolically parodying

Kracauer and Walter Benjamin on the Buber-Rosenzweig Bible," in *Permanent Exiles: Essays on the Intellectual Migration from Germany to America* (New York: Columbia University Press, 1985).

the temple situated on a hill (Jerusalem) that touches the heavens,[100] the
story of the tower of Babel narrated in Genesis 11:1–9 exemplifies here the
structural, internal limits of all translation. By relating how the "sons of
men"—or is it the sons of Shem, literally, the "names," as Derrida suggests, relying on the genealogical references in Genesis 10:31 and 11:10 that
frame the story (as well as on André Chouraqui's translation of it)?[101]—
attempted to give or make themselves a name, *one* name (one tongue, one
speech), lest they be "scattered abroad upon the face of the whole earth"
(Genesis 11:4), the fable of Babel would be "an epigraph for all discussions of translation."[102] *Babel* is the Hebrew for *Babylon,* which renders
the Akkadian *Babilium* or *Babilim* and was interpreted by the Babylonians
as "the gate of God" (recalling the pyramidal temple tower of the ziggu-
rat, which represented the symbolic power of Mesopotamia, and whose
top was seen as a gateway to heaven: in Cuneiform sources, *bâb-ilim,* the
"gate of the deity"). The biblical story that undermines this etymology by
replacing it with another one, relating *Babel* to the Hebrew verb *bâlal,* "to
confuse,"[103] narrates how the sons of men tried to manifest themselves—
imposing themselves on others, Derrida assumes—by universalizing their
idiom and how, finally, this endeavor was baffled—obstructed, or decon-

100. Cf. Northrop Frye, *The Great Code: The Bible and Literature* (San Diego: Harcourt
Brace Jovanovich, 1983), 158, 230.

101. *La Bible,* trans. André Chouraqui (Paris: Desclée de Brouwer, 1989), 33. See, for the
following, Jacques Derrida, "Des tours de Babel," in *P* 203–35 / trans. Joseph F. Graham, in *Difference in Translation,* ed. Joseph F. Graham (Ithaca: Cornell University Press, 1985), 165–248;
and Jacques Derrida, "Théologie de la traduction," in *DP* 371–94.

102. Jacques Derrida, *L'Oreille de l'autre: Otobiographies, transferts, traductions,* ed. Claude
Lévesque and Christie V. McDonald (Montréal: VLB, 1982), 134 / *The Ear of the Other: Oto-
biography, Transference, Translation,* ed. Christie V. McDonald, trans. Avital Ronell and Peggy
Kamuf (New York: Schocken Books, 1985), 100. As an "epigraph for all discussions of transla-
tion," the name *Babel* punctuates the text of Antoine Berman, *L'Épreuve de l'étranger: Culture et
traduction dans l'Allemagne romantique* (Paris: Gallimard, 1984) / *The Experience of the Foreign:
Culture and Translation in Romantic Germany,* trans. S. Heyvaert (Albany: State University of
New York Press, 1992). See also George Steiner, *After Babel: Aspects of Language and Translation*
(Oxford: Oxford University Press, 1975). Furthermore, in the study of visual culture, the motif
of Babel (as well as Derrida's reading of it) figures centrally in Miriam Hansen, *Babel and Baby-
lon: Spectatorship in American Silent Film* (Cambridge: Harvard University Press, 1991), esp. 184
ff. Yet another example is the debate in moral philosophy: see Jeffrey Stout, *Ethics after Babel:
The Languages of Morals and Their Discontents* (Boston: Beacon, 1988); and Pascal Bruckner,
La Vertige de Babel: Cosmopolitisme ou mondialisme (Paris: Arléa, 2000).

103. See the lemmata Babel, Babylonia, and *balal* in *Der kleine Pauly: Lexikon der Antike,*
vol. 1, Wilhelm Gesenius, *Hebräisches und Aramäisches Handwörterbuch über das Alte Testament* (Berlin: Springer, 1962), and Bruce M. Metzger and Michael D. Coogan, eds., *The Oxford
Companion to the Bible* (New York: Oxford University Press, 1993).

structed—by God himself. What remains is Babel, Bavel, Ba'bel, Ba Bel, Babble:

> And the Lord came down to see the city and the tower, which the sons of men had built. And the Lord said, "Behold, they are one people, and they have all one language; and this is only the beginning of what they will do; nothing that they propose to do will now be impossible for them. Come, let us go down, and there confuse their language, that they may not understand one another's speech." So the Lord scattered them abroad from there over the face of all the earth, and they left off building the city. Therefore its name was called Ba'bel, because there the Lord confused the language of all the earth. (Genesis 11:5–9, Revised Standard version)

Derrida suggests that God opposes *his* name—his untranslatable proper name—to that of the Shem and *thereby* enforces upon them the irrevocable multiplicity of languages. God, Adonai, indeed YHWH, is on his reading both a proper name and the index—the name—for the untranslatability of every proper name. With the confusion of tongues—and "confusion" is the signification that resonates in the name of the tower chosen by God, *Babel*, which Voltaire, in the *Dictionnaire philosophique* cited by Derrida, associates with "father" (*Ba*) and "God" (*Bel*)[104]—God destines the sons of men (the Shem, the names?) to master an irredeemable "destinerrance," "clandestination," or "desschemitization,"[105] neologisms that evoke the erring as well as the relative illegitimacy of their intended address and—in the case of "desschemitization"—not only this dissemination but also a "deschematization," "de-Shemitizing," and "derouting" from the path (*chemin*) taken.[106]

The Babelian multiplicity within language, the difference between different languages or dialects, is preceded and predetermined by a division and migration of language within one language and even within a single word, for example, a proper name or a poetic inscription.[107] Thus, when

104. Voltaire writes: "I don't know why it is said in *Genesis* that Babel means confusion; for *Ba* means father in the oriental languages, and *Bel* means god; Babel means the city of god, the holy city. The ancients gave this name to all their capitals" (Voltaire, "Babel," in *Philosophical Dictionary*, ed. and trans. Theodore Besterman [London: Routledge, 1972], 59).

105. Cf. Rosenzweig, *Der Stern der Erlösung*, 328: "Dass die Welt unerlöst ist, nichts lehrt es deutlicher als die Vielzahl der Sprachen."

106. See *P* 137 and the translator's note in *The Ear of the Other*, 103.

107. Cf. Jacques Derrida, *Schibboleth—pour Paul Celan* (Paris: Galilée, 1986), 52, 54 / "Shibboleth: For Paul Celan," trans. Joshua Wilner, in *Word Traces: Readings of Paul Celan*, ed. Aris Fioretos (Baltimore: Johns Hopkins University Press, 1994), 3–72, 29–31. Derrida here cites the

God is said to declare war on the "names," the very pronunciation of the proper name par excellence ("God," "I am who I am"), is from its very first revelation part of—and partitioned by—an economy of violence. God himself is divided by the division, the double bind, the deconstruction and dissemination that his name ordains (*P* 137).

To clarify, Derrida refers in *The Post Card, The Ear of the Other,* and *Ulysses Gramophone* to a Babelian motif that runs through James Joyce's *Finnegans Wake,* the greatest challenge to all translation: the idiomatic expression "And he war,"[108] which, because it condenses an irreducible linguistic duplicity of the English and German connotations of the word *war* evokes not only the *polemos* but also the irrecuperable temporality of the past.

Like the originary affirmation discussed above, the figure, myth or allegory of Babel, as examined by Derrida in "Des tours de Babel," is doubled or, rather, pluralized to the point of no return. He reads the story of Babel as a parable of the deconstruction of all linguistic, conceptual, or historico-political edifices, a deconstruction that, as his very title ("Des tours . . .") suggests, can only be narrated in endless "detours." Moreover, the name *Babel* indicates the modality of giving—of language, of being—as such: "There is," Derrida writes, "Babel everywhere";[109] there is—*es gibt*—Babel at any given moment, at any moment that gives rise to something determinate like a structure, an edifice, and also its deconstruc-

---

concluding lines of Celan's "Hinausgekrönt," from *Die Niemandsrose:* "And an earth rises up, ours, / this one. / And we'll send / none of our people down / to you, / Babel. [*Und es steigt eine Erde herauf, die unsere, / diese. / Und wir schicken / keinen der Unsern hinunter / zu dir, / Babel*]." See Paul Celan, *Gesammelte Werke,* ed. Beda Alleman and Stefan Reichert, in collaboration with Rolf Bücher (Frankfurt a. M.: Suhrkamp, 1983), 1:272 / *The Poems of Paul Celan,* trans. Michael Hamburger (New York: Persea Books, 1989), 211. Likewise, Franz Kafka writes: "Wir graben den Schacht von Babel. . . . Wenn es erlaubt gewesen wäre, den Turm von Babel zu erbauen, ohne ihn zu erklettern, es wäre erlaubt gewesen."

108. "And shall not Babel be with Lebab? And he war" (James Joyce, *Finnegans Wake* [Harmondsworth, Middlesex: Penguin, 1976; orig. pub. 1939], 258.11–12). For a subtle commentary on Derrida's reading, see Garrett Stewart, *Reading Voices: Literature and the Phonotext* (Berkeley: University of California Press, 1990), 244–49.

109. Derrida, *The Ear of the Other,* 149 / 196. See also Derrida, *D'un ton apocalyptique adopté naguère en philosophie* (Paris: Galilée, 1981), 10, cf. 71 / "On a Newly Arisen Apocalyptic Tone in Philosophy," trans. John P. Leavey Jr., in *Raising the Tone of Philosophy: Late Essays by Immanuel Kant, Transformative Critique by Jacques Derrida,* ed. Peter Fenves (Baltimore: Johns Hopkins University Press, 1993), 117, cf. 163.

That the figure of Babel is linked with an experience of—apparent—ontological infinitization is also clear from Jorge Luis Borges's famous story "The Library of Babel," in *Collected Fictions,* trans. Andrew Hurley (New York: Viking, 1998).

tion. Although Benjamin's "On Language as Such and on the Language of Man" explicitly speaks of Babel as well as the gift of language that it entails, Derrida focuses on "the task of the translator" to explore this motif of the "there is" (*il y a, es gibt*) of language as it pervades Benjamin's understanding of the impossible task (*Aufgabe*) and the "double postulation" of translation.

The task of the work of reconciliation and restitution of the essence of language is said to respond to a debt that, Derrida notes, can never be acquitted (*P* 211) and imposes the double bind of a law that both commands and interdicts translation and that therefore remains unfulfillable (*P* 210). This structural inadequation between different genres of discourse or even within a single discourse explains why figures, myths, and metaphors are necessary. Babel is the myth of the myth, the metaphor of the metaphor (*P* 203).

Babel thus stands for the paradoxical logic of iterability, of the incessant movement of repetition and alteration that marks all linguistic utterance: in short, of the "generalized singularity"[110] of all language and experience. Referring to Matthew Arnold's *Culture and Anarchy*, Derrida recalls the primal—"Babelian"—scene as being that of an ab-solute performative gesture, a "Get *Geist*," that is, as the most characteristic trait of the spirit that, because of the fact that it is irreducible to any constative and unforeseen by any history, remains without a proper beginning and marks itself at most by an invisible, incomparable "step" (or *pas*): "In the beginning—no [or: a step of a] beginning [*Au commencement—pas de commencement*]."[111] This is what Benjamin's metaphysics of language, in spite of its anti-Babelian stance, gives us to think: language's essence consists in the communication of communication, in the giving of the sign, rather than in any function of signification. This feature of language, as well as the task of translation it determines or prescribes, "opens," in Derrida's view, the way to the "performative dimension of utterances,"[112] before any explicit discussion of "speech acts."

Yet Derrida also takes an anti-Babelian stance. Not only does the no-

110. Derrida, *The Ear of the Other*, 104 / 138.

111. Derrida, *Of Spirit*, 126–27 n. 8 / 116 n.

112. *P* 215. On this singular displacement of the notion of the performative, see also Werner Hamacher's incisive analysis of the "imperformative" and "afformative" in "Afformativ, Streik: Entsetzung der Repräsentation in Benjamin's 'Zur Kritik der Gewalt,'" in *Was heisst darstellen?*, ed. C. Hart-Nibbrig (Frankfurt a. M.: Suhrkamp, 1991) / "Afformative, Strike: Benjamin's 'Critique of Violence,'" trans. Dana Hollander, in *Walter Benjamin's Philosophy: Destruction and Experience*, ed. Andrew Benjamin and Peter Osborne (London: Routledge, 1994).

tion of a "revelatory catastrophe" that is the unthinkable "condition for everything" — an originary being "lost" that is the consequence of an "initial disaster," "right near the beginning"[113] — play an important role in *The Post Card*, but the letters that comprise the first part of this text, entitled "Envois," set the scene for the "Babelization"[114] of the postal service and also testify to an ineradicable desire of the author of the sendings finally to overcome the distance between addressor and addressee and thus "to erase all the traits of language, coming back to the most simple."[115] Only between these two limits can a quasi-apocalyptic displacement of the structure of linguistic communication be advanced: "We are not angels, my angel, I mean messengers of whatever, but more and more angelic."[116]

The way in which this fall and this desire are thematized reveals some striking differences from Benjamin's metaphysics of language, however. First, the original language of which Derrida speaks was, more explicitly than Benjamin suggests, never there; it never existed in its purported purity, not even as an idea, not even as a postulate. Derrida leaves no doubt that there cannot be one unique, secret, or sacred — divine — name or language of names. The relation to God is at least triple, if not trinitary, that is to say, it is marked from the very outset by an *à dieu*, an *adieu*, and an *a-dieu*. If there were a single, singular name, exempt from the differential realm of language and experience, then this name would name nothing and nobody; it would not be a name, properly speaking, but an "absolute vocative,"[117] that is, a pure performative, which, precisely because of its purity, would perform nothing.

This being said, Derrida leaves no doubt that certain aspects of Benjamin's text could make one "uncomfortable," especially those that relate to the sacredness of the text and the messianic dimension of all translation. The sacred text seems to be the virtual original that one always has to postulate while translating. This original reminds one of what has remained untranslated and of what will remain untranslatable in the future.

113. Derrida, *La Carte postale: De Socrate à Freud et au-déla* (Paris: Flammarion, 1980), 16 and 23, cf., for the motif of Babel, 13, 154, 155, 179 / *The Post Card: From Socrates to Freud and Beyond*, trans. Alan Bass (Chicago: University of Chicago Press, 1987), 12 and 19, cf. for Babel 9, 142, 165.

114. Derrida, *Ulysse gramophone*, 62, cf. 66–67, 77–78.

115. Derrida, *The Post Card*, 114 / 125.

116. Ibid., 43 / 50.

117. See Geoffrey Bennington, "Derridabase," in Geoffrey Bennington and Jacques Derrida, *Jacques Derrida* (Paris: Éditions de Seuil, 1991), 102 / (Chicago: University of Chicago Press, 1993), 105.

The sacred thus takes on the meaning of an untranslatable rest, a proper name, an idiom, a certain literary or poetic remainder that does not let itself be translated in any common discourse or into discourse as such.[118] Yet precisely this absolute idiom calls, as it were, the secret name—our secret name—to which we respond, involuntarily, before and beyond any decision.[119]

In an even more radical sense than that of Benjamin, the translation that follows in the wake of Babel, as Derrida reads it, is not secondary to or derived from any originary language. In his view, its task is without any identifiable beginning, end, or "exit."[120] If a concise definition of deconstruction were possible, it would therefore contain at least this: the affirmation that there is always already *"plus d'une langue—*more than one language, no more of one language,"[121] not even the language of names— the affirmation, that is, that the pure essence of language (Benjamin's *reine Sprache*) is in itself, in its very idea, in advance, multiple ("more than one language, no more of one language").

"In the Beginning There Will Have Been Force": The Mystical Postulate, Justice, and the Law

Derrida's analysis of Benjamin's "Critique of Violence," in "Force of Law: The 'Mystical Foundation of Authority,'" politicizes his earlier readings by inscribing, by translating, their reflection on language into a more specific inquiry into the nature—that is, the foundation, conservation, and "destruction"—of the historico-juridical realm. This discussion is framed in a lecture first delivered at the October 1989 colloquium "Deconstruction and the Possibility of Justice," then reiterated at the April 1990 colloquium "Nazism and the 'Final Solution': Probing the Limits of Representation." These outward circumstances are essential to the internal structure of Derrida's Benjamin interpretation, which remains incomprehensible if one does not take into account Derrida's explicitly stated interest in the fact that Benjamin "is considered and considered himself to be, in a certain fashion, Jewish" (FL 973 n.). In "Force of Law" Derrida sets out to decipher the "enigma" of this "signature," especially in the second part of the lecture, which concerns "Critique of Violence" directly.

118. Derrida, *The Ear of the Other,* 148 / 195–96.
119. Ibid., 106–7.
120. Derrida, "On a Newly Arisen Apocalyptic Tone," 117, 125 / 9–10, 18.
121. Cf. J. Derrida, *Mémoires for Paul de Man,* 14–15, cited in *A Derrida Reader: Between the Blinds,* ed. Peggy Kamuf (New York: Columbia University Press, 1991), 241.

More than an analysis of the paradoxes of the proper name (to which I will return at the end of this chapter) is at stake here.

In particular, Derrida suggests that "Critique of Violence" relates the proper name—of God and indirectly of Benjamin himself—to the general problem of the law in connection with the state, parliamentary liberal democracy, and the general proletarian strike. Its exploration of these themes is "inscribed," Derrida writes, "in a Judaic perspective that opposes just, divine (Jewish) violence that would destroy the law to mythical violence (of the Greek tradition) that would install and conserve the law" (FL 973 n.). He questions this opposition between a force that founds a juridico-political order and one that preserves it, plus the demarcation between these two and a force that finally suspends them both. Benjamin's own text, he argues, ruins these conceptual dichotomies, like those set up in the early essays on language. Thus Benjamin's critique of the violence of the law is highly ambiguous: "at once" mystical, in the "overdetermined sense" that, Derrida acknowledges, interests him here, and "hypercritical" (FL 979).[122]

Based on a philosophy of the fall of history into language—into the law —this text is marked by an "archeo-teleological, indeed archeo-eschatological perspective that deciphers the history of *droit* as a decay (*Verfall*) since its origin" (FL 1015). Yet in its very critique of this derailment (or *Verfallsprozess; GS* 245 / II.1, 192), "Critique of Violence" blurs most of the familiar distinctions, so that the reader can no longer decide whether this text expresses "neo-messianical Jewish mysticism grafted onto post-Sorelian neo-Marxism (or the reverse)" (FL 979), whether its radical critique merely mentions or also intentionally uses a vocabulary that recalls the idiom of the "conservative" revolution associated with the name of Carl Schmitt and others. Further, what would it mean to read Benjamin as the "Kierkegaard"—the most "theological"—of the "speculative materialists"?[123]

Benjamin's fascination with a pure, nonviolent force seems to echo or anticipate the preoccupation with a Being that—as such—remains

<hr/>

122. See Rodolphe Gasché, "On Critique, Hypercriticism, and Deconstruction: The Case of Benjamin," *Cardozo Law Review* 13, no. 4 (1991): 1115–32.

123. See: Klaus-M. Kodalle, "Walter Benjamins politisicher Dezisionismus im theologischen Kontext: Der 'Kierkegaard' unter den spekulativen Materialisten," in *Spiegel und Gleichnis: Festschrift für Jakob Taubes*, ed. Norbert W. Bolz and Wolfgang Hübener (Würzburg, 1983); and Horst Turk, "Politische Theologie?: Zur 'Intention auf die Sprache' bei Benjamin und Celan," in *Juden in der deutschen Literatur: Ein deutsch-israelisches Symposium*, ed. Stéphane Mosès and Albrecht Schöne (Frankfurt a. M.: Suhrkamp, 1986).

irreducible to (and, in essence, incorruptible by) the realm of empirical or ontic beings. Finally, everything appears as though the proletarian and divine violence cannot but resemble or prefigure the politically lethal "destruction" that Derrida, beginning in his earliest writings, problematizes in Heidegger's thought of Being. ("*Ousia* and *grammē*" also gives a formal scheme for deconstructing the metaphysical presuppositions that structure and limit the critical and more than simply critical — indeed, "hypercritical" — potential of Benjamin's text.) Although, Derrida acknowledges, "Heideggerian *Destruktion* cannot be confused with the concept of Destruction that was also at the center of Benjaminian thought, one may well ask oneself what such an obsessive thematic might signify and what it is preparing or anticipating between the two wars, all the more so in that, in every case, this destruction also sought to be the condition of an authentic tradition and memory, and of the reference to an originary language" (FL 977 n.).[124]

Benjamin's singular configuration of heterogeneous mystic, messianic, theological, Marxist, and reactionary tropes seems to announce "a new historical epoch," "the beginning of a true history that has been rid of myth" (FL 975). This purported end of history (at least as we know it) allows a return to the language of names and appellation that, Benjamin postulates, preceded the Fall. Like the translation that aspires to reconstitute pure language (*reine Sprache*), the destruction (*Vernichtung*) of the violence of history in general and the state in particular is identified as a singular, paradoxical task (*Aufgabe*).[125] The task of critiquing the vio-

---

124. In this text as well, Derrida hints at the analogy between the sovereignty of "divine violence" and Heidegger's understanding of *Walten* and *Gewalt*: "It is this historical network of equivocal contracts that interests me in its necessity and in its very dangers" (FL 979). The analogy is crucial, given the final words of Benjamin's essay, which read: "Divine violence . . . may be called 'sovereign' violence [*Die göttliche Gewalt . . . mag die waltende heissen*]" (GS 252 / II.1, 203). In this context, Derrida only briefly refers to Heidegger's claim that justice, for example, in Heraclitus's notion of *Dikē*, also meant *Eris*, conflict, *polemos, Kampf*, and thereby injustice, *adikia* (see FL 927). For more extensive analyses, see "L'Oreille de Heidegger," PF 341–419, 145 n. 1, 359, 360–61, and 409 ("Au commencement, il y aura eu le *polemos*, un 'waltenden Streit'") / "Heidegger's Ear," 176–79; "*Istrice 2*. *Ick bünn all hier*," in *Points de suspension: Entretiens*, ed. Elisabeth Weber (Paris: Galilée, 1992), 320 / *Points . . . : Interviews, 1974–1994*, ed. Elisabeth Weber, trans. Peggy Kamuf et al. (Stanford: Stanford University Press, 1995), 310; and Howard Caygill, "Benjamin, Heidegger, and the Destruction of Tradition," in *Walter Benjamin's Philosophy: Destruction and Experience*, ed. Andrew Benjamin and Peter Osborne (New York: Routledge, 1994).

125. Cf. GS 246, 249 / II.1, 194, 199. Benjamin also speaks of the "delicate task [*zarte Aufgabe*] . . . beyond all legal systems [*Rechtsordnung*] and therefore beyond violence [*Gewalt*]" that characterizes the secrecy and delicacy of diplomacy (GS 247 / II.1, 195).

lence of the law as well as the history it presupposes or enforces consists in nothing less than abandoning—*giving up*—the law and history as such (or at least as we know them).[126] This conviction explains Benjamin's "rejection of *every* contemporary political tendency"[127] from his early remarks on Zionism in January 1913, when, corresponding with Ludwig Strauss, he associates politics with the pursuit of the lesser evil,[128] up to the "Theological-Political Fragment" of 1921, in which the messianic, divine realm (the *Reich Gottes*) is sharply distinguished from any realization of a profane, historical, and political telos and in which, following Ernst Bloch's *Geist der Utopie* (*Spirit of Utopia*), Benjamin concludes that *theodicy* can have only a religious meaning (cf. *GS* II.1, 203).

Derrida's text centers on an analysis of the paradox or even double bind that characterizes Benjamin's conception of the *Aufgabe* of a destruction of the historico-political realm of the law. To begin with, postulating a mystical ground of authority by suggesting, as Benjamin does, that the positing of the law is in itself an unjustified—mythical—violence seems to make proposing a critique of any given law very simple. No new law can found itself by appealing to existing and generally accepted laws that precede it. In Derrida's words: "Law (*droit*) is essentially deconstructible, whether because it is founded, constructed on interpretable and transformable textual strata . . . , or because its ultimate foundation is by definition unfounded" (FL 943).

Yet this very circumstance—which is, Derrida is quick to add, a "stroke of luck for politics, for all historical progress" (FL 943–45)—explains why it is also very difficult and always, in a sense, illegitimate, if not unjust, to criticize a given imposition of the law. Since no social authority can be deduced or criticized and overturned for good reasons without leading to infinite regress or to the arbitrary violence of a certain idiolect,[129] every successful revolutionary moment, every felicitous performative act

126. Or, as the aphorism from *Zentralpark* puts it: "Die Rettung hält sich an den kleinen Sprung in der kontinuierlichen Katastrophe" (*GS* I.2, 683).

127. Benjamin, *Correspondence*, 172 / 219.

128. Cf. *GS* III.3, 842: "Im tiefsten Sinne ist Politik die Wahl des kleinsten Übels. Niemals erscheint in ihr die Idee, stets die Partei." One should, of course, not confuse this critique of a political Zionism with Benjamin's sincere interest in the task of a "Kultur-Zionismus" (ibid., 838, cf. 843), which is never an end in itself but rather the supreme bearer of the spiritual idea ("vormehmster Träger und Repräsentant des Geistigen"; ibid., 839). The early "Dialog über die Religiosität der Gegenwart" (1913) relates this task to that of the "Literaten," the "Geknechteten" of our epoch (*GS* II.1, 28).

129. See Lyotard, *The Differend*, no. 203, 142.

that founds or destructs a law will at the same time invent or institute a new law or right that—retrospectively, *après coup*, after its own *coup de force*—seeks to legitimate the violence with which a preexisting order was overcome. Therefore, the law is always already constructed: that is, it accompanies itself with a legitimating fiction or myth: for example, the claim in Hegel's *Grundlinien der Philosophie des Rechts* (*Elements of the Philosophy of Right*) that its authority is precisely *not* historically determined or constructed but eternal, absolute, and therefore divine: "It is at any rate utterly essential that the constitution should *not* be regarded as *something made*, even if it does have an origin in time. On the contrary, it is quite simply that which has being in and for itself, and should therefore be regarded as divine and enduring, and as exalted above the sphere of all manufactured things."[130] Yet this fiction or fable, Derrida contends, does not imply any relativistic or pragmatist understanding of the conventionality of the law. The singularity of this founding and conserving performance consists precisely in that it precedes and constitutes all historically and socially determined conventions.

On what grounds, then, could anyone claim to be justified in criticizing this violence of the law if, by definition, the force of its grounding and preservation not only escapes the jurisdiction of all given right but also, paradoxically, exceeds the legality that it by its own right has called into being? How could one accuse a force that founds the realm of legitimation while itself remaining without any objective legitimation? This impasse, Derrida claims, defines the perilous moment of every political earthquake as well as every genuine juridical or ethico-political judgment and decision:

> These moments, supposing that we can isolate them, are terrifying moments. Because of the sufferings . . . that rarely fail to accompany them, no doubt, but just as much because they are in themselves, and in their very violence, uninterpretable or indecipherable. That is what I am calling "mystique." . . . This moment of suspense, this *ēpokhē*, this founding or revolutionary moment of law is, in law, an instance of non-law. But it is also the whole history of law. This moment always takes place and never takes place in a presence. It is the moment in which the formation of law remains suspended in the void or over the abyss, suspended by a pure performative act that would not have to answer to or before anyone. The supposed subject of this pure performative act would . . . be before a law not yet determined. (FL 991)

130. Hegel, *Elements of the Philosophy of Right*, 312 / 239.

At this point Derrida recalls the uncanny, tragicomic scene described in Kafka's parable "Vor dem Gesetz" ("Before the Law"), in which the man from the country cannot enter the law "because it is transcendent in the very measure that it is he who must found it, as yet to come, in violence" (FL 993). The theological figure of the transcendence of the law seems to be a figure for an absolute performativity that is pure to the degree that it precedes any given context or convention and, in that sense, never really takes place, cannot be pinpointed, or never arrives at any ontotheological, topological, let alone mere empirical presence:

> Here we "touch" without touching this extraordinary paradox: the inaccessible transcendence of the law before which and "prior" to which "man" stands fast only "appears" infinitely transcendent and thus theological to the extent that, so near him, it depends only on him, on the performative act by which he institutes it: the law is transcendent, violent and non-violent because it depends only on who is before it—and so prior to it—on who produces it, founds it, authorizes it in an absolute performative whose presence always escapes him. The law is transcendent and theological, and so always to come, always promised, because it is immanent, finite and so already past. (FL 993)

Yet the founding moment is never immune to the possibility of a certain perversion and therefore never pure—that is, strictly speaking, never foundational as such. Every performative, says *The Post Card,* is in essence, in its very structure, from its earliest inception, already a perversion of itself: a "perverformative." [131] Similarly, every retrospective projection of a fictive legitimation and subsequent conservation of the law—the necessity of constantly recalling and repeating the act with which it was founded—inscribes a peculiar drift into its purported pure and single origin. For when the founding violence, as Derrida writes, "must envelop the violence of conservation . . . and cannot break with it" (FL 997)—something, as Adorno had already noted, Benjamin does not take into consideration—then the very iterability of the law excludes in advance (or a priori and of necessity) the possibility of the sudden emergence of "pure and great founders, initiators, lawmakers ('great' poets, thinkers or men of State, in the sense Heidegger will mean in 1935, following an analogous schema concerning the fatal sacrifice of these founders)" (FL 1009).

Benjamin's demarcation between, on the one hand, the founding or positing violence at the beginning of—and, subsequently, within—the

131. Derrida, *The Post Card,* 136 / 148.

cycle of mythical forms and interpretations of positive right and, on the other hand, the nonviolent violence that demises or de-posits this dialectic marking all existing sociopolitical history is untenable as it stands. Against this supposition Derrida repeats the formal structure of the argument that governs his deconstruction, in "Ousia and grammē," of Heidegger's distinction between "vulgar" time and "authentic" temporality in *Being and Time.* Because the manifestation of the violence that Benjamin describes as "ethical [*sittlich*]" is to a certain extent an extrapolation and radicalization of the genuine revolt, the real revolutionary violence of the general proletarian strike, which destructs all right, one can easily see what the consequences of this deconstruction are. Following the logic of iterability, as explained in *Limited Inc,* the mere possibility of decay and petrification, betrayal and parody that endangers every act of preservation or commemoration also implies that all law has the structure of a ruin even before it is constructed (or destructed). The same could be said of any judgment or decision. Paradoxically, only this inescapable possibility—and therefore necessity[132]—of the ruination of the law accounts for the fact that the law can make itself felt, feared, or even loved and that, consequently, an act can take place at all.

For Benjamin, however, the critique of the violent instauration and conservation of the law can be based only on the postulation of an (at least) equally violent yet incommensurate annihilation of the sphere of law. The human—and, Benjamin adds, mythic—writing and rewriting of the law can only be confronted by a (divine) unwriting, not just of this or that prescription but of the law in its very generality. This violence above and beyond the founding and conserving violence is associated by Benjamin with the power and wrath of God, with, as Derrida formulates, "a wholly other 'mystical foundation of authority'" (FL 1021–23). This nonviolent violence interrupts the representational power of language—its present state of being just a technical means to an end, a vehicle for communication and information—and thereby recalls and restores its original destination of being a *pure manifestation* of "appellation, nomination, the giving or the appeal of presence in the name" (FL 973–75 n.).

At the end of "Critique of Violence," the recourse to a nonviolent divine force thus reconfirms the privilege or, rather, inevitability of a theo-

132. Derrida's "Signature Event Context" identifies the "risk" and the "exposure to infelicity" of all speech acts as a structural feature not just of a speech act but as the "necessary possibility" and, in that sense, the "*law*" of any mark (*Limited Inc,* ed. Gerald Graff [Evanston: Northwestern University Press, 1988], 15 / 41).

logical figure that the early essay "On Language as Such and on the Language of Man" posits as the origin and essence of language. There is a correspondence between and mutual implication of the mystic abyss from which language emerges (or to which it, in the originary split or dissemination, always remains exposed) and the destinal violence through which history as violence is suspended. Derrida insists on this correlation of two virtual extremes or limits between which the drama of language and history takes place: "Who signs? It is God, the Wholly Other, as always, it is the divine violence that always will have preceded but also will have *given* all the first names" (FL 1037). God signs first and last, He opens and seals the event of language and is in that sense its alpha and omega.

This structural analogy between the event that takes place at the origin of language and what happens in the destruction of the law can also be articulated in other respects. Both violences attempt to overcome a fundamental arbitrariness or undecidability (*Unentscheidbarkeit*). Derrida points out that Benjamin establishes this analogy explicitly by comparing the impossibility of coming to a real, let alone just, decision within the order of right to the situation in which emerging human language can be nothing but a means of communication and thus an undiscriminating "prattle" (*Geschwätz*; cf. GS 72 / II.1, 154). The fact that conserving violence obliterates and perverts the mythical founding violence blurs crucial distinctions and corrupts the legitimacy or, rather, justice of decisions. The possibility of deciding resides only in the double manifestation of the divine violence that once opened the event of language and now cannot but destroy the mythological order of right that was the consequence of language's fall, thereby inaugurating a new historical epoch, an era marked by a justice (*Gerechtigkeit*) beyond the order of law and right, beyond their generality or even universality. Only the sudden, striking force of divine violence guarantees — or, perhaps, simply stands for — the "irreducible singularity of each situation" (FL 1023). Yet precisely that singularity explains why divine violence can manifest itself only in incommensurable, incomparable effects, which preclude any conceptual determination, which we can neither affirm nor deny on rational grounds, and which, for that reason, retain once more a certain undecidability.

The same paradox appears if one realizes that the pure violence of God and the violence of the general proletarian strike can never completely escape contamination from the dialectic — the rising and falling, the *Auf und Ab* (GS 251 / II.1, 202) — of the mythological foundation of right and its historical conservation. Neither divine nor proletarian violence can hope to situate itself comfortably beyond the fundamental undecidability that it—now and then, for a moment only—seems to interrupt. Neither can force a decision or enforce a judgment without, at the same time, exposing itself to a reiteration and thereby a (possible) perversion which reinscribes nonviolent violence in the order from which it appeared to break away.[133] For analogous reasons, Benjamin's distinction between different types of strikes—the partial and the general, the political and the proletarian—can only point to two limit situations that could never take place in their purity, but in their suggestive force reveal two permanent "temptations" (FL 995)[134] of all deconstruction: namely, the reformation of the existing political order into another, perhaps more just, state versus its violent (or peaceful) total destruction in a revolt more radical than any coup d'état. Neither of these strategies of (piecemeal or abrupt, limited or total) transformation and anarchic rupture can, of course, fully capture the intent, let alone the import, of "deconstructive" displacement. Yet no such deconstructive gesture can ever immunize itself against these extreme possibilities.

More than merely invoking the "generalized singularity" of all linguistic utterance and of all juridico-political intervention—"The sudden reference to God above reason and universality, beyond a sort of *Aufklärung* of law, is nothing other than a reference to the irreducible singularity of each situation" (FL 1023)—Benjamin's reference to God at the very end of his essay makes at least one of these temptations explicit. Not only is

133. In a seemingly different context, Jean-François Lyotard, as if he were providing in passing yet another reading of "Critique of Violence," insists that for essential reasons the genres neither of myth, divine right (here, *droit*), deliberative consensus, nor proletarian communism could ever hope to forge an autoreferential narration, an ultimate redemption, a free linking of heterogeneous phrases, let alone a destruction of all "genres of discourse." These different names all stand for irreconcilable ways of instituting the litigations for irresolvable differends that are given with the *Ereignis* of language as such (whether before or after the fall, whether its phrases are silent or not, human or not). Between all phrases—and no phrase is first or last— an abyss of Not-Being opens up. Yet Lyotard refuses to grant a mystical profundity to this abyss that, to give just one example, drives constatives and moral imperatives apart. If, for example, the tradition of Kabbalah can be said to do more justice to the occurrence, the happening, the taking place—the *Arrive-t-il?*—of the *Ereignis* of Being or, rather, of *There is's* than, say, mythical narratives, this is not a sufficient reason to make the dispersion to which it testifies into a new first principle. The very idea of an original or originary splitting would always already presuppose the idea of a lost totality and thereby risk the diffusion of a certain nostalgia. (Wording taken variously from *The Differend*, 141, 155, 171–72, 65–66, 128, 104–6, 79, 138, 109–10 / 204, 223–24, 246–47, 102, 187, 155–58, 120–21, 200, 162–63.) The "mystical postulate" would be less vulnerable to this possible objection in its Derridean than in its Benjaminian form.

134. Cf. FL 997.

what he writes about divine violence, as Derrida remarks, "not always incompatible with the theological basis of all jusnaturalisms" (FL 985), that is to say, of precisely the theories of law that he had earlier dismissed as dogmatic, but in its very "critique of Aufklärung" in the name of a purported originary or ultimate authenticity, in its reliance on a theory of the fall of language, the text hinges on the divine signature and seal. Thus it brings out what, Derrida writes, is "most redoubtable," "intolerable" even "beyond" the undeniable and dangerous affinity with "the worst" characteristic of any critique of Aufklärung, parliamentary representation, and so on, regardless of its intentions (FL 1044). Derrida does not hesitate to draw the ultimate consequence from this disturbing analogy: "One is terrified at the idea of an interpretation that makes of the holocaust an expiation and an indecipherable signature of the just and violent anger of God" (FL 1045).[135]

That this association is not as far-fetched as it may seem is made clear, Derrida stresses, by the single biblical example Benjamin gives to distinguish divine violence from mythological violence: God's "anger [Zorn]," cited as one of the most visible manifestations of a violence that is not a means to an end (GS 248 / II.1, 196), as well as his severe judgment on the followers of Korah, who rebelled against the authority of Moses and were struck without distinction, disappearing alive into the abyss under the earth, the kingdom of death, annihilated without leaving any trace or remainder of their destruction (Numbers 16:1–35), "without bloodshed," as it were. This "bloodless" character of their destruction, Benjamin contends, shows its expiatory character. Derrida comments:

> The mythological violence of droit is satisfied in itself by sacrificing the living, while divine violence sacrifices life to save the living, in favor of the living. In both cases there is sacrifice, but in the case where blood is exacted, the living is not respected. Whence Benjamin's singular conclusion, and again I leave to him responsibility for this interpretation, particularly for this interpretation of Judaism: "The first (the mythological violence of droit) demands (fordert) sacrifice, the second (divine violence) accepts it, assumes it (nimmt sie an)." (FL 1027–29)

Here Derrida's reading is both at its most outspoken and its most cautious, marked by a repeated "perhaps" while raising doubts about the ultimate

135. On an equally disturbing "genocidal passage" in Baudelaire, see Given Time, 130–31 n. 14 / 166–67 n. 1.

responsibility of Benjamin's text as well as of any reading that would all too quickly comply with its interpretation of the task of destruction:

> It is at this point that this text, despite all its polysemic mobility and all its resources for reversal, seems to me finally to resemble too closely, to the point of specular fascination and vertigo, the very thing against which one must act and think, do and speak, that with which one must break (perhaps, perhaps). This text, like many others by Benjamin, is still too Heideggerian, too messianico-marxist or archeo-eschatological for me. . . . [W]e must . . . formalize, judge the possible complicity between this discourse and the worst (here the final solution). In my view, this defines a task and a responsibility the theme of which . . . I have not been able to read in either Benjaminian "destruction" or Heideggerian "Destruktion." It is the thought of difference between these destructions on the one hand and a deconstructive affirmation on the other that has guided me . . . in this reading. It is this thought that the memory of the final solution seems to me to dictate. (FL 1045) [136]

The task of deconstruction, then, is to explore a reading that would be "neither . . . Heideggerian nor Benjaminian" (FL 977 n.). Although one must admire the "heart" and "courage" of a thinking that does not ignore that one cannot be just or responsible "except in exposing oneself to all risks, beyond certitude and good conscience" (FL 1025), the specific form this thinking takes in Benjamin should make one extremely cautious. To

---

136. Starting out from a different horizon, Samuel Weber concretizes the *Auseinandersetzung* between Walter Benjamin and Carl Schmitt. See Samuel Weber, "Taking Exception to Decision: Walter Benjamin and Carl Schmitt," in *Enlightenments: Encounters between Critical Theory and Contemporary French Thought*, ed. Harry Kunneman and Hent de Vries (Kampen: Kok Pharos, 1993). Weber shows their writings to be marked by a similar "methodological extremism," one that opens yet another perspective on the question of "what is involved in thinking the irreducibility of the norm," that is to say, in thinking its independence from any generality. Although Schmitt's theory of decision (especially of the sovereign's privilege in determining the *Ausnahmezustand*) and Benjamin's analysis of the historicality of the German *Trauerspiel* both adopt a language of interruption and suspension that is not so much a negation of the present order of things as the affirmation of its dependence on a certain transcendence that exceeds and grounds the juridical realm, their secularization of theological concepts into political categories reveals striking differences. These differences, Weber demonstrates, show the profound distinction between a theory of authentic, ultimate, and punctual decidability, on the one hand, and a staging of infinite revision and displacement, on the other. This analysis anticipates the one Derrida proposes in *Politics of Friendship*, to which I will return in the final chapter of this book. On the relationship between Benjamin and Schmitt, see also Susanne Heil, *"Gefährliche Beziehungen": Walter Benjamin und Carl Schmitt* (Stuttgart: J. B. Metzler, 1996); and Giorgio Agamben, *Potentialities: Collected Essays in Philosophy*, ed. and trans. Daniel Heller-Roazen (Stanford: Stanford University Press, 1999), 160 ff.

the degree that, in Benjamin's discourse, an authentic originarity and destruction are knotted together and mirror each other, his text should be
confronted with another logic, one that would no longer be caught up
in this metaphysical specularity, and that might therefore be more effective in resisting the worst. Derrida calls this other logic—which is, like
Benjamin's, the logic of a radical otherness—a logic of the specter. Unlike the specularity of the "performative" of divine founding and annihilation that marks Benjamin's interpretation of the mystical postulate, the
spectral logic that Derrida invokes precludes the possibility of any ontological or textual resting point, even the one presupposed by theories that
claim that meaning is subjected to a permanent "drifting." Speaking of the
"athesis" of *Beyond the Pleasure Principle* in "To Speculate—on Freud," in
The Post Card, Derrida points out that the postulate of the "drifting" of
meaning implies "too continuous a movement: or rather too undifferen-
tiated, too homogenous a movement that appears to travel away . . . from
a supposed origin" that would be indivisible.[137]

This ultimate anti-Babelian stance marks the difference between Benjamin and Derrida. The "fall" in "On Language as Such and on the Language of Man" and the "destruction" in "Critique of Violence" are irreconcilable with the originary catastrophe that haunts Derrida's concept of
the language and politics of deconstruction. But one would need many
more detours to articulate in detail the differences and the disturbing affinities between the ghost of the worst that Derrida detects in Benjamin's
text and the motif of the holocaust in his own *The Post Card.* There Derrida
speaks, for example, of a necessity to burn everything and to destroy the
archive of the correspondence, which would be, not a deplorable accident,
but a necessary condition—a chance—for the "affirmation to be reborn
at every instant, without memory."[138]

Here, I would claim, a structural or formal parallel outweighs the necessary differentiation between these two thinkers of the *à dieu.*[139] Why this
must be so is clear from the central motif of *Specters of Marx:* the fact that
the decision between the extremes—between the specters, that is—must

137. Derrida, *The Post Card,* 261 / 279.
138. Ibid., 23, cf. 26 / 28, cf. 31.
139. As the reading of Levinas in Chapter 2 has established, a reference to *Otherwise Than
Being* would be in place here, too. Levinas articulates a catastrophic notion of responsibility
that seems much closer to Benjamin's disturbing "destructive" notion of justice than the ethical
first philosophy of *Totality and Infinity,* to which Derrida refers in *Force of Law* and *Specters of
Marx.* This resemblance, however, is not based on any direct influence from Benjamin.

remain obfuscated, indeed to a certain extent unjustifiable, because and so long as "the time is out of joint":

> If right or law stems from vengeance, as Hamlet seems to complain that it does—before Nietzsche, before Heidegger, before Benjamin—can one not yearn for a justice that one day, a day no longer belonging to history, a quasi-messianic day, would finally be removed from the fatality of vengeance? Better than removed: infinitely foreign, heterogeneous at its source? And is this day before us, to come, or more ancient than memory itself? If it is difficult, in truth impossible, *today*, to decide between these two hypotheses, it is precisely because "The time is out of joint": such would be the originary corruption of the day of today.[140]

À *Dieu:* The Divine Signature

Michel de Certeau's writings on mysticism provide a historical context and inspiring example for the systematic concerns that have guided us so far. In the introduction to *The Mystic Fable,* de Certeau locates the point of departure for what he terms "mystic speech" in the terminology that characterizes a decidedly Christian discourse that, he claims, comes into its own in the sixteenth and seventeenth centuries. Yet, as Derrida's subsequent analyses in "A Number of Yes," "Force of Law," and "Des tours de Babel" convincingly show, the philosophical underpinnings of the mystic discourses singled out by de Certeau are of the utmost relevance far beyond their confessional scope. Not only do they help explain what is at stake in the relation between mystic speech and philosophy, they cast an interesting light on the theoretization (with and against theories of the speech act) of a performative that is, if not pure, then at least ab-solute in an etymological sense of the word, one that involves both the performative's inevitable self-contradiction and the fact that such self-contradiction is due to a structure of "perverformativity" that can only be affirmed, for better and for worse. Moreover, the analysis of mystic speech demonstrates the intimate link between the *via negationis* and *via eminentiae,* between the discovery of an immemorial loss and the celebration and infinite recovery of this loss, of the One that is no longer One, or one, just one, one of a kind, but exiled from itself, indeed, as the one haunting itself. In de Certeau's words, which seem to anticipate some of the preoccupations of Derrida's later writings:

---

140. Derrida, *Specters of Marx,* 21–22 / 47.

One sole being is lacking, and all is lacking. This new beginning orders a sequel of wanderings and pursuits. One suffers the pangs of absence because one suffers the pangs of the One.

The One is no longer to be found. "They have taken him away," say so many chants of the mystics who inaugurate, with the story of his loss, the history of his returns elsewhere and otherwise, in ways that are the effect rather than the refutation of his absence. While no longer "living," this "dead" one still does not leave the city—which was formed without him—in peace. He haunts our environs. A theology of phantoms would doubtless be capable of analyzing how he reappears on another stage than the one from which he vanished. Such a theology would be the theory of this new status. Hamlet's father's ghost once became the law of the castle in which he was no longer present. Similarly, the absent one who is no longer in heaven nor on earth inhabits a strange third region (neither one nor the other). His "death" has placed him in that limbo. Speaking in approximate terms, this is the region the mystic authors designate for us today. (*MF* 2 / 9-10)

This motif of spectrality, of the ghost that haunts *Hamlet*—a text in which the French phrase *adieu* resounds three times—plays a crucial role in Derrida's *Specters of Marx*. There it provides the key to an analysis of mourning and of an irreducible messianicity that escapes ontology and calls for its transformation into a *hauntology*, which, far from obeying any new or old logos, seems *nothing but* the very wakefulness of the wake, the apocalyptics of apocalyptics, the eschatology of eschatology, the last— and least—become first.

Remarkably, in the same context de Certeau compares the scholar of mysticism—more precisely, of the mystical, *la mystique*—to the man from the country who, in Kafka's parable "Before the Law," sits and waits indefinitely before the gate to the Law, only to see a quasi-divine "radiance" shine forth from its inner halls when the instant of his death is imminent. De Certeau comments on this passage as follows, sounding, again, a theme familiar to those who have read Derrida's "Force of Law" in conjunction with his earlier "Préjugés—devant la loi" ("Before the Law") and later *The Gift of Death* and *Aporias:* "That brightness, Kafka's allusion to the *Shekhina* of God in the Jewish tradition, may be the very radiance of a desire that has come from 'elsewhere.' But it gives itself up neither to work nor to age. It is testamentary: a kiss of death."[141] Can the mystics

---

141. *MF* 3 / 11. For a detailed critique of such an interpretation, see Hartmut Binder, *"Vor dem Gesetz": Einführung in Kafkas Welt* (Stuttgart: J. B. Metzler, 1993).

then be seen as those who are condemned to remain external to the Law, not by facing it (as "we," like the man from the country, do), but by holding it in reverence while indefinitely deferring it — like an endless series of heralds who are less representatives or delegates than doorkeepers, guardians? Their testimony — mystic speech — lives by its very distance from the Law and keeps that distance intact. Paradoxically, it increases this distance to the degree that it overcomes it. In this respect, the elliptical and allusive formulation of de Certeau's model of mystic speech resembles in its formal structure the metaphysical desire of which Levinas writes, starting in his earliest work. Moreover, it mimics Derrida's relentless examination of the aporetics at the bottom of the thought of the trace (here, *la trace de l'autre*, that is to say, of an other that is not just *autrui* or, for that matter, *Autrui*).

As I indicated earlier, de Certeau's model of mystic speech, including the way it is adopted and formalized, generalized as well as singularized by Derrida, is marked by its insistence on the necessity of affirming an absolute yet impure performativity or "perverformativity," whose structure is ultimately incomprehensible in terms of speech act theory as we know it. In this, it differs from most other analyses of "God-talk" or "divine speech."[142]

I have argued throughout that the passion for which this performativity stands reveals what might be called the promise of deconstruction. By this I mean not only what, in deconstruction, "has a future," a future that it cannot avoid and that has all the characteristics of a fatality — *la Nécessité*, in Derrida's words — but also what, like chance itself, has the best chance of provoking new rounds of discussion on deconstruction, in the wake of deconstruction, and beyond. In speaking about the promise of deconstruction, I mean first that the mystical postulate and all its related motifs resemble in their very structure the figure of the promise — a promise that must be kept, but that cannot be kept as such (a *Versprechen* that, as de Man, parodying Heidegger, suggests, *sich verspricht*).[143] Moreover, along the lines drawn by de Certeau, the promise of deconstruction could be that of a discourse that doubles (shadows and haunts) as much as it respects the formal structure of a traditionally dogmatic, negative, affirmative, hyperbolic, or mystical theology. The argumentative thrust and the rhetorical

142. See, e.g., Nicholas Wolterstorff, *Divine Discourse: Philosophical Reflections on the Claim That God Speaks* (Cambridge: Cambridge University Press, 1995). Chapter 9 offers a critique of Derrida "in defense of authorial-discourse interpretation" (ibid., 153–70).

143. These passages are recalled by Derrida in *Of Spirit* and *Mémoires*.

procedures of deconstruction are likewise obsessed by a similarly positioned or, rather, de-positioned address, addressee, and addressor, each of which retreats from the realm of beings and Being as such, including the most general and the highest Being beyond Being. Therefore this structure can no longer adequately be described in an ontico-empirical or "onto-theo-teleo-logical" fashion. Yet no other purely heterological discourse — a language of prayer, lamentation, celebration, a "language of angels," for example — could be conceived that would finally be appropriate to its object. Here the aporia resides.

Neither in his reading of Benjamin's early essays on language nor in his lecture on "Critique of Violence" does Derrida refer to de Certeau's study of the absolute, performative structure of the mystical fable. In "Force of Law" the very formulation "the mystical foundation of authority" is, like the expression "In the beginning there will have been force," taken from Pascal and, indirectly, from Montaigne (*Essays*, book 3, chapter 13), whose idea that the law founds "the truth of its justice" on "legitimate fictions" (*Essays*, book 2, chapter 12) is cited in the epigraph to Derrida's reading of Kafka's "Before the Law." [144] Derrida's analysis of these expressions moves far beyond the common interpretation that reduces (human) law to a façade for dubious powerful interests, to a might that would dictate all right. Simultaneously, these passages are subtracted from the Christian pessimism that inspired Pascal at least in part, [145] and that sees in natural laws merely a sign of the corruption that had befallen human reason since the first — original — sin (one that, if traditionally interpreted, is not as radically defined as "radical evil" in Kant's *Religion within the Boundaries of Mere Reason* or "despair" and the "continuance of sin" in Kierkegaard's *The Sickness unto Death*, both of which come closer to Derrida's own conception of the irresponsibility that is at once a risk and a chance, and which Kierkegaard calls the "possibility of offense").

Derrida seems to suggest that only insofar as the expression "mystical foundation of authority" can been stripped of its theological overtones will it be of help in establishing the premises of a indispensable critique of juridical ideology. Yet his interest in the remarkable resemblance between Pascal's notion of a divine annihilation of all our justice and Benjamin's

144. See Jean-François Lyotard et al., *La Faculté de juger* (Paris: Minuit, 1985), 87.

145. See FL 941: "Perhaps the Pascal *pensée* that, as he says, 'puts together' justice and force and makes force an essential attribute of justice (by which he means *droit* more than justice) goes beyond a conventionalist or utilitarian relativism, beyond a nihilism, old or new, that would make the law 'a masked power.'" See also FL 937.

critique of mythical violence (FL 941)[146] points toward a thematics that reaches far beyond a desedimentation of the existing orders of law and right. To be sure, whereas for Pascal the "infinite abyss" of the human condition—the void and vanity that characterize a situation in which there is no longer any true justice—can in principle be filled (again) with an infinite object, God, Derrida insists that the "measure" of our "tragic lot" comes into view only when we realize that even such an infinite object, even God himself, is "impotent" to master the "aleatory" dimension and the "chance" of this situation, this "atrocious lottery" of all destination.[147] Thus in the postscript to "Force of Law"—as he puts it, "in saying *adieu* or *au-revoir* to Benjamin" (FL 1037)—he concludes that Benjamin's text, as well as its ultimate signature, should be considered "dated." Every signature takes place at a given singular time (and place), perhaps even more so when the signature "slips in among several names of God and only signs by pretending to let God himself sign" (FL 1040). Would this being "dated" also mean that the divine signatory with which Benjamin seals his text is at bottom a ruined notion, an idea that has outlived itself and is now out of date?

The formulation "mystical postulate" is the index of a much older and, perhaps, even more fundamental problem, which is thematized in Derrida's writings long before being addressed and analyzed in quasi-theological terms. Thus, in his early remarks in response to Michel Foucault's reading of the first of Descartes's *Meditationes de prima philosophia* (*Meditations on First Philosophy*), Derrida hints at the "silence" as well as the *coup de force*—that is to say, the "without foundation [*sans-fond*]" or "non-sense [*non-sens*]"—that, again paradoxically or, rather, aporetically, can be said to "found," distribute, and diffuse the relationship between the ego and madness (*WD* 54, 57 n. 26 / 84, 88 n. 1).[148] Likewise, radicalizing

146. Cf. FL 1021, 1023.

147. Derrida, *The Post Card*, 81 / 90.

148. Derrida's reading of Descartes's *Meditations* and Foucault's *Madness and Civilization* revolves around the structure that has interested us here. This discussion premeditates the association of Rosenzweig's and de Certeau's "yes" as the "inaudible companion" and "hidden ground" of and in speech that I pointed out earlier. This *almost* Kantian, quasi-transcendental reading of the "yes" as that which accompanies all our representations, together with the performative stance developed throughout "Force of Law," effectively resists the dilemma of foundationalist and antifoundationalist positions. Derrida's line of thinking here also runs counter to the models of critique, genealogy, and archaeology. Foucault responded to Derrida's reading in the second (1972) edition of his book in an appendix entitled "Mon corps, ce papier, ce feu," *Folie et déraison: Histoire de la folie à l'âge classique* (Paris: Plon, 1972) / "My Body, This Paper, This Fire," trans. Geoff Bennington, *Oxford Literary Review* 4, no. 1 (1979): 9–27. An oblique

Freud's notion of originary repression (*Urverdrängung*), Derrida speaks of a trace out of nothing, almost ex nihilo, as it were, *à partir de rien* (*WD* 230 / 339). Then there is the rethinking of an originary affirmation that, in the later work of Heidegger, unsettles the "questioning attitude" that forms the questionable point of departure for *Being and Time*.[149] In all these instances, I would submit, most of the characteristic features of the "mystical postulate" are already indicated and anticipated.

Yet the explicit formulation of this dependency on quasi-theological or religious terms adds something decisive to these earlier, more formal if not formal-indicative, analyses. Not only does the adjective *mystical* remind us of a certain ethico-political overdetermination of these groundless grounds (which is an inevitable risk), but the expression "mystical postulate" also underscores the singular performativity of any affirmation of these grounds. It thereby corrects or counterbalances the classical transcendental and ontological fixation on the conditions of the possibility of any thing in general. Likewise, its second term, *postulate*, remains a highly problematical and at best provisional expression, caught up in the very performative contradiction it seeks to describe. Whereas a "postulate," after Kant, is generally considered to be a *theoretical* axiom or proposition, whose referent cannot be established by any procedure through which knowledge is acquired, the "postulate" discussed above is the silent and violent "act" of any such postulation. It is a gesture that — like the addressing, signing, and sealing of a text — manifests itself first and foremost in a nonconstative, pre- or post-predicative manner. It comes as no surprise, therefore, that Derrida concludes his reading by noting that the final words of Benjamin's text, its "ultimate address," as it were, *resound* like "the *shophar* at night or on the brink of a prayer one no longer hears or does not yet hear" (FL 1037). This essential uncertainty at the heart of all attestation marks his text with an ineffaceable *à dieu, adieu,* and *a-dieu,* which, paradoxically, is its sole chance of being salvaged.[150]

---

response to this riposte can be found in Derrida's "'Être juste avec Freud': L'Histoire de la folie à l'âge de la psychanalyse," in *Résistances de la psychanalyse* (Paris: Galilée, 1996) / "'To Do Justice to Freud': The History of Madness in the Age of Psychoanalysis," trans. Pascale-Anne Brault and Michael Naas, *Critical Inquiry* 20 (1994): 227- 66.

149. In the essay on de Certeau, Derrida reiterates the analysis of the *Zusage* (cf. P 645–46) that plays such an important role in *Of Spirit*.

150. In a letter to Scholem in April 1931, Benjamin describes his perilous situation as that of someone "who has been shipwrecked, who carries on while drifting on the wreckage, by climbing to the peak of the mast that is already crumbling. But he has a chance of sending out an SOS [*ein Signal*] from up there" (Benjamin, *Correspondence*, 378 / 532).

Chapter 4
Hospitable Thought

Before and beyond Cosmopolitanism

IN DERRIDA'S UNDERSTANDING of religion, ethics, and politics, the leitmotif of unlimited, infinite, or absolute responsibility is repeatedly unfolded, depending on context or specific occasion. In his recent writings, above all *Adieu to Emmanuel Levinas,* responsibility takes the form of hospitality, a welcoming of the other as (the) totally other or, rather, Other. Such hospitality, he shows, at once must and cannot both maintain its status as an unlimited, infinite, or absolute demand and translate itself into concrete (empirical, ontic, positive) laws, a duality that illuminates the structure and the paradoxical intelligibility of experience in general.

To situate Jacques Derrida's contribution to the understanding of religion in its complex relation to ethics and politics, one must begin by recalling first Levinas's and then Kant's definition of these terms. Following Derrida's philosophical itinerary, one moves almost invisibly from an engagement with Levinas to a confrontation with Kant (this is in fact the itinerary we have traced from *Theology in Pianissimo* through *Philosophy and the Turn to Religion* to the present study). Only by carefully comparing the radically distinct yet intimately related philosophical projects for which the proper names *Levinas* and *Kant* stand can one begin to situate the convoluted thematic and argumentative approach to ethics, politics, and, in particular, religion that Derrida unfolds in increasing detail and consequence in the philosophical trajectory running from his earliest to his latest writings. His discussions, first of Levinas (in "Violence and Metaphysics," arguably the most powerfully argued chapter of *Writing and Difference,* and "At This Very Moment in This Work Here I Am," arguably the most enigmatic essay in *Psyché*) and subsequently Kant (especially in *The Truth in Painting,* "Of an Apocalyptic Tone Recently Adopted in Philosophy," *Du droit à la philosophie,* and *Politics of Friendship*) set the tone for a remarkable recasting of our understanding of the ethical and the political in light of the religious, its chances, and its perils. Finally, in *Adieu to Emmanuel Levinas,* together with the pamphlet *Cosmopolites de tous les*

pays, encore un effort! (*Cosmopolitans of All Nations, Yet Another Effort!*),
the names—and arguments—of Levinas and Kant are brought together
into a single configuration and presented as two complementary views on
the same problem. This movement from the concept of the ethical by way
of the political to that of the religious is confirmed by one of the latest
of Derrida's sustained discussions of religion, "Faith and Knowledge: The
Two Sources of 'Religion' at the Limits of Reason Alone," a study whose
subtitle echoes that most Kantian of titles, *Religion within the Boundaries
of Reason Alone.* Indeed, Derrida's different approaches could be seen as
so many endeavors to rewrite Kant's famous essay.

Any such genealogy is inevitably too schematic, however. It suggests
a linear development of concepts and themes where there is in fact a far
more convoluted trajectory, in which what seems a single leitmotif—unlimited, infinite, or absolute responsibility—is unfolded only to be folded
in again, in varying ways depending on the context, the specific occasion of an interrogation, or the urgency of a certain clarification. Derrida insists, time and again, that responsibility, although unrestricted and
hence categorical or even transcategorical and excessive, relies on a general structure of iterability in which it is singularly traced and retraced and
only thus attains a certain *ideality.* What might thus be considered Derrida's single most wide-ranging insight—infinite responsibility, as Levinas would have said, and its necessary betrayal in repetition—is presented
in an in principle incomplete series of "examples" or, better, instantiations whose plurality respects the uniqueness of pragmatically determined
situations. The latter also include the idiom of those addressed.

Hence, in a technical sense the analysis of each of the notions that
interest us here—religion, ethics, politics—regardless of (or, rather,
thanks to) their conceptual and empirical specificity revolves once again
around a critical reassessment of the concept, so central to Derrida's earlier
work, of the historical. Ethics, politics, and religion are analyzed neither as
transcendental terms (i.e., categories, ideas, or existentials) nor as simple
or pure transcendence, but in view of what is called their transcendental historicity. This fundamentally Husserlian concept, studied systematically by Derrida in his introduction to Husserl's *L'Origine de la géo-
metrie* (*Origin of Geometry*) and broached even earlier in his dissertation
Le Problème de la genèse dans la phénoménologie de Husserl [*The Problem
of Genesis in the Phenomenology of Husserl*], forms the interpretive key
to the discussion of ethicity (as distinguished from this or that ethics or
morality), of the political (*le politique;* as opposed to a politics, *la poli-*

tique, in the concrete and pragmatic sense of the word), and of reveal-ability or messianicity (as differentiated from the purported revelations and messianisms that punctuate the history of religion, more precisely, the religions of the Book). In all these concepts—which to a certain extent are "non-synonymous substitutions," to cite a helpful formulation from "Différance"—a certain motif of idealization touches upon the realm of the empirical (the world of phenomena, according to Kant; the domain of the ontic, following Heidegger) in the most unexpected ways. The two extreme poles of our experience and our language—the ideal and, say, the real—are thereby presented as abstractions from a more complex process of constant *resignification* (since no signification was ever first). They are described as being in permanent need of *negotiation,* as having in fact and for structural reasons been negotiated from the very outset, and hence as never having been given as such, in all purity. Responsibility, the whole drama of decision and of testimony, act, and passion, would thus consist in reiterated engagement with this difficulty—or aporia—of engaging (i.e., negotiating, economizing, betraying, and implicating) the ethical, the political, and the religious. It consists in compromising the absolute, distributing infinite—yet also infinitely pervertible (and, one should add, in itself, when left to itself, also perverse)—justice by translating it into an inescapably limited set of principles and rules, laws and customs.

This translation and consistent reinscription of ethical responsibility and justice (*la justice*) into the realm of rights (*le droit*) cannot be guided or inspired by an ideal of infinite approximation, as Kant believed. Nor does it obey a Levinasian logic of oscillation between the invisible and visible, that is to say, between ethical Saying (*le Dire*) and the ontological and historico-political Said (*le Dit*), which, again in Levinas's view, finds its empirical expression in the state and its institutions, reason and the system. A different, more aporetic relationship between the infinite and the finite is at work here, one that Derrida spells out in relentless and increasing consequence. The questions raised in "Violence and Metaphysics" about a certain—residual, some would say absolute—empiricism, as well as the proposal, made in "At This Very Moment in This Work Here I Am," to introduce the notion of seriature (*sériature*), exemplify this concern. They all lead to a formalization of the co-implication of responsibility and ethics, ethics and the political, the political and politics, politics and religion (as well as the religious), regardless of the no less stringent difference between them. Yet, paradoxically, as soon as one concept or one realm (ethics, politics, religion) receives its distinctive articulation, it is folded back (reverse implication, once again) into those from which it set itself apart.

Turning Around Religion: The Conditions of Responsibility

In the renewed meditation on Levinas and Kant in *Adieu to Emmanuel Levinas,* Derrida lets himself be guided by a question that he "will in the end leave in suspense, being content simply to situate some of its premises and points of reference," a question that concerns "the relationships between an *ethics* of hospitality (an ethics *as* hospitality) and a *law* or a *politics* of hospitality, for example, in the tradition of what Kant calls the conditions of universal hospitality in *cosmopolitical law:* 'with a view to perpetual peace'" (*AL* 19–20 / 45). Derrida goes on to specify at some length the difficulty in thinking and acting upon the complementary relationships between these two meanings and forms of hospitality. As he notes, here we are dealing with relationships whose modality is at odds with those of philosophical (metaphysical, ontological, and transcendental) conditioning or possibilization, indeed, radically distinct from any form of deduction, empirical causation, and psychological motivation. Even saying that they are complementary would be saying too much or too little, since what is at issue are two relational terms or poles—schematically, the *idea* and the *law* or, rather, *laws* of hospitality—that mutually imply and exclude each other, in an enigmatic and fundamentally aporetic way. To understand what Derrida means by this, it is worth quoting him *in extenso:*

> The classical form of this question would perhaps be found in the figure of a founding or legitimating foundation. It might be asked, for example, whether the ethics of hospitality that we will try to analyze in Levinas's thought would be able to found a law and a politics, beyond the familial dwellings, within a society, nation, State, or Nation-State.
>
> This question is no doubt serious, difficult, and necessary; but it is already canonical. We will try to subordinate it to another suspensive question, to what might be called a sort of *epochē.* Which one?
>
> Let us assume, *concesso non dato,* that there is no assured passage, following the order of a foundation, according to a hierarchy of founding and founded, of principal originarity and derivation, between an ethics or a first philosophy of hospitality, on the one hand, and a law or politics of hospitality, on the

other. Let us assume that one cannot *deduce* from Levinas's ethical discourse on hospitality a law and a politics, some particular law or politics in some determined situation today, whether close to us or far away. . . . How, then, are we to interpret this impossibility of founding, of deducing or deriving? Does this impossibility signal a failing? Perhaps we should say the contrary. Perhaps we would, in truth, be put to another kind of test by the apparent negativity of this lacuna, by this hiatus between ethics (first philosophy or metaphysics — in the sense, of course, that Levinas has given to these words), on the one hand, and, on the other, law or politics. If there is no lack here, would not such a hiatus in effect require us to think law and politics otherwise? Would it not in fact open — like a hiatus — both the mouth and the possibility of another speech, of a decision and a responsibility (juridical and political, if you will), where decisions must be made and responsibility, as we say, *taken*, without the assurance of an ontological foundation? According to this hypothesis, the absence of a law or a politics, in the strict and determined sense of these terms, would be just an illusion. Beyond this appearance or convenience, a return to the conditions of responsibility and of the decision would impose itself, between ethics, law, and politics. (*AL* 20–21 / 45–47).

Derrida's hypothesis seems to rest on the very *epochē* — the same suspension of judgment, an in-decision, if not in-difference, a scruple, rather, *Scheu* and *Gelassenheit* — with which "Faith and Knowledge" associates the concept and experience of "religion" (or at least one of its two "sources"). What is said of hospitality and its two meanings resembles the characterization of the two "sources" of "religion" and their relation. All that remains of "religion," apart from the sacrificial, dogmatic, and obscurantist tendencies that animate its historical manifestations (that is to say, its idiosyncrasies, idolatries, and blasphemies), would be this inability or unwillingness and hesitation to choose which comes first: the transcendental, ideal, and pure condition of possibility for the religious (natural, rational, or moral religion and its transcendental, some would say mystical, concept of God as the ground of all possible attribution) *or* its supposed empirical and ontic instantiations (historical revelations, positive religions, and their rituals, practices, doctrines), which, being conditioned, in a way condition their condition in turn. This hesitation to choose between the most formal and the more concrete features of "religion," between its abstract concept and its material substratum, between its idea (or ideality) and its phenomenality, effectively strips the religious of both orthodox and heterodox determinations. Neither faith nor knowledge, neither ethics nor politics, it pervades, inspires, and unsettles both. For good and for ill.

The originality of authors such as Levinas and Kant, in Derrida's view, consists in exposing the concepts of the ethical and the political, in their ancient, modern, and contemporary determinations, to the "religious" tradition, understood against the historical background of the "positive" religions of the Book, especially Judaism, Christianity, and, more indirectly—we will come to that—Islam. Despite (or thanks to?) this exposure—which is a reinscription of sorts—these concepts are rethought and rewritten in the most unexpected ways. This procedure—as we have argued, a turn to religion of sorts—forces the notions of the ethical and the political into a relation of simultaneous proximity to and distance from a concept and phenomenon (namely, "religion") that they affirm and generalize or even universalize, but thereby also trivialize by stripping it of its ontological and axiological privilege. *To turn around religion here also means to turn religion around.*[1]

All this is implied from the outset in the enigmatic title *Adieu*, which Derrida borrows from Levinas, even though he gives it a significant and almost contrary twist of his own ("pronouncing this word of *adieu*, this word *à-Dieu*, which, in a certain sense, I get from him, a word that he will have taught me to think or pronounce otherwise"; *AL* 1 / 11). The complexity and aporetic structure of this movement, a conversion and aversion of sorts,[2] is captured by the fact that it evokes the ambiguity of a movement toward God (*à Dieu*), toward the word or the name of God, and a no less dramatic farewell (*adieu*) to at least the canonical, dogmatic, and onto-theological interpretations of this notion called "God." As if noth-

---

1. See my "Theotopographies: Nancy, Hölderlin, Heidegger," *Modern Language Notes*, 109 (1994): 445–77; and "Winke," in *The Solid Letter: New Readings of Friedrich Hölderlin*, ed. Aris Fioretos (Stanford: Stanford University Press, 1999), 94–120.

2. Levinas speaks of a "reverting" or *retournement* in *Otherwise Than Being*, 121 / 155. The term *aversion* is Ralph Waldo Emerson's (see, e.g., "Self-Reliance") and has been analyzed indefatigably by Stanley Cavell. When used in tandem with *conversion*, the term reminds us of the doubleness of the turn that resonates through the writings of Paul and Augustine, as read by the early Heidegger, not to mention the deployment of the *à-Dieu* by Levinas and Derrida. The term *conversion* appears in a passage in which Derrida observes that through "discrete though transparent allusions" Levinas draws our attention to the massive displacement of people who in the twentieth century have been forced to seek refuge, to go into exile, to immigrate, etc.; their many examples, he writes, "call [*appellent*] for a change in the socio- and geo-political space—a juridico-political mutation, though, before this, assuming that this limit still has any pertinence, an ethical conversion" (*AL* 70–71 / 131).

ing save its names were untouched, and, as it were, left intact. As if the sacred name were not so much lacking (as Heidegger, misreading Hölderlin, believed), as to be found in a certain integrity—an absoluteness, safe and sound—of a host of idiomatic, singular, yet infinitely substitutable names.

This turn to—or around—religion should not be confused with the many attempts, old and new, to reduce the problem of ethics and morality to that of articulating a distinct (concrete, empirical, and ontic) conception of the good or the good life, from Aristotle to Hegel, or from Alasdair MacIntyre to Charles Taylor. Nor should we identify all too quickly the steps taken by Levinas and Kant, as Derrida reads them, with attempts to mobilize a "political theology." Their itinerary differs in many regards from that of historical messianisms and theodicies, and it occupies a universe different from that of Carl Schmitt, Walter Benjamin, Jakob Taubes, and the "liberation"—or genitive—theologies of recent decades. An alternative turn to—and away from—religion is at work in the texts that concern us here.

Their procedure, which I term *reverse implication*, folds the transcendental (indeed, the quasi- or simili- or ultra-transcendental) back into the empirical and the historical, in a radical movement whose direction goes against the grain of the phenomenological—and hence transcendental—reduction in its idealist and merely provisional interruption or bracketing of the psychologisms, sociologisms, biologisms, and all other naturalistic reductionisms that pervade the realist interpretation of the world and ourselves. Only with this conversion of the gaze does responsibility become possible—and necessary—again.

Husserl and Heidegger compared this turning around of the natural attitude to religious conversion, and modeled it after a certain kenosis of discourse. Reverse implication converts, and hence doubles, that conversion once again, thereby both intensifying and trivializing the gesture of faith. It multiplies that gesture and folds it back upon itself. The difference is hard to tell. From a Levinasian or Kantian perspective, this would be a disconcerting conclusion. Or so it seems.

Derrida reads these authors in a more unexpected way, bringing out a simultaneous allegiance and radical distantiation, contrary gestures that, he shows, are inevitable when dealing with ethics, politics, religion, and their traditional resources—gestures, moreover, that cannot be held apart easily, if at all. Any discourse, like those proposed by Levinas and Kant, that would set out to question these notions—the ethical, the political, the religious—would be bound to affirm them all over again, for to engage them is to say the same thing completely otherwise, in a proximity that approaches identification and tautology, yet implies an allegory or heterology as well.

These mutually exclusive yet simultaneous movements are prefigured and formalized in the *terminus technicus* that Derrida introduces and justifies in "Signature Event Context," then elaborates in *Limited Inc*, where he discusses the concept of iterability, and in *Of Spirit*, where he speaks of an originary affirmation, acquiescence, and reiteration at the root of even the most violent negation. Nowhere are these contradictory yet mutually dependent movements expressed more poignantly than in the figure of the *adieu*, whose ambiguity makes all the difference in the world, even though it expresses, repeats, and displaces the function of the more formal terms *iterability* and *originary affirmation*.

Why, then, is the reference to religion and to God (*à Dieu*) necessary or useful at all? Why is the analysis of the formal and supposedly universal structure of iterability (paradoxically, aporetically) contingent upon invoking a particular tradition, here that of the religions of the Book, especially since that structure is also held to have made these religions possible in the first place? What are we to make of this circular relation, which seems to undercut what Derrida, in *Aporias*, has called the "logic of presupposition," that is to say, not only foundationalism and reductionism, but, with far more consequence, any assumption of possibilization, of conditions of possibility and the like? Did not the latter form the heart of all (quasi-, simili-, ultra-) transcendental discourses that sought to escape the predicament of empiricism pure and simple?

Two Concepts of Hospitality

In *Adieu to Emmanuel Levinas,* Derrida rearranges Levinas's reassessment of ethics, politics, and religion around the notion of *hospitality,* a term that seems increasingly relevant in the present age, when "globalization," mobility, immigration, minority rights, democracy, and the complexities of multicultural citizenship are hotly contested issues. These issues are intimately related to the challenges imposed by new mediatizations, the new technological media that transform our experience and understanding of the public sphere and of privacy, of national belonging and virtual communities, in radical ways. That these recent challenges have tremendous consequences for religion in almost all of its manifestations, Western and non-Western, has been sufficiently documented and need not concern us here.[3]

Levinas rethinks the notions of ethics, politics, and religion around hospitality, Derrida shows, by the qualification, definition, or rather *infinition* of hospitality as absolute hospitality, a welcoming of the other as (the) totally Other, as the other in whose trace, transcendence, and dimension of height we find the sole access to—indeed, the very desire for and fear of—God. The immense relevance of a Levinasian ethics for the most urgent questions that dominate the contemporary political debate on the displacement if not the demise of the nation-state, multilingualism, and the like becomes particularly clear, Derrida seems to suggest, if we understand this philosophical thought as an ethics of hospitality, or even ethics *as* hospitality. What, then, is the significance of the Levinasian conception of ethics—the relation to the other pure and simple, to the *tout autre*—for questions of rights and jurisprudence, and especially for all the apparently unprecedented burning issues for which the inherited doctrines of law, recent conventions in international relations, and the ancient, modern, and current understanding of cosmopolitanism (from Cicero through Kant, up to Rawls, Habermas, and Nussbaum) seem, all of a sudden, so ill prepared? This question is all the more urgent because the translation from one perspective into the other—or the negotiation of one with the other—seems highly questionable, indeed, impossible.

As Derrida asserted in "Violence and Metaphysics" and "At This Very Moment in This Work Here I Am," for Levinas the very notion of ethics is devoid of principles and rules, maxims and practices, and appears to be merely a word—one for which there are an infinite number of substitutes—for the infinitizing relation to the infinite other, the welcome offered to or received from the Other. Derrida's previous readings had shown that for Levinas this relation is one of transcendence, eschatology, and the messianic, of a saintliness that does not even claim to be, that is otherwise than Being, that finds no halt and no limit in beings or in Being. At an earlier stage of his thought, in *Totality and Infinity*, Levinas had conceived of this relation in terms of an infinity of Being in order to stress its exteriority with regard to the finite—Adorno would say, "false"—totality that had been, quite literally, the idée fixe of Western ontology. Ethics qua hospitality thus instantiates a relation to the other (*l'Autre;* first of all, the other human being, *autrui,* who comes to me from a dimension of

3. See de Vries and Weber, eds., *Religion and Media.*

height, as *Autrui*) that does not close itself off in a totality. What is at issue, therefore, is a *relation without relation*, to use a formulation introduced by Maurice Blanchot and echoed by both Levinas and Derrida.

For the Levinas of *Totality and Infinity*, these terms are possible definitions (or, again, *infinitions*) not only of "religion" but, more specifically, of a "religion of adults," as the opening essay of *Difficult Freedom* has it. This is characterized by a sober rigor that resists not only the conceptual appropriation of the philosophies of the Same and the neuter (from Parmenides and Spinoza through Hegel up to Heidegger), but also the raptures and rhythms of mythico-mystical participation, of diffuse totalities, that encapsulate the self in the other. The later Levinas, however, increasingly characterizes this religious posture in terms of a saintly madness (obsession, trauma, etc.).

Adieu opens with a moving and conceptually astute address spoken by Derrida at Levinas's funeral in 1995, then rereads *Totality and Infinity*, together with some lesser-known Talmudic readings and short essays, in view of their contribution to an ethics and politics of hospitality, specifically, to contemporary debates on, for example, "cities of refuge" and the continuing Arab-Israeli conflict. *Adieu* can, moreover, be read as a supplement to Derrida's own engagement with the concepts "messianicity" and "friendship" in *Specters of Marx* and *Politics of Friendship*. It seeks to determine how the politics of friendship — especially as linked to the notion of democracy, in its ancient and modern liberal guises — ties in with the discussion of hospitality introduced by this book and by the accompanying pamphlet *Cosmopolitans of All Nations, Yet Another Effort!* It is no accident that the notions of hospitality, friendship, and democracy to come surface in a text named *Adieu*, under the heading of this intriguing turn toward and away from religion, toward and away from its turns of phrase and everything for which they stand, the best and the worst. There could be no better entry into the abyssal logics of this curious phrase — of its semantic potential, where given meanings and possibilities are charged with unforeseen effects — than an analysis of the welcome granted to and given by the *tout autre*. *Adieu* draws attention to the fact that Levinas's oeuvre, especially *Totality and Infinity*, is "an immense treatise of hospitality" (*AL* 21 / 49), indeed, on or of metaphysics as hospitality: "The metaphysical event of transcendence — *the welcome of the Other, hospitality*" (*TI* 254 / 232). Levinas's book enacts hospitality as much as, or more than, it thematizes hospitality. It shows certain concepts or notions welcoming each other, signing up with each other, calling each other forth, and accepting an invitation to enter into a series that is in principle infinite.

Derrida now sees the absolute and ultimately unphilosophical empiricism that, in the final pages of "Violence and Metaphysics," he had detected in Levinas's project up to *Totality and Infinity* as giving way to a different logic and rhetoric—a series of linkages that allows no single concept or figure of speech to be privileged ontologically, axiologically, aesthetically, theologically, or ethically and religiously. Instead, in principle if not de facto, it treats all alike and "appears to proceed, indeed to leap, from one synonym to the next" (*AL* 22 / 50-51). Such a procedure undercuts and outwits both any empiricism, however absolute, and any insistence on a *primum intelligibile*, any first philosophy, however ethical. In this more hospitable reading, we are no longer dealing with an ethical transcendental philosophy or metaphysics but with a mode of argumentation less reminiscent of the *via negativa* of apophatic theologies than of the hyperbolic affirmations and exaggerations of the *via eminentiae*, a tradition Levinas invokes in his later writings, especially at the end of *Otherwise Than Being*. One must ask, however, whether these two theological approaches—which strip dogmatic theology of its metaphysical presuppositions and onto-theology or, what comes to the same thing, stretch it to its outer limits—do not go hand in hand, historically and systematically speaking. Apophatic—and anthropophatic—thinkers from Pseudo-Dionysius to Cusanus, Hans Urs von Balthassar, and Jean-Luc Marion have always insisted that this is so.

In another attempt to explain this peculiar logic, Derrida identifies it with an "apposition," a "movement without movement" (ibid.), which could be taken either for no movement at all, for a perpetual movement on the (one and the same?) spot or, even more puzzling, for both of these—movement and stasis, repetition and repetition of the same—at once. We are dealing here, Derrida continues, with a "play of substitution" that—paradoxically, aporetically—"would replace the unique with the unique" (*AL* 65 / 119); in other words, in Levinas's project, the "*thinking of* substitution" orients itself toward "a logic that is hardly thinkable, almost unsayable, that of the possible-impossible, the iterability and the replaceability of the unique in the very experience of unicity as such" (*AL* 70 / 128). What does this mean? And what would be the consequences of adopting such a model for thought, for ethics, politics, and the like?

Hospitality, we learn, can be neither thematized nor crudely historicized, psychologized, or politicized. Yet it "is," the *concretissimum* par excellence: it unfolds as the openness of intentionality, as the welcome offered to the totally other. As such it is already implied or at work in any account one might want to give of it. What remains or becomes of the welcome and hospitality if its meaning is stripped of its most common, familial, and juridico-political connotations? When the ethics of pure prescription — originally intended as an ethical transcendental and first philosophy — is identified with the elusive notion of an infinite and absolute hospitality, the homology between the word *hospitality* and its use and abuse in the most pressing institutional and international concerns of our days must give us pause, must make us think, indeed think twice, gesturing in two directions at once. What, precisely, is the relationship between a hospitality vis-à-vis the other that is understood philosophically, and politics and law, between an emphatic notion of responsibility and a down-to-earth set of rights and rules, a jurisprudence? This is the problem of *le droit* as opposed to *la justice*, as Derrida has it in "Force of Law," or of justice as opposed to the wisdom of love, to cite the final chapter of Levinas's *Otherwise Than Being*. How can one inspire and enable, orient but inevitably also limit the other? Here, it seems, we are dealing with two concentric circles that revolve around each other and draw ever closer (the image invoked both by Kant in *Religion within the Boundaries of Mere Reason* and by the ancient Stoic conceptions of cosmopolitanism), but also with two focal points that figure as the mutually constitutive poles of a mathematical ellipse, a circle whose center is split down the middle.[4] The question remains: How does one pole affect, orient, and correct the other?

In *Adieu*, Derrida explicitly raises this question and reminds us that no unilinear, hierarchical order of foundation, derivation, or causation regulates the relation between these two orders. A completely different logic is at work, one that differs radically from the "logic of presupposition" Derrida takes to task in *Aporias*, in a discussion of Heidegger's *Being and Time*.[5] Early in *Adieu*, we found, Derrida notes that, according to the "canonical" form of philosophical questioning, absolute hospitality, on the one hand, and the hospitality of rights and laws, on the other, must always exist in a relation of subordination, of justification, with one enabling the other. Following the classical and modern schemat-

---

4. See my *Philosophy and the Turn to Religion*, chap. 6.
5. Ibid., chap. 3.

ics, the two orders in question could not be co-originary, co-extensive, co-existent, co-temporaneous, since each is, as it were, the possibility— in fact, the transcendental or the empirical condition of possibility—of the other. Metaphysical, idealist, or rationalist accounts do not fundamentally differ from naturalist, materialist, and culturalist explanations in this regard.

By contrast, the other logic that Derrida sees at work in Levinas's thoughts on hospitality leaves in suspense the question of what comes first. It does so in a paradoxical gesture that bears a remarkable resemblance to the classical procedure of the phenomenological *epochē*.[6] One can thus say of hospitality in its two modes and of their implied ethics and politics what Derrida says of literature in a different context: namely, that it instantiates a "phenomenological conversion of the gaze," a "nonthetic experience, of belief, of position, of naiveté, and of what Husserl called the 'natural attitude.'" In so doing, the language of hospitality, like that of literature, dislodges phenomenology from its supposed "certainties."[7] Levinas's oeuvre can thus be read as a phenomenology that liberates itself from all "presuppositions": to begin with, the ontological concept of the phenomenon and of logos that Heidegger, faithful and unfaithful to Husserl, develops in paragraph 7 of *Being and Time,* but also from an understanding of the transcendental in terms of conditions of possibility and of the movement of possibilization.

As I have argued in *Philosophy and the Turn to Religion,* this "phenomenological conversion of the gaze" implies emphasizing a certain Christianity or "Christian logic." Surely, in the context of our present discus-

6. Again, this suspension is produced in phenomenology *from within and without:* as a "phenomenological interruption of phenomenology" (*AL* 102 / 178, cf. 61 / 113–14). Paradoxically, while drawing on its own resources, the phenomenological description thus touches upon an alterity that it can no longer contain but must welcome as other — indeed, as its other. In the discourse of philosophical phenomenology, the attestation of this other always risks reducing the relation to the *tout autre* to that with an "impersonal neutrality." One can escape this risk only in an endless oscillation between the Saying (*le Dire*), the Said (*le Dit*), and the Unsaying (*le Dédire*). According to Levinas, this movement obeys the same rhythm as the skepticism that follows *philosophia perennis* as its inescapable shadow (and, Levinas claims, as its legitimate heir). For Derrida, this scansion is dictated by the aporetics that marks any philosophy from the very first act of constitution, as well as all subsequent attempts to legitimate it. To respond to it in a responsible way demands that one enter into an infinite — and infinitely compromising — series of steps of impossible yet necessary negotiation.

7. Jacques Derrida, "'This Strange Institution Called Literature': An Interview with Jacques Derrida," in *Acts of Literature,* ed. Derek Attridge (New York: Routledge, 1992), 46.

sion of *Adieu to Emmanuel Levinas,* that cannot mean reading Levinas as a Christian, as if—while reading, interpreting, philosophizing, in a scholarly fashion—one could assume the "position" of a Christian (even supposing one identifies oneself as Christian or as a Christian). Nor could it mean reading Levinas as if he were himself—as a philosopher, let alone in a more personal (biographical or existential) sense—Christian, or a Christian. He, like so many other thinkers who have interested us here, was not. To read Levinas in light of a certain Christianicity (or "Christian logic") can only mean opening oneself up to the isolated and more systematic Christian motifs and theologemes that Levinas (like others) engages throughout his writings, in more than a merely, or simply, polemical way. True, "Polemics" is the title of one of the central sections of *Difficult Freedom.* Yet any careful reading of the essays it collects soon complicates the assumption that Levinas's distance from Christianity is easy to determine. While there remains in Levinas (and many others) an asymmetry between his critique and his affirmation of certain essential aspects of Christian dogma, of theologemes and figures of thought (to say nothing of liturgy, prayer, and practices in a more wider sense), a whole series of oblique and explicit references to Christian tropes recur throughout writings whose *philosophical* ambition—and weight—cannot be in doubt. More than interpretive and, historically speaking, undeserved generosity is at stake here, because invocations of the Christian—of Christianity, Christianicity, and their "logic"—punctuate these writings at what are argumentatively crucial points. This observation alone should caution us to steer clear of facile distinctions and oppositions.

If that is so, the question of "how to read Levinas as a Christian, or in a Christian way," is somewhat misguided, not only because one cannot read and interpret philosophically by being a Christian, or because Levinas did not think of himself in those terms. The more serious—the methodological and systematic—reservation is that Levinas's position, as Derrida sketches it, subverts any dichotomy between Christianity, the history of onto-theology and political theology, and its ethico-religious Jewish other. Just as Levinas does not opt for one of the two modes of hospitality but is interested above all in their relation (a relation, we suspect, without relation), both the Judaic and the Christian form mutually exclusive yet equally constitutive elements of the drama of human responsibility. This may be the legacy of Rosenzweig's *Star of Redemption,* which thinks of redemption along similar lines, endowing both Judaism and Christianity with a fundamental yet radically distinct role in keeping to a, so to speak, paradigmatic idea as well as to "its" historical manifestation.[8]

Another element further complicates our understanding of these things. The hesitation to choose between Judaism and Christianity or, more precisely, the reluctance to reduce the one necessary possibility to the other, comes down to a certain "scruple," which Derrida, in "Faith and Knowledge," associates with a central meaning of "religion." Is this epochē Jewish or Christian? Or both? Here we find yet another articulation of the "religion of adults," a concept Levinas introduces at the outset of *Difficult Freedom*. What would such hesitation to choose between two alternatives mean?

Hospitality as "Culture Itself"

Derrida shows that Levinas's conception of hospitality differs radically from the one Kant develops, notably in "Idee zu einer allgemeinen Geschichte in weltbürgerlicher Absicht" ("Idea for a Universal History with a Cosmopolitan Purpose"), published in the *Berlinische Monatschrift* in 1784, and in "Zum ewigen Frieden: Ein philosophischer Entwurf" ("Toward Perpetual Peace: A Philosophical Sketch"), which dates from 1795.[9]

8. I have been insisting on a deconstructive logic of substitution that enables one to understand why a certain ideality—any ideality—and a certain historicity (every historicity) must always go hand in hand, while excluding each other all the same. Nonetheless, I do not think that the term *deconstructive* is decisive here in describing Levinas's position. That position might also be characterized as dialectical, provided one strips this term of its overly Hegelian determination. Indeed, as I have argued elsewhere, Levinas's position resembles the one Adorno, in "Fortschritt" (in *Stichworte: Kritische Modelle 2* [Frankfurt a. M.: Suhrkamp, 1969 / "Progress," in *Critical Models: Interventions and Catchwords*, trans. Henry W. Pickford [New York: Columbia University Press, 1998]), attributes to St. Augustine's *De Civitate Dei* (*City of God*). See my *Theology in Pianissimo*.

9. Immanuel Kant, "Idee zu einer allgemeinen Geschichte in weltbürgerlicher Absicht," in *Werke*, ed. Wilhelm Weischedel (Darmstadt: Wissenschaftliche Buchgesellschaft, 1983), 9:33–50 / "Idea for a Universal History with a Cosmopolitan Purpose," in *Political Writings*, trans. H. B. Nisbet, ed. Hans Reiss, *The Cambridge Edition of the Works of Immanuel Kant* (Cambridge: Cambridge University Press, 1991); idem, "Zum ewigen Frieden: Ein philosophischer Entwurf," in *Werke*, ed. Weischedel, 9:195–251 / "Toward Perpetual Peace: A Philosophical Project," in *Practical Philosophy*, trans. and ed. Mary J. Gregor, *The Cambridge Edition of the Works of Immanuel Kant* (Cambridge: Cambridge University Press, 1996). See Reinhard Merkel and Roland Wittmann, eds., *"Zum ewigen Frieden": Grundlagen, Aktualität und Aussichten einer Idee von Immanuel Kant* (Frankfurt a. M.: Suhrkamp, 1996). Yet another relevant text is, of course, Kant's "Über den Gemeinspruch: Das mag in der Theorie richtig sein, taugt aber nicht für die Praxis," in *Werke*, ed. Weischedel, 9:127–72, esp. pp. 165–72, the section "Vom Verhältnis der Theorie zur Praxis im Völkerrecht in allgemein-philantropischer, d.i. kosmopolitischer Absicht betrach-

Levinas starts out from a nonnatural yet originary—or, better, preorigi-nary—peace rather than from a natural state of war, as Kant does. Unlike Kant, Levinas does not portray peace as the interruption of war. Regard-less of its anteriority and primacy, he insists that this peace still needs to come here and now; it cannot be thought or lived as indefinitely post-poned or to be approximated in a distant future, as it would if we were dealing with a regulative idea.

Unlike Kant's cosmopolitanism, which is ultimately based on juridico-political presuppositions and thus limits universal hospitality to a merely (or primarily) juridical, cosmopolitical arrangement of citizens and states (*AL* 68 / 124 and, notably, 87–88 / 156), Levinas's notion of hospitality re-volves from the outset around a before or beyond of the political. The political is neither its first nor its final point of reference, nor its privi-leged model. At times it seems that for Levinas hospitality is to be found everywhere but in the political, regardless of its conservative or progres-sive, restorative or revolutionary, anarchist or utopian appropriations. The political *in toto* seems to be relegated to the realm of a history whose teleology and premature judgment constitutes no more than a finite—or false—totality.[10]

Derrida observes that if the modality of transcendence is thus de-scribed in what seems an un- or apolitical way, one must ask whether there can still be any correspondence, analogy, or elective affinity, how-ever indirect or figural, between absolute hospitality as a pre- or meta-ontological relation to the other, on the one hand, and hospitality as an

---

tet" / "On the Common Saying: That May Be Correct in Theory, but It Is of No Use in Practice," in *Practical Philosophy*, trans. and ed. Gregor 304–9.

Rawls presents his *The Law of Peoples* as an interpretation, explication, and extrapolation of Kant's idea of the *foedus pacificum*, as presented in "Perpetual Peace" (John Rawls, *The Law of Peoples* [Cambridge: Harvard University Press, 1999], 10, 21, 36, 54, 86), and as a further elaboration of the rather summary account of the context in international law of a discussion of just wars in *A Theory of Justice*. See Rawls, *A Theory of Justice*, rev. ed. (Oxford: Oxford Uni-versity Press, 1999), 331 ff. The guiding question in both contexts is: how can the idea of the social contract, reformulated in terms of "justice as fairness," be extended in the direction of a "Society of Peoples," more precisely, "well-ordered" (that is to say, "reasonable liberal" and "decent") peoples, as distinguished from peoples from "outlaw states," "societies burdened by unfavorable conditions," and "benevolent absolutisms" (*The Law of Peoples*, 4). Such an exten-sion is, Rawls believes, a "realistic utopia," and political philosophy asks the question whether and "under which conditions" it is possible. More precisely: "Political philosophy is realisti-cally utopian when it extends what are ordinarily thought of as the limits of practical political possibility" (ibid., 6). Yet this extension of limits is hardly what Levinas, in the context that interests us here, has in mind.

10. On these notions, see my *Theology in Pianissimo*.

ethics and politics of practices and rules, laws and rights, nations and states, citizens and institutions, on the other. One striking example of such a possible, necessary, yet in the end also impossible translation, transfiguration, or schematization can be found in the tradition of the "cities of refuge" (*villes-refuges*), of which Levinas reminds us in one of his Talmudic writings, reading the treatise *Makkoth* 10a.[11] I will return to it below.

Derrida takes up this motif in an almost pragmatic fashion, with reference to the juridical consequences of immigration and the eruption of ethnic conflict, in *Cosmopolitans of All Nations, Yet Another Effort!* This supplement to *Adieu*'s discussion of the Levinasian politics of hospitality precedes an address (given to a congress) devoted to the cities of refuge that took place in Strasbourg in 1996, under the auspices of the Council of Europe at the initiative of the International Parliament of Writers. Its argument resembles that of another short text, "Le Droit à la philosophie du point de vue cosmopolitique" ("The Right to Philosophy from a Cosmopolitical Point of View"). Both texts rehearse the nuclear structure of formal arguments expounded at greater length in *Adieu* and *Du droit à la philosophie*, rephrasing them in the context of a concrete political and institutional debate. *Cosmopolitans* addresses the juridical consequences of immigration in the global market and the eruption of ethnic conflict; "The Right to Philosophy from a Cosmopolitical Point of View" speaks to the future of higher education in an international context dominated by the information or networked society and the demise of the nation-state and its cultural hegemony.

Does Levinas's notion of hospitality thus allow itself to be transposed to a more pragmatic, everyday politico-juridical context? If so, how? To say that the idea of absolute hospitality serves as a necessary or imperative criterion for the many laws of hospitality is to say too little. It immediately raises the question of when, where, under which circumstances, and in what measure this general principle or rule, if that's what it is, applies. Always, everywhere, immeasurably? Is this all we can say in good faith? Is there nothing more to *say* from here on, but everything to *show*, instantly, without any further possible proof or mediation?[12] And should

---

11. See Emmanuel Levinas, *L'au-delà du verset: Lectures et discours talmudiques* (Paris: Minuit, 1982), 51–70 / *Beyond the Verse: Readings and Lectures*, trans. Gary D. Mole (Bloomington: Indiana University Press, 1994), 34–52.

12. The way in which notions like absolute hospitality resist "criteriological" interpretation reminds us of the alternative reading that Stanley Cavell has proposed of Wittgenstein's *Philosophical Investigations*, notably in *The Claim of Reason*.

one not raise the same questions when speaking, not of hospitality, but of friendship, brotherhood, and messianicity, all of which scarcely differ in their structure or supposed content—since there is none, since their "normativity" (not Derrida's term, to be sure) contains in principle nothing or almost nothing that can be described? In Levinas, as in Kant and Derrida, all these notions are formalized to the point of becoming *almost* pure abstractions, *almost* substitutable without further remainder. We seem to be dealing here with an infinite series of finite, nonsynonymous substitutions: hospitality-without-hospitality, friendship-without-friendship, brotherhood-without-brotherhood, messianicity-without-messianism, and so on, *as we know it*. What, then, marks the difference between them?

To answer these questions, we must revisit the premises, impetus, and direction of Levinas's argument. Derrida's view is both extremely close to and at a certain distance from that of Levinas, just as it is both near to and removed from Kant (see Chapter 1). These thinkers' writings can be translated *almost* completely into one another, to the point of becoming *almost* interchangeable. While this resemblance is remarkable, on second reading they take different directions, as well. Their relation to one another is "sagital," to use Foucault's term; they touch upon each other, tangentially; their congruity is not that of an overlapping minimal consensus but an intersection that is a chiasmic crossing, an instantaneous substitution of one for the other at an indeterminate point of in-difference, albeit one from which all that matters will take its departure.

Levinas insists on a certain primacy of the other—of *autrui*, the other human being—but the very otherness of this other demands a welcoming, *le mot d'acceuil*, that, not unlike the notion of hospitality, is co-temporaneous, co-extensive, or co-originary with the appeal that comes from the face to face. At times, even in Levinas's own exposition, this circumstance works *almost* against an interpretation of ethics as first philosophy. The face to face is thought against the backdrop of hospitality or the welcome, not the other way around: "There is no face without welcome. . . . We must first think the possibility of the welcome in order to think the face and everything that opens up or is displaced with it: ethics, metaphysics or first philosophy, in the sense that Levinas gives to these words. // The welcome determines the 'receiving,' the receptivity of receiving as the ethical relation" (*AL* 25 / 55). The welcome, hospitality, and the face to face are thus not simply synonyms for the absolute relation to the absolute, to what absolves itself from any horizon of objectification and thematization. Derrida notes that all these terms are at once "associated and dissociated" (*AL* 19 / 44), according to a subtle law whose elementary form is preethical, prepolitical, and prereligious, albeit not in any chronological, logical, or ontological sense of this prefix. It is as meta- and non-ethical as it is quasi-, simili-, and ultra- or hyper-ethical, since the very articulation and expression, genesis and meaning of this law remain contingent upon the domains and practices that it, paradoxically, sets to work by enabling their repetition and change, iterability and idealization.

How should we understand the tension between the primacy of the welcome, hospitality, and openness, on the one hand, and the singular concreteness, the *concretissimum,* of the face, on the other? The face to face must somehow *also* come first if it is to be considered the *primum intelligibile,* without further quality or mediation, since it is straightforwardness and uprightness (*droiture*) itself. This insight involves a tension that Levinas never revokes. Indeed, if there were no tension here, why distinguish and multiply these terms at all? Why speak of a welcome or of hospitality if the notion of the face or the face to face itself (or in itself) already welcomes everything that gives itself to be thought in the other synonyms (or nonsynonymous substitutions) that, with Derrida's help, we have come to assess only now? What motivates, justifies, or triggers the emphasis on these figures and privileges them over so many possible, and seemingly equally decisive, others?

Stressing this tension points toward the conclusion that the ethical relation — in Levinas's sense of an ethics that precedes and circumvents or exceeds imperatives and rules, maxims and virtues, as the *ethicity of ethics* — is made possible, opened up, welcomed, and received, or at least qualified and carried away by something else (some other law or laws), just as it, in turn, makes this something possible. Should we not conclude that ethics, even Levinas's meta-ethics, therefore does *not* come first — or that in coming first it is not alone — since in its very primacy it seems already shadowed (Derrida would say "haunted" or "doubled") by what it is not, not yet, or no longer? The *meta-meta-ethical* perspective that results is, if not the empirical and ontic *positum* of a concrete history, then at least the singularity of a testimony that in its very unicity and uniqueness — a *hapax legomenon,* of sorts — is nonetheless infinitely repeatable. Indeed, as Kierkegaard already knew, it is given to us in repetition alone.

At times, Derrida suggests, ethics seems for Levinas to have primacy over everything else. This happens whenever ethics is said to find its element, modality, and destination in hospitality, to the extent that one might speak of hospitality when speaking of ethics and vice versa:

> If the category of the *welcome* everywhere determines an opening that would come even before the première [*une ouverture avant-première*], before the opening, it can never be reduced to an indeterminate figure of space, to some sort of aperture [*apérité*] or opening to phenomenality (for example, in the Heideggerian sense of *Erschliessung, Erschlossenheit,* or *Offenheit*). The welcome orients, it *turns* the *topos* of an opening of the door and of the threshold toward to other; it offers it to the other *as* other, where the *as such* [comme tel] of the other slips away from phenomenality, and, even more so, from thematicity. (*AL* 53–54 / 100)

What does it mean to say that interiority and economy presuppose a welcome, that there is an "absolute precedence [*préséance absolue*] of the welcome" (*AL* 43 / 81), or that this welcome (*acceuil*) accomplishes itself in a gathering or "recollection [*recueillement*]" (*AL* 36 / 70)? Does Levinas not put into question the presupposition of a "general structure" (*AL* 35 / 70) of opening, of a welcome supposedly enabling or defining the face to face, when he writes, in *Totality and Infinity,* that the welcome, the *visage* or the "opening of the I [*l'ouverture du moi*]," signals "the philosophical priority of the existent over Being [*de l'étant sur l'être*]" (*TI* 51 / 22)? Or is the welcome qua general structure tied to a particular being and hence an ontic — or preontological — instance, whose singularity outwits any ontological category or even existential (i.e., *Existenzial*)? Would this important differentiation, surely intended by Levinas himself, make any difference in the attempt to move away from the metaphysical and transcendental logic of presupposition and of possibilization? Is the traditional (or is it modern?) order of prioritization simply reversed, substituting for the primacy of the ontological that of the ontic? Or does the logic of substitution that Levinas eventually adopts finally displace transcendental architectonics altogether? Do Kant, Heidegger, and the Levinas of *Totality and Infinity* fall under the same verdict of having too sharply distinguished and then hierarchized or secondarized specific conditions and possibilities in light of the supposed conditions of their possibility? Have they ignored the condition(ing) of these conditions of possibility (and their conditioning and possibilization)? Whether one takes one's point of departure from the general and the necessary, from the abstract and the formal, or from their supposed opposites (the singular and the concrete, the empirical and the ontic, existents rather than existence), the difference matters little. But without these distinctions, could one think, speak, analyze, or act at all?

An ambiguity or, rather, aporia here will be reiterated in the analysis of "the third" (*le tiers*), at once the interruption and the very implication and accomplishment of the face to face, the substitution for the ethical of justice, including distributive justice, rights and laws, politics, and the System, to cite the institutions that Levinas discusses in the final pages of *Otherwise Than Being*. On the one hand, the welcome and the face to face are virtually synonyms: both stand for the relation to the other, intentionality par excellence, but also the expression and expressiveness that disrupts, inspires, and reorients all phenomenological conceptions of the intentionality of consciousness (and the proper body). On the other hand, the welcome *welcomes* the face — and, on Derrida's reading, not the face alone, but, following the tauto-heterological dictum *tout autre est tout autre,* every other, including the self, *le Même* — by characterizing and *redescribing* it, more abstractly and formally, as the unconditional or radical openness toward what it cannot contain, anticipate, and hence "welcome" as such even though every welcome is geared toward it. This ambiguity is nowhere clearer than in the following: "discourse, justice, ethical uprightness have to do first of all with *welcoming*," which is immediately qualified by the assertion that the welcome "is always a welcome reserved for the face" (*AL* 35 / 70).

The tension between ethics as the first welcome and the welcome or hospitality that enables this first welcome, but whose possibility must also be thought — paradoxically, aporetically — as first *as well* announces itself in Levinas's writings in at least two more ways. First, in many contexts Levinas places the ethical against the backdrop of another opening, not of Being but of an otherwise than being, more precisely, *an otherwise than otherwise than being,* an infinity that is infinitely other than the infinity *Totality and Infinity* speaks of: the sonorous anonymity of the *il y a,* the counterpart to, no less than a modality of, the transcendence of the trace of God, the *illéité*. Second, there is the passage, cited by Derrida, where Levinas states that the face, its epiphany, comes to us (or comes over us) out of a "dimension of height," thereby suggesting that this dimension of height is not simply identical with the face, whose epiphany it makes possible or determines in advance. Moreover, the word *dimension* is not just any term, but a *terminus technicus* used by the later Heidegger to indicate the revealability (*Offenbarkeit*) of Being, in whose horizon all beings, all mortals, and all gods must of necessity appear if they are to manifest themselves at all. But let me leave these elliptical references,[13] and return to the earlier question of how the structure of hospitality relates to the ethical and the political and sheds a fresh light on the notion of religion, taken here in Levinas's definition as a relation without relation to the other that does not close itself off in a totality.

In Levinas, the break with totality and everything for which it stands occurs on two levels, which should be carefully distinguished, even though one is subsequently inscribed in, even elevated into the other. The first, relative break with totality takes place in what *De l'existence à l'existant* (*From Existence to Existents*) calls the *hypostase* and *Totality and Infinity* describes at length in terms of interiority. As Derrida notes, the chapter "Interiority and Economy" poses the gravest problems for the "architectonics" (*AL* 39 / 78) of Levinas's thought.

Interiority—in its self-centeredness, natural atheism and egoism, intimacy, and *égoïsme à deux*—would seem a condition of possibility for any hospitality toward the other that might subsequently be inspired or demanded by this other. Does not a movement of ontological pluralization result from the contraction of God and thus become a preethical instance—meta-ethically here, in the sense Rosenzweig deploys in *The Star of Redemption*—without which separation, the condition for any hospitality, could not be absolute? A certain order of the same (*le Même*) would thus be as much a condition of possibility for the relation to the other as is the unwelcome accusation come from that other, which cannot but be welcomed, one way or the other. We find these considerations hinted at where Derrida speaks of a "law of hospitality" that is paradoxical and an extreme formalization of the notion of hospitality: "The *hôte* who receives (the host), the one who welcomes the invited or received *hôte* (the guest) . . . is in truth a *hôte* received in his own home. He receives the hospitality that he offers *in* his own home; he receives it *from* his own home—which, in the end does not belong to him" (*AL* 41 / 79). In a different context, Derrida acknowledges that the *chez-soi* is a "condition of the opening [*ouverture*] of hospitality."[14] The home or dwelling finds its counterpart in the cities of refuge, which are pragmatically constituted but principled pockets or niches that fold themselves into the political order, the result of hypocrisy as much as of skilled negotiation. The former, Levinas noted in

13. The first I have discussed in Chapter 2, above, the second, in my "Theotopographies: Nancy, Hölderlin, Heidegger."

14. Jacques Derrida and Bernard Stiegler, *Échographies: De la télévision* (Paris: Galilée / Institute national de l'audiovisuel, 1996), 93.

the opening pages of *Totality and Infinity,* can itself be seen as an indication of moral progress.

For the Levinas of *Totality and Infinity* and even *From Existence to Existents,* there seems to be a rupture with the ontological, or at least with its diffuse, mythical, or conceptual totality, that remains ontological and that is the *conditio sine qua non* for welcoming a rupture—the second, absolute break—that goes even further. Some remarks made by Levinas in *Of God Who Comes to Mind* can best be seen less as a concession or a *retractatio* than as hinting at a turn that takes place after *Totality and Infinity.* This helps situate a tantalizing problem to which Derrida refers only in a footnote: "What about the 'I,' safe and sound, in the unconditional welcoming of the Other? What about its survival, its immunity, and its safety in the ethical subjection of this other subjectivity?" (*AL* 136 n. 10 / 59 n. 2). At times, Derrida suggests that a certain "protection [*sauvegarde*]" (*AL* 136 n. 10 / 58 n. 2) deserves as much (*autant*) attention as the *accueil.* This motif could easily be transposed beyond the dwelling (*la demeure*) to the polis, the city of refuge, the nation, the state, the community or commonwealth of states, and the politics of friendship.

Derrida says as much when he formalizes the internal contradiction of hospitality by stating that this aporetics is implied in the link between the meaning of hospitality and the whole semantic field of *oikonomia.* It is no accident, he notes, that Kant, in the Third Definitive Article of "Toward Perpetual Peace," translates *Hospitalität* as *Wirtbarkeit* (a term rendered in a recent translation as "hospitableness,"[15] which loses its directly "economic" connotations). Treating the stranger as a friend, inviting him or her to one's home as a guest—this openness with regard to and for the other also implies, paradoxically, indeed aporetically, that in going out to the other and in giving (of) oneself one simultaneously keeps to oneself. To open one's doors unconditionally, one must reign over the house in full authority. Before one can solicit the other to step across a threshold and become a guest, this threshold (of the house, the family, the temple, the nation, a language community, and so on) must be in place and be maintained for the welcome to be what it is. And yet the threshold is also what forever ipso facto puts a limit to the acceptance of the other. What constitutes hospitality in its essence or structure destructures it in every instance. Wherever it shows its face, hospitality deconstructs itself. From the moment it goes into effect, its effect is interrupted. Yet in this apo-

15. Kant, "Toward Perpetual Peace," 328 /213.

ria it finds an effectivity of its own. Derrida adds that hospitality must also *work against itself*, in a process of "auto-immunization." Although Levinas never says so, *a certain egoism is good for the other*, is *necessary for being good to the other*, indeed for being *separate from and other than the other*. We encountered this term — "auto-immunization" — earlier in reading "Faith and Knowledge," where it is attributed to paradoxes that underlie the "return" of "religion."[16] The dynamics in the present context is the same; while we may — and, indeed should — know all there is to know of hospitality, of its laws, conditions, and limitations, hospitality is nowhere given to knowledge as such, in its purity or intact, coinciding with itself or localizable in a determinate place or act.

Seen in this light, the notion of hospitality, like those of the welcome, friendship, eschatology, the messianic, democracy, cosmopolitanism, and, last but not least, religion, *schematizes* a responsibility that precedes all of its subsequent translations, substitutions, and eventual concretizations. Is this Kantian solution — invoking the mediating function of the *schema* between form and content — the answer to our question of how the first, absolute or quasi-transcendental mode of hospitality (or all the other notions) relates to its second, more outspoken empirico-pragmatic counterpart? Not quite; things are more complicated than it would seem at first glance.

Pointing out that the ethical relation is engraved with sheer gravity in the traumatism and obsession of the one for the other, substitution, being hostage, in one's own house, Derrida notes that this relation is justly described in terms of a *visitation*. The general structure of the welcome of all intentionality and, indeed, of experience as such finds its prime example in the figure of revelation qua visitation. But this transcription is not as simple or unilinear as it would seem at first sight:

> In the words *visit* and *visitation*, is it really a question of *translating* this trace of the other into the vocabulary of hospitality, as we have seemed to assume? Must one not, on the contrary, refer the phenomenon and the possibility of hospitality back to this passing [*passée*] of visitation so as, first of all, to re-translate them? Does not hospitality *follow*, even if just by a second of secondariness, the unforeseeable and irresistible irruption of a visitation? And will

16. I refer to the unpublished lecture "Les Lois de l'hospitalité," which Derrida presented in Frankfurt an der Oder on June 20, 1996. For the complex of immunization and auto-immunity, see P. B. Medawar, *Aristotle to Zoos: A Philosophical Dictionary of Biology* (Cambridge: Harvard University Press, 1983), 153–56.

not this inverse translation find its limit, the limit of the liminal itself, there where it is necessary to arrive, that is, at the place where, as past visitation, the trace of the other passes or has already passed the threshold, awaiting neither invitation nor hospitality nor welcome? This visit is not a response to an invitation; it exceeds every dialogical relation between host and guest. It *must,* from all time, have exceeded them. Its traumatizing effraction must have preceded what is so easily called hospitality — and even, as disturbing and pervertible as they already appear, the laws of hospitality. (*AL* 63 / 115–16).

A certain ambiguity, therefore, remains in place and, perhaps, de rigueur. Although the structure and vocabulary of hospitality find their condition of possibility in a certain revealability (*Offenbarkeit,* as Heidegger would have it) and hence — by reverse implication — in the revelations (*Offenbarung,* or accounts thereof) of the religions of the Book, the opposite holds true as well. Hospitality is made possible by what it makes possible, and vice versa. It is conditioned by what it conditions, in turn. There is no way out of this paradox; indeed, it is an aporia that marks the limit of thought and necessitates and demands a certain suspension or *epochē* of philosophical or, more narrowly, phenomenological reflection. In the self-restraint or self-critique that this limit imposes (or enables — and nothing else does), philosophy, responsibility, indeed existence, the experience of factical life experience (as the early Heidegger would have said)[17] come into their "own." This pause, halt, reticence, or scruple, Derrida suggests from "Faith and Knowledge" on, might well constitute the very heart and impetus of "religion," "at the limits of reason alone."

We should differentiate carefully here. Derrida leaves no doubt that the quasi-transcendental and juridico-political concept of hospitality finds its prefiguration and semantic resources, its analogues and paradigms, in the tradition of the religions of the Book. This tradition, moreover, is not just that of Judaism and Christianity, as Levinas, following Rosenzweig, seems to imply. On the contrary, the very formulation recalls an Islamic expression, the "peoples of the Book." Referring to "Judeo-Christian spirituality," Derrida remarks:

> It will one day be necessary, first of all [*d'abord*] so as to recall and understand Islam, to question patiently many of the affinities, analogies, synonymies, and homonymies, be they the result of a crossing of paths, sometimes unbeknownst to the authors, or of necessities that are more profound, though

often perplexing and oblique. The most pressing (and no doubt least noticed) example in France is to be found in another thought of substitution, one that, under this very name, traverses the entire oeuvre and adventure of Louis Massignon. Inherited from Huysmans—whom Levinas in fact evokes early on in *From Existence to Existents* . . .—and at work throughout the tradition of a certain Christian mysticism (Bloy, Foucauld, Claudel, the author of *The Hostage,* etc.) to which Massignon remains faithful, the word-concept "substitution" inspires in Massignon a whole thought of "sacred hospitality," a foundational reference to the hospitality of Abraham, or Ibrahim, and the institution, in 1934, of *Badaliya*—a word that belongs to the Arab vocabulary of "substitution." (*AL* 145–46 n. 71 / 128 n. 1, trans. modified)

These parallels are not limited to isolated authors that one should read in light of—and as correction to—each other, in preparation for a not more inclusive but hospitable thought of substitution. More than a Judeo-Christian-Islamic consensus and its "logic" is at stake here. This is clear from Derrida's recent interventions: for example, at the Rencontre de Rabat avec Jacques Derrida, which took place in 1996 in Morocco and was published under the title *Idiomes, nationalités, déconstructions* (*Idioms, Nationalities, Deconstructions*).[18] Here, under the heading of a rigorously assumed "'être-avec' les musulmans"—"'being-with' Moslems," echoing, concretizing, and, as it were, ontically correcting the expression *Mitsein,* which punctuates Heidegger's analysis of the ontological structures of sociality in *Being and Time*), Derrida speaks of the structural similarities and idiomatic and national dissimilarities enabling or imperiling the chances of a common heritage that, in the course of an often violent history, has been assumed and diffused in various ways. These improvised analyses were formulated in a context of debate that was set the following task by the volume's editor: "(1) Open an avenue for an explication with Islam in its anthropological and metaphysical constitution. (2) Reinterrogate the opposition between Islam and Europe, in view of a reinterpretation of their relations."[19] Such an undertaking, Derrida seems to suggest,

18. Jacques Derrida, "Fidélité à plus d'un: Mériter d'hériter où la généalogie fait défaut," in *Idiomes, nationalités, déconstructions: Rencontre de Rabat avec Jacques Derrida, Cahiers Intersignes,* no. 13, ed. Fethi Benslama (Paris and Casablanca: Toubkal & Intersignes, 1998). Here we find another reference to Massignon (ibid., 228), as well as to the interpretation of the origin or source of the "religious," to be distinguished from "relation," this time in "suspense, abstention, shame [*pudeur*], reserve, respect, the secret, the mystery, the mystical, the separation, holiness, sacrality, immunity" (ibid., 227). See also Louis Massignon, *Parole donnée* (Paris: Seuil, 1983).

19. Fehti Benslama, "Éditorial," in *Idiomes, nationalités, déconstructions,* 12 n. 11. The third

does not mean indulging in the celebrated — or decried — untranslatability of some religious or national idiom. On the contrary, Derrida writes:

> My temptation — today as always, without doubt — would dictate two fidelities: to respect the untranslatable irreducibility of the idiom, certainly, but at the same time to apprehend that untranslatability otherwise. The latter would no longer be a hermetic limit, the impenetrable opacity of a screen, but, on the contrary, a provocation to translation. Already an engagement to translate in the experience of the untranslatable as such. To apprehend the untranslatable, to apprehend as such, is to read, to write, in the strong sense of the word, to be sure; it is the body-to-body with the idiom. . . . From the outset the "poem" inscribes itself in a network [réseau] of possible translations. Let's call here "poem" the unicity of the signature, the occurrence, the event of such a discursive performance, where meaning no longer lets itself be separated from a phrase, of a vocabulary and a grammar. I do not oppose thereby the translatable to the untranslatable. I always search, in the "sacred" respect for the idiom, for a universal political chance, a universality that is not the crushing of the idiom. Is that possible?[20]

That is only possible, Derrida goes on to suggest, on the condition that one redefine the understanding of *being-with*, whose very possibility consists in noncoincidence — indeed, differentiality — within the idiom itself. This difference with respect to itself is the space or *lapsus* that at once conditions and calls for translation.

The "sacred" respect for the idiom and its "universal political chance" — this formulation, Derrida hastens to add, presupposes a preceding transcendental structure of which the idiom would be merely a concrete, ontico-empirical exemplar. Yet any transcendentality will be folded back into the idiom that it, in turn, paradoxically also reveals. This reverse implication of the general in the singular and vice versa is responsible for the fact that there is no universality or idiomaticity, *stricto sensu*. Derrida writes: "I would not say by this that there is *first* the possibility of this respect, some general religion that would come here to take the idiom for one of its exemplary themes or objects. This experience of the idiom, this desire of the idiom to be safe, this salvation of the idiom to be guarded

---

task consists in mobilizing the analytical resources of psychoanalysis. For a more general account of the relationship between Islam and the West that steers clear of essentialist and homogeneous portrayals, see Aziz Al-Azmeh, *Islam and Modernities* (London: Verso, 1996; orig. pub. 1993).

20. Derrida, "Fidélité à plus d'un," 224.

intact, immune, sacrosanct, is itself the origin of religion."[21] The idiom
or revelation reveals the structure of revealability at least as much as it is
revealed by it.

There are many reasons to attribute to hospitality—the general structure of absolute hospitality—a certain prevalence, one resembling the primacy of ethicity over moral principles, practical rules, and juridical prudence. This is clear from the following passage, in which Derrida reminds
us that hospitality stands not only for the ethicity of ethics, but also for
openness to what threatens the very possibility of ethics (and ethicity):
namely, hostility or worse. I will return to this flip side of all hospitality,
including absolute hospitality, below. As we will see, it plays an important
role in the pages Derrida devotes to Carl Schmitt, notably in *Politics of
Friendship*. Derrida echoes this interpretation by drawing the consequence
of Levinas's own analysis:

> Intentionality is hospitality, then, says Levinas quite literally. The force of this
> copula carries hospitality very far. There is not some intentional experience
> that, here or there, would or would not undergo the circumscribed experience
> of something that would come to be called, in a determining and determinable
> fashion, hospitality. No, intentionality opens, from its own threshold, in its
> most general structure, as hospitality, as welcoming of the face, as an ethics of
> hospitality, and, thus, as ethics in general. For hospitality is not simply some
> region of ethics, let alone . . . the name of a problem in law or politics: it is
> ethicity itself, the whole and the principle of ethics. And if hospitality does not
> let itself be circumscribed or derived, if it originarily [*originairement*] conveys
> the whole of intentional experience, then it would have no contrary: the phe-
> nomena of allergy, rejection, xenophobia, even war itself would still exhibit
> everything that Levinas explicitly attributes to or allies with hospitality. . . .
> Whether it wants to or not, whether we realize it or not, hostility still attests
> to hospitality. (*AL* 50 / 94)

Where does this leave us? As I see it, this statement allows two possible interpretations. First, we seem to touch here, once more, upon a
certain generalization of the concept of hospitality—as the welcoming of
the best *and* the worst and of everything in between, one that entails the
simultaneous trivialization and intensification of its meaning. If hospitality, in its very absoluteness, is somehow, in a singular way, *everywhere*—

21. Ibid., 265 n. 2.

in hospitality *and* in hostility, in friendship *and* enmity, in our relation to other human beings *and* in the openness to any intentional (ideal, material, animal) object whatsoever—then it is also *nowhere* to be found, or at least never as such, in its integrity, intact. This is, perhaps, what is implied by the adjective *absolute*, which indicates the fact—a fact of reason, of sorts—that hospitality thus (we can no longer say "properly") understood absolves itself from any conceptual or empirical fixation or determination—for good and ill, since this necessity is its risk no less than its chance. Such ambiguity and its accompanying uncertainty raise the stakes involved in any welcome, in the openness to any future. While dealing with the best, one may in fact be facing the worst, and allowing for the possibility of the worst is a necessary condition of the best. Mutatis mutandis, the same would hold true for the intermediary and less dramatic range of possible positions that makes up the spectrum of the ethical, the political, the juridical—in short, of the pragmatic.

But there is more. As Derrida points out, we can speak of a history of hospitality because of the co-extensiveness, co-existence, and co-implication of ethics and hospitality—as well as of these two and a hospitality to the possibility of the worst. In this emplotment (in French, *intrigue*) or divine comedy, an infinite responsibility leaves its mark in the finite according to an infinition, a folding of the infinite into the finite, which at each step emphasizes a positive, superlative excess of meaning or signifyingness at least as much as a certain negation. The "in" in "infinity," Levinas stresses, does not point toward a privation but indicates the place where the other takes hold and hollows one out in a process of relentless singularization, substitution, and so on. This is a *kenosis* and *incarnation* of sorts, but one that instantiates, diffuses, and disseminates itself before and beyond the concrete—the supposedly historical and divine—features of one Son of man (or *Dieu-homme*), without leaving its trace in the nonhuman, the living, the nonliving, or the machinal (hence Levinas's radically asymmetric yet intersubjectivist humanism, different from dialogical thought and theories of communicative action, but a *humanisme de l'autre homme*, nonetheless). In consequence, only in the order of the finite—not in some transcendent or purely transcendental world—does responsibility come to pass. But the finite is not all.

In history, the concepts of hospitality (messianicity, friendship) and of ethics, together with their respective sociopolitical manifestations, institutions, or instantiations, revolve around each other, correct each other, supplement and at times interpenetrate each other, to the point of confusion:

> Hospitality is culture itself and not an ethics among others. Insofar as it
> touches upon the *ethos,* that is to say, upon the dwelling [*la demeure*], the
> home [*chez-soi*], upon the familiar place of residence as much as upon the way
> of being there, upon the manner of relating oneself to oneself and to others, to
> others as those who are one's own or as those who are strangers, *ethics is hospi-*
> *tality,* it is in part co-extensive with the experience of hospitality, in whatever
> way one opens or limits it. But for the same reason, and because being-at-
> home [*l'être-soi chez soi*] (ipseity itself) supposes a welcome or an inclusion
> of the other that one seeks to appropriate, control, master according to differ-
> ent modalities of violence, there is a history of hospitality, an always-possible
> perversion of the Law of hospitality (which can appear unconditional) and of
> the laws that come to limit and condition it and inscribe it in a rule of law [*un*
> *droit*].[22]

Without this inevitable translation—and betrayal—the very notion of universal hospitality would remain an empty and even irresponsible dream. Conversely, if hospitality were reduced to the laws and examples that make up its history, whether individually or as a sum total, then its concept and practical instantiations would lose their critical potential and universalistic import. Neither as an absolute idea nor as a concrete example—neither as the Law nor as a series of particular laws—is hospitality ever given as such, in its purity or integrity. This is why the relationship between hospitality and all the notions, concepts, rules, and practices of hospitality—including the very concept of hospitality—is from the outset aporetic and must irrevocably remain so, if it is thought responsibly—that is to say, hospitably.

The transposition of absolute hospitality into the field of economics (and thereby into its self-contradiction) does not involve only the inevitable negation and negotiation of an an-archical idea of justice and its

22. Jacques Derrida, *Cosmopolites de tous les pays, encore un effort!* (Paris: Galilée, 1997), 42–43. See also Jacques Derrida and Anne Dufourmantelle, *De l'hospitalité* (Paris: Calmann-Lévy, 1997), 53 / *Of Hospitality,* trans. Rachel Bowlby (Stanford: Stanford University Press, 2000), 53, 55. On the notion of an inevitable "pervertibility"—a radical propensity (*Hang*) toward evil, to use Kant's famous formulation—as a possibility and condition of all perfection, intrinsic to the very concept of perfectibility, see *AL* 34 / 68–69. See also Derrida, "Une hospitalité à l'infini," in *Manifeste pour l'hospitalité: Autour de Jacques Derrida,* ed. Mohammed Seffahi (Paris: Paroles d'aube, 1999), 104 ff.

betrayal by numbers, in the very distribution and thereby limitation of justice—in virtue, precisely, of its limitless demand. Another ontological interruption of the ethical—in and as politics and economy in the common meaning of these words—is equally necessary. The unjustifiable mitigation of justice that takes place in the distribution of justice—of rights and the law, permits and goods—finds a partial justification in that it counterbalances the supposed purity and absoluteness of the responsibility toward the one other, who had seemed to come absolutely first. Seen in this light, the figures of the immigrant and the seeker of asylum evoke not only the stranger but also the third, the one who not only deepens my responsibility but also *gives me a break* and thus makes responsibility, if not bearable or masterable, then at least less violent. The third neither mediates nor mitigates the immediacy of the one for the other—*l'un pour l'autre,* to the point of substitution—that for Levinas constitutes the heart of responsibility, if not of ethics in the traditional and modern philosophical sense, of saintliness and the fear of God. In its interruption of the immediacy of the one for the other, the third is, Derrida notes, itself in turn immediate; it introduces—not after the fact but from the outset of any relation to the other (to *autrui*) as other—*more than one other for the one.* Pushing his interpretation far beyond commentary, Derrida concludes that it is "as if the unicity of the face were, in its absolute and irreducible singularity, plural *a priori*" (*AL* 110 / 190).[23] Only by way of this singular plurality in the very heart of singularity does the appearance of the third in principle "protect against the vertigo [*vertige*] of ethical violence itself" (*AL* 33 / 66). This would be the logic, the argument, or—in Kantian and Husserlian parlance—the "deduction" at work in Levinas's text; without ever being acknowledged, thematized, or formalized as such. To the extent that Levinas offers an "ethical transcendental philosophy" by deducing sociality—the political, laws and rights, the state, and so on—from the structure of "thirdness [*tertialité*]," that is to say, of the one who as a witness (*terstis*) interrupts the complacency of the duality or dialogue of the *I-Thou* or the obsession-substitution-hostage-taking of the *one-for-*

23. Derrida bases this interpretation on Levinas's formulation "The revelation of the third party, ineluctable in the face, is produced only through the face" (*TI* 305 / 282). *Totality and Infinity* already hints at the logic of substitution developed in the central chapter of *Otherwise Than Being,* taken here to imply an a priori and singular pluralization—or infinitization—of the experience of the relation to the other as other. Derrida stresses that this logic of "infinitization" is also a "Christian logic" in a discussion of the Christian origins of the idea of fraternity and its adoption by the French Revolution (see *PF* 268 n. 10 / 263–64 n. 1).

the-other, his analysis allows for a radical possibility whose consequences are far-reaching. Derrida spells them out:

> The deduction proceeds in this way right up to "the political structure of society, subject to laws," right up to "the dignity of the citizen," where, however, a sharp distinction must remain between the ethical subject and the civic one. But this move out of purely ethical responsibility, this interruption of ethical immediacy, is itself immediate. The third does not wait; its illeity calls from as early as the epiphany of the face in the face to face. For the absence of the third would threaten with violence the purity of ethics in the absolute immediacy of the face to face with the unique. Levinas does not say it in exactly this way, but what is he doing when, beyond and through the dual of the face to face between two "uniques," he appeals to justice, affirming and reaffirming that justice "is necessary," that the third is "necessary"? Is he not trying to take into account this hypothesis of a violence in the pure and immediate ethics of the face to face? A violence potentially unleashed in the experience of the neighbor and of absolute unicity? The impossibility of discerning here between good and evil, love and hate, giving and taking, the desire to live and the death drive, the hospitable welcome and the egoistic or narcissistic closing up within oneself?
>
> The third would thus protect against the vertigo of ethical violence itself. For ethics could be doubly exposed to such violence: exposed to undergo it but also to exercise it. Alternatively or simultaneously. (*AL* 32–33 / 65–66)

This is not all. The interruption of the third, while being an interpellation in its own right, given that the third is an other (*autrui*) for me (and hence my neighbor) as well, also constitutes a violation of sorts. It can be treated, judged, and responded to, as such. It divides and diminishes — but also intensifies and exalts — the absolute relationship between the one "me" and the one "other." Both the mediating or mitigating and the hyperbolic effects of "thirdness" (and what other function could *tertialité* have?) violate the purity of the ethical, that is to say, the absolute relationship between uniques or absolutes. The introduction of the third in the one-for-the-other is the drama of this relationship's insufficiency or even exclusivity and hence, paradoxically, of its *being not absolute enough.* In and for itself, the ethical relationship could not rest in itself. Even in its obsessive and traumatic structure — substitution and alienation where no identity, no *idem,* but only an *ipse* remains in place or intact — its restlessness would mean too much peace of mind, uneven reciprocity, *égoisme à deux.* And yet in the one for the other, face to face with the other, I am, in a way, facing all others. The introduction of the third—justice in Levinas's sense—is therefore as much the promise and enactment as the interruption and violation (Derrida says "perjury") of ethical responsibility.

The Torah before and beyond Revelation

Levinas's text thrives on an ambiguity (paradox, aporia) that marks its decidedly philosophical signature and subtracts it from any dogmatic doctrine and, more generally, from all theological, confessional, or edifying discourse. Its argumentative thrust is that of a phenomenological *epochē*, a transcendental reduction, and even, more indirectly, a certain *scepsis*. Yet the movement also gestures in the direction of a formal definition of *religion* stripped of all of this concept's onto-theological determinations. Already in *Totality and Infinity* (and not just in *Otherwise Than Being* or beginning with the essay "La Trace de l'autre" ["The Trace of the Other"]), Derrida shows, Levinas takes a "step back" from the dominant tradition of Western metaphysics in its "onto-theological constitution," far more radically than Heidegger ever attempted. Thus, Derrida writes of the "welcome" that it

> designates, along with the "notion of the face," the opening of the I and the "philosophical priority of the existent over Being." This thought of welcoming thus also initiates a discreet but clear and firm contestation of Heidegger, indeed of the central motif of gathering oneself, of recollection [*recuillement*], or of gathering together (*Versammlung*), of the collecting (*colligere*) that would be accomplished in recollection. There is, of course, a thinking of recollection in Levinas, particularly in the section of *Totality and Infinity* entitled "The Dwelling." But such recollection of the "at home with oneself [*chez-soi*]" already assumes the welcome; it is the *possibility of welcoming* and not the other way around. It makes the welcome possible, and, in a sense, that is its sole destination. One might then say that the welcome to come is what makes possible the recollection of the at home with oneself, even though the relations of conditionality appear impossible to straighten out. They defy chronology as much as logic. The welcome also, of course, supposes recollection, that is, the intimacy of the *at home with oneself* and the figure of woman, feminine alterity. But the welcome [*l'accueil*] would not be a secondary modification of collecting [*cueillir*], of this *col-ligere* that is not without link or ligature to the origin of religion, to this "relation without relation" for which Levinas *reserves,* as he says, the word "religion" as the "ultimate structure": "For the relation between the being here below and the transcendent being that results

in no community of concept or totality—a relation without relation—we reserve the term religion." The *possibility* of the welcome would thus come—so as to open them up—*before* recollection, even before *collecting,* before the act from which everything nonetheless seems to be derived. (*AL* 28-29 / 58-60)

The reference to "religion" in this context recalls three motifs, all of which draw on different semantic and figural archives and allow for contrary analytical possibilities. In addition to Blanchot's motif of the "relation without relation"—independent of all echoes out of the more widely apophatic tradition extending from Pseudo-Dionysius through Meister Eckart and Heidegger up to Marion and, at a certain distance, to Derrida—there is the element of "gathering," which Derrida explores at more length in "Faith and Knowledge." There is also the moment of the halt and the scruple, the impossibility of deciding between possibilities with the help of criteria or once and for all (a motif introduced in "Faith and Knowledge" as well). But the text demands yet another reading.

The structure of openness, of the welcome, seems premised upon experiences that can be better understood against the backdrop of religious idiom. Levinas inscribes the formal, abstract, and absolute structure of the welcome into a particular (and, in part, inevitably particularist) idiom, that of a revealed, positive, and ontic religion, related to a language, a people, a nation. Likewise, Levinas inscribes the welcome into a phenomenology of femininity; a femininity, Derrida reminds us, that, while taken seriously as a philosopheme, is at the same time traditionally and androcentrically defined. Hence this second reinscription demands a double reading—one that at once generalizes or intensifies and trivializes the perspective of the first.

Derrida cites some passages from Levinas's early texts in which these two reinscriptions of the quasi-transcendental structure of the welcome into the empirical—here religion and the feminine—go hand in hand. In both instances, we are dealing with a process of folding and reverse implication of the one in the other; for there is a transformation (one is tempted to say, "transubstantiation") of the empirical into the ontologico-transcendental, following a procedure of phenomenological concretization, on the one hand, and of formal indication, on the other. Are the two instances of equal weight, equally revealing? Or does their respective or simultaneous privileging depend on *strategic* or *pragmatic*—more precisely, *programmatological*—considerations alone? No direct answer is given, but clearly neither religion nor femininity—if these two concepts can be clearly separated—is accorded an *essential* or *principal* status. They are not written in stone, not based on some a priori or anthropological constant belonging to "the living" as such. Religion and sexual difference are not mere facts of life, which is not to say that they are mere ideological constructs. Derrida cites Levinas:

> To dwell is not the simple fact of the anonymous reality of a being cast into existence as a stone one casts behind oneself; it is a *recollection*, a coming to oneself, a retreat home with oneself as in a *land of asylum or refuge*, which answers to a *hospitality*, an expectancy, a *human welcome*. In *human welcome* the language that keeps silence remains an essential possibility. Those silent comings and goings of the feminine being whose footsteps reverberate the secret depths of being are not the turbid mystery of the animal and the feline presence whose strange ambiguity Baudelaire likes to evoke. (*TI* 155–56 / 129)

The fact or, rather, the analytical necessity that the one (a host) who welcomes an other (a guest) is already, *him*self welcomed in *his* own home—the structural insufficiency of the welcome that is made possible by what it makes possible—is thus exemplified and redescribed with the help of a biblical reference and with an uncharacteristic acknowledgment of its overdetermination in terms of sexual difference, more exactly, of femininity. The phrase "a *land of asylum or refuge*" alludes to Leviticus 25:23 and, Derrida reminds us, to a topos found also in Rosenzweig's *The Star of Redemption* (*AL* 42 / 80).

Discussing biblical and contemporary examples of hospitality in Israel's dealings with its neighbors, Egypt in particular—instances analyzed by Levinas in *À l'heure des nations* (*In the Time of Nations*) and in *Au-delà du verset* (*Beyond the Verse*)—Derrida reminds us of a similar independence and dependence of the structure of welcome with regard to the Torah and the revelation at Sinai. He notes,

> Levinas orients his interpretation toward the equivalence of *three concepts*—*fraternity, humanity, hospitality*—that determine an experience of the Torah and of the messianic times even *before* or outside of the Sinai. . . .
>   What announces itself here might be called a structural or *a priori* messianicity. Not an ahistorical messianicity, but one that belongs to a historicity without out a particular and empirically determinable incarnation. Without revelation or without the dating of a given revelation. (*AL* 67 / 121–22)

Can the hospitality inspired and dictated by the Torah be recognized before—and, therefore, independently of—the specific historical occurrence of a revelation or account thereof? Can this Torah have any universal meaning for the individuals, peoples, and nations for whom "the name, the place, the event *Sinai* would mean nothing" (*AL* 65 / 119)? Can hospitality, or a "structural messianicity," ever stand on its own and be comprehended *without* the cultural and political instantiations of its historical forms, punctuated by the many names, proper and common, that haunt the religions and the peoples of the Book? This seems to be a decisive and recurring question in Derrida's most recent work on the relation between revelation and revealability, messianism and messianicity, even though it is never answered in any decisive way, since the problem and trial of a certain indecision—yet another *religio,* again interpreted as a *halt* and *scruple*—is at stake here.

If the dwelling is already hospitable, then the term *hospitality* indicates a general structure whose very form is a welcome of any alterity per se. This mode of relating to the other qua other (regardless of the concrete nature of that singular other), must then be analytically distinguished from the other (*autrui, le visage*), even though it welcomes that other already, first of all, and most of all. Hospitality is the prime characteristic of the relation to the other—paradoxically, of the relation to the other *as* other—it is its inflection: in Levinas's words, the "curving" of the very space of sociality, an inflection that is also a "strange violence" (*PF* 231 / 258). This "violence of the face" assumes an ambiguous role in Levinas's thought. What is more, the figure of curvature (of *courbure,* in French, or *Krümmung,* in German) has a significant function in Kant's characterization of the problem of radical evil. Everything boils down to distinguishing between two curvatures, those of goodness and evil, whose radical difference escapes all demonstration but can, as it were, only be *shown.*

Levinas insists throughout his work that the proximity of the other (the neighbor, the stranger) is that of a "nonformal alterity." What, then, does it mean to be hospitable to the other? It can only mean that the term *hospitality* is used, cited, mentioned in a way that is at once formal and nonformal, pre- or meta-ethical: that is to say, not yet or not quite ethical, the condition and the preamble, the *antechamber,* the threshold, the *parvis* of the ethical—and of the religious as well. One is inextricably bound up with the other. As in the Husserlian motif of transcendental historicity, the moment that in traditional and modern philosophical parlance is called the transcendental *and* its particular—empirical, historical, ontic, positive—instantiations are intertwined: one calls forth the other, one calls for the other, to the point where, for all their separation, they become virtually indistinguishable. This is evoked by the terminology of the quasi-, the simili-, or the ultra-transcendental or by the "passage through the transcendental" — all of which indicates simply that neither the transcendental nor the empirical can claim any independent existence or discursive and differential function as such. Like the a priori and the a posteriori (schema and content, etc.), they are merely analytical distinctions, without any *fundamentum in re*, but nonetheless distinctions without which no conceptual analysis, no language, would be possible. Levinas therefore seems to locate hospitality at once inside and outside the ethical relation when he says that the home "already and henceforth is *hospitable for its owner.* This refers us to its essential interiority, and to the inhabitant that inhabits it *before every inhabitant, the welcoming one par excellence, welcoming in itself — the feminine being"* (*TI* 157 / 131).

Yet if hospitality situates itself at once inside and outside the ethical relation — along with many other terms, many other synonyms — what, then, constitutes its absolute or relative privilege and priority, *here and now,* at this particular juncture in the reception of Levinas's work? Since we are dealing with a hospitality that is not empirical, visible, or thematic — one that, as Derrida rightly points out, hardly ever occurs literally under this name, whether in the texts under consideration or elsewhere in Levinas's oeuvre — neither historico-political nor philological or hermeneutical grounds can be of help. The primacy or prevalence of hospitality in these readings is not (cannot and should not be) motivated by the current worldwide tendencies toward globalization, marked by migration, forced displacements, the decline of the nation-state, and "crimes against hospitality" (*AL* 71 / 132), all of which seem to give the category of hospitality a new prominence and a new urgency. The notion of hospitality is taken here (as much as possible, with an unsurpassable analytical gesture) to be a category beyond all categories, which not only resists definition in common political and juridical terms but, because it is sui generis, must in principle subtract itself from any conceptual determination as well.

Nonetheless, Derrida suggests that "by means of discrete though transparent allusions, Levinas oriented our gazes toward what is happening today" (*AL* 70 / 131). Indirectly, Levinas thus seems to address the present situation in many modern states, in Europe and elsewhere, in which ever more refugees "call for a change in the socio- and geo-political space — a juridico-political mutation, though, before this, assuming that this limit still has any pertinence, an ethical conversion" (*AL* 71 / 131). This resonance between the phenomenological and more than simply phenomenological analysis of the relation to the other, on the one hand, and the contemporary political world order, on the other, does not stand on its own. One is reminded of how Levinas—unlike Heidegger and long before the publication of Derrida's reflections on media, in *The Post Card, Of Spirit,* and *Ulysses gramophone,* which speak of an *être au téléphone*— portrays modern technology as a virtual ally in the process of decontextualization and deterritorialization that makes us face the other—and others—as if for the first time. This motif is not completely absent from Derrida's thoughts on the interplay, even the interface of religion and the new media, as well as the motif of teletranscendence, which Derrida analyzes at length in "Faith and Knowledge" and, more indirectly, in *Échographies: De la télévision (Echographies: Of Television).*[24]

But why hospitality? If in the course of a certain procedure of formalization, desertification, kenosis, and *epochē* concepts or figures start to resemble, mimic, and welcome each other, why and how can we choose one over the other (as we must)? Can we do so without resorting to merely occasionalist, pragmatic, or empirical criteria? Hospitality as a general structure of welcome, of openness, of possibility, of a possibility for better and for worse would be unthinkable without the legacy of the phenomenological tradition and without a certain Heidegger. Levinas is the first to acknowledge this. Yet he proposes at least three further qualifications—indeed, curvatures—of the general structure of intentionality that undo its apparent indifference. Or so it seems, for they in turn introduce a certain ambiguity and indeterminacy that ties the respective alterity—and, as it were, specific difference—back to a foil of indifference, without allowing us to ascertain which comes first.

First, hospitality qua openness is tied, not to a being concerned with its own being, but to the welcoming of the other, of *autrui,* the other human being, in the epiphany of whose face God leaves his trace. Derrida seems to be at once close to and at a certain distance from Levinas here. For Derrida hospitality (as the openness of intentionality) is openness to any event and any phenomenon whatsoever, albeit one that exceeds the bounds of sense that delimit the world of objects and empiricity, whereas Levinas restricts hospitality to the ethical, the metaphysical, the religious, the eschatological, and the messianic (notions that should be used with great care and whose definition is subjected to a rigorous procedure of *infini-*

---

24. I have discussed these matters in the introduction to *Philosophy and the Turn to Religion.* They are further substantiated in de Vries and Weber, eds., *Religion and Media.*

tion). It's just that hostility, war, and worse—the neutral sonority of the *il y a*—overcome and haunt the peace of hospitality as co-originary possibilities. For Levinas, the extremes of welcome and respect versus allergy vis-à-vis the other do not inhabit the same concept. Hence the conceptual necessity of distinguishing, as Derrida does, between a good and a bad hospitality, an openness to the good and to the bad. The boundaries between the two hospitalities are far from stable, however. Transposed into the idiom of hospitality, the relation to the visage is a "visitation": "The trace of this visitation disjoins and *disturbs* [dérange], as can happen during an unexpected, unhoped-for, or dreaded visit, expected or awaited beyond all waiting, like a messianic visit, perhaps" (*AL* 62 / 114–15). Its revelation might be an illusion; its promise, a threat.

Second, as we have seen, Levinas defines hospitality in terms of an understanding of the feminine—"Woman" as "hospitable welcome par excellence" (*TI* 157 / 131)—that, as Derrida shows in an interpretative tour de force, despite its androcentric resonances and obvious perils, allows Levinas's text to be turned into something like a "feminist manifesto" (*AL* 44 / 83). Taking up an earlier discussion of Levinas's ambivalent treatment of the question of the feminine in *Le Temps et l'autre* (*Time and the Other*) and then in the sections of *Totality and Infinity* that deal with interiority, economy, the dwelling, and the phenomenology of eros, Derrida claims that here once more one could be tempted to read Levinas against the grain:

> For this text defines the welcome par excellence, the welcome or welcoming of absolute, absolutely originary, or even pre-originary hospitality, nothing less than the pre-ethical origin of ethics, on the basis of femininity. That gesture reaches a depth of essential or meta-empirical radicality that takes sexual difference into account in an ethics emancipated from ontology. It confers the opening of the welcome upon "the feminine being" and not upon the *fact* of empirical women. The welcome, the anarchic origin of ethics, belongs to "the dimension of femininity" and not to the empirical presence of a human being of the "feminine sex." (*AL* 44 / 83–84)

The feminine, the discrete other, in Levinas's words—but also the feminine (*le féminin*) or, rather, the "dimension of femininity" is both a presence-absence "with which is accomplished the *hospitable welcome par excellence*" (*TI* 155 / 128) and, according to Levinas, its most revealing "modality" (*AL* 36 / 71). Femininity welcomes the welcome and is its best example; it welcomes itself as much as it is welcomed by what it welcomes.

This paradox or aporia makes clear that no structure of possibilization—whether ontic or transcendental—is at work here. Neither comes first or last, and Derrida therefore concludes by asking: "Need one choose here between two incompatible readings, between an androcentric hyperbole and a feminist one? Is there any place for such a choice in ethics? And in justice? In law? In politics? Nothing is less certain" (*AL* 44 / 84).

Third, hospitality is thought as an *à dieu* that in its formal characteristics resembles the utmost possibility of the being-toward-death of which *Being and Time* speaks, adding a different tone and exposing this possibility, as Levinas insists (without, perhaps, foreseeing the full implications of his formulations),[25] to a different climate. What happens when the notion of hospitality—as a universal, categorical, a priori hospitality—is inscribed or finds its most exemplary figure in the idea of the Infinite, in an idea that exceeds the very formalization of excess, of thinking more than one thinks, which can capture it only in part? Derrida cites *Totality and Infinity:* "To approach the Other in discourse . . . is to *welcome* . . . his expression, in which at each instant he overflows the idea a thought would carry away from it. It is therefore to *receive* from the Other beyond the capacity of the I, which means exactly: to have the idea of infinity" (*TI* 51 / 22). What does it mean that this relation without relation is evoked or redescribed in terms whose religious overdetermination or resonance cannot be accidental, given that Levinas always insists on the difference between philosophical and confessional writings, or philosophical and Talmudic readings? What does it mean that for Levinas the offering of hospitality entails belonging to the messianic order (*AL* 72 / 132) and that hospitality and fraternity are *"already a memory of the 'Word of God'"* (*AL* 69 / 126, trans. modified)? Derrida points out that this *souvenir* is immemorial, preceding any spoken or written word, and thus older even than Sinai. Still, what does it mean to say "the Saying *à-Dieu* would signify hospitality" (*AL* 105 / 182)?

One answer might be that the notion "God"—even more so than, say, "the feminine"—is a unique designator for an Other that is uniquely substitutable. In Derrida's recent writings, this proceeds according to a logic summed up in the formula *tout autre est tout autre,* though in Levinas it restricts itself to a logic of asymmetrical substitution, according to which I alone am responsible for all others if not for everything other.[26] Yet it

25. See Derrida's subtle riposte in "Violence and Metaphysics" and my analysis of these passages in "Theotopographies."

26. Of course, things are more complicated, even in Levinas's text. In *Adieu* Derrida ob-

does not suffice to define Levinas's thought as an ethics, let alone as an ethical first—or transcendental—philosophy. What is called ethics here exceeds all ancient and modern conceptions of the ethical and touches, not only on an opening of hospitality that is at least as originary, but also, supposing there is any decisive difference, on religion. Derrida speaks of an "ethics before and beyond ontology, the State, or politics [*la politique*], but also ethics beyond ethics" (*AL* 4 / 15).

At this point, Derrida concludes, we must confront the task of dissociating, "with all the consequences that might follow, a structural messianicity . . . from every determinate messianism: a messianicity before or without any messianism incorporated by some revelation in a determined place that goes by the name of Sinai or Mount Horeb" (*AL* 118-19 / 204). What are the consequences of doing so? Derrida suggests that Levinas offers us the possibility of dreaming, "in more than one sense" of "a revelation of the Torah from before Sinai" or, more carefully, a "*recognition* [reconnaissance]" of the Torah even "before this very revelation" (*AL* 119 / 204). But what does "dreaming"—dreaming "in more than one sense"— mean here? What is the difference between dreaming and the wakefulness and vigilance so often invoked by both Levinas and Derrida? In what sense can (must, should) politics—including or especially a politics of hospitality—"dream"?

Unlike ethics, the welcome—hospitality wherever it comes to pass, if at all—has to do with "the saintliness of the saint." Indeed, for Levinas "'ethics,' the word 'ethics,' is only an approximate equivalent, a makeshift Greek word for the Hebraic discourse on the holiness of the separated (*kadosh*). Which is not to be confused—especially not—with sacredness. But in what language is this possible?" (*AL* 61 / 113). Derrida leaves no doubt that a "recognition of the Torah before Sinai," a recognition "before all revelation" (*AL* 65 / 119), is at issue here. But why, then, invoke tradition, religion in its historical overdetermination, in the first place?

---

serves that its central phrases—such as the one stressing that intentionality is the "attentiveness toward the word or the welcoming of the face, hospitality and not thematization"—open themselves to a "chain of equivalents." In so doing, they raise a key problem that ties our understanding of ethics and politics qua hospitality to a radical rearticulation of ontology and semantics in terms of a relation of what is not in itself related at all. Derrida implies as much when he writes: "But what is the copula doing in this serial proposition? It binds together phenomena of unbinding [*déliaison*]. It assumes that this approach of the face—as intentionality or welcome, that is, as hospitality—remains inseparable from separation itself" (*AL* 46 / 88). This establishment and engagement of a relation without relation forms the very definition of religion as introduced by Levinas and adopted by Derrida.

Why and how is it that only a proper name like *Sinai*—no more enigmatic than the noun *visage*—can remind us of what would have come before Sinai and everything for which it stands? Why speak of "hospitality" or the "face" when mere allusion to openness, revealability, and historicity might suffice to analyze the formal features of the relation without relation that precedes ontology, onto-theology, and the revelations of "positive" religions? Why speak of "religion" as the definition of this relation without relation at all? Why invoke the *adieu*, both *à Dieu* as the relation to the totally other and *a-dieu*, the relation to the other of this other, to the possibility of the *il y a* and worse?[27]

The most important difficulty seems to be that we cannot be sure whether we should translate the trace of the other invoked by the revelation and visitation associated with the name and place of Sinai into the vocabulary of hospitality, as Derrida says, he had "seemed to assume": "Must one not, on the contrary, refer the phenomenon and the possibility of hospitality back to this passing [*passée*] of visitation so as, first of all, to retranslate them? Does not hospitality *follow*, even if just by a second of secondariness, the unforeseeable and irresistible irruption of a visitation?" (*AL* 63 / 116). If such an inverse translation truly touches upon or presupposes a visitation, that visitation will already have preceded any hospitality or laws of hospitality and will have done so immemorially. It will be a trauma or, rather, a traumatic aftereffect, which is never given as such, never presents itself in person, but only as an echo or hearsay (*ouï-dire*). Though Levinas clearly defines fraternity, humanity, and hospitality as notions that, in the final analysis, "already bring back a memory of the

---

27. The *à-Dieu* receives at least three characterizations, inflections of its formal structure or traits of its *concretissimum*. (1) As Derrida recalls, Levinas stresses an intrinsic link between the *à-Dieu* and the love for the stranger (*AL* 104 / 180). (2) The stranger, properly speaking, is an other who in being welcomed is devoid of all determinate—or visible—properties and therefore takes on an almost "spectral aura." The visitation of Other qua Other has, Derrida notes, a "phantomatic character": the *Gast* is a *ghost* (*AL* 111 / 192). (3) Stretching his interpretation to the limit, Derrida concludes that one would "neutralize" Levinas's idiom if one were to reduce the meaning of the *à* to that of "the idea of infinity in the finite," for this would all too easily lead to "forgetting death," to forgetting that Levinas's thinking is "from the beginning to the end" nothing but a "meditation on death" (*AL* 120 / 206). The thinking of the *à-Dieu* is, in the final analysis, a thought of the *adieu*. It engages the whole of the philosophical tradition and its memento mori, from Plato's *epimeleia tou thanatou* up to Heidegger's *Sein zum Tode*. So does its radical—theopolitical—counterpart, the thought of hostility as formulated by Carl Schmitt. See *PF* 123 ff. / 145 ff., esp. 135 n. 18 / 145 n. l, where Derrida writes: "Does the being-for-death of *Dasein* include, in the structure of its essence, war and combat (*Kampf*) or not?" For an elaboration of and tentative answer to this question, see Derrida's "Heidegger's Ear," and my analysis on pp. 358 ff., below.

'Word of God,'"[28] this memory comes before any memory, before every taking place, and thus eludes all archivization. The most one could say is that the name and the place of Sinai seem to signal precisely this "allegorical anachrony" (*AL* 69 / 126). Here we confront a procedure of simultaneous formalization, generalization, and trivialization, a double strategy that at once engages with and is indifferent to the positive, empirical, or ontic singularities — that is to say, the names and places — of which the history of religion is composed, *in part*. In part, because these singularities also gesture toward — presuppose — what makes them possible in the first place and, paradoxically and aporetically, is made possible by them in turn.

Complementary Alternatives

If hospitality is ultimately unthinkable without reference to the notion of religion, not only in Levinas's sense of the word, what light does that shed on other traditions of hospitality? Elsewhere, in the service of a new cosmopolitanism, Derrida invokes: Greek Stoicism as transmitted by Cicero and Seneca; the biblical, medieval, and Talmudic figure of the cities of refuge; and, most rigorously, Kant's Third Definitive Article in "Toward Perpetual Peace," according to which "Cosmopolitan right shall be limited to conditions of universal hospitality."[29]

---

28. Levinas, *A l'heure des nations* (Paris: Minuit, 1988), 112–13 / *In the Time of Nations*, trans. Michael B. Smith (London: Athlone, 1994), 97. See also *TI* 214 / 189: "The very status of the human implies fraternity and the idea of the human race. . . . [I]t involves the commonness of a father [*la communauté de père*], as though the commonness of race [*du genre*] would not bring together enough."

29. On the Stoic influences on Kant's conception, see Martha C. Nussbaum, "Kant and Cosmopolitanism," in *Perpetual Peace: Essays on Kant's Cosmopolitan Ideal*, ed. James Bohman and Matthias Lutz-Bachmann (Cambridge: MIT Press, 1997). Nussbaum, following an elaborate suggestion made by Klaus Reich, argues that Cicero's *De Officiis* decisively influenced Kant during the composition of the *Groundwork of the Metaphysics of Morals* and the later writings. Of lesser importance was Seneca's *Epistulae Morales*, although Nussbaum notes that the conclusion of the *Critique of Practical Reason*, concerning awe before "the starry sky above and the moral law within," clearly echoes Seneca's Letter 41, "expressing awe before the divinity of reasons within us" ("Kant and Cosmopolitanism," 36). There is, perhaps, a remote influence from Epictetus and Marcus Aurelius. Nussbaum recalls that the term *kosmou politēs* may have a Cynic origin, since Diogenes Laertius, in his *Life of the Philosophers*, has Diogenes the Cynic respond to the question whence he came, "I am a *kosmopolitēs*" (Nussbaum, "Kant and Cosmopolitanism," 53 n. 11). Concerning Kant's adoption of certain Ciceronian motifs, Nussbaum says: "There are close parallels between the two thinkers' 'discussions' of the hospitality right ([*De Officiis*] II, 64), and between their extremely stringent accounts of proper moral conduct during wartime and especially of justice to the enemy ([*De Officiis*] I, 38 ff.) . . . Kant is again close to the Stoic analysis when he speaks of the right of all human beings to 'communal pos-

Derrida reminds us that a certain right to immunity and thus a limited practice and jurisprudence of hospitality is already discussed in Numbers 35:9–32, I Chronicles 6:42 and 52, and Joshua 20:1–9.[30] He also notes

session of the earth's surface,' and of the possibility of 'peaceful mutual relations which may eventually be regulated by public laws, thus bringing the human race nearer and nearer to a cosmopolitan constitution'" ("Kant and Cosmopolitanism," 37).

On the current debate concerning the conceptual and pragmatic rearticulation of cosmopolitanism, see also Martha C. Nussbaum with respondents, in *For Love of Country: Debating the Limits of Patriotism,* ed. Joshua Cohen (Boston: Beacon Press, 1996), as well as Martha C. Nussbaum, *Cultivating Humanity: A Classical Defense of Reform in Liberal Education* (Cambridge: Harvard University Press, 1997). Further, with more explicit reference to Kant: Heiner Bielefeldt, "Towards a Cosmopolitan Framework of Freedom: The Contribution of Kantian Universalism to Cross-Cultural Debates on Human Rights," *Jahrbuch für Recht und Ethik / Annual Review of Law and Ethics* 5 (1997): 349–62; and idem, *Philosophie der Menschenrechte: Grundlagen eines weltweiten Freiheitsethos* (Darmstadt: Wissenschaftliche Buchgesellschaft, 1998), 14 ff. and 175 ff.

30. See *Cosmopolites de tous les pays, encore un effort!,* 44. Derrida draws on Levinas, "Cities of Refuge," in *Beyond the Verse,* 34 ff., "Les Villes-refuges," in *L'au-delà du verset,* 51 ff.; and Daniel Payot, *Des villes-refuges: Témoignage et espacement* (Paris: L'Aube, 1992), 65 ff. Both the biblical verses and the Talmudic commentary inspiring Levinas's reading emphasize that the cities of refuge, the six special cities allotted to the Levites, exist for those who are responsible for a crime of which they are objectively though not subjectively guilty: "And the Lord said to Moses. 'Say to the people of Israel, When you cross the Jordan into the land of Canaan, then you shall select cities to be cities of refuge for you, that the manslayer who kills any person without intent may flee there. The cities shall be for you a refuge from the avenger, that the manslayer may not die until he stands before the congregation for judgment'" (Numbers 35:9–12). Crucial here is the difference between manslaughter and murder, both of which provoke the rage of the avenger. Whereas in the Bible these laws are in part a concession to the tribal tradition of blood vengeance—which is not condemned as such, but mitigated and regulated—in Levinas they receive a different significance. For Levinas the protection of those who are half-guilty (and half-innocent) against aggression by the wronged is first of all a reminder of the partly unjustifiable nature of the modern polis, the modern metropolis, whose inhabitants are perhaps not fully without responsibility for the violence outside its walls. Yet in all of its hypocrisy the "political civilization"—in Kant's words, the *status civilis*—for which these cities stand is "better" than the *status naturalis,* driven by passions and free desires; it protects the "subjective innocence" of humanity and to some extent "forgives objective guilt" ("Cities of Refuge," 52 / 70), without ever permitting it a good conscience.

What is more, Levinas observes, the fact that the half-guilt of those who involuntarily or unintentionally commit crimes is not denied or erased blurs the radical distinction between manslaughter and murder, between noncriminals and criminals, and, we might add, between different shades or gradations of violence. Like citizens of modern states, who have taken refuge as if in cities protected by high walls, the limit between intentionality and the lack thereof is blurred. We live, not in full conscience of what is good and just, but rather in the intermediary state of a *clair-obscur*. That is why spiritual life—the city of refuge that is (the study of) the Torah—can never separate itself from the question of justice (or, as Derrida would say, *le droit*), that is to say, from walls of protection and everything they entail. This is not to ignore that the city of refuge remains premised on "ambiguous situations" (ibid., 46 / 64), which must eventually defer to (and can only be experienced as ambiguous when contrasted with) the "absolute

that the tradition of cosmopolitanism infuses the letters of Paul, where it "radicalizes and literally 'politicizes' the first injunctions of every Abrahamic religion," inventing their subsequent "modern names."[31] In Ephesians 2:19, for example, Paul declares that through the unifying peace of Christ those who believe are no longer "strangers [*xenoi, hospites*]" and "sojourners [*paroikoi*]," divided by hostility, but "fellow citizens [*sympolitai, cives*]" and "members of the household [*oikeioi, domestici*]" of God. Likewise, the contemporary appeal for a charter of cities of refuge could, perhaps, be seen as the "secularized version of that Pauline cosmopolitanism."[32] Here we can discern a complex genealogy of what *The Gift of Death*, referring to the work of Jan Patočka, calls the "secrets of European responsibility." Moreover, Kant's insistence that universal hospitality is a natural right, albeit one that is subsequently qualified and restricted, be-

---

vigilance" (ibid.) for which the Torah—yet another inner, concentric circle at the heart of a city—stands.

Here Levinas provides a remarkable critique or correction of the filial schema of responsibility qua fraternity. The latter, Levinas notes, rests upon the same ambiguity as the venerable tradition of the cities of refuge, which are still deeply steeped in tribal laws of bloody retribution. Again, blood vengeance is implicitly tolerated by these texts, if only and so long as there is also a possibility of refuge. In the Talmudic commentary, Levinas points out, the first city mentioned is identified with Reuben, who prevents his brother Joseph from being murdered. In other words: "The ancient status of the city of refuge—the ambiguity of a crime which is not a crime, punished by a punishment which is not a punishment—is related to the ambiguity of human fraternity which is the source of hatred and pity" (ibid., 46–47 / 65). The passage, Levinas concludes, solicits the thought of "another humanity [*une autre humanité*]" (ibid., 47 / 65). The latter is not thought along the lines of sanguinity and phallocentric equality, but is modeled after the asymmetry of the relationship between master and pupil, communicating with each other regardless of the multitude in which they find themselves—in other words, according to "a universality structured differently from the universality of the general and the abstract" (ibid., 49 / 67).

One could imagine yet another reading, midway between those proposed by Levinas and by Derrida. According to this interpretation the biblical image of the cities of refuge would signal a body politic that extends a certain hospitality—at least for a limited time ("until the death of the high priest who was anointed with the holy oil"; Numbers 35:25)—regardless of the subjective motive of those who seek it out as a safe haven: that is to say, for reasons of political and religious persecution or on economic or cultural grounds alone. Current laws of immigration exempt the latter category from consideration for a more extended stay, let alone for naturalization. A necessarily limited number of "cities of refuge" that disregard the more severe formal restrictions adopted by states and federations might signal the arbitrariness of these rules and regulations and establish freer spaces for experimentation with different practices of integration inside and beyond the boundaries of the national state.

31. Derrida, *Cosmopolites de tous les pays, encore un effort!*, 48. Alain Badiou, *Saint Paul: La Fondation de l'universalisme* (Paris: Presses Universitaires de France, 1997), offers a different reading of Paul's engagement with a certain universalism.

32. Derrida, *Cosmopolites de tous les pays, encore un effort!*, 50.

trays "the traits of a secularized theological heritage."[33] Hospitality shares these theologico-political traits with every theory of natural rights and contractual civic duties. Yet this "religious" tradition is highly ambiguous. Though it may call violence and intolerance to a halt, it is more often than not their main instigator and the source of exclusion. This is so not only empirically or historically, but as a possibility inscribed in the visitation by the other. Such visitation is not an act of peace, but a passion that deserves to be called "violent." Commenting on *Otherwise Than Being,* Derrida explains this as follows: "In the assignation of responsibility, the election of the hostage seems not only more 'originary' (in truth, as always, more originary than the origin) but violent, indeed traumatizing—more so, it seems, than the sometimes pacifying vocabulary of the welcome and of the hospitality of the host might suggest" (*AL* 59 / 109).

This insight that the promise resembles a threat, as Derrida makes clear in "Avances,"[34] or that the face of the other, in its invisibility and being without predicate, takes on an almost "spectral" or phantomatic character (*AL* 111 / 192) is at odds not only with the premises of those theorists who treat the promise as a speech act (*AL* 89 / 158) and the moral philosophies or discourse ethics built upon them, but also with the interpretation that Levinas himself seems at times to give his own project, in terms of an ethical first philosophy or, as has been extrapolated, an ethical transcendental philosophy. Clearly, things are more complicated. As Derrida points out, the radicality of this perspective can hardly be overestimated. It marks a significant but subtle divergence from the Kantian view.

> The closing of the door, inhospitality, war, and allergy already imply, as their possibility, a hospitality offered or received: an original or, more precisely, pre-originary declaration of peace. Here is perhaps one of the most formidable traits in the logic of an extremely complex relation with the Kantian legacy that . . . distinguishes ethical or originary peace (originary but not natural: it would be better to say pre-originary, an-archic), according to Levinas, from "perpetual peace" and from a universal, cosmo-*political,* and thus political and juridical hospitality, the hospitality that Kant reminds us must be instituted in order to interrupt a bellicose state of nature, to break with a nature that knows only actual or virtual war. Instituted as peace, universal hospitality must, according to Kant, put an end to natural hostility. For

---

33. Ibid., 52.
34. Jacques Derrida, "Avances," in Serge Margel, *Le Tombeau du dieu artisan* (Paris: Minuit, 1995).

> Levinas, on the contrary, allergy, the refusal or forgetting of the face, comes to inscribe its secondary negativity against a backdrop of peace, against the backdrop of a hospitality that does not belong to the order of the political, or at least not simply to a political space. (*AL* 48-49 / 92)

Paradoxically, for Levinas — in contrast to many modern contract theories and their postulation of an originary war of all against all — everything begins with peace. He describes the uncertain modality of this originary or, rather, preoriginary peace, but does so in a terminology that suggests nothing peaceful. Whereas in Kant's "Toward Perpetual Peace" peace consists in a process of infinite approximation and gradual movement away from the state of war (*Zustand des Krieges*) that defines the state of nature (*status naturalis, Naturzustand*), although war threatens to return at any moment,[35] Levinas insists on a peace *here and now,* to which even the most outrageous hostility, even war, continues obliquely to attest. Here, Derrida comments in an ironic reversal of von Clausewitz's dictum, war is the continuation of peace by other means. This peace, which manifests itself at any given moment, in one way or another, is far from being idyllic. It is neither ontological, nor instituted politically and juridically (*gestiftet,* as Kant would have it), but genuinely metaphysical and, in the precise sense Levinas gives to the word, religious. While it should not be confused with the image of the graveyard with which Kant opens his essay, it is nonetheless characterized by trauma, even by a certain violence. Levinas's conception of peace, therefore, is "anything but political irenism" (*AL* 95 / 168). And yet, it is hardly the position we have analyzed in Schmitt. As Derrida points out:

> Levinas never speaks of Schmitt. This theoretician of the political is situated at the opposite extreme from Levinas, with all the paradoxes and reversals that such an absolute position might harbor. Schmitt is not only a thinker of hostility (and not of hospitality); he not only situates the enemy at the center of a "politics" that is irreducible to the ethical, if not to the juridical. He is also, by his own admission, a sort of Catholic neo-Hegelian who has an essential need to adhere to a thought of totality. This discourse of the enemy as the discourse of totality, so to speak, would thus embody for Levinas the absolute

---

35. See also Jürgen Habermas, "Kants Idee des ewigen Friedens — aus dem historischen Abstand von 200 Jahren," in *Die Einbeziehung des Anderen: Studien zur politischen Theorie* (Frankfurt a. M.: Suhrkamp, 1996); "Kant's Idea of Perpetual Peace, with the Benefit of Two Hundred Years' Hindsight," trans. James Bohman, in *Perpetual Peace: Essays on Kant's Cosmopolitan Ideal,* ed. James Bohman and Matthias Lutz-Bachmann (Cambridge: MIT Press, 1997).

adversary. More so than Heidegger, it seems. For Heidegger does not give in either to "politism" or to the fascination of a (supposedly Hegelian) totality. The question of being, in its transcendence (*epekeina tes ousias,* a phrase that Heidegger also often cites), goes beyond the totality of beings. The passage beyond totality was thus, at least in its formality, a movement whose necessity Heidegger, no less than Rosenzweig, recognized. Whence the stained and precarious filiation of a heritage. (*AL* 147 n. 95 / 161–62 n. 1)

In the same vein, Derrida notes, Schmitt adheres to the "traditional and predominant way of determining the subject" and is hence, unlike Levinas, "incapable of accounting for the slightest decision" (*AL* 135–36 n. 8 / 52 n. 2; cf. *PF* 68–69 / 86–88).

But how can one maintain that peace and hospitality lie at the bottom of even conflict and war, when the elusive and almost phantomatic quality of the relation to the face in itself contains the features of obsession and trauma, even of a certain violence? What if the sonorous and senseless *il y a* haunts and doubles the divine *illeité* to the point of becoming virtually indistinguishable from it? Derrida distinguishes between two radically different, opposed, and juxtaposed modes of welcome offered to or received from the other. For this relation to be what it is—a relation (without relation, again in the Levinasian definition of religion) and not any programmatic exchange of moves—there *must be* (il faut) at least the possibility that the relation to the other will pervert itself: "This possible hospitality to the worst is necessary so that good hospitality might have a chance" (*AL* 35 / 69). Following the lines of thought set out in *The Gift of Death,* Derrida analyzes this difficulty by pointing to the "intolerable scandal" that *justice begins with a perjury,* that ethics is violently interrupted by the third—the other of the other, the other in the other, given with this very other—while this interruption also interrupts an at least virtual violence of the ethical, which, *left to itself,* resembles the worst. In spite of his insistence on the "non-violent transitivity" (*TI* 51 / 22) in which the epiphany of the face is produced, Levinas would seem to subscribe to this analysis, at least implicitly, evoking the *il y a* as a modality of transcendence, *illéité.* Hospitality, then, opens in two directions, circles around two foci, stems from two sources. It signals both a welcome—of the gift of the other, giving oneself (up) to the other—and an abandonment, desertion, even desperation. In the final pages of *Adieu,* Derrida speaks of the link between Levinas's ethics of hospitality and this nonreciprocity in the relation to Other: "What would faith or devotion be when directed toward

a God who would not be able to abandon me? Of whom I would be absolutely certain, assured of his concern? A God who could but give to me
or give of himself to me? Who could not not choose me?" (*AL* 104 / 181).
The relation to the other is thus as much premised on a gesture toward
the totally other, on the *à dieu* (or *à Dieu*) as it remains exposed to the departure of (and from) this other, that is to say, on the *adieu* (as well as the
a-dieu, the *il y a,* the demonic, the worst). But what, exactly, necessitates,
motivates, or justifies emphasis on one movement rather than the other?

The notion of hospitality points both ways. We must attribute to it a
certain transcendental or quasi-transcendental status, but where it is left to
itself and does not translate and betray itself in concrete (empirical, positive) laws, which—inevitably—offer less than the universal or absolute
openness it calls for, it betrays itself. Any concrete form hospitality might
take is of necessity absolutely distant from the universal and measureless
measure, which allows for no gradual approximation. But without such
form, it resembles and indeed welcomes or solicits the worst. This is why a
good conscience, the reluctance to dirty one's hands, to compromise, or to
negotiate, is irresponsible. Hospitality, taken in its emphatic, absolute, or
all-encompassing sense is caught in a familiar aporetics: rather than give
itself in a simple all or nothing, it is all *and* nothing. It must partition itself
in order to remain whole (or wholesome); it must be forgotten and done
away with in order to be remembered and lived up to.

If the modality of transcendence must be described in this way, can
there still be any correspondence or analogy between hospitality as a pre-
or meta-ontological relation to the other and hospitality as an ethics and
politics of practices and rights, of nations and states, citizens and institutions? Why not simply side with Kant and move from the originari-
ness of displacement and abandonment—of war—rather than take one's
point of departure from a peace that, for all its anteriority, always still
needs to come here and now? A peace moreover, that is characterized by
a peculiar—nonempirical and transcendental—violence of its own, one
that may, indeed, inspire or ignite all the other violences that we know of?

Derrida makes clear that the Kantian conception is less radical, since it
limits hospitality—universal hospitality—to a mere political and juridical, a cosmopolitical arrangement of citizens and states (*AL* 68 / 124 and,
notably, 88 / 156–57). Levinasian hospitality, by contrast, involves a "beyond of the political." But what could speak, philosophically or phenomenologically, for emphasizing or privileging a certain hospitality to the
good, the best, the just? This question also pertains to the notion—in-

deed, the politics—of friendship. Once more, we are dealing with what Derrida, in "Différance," calls "nonsynonymous substitution." The relation between them—like the openness and alterity they seek to convey—resembles a relation without relation, to the point that the word *relation* becomes almost inappropriate (or is, in the end, no better than any other term). Why, then, discuss one term—one "synonym"—rather than another? How and when can we move from one to the next? At times it seems that the answer to these questions could only be pragmatic or, if not empirical and contingent, then based on a testimony and confession in which a certain chance and necessity are simultaneously affirmed. On other occasions, however, the answer is left in abeyance.

Levinas's heritage seems to inspire two different kinds of politics, which are complementary alternatives. Each entails certain risks and dangers, and each situates itself uneasily vis-à-vis the current debates between liberals, communitarians, multiculturalists, and others. These alternative models coexist in Levinas's double and at bottom aporetic position with respect to the politics of Zionism. This position, Derrida clarifies, enables us "*on the one hand,* to interpret the Zionist *commitment,* the promise, the sworn faith and not the Zionist *fact,* as a movement that carries the political *beyond* the political, and thus is caught between the political and its other, and, *on the other hand,* to think a peace that would not be purely political" (*AL* 79 / 144).

In both options we are dealing with a new and broadly defined politics of hospitality and generosity: one that welcomes the other *as such* or *in principle.* This politics should not be confused with modern, liberal-democratic concepts and practices of tolerance, as Derrida points out.[36]

36. To accept the strangers among us as strangers implies engaging in a political virtue at the heart of the *res publica* that, Derrida notes, cannot be reduced to tolerance, "unless this tolerance itself requires the affirmation of a 'love' without measure" (*AL* 72 / 133). For Levinas, Derrida points out, this demand regulates the relationship between Israel and other peoples and is therefore the heart of *Jewish thought.* Moreover, following a singular logic of election, particularity, and universality, it "opens the way to the humanity of the human" (ibid.). At stake is a logic of exemplarity that relates the singular to the general, indeed, the universal—and vice versa—and that here finds its most revealing name in Sinai. The name *Sinai,* Derrida suggests, is at once the unique inscription of a particular history, of a place and time and destiny, whose idiom and idiosyncrasy—*hapax legomenon*—one should never forget, and the metonymy for much (indeed, virtually everything) else, in the Middle East and worldwide, in the past, present, and future. In fact, Derrida goes on to suggest, it stands for all the borderlines drawn between this people and others, other peoples and yet others, peace and war, the nation-state and all the many displaced persons whose status (that of being alien, refugee, exiled, immigrant, deported, stateless, *sans papiers,* etc.; cf. *AL* 64 / 117–18 and *Cosmopolites de tous les pays, encore un*

The latter remain premised on a certain Christianity (or Christianicity) that goes hand in hand with an ultimate "indifference" to the political and thus differs from "pre- or post-Christian Judaism" (*AL* 75 / 137), from what could be called a politics of negotiation. Interestingly, Derrida observes that in Judaism, as interpreted by Levinas, the disjunction between what Augustine called the *civitas terrena* and the spiritual *civitas Dei* has a less "clear-cut character" than in Christianity, and that precisely because of this *"political spirit of indifference"* Christianity "so often became a State religion."[37]

How can we distinguish between such Christian indifference and the "instantaneous meantime [*l'entretemps instantané*] of decision" (*AL* 116 / 200), a silence not unrelated to the "nonresponse [*sans-réponse*]" that, for Levinas, defines death? On Derrida's reading, death and the toward-death, again in all the ambiguity of the *à-Dieu* and *adieu*, casts its shadow on the both impossible and imperative translation of the ethical — more exactly, of sanctity — into the many rules, norms, and rights of the juridico-political. (The very concept of ethics already constitutes the first translation — and betrayal — of responsibility.) The "hiatus" between responsibility and the juridico-political is, Derrida writes, not merely an "empirical contingency" but a fact of reason, in the sense Kant attributes to the word *Faktum:* the "heterogeneity" or "discontinuity" between these "two orders" (*AL* 116–17 / 201). The distinction, which is not simply that between the Kantian intelligible/noumenal realm of the thinkable and the sensible/phenomenal realm of possible experience, makes the search for schemas at once possible (even necessary or imperative) and, from the outset, impossible. In this difficulty of defining the political in contradistinction to the ethical and the religious (and to hospitality in the emphatic, hyperbolical, and absolute sense of the word), Derrida is himself at

---

effort!, 14) should not be reduced to a single category, whether that of the stranger or the guest, but should be thought, respected, and welcomed in its specificity as well as *absolutely*. Every single one of them demands and already signals an inflection and curvature of the social space and the body politic, its institutions, its laws, its customs, its ideals, its contracts, its treaties, etc. It is, Derrida concludes, toward the "violence" and the "distress" (*AL* 64 / 118) of all the endless conflicts that loom — and, more often than not, eventually manifest themselves — here, on an unprecedented scale, that Levinas's analyses orient themselves, "whether he spoke of it directly or not, in one way or another" (ibid.). Derrida speaks most directly about the more practical side of hospitality in "Manquements du droit à la justice (mais que manque-t-il aux 'sans-papiers'?)," in Jacques Derrida et al., *Marx en jeu* (Paris: Descartes & Cie, 1997). See also idem, *Sur parole*, 63–74.

37. Levinas, *Beyond the Verse*, 177 / 209. See in this context also Adorno's discussion of St. Augustine in "Progress" and my *Theology in Pianissimo*.

once close to Judaism (in Levinas's sense), and to Christianity (in its early Christian and Augustinian—and perhaps early Heideggerian—determinations). At times Derrida seems to dream of a conception of the political (of a politics of hospitality and of friendship) that situates itself beyond the Greek and modern "post-Hegelian" tradition, just as Levinas is not afraid of espousing, here and there (though never without qualifying the terms involved), a "messianic politics" (*AL* 74 / 136). In most contexts, however, this beyond of the political becomes more and more difficult to situate. In consequence, Derrida writes, one may ask oneself whether "the alternative between the State of Caesar and the State of David is an alternative between a politics [*une politique*] and a beyond of the political [*du politique*], or an alternative between two politics, or finally, *an* alternative among *others,* where one could not exclude the hypothesis of a State that would be neither of Caesar nor of David, neither Rome nor Israel nor Athens" (*AL* 74 / 136).

This unclarity is neither weakness nor deplorable and, in principle, avoidable inconsistency. Levinas's conception of the political, Derrida writes, "seems to defy any topological simplicity" (*AL* 75 / 138). Like the concept of hospitality (and those of friendship and the messianic), the very idea of the political—and the very practice of politics—can no longer be assigned to a specific place, a topos, a nation, a land. Rather, both are at once within and outside the classical and modern coordinates that determine the realm or the space of the political, especially its connection with the concept of the state or nation. This is clearly expressed in the title of a late Talmudic reading by Levinas: "Au-delà de l'État dans l'État" ("Beyond the State in the State"),[38] on which Derrida comments: "*Beyond-in:* transcendence in immanence, *beyond* the political, but *in* the political. Inclusion opened onto the transcendence that it bears, incorporation of a door [*porte*] that bears [*porte*] and opens onto the beyond of the walls . . . framing it [*l'encadrent*]. At the risk of causing the identity of the place as well as the stability of the concept to implode" (*AL* 76 / 138).

As the earlier reference to Rosenzweig already indicated: mutatis mutandis, this nonlocalizable quality of the ethical (the political, the re-

38. Emmanuel Levinas, *Nouvelles Lectures talmudiques* (Paris: Minuit, 1996). See also "The State of Caesar and the State of David," in *Beyond the Verse.* On Levinas's "politics," see Marie-Anne Lescourret, *Emmanuel Levinas* (Paris: Flammarion, 1994), 338 ff.; Olivier Mongin, "La Parenthèse politique," in *Emmanuel Levinas: L'Ethique comme philosophie première,* ed. Jean Greisch and Jacques Rolland (Paris: Cerf, 1993); and Guy Petitdemange, "Emmanuel Levinas et la politique," ibid.

ligious—the difference matters little) holds true for its relation to history —in its process, totality, and historicity (or *Geschichtlichkeit*)—as well. Situated between "two models of redemption," the eternal paradigm of Judaism and the historical manifestation and incarnations of Christianity, two models whose "complimentarity" and then "opposition" do not exclude but, on the contrary, imply a certain "symmetry," responsibility navigates between two extremes. These extremes, however, are no longer alternatives but mutually constitutive—and corrective—of a single drama. Two sources of morality and religion, once more. This seems the message of the third book of *The Star of Redemption*, powerfully interpreted by Stéphane Mosès in his *Système et Révélation* (*System and Revelation*) and endorsed by Levinas on more than one occasion.[39] Significantly, this drama made up by Judaism and Christianity is not described from within, by spelling out the self-understanding and rivalry of theologies, dogmas, and sacred texts, but from the external perspective of the contrast between their respective forms of life and sociality. Nonetheless, they constitute not mere historical—or positive—religions but, as it were, "*two categories of being.*"[40] From the outset—and, one wonders, also at the end?—the truth is not just one, undivided, identical with itself, monological (or even mono-theistic?). On the contrary, there is an originary—and, one wonders, ultimate?—"*multiplicity* of reality [*du réel*]."[41] Hence, as Kant knew, a dual citizenship, the necessary possibility of belonging to two different worlds at once.[42]

Though it is difficult and perhaps impossible to *think* this tension, we

39. See the conversation transcribed in Gotthard Fuchs and Hans Hermann Henrix, eds., *Zeitgewinn: Messianisches Denken nach Franz Rosenzweig* (Frankfurt a. M.: Verlag Josef Knecht, 1987), esp. 166, as well as Mosès, *Système et Révélation*, 228 ff., and Levinas's preface (ibid., 7–8), which speaks of a "surprising idea of Truth that by its very essence splits itself [*se scindant*] between Christianity and Judaism, two adventures of the spirit that would both—and with equal validity [*au même titre*]—be necessary for the truth of Truth [*la vérité du Vrai*]. A philosophical and theological position without precedent in the history of thought, an anticipation [or presentiment, *pressentiment*] of the ecumenical tendencies today, completely free from all syncretism."

40. Mosès, *Système et Révélation*, 231.

41. Ibid. And yet, as Mosès notes, we are not dealing here with some metaphysical dualism, separating the determinism of the sensible world from the freedom of the intelligible realm, but with a "rigorous symmetry of a chiasma" (ibid., 233).

42. Pascal seems to suggest as much when he writes: "If God had permitted only one religion, it would have been too easily recognizable." However, he immediately adds: "But, if we look closely, it is easy to distinguish the true religion amidst all this confusion." (See Blaise Pascal, *Pensées*, trans. A. J. Krailsheimer [Harmondsworth, Middlesex: Penguin Books, 1966], 102.)

live and instantiate it every day. It is at the heart of each decision and thus of the very structure of everydayness as such. As in Kant's writings on the different historical forms of religion that form concentric circles relating (without relating) to the innermost circle of "moral religion" — in Kant's view, religion proper, the disposition that regards the duties dictated by moral law as divine commands — so the relation between absolute hospitality and the laws of hospitality has a merely formal (or formally indicative?) nature. Here we touch again upon the central problem of transcendental historicity: any event, occurrence, or action is as if suspended between two interdependent elements — the singular or particular and the universal, the empirical or ontic and the intelligible or ontological, the absolutely concrete and the absolutely abstract. What, in this context, does that mean?[43]

43. It cannot mean, I think, that one should interpret, for example, cosmopolitanism in a manner that relies too heavily on its original Stoic imagery and metaphysical premises, as does Martha Nussbaum in "Kant and Cosmopolitanism," "Patriotism and Cosmopolitanism" (in *For Love of Country*, ed. Cohen), and *Cultivating Humanity*, but also in *The Therapy of Desire: Theory and Practice in Hellenistic Ethics* (Princeton: Princeton University Press, 1994). Genuine differences between Nussbaum's adaptation of the Stoic motif and its rearticulations in Derrida, no less than in Kant's idea of the coming about of the kingdom of ends, are:

(1) Nussbaum adopts the metaphor of concentric circles as if world citizenship consisted in drawing strangers into one's own circle of affection and loyalty or, conversely (but this comes down to the same), in expanding one's own circle until it coincides with the outer circle of humanity as such (cf. *Cultivating Humanity*, 60–61). Both Kant and Derrida, however, take these circles to be in principle distinct, heterogeneous, even though they necessarily refer to and imply one another. Whether the heterogeneity in question is ultimately served by or compatible with the figure of concentricity — that is to say, of two figures that match each other at least in form if not in diameter, regardless of whether one should conclude with Derrida and against Kant that each of the circles in question contains the other as much as it is contained by this other — raises consequences ignored by Nussbaum. She relies here heavily on a classical topos: "Hierocles, a Stoic of the first and second centuries A.D., using an older metaphor also in Cicero's *De Officiis* [*De Officiis*, I, 50 ff.], argued that we should regard ourselves not as devoid of local affiliation but as surrounded by a series of concentric circles. The first circle is drawn around the self; the next takes in one's immediate family; then follows the extended family; then, in order, one's neighbors or local group, one's fellow city dwellers, and one's fellow country men. Outside all these circles is the largest one, that of humanity as a whole. Our task as citizens of the world will be to 'draw the circles somehow toward the center,' making all human beings more like our fellow city dwellers, and so forth" ("Kant and Cosmopolitanism," 32–33).

(2) The same could be said of the "organic imagery" according to which "all human beings are limbs of a single body" (ibid., 64). The reference here is to Marcus Aurelius's *Meditations*, but it allows one to formulate some suspicions concerning the unquestioned category of "humanity" or the "human" along lines set out by Derrida's "The Ends of Man" ("Les Fins de l'homme"). The same holds for the passage from Terence's *Heautontimoroumenos* taken up by Cicero in *De Officiis* and cited by Kant in the *Metaphysics of Morals*: "Homo sum: humani nihil a me alienum putto" ("I am a human being: I think nothing human alien to me"; cited after Nuss-

On the one hand, there must be a translation and retranslation of the absolute welcome into the many laws that follow upon it — *"This relation is necessary* [Il faut ce rapport]," Derrida writes — and not every "deduction" is equally valid, responsible, or just. And yet, Derrida insists, "Even in its 'hypocritical' nature, 'political civilization' remains 'better' than barbarism" (*AL* 115 / 198). On the other hand, only the *"formal* injunction of the deduction remains irrecusable" (ibid.). This means that the ethics of absolute hospitality or ethics qua hospitality demands and implies or even necessitates a politics of sorts, without ever being able to stipulate (let alone deduce) which politics, in whatever particular context, let alone in all possible contexts, this ought to be. In other words, justice (*la justice*) becomes injustice if it does not expose itself to the betrayal of rules and rights (i.e., *le droit*). This being said, however, it must immediately be added that "the political or juridical *content* that is thus assigned itself remains indetermined, still to be determined beyond knowledge, beyond all presentation, all concepts, all possible intuition, in a singular way, in the speech and responsibility *taken* (up) by each person, in each situation, and on the basis of an analysis that is each time unique — unique and infinite, unique but *a priori* exposed to the substitution, unique and yet general, interminable in spite of the urgency of the decision" (*AL* 115 / 199).

Here two perspectives on the ethical interlock. Being two sides of the same coin, they at once mutually imply and exclude each other. These two perspectives, Derrida writes in *De l'hospitalité* (*Of Hospitality*), one unconditional or hyperbolical and one conditional (a distinction that roughly corresponds to Kant's distinction between categorical imperatives and

baum, "Kant and Cosmopolitanism," 33). As Nussbaum points out, the way in which Kant, in the *Metaphysics of Morals*, connects the formula of universal law to that of humanity constitutes a "nonteleological recasting of the argument of *De Officiis,* where Cicero interprets the Stoic idea of life in accordance with nature as entailing a universal respect for humanity" (ibid., 36). These two premises, of course, also have consequences for the discussion of the university that formed our point of departure. See my "De Universiteit als kosmopolis: Martha Nussbaum's 'Cultivating Humanity,'" *Tijdschrift voor Literatuurwetenschap* 3 (1998): 210–22. Universal respect for humanity takes a different form, though, in Levinas and in Derrida. Whether it is seen in light of a *humanisme de l'autre homme,* to cite a well-known title by Levinas (Montpellier: Fata Morgana, 1972), and thus in view of another (*autrui,* the neighbor, in whose face God and the third, all others, already leave their trace), or whether the human is exposed to the beyond of an all-too-self-sufficient humanism, the value of the human, even of humanity, is no longer taken for granted in its classical and modern determination. Both Levinas and Derrida are aware of the uncanny fact that a certain experience of the *in*-human — a *horror religiosus,* of sorts — forms a condition of possibility for, no less than the risk incurred in, any genuine articulation of or encounter with the human and with humanity "as such."

hypothetical maxims), form the "two regimes of a law of hospitality," between which the very concept and practice of the ethical and of ethics (one
might add, of the political and of politics, of the religious or religiosity
and of religion as a historical, positive, ontic phenomenon, of messianicity and of messianism, of Christianicity and of Christendom) is perma-
nently "stretched [*tendue*]," [44] unable to coincide with itself and ever to be
just *just*. In this view, then, there are structural reasons why a good conscience, but also radical idealism and sober or cynical pragmatism, are
ipso facto signs of bad faith and perhaps not even possible in full rigor:
there are two sources of any action, of any decision, not just of "religion."
Put otherwise, the primal, irreducible, or irrevocable duality of the two
sources of religion and morality at the limits of mere reason would illuminate (and, in part, obscure) the intelligibility of the structure of experience
in general.

Derrida concludes, again in an almost Kantian style of argumentation,
that this reciprocal "distinction" and "indissociability" does not "para-
lyze" [45] the demand for hospitality, for its ethics and politics, but, on the
contrary, solicits (inspires, provokes) such an ethics and politics to come
into their own, without ever allowing them effectively to do so. Derrida's
view is, as I said, *almost* Kantian here, since the structure in question is not
that of an infinite approximation, as if absolute hospitality were nothing
but a regulative idea. On the contrary, we betray this idea not just here
and now, under the conditions of finitude and the phenomenal (rather
than noumenal) order—which ipso facto imposes a limitation upon any
aspiration, any metaphysical desire, and any boundless duty, any imperative that is truly categorical—but, as it were, at every single step along the
way, ad infinitum. Otherwise than Kant would have it, this idea—necessarily invoked and necessarily betrayed—is not even properly thinkable,
or, what amounts to the same thing, it is thinkable only aporetically. This
means, as the final pages of Kant's *Grundlegung zur Metaphysik der Sitten*
(*Groundwork of the Metaphysics of Morals*) remind us, not understanding its incomprehensibility, but understanding that there is something incomprehensible about it. The kingdom of ends stands under the same
dictate. Because of this situation, we experience trial and experiment—
l'épreuve, as Derrida writes in "Force of Law"—in the no-man's-land of
an in-between, forever forced to resort to an infinite series of substitutable

44. Derrida, *Of Hospitality*, 135, 137 / 119, 121.
45. Ibid., 147 / 131.

"intermediary schemas" (of symbols, in Kantian parlance), which mediate, albeit in a nondialectical and fundamentally nonhermeneutical fashion (i.e., beyond or before any *Vermittlung*), the singular instance. The last, Kant says, gives itself to sensible intuition alone, as does the universality evoked by the very concept, idea, or notion of, for instance, hospitality (or the messianic, democracy, friendship, etc.).[46]

Hospitality qua Friendship

In Derrida's teaching and writings in recent years, the philosopheme hospitality is more than a philosophical category. Less a category sui generis than a category beyond category, more or less than a category, this notion tests the limits of the concept of the political as we know it, tied to nation, land, geopolitics or topolitology, consanguinity, fraternity, or a concept of community that, with few exceptions, slips into a notion of fusion and communion.[47] Derrida's considerations seem premised on the desire and the dream that the relation to the other not exhaust itself, that it neither begin nor end in the contextually specific determinations of given historical and sociopolitical formations and institutions. Since the relation to the other is a relation without relation, a structure of intentionality — as Levinas would say, turning the language of phenomenology against its im-

46. Ibid. and also *PF* 277 / 308.

47. Exceptions would, perhaps, be: the writings of Maurice Blanchot, notably *La Communauté inavouable* (Paris: Minuit, 1983) / *The Unavowable Community*, trans. Pierre Joris (Tarrytown, N.Y.: Station Hill Press, 1988); Jean-Luc Nancy, *La Communauté désoeuvrée* (Paris: Christian Bourgeois, 1986, 1990) / *The Inoperative Community*, trans. Peter Connor, Lisa Garbus, Michael Holland, and Simona Sawhney, ed. Peter Connor (Minneapolis: University of Minnesota Press, 1991); and Giorgio Agamben, *La comunità che viene* (Turin: Einaudi, 1990) / *The Coming Community*, trans. Michael Hardt (Minneapolis: University of Minnesota Press, 1993). Derrida does not hesitate to signal, as he did in "Eating Well," his hesitation about the very concept of community and that on which, even in these authors, it still seems to rely: "There is still perhaps some brotherhood in Bataille, Blanchot and Nancy, and I wonder, in the innermost recess of my admiring friendship, if it does not deserve a little loosening up, and if it should still guide the thinking of the community, be it a community without community, or a brotherhood without brotherhood" (*PF* 48 n. 15 / 57 n. 1). A similar reservation should stand guard over our interpretation of the mythical story of the murder of Father by the brothers, as related in Freud's *Totem and Taboo* and as read by Derrida in "Before the Law." The investigation in *Politics of Friendship* (see *PF* 137 n. 25 / 153 n. 1) can also be seen as a belated rejoinder and salute to the projects of the short-lived Center for Philosophical Research into the Political, directed by Philippe Lacoue-Labarthe and Jean-Luc Nancy. Its results, originally published by Galilée in 1981 and 1983 and by Flammarion in 1979, have now been collected in English in Philippe Lacoue-Labarthe and Jean-Luc Nancy, *Retreating the Political*, ed. Simon Sparks (London: Routledge, 1997). Conversely, Nancy clarifies his position on the concepts of brotherhood and community in *Being Singular Plural*, 25, 198 n. 28 / 44 and 44 n. 3.

plied ontological premises—whose noesis and noema absolve themselves from this very relation, that is to say, from all reciprocity and all correlation, we are dealing here with what limits and exceeds, permeates and redirects, inflects, or curves the order of historicity and sociality, indeed of phenomenality, in toto.

Responsibility is seen here, not as the domain of ethical rules and maxims, of norms and customs, but as the structure of sociality as such. Levinas stresses that the intersubjectivity to which the relation between self and other is limited is based on an asymmetry, a nonreciprocity that produces a curvature of the social space that precedes (albeit it not chronologically or logically but in a genuinely phenomenological sense) and thus orients the concept and practice of all contractual agreement.

What is more, responsibility is not only taken or assumed, but above all assigned, and this before it receives any concrete content, before it is taken as an imperative, even as the general law of the imperative called "categorical." This, together with the prevalence of the other over the relation to the self and the Same that it entails, can be found in Levinas's "La Philosophie et l'idée de l'infini" ("Philosophy and the Idea of the Infinite"): "The situation in which one is not alone is not reducible to the fortunate meeting of *fraternal* souls that greet one another and converse. This situation is the moral conscience, the exposedness of my freedom, the exposedness of my freedom to the judgment of the other. It is a disalignment [*dénivellement*] which has authorized us to catch sight [*d'entrevoir*] of the dimension of height and the ideal in the gaze of him to whom justice is due." [48] This is not to say that fraternity has no importance for Levinas, but the general direction of his interrogation into the ethical seems clear. [49] What is said of the relation to the other (distinguished, in Levinas's formulation, from brotherhood) holds true for the notion of friendship as Derrida analyzes it in *Politics of Friendship*.

In the course of the deconstructive genealogy pursued there—a gene-

---

48. Emmanuel Levinas, "La Philosophie et l'idée de l'infini," in *En découvrant l'existence avec Husserl et Heidegger*, 178 / "Philosophy and the Idea of the Infinite," in *Collected Philosophical Papers*, 59 (my italics).

49. In *AL* 67 and 144–45 n. 69 / 122–23 and 122–24 n. 1, Derrida registers reservations about the fraternalist paradigm that continues to hold sway in Levinas and recalls notable passages in which he speaks of fraternity: e.g., *TI* 214 and 278–80 / 189 and 255–57; *Otherwise Than Being*, 140, 152, and 166 / 179, 194, and 211, as well as *In the Time of the Nations*, 97 / 113. Derrida discusses these matters further in *PF* 304–5 / 338, focusing especially on Levinas's reception of Kant's analyses of friendship in *Metaphysics of Morals*. I will return to this at the end of this chapter.

alogy, Derrida insists, that is not imposed on a body of historical material but systematically reconstructs a development, a self-deconstruction, already well under way from the very first moment the word and concept were introduced [50] — friendship is patiently uncoupled from its dominant Greek, Christian, and modern interpretations. In the process, Derrida pits what remains to us of friendship against all the fraternalist and phallocentric schemas of *philia,* of charity, which can be seen as so many arrested forms of the concept, idea, and ideal of ancient democracy, its modern liberal successors, and, most of all, a "democracy" still and forever to come.

In its opening pages, *Politics of Friendship* invokes the dream of a friendship that would no longer "belong to a *familial, fraternalist* and thus *androcentric* configuration of politics" (*PF* viii / 12), but instead signal a totally different relation to the other and to others. With such responsibility and hospitality qua friendship in mind, one might ask:

> Would this still deserve the name "politics"? . . .
>
> The concept of politics rarely announces itself without some sort of adherence of the State to the family, without what we will call a *schematic* of filiation: stock, genus or species, sex (*Geschlecht*), blood, birth, nature, nation — autochthonal or not, tellurian or not. This is once again the abyssal question of the *phusis,* the question of being, the question of what appears in birth, in opening up, in nurturing or growing, in producing by being produced. Is that not life? That is how life is thought to reach recognition.
>
> If no dialectic of the State ever breaks with what it supersedes and from which it arises (the *life* of the family and civil society), if politics never reduces within itself this adherence to familial generation, if any republican motto almost always associates fraternity with equality and freedom, as for democracy, it is rarely determined in the absence of confraternity or brotherhood.
>
> Literally or through a figure, but why this figure? (*PF* viii / 12–13; see also *PF* 104 / 127)

Apart from the concern for a particular (indeed, particularist) filiation that overshadows the philosophical concept of *philia* and its possibili-

---

50. Derrida leaves it unclear whether the most recent transformations brought about (or registered) by the media technologies — transformations that are not without repercussions for the fate of friendship, hospitality, etc. — constitute something radically new or not. He says that "a new stage has opened up (but have we not known that for such a long time?)" and continues, in a little polylogue: "Fundamentally, one will say that there is nothing new here, despite the leap of technological mutation which also produces structural effects. — Certainly, but the novelty of these structural effects must not be neglected; this is the entirety of the 'concrete' in politics" (*PF* 144 / 166).

ties (here, universalism), Derrida emphasizes a theologico-political overdetermination in the finite horizon of this concept that he associates with a
certain Christianization: "The philosophical horizon of *philia* (with everything it supposes, of course) carries in its determination, in the very form
of its finity *qua* horizon, the potential but inexorable injunction of its infinitization, hence also that of its *Christianization*" (*PF* 233 / 260). What
does this fundamentally "Christian logic" (268 n. 10 / 264 n. 1) mean?

Not merely that the concept of friendship lends itself to an in principle endless series of equally possible yet nonsynonymous substitutions,
including the one that would turn friendship into or toward an absolute,
positive infinity — God, for example. A crucial reference in this context is
to book 4 of St. Augustine's *Confessions* and, a little further in Derrida's
text, to Aristotle's *Nicomachean Ethics*. In the *Confessions*, Derrida points
out, Augustine transposes friendship onto the confessional model.[51] There
is, Derrida writes, an "infinitization *qua* conversion *in God,* if this can be
said, of this model of fraternal friendship":

> That which is turned towards God, towards His face, entrusted to God, trust-
> ing in God, assembled in and affected by God, in the dwelling place of *God,*
> in the home — that is, in the family or in the filiation of God, in this "God of
> virtues" whom we pray to *convert* us and to *turn* us towards Him (*"Deus vir-
> tutum converte nos et ostende faciem tuam"*), is not only the friendship of the
> friend but the enmity of the enemy. The enemy, too, must be loved according
> to God. The friend should be loved *in God,* the enemy must be loved not — to
> be sure — in God, but *because of* God. . . . Augustine says this at the heart of
> the *Confessions:* "Blessed are those who love you, and their friends in you and
> their enemies for your sake [*Beatus qui amat te et amicum in te et inimicum
> propter te*]." (*PF* 187–88 / 215)

In the *Nicomachean Ethics,* by contrast, Aristotle emphasizes that the concept of friendship finds in the divine and its perfection (rather than infinity) not so much its telos as its end in the sense of its structural limit.
The divine is not the element, justification, or cause of friendship, as in
Augustine, but its intrinsic aporia. Although one must wish the friend to
be a god, the fulfillment of this wish would annihilate the possibility of
the friendship. A distant, impassive, and self-sufficient object cannot be
addressed as a friend or call upon one as a friend. Its *autarkeia* precludes

51. This is noted in passing in *Sauf le nom* and "Circumfession." See also my discussion of
the confessional mode in *Philosophy and the Turn to Religion,* 343 ff.

proximity, the acknowledgment of alterity, and any thought other than the divine *noēsis noēseōs*—and thus the mortality that makes friendship an exclusively human affair (*PF* 222–23 / 250–51).

On the one hand, the concept of friendship leads inevitably to "a thought of alterity which makes true or perfect friendship not only inaccessible as a conceivable *telos*, but inaccessible *because it is inconceivable* in its very essence, and hence in its *telos*" (*PF* 222 / 249–50). On the other hand, this impossible referent informs a whole tradition on friendship, as well as Derrida's deconstructive genealogy of it: "Perhaps because we have an idea of friendship and what it should be, in the ideality of its essence or the culminated perfection of its *telos* (*teleia philia*), an idea of invincible friendship in the face of all skepticisms, perhaps it is *in the name of friendship* that we must indeed acknowledge (*constater*) that if there is friendship, if there is indeed a promised friendship, alas, 'there is no friend'" (*PF* 235 / 262–63).

The concept of friendship functions here as an idea, albeit not in the Kantian, regulative sense of the word. Friendship cannot be approximated in any incremental way, nor does it give itself to intuition all at once. On the contrary, the idea—more precisely, the name, only the name, *sauf le nom*—of friendship stands here as an index (yet another nonsynonymous substitution) of an aporia that offers much to think about and to act upon, one whose theologico-religious reverberations, Derrida demonstrates, are difficult to ignore. The irreducibility of the theologico-political is no mere obscurity, nor the consequence of a formal approach or of identifying all legal indeterminacy with the theological. On the contrary, its irreducibility is determined less by general or systemic structures than by singular instances and instantiations, whose events and proper names punctuate history at every juncture. In them, the theologico-political, together with the horizon (the idea and cultures) of death and immortality, forms the "irreducible element," as Lefort notes, of modern democracies. In what sense is this "element" invaded by the question, that is to say, the possibility and the reality—or, as Schmitt says, the "real possibility [*die reale Möglichkeit*]"—of violence?

The Theologico-Political Once More: Absolute Hostility

The absolute hospitality toward (and of) the other, signaled by the very indeterminacy of the political (of the juridical, indeed, of any decision, intentionality, or experience in general), is at once close to and at an infinite remove from its opposite, absolute hostility. The middle part of *Politics of Friendship* elaborates the structural resemblance between the two extremes—the best and the worst, once more—in a lengthy discussion of the work of Carl Schmitt. Schmitt's political theology (which, as we have seen in the previous chapter, was a major source of inspiration and contestation for Walter Benjamin), serves here to contrast the positions ascribed earlier to Kant and Levinas, positions that contrast at least as much as they coincide. Moreover, the introduction of Schmitt returns Derrida to questions broached earlier in "Force of Law." The reservations about Benjamin that Derrida formulates there (see Chapter 3, above) now are corroborated in an even more critical exposition of Schmitt.

Derrida recalls that Schmitt bases the concept of the political on the discrimination between friend and foe, and the principle of sovereignty on the question of who decides on the "state of exception." Instead of a constitutionally framed process of in principle endless deliberation and consultation—structured by a system of checks and balances, the division of legislative, executive, and judicial power, representative democracy, and an adequately informed public debate—the political, Schmitt *believes* (for what else could be the status of his overall claim?), is premised on the *ultima ratio* of violence and the decision to declare or cease war. Even the most peaceful regime, even the most benign and banal pragmatic arrangements of everyday life and the body politic, finds its final resort, if not justification, in this extreme possibility of the commerce between agents called the political. Schmitt invests this possibility—a difference and differend of sorts—with a quasi-theological determination.

We are not simply dealing here with the "transformation of the divine into the civic" that Patrick Riley retraces in his *The General Will before Rousseau.*[52] In Schmitt, there is a different logic of original supplementarity: not a translation without remainder, but one tied backward to something (some "thing," *das Ding, la Chose*) irreducible, namely, to *"absolute hostility*, as philosophy's thing" (*PF* 146 / 168). This nonnatural remainder is qualified by concepts and images taken from a theologico-mystical tradition that is invoked and cited—some would say, strategically deployed (but why, or with what purpose, exactly?)—yet at the same time infinitely displaced, generalized, and trivialized all in a single stroke.

Politics of Friendship suggests that, although friendship is defined in contradistinction to a hostility deemed absolute, this hostility inhabits friendship as an intrinsic possibility—perhaps its innermost. Indeed, Der-

52. Riley, *The General Will before Rousseau.*

rida shows, not only can friendship revert to hostility, but there is a possible (i.e., not necessarily actual) hostility *among* friends. The very idea of friendship turns against itself, even where it is not merely aspired to but comes into its own. Friend and foe revert to, and potentially reverse into, each other. The distinction that grounds the political—sovereignty and the state—is not one.

Derrida suggests that this terrible ambiguity finds expression in the concept of "stasis" or "status" in Schmitt's *Der Begriff des Politischen* (*The Concept of the Political*), where we read that "the State is Status, status *par excellence*, sheer status [*der Status schlechthin*]." Schmitt recalls that the notion "stasis" refers both to stability as opposed to movement, that is to say, *kinesis*, and to political unrest, trouble, or revolution as distinct from *polemos*. For Schmitt, Derrida points out, this radical ambiguity—an ambivalence at the very root of the *polis* or *politeia*—is grounded in what is at once an onto-theological presupposition and a self-deconstructing principle, namely, the assumption that the divine principle, the One (*to hen, das Eine*), does violence to itself, is divided in and against itself.

This theological motif, Schmitt recalls in the postface to *Politische Theologie II* (*Political Theology II*), stems from Gregory of Nazianzus, patriarch of Constantinople, who writes: "The One—*to hen*—is always in rebellion—*stasiatson*—against itself—*pros heauton* (*Oratio theol.*, III, 2)." [53] Reference to this passage marks Schmitt's shift of focus, in his later writings, toward a "political Christology," [54] thereby modifying and radicalizing his earlier analysis of the political and of exception, sovereignty, and decision, in sociological and legal conceptual terms, which supplemented a still relatively abstract and formal approach to the theologico-political. This shift in Schmitt resembles, in a way, Derrida's itinerary from "Force of Law" to *Politics of Friendship* and "Faith and Knowledge," from the first discovery of the mystical postulate (in the wake of de Certeau's "fable") or of originary affirmation (in the analysis of Heidegger's *Zusage* or "acquiescence," in *Of Spirit*) toward a messianicity, Christianization, and "globalatinization."

Of course, the mystical postulate and originary affirmation are not pure or simple "postulations," but performative or, rather, "perverformative" instances already divided in and against themselves. But the ulterior

---

53. Carl Schmitt, *Politische Theologie II: Die Legende von der Erledigung jeder Politischen Theologie* (Berlin: Duncker & Humblot, 1990; orig. pub. 1970), 116.

54. Ibid., 11. See also Taubes, *Die politische Theologie des Paulus*, 86–97, 132–42.

motifs—Schmitt's reference to a "political Christology," Derrida's invocation of a process of *mondialatinization*—hint at overt historical concretization and singularization. What is more, these later motifs are imbued
with a far more articulated structural complexity, whose semantic or analytical potential may serve a certain purpose—limited and contextually
defined, if not simply strategic or pragmatic—at least at this particular
juncture in Western and non-Western societies. Derrida acknowledges as
much when he writes:

> As for the stasiology evoked ... (which would be working either at the heart of
> the One, or in the center of a Trinity or Holy Family), this is a motif which—
> in different words, in another style and in view of other consequences—could
> very well describe one of the subterranean but utterly continuous themes of
> this essay: how the One divides and opposes itself, opposes itself by posing
> itself, represses and violates the difference it carries within itself, wages war,
> *wages war on itself, itself becoming war* [se fait la guerre], *frightens itself, itself
> becoming fear* [se fait peur], and *does violence to itself, itself becoming violence*
> [se fait violence], transforms itself into frightened violence in guarding itself
> from the other, for *it guards itself from, and in, the other* [il se garde de l'autre],
> always, Him, the One, the One "different from itself." (*PF* 109 n. 13 / 110 n. 2)

The analysis of absolute hostility at the very heart of the political or of
any order (authority, command, obligation, etc.)—or the hostility at the
heart of the absolute in and for itself—cannot be limited to any metaphysical or theological exposition or deconstruction thereof. Derrida carefully
points out that hostility, the possible or real distinction between friend
and foe, should be understood against the backdrop of an institutional
development in the West. Thus, for Schmitt the idea of a "*private* enemy"
would be absurd. For all its dependence on the self-deconstructing One—
the One plus or minus One, no longer exactly One, or more than One,
plus d'Un—hostility, the very postulation of an enemy, is contingent upon
the historical emergence of a public sphere that defines, constitutes, and
orients the political, together with the primary distinction between friend
and foe. Because this public sphere is a social and cultural construct—a
symbolic and phantasmagoric universe whose anthropological and collective psychological determinants are of an empirical nature and demand,
in part, a naturalist interpretation—we are dealing, once more, with a
mutual implication (in Heidegger's words, with a co-originariness) of the
ontic and the ontological, here, the onto-*theo*-logical.

Unlike Schmitt (and Kant), Derrida, like Levinas, ties both hospitality in its emphatic, absolute sense and its counterpart, absolute hostility (that is to say, war and the worst violence), to a "publicness'" or manifested-ness that exceeds the classical and modern distinction between the public and the private. In consequence, hospitality and hostility can no longer be grasped in terms of the political (or the societal) per se; they no longer fit the concept and the method of a "sociology of juridical concepts" as defined by Schmitt. They remain at odds with the idea of the political or everyday politics as conceived by contemporary liberal and communi-tarian theories of democracy, cosmopolitanism, multicultural citizenship, and so on. Indeed, hospitality and hostility, in Derrida's and Levinas's views, are more elusive and paradoxical notions than either Schmitt or his democratic opponents could accept. The relation to alterity of which they distinctively speak — in Levinas, the relation to the other, to the neighbor or *autrui;* in Derrida, the relation to the *sans papiers* and to nonhuman ani-mality — entails an aporetic structure that undermines not only Schmitt's simple ascription of the enemy, but the positions of his democratic, "non-decisionist," conversationalist, and neo-contractarian contenders as well. Derrida's and Levinas's analyses put into question postulations of a non-violent and nonarbitrary intersubjectivity based on reciprocity and the very definition of the ideal speech situation, as in Habermas, and of the veil of ignorance, as in Rawls, to cite two of the most significant represen-tatives of modern democratic theory and political liberalism.

Moreover, the relation to the other, as evoked by Derrida and Levi-nas, escapes the fusionist or participatory notions presupposed by neo-Aristotelian or narrativist (i.e., nonprocedural and nonformal) theories of community and solidarity (e.g., Alaisdair MacIntyre and Charles Taylor), as well as the heterogeneous projects that go by the name of "the politics of identity." None of these political philosophies can measure up to the com-plexity of the contemporary political landscape that guides Derrida's dis-cussion of these themes. Referring critically to Schmitt, Derrida notes that there is a significant "disorientation of the political field, where the prin-cipal enemy now appears unidentifiable! . . . Where the principal enemy, the 'structuring' enemy, seems nowhere to be found, where it ceases to be identifiable and thus reliable — that is, where the same *phobia* projects as a mobile multiplicity of potential, interchangeable, metonymic enemies, in secret alliance with one another: conjuration" (*PF* 84 / 103). There is a decentering, therefore, of the heart, the anchorage, and the very struc-ture of the political. Derrida turns this observation, which seems at least formally and nominally to follow the analysis proposed by Schmitt — for absolute hostility multiplies here and is disseminated beyond the point of recognition, unrecognizable in any Hegelian or formal-pragmatic theory of recognition (*Anerkennung*) — not against a supposed de-politicization inherent in the parliamentary democracy Schmitt decries, but against the metaphysical presupposition on which his conception ultimately rests. One element of this critique is the suspicion that a certain generalization and universalization of hostility leads to both trivializing and inflating this central concept. To invoke hostility as a possible risk in every corner of the "political field," at every instance of political decision — to say, in short, that every friend is a possible enemy, and all peace possibly a cover-up for the perpetuation of war under different conditions and with different means — would invalidate any direct link between the concept of the political and the designation (or, rather, targeting) of any specific (say, national, race, or class) enemy. Where "every other is totally other," no other can be discriminated — or be discriminated against — on ontological and axiological grounds. Where that happens, it results from particular judgment that lacks all metaphysical justification or warrant and is therefore by definition vulnerable to critique and revision. The concept of hostility — and hence the very concept of the political, as defined by Schmitt — is therefore deconstructable and, as a matter of fact, deconstructs itself. As a possible access to the analysis of the political, when stripped of its most dubious associations, it is also a figure of the impossible, of the possibility of an eminent — indeed, absolute — impossibility, but also of the impossibility of the very concept of the possible. This brings me to the second element of Derrida's analysis.

Derrida subtly assesses Schmitt's invocation of a certain regime of the possible and of the political being toward death. Here Schmitt comes closest to Heidegger. Or so it seems. Beyond these thematic and structural parallels lies a secret correspondence and divergence between the writings of these two thinkers — as so often, a chiasm. Its crux is the motif of *possibilism*, here, of death as the possible par excellence, a notion introduced and discussed at some length in *Philosophy and the Turn to Religion*.[55] This

---

55. See *Philosophy and the Turn to Religion*, chaps. 3 and 4. Derrida, "Heidegger's Ear," discusses a question the main text of *Politics of Friendship* leaves in suspense: "Does the being-for-death of *Dasein* include, in the structure of its essence, war and combat (*Kampf*) or not?" (*PF* 135 n. 18 / 145 n. 1). In the chapter "On Absolute Hostility" in *Politics of Friendship*, Derrida takes up the inverse perspective, stressing that between Heidegger's analytic and Schmitt's politics of a certain being toward death a "divergence prevails": "This may seem paradoxical, but the real possibility of putting-to-death [*la mise à mort*], which is an irreducible condition of the political, and indeed the ontological structure of human existence, means for Schmitt

motif allows us to reformulate the logic of the *à dieu, adieu, a-dieu* in terms of the inevitable, even necessary openness of the "theologico-political" to violence, to the possible being toward death in and of the polis—in other words, to the possible political death that determines the life of all politics, indeed, of the body politic as such, as long as it lasts.

But what does the "possible" mean for Schmitt? And in what sense does this modifier used as a substantive—a category, in Kantian (and Aristotelian) parlance—differ from Heidegger's use of the term in *Being and Time* and the later writings? What does being toward the "possible" entail, politically speaking? In *The Concept of the Political,* Schmitt presents as a central axiom that it

> cannot be denied that nations group themselves according to the friend and enemy opposition, that this opposition still remains actual today, and that it subsists in a state of real virtuality [*als reale Möglichkeit*] for every people having political existence. . . . The enemy can only be an ensemble of grouped individuals, confronting an ensemble of the same nature, engaged in at least a virtual struggle, that is, one that is effectively possible. [*Feind ist nur eine wenigstens eventuell, d.h., der realen Möglichkeit nach kämpfende Gesamtheit von Menschen die einer ebensolchen Gesamtheit gegenübersteht.*] (Cited after PF 85–86 / 105)

According to Schmitt and the authors he bases himself upon, notably Machiavelli and Hobbes, the sole presupposition of the political, of the state and its state of exception, and hence of sovereignty is this genuine reality or possibility of distinguishing between friend and foe ("die reale Wirklichkeit oder Möglichkeit der Unterscheidung von Freund und Feind"). In *Politics of Friendship,* Derrida explores the "logic" of this presupposition. What lies at the source of political authority is not simply the

---

neither an ontology of death or of dying nor a serious consideration of nothingness (*néant*) or of a *Nichtigkeit;* nor, in another code, the position of a death principle or instinct. Putting to death [*La mise à mort*] proceeds from an oppositional negativity, but one which belongs to life through and through, in so far as life *opposes itself in affirming itself.* . . . This affirmation of life (in the war *of life against life*) culminates precisely in a condemnation of modern technologism which would strive to neutralize the political (and the politicity of technics) by relying on the antithesis between mechanical and organic as the antithesis between the dead and the living [*le vif*]" (*PF* 136 n. 18 / 145 n. 1, trans. modified). As Derrida suggests earlier in the text, a confrontation with Freud's 1915 essay "Zeitgemässes über Krieg und Tod" ("Timely Thoughts on War and Death") would be necessary here (see *PF* 143–44 n. 1 / 135 n. 17). For a sustained reading of this text in the context of the question of violence, see Samuel Weber, "Wartime," in *Violence, Identity, and Self-Determination,* ed. de Vries and Weber; and Jacques Derrida, *États d'âme de la psychanalyse: Adresse aux états Généraux de la Psychanalyse* (Paris: Galilée, 2000).

abstract, indeterminate, or indifferent postulate that Montaigne, Pascal, Benjamin, de Certeau, and Derrida in their footsteps describe as "mystical." The logic of the theologico-political also entails a "*hyperbolic* build-up that is perhaps the very origin of good and evil, both beyond being (the *Republic* once defined the Good by this hyperbole that ranges beyond being): a hyperbole at the origin of good and evil, common to both, a hyperbole *qua* the difference between good and evil, the friend and the enemy, peace and war. It is this infinite hyperbole common to the two terms of the opposition, thereby making them pass into one another, that makes one's head spin" (*PF* 112 / 131). Here we would seem to be dealing with "a theory of absolute ambivalence," one that for all its susceptibility to theological appropriation—insisting on the theory's Christianicity and, as we will see, a certain Catholicism—nonetheless reminds us, Derrida suggests, of the "Empedoclean tradition of Freud—that is, one hospitable to the death instinct" (*PF* 113 / 132).

Derrida points out that in many passages throughout Schmitt's work the violence of war and hostility is silently taken to be a matter of fact. Schmitt chooses to ignore or deny the "abyss" that must be crossed in the passage—a transition that is far from self-evident—from the "possibility" to the "eventuality," then to the "effectivity-actuality" (*PF* 86 / 105) of war. Schmitt's text is premised on an "allegation of presence" expressed, Derrida notes, in emphasis on the "*combating* [kämpfende] collectivity" that constitutes any community in its essence, regardless of whether a public enemy is at hand or not:

> As soon as war is possible, it is taking place, Schmitt seems to say; presently, in a society of combat, in a community presently at war, since it can present itself to itself, as such, only in reference to this possible war. Whether the war takes place, whether war is decided upon or declared, is a mere empirical alternative in the face of an essential necessity: war is taking place; it has already begun before it begins, as soon as it is characterized as *eventual* (that is, announced as a non-excluded event in a sort of contingent future). And it is *eventual* as soon as it is *possible*. Schmitt does not wish to dissociate the quasi-transcendental modality of the possible and the historico-factual modality of the eventual. He names now the eventuality (*wenigstens eventuell*), now the possibility (*Möglichkeit*), without thematizing the criterion of distinction....
> As soon as war is possible-eventual, the enemy is present; he is there, his possibility is presently, effectively, supposed and structuring. His being-there is effective, he institutes the community as a human community of combat, as

a *combating* collectivity (kämpfende *Gesamtheit von Menschen*). The concept of the enemy is thereby deduced or constructed a priori, both analytically and synthetically—in synthetic a priori fashion, if you like, as a political concept or, better yet, as the very concept of the political. From then on, it is important that the concept be purified of all other dimensions—especially of everything opposed to the political or the public, beginning with the private: anything that stems from the individual or even the psychological, from the subjective in general. In fact, this conceptual prudence and rigor are bound to imply, as is always the case, some sort of phenomenological procedure. Following what resembles at least an eidetic reduction, all facts and all regions that do not announce themselves *as* political must be put in parentheses. All other regional disciplines, all other knowledge—economic, aesthetic, moral, military, even religious knowledge—must be suspended, although the theological-political tradition has to remain in operation for essential reasons . . . in this apparently secular thought of the political. (*PF* 86–87 / 105–6)

Is this why Derrida stresses that Schmitt's "axiom" that the political is based on the always-present possibility or real virtuality of hostility is at once "posited in a 'Nietzschean' posterity"—that is, formulated hypothetically and punctuated by an indelible "perhaps"—and "attuned to a fundamentally Christian politics" (*PF* 84 / 103)? According to Derrida, Schmitt is a "traditionalist and Catholic thinker of European law" (*PF* 88 / 108), whose theses are simultaneously marked by a certain "originality" and "ragingly conservative in their political content . . . reactive and traditionalist in their philosophical logic" (*PF* 83–84 / 101–2). Through him, a certain potential and promise for thought can be discerned in the apparently obsolete forces of the past. This chance, which is a risk as well, remains to be further determined,[56] especially in relation to the "permanence of the theologico-political,"[57] to borrow Lefort's suggestive phrase, and the possibility of violence—indeed, of war—that looms within it. Not only are these elements intrinsically related, in the intellectual and political history of the West, at least; they hinge on a certain filiation and engagement with a primarily Christian heritage that has come to super-

56. See also Meier, *The Lesson of Carl Schmitt*. In the preface to the American edition, Meier briefly takes issue with Derrida's interpretation.

57. Claude Lefort, "Permanence du théologico-politique?," in *Essais sur le politique: XIXe–XXe siècles* (Paris: Seuil, 1986) / "The Permanence of the Theologico-Political?" in *Democracy and Political Theory*, trans. David Macey (Minneapolis: University of Minnesota Press, 1988).

sede its Judeo-Greek-Roman predecessors and to dominate its Islamic and more heterodox counterparts.

The Christianization of the Political

Where does the Christianization of the political, in particular, of friendship and fraternity, begin? Where, if anywhere, does it end? Do these questions fall within the scope of historical or of systematic research? Do they call for demarcations that could, in principle, be established with full rigor? If not, why speak of "Christianization" or "Christianicity" at all?

Between Aristotle and St. Augustine, Derrida reminds us, stands Cicero, whose thoughts on friendship in *De amicitia* (*On Friendship*) have influenced the canonical interpretation of this concept, just as his considerations in *De officiis* (*On Duties*) have prepared for the conception of cosmopolitanism and the right to hospitality it entails. Indeed, Derrida observes, the two motifs—friendship and hospitality—are intimately connected and form the matrix for later articulations (see *PF* 98 / 120). Cicero's texts thus demonstrate that in the Stoic definition of friendship and hospitality, especially in its subsequent translations, the Greco-Roman and Christian motifs are difficult, even impossible, to disentangle. This circumstance, Derrida observes, undermines "customary periodizations." One author does not simply succeed another; the different authors that make up a tradition are as much each other's contemporaries as they are separated in time: "The fact that Saint Augustine and Montaigne (among others) continue to develop, deploy and make explicit Ciceronian motifs, to claim authority for themselves in the letter of these texts while undoubtedly submitting them to a sort of infinite transplantation, to an uprooting and a transplantation *of the infinite,* is enough to cause us to suspect something untimely, some non-identity with self, in each of the presumed models: Greek, Roman, Christian" (*PF* 188 / 215).

No linear genealogy can account for the fate of *philia,* in its at once intrinsic and arbitrary relation to the naturalistic, not to mention biologistic, and religious (thus infinitizing) determinations that have shaped and transported it through its convoluted history. Does the naturalistic determination determine more than the religious one? Are the two each other's opposites? Can they be separated at all? Though Derrida's major concern in *Politics of Friendship* is with the naturalistic schema, which remains even where the meaning of friendship qua fraternity is de-naturalized, a preoccupation with religion—with infinitization and Christianization—

forms an equally important thread. The central thesis of *Politics of Friendship* presupposes the analysis of messianicity in *Specters of Marx* and of fictional filiation (the One that does violence to itself) in *Archive Fever*. It also anticipates the discussion of religion and testimony in *On the Name* (notably *Sauf le nom*) and "Faith and Knowledge." The latter texts stress the persistence and hegemony of a certain Christian schematics, whether under the name of a kenosis of discourse that characterizes — and over-determines — a certain moment of abstraction in apophatic, heterodox, and decisively modern conceptions of language, or under the heading of "globalatinization," which signals the Christian — more precisely, Roman — shaping of the Western world, in its political institutions no less than in its emphatic, ontological self-understanding as a *Welt* in the later Heidegger's deployment of this word (notably in the *Beiträge zur Philosophie* [*Contributions to Philosophy*]).

The term *Christianization*, introduced in *Politics of Friendship*, is borrowed from Émile Benveniste's *Le Vocabulaire des institutions indo-euro-péennes* (*Indo-European Language and Society*). It signals that the ancient interpretation of the concept of brotherhood in terms of "natural kinship" is displaced by the profound transformation brought about in the Greek and Roman world by the Christian religion, by its orthodoxies and hetero-doxies, all centered on the "exclusively religious sense," as Benveniste puts it, of what seems a nonnatural kinship of brothers (and sisters) in spirit (or in Christ):

> Such is this complex history in which we see that, when a culture is trans-formed, it employs new terms to take the place of traditional terms when they are found to be charged with specific values. . . . As a term of kinship, Latin *frater* has disappeared. . . . The reason for this is that in the course of Christian-ization, *frater*, like *soror*, had taken on an exclusively religious sense, "brother and sister in religion." It was therefore necessary to coin a new term for natu-ral kinships, *frater* and *soror* having become in some way classificatory terms, relating to a new classificatory relationship, that of religion. (cited after *PF* 96 / 118–19)[58]

According to Benveniste, this transposition of the term *brother* (*frater*) hardly means a loss of semantic stability. Here, as so often in his discus-

---

58. The quote is from Émile Benveniste, *Le Vocabulaire des institutions indo-européennes* (Paris: Minuit, 1969), 1:220 / *Indo-European Language and Society*, trans. Elizabeth Palmer (London: Farber & Farber, 1973), 179.

sions of historical linguistics and semantics, Derrida critically engages an unquestioned presupposition. This engagement takes the form of a seemingly simple question, whose answer is left suspended, in a gesture not unrelated to the issue at hand (i.e., *religio,* and thus a certain scruple): "Why are these two kinships (said to be 'natural' or of an 'exclusively religious' nature) still kinships or classificatory kinships? What is the analogy? How does the tropical or homonymic passage from one register to the other take place? . . . What does 'religious' mean? And what does 'natural' mean, when one knows that no classificatory kinship is devoid of all religiosity?" (*PF* 97 / 119). In more than one context, *Politics of Friendship* dwells on this motif of a supposedly "Christian semantics of fraternity," in other words, on "the Christianization of fraternization, or fraternization as the essential structure of Christianization" (*PF* 96 / 118). The history of fraternity, Derrida says a little later in the text, plays itself out in a "Christian space" or is punctuated by a "Christian scansion" (*PF* 156 / 179). Derrida remarks of this hegemony of a certain Christianization and the infinitism it presupposes and provokes: "The privilege we are bestowing here on the latter . . . would be justified—provisionally—only by the role it played, in the theologico-political graft between the Greek and Christian worlds, in the construction of models and the political discourse of modern Europe" (*PF* 233 / 260).

Even the "model" of democracy, in its past, present, and future determination, is seen as related to "the tradition of the Decalogue, notably in its Christianization" (*PF* 279 / 310). Does that mean democracy is exposed to—and imperiled by—this heritage? Or does it mean, rather, that democracy cannot exist, come into existence, or survive unless it lets itself be inspired and called forth by a tradition that precedes, overshadows, and sustains it: that of the theologico-political and the mystical postulate, which equally proclaim and threaten the life of the polity? If this is so, then the place and function of the religious is much the same as the one ascribed to democracy "itself" (as word, idea, and practice). Derrida writes:

> What remains or still resists in the deconstructed (or deconstructible) concept
> of democracy which guides us endlessly? Which orders us not only to engage
> a deconstruction but to keep the old name? And to deconstruct further in the
> name of a *democracy* to come? That is to say, further, which enjoins us still to
> inherit from what—forgotten, repressed, misunderstood, or unthought in the
> "old" concept and throughout history—would still be on the watch, giving

off signs or symptoms of a stance of survival coming through all the old and tired features? (*PF* 104 / 127)

And toward the end of the book:

> Is it possible to think and to implement democracy, that which would keep the old name "democracy," while uprooting from it all these figures of friendship (philosophical and religious) which prescribe fraternity: the family and the androcentric ethnic group? Is it possible, in assuming a certain faithful memory of democratic reason and reason *tout court*—I would even say, the Enlightenment of a certain *Aufklärung* (thus leaving open the abyss which is again opening today under these words)—not to found, where it is no longer a matter of *founding*, but to open out to the future, or rather, to the "come," of a certain democracy? . . .
>
> Is it possible to open up to the "come" of a certain democracy which is no longer an insult to the friendship we have striven to think beyond the homo-fraternal and phallogocentric schema? (*PF* 306 / 339–40)

Remarkably, this seems, if not possible, at least imperative. Derrida argues throughout that a certain deployment of the numerical (and thereby, as so often, of a technicity and artificiality) is needed here. Speaking of "the possibility and the duty for democracy itself to de-limit itself," he writes:

> Delimitation not only in the name of a regulative idea and an indefinite perfectibility, but every time in the singular urgency of a *here and now*. Precisely, through the abstract and potentially indifferent thought of number and equality. This thought certainly can impose homogenizing calculability while exalting land and blood, and the risk is as terrifying as it is inevitable—it is the risk today, more than ever. But it perhaps also keeps the power of universalizing, beyond the State and the nation, the account taken of anonymous and irreducible singularities, infinitely different and thereby indifferent to particular difference, to the raging quest for identity corrupting the most indestructible desires of the idiom. (*PF* 105–6 / 129)

As the reference to Christianization already makes clear, Derrida seems to imply that, for some time to come, reference to democracy will go hand in hand with reference to the religious, to its idiom and its gestures rather than to its dogmatic and doctrinal content. These and further stipulations—the significance of the numerical and of calculation together with the ever more prominent performativity of the theologico-political—converge in Derrida's analysis of the much decried return to religion. As I have indicated elsewhere,[59] Derrida's "Faith and Knowledge" highlights the interface between the "return of religion" and the teletechnologies to which it reacts, but which it also uses as more than a vehicle alone. In a sense yet to be determined, religion forms the prime model of teletranscendence. The exponential growth in the importance of the new media enhances our understanding of the mediatic element in and mediatizing function of religion and symbolic systems in general, revealing, on the flip side of harmonizing, anti-Babelian interpretations: polysemy rather than dissemination, the return of the repressed instead of spectralization, repetition and mimesis of the same as opposed to its re-iteration and displacement, approximation to the possible but not the invention of the impossible, pluralism and tolerance over and against the multicultural, and the attestation of the self as already another for this very self.

Derrida calls this seemingly irreversible process—the diffusion of particularism via the media plus the fetishization and the becoming virtually absolute of the universal media themselves—"globalatinization." The term seeks to capture one way in which the reappearance of religion on the geopolitical stage is intrinsically linked to a wide-ranging transformation of the public sphere in which the teletechnological media are both vehicle and symptom.

Derrida's genealogy and deconstruction of the concept and imperative of *philia* seek to strip it of naturalistic, conventional, and ontological determinations.[60] In the process, its canonical interpretations are relentlessly historicized and contextualized. By contrast, the notion of a friendship (but also of a hospitality and a democracy) to come is inscribed at and possibly beyond the margin of history and politics as we know them. This double procedure is no naive endorsement of utopianism. Derrida's analysis reflects the logic of deconstruction's relation to the political and

59. See the introduction to my *Philosophy and the Turn to Religion* and "In Media Res," my contribution to *Religion and Media*, ed. de Vries and Weber.

60. See Derrida and Stiegler, *Échographies*, 20, where Derrida contrasts the coming of the *arrivant absolu* with a new birth, which is always somehow anticipated or prepared. Derrida seems to depart here from his earlier characterizations, in *Of Grammatology* and elsewhere, of the birth of a child as the figure without figure for the futurity—also the monstrosity—of the "to come" (*l'à venir, l'avenir*). I will return to this below. Another example of the tendency to denaturalize or, if one wishes, to *de-ontotopologize* the concept of friendship and in its wake—or as its privileged form and example—hospitality is the attempt to "redefine and develop the right of asylum without repatriation and without naturalization" (Derrida, *Cosmopolites de tous les pays, encore un effort!*, 21–22).

to transformative changes in general—for better and for worse, it rides waves already in motion. As Derrida writes, here we are following a genealogical analysis "in the course of a deconstruction—the course of the world" (*PF* 105 / 128).[61] Friendship, thus understood, is a limiting, self-transgressing concept. As Derrida formulates it: "The relative invariance of this model is *itself* fractured and fractures *itself*" (*PF* 290 / 322). Friendship, like other concepts, words, and figures singled out in Derrida's recent writing, obeys a contradictory logic—at once instituting or founding and undermining or destabilizing all of the conceptual oppositions that have come to organize the Western categorization of human experience in its striving for a certain totality: "singular/universal, private/public, familial/political, secret/phenomenal, etc." (ibid.). Yet, Derrida continues, the hegemonic model is also transgressive in that it cannot fail to point beyond its delimitations: "The Greco-Roman model, which seems to be governed by the value of *reciprocity,* by homological, immanentist, finitist—and rather politist—concord, bears within itself, nevertheless, potentially, the power to become infinite and dissymmetrical" (ibid.).

Conversely, the very idea of friendship seems already to entail a factual—historical, quasi-empirical, or pragmatic—negotiation that lies outside the concept of absolute responsibility as such. Responsibility consists in responsiveness to *every* other as totally other. In Levinas's universe this means every other human being, every neighbor, every *autrui*. But in Derrida's reading, *tout autre est tout autre* entails and engages every other *tout court*. Every other *tout autre*—whether human, divine, or inhuman, whether animal or otherwise—ought, so the argument goes, in principle to be encountered as *tout autre,* as totally (or every bit) other. But why then privilege friendship, hospitality, democracy, and, last but not least, religion?

Friendship—like love, though also like hospitality, democracy, and the messianic—would seem to apply only where my relation to one or more others is not primarily that of absolute responsibility, but has taken the relatively stable form of a relationship that measures itself against one or more "third" persons. As in the distinction between absolute responsibility and its common interpretation in terms of an ethics of norms and rules, or in the differentiation between an absolute hospitality and its juridico-political determination, the distance between the idea of friendship and its historical fixation must forever be maintained. The concepts of friendship and hospitality could be said to schematize (or, as Kant puts it, to symbolize) a relation that no actual or concrete form or fact of friendship or hospitality can ever contain in full rigor or without contradiction. This is why friendship and all its nonsynonymous substitutions are aporetic at the core.

Derrida leaves no doubt, in *Politics of Friendship, Adieu,* and *Of Hospitality,* that one must be cautious about translating the motif of hospitality, not to mention absolute hospitality, into contemporary "illustrations" (see *PF* 272–73 / 302–3).[62] Readers of such philosophical considerations invent the relevant mediations that would allow one to imagine or experience the link — but also the tension — between the idea of hospitality and its pragmatic forms of enactment, engagement, and implementation. This link *must* take place, however, and it will always be a relation without relation, which can only be thought and lived aporetically, intermittently, and by way of a perpetual trial and error, back and forth, for better and for worse. Nonetheless, in the process a certain vindication or, as Derrida writes, *verification* or *authentication* of the nontrue, thus a certain "becoming-true of illusion," of the "simulacrum" may take place, albeit in the most indirect, fragile, or provisional ways (*PF* 274–75 / 305–6).[63]

A certain "heteronomic and dissymmetrical [*dissymétrique*] curving of a law of originary sociability" (*PF* 231 / 258) is evoked here (again to cite Levinas, to whom Derrida obliquely refers). Of this quasi-formal structure, we can only give examples — an in principle endless series, whose rhythm, relative weight, and order of appearance vary according to differences in historical and pragmatic context. This is what the singularization and differentialization (rather than the mere differentiation) of the general and the universal[64] — a process that is at the same time a gener-

62. Yet there are many of them, also and especially in Derrida's recent interventions concerning the *sans papiers,* the question of forgiveness, the death penalty, etc.

63. This aspect seems to be lacking from Jacob Rogozinski's interesting article "'Il faut la vérité' (notes sur la vérité *de* Derrida)," in *Rue Descartes* 24 (1999): 13–39.

64. This distinction draws on one made in "Différance" in discussing Hegel's concept of *Differenzierung,* a concept that informs not only dialectical philosophies of history in their idealist, Romantic, and materialist guises, but also Weberian paradigms of modernization qua rationalization, of rationalization qua differentiation, and of differentiation qua secularization, individualization, etc. Both strands of thought have left their traces in the work of the early and late Frankfurt School, though they have also been severely criticized within this tradition, albeit on different grounds. Two examples may suffice: Jürgen Habermas, *Zur Rekonstruktion des historischen Materialismus* (Frankfurt a. M: Suhrkamp, 1976), and José Casanova, *Public*

alization and virtual universalization of the singular, a serialization and infinite substitution of sorts—implies at the level of conceptual analysis. This movement is not a mere theoretical procedure, but structures the realm of the ethical and the political, at every step of the way.

From here it is a small step to Derrida's analysis of the nonnaturalness and the legal fictitiousness of all filiation. One way to read *Politics of Friendship* is to underscore that it is not so much a thematic and historical investigation (for example, of "friendship") as an exploration of the systematic ways in which a concept lets itself be adopted—and abducted—by certain hegemonic traditions that invest its interpretation with a certain canonicity. However, the appearance of the general or even universal validity of the latter is in fact the expression of a particular—and all too often particularist—politics that mistakes itself for the natural order of things and, in so doing, mobilizes "a *discourse* on birth and on nature, a *phusis* of genealogy (more precisely, a discourse and a phantasm on the genealogical *phusis*)" (*PF* 91 / 112-13). This strategy, Derrida stresses, informs all nationalisms, all ethnocentrisms, all racisms:

> A genealogical tie will never be simply real; its supposed reality never gives itself in any intuition, it is always posed, constructed, induced, it always implies a symbolic effect of discourse—a "legal fiction," as Joyce put it in *Ulysses* on the subject of paternity. . . . All politics and all policies, all political discourses on "birth," misuse what can in this regard be only a belief, some will say: what can only remain a belief; others: what can only tend towards an act of faith. Everything in political discourse that appeals to birth, to nature or to the nation—indeed, to nations or to the universal nation of human brotherhood—this entire familialism consists in a re-naturalization of this "fiction." What we are calling here "fraternization," is what produces symbolically, conventionally, through authorized engagement, a *determined politics*, which, be it left- or right-wing, alleges a real fraternity or regulates spiritual fraternity, fraternity in the figurative sense, or the symbolic projection of a real or natural fraternity. (*PF* 92-93 / 114; cf. 149 / 171 and 168 n. 25 / 171-72 n. 3)

The mechanism of this politics of naturalization—which is also a naturalization of politics (one far more fatal than the aestheticization of politics discussed in Lacoue-Labarthe's *La Fiction du politique* [*Art and Politics*])

Religions in the Modern World, which I discuss in "In Media Res," in *Religion and Media*, ed. de Vries and Weber.

—takes place even where a certain naturalism of fraternity is explicitly denied.[65] We must envision a complex, paradoxical, indeed aporetic way in which a certain return of the "natural" at the heart of the political must be possible or even required.

A Black Swan: Friendship from a Metaphysical and a Pragmatic Point of View

Toward the end of *Politics of Friendship,* in a succinct discussion of the *Metaphysics of Morals* and *Anthropology from a Pragmatic Point of View,* Derrida points out that for Kant a privileged example of morals can be found in the figure of friendship. Yet the ways in which friendship serves as a symbolic presentation or imaginative scheme of morality in the *Metaphysics of Morals* are far from obvious or even coherent. According to Kant, friendship is based on the morally good will. As Aristotle already knew, it is the result and sign of goodness among men—in Kantian parlance, of moral dispositions that are reciprocated.[66] Yet friendship should not

65. Derrida's example is Montaigne's essay on friendship: "Montaigne insists on this point: friendship is not and must not be a *natural* fraternity, but a fraternity of alliance, adoption, election, oath. Why, then, this 'natural' figure? Why this adherence or this reference again to a natural bond, if one has set out to de-naturalize? Why does the natural schema remain? This is our question" (*PF* 191 n. 6 / 205 n. 1). And a little earlier in the text: "Has anyone ever met a brother? . . . In nature?" (*PF* 93 / 114; cf. 149 / 171). One should wonder what the friendship of the friend is if one withdraws it from its dominant determinations in the Greek or Christian world, from the fraternal (fraternalist) and phallocentric schema of *philia* or charity, as well as from a certain arrested form of democracy. Here one would stumble upon an Augustinian trope that is not thematized in *Politics of Friendship* in so many words, but that deserves mention in light of the important role of Augustine in determining the structure of autobiography (see *The Ear of the Other*), confession (see "Circonfession," in Geoffrey Bennington and Jacques Derrida, *Jacques Derrida* [Paris: Seuil, 1991] / "Circumfession," trans. Geoffrey Bennington, in Bennington and Derrida, *Jacques Derrida* [Chicago: University of Chicago Press, 1993]), and modes of seeing (Derrida, *Mémoires d'aveugle: L'Autoportrait et autres ruines* [Paris: Réunion des musées nationaux, 1990] / *Memoirs of the Blind: The Self-Portrait and Other Ruins,* trans. Pascale-Anne Brault and Michael Naas [Chicago: University of Chicago Press, 1993]). *Sauf le nom* determines the place of "friendship" in Augustine as follows: "Friendship and translation, then, and the experience of translation as friendship, that is what you seem to wish we were speaking about. It is true that one imagines with difficulty a translation, in the current sense of the term, whether it is competent or not, without some *philein*, without some love or friendship, without some 'lovence' [*aimance*] . . . , borne [*portée*] toward the thing, the text, or the other to be translated. Even if hatred can sharpen the vigilance of a translator and motivate a demystifying interpretation, this hatred still reveals an intense form of desire, interest, indeed fascination" (*Sauf le nom [Post Scriptum]* [Paris: Galilée, 1993], 39–41 / trans. John P. Leavey Jr., in *On the Name,* ed. Thomas Dutoit [Stanford: Stanford University Press, 1993], 47.

66. For an analysis, see Christine M. Korsgaard, *Creating the Kingdom of Ends* (Cambridge: Cambridge University Press, 1996), 190 ff.

be confused with respect for the pure form of the moral law as such. In Derrida's words:

> There is no friendship without "the respect of the other." The respect of friendship is certainly inseparable from a "morally good will" (the tradition of *virtue* in the *protēphilia,* from Aristotle to Cicero and Montaigne). However, it cannot, for all that, be simply conflated with *purely moral* respect, the one only due to its "cause," the moral law, which finds in the person only an example. To respect the friend is not exactly to respect the law. One can have friendship for a person: an example of respect for the moral law. One has no friendship for law, the cause of moral respect. (*PF* 252 / 283)

As an imaginative schema of symbolic representation, friendship is premised upon bodily incarnation. It must keep its distance from both the attraction that constitutes love and the purity of dispassionate respect. Friendship takes up an intermediary position between love and respect, and — like "positive" forms of historical, revealed religion (even like the veiled body of the goddess Isis, which aesthetically presents the moral law) — serves as an insufficient yet necessary paradigmatic figure for the relation at the heart of individual conduct and the body politic. For there to be a kingdom of ends, a certain balance must prevent intersubjective relation and the community as a whole from either falling apart (due to too much distance between its members) or collapsing into simple fusion (as a result of too much attraction):

> In speaking of laws of duty (not laws of nature) and, among these, of laws for human beings' external relations with one another, we consider ourselves in a moral (intelligible) world where, by analogy with the physical world, *attraction* and *repulsion* bind together rational beings (on earth). The principle of *mutual love* admonishes them to constantly *come closer* to one another; that of the *respect* they owe one another, to keep themselves *at a distance* from one another; and should one of these great moral forces fail "then nothingness (immorality), with gaping throat, would drink up the whole kingdom of (moral) beings like a drop of water." [67]

Susan Shell, in an interesting comment on this passage, points out that "of the two forces taken in isolation, attraction would seem to pose the greater

---

67. Immanuel Kant, *Metaphysik der Sitten,* in *Werke,* vol. 7, ed. Wilhelm Weischedel (Darmstadt: Wissenschaftliche Buchgesellschaft, 1983), 585 / *The Metaphysics of Morals,* in *Practical Philosophy,* trans. and ed. Mary J. Gregor, *The Cambridge Edition of the Works of Immanuel Kant* (Cambridge: Cambridge University Press, 1996), 568–69.

danger, for repulsion without attraction would lead to infinite dispersion, *not* the abyssal collapse."[68]

Despite privileging distance over proximity, Kant does seek to mitigate the infinitization of absolute respect by counterbalancing it with the force of attraction and by invoking—well before Levinas—the third person, who is an object neither of respect nor of love. Friendship, as Kant discusses it in the section that concludes the elements of ethics (*Tugendlehre*) of the *Metaphysics of Morals*, is, for all its potential instability and conceptual unclarity, "the most intimate union [*die innigste Verbindung*] of love with respect." In Kant's definition: "*Friendship* (considered in its perfection) is the union of two persons through equal mutual love and respect." How can friendship be possible—let alone realized—without endangering the balance between attraction and repulsion, between love and respect, in one way or another?

In a sense, it cannot. Kant leaves no doubt that friendship in its perfection remains an idea. It appears as seldom as a "black swan" or the *friend of human beings*, the *Menschenfreund*, who considers all others to be in principle (and de facto?) equally deserving of love and respect.[69] In Kant's text, this friend of humankind takes on almost messianic qualities. This concept should be sharply distinguished from the idea and practice of philanthropy, which, for all its welcoming of the other, is tainted by a structural limit. Kant writes: "It is readily seen that friendship is only an idea (though a practically necessary one) and unattainable in practice, although striving for friendship (as a maximum of good disposition toward each other) is a duty set by reason."[70] The gravest difficulty here is to determine whether "if the *love* of one is stronger, he may not, just because of this, forfeit something of the other's *respect*, so that it will be difficult for both to bring love and respect subjectively into that equal balance required for friendship."[71] Again, Kant seems to privilege distance over proximity in stressing the importance of a "limitation on confidence [*Vertraulichkeit*]" and adding that friends should "not be too familiar with one another."

Derrida notes that Kant's analogy of the mechanical—indeed, mechanicist Newtonian—balance of attraction and repulsion is questionable in more ways than one. Love, like respect, is characterized by distance

68. Shell, *The Embodiment of Reason*, 158–59.
69. Kant, *The Metaphysics of Morals*, 587 / 612.
70. Ibid., 585 / 608–9.
71. Ibid., 585 / 609.

and distantiation, and respect always draws upon an affect whose aspirations to (or origins in?) fusion are difficult to suppress. Rather than pursue such questions, however, Derrida points out that Kant's excursus on friendship, for all its complexities, inscribes itself in the long tradition of *philia* qua fraternization premised in a certain history of Christianization. It further testifies to what Derrida has called the nonhistory of the arch-originary—the brotherly—murder of the Father that Freud relates in *Totem and Taboo*.[72]

Kant betrays his "desire for *one* family" (*PF* 262 / 294) in the figure of the *Menschenfreund,* the friend of all humankind, whose occurrence —signaling the happy balance of love and respect in friendship—is as rare, we found, as that of a black swan. As so often in the genealogy of friendship, Kant's prime example of *philia* is once more identified with the brother, without further justification. Far from giving the filiation of friendship a new or decisive twist, Kant—like Aristotle, Cicero, Montaigne, and so many others (with the possible exception of Nietzsche and Blanchot)—immediately inscribes friendship into a history of fraternization and Christianization, though nothing in the concept of the friend, let alone the friend of humankind, links it necessarily or intrinsically to brothers or brotherhood. This surreptitious moment—reminiscent of all the slippages that punctuate Kant's demarcation between the noumenal (or intelligible), the symbolic, and the phenomenal (or empirical)—reminds us of the general law that there be some transcription, inscription, or incarnation of the moral principle in the realm of experience. Despite its purity the moral law, to the extent that it can be linked to the notion of the friend and of friendship, touches upon the contingencies of an anthropology, one that Kant considers from a pragmatic point of view.

However, Derrida continues, the central notion that "all men are here represented as brothers under one universal father" can receive an infinite variety of nonsynonymous substitutions. Thus, the place taken by the brother or human brotherhood is "there," as it were, only to "receive" a host of different possible "inscriptions." What seemed an unjustifiable restriction of friendship to brotherhood can also give way to the most hospitable of thoughts. Therefore, after having quoted from Kant's discussion in the *Metaphysics of Morals,* Derrida notes:

72. Derrida discusses these matters at length in his reading of Kafka's "Vor dem Gesetz" ("Before the Law"), again in the context of Kant's moral philosophy and its constitutive aporias. A reading of Kant in light of Freud and vice versa appears also, much earlier, in *Glas.*

Let us recall that this discourse concludes the *Elements of Ethics* and belongs to
a *Doctrine of Virtue*. The determination of friendship *qua fraternity* therefore
tells us something essential about ethics. It also tells us something irreducible
about the essence of virtue. It tells us its universal political horizon, the cosmopolitical idea of all virtue worthy of the name. This would be reason enough
to place fundamental value on this "doctrine." But this text, this *presentation*
of the doctrine, is of import to us also because it locates, with remarkable precision, the place of the brother, the brother *qua* place. Especially *qua* topical
place. Indeed, Kant says: "All men are here represented as brothers under one
universal father."

It could be said that this is merely a representation, a presentation, a manner of speaking, an image or a schema of the imagination *in view of* the idea
of equality and *in view of* responding to the obligation attached to it. . . . To
be sure. Or it will be said: no more than those who, throughout history, have
linked friendship to fraternity . . . does Kant confuse this fraternity with the
fraternity called "natural," strict, literal, sensible, genetic, etc. To be sure. But
. . . *qua* sensible or imaginal schema, in its very necessity, it remains linked to
sensible or imaginal fraternity, to the *virility* of the *congeneric*. And this adherence has become indivisible, it is *posited* as such, it sees itself as necessary,
it does not wish to be conventional, or arbitrary, or imaginary. Failing which,
Kant could have proposed another figure to speak of human community or of
the universal equality of finite beings. He could have diversified the examples
to name the link of kinship . . . why did he not speak of the sister?

The *anthropological* schema of the family is doing all the work here. It is the
desire for *one* family. . . . At the center of *this* familial schema, at the center
of what can again be called *oikeōtes*, the brother occupies a unique place, the
place of the irreplaceable. In this place of the irreplaceable, a "pure practical
reason" is welded indivisibly to an anthropology, and even . . . to a *pragmatic
anthropology*.

We must know that the place of the irreplaceable is quite a singular place
indeed. If it is irreplaceable, as the place, as the *khōra*, it is so as to receive
substitutable inscriptions. It is the place of possible substitution. It can never
be confused with that which occupies it, with all the figures which come to
be inscribed therein and pass themselves off as the copies of a paradigm, the
examples of an irreplaceable exemplar.

Is it not from the place of this very place that we gaze over the *horizon*,
awaiting the black swan that does not come every day of the week? . . . Is it not
from off this bank and under this horizon that a political phallogocentrism

has, *up to this point*, determined *its* cosmopolitical democracy, *a* democracy, *qua* cosmo-phratrocentrism?

Up to this point, at least *up until now*, through countless tremors. Some of them, in the past, have been so violent that, at least *up to this point*, they have not even been interpreted. . . . These tremors have only just begun, for the history we have been speaking of is only several thousand years old: the time of a twinkling of an eye. (*PF* 262–63 / 293–94)

The question here concerns "hegemony," a hegemony that is neither simply cultural, nor political, nor all-determining, but one that nonetheless makes all the difference in the world (of culture, politics, etc.). Everything depends on a subtle, infinite interpretation of balances and imbalances, on calculation, strategies, and the like. Derrida notes: "When one speaks of hegemony—that is, the relation of forces—the laws of structure are tendential; they are determined not (do not determine) in terms of *yes or no*, hence in terms of simple exclusion, but in those of differential force, *more or less*" (*PF* 293 / 325).

Derrida refrains from contrasting the narrative of *humanization* qua *fraternization*—which in Kant portrays the ascent of humanity and the elevation of the moral law as a sublimity that finds its exemplary figure in friendship defined as brotherly love—with a set of alternative "illustrations" of the politics implied, enabled, or obstructed by both the hegemonic concepts of friendship and its possible reconceptualization. In a long parenthesis, he both notes the manifold pertinences of such analyses for the contemporary geopolitical scene and indicates that one should not dwell on them at too great length because of the "sobriety" (*PF* 272 / 302) on which any philosophical text—being addressed to modern, adult readers—ought in the end to be based. Each of us could—and should—be aware of the "mediations" needed here between more abstract and formal and more concrete or pragmatic considerations, though these concerns can never be completely separated:[73]

---

73. If this interpretation of Derrida's parenthetical remark is correct, one notices the similarity between this "sobriety"—an *epochē* of sorts—and the reluctance, voiced by Habermas and others, to concretize an image of the "good life" (of *Sittlichkeit*, say) beyond the formal conditions of "morality." Derrida is speaking about the structural traits of a friendship and democracy to come that by far exceeds the "merely" discursive requirements that, according to theoreticians of transcendental and formal pragmatics (Apel, Habermas, and others), define the moral point of view: the ideal speech situation, the equal position of the interlocutors, etc. For one thing, in Derrida's account any plausible conception of such a speech situation would

Be it a matter of new forms of warfare, of what is confusedly called the "return" of the "religious," of nationalism, of ethnocentrism . . . ; upheavals of "number," of demographic calculation in itself and in its relations to democracy, or to a democratic "model" which will never have been inscribed in the culture or religion of an *immensely ever-growing majority* of the world's population; unprecedented statistics on what can no longer even be tranquilly called "immigration" and all forms of population transfer; the restoration or calling into question of citizenship in terms of territory or blood; unheard-of forms of theologico-political intervention on a worldwide, inter- or trans-state scale; the refoundation of state structures and international law (in progress or to come, etc.) — the list would be endless; *all* the themes broached here are, to all intents and purposes, situated at the articulation between these "present-day examples" and the history of problematics that we are striving to reconstruct or deconstruct. But they demand, above all, implicitly or explicitly, a new topic of these articulations. (*PF* 272 / 302–3)

Only one topical instance of such rearticulation is given: the question concerning what, here and now, could count as truly humanitarian. This question takes a less abstract and more institutional and political, if not downright pragmatic, form than in Kant's "Formula of Humanity" and is at once more elusive, demanding, and down to earth than his reference to an ultimate and ideal kingdom of ends.[74] In setting out the example of the "humanitarian," Derrida mentions

> its ever more specific organizations, the accelerated multiplication of its interventions, its both continental and international scope, its complex relations with governmental and non-governmental institutions, its medical, economic, technical, militaro-policing dimensions, the new rights that this "humanitarianism" seeks between the usual "United Nations" type of intervention and the right to interfere, to invent, etc. — all of this demands a conceptual and practical reformulation. But this cannot be done without a systematic, and *deconstructive*, coming to terms with the tradition of which we are speaking here. For example, what would the definition of "humanitarian" be in its unheard-of forms with respect to what Kant calls . . . "the friend of man," a concept Kant intends to keep separate from that of the "philanthropist"? In what respect does the humanitarian participate in this process of fraternizing

---

have to include at least a reference to and consideration of past and future generations, and not of the *animal rationale* alone.

74. See Korsgaard, *Creating the Kingdom of Ends*, 106–32.

humanization that we are questioning here? Another question: what would be today, in a new system of law, a crime against humanity? Its recent definition is no longer sufficient. (*PF* 272–73 / 303)

Here, I cannot pursue further these topical questions, which lend themselves equally to concrete intervention and to phenomenological description.[75] In *Politics of Friendship,* Derrida limits his analysis to reassessing the formal structure and intrinsic aporia that characterize the concept of friendship (like those of hospitality, hostility, responsibility, and democracy). The book ends with a plea for a friendship that—like democracy—remains still and forever to come. But the emphasis is clearly on what the early Heidegger, in his 1920–21 lectures on the phenomenology of religion and his 1927 lecture "Phenomenology and Theology" calls their "formally indicative" use. Their function is above all critical—in the sense that they figure as warning signs not to prejudge—or *corrective*. This procedure (the method, I would claim, of all genuinely hospitable thought) is also that of Kant, especially where he insists that philosophy can do no more than spell out certain negative protocols.[76] Derrida recalls that the two central dimensions of the relation to the other, respect and responsibility (based on the spatial figure of distance and the gaze, on the one hand, and on the temporal and the word, that is, on proximity, on the other) both intersect (*se croisent*) and cross each other out in the ethics or virtue of friendship (*PF* 276 / 306). Friendship signals at once a singular relation and a passage toward universality. This is nowhere clearer than in the confidentiality or secret that friendship makes possible and that makes friendship possible, but that also threatens it in its exclusivity.[77] We have

75. For a phenomenological concretization of the gift without return in mediatized forms of "solidarity" in "caritative" or "humanitarian" actions for collective fundraising, see Jean-Luc Marion, *Étant donné: Essai d'une phénoménologie de la donation* (Paris: Presses Univérsitaires des France, 1997), 126–27. Marion insists on the quotidian—almost banal—character of these phenomena as well as on the fact that the gift can (and, perhaps, in the final analysis must?) be given "*without regard for the face of the other* [sans égard au visage d'autrui]" (ibid., 127). This, together with the circumstance that the gift (1) takes place in relative or absolute "ignorance" of its effective destination and (2) always runs the risk of derailment or even "delirium" (ibid., 127 n. 1), means that, *phenomenologically speaking*, the gift is not derived from the ethical relation (to the other or, in Levinasian parlance, to the *visage*): "The donation of the gift does not depend on ethics but, inversely, ethics undoubtedly supposes the donation of the gift" (ibid., 128).

76. See the final chapter of *Philosophy and the Turn to Religion*.

77. On the problem of the secret, see also *PF* 145 / 166, where Derrida speaks about the new technologies that affect the distinction between the private and the public and thus the very concept of the political, in order "to recall that a reflection on the politics of friendship should

already encountered the reason for this, time and again, in Levinas. As in any relation between a self and an other, over the friendship of two always hovers the possible or actual friendship with a third (*le tiers*); in Derrida's word, a "beyond the face to face of singularities" (*PF* 276 / 306).

In its very structure, this necessary yet impossible inclusion into moral friendship of the other friend, the friend of the other—in the language of calculation, of the *plus d'un, N + 1*—confirms and parallels the tension or aporia between "hospitality" and hospitality, justice and right, or, to cite Kant, religion proper and its historical, revealed, or "positive" forms. Neither of these poles is stable or can be identified in itself or as such; they can be alluded to only as extremes of a spectrum whose limits absolve and abstract themselves from the visible and the thinkable.

The third reminds us that the other is not just my other, let alone a specular reflection of myself or another oneself. Nor is this appearance of the third merely the annihilation of the singular structure of symmetry between two singularities that constitutes moral friendship. The third friend signals a fundamental aporia. While the third signals the universality of the law, its appeal is no less singular than that of the vertiginous singular relation to any single *autrui* that it comes to interrupt—in the name of the law, but as a singular instance that contradicts the very generality of this law. Such is the aporia of responsibility, of ethics and politics, of justice and rights. Such also is the aporia of the friendship that is necessarily based on the possibility, if not the presence, of a third (of a friend of the friend, of a friend of this friend, ad infinitum).

This reading of the concept of friendship, like the reading of the concept of hospitality, reinforces our suspicion that canonical interpretations of the relation to the other in terms of friendship—notably, as brotherhood (thus ipso facto excluding the feminine, friendship between women, and heterosexual friendship by forging a line of demarcation between *philia* and *eros; PF* 277 / 308)—are not the only possible, let alone the most responsible, substitutions for the structural opening toward the other. As a matter of fact, they may not even be the most viable, opportune, or prudent in the present global political constellation. Whence comes their historical and, apparently, philosophical "force" (ibid.)? If they are only figures, which should not be understood literally or taken too seriously, what explains their persistence, recurrence, and apparent necessity (for ex-

---

not be distinguishable from a meditation on secrecy, on the 'meaning,' the 'history,' and the 'techniques' of what is still referred to today, with the old Latin word, *secret*."

ample, in classical, modern, and contemporary conceptions of the political and of democracy)?

Kant thematizes the balance between the opening toward the other and its privileged examples most clearly in his discussion of the relation without relation between the moral religion of reason and historical, positive, ontic, and "revealed" religion within the context of secrecy (here, censorship). It is difficult to read these expositions on religion, in *Religion within the Boundaries of Mere Reason* and the first part of *The Conflict of the Faculties,* without thinking of similar relations between *Offenbarkeit* and *Offenbarung* in Heidegger, between messianicity and messianisms in Derrida, and between "hospitality" and hospitality in Levinas. Mutatis mutandis, the discussion of friendship in *Politics of Friendship* can be seen against the same backdrop. Here as well, we find recurring reference to the theologico-political or to a certain "infinitization" and even "Christianization" in the history of the concept and politics of friendship (cf. *PF* 233 / 260).

Thus, when Kant writes that the series of forms that makes up the history of religion is betrayed in various degrees (but how, exactly?) by an "admixture of paganism," the implications of this conceptual and figural scheme hold true for the concept and politics of friendship as well. Like moral religion, friendship must enter — be instantiated and, as it were, encountered in — a series of nonsynonymous substitutions, here of an openness toward the other, an openness, however, that can never be described, evoked, engaged, or even respected without at the same time inscribing it into a specific idiom that will de facto betray it. To be sure, this idiom is never merely arbitrary, but a fatality and necessity of sorts. Without the risk of betrayal — of paganism, idolatry, blasphemy, infidelity — neither moral religion nor friendship could ever come into its own or be lived "as such." And because of this risk of betrayal, it can *stricto sensu* never be had or given untainted, in its purity — safe and sound. It must lose itself in order to gain itself, but it never gains (or, for that matter, loses) itself as such.

This is not to deny but perhaps rather to imply that friendship — and, again, the same holds true for moral religion, in Kant's view — must be thought, experienced, or lived "*qua* the experience of a certain ahumanity, in absolute separation, beyond or on this side of the commerce with gods and man," for any genuine attempt to rearticulate the idea of friendship should exceed the "measure of man without becoming a theologeme" (*PF* 294 / 326–27, trans. modified). Such is the status of morality, religion, hos-

380 Religion and Violence

pitality, and friendship. Could any politics or even any concept of politics ever correspond to such an idea?

The answer to this question is neither yes nor no. A translation is both necessary and imperative, but no single translation will do. The question of friendship, no less than that of hospitality, seems to revolve around a single structural difficulty, a single aporia that, as Derrida says, speaking of justice in "Force of Law," "distributes itself infinitely" in the most diverse contexts. This difficulty is intimately linked up with the tradition called the religious, in which it finds its most illuminating expression and also, perhaps, its driving force.

That the very concept or notion of friendship—especially in its perfection, as exemplified by the *Menschenfreund*—borders upon the religious and the messianic (or is it a certain messianicity?) should be clear. The *Menschenfreund* bears a striking resemblance to the figure of Christ as interpreted by Kant in *Religion within the Boundaries of Mere Reason*. Yet Kant hastens to point out that the *Menschenfreund*—unlike, say, the idea of an intelligent creator of this world (i.e., God) or the synthesis of moral virtue and empirical happiness (in the highest good, or *summum bonum*)—is not an "Ideal," that is, not an idea of *reason* proper.[78]

This religious strain can be discerned elsewhere as well. In a discussion of Nietzsche's *Zarathustra*—notably, its evocation of a friendship to come, apparently beyond the Greek and Christian determinations of the concept—Derrida reminds us of the shadows the New Testament Gospel

---

78. Kant, *The Metaphysics of Morals*, 587 / 612. If friendship is neither a coherent concept nor—in Kant's sense—an *Ideal*, is it "religious," in the sense Levinas and, up to certain point, Derrida and Blanchot give to this term? Again, the answer to this question can be neither simply affirmative nor outright negative. A related example, taken from *Politics of Friendship*, may illustrate this. While expressing reservations about Blanchot's definition of Judaism as "more than a culture and even more than a religion, but, rather, the foundation of our relationship with the other [*autrui*]," and while making no secret of his uneasiness about this author's use of the word *community* (avowable or unavowable, inoperative or not), Derrida raises the following questions: "Where did my reticence come from? And is it not fundamentally the essential part of the disquiet which inspires this book [i.e., *Politics of Friendship*]? Is this reserve, with respect to the above definition of Judaism, insufficiently Jewish, or, on the contrary, Jewish to the point of hyperbole, more than Jewish? What, then, once again, does 'Judaism' mean?" (*PF* 304-5 / 338, trans. modified). Let us recall in passing that for Kant, in *Religion within the Boundaries of Mere Reason*, the meaning of Judaism is an eminently—indeed, exclusively—political one. (See Chapter 1.) A little earlier in *Politics of Friendship*, Derrida recalls the motif of the "literary community," which would constitute the (last) resistance against "theologico-political systems," whose authority tolerates neither a subversive word nor an unconditional idea of democracy, but is based on the dangerous premise of an "absolute theologization *qua* [comme] absolute politicization" (*PF* 302-3 / 335-36).

casts over the "neo-evangelical" (*PF* 288 / 321) stances that characterize the announcement of the superman, now that all gods are dead. For all Nietzsche's rejection of the doctrine of loving one's neighbor, there remain indelible resemblances to some of the Gospels' central concerns:

> If this Gospel word promises spiritual fraternity, beyond milk and blood (but owing to other blood, to another eucharistic body . . .); if the word of Christ thus promises the true filiation of brothers of the "father who is in heaven," is this not in terms of a love of neighbor which prescribes, *as does Zarathustra*, the love of one's enemies? One becomes a brother, in Christianity, one is worthy of the eternal father, only by loving one's enemy as one's neighbor or as oneself. . . . Let us cite here only Matthew, aware nevertheless that we are here on the brink of a work of infinite reading:
>
> > You have heard the commandment, "You shall love your countryman but hate your enemy." My command to you is: love your enemies, pray for your persecutors. This will prove that you are sons of your heavenly Father, for his sun rises on the bad and the good, he rains on the just and the unjust. If you love those who love you, what merit is there in that? Do not tax collectors do as much? And if you greet your brothers only, what is so praiseworthy about that? Do not pagans do as much? In a word, you must be made perfect as your heavenly Father is perfect. (*PF* 285 / 317; Matthew 5: 43–48)

We are not dealing, therefore, with the continuing relevance of religion for a philosophy that one could still consider to be Protestant, as one might imagine for Kant. On the contrary, the return of the religious can be discerned in places where one would least expect it.

The analogy between the structural function of Derrida's friendship to come and Kant's messianic paradigm does not stop here. Both are indices of a transcendental historicity that indicates how and why the quasi-transcendentality of friendship in its perfection or "to come" (and without this notion no perfectibility could be hoped for) cannot stand on its own but demands its own interruption and, as it were, instantiation. Implicitly referring to the appendix (par. 48) to the second and final part of the *Doctrine of the Elements of Ethics* ("Duties of Virtue to Others," as distinguished from those to oneself), once again in the context of cosmopolitanism, of "citizens of the world," Derrida speaks of *verification* and *authentication*. These terms translate and transpose Kant's invocation, not of "what is best for the world [*das Weltbeste*]," but of an indirect cultivation of the "disposition of reciprocity—agreeableness, tolerance, mutual love and respect (affability and propriety, *humanitas aesthetica et deco-rum*)."[79] Kant adds: "To bring this out is itself a duty of virtue [*Tugend-pflicht*]."[80] Kant is fully aware that these cultivated dispositions form, in essence, neither the heart nor the essence of morality (nor that of moral religion). Yet what seems indifferent here makes all the difference in the world. Kant writes:

> These are, indeed, only *externals* or by-products (*parerga*), which give a beau-tiful illusion resembling virtue that is also not deceptive since everyone knows how it must be taken. *Affability, sociability, courtesy, hospitality,* and *gentleness* (in disagreeing without quarreling) are, indeed, only tokens; yet they pro-mote the feeling for virtue itself by striving to bring this illusion as near as possible to truth. By all of these, which are merely the manners one is obliged to show in social intercourse, one binds others too; and so they still promote a virtuous disposition by at least making virtue fashionable [*beliebt*].[81]

Like an aesthetic presentation of the moral law, which can never ground or precede it but may induce a sentiment conducive toward it—as I have shown in the final chapter of *Philosophy and the Turn to Religion*—the *parerga* of sociality serve as a semblance, an illustration, a pedagogical and strategic device. Like the *parerga* of historical and positive religion with their "admixtures of paganism," albeit far more directly and, we should add, correctly (but why and how exactly, given the ultimate and therefore equal indifference of *all parerga?*), they bring the law "as near as possible" to truth and enable it to come into its own. Derrida's terms "verification" and "authentication" seem to suggest something more, however.[82] This can be explained, up to a point, by recalling that he explicitly refers to Kant's *Anthropology from a Pragmatic Point of View,* in particular to its didactic discussion of the salutary effect of keeping up certain social ap-pearances, which, although illusory, can be beneficial to all involved. Kant thus, Derrida observes, establishes a certain history "which begins in a

79. Kant, *The Metaphysics of Morals*, 588 / 613.
80. Ibid.
81. Ibid., 588 / 613–14.
82. One is again reminded of the epigraph to Derrida's "Préjugés—devant la loi" ("Before the Law"), taken from Montaigne, an author omnipresent in *Politics of Friendship* as the source of the dictum, attributed to Aristotle, "Oh my friends, there is no friend," which punctuates the text with its peculiar rhythm: "Science does likewise (and even our law, it is said, has legitimate fictions on which it bases the truth of its justice)" (Montaigne, *Essays* 2.12; cited after Derrida, "Before the Law," trans. Avital Ronell and Christine Roulston, in *Acts of Literature,* ed. Derek Attridge [New York: Routledge, 1992], 183–87).

non-truth and *should end up making non-truth true*" (*PF* 274 / 304). He cites Kant's *Anthropology from a Pragmatic Point of View:*

> *Politeness* ([Höflichkeit] politesse) is an appearance of affability which instills affection [*Liebe*]. *Bowing and scraping* (compliments) and all courtly gallantry, together with the warmest verbal assurance of friendship, are not always completely truthful. "My dear friends," says Aristotle, "there is no friend." But these demonstrations of politeness do not deceive because everyone knows how they should be taken, especially because signs of well-wishing and respect, though originally empty, gradually lead to genuine dispositions of this sort.
>
> Every human virtue in circulation is small change; only a child takes it for real gold. Nevertheless, it is better to circulate pocket pieces than nothing at all. In the end, they can be converted into genuine gold coin, though at a *considerable loss*. To pass them off as nothing but counters which have no value . . . , all this is high treason perpetrated upon humanity. Even the appearance of the good in others must have value for us, because in the long run something serious can come from such a play with pretenses [*Verstellungen*] which gain respect even if they do not deserve to. Only the illusion of the good inside ourselves must be wiped out, and the veil with which self-love conceals our moral infirmity must be torn away. The appearance is deceptive if one pretends that one's guilt can be erased, simply cast off, by doing something that is without moral value, or one can convince oneself of being in no way in the wrong.[83]

Following this Kantian genealogy of morals, the history of humanity would consist in the "becoming-true of illusion," an illusion that does not deceive so long as one does not deceive oneself by believing that one (is the only one who) lives in the truth, in truth, truthfully, etc. Again, this genealogy construes — i.e., constructs and deconstructs — history as being made up of the narrations that one relates to oneself and to others, which form as many "truths in the garments of a lie." Yet instead of leading to radical suspicion vis-à-vis the intentions and effects of morality and virtue *tout court,* this perspective allows for a gradual process of verification and authentication through which humanity may live up to the highest of its

83. Immanuel Kant, *Anthropologie in pragmatischer Hinsicht,* in *Werke,* ed. Wilhelm Weischedel (Darmstadt: Wissenschaftliche Buchgesellschaft, 1983), 10:444–45 / *Anthropology from a Pragmatic Point of View,* trans. Victor Lyle Dowdell, rev. and ed. Hans H. Rudnick (Carbondale: Southern Illinois University Press, 1978), 39. Derrida cites these passages almost completely in *PF* 274–75 / 304, 305–6.

expectations. We are dealing with a *perspectivism from an infinitist point of view*, a *pragmatism in view of the absolute, or in view of an absolute task*. Opting for anything less, Kant stresses, constitutes a betrayal of and even crime against humanity, against its very idea (and ideal). On this reading, then, the terms *genealogy* and *perspectivism* draw attention to certain surprising parallels: "This Kantian history of truth *qua* the history of an error could be converted by a good philosophical computer into Hegelian software, then into Nietzschean" (*PF* 274 / 305).

Derrida places much weight on Kant's invocation of currency as the central figure to explain how virtue circulates in social intercourse.[84] This analysis, which differs dramatically from other accounts of the function of money in the social construction of identity in modern societies (from Marx and Kolakowski up to Levinas), makes good on a suggestion made in a similar context. At the end of a long exposition on counterfeit money in Baudelaire, *Given Time* introduces Kant into a discussion of the problem of radical evil, just as in *Politics of Friendship* counterfeit money serves as a clue to understanding history—even transcendental historicity—as the eventual "becoming-true of an illusion." Derrida writes:

> The crime against humanity—what Kant will call "high treason against humanity"—consists in not taking into account a history, precisely, of this history that makes that which was only appearance, illusion, "small change" (*Scheidemünze* . . .) become true and serious. The crime against humanity would be to disdain currency, however devalued, illusory, or false it may be; it would be to take counterfeit money for counterfeit, for what it is, and to let it come into its truth as counterfeit money. The crime would be not to do everything in one's power to change it into gold—that is, into virtue, true friendship. (*PF* 275 / 305)

This final statement, I believe, encapsulates the argument of both this book and my earlier *Philosophy and the Turn to Religion*. Mutatis mutandis, the principle that transforms counterfeit money into gold and, in turn, suspects all gold of being counterfeit after all is at work not only in Kant's discussion of the relation between the pure form of moral religion (or morality), but also in the many revealed forms of religion. The latter, we can now conclude, *make up* all history. Indeed, they make up all sociality as we know it, to the extent that it belongs to the realm of experience. The

84. One is reminded of reflections that Levinas put forward under the title "Philosophie et argent."

beyond of this realm can be found only in the transformation—indeed, the purification and authentication—of current concepts and practices, changing small change into gold. This is alchemy of sorts, the enigma of existence proper. Yet it is also reminiscent of the doing and bringing about of the truth, the *veritatem facere,* whose performativity St. Augustine sees at the heart of testimony and confession. And it is as if the New Testament's "as if it were not (*hoos me*)," singled out by the early Heidegger in his phenomenological interpretation of Paul's letters, and the "as if it were" of Kantian verification, analyzed by Derrida in the final pages of *Politics of Friendship,* were thus two sides of one and the same coin, tossed up in the air for us to catch.

A FINAL QUESTION REMAINS. Should the same procedure not also apply to the supposed naturalness of filiation in the canons of friendship and brotherhood—of *philia* qua fraternization? Should we not also refrain from taking this naturalness for counterfeit alone and transform it into gold, into the quasi-naturalness—or second nature?—of authenticated relations made true? The deconstructive reading that allows us the critical genealogy and de-mystification of fraternity would thus also permit and—following Kantian logic—perhaps even prescribe a certain *renaturalization* or *defictionalization* of this concept and the nonsynonymous substitutions it calls forth. But a second nature—like a second naiveté—is not the same as the first. It is a nonnatural relation—without relation, that is, in any strict, determinable, or noncontradictory sense of the word—to the "natural" as such. Or, rather, in being assumed and affirmed *as the same* in the process of authentication and verification, it is no longer quite the same in any strict ontological or axiological sense. The tautology proposed and enacted is a heterology as well.

The temporal and performative structure of this *making it so* remains the same. Like the paradoxical invocation whose scansion dictates the rhythm of *Politics of Friendship*—"Oh my friends, there is no friend"—it is characterized by proleptic gestures that Derrida chooses to call, here and elsewhere, a "messianic teleiopoesis" (*PF* 235 / 262). Its singular futurity—a futurity that it must first establish—recalls in many respects not so much a performative contradiction (which assumes what it denies, as if the times in which these two opposite gestures take place were one and the same), but an absolute performative, which initiates (and consists in nothing but the creation of) the very conditions of its own (im)possibility.

Taking supposed counterfeit for gold also ties in with the procedure of hyperbole, exaggeration, and emphasis that Levinas, in the final pages of *Otherwise Than Being,* associates with the *via eminentiae.* This has nothing to do with a pragmatic "what it is better for us to believe," but everything to do with a dialectical reversal that does not halt in the movement of re-signification, authentication, verification, and making it so. No halt: the performativity in question is also a perverformativity; it misses steps at every step along the way. Or at least it risks doing so.

Like a certain death, the instance and instantiation of welcoming the other is thus always pending or in abeyance (*en instance,* as Blanchot writes).[85] Moreover, as I have argued throughout, it is crucial for the very structure of the *à dieu* or *adieu* that one cannot and must not know whether one is — or "walks" — actually or potentially with (and in the presence or the name of) God, god, or gods; whether in turning toward these figures of the good or the best one has not ipso facto turned oneself to what is taken to be their opposite: radical evil, the worst, the *a-dieu,* as it were. But why stick to this figure at all? Here, I have insisted, only a pragmatic sensibility (a judgment, decision) can fill in a conceptually or analytically unbridgeable gap. Philosophy — and any philosophical ethics and politics — should begin by affirming the inevitability of this gap, just as it must affirm stepping over it, something that can never fully be justified for all contexts and all times. Therefore, this step can never be made in good conscience. *For systematic or internal reasons, good conscience is bad faith.*

We touch here upon a conceptual necessity that has been confirmed by analysis of all the concepts we have been tracing (hospitality and friendship, but also messianicity, Christianicity, the mystical postulate, etc.). This double postulation — yet another double bind — manifests itself not only in the writings of Kant and of Levinas,[86] but everywhere a concept

85. See my "Lapsus Absolu."

86. Derrida has suggested more than once that there is virtually nothing in Levinas's oeuvre to which he would not fully subscribe in one way or another. To be sure, Derrida often writes, "Levinas does not say this, or he does not say it in this way" (*AL* 25 / 54), or, "in a language that is no longer literally that of Levinas" (*AL* 48 / 91). *Adieu* is thus admittedly an attempt to "pronounce" Levinas's *à Dieu* "otherwise" (*AL* 1 / 11). One might wonder what concrete or abstract form philosophy assumes when in the most subtle of its readings it finds — in principle — *nothing to disagree with,* when every question that it must nonetheless raise takes the shape, not of a criticism, let alone an objection, but of a *question-prière* (*AL* 13 / 26), that is to say, of homage and affirmation at least as much as, indeed, an *adieu.* With an oblique reference to Levinas's response to his own work, the essay "Tout autrement," in *PN* 55–62 / 81–89, Derrida

or an idea comes to orient a discourse, a practice, or a tradition, however temporarily and always with the possibility—indeed the necessity
—of further substitution, for better and for worse. This inevitability of
translation and negotiation is not often acknowledged, let alone directly
theorized. It operates, as it were, in disguise, unwittingly, unintentionally—and it is often met with a considerable lack of tolerance, hospitality,
friendship, or even democratic citizenship.

Friendship and democracy to come at times seem to serve as micro-
(or meso-) and macro-political instantiations or figurations of a hospitality that is prior to them or that lies forever beyond the horizon and
scope of their possible translations. Then again, friendship and democracy to come keep a critical distance from all known and as yet unknown
transfigurations of anthropological and sociohistorical schemas and institutions, such as the family and the *polis*—though all these cast their shadows on whatever it "is" that is given to be thought here. *As such,* friendship
"is" hospitality, hospitality "is" democracy. Yet each of these notions remains merely a nonsynonymous substitution for what cannot be thought,
experienced, or lived in its integrity, as something *safe and sound,* but
which gives "itself" in no more than a name, more precisely, in a host of
names. As a matter of fact—and *of necessity*—the "thing itself" cannot be
had and belongs neither to the realm of the possible nor to that of the
impossible, or to both at once. This absurdity—whose very incomprehensibility can be comprehended, although it cannot be understood in itself
(neither in its structure nor in its content, if there is one)—can only be
believed or *assumed in an act or a leap of faith.* This, nothing else, motivates the turn to religion, so unavoidable in philosophy and the analysis
of culture, of which we have been speaking all along, indirectly, in one
form or another.

---

notes: "The hypothesis I am venturing here is obviously not Levinas's, at least not in this form,
but it seeks to move in his direction—perhaps to cross his path once more. 'At the heart of a
chiasm,' as he said one day" (*AL* 67 / 122).

I hope that the questions raised in this chapter have respected the same subtle logic. If the
preceding remarks have taken the form of questions—questions addressed to Jacques Derrida
and, more hesitatingly, to Emmanuel Levinas, or at least to the Levinasian heritage of which I
take *Adieu to Emmanuel Levinas* to be a prime example—then none of these questions could
have been formulated without reading Derrida reading Levinas (and without reading Derrida
via Levinas) in the first place. None of these issues is not already implicitly—and often explicitly—raised by Derrida and Levinas themselves. Yet questions they remain. And homage,
also.

Final Considerations: Cosmopolitanism and the Institution of Philosophy

Religion, in its peculiar, almost contentless form of a relation without relation to the totally other, as à Dieu, allows no fixation or determination of that other. The other could just as well be the self, the same, the Self, or the Same, qua other or otherwise. When dealing with the truly other, we do not know, indeed we can and must not know, whether the other is what we are, in fact or in principle, dealing with. Where the other is at issue, we might just as well be confronted with the other of the other, the other than other, or other at least than any preconceived notion or idea of that particular (or, rather, singular) other. Since we cannot not speak of "this" or "that" other (which one?), while speaking toward the other, no relation to the radically or absolutely other (i.e., every other), that is to say, no religion thus formally defined can avoid opening itself up from the outset to an (in principle infinite) series of (nonsynonymous) substitutions for the infinite that diffuse and disseminate but also undercut and dislocate its aspirations, doctrines, and practices. On this necessary, transcendental betrayal of its original intent and purport—through this "admixture of paganism," idolatry, blasphemy, and parody that threatens at every step, before a single word has been uttered—religion's historical effectiveness stands or falls. The same could be said of its empirical forces, economy, politics, ethics, and aesthetics. No experience can take place without this iterability, which inscribes an indelible change into the heart and the rhythm of any repetition. In other words, any à Dieu is marked, indeed, stigmatized by its proper adieu and à-dieu.

The occurrence of any genuine event—including any historical event—must be awaited and experienced with an "absolute hospitality" as the perfect "stranger,"[87] the arrival of whatever and whomever it is that arrives (even if it be the worst). The arrivant must be structurally (essentially, constitutively, pragmatically) indeterminate for there to be something new—or possible—at all. Neither the nature of this instance nor the exact modality of its instantiation can be anticipated in advance, intuited in the present, or understood in retrospect. This is where hospitality must run the risk of its opposite, of hostility. As Derrida notes—drawing on Schmitt's The Concept of the Political and Political Theology, while questioning his metaphysical, possibilist presuppositions, not to mention his

87. Derrida and Stiegler, Échographies, 20.

actual and activist stances — this uncertainty pervades the emergence and definition of any public sphere, and not in modernity alone (*PF* 85 / 105).

Even the figure of "birth [*la naissance*]"[88] — cited in the opening pages of *Of Grammatology* as the figure par excellence of futurity, being distinguished by its novelty, monstrosity, or formlessness — falls short of respecting the absolute welcome due to the *arrivant*. This rethinking of futurity as a negotiation of absolute hospitality implies that the laws and customs of hospitality within the polity should be detached from all biological predetermination, and thus from certain ways of deciding how one belongs to a nation.

In an early text entitled "Signature," published in *Difficult Freedom*, Levinas speaks of the French nation as one to which one can belong by choice rather than by birth. This remark, made almost in passing and without further elaboration of its consequences, should be inserted into the dossier of recent debates on citizenship, multicultural and otherwise.[89] It also has consequences for rethinking claims to civil rights by nonhumans or other than humans, a claim made quite explicitly — and quite convincingly — by the sentient automatons that revolt against their arbitrary and imposed finitude in the film *Bladerunner,* to give just one example. This issue would involve the status of "the living in general" as well.

As Derrida observes, in Kant and others hospitality has always been an anthropological notion, in addition to (or perhaps by virtue of?) being above all a juridical concept. Might one (should one not?) also welcome or let oneself be welcomed by other — non-, infra-, or superhuman — others, such as God, animals, plants, and (although Derrida doesn't say so) minerals or inanimate objects?[90] Hospitable thought should surely include them and will always already have done so, where it thinks at all. But is "hospitality" (or, for that matter, "friendship" or "democracy") still the right name for this openness of intentionality, although hardly of intentionality alone?[91] Surely, such hospitality could not simply be a matter of

88. Ibid.

89. See on this topic Rogers Brubaker, *Citizenship and Nationhood in France and Germany* (Cambridge: Harvard University Press, 1992), and Will Kymlicka, *Multicultural Citizenship: A Liberal Theory of Minority Rights* (Oxford: Oxford University Press, 1995). One should rethink these debates in light of the considerations that govern the question "Who comes after the subject?" See Eduardo Cadava, Peter Connor, and Jean-Luc Nancy, eds., *Who Comes after the Subject?* (New York: Routledge, 1991).

90. See Jacques Derrida, "L'Animal que donc je suis," in *L'Animal autobiographique: Autour de Jacques Derrida,* ed. Marie-Louis Mallet (Paris: Galilée, 1999).

91. Here I draw roughly on some remarks in the lecture "Les Lois de l'hospitalité."

expanding one's horizon, widening one's inner circle so as to include as many "others" as possible, drawing them into one's own orbit, as if concentricity (Kant's metaphor) or a certain organicist image (in Stoicism and in Martha Nussbaum's writings on cosmopolitanism and the need to cultivate humanity) were the necessary presupposition of any encounter whatsoever. Rather, a different mode of relating (without relating) and negotiation (without consent or compromise) would be, if not possible, then at least required: "One belongs to the messianic order when one has been able to admit others among one's own," Levinas writes.[92] Derrida comments:

> That a people, as a people, "should accept those who come and settle among them — even though they are foreigners," would be the proof [gage] of a popular and public commitment [engagement], a political res publica that cannot be reduced to a sort of "tolerance," unless this tolerance requires the affirmation of a "love" without measure. Levinas specifies immediately thereafter that this duty of hospitality is not only essential to a "Jewish thought" of the relationships between Israel and the nations. It opens the way to the humanity of the human in general. There is here, then, a daunting logic of election and exemplarity operating between the assignation of a singular responsibility and human universality — today one might say humanitarian universality insofar as it would at least try, despite all the difficulties and ambiguities, to remain, in the form, for example, of a non-governmental organization, beyond Nation-States and their politics. (AL 72–73 / 133–34)

Here lies Levinas's invaluable contribution to the present understanding of the paradox Hannah Arendt formulated in The Origins of Totalitarianism under the heading "The Decline of the Nation-State and the End of the Rights of Man." As a matter of fact, this whole problematic centrally informs all the questions that have interested us throughout this chapter, in particular the modes of relationship between hospitality as a descriptive (or, rather, normative) term for the relation to the other tout court and the laws of hospitality that form its instantiation.[93]

---

92. Levinas, In the Time of the Nations, 98 / 113–14.

93. Hannah Arendt, "The Decline of the Nation-State and the End of the Rights of Man," in The Origins of Totalitarianism (San Diego, Calif.: Harcourt Brace Jovanovich, 1979; orig. pub. 1951). See also Seyla Benhabib, "'Nous' et 'les Autres': The Politics of Complex Cultural Dialogue in a Global Civilization," in Multicultural Questions, ed. Christian Joppke and Steven Lukes (Oxford: Oxford University Press, 1999).

Of Hospitality and *The Right to Philosophy from a Cosmopolitical Point of View* concisely and compellingly clarify the need for this different mode of relating and negotiation.[94] The former text will allow us to recapitulate our basic arguments. The latter dwells upon philosophy's relation to the institution and the latter's relation to the concepts of hospitality and world citizenship. It speaks to the future of higher education in an international context determined by the information or networked society and the demise of the nation-state, and it will permit us to circle back to the considerations that opened this study, namely, the relationship between the institution of philosophy—or the philosophical institution, in particular, the university—and the matters that have occupied us throughout (religion and violence, censorship and tolerance, hospitality and friendship).

The format of *Of Hospitality,* the protocol of one of Derrida's recent seminars, reflects a dialogue, juxtaposing notes and queries by Anne Dufourmantelle, in the guise of a running commentary and an "invitation to answer." This short work traces the heritage of the notion of "hospitality" from Sophocles's Theban tragedies *Oedipus at Colonus* and *Antigone* through Plato's dialogues up to Kant, Hegel, Klossowski, and Massignon. Other stages along the way are the Bible and discussions on the nature of telecommunication, e-mail, and the Internet. This conjunction is of some importance, since one of the most provocative suggestions in Derrida's discussion of "hospitality" (like that of "messianicity," "faith," and their nonsynonymous substitutions) is to establish unexpected links between, say, the "resistance" of Sophocles's "semantics," explored already at length in *Glas,* and the present public space, structured and transformed in the age of information, the new geopolitics, the politics of immigration, the technologies of life, the reinvention of identities, the family, citizenship, privacy, and so on.

Of Hospitality, like the other texts we have discussed, reassesses the history of concepts (that of the stranger, the guest, the host, the enemy, the friend) against the backdrop of what Derrida calls the unsolvable, "nondialectizable antinomy"[95] of the relationship between the Law of hospitality (in the unconditional, hyperbolical, categorical, or absolute sense

---

94. Jacques Derrida, *Du droit à la philosophie du point de vue cosmopolitique.*

95. See also *AL* 118–19 / 203–4, which addresses the contradiction internal to the Levinasian Saying or *Dire,* its "ContraDiction," the "intimate caesura" that is also its "inspiration" and "respiration."

of the word) and the many laws of hospitality, its many concrete juridico-political instantiations. The latter necessarily betray the former, which, in turn, is nothing without—before or beyond—them, even though the two share no common measure. This circumstance, the circumvention or destabilization of any stance or stasis,[96] explains why the event of decision, indeed all historicity and all futurity, is punctuated and driven by a rhythm whose aporetics no philosophy can disentangle, straighten out, or flatten. The curvature, for good and ill, is too resistant for that. This aporetics is due to the fact that the absolute welcoming of the absolute coming does not let itself be translated into a hospitality of laws and rights, of maxims and rules. The inevitable, indeed necessary, negotiation is here inevitably, of necessity, also impossible. The difficulty does not stop here. The very notion of a genuine coming of the event is already premised upon an inescapable internal contradiction. In Derrida's exposition this additional difficulty takes roughly two forms.

First, the *viens!*—the absolute coming that solicits, requires, and signals itself in and as an absolute welcoming—may not come at all. What is coming may be a not-coming, a noncoming, which may, worst of all, annihilate the possibility and the very eventuality of all present and future (or even past?) coming—the nonarrival of Elijah, which is yet another figure for *la déconvenue absolue*.[97]

Second, we can never exclude the possibility that there is no (more) such thing: no proper modality, no time and space for the event or the "come" to signal itself in its absoluteness, which manifests itself (as is etymologically appropriate) by untying itself from all semantically, pragmatically, or even differentially determined and structured contextuality. Derrida says explicitly that *not* to anticipate and thus to program or grasp and clutch at the event in its coming is "almost" impossible: "If there had been a horizon of waiting, anticipation, programmation, there would have been no event, no history (a hypothesis that, paradoxically, and for the same reasons, one can never exclude in good reason [*en toute ratio-nalité*]: it is almost [*presque*] impossible to think the absence of an hori-zon of waiting [*l'absence d'un horizon d'attente*]."[98] The passage recalls an

---

96. On the notion of stasis, see the discussion of Schmitt in *PF* 108–9 n. 13 / 109–10 n. 1.
97. Derrida and Stiegler, *Échographies*, 22.
98. Ibid., 20. "Clutching" refers to the vocabulary used by Stanley Cavell, who adopts it from Ralph Waldo Emerson (see *This New Yet Unapproachable America: Lectures after Emerson and Wittgenstein* [Albuquerque, N.M.: Living Batch Press, 1989]).

earlier exclamation made by Derrida in his pivotal essay on Lévi-Strauss in *Writing and Difference:* it is impossible — or almost impossible — to think a structure without a center. Could one think hospitality (cosmopolitanism, friendship, democracy) without this seemingly inevitable presupposition of one center, of a horizon of expectation, and so on?

But, again, why is this structure, in its double complexity (the absolute welcome being aporetic in itself no less than in its relation to the hospitality of rights and rules), grafted upon a religious idiom and imagery that it must have made possible in the first place? How can what comes later come first or how, to use a philosophical language, can the a priori become the a posteriori, and vice versa? Derrida raises this question as follows:

> The most difficult thing is to justify, at least provisionally, pedagogically, this attribute "messianic": at issue is an *a priori* messianic experience, but *a priori* exposed, in its very awaiting, to what will only be determined *a posteriori* by the event. Desert in the desert (one gesturing toward the other [*faisant signe vers l'autre*]), desert of a messianic without messianism, where, without doctrine and without religious dogma, this arid waiting devoid of any horizon retains from the grand messianisms of the book only the relation [*le rapport*] to the one who arrives [or the arrival, *l'arrivant*], who [or that] can arrive — or never arrive — but about whom [which] I ought, by definition, not to know anything in advance.[99]

This passage economically recapitulates the central question of the relationship between and co-implication of ideality and empiricity — a co-implication that, we have found, is implicit in Husserl's motif of transcendental historicity, Heidegger's conception of formal indication, and Derrida's understanding of the programmatological, of invention, institution, negotiation, and so on[100] — all of which evoke the logics and aporetics

---

99. Derrida and Stiegler, *Échographies,* 21.

100. A certain interpretation of pragmatism might perhaps be added to this list, pace Bennington, Gasché, and Rorty, who differ across a single divide. Rorty, in "Derrida and the Philosophical Tradition," republished in his *Truth and Progress: Philosophical Papers* (Cambridge: Cambridge University Press, 1998), 331, argues against "the idea that we can engage in two distinct sorts of activity: empirical inquiry into causal conditions of actuality and philosophical inquiry into transcendental conditions of possibility." Rorty continues: "If you are a nominalist, any exploration of presuppositional relations between concepts in which you may engage will take the form of an argument that you could not use some words in certain ways if you did not use some words in certain other ways." In a footnote, Rorty further sums up this view by saying that "the only good transcendental argument is a parasitism argument." (Rorty refers to his defense of this claim in different essays: "Transcendental Argument, Self-Reference,

of signification and resignification in general, and of a particular cultural formation, namely, "religion," in particular. Indeed, the passage summarizes the problematic that has occupied us throughout: Why is it that, *in this day and age*, pressing questions of ethics and politics, of multicultural citizenship and education, of institutions and the new media, of knowledge, science, and the technologies of life, appear through the prisms of "religion" and "faith"? What explains this structural resemblance and, as Max Weber expressed it, "elective affinity" between such questions and this ancient archive, whose semantic and figural resources will, no doubt, dry up one day or, rather, disseminate and *diffuse* themselves beyond recognition? In what, to cite Lefort once more, lies the "permanence of the theologico-political" and where, if anywhere, does its limit—its end or closure—announce itself? Finally, what new and unprecedented forms does its violence—albeit its "violent" interruption of violence, in other words, the "mystical foundation" of its authority and its dream and imposition of an "eternal peace"—take?

---

and Pragmatism," in *Transcendental Arguments and Science*, ed. Peter Bieri et al. [Dordrecht: Reidel, 1979]; "Strawson's Objectivity Argument," *Review of Metaphysics* 24 [December 1970]: 207–44; and "Verificationism and Transcendental Arguments," *Nous* 5 [Fall 1971]: 3–14.)

   Several questions could be raised at this point. First, how does the transcendental argument that Rorty calls the parasitism argument differ in its structure and philosophical pertinence from Derrida's (but also Gasché's and Bennington's) indefatigable reinterpretation of the transcendental with the help of the prefixes "quasi-," "simili-," "ultra-," and the like? Second, is the presuppositional relation between concepts of which Rorty speaks not the relation between different concepts that enter into a series of in principle infinite—and also infinitely finite and nonsynonymous—substitutions in Derrida's writings, as in those of Levinas? Or does it bear instead on the principal distinction—a transcendental or quasi-transcendental distinction of sorts—that we have been discussing in this chapter and throughout, namely, that between the two concepts of hospitality, but also between friendship qua fraternity and friendship to come, between messianism and messianicity, democracy and democracy to come, etc.? Or are both of these interpretations equally valid?

   In Rorty's view these sequences of invocations—from hospitality to friendship and beyond, but also these concepts taken in their quasi-transcendental, indeconstructible sense of being *ideas* that, far from being regulative, remain forever to come—are in fact as many different ways of doing things with words according to the different uses we find for them in different pragmatic contexts. This seems exactly what Derrida suggests. What difficulty, then, is there in maintaining that some words—as it turns out, different words all the time—adopt a transcendental, quasi-transcendental, function of sorts, and, it seems, *inevitably* so? To argue otherwise implies the belief that the functioning of words can be limited to the contexts in which they happen to function, each time, indeed, with a pragmatic purpose. Words, however, spin out of control and take on meanings that are often more far-reaching and loftier than is philosophically—and pragmatically—justifiable. Iterability, ideality, reidentification, and resignification (and they are the vehicle of any semantic or differential-structuralist or pragmatic theory of language) mean nothing else.

Answering these questions involves grappling with the issue of how the mutual co-implication of structure and event, of the universal and the singular, relates to the universalism of a democracy, a friendship, and a cosmopolitanism forever to come. In conclusion, Derrida's *The Right to Philosophy from a Cosmopolitical Point of View* (whose title plays with the title of Kant's *Idea for a Universal History with a Cosmopolitan Purpose* as well as that of Derrida's own *Du droit à la philosophie*) will allow us to confront this issue by revisiting Derrida's main argumentative steps and will link the central concerns of this final chapter back to the discussion of the institution of philosophy with which we started out.

In *The Idea for a Universal History,* Kant sets the right to philosophy, together with the paradoxical fact that philosophy is both a particular discipline and given with European institution (notably of the university) as such, against the backdrop of an original nonsociability (*Ungesellig-keit, Unvertragsamkeit*) that he takes to be the "historicity itself of history." This nonsociability is characterized by a "detour of violence" (*DPC* 26) through which nature — teleologically and, it would seem, on its own account — produces the need for the contractual and institutional arrangements of modern states. Reason, together with its transcendental illusions, is intertwined with this ruse of nature. The same holds true of the curvature that, as an inescapable possibility or propensity, inflects all human conduct: namely, radical evil. To Derrida's taste, this conception is at once too "naturalistic" and too teleological or, as he puts it, too "teleologico-European" (*DPC* 46). The conception of cosmopolitanism propounded in Kant's essay is limited because Kant views the interpenetration of reason and history in Occidentalist terms. The ruse of nature is an essentially Graeco-Latin-European affair. This reflects also on the question of the relation between philosophy and the institution. Kant's essay, according to Derrida, must above all be read as a "treatise on education" (*DPC* 46).

As we have seen, Kant insists on the universal freedom of moral religion and of the philosophy that corroborates its truth and gives it its voice. Yet philosophy cannot and ought not go beyond the limits of transcendental theology, even though it can — indeed, cannot but — demonstrate the reasonableness of the desire and need (*Bedürfnis*) to take steps toward the empirical, the historical, the ontic: in short, toward the aesthetic and symbolic presentation or schematization of the intelligible in the phenomenal world. Argument can prove the necessity of this transition, but how it happens in any concrete instance or instantiation can only be shown. Here, the intelligible reaches its limit.

Derrida takes this differentiation or, rather, dissemination of the philosophical one step further by drawing it into the heart of the intelligible
itself—indeed, inscribing it there. What comes later comes first, according to an aporetic logic that undercuts the very premises of any *prima
philosophia,* of all transcendental thought, whether quasi-, simili-, ultra-,
or not, and thereby of all conditioning, causal and otherwise, all possibilization, and so on. Its instances and singular instantiations have to be
thought differently.

The philosophical, he notes, even in its Graeco-European determination, has always already been "bastard, hybrid, grafted, multilinear, poly-
glot" (*DPC* 33). The same holds true of the conceptions—the very ideas—
of democracy and rights (*le droit*). Neither lets itself be thought and acted
upon when framed in conceptual and practical oppositions—or when reduced to harmonious, unified, and syncretist views—which are not their
own. Derrida writes:

> In philosophy as well as elsewhere, Eurocentrism *and* anti-Eurocentrism are
> symptoms of missionary and colonial culture. A concept of cosmopolitanism
> that would still be determined by that opposition would not only concretely
> limit the development of the right to philosophy but would not even do jus-
> tice [*ne rendrait même compte*] to what goes on in [*se passe en*] philosophy.
> In order to think toward what goes on or could still go on under the name of
> philosophy (a name that is at once very grave [*grave*] and without importance,
> depending on what one makes of it [*selon ce qu'on en fait*]), we must reflect
> on what can be the concrete conditions of the respect for and the extension
> of the right to philosophy. (*DPC* 33–34)

Derrida mentions several preconditions, drawing in part on considerations charted earlier in *Du droit à la philosophie* (notably in his contribution to the preparatory texts of the *Greph* and the Collège International
de Philosophie). His observations all pertain to the "institutions of philosophy": that is to say, its multiple or reiterated founding acts no less
than its organizational and curricular structure and orientations, its internal discursive strategies as much as its external, geopolitical, inter- and
transnational divisions.

First, he observes that the pursuit of philosophy demands an "access to
places and names" other than those that have come to indicate the dominant division between the "Continental" and "analytical" traditions. Not
only has this division become obsolete, its supposed geopolitical hegemony (based on the phantasma of an Anglo-Saxon empiricist rigor ver-

sus a German-French speculative or dialectical and hermeneutic imagination) was from the outset more convoluted and internally divided than was often admitted.

Second, not only does the right to philosophy require the progressive, if only virtual, inclusion of all by all (regardless of canons, methods, and themes), unconditional respect for the unlimited access of others to all others also requires a babelian dissemination of languages, well beyond the traditional philosophical idioms of Greek and Latin, German, French, and Arabic:[101]

> Philosophy must be practiced, in ways that are not simply amnesiac, in languages which are without a relation of filiation to its roots. . . . There can be no question of withdrawing philosophy from language and from what forever binds her to an idiom [*ce qui à jamais la tient à de l'idiome*]; it is not a matter of promoting a philosophical thought that is abstractly universal and does not inhere in the body of the idiom, but *on the contrary* of putting it to work in a way that is each time original, in a nonfinite multiplicity of idioms that produces philosophical events neither particularist and untranslatable nor abstractly transparent and univocal in the element of an abstract universality. (*DPC* 43)

After stressing once more that such a proliferation and dissemination is intrinsically linked to the idea of a democracy still and forever to come, Derrida makes a third and final observation. Here he touches upon the pragmatic restraints with which the pursuit of philosophy—of the right to philosophy—must engage, in an endless process of negotiation: "While philosophy does not let itself be summed up [*ne se resume pas à*] by its institutional and pedagogic moments, it goes without saying that all differences in tradition, style, language, and philosophical nationality are translated or incarnated in institutional or pedagogical models, are often even produced by these structures (school, college, lyceum, university, institutions of research). That is the place of debates, of concurrences, of war and communication" (*DPC* 43).

The inevitable—enabling and limiting—idiomaticity of the many instantiations of philosophy is thus above all institutional. Here, Derrida concludes, we find a last condition of and restraint upon the possibility of

101. This linguistic element informs all those previously mentioned and is the central question raised by Derrida in *Le Monolinguisme de l'autre; ou, La Prothèse de l'origine* (Paris: Galilée, 1996) / *Monolingualism of the Other; or, The Prosthesis of Origin*, trans. Patrick Mensah (Stanford: Stanford University Press, 1998).

what should, in fact and in principle, be an unrestricted right to philosophy. Here we touch again upon the question of measuring and calculating the incalculable, which is a matter not only of budgets and available means but also, Derrida argues in *Du droit à la philosophie,* of censorship in one guise or another. These conditioning factors, though historically, politically, and culturally variable, impose a certain conjectural or aleatory rhythm upon even the most responsible and open thought, including — or, rather, especially — where the right to philosophy is respected, even absolutely, as it must be.

As Kant already knew, respect for the best has no existence — no chance, no necessity — outside or independent of the many multifaceted institutional, that is to say, political and cultural, forms that punctuate the path of humankind on its postulated progression toward the better and the best. Of this, I have suggested, the history of religion forms the most salient example. In this history, in order to mitigate the propensity toward radical evil, that other curvature in the order of things, one must run the risk of indispensable yet disposable errors, that is to say, idolatries and blasphemies. To risk less is to risk the worst. What's more, to risk less than the worst is to risk the worst of the worst, the evil of evil, more radical than radical evil: the indifference of in-decision or, worse still, the complacency of good conscience.

Bibliography

Adorno, Theodor W. "Fortschritt." In *Stichworte: Kritische Modelle 2*. Frankfurt a. M.: Suhrkamp, 1969. Translated by Henry W. Pickford under the title "Progress," in *Critical Models: Interventions and Catchwords* (New York: Columbia University Press, 1998), 143–60.

———. *Negative Dialektik*. Vol. 6 of *Gesammelte Schriften*, ed. Rolf Tiedemann in cooperation with Gretel Adorno, Susan Buck-Morss, and Klaus Schultz. Frankfurt a. M.: Suhrkamp, 1997. Translated by E. B. Ashton under the title *Negative Dialectics* (New York: Continuum, 1973).

———. "Säkularisierung der Theologie um ihrer Rettung willen." In *Über Walter Benjamin*, ed. R. Tiedemann. Frankfurt a. M.: Surhkamp, 1970.

Adriaanse, Hendrik Johan. "After Theism." In *Posttheism: Reframing the Judeo-Christian Tradition*, ed. Henri Krop, Arie L. Molendijk, and Hent de Vries, 33–61. Louvain: Peeters, 2000.

———. "Het morele godsbewijs, in het bijzonder bij Kant." *Wijsgerig Perspectief* 5 (1983–84): 173–80.

Agacinski, Sylviane. *Aparté: Conceptions et morts de Søren Kierkegaard*. Paris: Aubier Flammarion, 1977. Translated with an introduction by Kevin Newmark under the title *Aparté: Conceptions and Deaths of Søren Kierkegaard* (Tallahassee: Florida State University Press, 1988).

Agamben, Giorgio. *La comunità che viene*. Turin: Einaudi, 1990. Translated by Michael Hardt under the title *The Coming Community* (Minneapolis: University of Minnesota Press, 1993).

———. *Homo Sacer: Il potere sovrano e la nuda vita*. Turin: Einaudi, 1995. Translated by Daniel Heller-Roazen under the title *Homo Sacer: Sovereign Power and Bare Life* (Stanford: Stanford University Press, 1998).

———. *Moyens sans fins: Notes sur la politique*. Paris: Payot and Rivages, 1995.

———. *Potentialities: Collected Essays in Philosophy*. Ed. and trans., with an introduction, by Daniel Heller-Roazen. Stanford: Stanford University Press, 1999.

———. *Quel che resta di Auschwitz*. Turin: Bollati Boringhieri, 1998. Translated by Daniel Heller-Roazen under the title *Remnants of Auschwitz: The Witness and the Archive* (New York: Zone Books, 1999).

Al-Azmeh, Aziz. *Islam and Modernities*. London: Verso, 1996; orig. pub. 1993.

Arendt, Hannah. *Lectures on Kant's Political Philosophy*. Ed. Ronald Beiner. Chicago: University of Chicago Press, 1982.

———. *On Violence*. San Diego: Harcourt Brace Jovanovich, 1970.

———. *The Origins of Totalitarianism*. San Diego: Harcourt Brace Jovanovich, 1979; orig. pub. 1951.

———. "Walter Benjamin." In *Men in Dark Times*, 153–206. San Diego: Harcourt Brace Jovanovich, 1968. Subsequently published in German in *Walter Benjamin, Bertolt Brecht: Zwei Essays* (Munich: Piper, 1971), 7–62.

Asad, Talal. *Genealogies of Religion: Discipline and Reason in Christianity and Islam*. Baltimore: Johns Hopkins University Press, 1993.

Assmann, Jan. *Herrschaft und Heil: Politische Theologie in Altägypten, Israel und Europa*. Munich: Carl Hanser, 2000.

Attridge, Derek, ed. *Acts of Literature*. New York: Routledge, 1992.

Attridge, Derek, and Daniel Ferrer, eds. *Post-Structuralist Joyce: Essays from the French*. Cambridge: Cambridge University Press, 1984.

Austin, J. L. *How to Do Things with Words*. 2d ed. Ed. J. O. Urmson and Marina Sbisà. Cambridge, Mass.: Harvard University Press, 1994; orig. pub. 1962.

Bader, Veit. "Religious Pluralism: Secularism or Priority for Democracy?" *Political Theory* 27, no. 5 (1999): 597–633.

Badiou, Alain. *Saint Paul: La Fondation de l'universalisme*. Paris: Presses Universitaires de France, 1997.

Bahti, Timothy. "Histories of the University: Kant and Humboldt." *Modern Language Notes* 103, no. 2 (1987): 437–60.

———. "The Injured University." In *Logomachia*, ed. Rand, 59–76.

Baldwin, John W., and Richard A. Goldthwaite, eds. *Universities in Politics: Case Studies from the Late Middle Ages and Early Modern Period*. Baltimore: Johns Hopkins University Press, 1972.

Balibar, Etienne. *La Crainte des masses: Politique et philosophie avant et après Marx*. Paris: Galilée, 1997.

Barth, Karl. *Der Römerbrief: Zweite Fassung (1922)*. Zürich: Theologischer Verlag Zürich, 1989.

Beck, Lewis White. *A Commentary on Kant's "Critique of Practical Reason."* Chicago: University of Chicago Press, 1960.

Beiner, Ronald, and William James Booth, eds. *Kant and Political Philosophy: The Contemporary Legacy*. New Haven: Yale University Press, 1993.

Beinin, Joel, and Joe Stork. *Political Islam: Essays from the Middle East Report*. Berkeley: University of California Press, 1997.

Beiser, Frederick C. *The Fate of Reason: German Philosophy from Kant to Fichte.*
Cambridge: Harvard University Press, 1987.

Benhabib, Seyla. "The Embattled Public Sphere: Hannah Arendt, Jürgen Habermas, and Beyond." *Theoria* (December 1997): 1–24.

———. "'Nous' et 'les Autres': The Politics of Complex Cultural Dialogue in
a Global Civilization." In *Multicultural Questions,* ed. Christian Joppke and
Steven Lukes, 44–62. Oxford: Oxford University Press, 1999.

Benjamin, Walter. *Briefe.* Frankfurt a. M.: Suhrkamp, 1978; orig. pub. 1966. Translated by Manfred R. Jacobson and Evelyn M. Jacobson under the title *The Correspondence of Walter Benjamin: 1910–1940,* ed. Gershom Scholem and Theodor W. Adorno (Chicago: University of Chicago Press, 1994).

———. *Gesammelte Schriften.* Ed. Rolf Tiedemann and Hermann Schweppenhäuser. Frankfurt a. M.: Suhrkamp, 1980. Translated in part under the title
Walter Benjamin: Selected Writings, Michael W. Jennings, General Editor;
vol. 1: *1913–1926,* ed. Marcus Bullock and Michael W. Jennings (Cambridge:
Harvard University Press, 1996); vol. 2: *1927–1934,* trans. Rodney Livingstone
and others, ed. Michael W. Jennings, Howard Eiland, and Gary Smith (Cambridge: Harvard University Press, 1999).

———. *The Origin of German Tragic Drama.* Trans. John Osborne. London:
Verso, 1994.

———. "Rastelli erzählt . . . ." In *Gesammelte Schriften,* ed. Rolf Tiedemann and
Hermann Schweppenhäuser, 4.2:777–80. Frankfurt a. M.: Suhrkamp, 1980.
Translated by Carol Jacobs under the title "Rastelli Narrates," in Carol Jacobs,
*The Dissimulating Harmony: The Image of Interpretation in Nietzsche, Rilke,
Artaud, and Benjamin* (Baltimore: Johns Hopkins University Press, 1978), 117–
19.

Benn, S. I., and R. S. Peters. *Social Principles and the Democratic State.* London:
George Allen & Unwin, 1977; orig. pub. 1959.

Bennington, Geoffrey. "Derridabase." In Geoffrey Bennington and Jacques Derrida, *Jacques Derrida,* 7–292. Paris: Seuil, 1991. Translated by Geoffrey Bennington under the same title in idem, *Jacques Derrida* (Chicago: University of
Chicago Press, 1993), 3–316.

———. "The Frontier: Between Kant and Hegel." In *Enlightenments: Encounters
between Critical Theory and Recent French Thought,* ed. Harry Kunneman and
Hent de Vries, 45–60. Kampen: Kok Pharos, 1993.

Benveniste, Émile. *Le Vocabulaire des institutions indo-européennes.* Paris: Minuit,
1969. Translated by Elizabeth Palmer under the title *Indo-European Language
and Society* (London: Farber & Farber, 1973).

Berlin, Isaiah. *The Magus of the North: J. G. Hamann and the Origins of Modern Irrationalism.* London: John Murray, 1993.

Berman, Antione. *L'Épreuve de l'étranger: Culture et traduction dans l'Allemagne romantique.* Paris: Gallimard, 1984. Translated by S. Heyvaert under the title *The Experience of the Foreign: Culture and Translation in Romantic Germany* (Albany: State University of New York Press, 1992).

Berman, Harold J. *Law and Revolution: The Formation of the Western Legal Tradition.* Cambridge: Harvard University Press, 1983.

Biale, David. *Gershom Scholem: Kabbalah and Counter-History.* 2d ed. Cambridge: Harvard University Press, 1982.

Bielefeldt, Heiner. *Philosophie der Menschenrechte: Grundlagen eines weltweiten Freiheitsethos.* Darmstadt: Wissenschaftliche Buchgesellschaft, 1998.

———. "Towards a Cosmopolitan Framework of Freedom: The Contribution of Kantian Universalism to Cross-Cultural Debates on Human Rights." *Jahrbuch für Recht und Ethik / Annual Review of Law and Ethics* 5 (1997): 349–62.

Bielefeldt, Heiner, and Wilhelm Heitmeyer, eds. *Politisierte Religion: Ursachen und Erscheinungsformen des modernen Fundamentalismus.* Frankfurt a. M.: Suhrkamp, 1998.

Binder, Hartmut. *"Vor dem Gesetz": Einführung in Kafkas Welt.* Stuttgart: J. B. Metzler, 1993.

Birus, Hendrik, "'Ich bin, der ich bin': Über die Echos eines Namens (Ex. 3, 13–15)." In *Juden in der deutschen Literatur: Ein deutsch-israelisches Symposium,* ed. Stéphane Mosès and Albrecht Schöne, 25–53. Frankfurt a. M.: Suhrkamp, 1986.

Blanchot, Maurice. *La Communauté inavouable.* Paris: Minuit, 1983. Translated by Pierre Joris under the title *The Unavowable Community* (Tarrytown, N.Y.: Station Hill Press, 1988).

———. *The Instant of My Death / Jacques Derrida, Demeure: Fiction and Testimony.* Trans. Elizabeth Rottenberg (Stanford: Stanford University Press, 2000).

Bohatec, Josef. *Die Religionsphilosophie Kants in der "Religion innerhalb der Grenzen der blossen Vernunft."* Hildesheim: Georg Olms Verlagsbuchhandlung, 1966; orig. pub. 1938.

Bohman, James, and Matthias Lutz-Bachmann, eds. *Perpetual Peace: Essays on Kant's Cosmopolitan Ideal.* Cambridge: MIT Press, 1997.

Borges, Jorge Luis. "The Library of Babel." In *Collected Fictions,* trans. Andrew Hurley, 112–18. New York: Viking, 1998.

Borries, Kurt. *Kant als Politiker: Zur Staats- und Gesellschaftslehre des Kritizismus.* Leipzig, 1928.

Brandt, Reinhard. "Zum 'Streit der Fakultäten.'" In *Neue Autographen und Dokumente zu Kants Leben, Schriften und Vorlesungen,* ed. R. Brandt and Werner Stark, *Kant Forschungen,* 1:31–78. Hamburg: Felix Meiner, 1987.

Bröcker, Michael. "Sprache." In *Benjamins Begriffe,* ed. Michael Opitz and Erdmut Wizisla. Frankfurt a. M.: Suhrkamp, 2000.

Brubaker, Rogers. *Citizenship and Nationhood in France and Germany.* Cambridge: Harvard University Press, 1992.

Bruckner, Pascal. *Le Vertige de Babel: Cosmopolitisme ou mondialisme.* Paris: Arléa, 1994.

Butler, Judith. *Excitable Speech: A Politics of the Performative.* New York: Routledge, 1997.

Butler, Judith, Ernesto Laclau, and Slavoj Žižek, *Contingency, Hegemony, Universality: Contemporary Dialogues on the Left.* London: Verso, 2000.

Cadava, Eduardo, Peter Connor, and Jean-Luc Nancy, eds. *Who Comes after the Subject?* New York: Routledge, 1991.

Calhoun, Craig, ed. *Habermas and the Public Sphere.* Cambridge: MIT Press, 1992.

Callois, Roger. *L'Homme et le sacré.* Paris: Gallimard, 1950.

Canivez, Patrice. *Weil.* Paris: Les Belles Lettres, 1999.

Carlson, Thomas A. *Indiscretion: Finitude and the Naming of God.* Chicago: University of Chicago Press, 1999.

Casanova, José. *Public Religions in the Modern World.* Chicago: University of Chicago Press, 1994.

Castells, Manuel. *The Information Age: Economy, Society, and Culture.* Vol. 1: *The Rise of the Network Society* (Oxford: Blackwell, 1996); vol. 2: *The Power of Identity* (1997); vol. 3: *End of the Millennium* (1998).

Cavell, Stanley. "Benjamin and Wittgenstein: Signals and Affinities." In *Philosophie in synthetischer Absicht / Synthesis in Mind,* ed. Marcelo Stamm, 565–82. Stuttgart: Klett- Cotta, 1998.

———. *The Claim of Reason: Wittgenstein, Skepticism, Morality, and Tragedy.* New York: Oxford University Press, 1979.

———. "Kierkegaard's *On Authority and Revelation.*" In *Must We Mean What We Say?,* 163–79. Cambridge: Cambridge University Press, 1976.

———. *A Pitch of Philosophy: Autobiographical Exercises.* Cambridge, Mass.: Harvard University Press, 1994.

———. *This New Yet Unapproachable America: Lectures after Emerson and Wittgenstein.* Albuquerque: Living Batch Press, 1989.

Caygill, Howard. *Art of Judgment.* Cambridge: Basil Blackwell, 1989.

———. "Benjamin, Heidegger, and the Destruction of Tradition." In *Walter Ben-*

jamin's Philosophy: Destruction and Experience, ed. Andrew Benjamin and
Peter Osborne, 1–31. New York: Routledge, 1994.

———. *A Kant Dictionary.* Oxford: Blackwell Publishers, 1999; orig. pub. 1995.

Celan, Paul. *Gesammelte Werke.* Ed. Beda Alleman and Stefan Reichert, in collaboration with Rolf Bücher. Frankfurt a. M.: Suhrkamp, 1983.

———. *Poems of Paul Celan.* Trans. Michael Hamburger. New York: Persea Books,
1989.

Certeau, Michel de. *À partir de Michel de Certeau: De nouvelles frontières. Rue
Descartes,* no. 25. Collège International de Philosophie. Paris: Presses Universitaires de France, 1999.

———. *La Culture au pluriel.* Ed. Luce Giard. Paris: Seuil, 1994. Translated, with
an afterword, by Tom Conley under the title *Culture in the Plural,* intro. Luce
Giard (Minneapolis: University of Minnesota Press, 1997).

———. *L'Écriture de l'histoire.* Paris: Gallimard, 1975. Translated by Tom Conley
under the title *The Writing of History* (New York: Columbia University Press,
1992).

———. *La Fable mystique, 1: XVIe–XVIIe siècle.* Paris: Gallimard, 1982. Translated by M. B. Smith under the title *The Mystic Fable,* vol. 1: *The Sixteenth and
Seventeenth Centuries* (Chicago: University of Chicago Press, 1992).

———. *La Faiblesse de croire.* Ed. Luce Giard. Paris: Seuil, 1987.

———. *Heterologies: Discourse on the Other.* Trans. B. Massumi. Minneapolis:
University of Minnesota Press, 1986.

———. *L'Invention du quotidien I: Arts de faire.* Ed. Luce Giard. Paris: Gallimard,
1990.

———. *La Prise de parole, et autres écrits politiques.* Paris: Seuil, 1994. Translated,
with an afterword, by Tom Conley under the title *The Capture of Speech and
Other Political Writings,* intro. by Luce Giard (Minneapolis: University of Minnesota Press, 1997).

Certeau, Michel de, Luce Giard, and Pierre Mayol. *L'Invention du quotidien II:
Habiter, cuisiner.* Ed. Luce Giard. Paris: Gallimard, 1994.

Chalier, Catherine, and Miguel Abensour, eds. *Emmanuel Levinas, Cahier de
l'Herne.* Paris: Éditions de l'Herne, 1991.

Châtelet, François, Jacques Derrida, Jean-Pierre Faye, and Dominique Lecourt,
eds. *Le Rapport bleu: Les Sources historiques et théoriques du Collège International de Philosophie.* Paris: Presses Universitaires de France, 1998.

Chrétien, Jean-Louis. *Le Regard de l'amour.* Paris: Desclée de Brouwer, 2000.

Christin, Olivier. *La Paix de la religion: L'Autonomisation de la raison politique au
XVIe siècle.* Paris: Seuil, 1997.

Ciaramelli, Fabio. "From Radical Evil to the Banality of Evil: Remarks on Kant and Arendt." In *Postmodernism and the Holocaust,* ed. Alan Milchman and Alan Rosenberg, 101–12. Amsterdam: Rodopi, 1998.

Cicero, Marcus Tullius. *On Duties.* Ed. M. T. Griffin and E. M. Atkins. Cambridge: Cambridge University Press, 1991.

Coady, C. A. J. *Testimony: A Philosophical Study.* Oxford: Oxford University Press, 1992.

Cohen, I. Bernard. *Revolution in Science.* Cambridge: Harvard University Press, 1985.

Cohen, Thomas, ed. *Jacques Derrida and the Future of the Humanities.* Forthcoming from Cambridge University Press.

Connor, Peter Tracey. *Georges Bataille and the Mysticism of Sin.* Baltimore: Johns Hopkins University Press, 2000.

Courtine, Jean-François. *Nature et empire de la loi: Études suaréziennes.* Paris: Vrin, 1999.

Davidson, Arnold I. "Religion and the Distortions of Human Reason: On Kant's *Religion within the Limits of Reason Alone.*" In *Pursuits of Reason: Essays in Honor of Stanley Cavell,* ed. Ted Cohen, Paul Guyer, and Hilary Putnam, 67–104. Lubbock: Texas Tech University Press, 1993.

Deleuze, Gilles. *Proust et les signes.* Paris: Presses Universitaires de France, 1964.

Derrida, Jacques, *Adieu à Emmanuel Levinas.* Paris: Galilée, 1997. Translated by Pascale-Anne Brault and Michael Naas under the title *Adieu to Emmanuel Levinas* (Stanford: Stanford University Press, 1999).

———. "L'Animal que donc je suis." In *L'Animal autobiographique: Autour de Jacques Derrida,* ed. Marie-Louis Mallet, 251–301. Paris: Galilée, 1999.

———. *Apories.* Paris: Galilée, 1993. Translated by Thomas Dutoit under the title *Aporias* (Stanford: Stanford University Press, 1993).

———. *L'Autre Cap.* Paris: Minuit, 1991. Translated by Pascale-Anne Brault and Michael B. Naas under the title *The Other Heading: Reflections on Today's Europe* (Bloomington: Indiana University Press, 1992).

———. "Avances." In Serge Margel, *Le Tombeau du dieu artisan,* 7–43. Paris: Minuit, 1995.

———. "Canons and Metonymies: An Interview with Jacques Derrida." In *Logomachia: The Conflict of the Faculties,* ed. Richard Rand, 197–218. Lincoln: University of Nebraska Press, 1992.

———. *La Carte postale: De Socrate à Freud et au-delà.* Paris: Flammarion, 1980. Translated by Alan Bass under the title *The Post Card: From Socrates to Freud and Beyond.* Chicago: University of Chicago Press, 1987.

———. "Circonfession." In Geoffrey Bennington and Jacques Derrida, *Jacques Derrida,* 7–291. Paris: Seuil, 1991. Translated by Geoffrey Bennington under the title "Circumfession" in idem, *Jacques Derrida* (Chicago: University of Chicago Press, 1993), 3–316.

———. "Comment ne pas parler: Dénégations." In *Psyché: Inventions de l'autre*, 535–95. Paris: Galilée, 1987. Translated by Ken Frieden under the title "How to Avoid Speaking," in *Languages of the Unsayable: The Play of Negativity in Literature and Literary Theory*, ed. Sanford Buddick and Wolfgang Iser, 3–70 (New York: Columbia University Press, 1989).

———. *Cosmopolites de tous les pays, encore un effort!* Paris: Galilée, 1997.

———. "Déclarations d'Indépendance." In *Otobiographies: L'Enseignement de Nietzsche et la politique du nom propre*, 13–32. Paris: Galilée, 1984. Translated by Thomas Keenan and Thomas Pepper under the title "Declarations of Independence," *New Political Science* 15 (1986): 7–15.

———. *De l'esprit: Heidegger et la question.* Paris: Galilée, 1987. Translated by G. Bennington and R. Bowlby under the title *Of Spirit: Heidegger and the Question* (Chicago: Chicago University Press, 1989).

———. *De la grammatologie.* Paris: Minuit, 1967. Translated by Gayatri Chakravorty Spivak under the title *Of Grammatology* (Baltimore: Johns Hopkins University Press, 1976).

———. *A Derrida Reader: Between the Blinds.* Ed. Peggy Kamuf. New York: Columbia University Press, 1991.

———. "Des tours de Babel." In *Psyché: Inventions de l'autre*, 203–36. Paris: Galilée, 1987. Translated by Joseph F. Graham under the same title in *Difference in Translation*, ed. Joseph F. Graham, 165–248 (Ithaca: Cornell University Press, 1985).

———. *La Dissémination.* Paris: Seuil, 1972. Translated, with an introduction, by Barbara Johnson under the title *Dissemination* (Chicago: University of Chicago Press, 1981).

———. *Donner la mort.* In *L'Éthique du don: Jacques Derrida et la pensée du don*, ed. Jean-Michel Rabaté and Michael Wetzel, 11–108. Paris: Métailié-Transition, 1992. Translated by David Wills under the title *The Gift of Death* (Chicago: University of Chicago Press, 1995).

———. *Donner le temps, 1: La Fausse Monnaie.* Paris: Galilée, 1991. Translated by Peggy Kamuf under the title *Given Time* (Chicago: University of Chicago Press, 1994).

———. *Du droit à la philosophie.* Paris: Galilée, 1990.

———. *Du droit à la philosophie du point de vue cosmopolitique.* Paris: Unesco, Verdier, 1997.

———. *D'un ton apocalyptique adopté naguère en philosophie.* Paris: Galilée, 1983. Also in *Les Fins de l'homme: A partir du travail de Jacques Derrida*, ed.

P. Lacoue-Labarthe and Jean-Luc Nancy (Paris: Galilée, 1981). Translated by John P. Leavy Jr. under the title "On a Newly Arisen Apocalyptic Tone in Philosophy," in *Raising the Tone of Philosophy: Late Essays by Immanuel Kant, Transformative Critique by Jacques Derrida*, ed. Peter Fenves, 117–71 (Baltimore: Johns Hopkins University Press, 1993).

———. "Economimesis." In S. Agacinski et al., *Mimesis: Des articulations*, 57–93. Paris: Aubier Flammarion, 1975.

———. *L'Écriture et la différence*. Paris: Seuil, 1967. Translated by Alan Bass under the title *Writing and Difference*. Chicago: University of Chicago Press, 1978.

———. *États d'âme de la psychanalyse. Adresse aux États Généraux de la Psychanalyse*. Paris: Galilée, 2000.

———. "'Être juste avec Freud': L'Histoire de la folie à l'âge de la psychanalyse." In *Résistances de la psychanalyse*, 93–146. Paris: Galilée, 1996. Translated by Pascale-Anne Brault and Michael Naas under the title "'To Do Justice to Freud': The History of Madness in the Age of Psychoanalysis," *Critical Inquiry* 20 (1994): 227–66.

———. "Fidélité à plus d'un: Mériter d'hériter où la généalogie fait défaut." In *Idiomes, nationalités, déconstructions: Rencontre de Rabat avec Jacques Derrida, Cahiers Intersignes*, no. 13, 221–65, ed. Fethi Benslama. Paris and Casablanca: Toubkal & Intersignes, 1998.

———. "Foi et savoir: Les Deux Sources de la 'religion' aux limites de la simple raison." In *La Religion*, ed. Jacques Derrida and Gianni Vattimo, 9–86. Paris: Éditions du Seuil, 1996. Translated by Samuel Weber under the title "Faith and Knowledge: The Two Sources of 'Religion' within the Limits of Mere Reason," in *Religion*, ed. Derrida and Vattimo (Stanford: Stanford University Press, 1998), 1–78.

———. *Force de loi: Le 'Fondement mystique de l'autorité.'* Paris: Galilée, 1994. Translated by Mary Quaintance under the title "Force of Law: The 'Mystical Foundation of Authority,'" *Cardozo Law Review* 11 (1990): 919–1045.

———. *Glas*. Paris: Galilée, 1974. Translated by John P. Leavy Jr. and Richard Rand under the same title (Lincoln: University of Nebraska Press, 1986).

———. "'Il faut bien manger'; ou, Le Calcul du sujet." In *Points de suspension*, ed. Elisabeth Weber, 269–301. Paris: Galilée, 1992. Translated by Peter Connor and Avital Ronell as "'Eating Well,' or the Calculation of the Subject: An Interview with Jacques Derrida," in *Who Comes after the Subject?*, ed. Eduardo Cadava, Peter Connor and Jean-Luc Nancy, 96–119 (New York: Routledge, 1991).

———. "Interpretations at War: Kant, le juif, l'Allemand." In *Phénoménologie et politique: Mélanges offerts à Jacques Taminiaux*, 209–92. Brussels: Ousia, 1990.

Translated as "Interpretations at War: Kant, the Jew, the German," *New Literary History* 22, no. 1 (1991): 39–95.

———. Introduction to Edmund Husserl, *L'Origine de la géométrie*, trans. and intro. Jacques Derrida, 3–171. Paris: Presses Universitaires de France, 1974.

———. *Le toucher, Jean-Luc Nancy.* Paris: Galilée, 2000.

———. *Limited Inc.* Ed. Gerald Graff. Evanston: Northwestern University Press, 1988. Translated (into French) under the title *Limited Inc,* ed. and trans. Elisabeth Weber (Paris: Galilée, 1990).

———. "La Main de Heidegger (*Geschlecht II*)." In *Psyché: Inventions de l'autre,* ed. Elisabeth Weber, 415–52. Paris: Galilée, 1987. Translated by John P. Leavy Jr. under the title "Geschlecht II: Heidegger's Hand," in *Deconstruction and Philosophy: The Texts of Jacques Derrida,* ed. John Sallis, 161–96 (Chicago: University of Chicago Press, 1987).

———. *Mal d'archive: Une impression freudienne.* Paris: Galilée, 1995. Translated by Eric Prenowitz under the title *Archive Fever: A Freudian Impression* (Chicago: University of Chicago Press, 1996).

———. *Marges de la Philosophie.* Paris: Minuit, 1972. Translated by Alan Bass under the title *Margins of Philosophy* (Chicago: University of Chicago Press, 1982).

———. "Marx & Sons." In *Ghostly Demarcations: A Symposium on Jacques Derrida's 'Specters of Marx,'* ed. Michael Sprinker, 213–69. London: Verso, 1999.

———. *Mémoires d'aveugle: L'Autoportrait et autres ruines.* Paris: Réunion des musées nationaux, 1990. Translated by Pascale-Anne Brault and Michael Naas under the title *Memoirs of the Blind: The Self-Portrait and Other Ruins* (Chicago: University of Chicago Press, 1993).

———. *Mémoires pour Paul de Man.* Paris: Galilée, 1988. Translated by Cecile Lindsay, Jonathan Culler, and Eduardo Cadava under the title *Memoires for Paul de Man* (New York: Columbia University Press, 1986).

———. "Mochlos; or, The Conflict of the Faculties." In *Logomachia,* ed. R. Rand, 1–34. Lincoln: University of Nebraska Press, 1992.

———. *Le Monolinguisme de l'autre; ou, La Prothèse de l'origine.* Paris: Galilée, 1996. Translated by Patrick Mensah under the title *Monolingualism of the Other; or, The Prosthesis of Origin* (Stanford: Stanford University Press, 1998).

———. *Moscou aller-retour.* Paris: L'Aube, 1995. "Back from Moscow, in the USSR," in *Politics, Theory, and Contemporary Culture,* ed. Mark Poster, 197–235 (New York: Columbia University Press, 1993).

———. "Nombre de Oui." In *Psyché: Inventions de l'autre,* 639–50. Paris: Galilée, 1987. Translated by B. Holmes under the title "A Number of Yes," *Qui parle* 2, no. 2 (1988): 120–33.

————. "Onto-Theology of National-Humanism (Prolegomena to a Hypothesis)." *Oxford Literary Review* 1–2 (1992): 3–23.

————. *L'Oreille de l'autre: Otobiographies, transferts, traductions.* Ed. Claude Lévesque and Christie V. McDonald. Montreal: VLB, 1982. Translated by Avital Ronell and Peggy Kamuf under the title *The Ear of the Other: Otobiography, Transference, Translation,* ed. Christie V. McDonald (New York: Schocken Books, 1985).

————. "L'Oreille de Heidegger: Philopolémologie (*Geschlecht* IV)." In *Politiques de l'ámitié,* 341–419. Paris: Galilée, 1994. Translated by John P. Leavy Jr. under the title "Heidegger's Ear: Philopolemology (*Geschlecht* IV)," in *Reading Heidegger: Commemorations,* ed. John Sallis, 163– 218 (Bloomington: Indiana University Press, 1991).

————. "Pas." In *Parages,* 20–116. Paris: Galilée, 1986.

————. *Passions.* Paris: Galilée, 1993. Translated by David Wood under the same title in *On the Name,* ed. Thomas Dutoit (Stanford: Stanford University Press, 1995).

————. Contribution to *Penser l'Europe à ses frontières: Strasbourg, 7–10 novembre 1992,* 19–36. Paris: L'Aube, 1993.

————. "+ R (par dessus le marché)." In *La Vérité en peinture,* 200 ff. Paris: Flammarion, 1978. Translated by Geoffrey Bennington and Ian McLeod under the title "+ R (into the Bargain)," in *The Truth in Painting,* 149–82 (Chicago: University of Chicago Press, 1987).

————. *Points de suspension.* Ed. Elisabeth Weber. Paris: Galilée, 1992. Translated by Peggy Kamuf and others under the title *Points . . . : Interviews, 1974–1994,* ed. Elisabeth Weber (Stanford: Stanford University Press, 1995).

————. "Politics of Friendship: An Interview with Jacques Derrida." In *The Althusserian Legacy,* ed. A. Ann Kaplan and Michael Sprinker, 183–231. London: Verso, 1993.

————. *Politiques de l'amitié.* Paris: Galilée, 1994. Translated by George Collins under the title *Politics of Friendship* (London: Verso, 1997).

————. *Positions.* Paris: Minuit, 1972. Translated by Alan Bass under the title *Positions* (Chicago: University of Chicago Press, 1981).

————. "Préjugés— devant la loi." In Jean-François Lyotard et al., *La Faculté de juger,* 87–139. Paris: Minuit, 1985. Translated by Avital Ronell and Christine Roulston under the title "Before the Law," in *Acts of Literature,* ed. Derek Attridge, 183–220 (New York: Routledge, 1992).

————. *Psyché: Inventions de l'autre.* Paris: Galilée, 1987.

————. "Les Pupilles de l'Université: Le Principe de raison et l'idée de l'Université." In *Du droit à la philosophie,* 461–98. Paris: Galilée, 1990. Translated by

Catherine Porter and Edward P. Morris under the title "The Principle of Reason: The University in the Eyes of Its Pupils," *diacritics* 13, no. 3 (1983): 3–20.

———. *Résistances de la psychanalyse.* Paris: Galilée, 1996. Translated by Peggy Kamuf, Pascale-Anne Brault, and Michael Naas under the title *Resistances of Psychoanalysis* (Stanford: Stanford University Press, 1998).

———. *Sauf le nom (Post Scriptum).* Paris: Galilée, 1993. Translated by John P. Leavey Jr. under the same title in *On the Name,* ed. Thomas Dutoit, 35–85 (Stanford: Stanford University Press, 1993).

———. *Schibboleth—pour Paul Celan.* Paris: Galilée, 1986. Translated by Joshua Wilner under the title "Shibboleth: For Paul Celan," in *Word Traces: Readings of Paul Celan,* ed. Aris Fioretos, 3–72 (Baltimore: Johns Hopkins University Press, 1994).

———. *Spectres de Marx: L'État de la dette, le travail du deuil et la nouvelle Internationale.* Paris: Galilée, 1993. Translated by Peggy Kamuf under the title *Specters of Marx: The State of the Debt, the Work of Mourning, and the New International* (New York: Routledge, 1994).

———. *Sur parole: Instantanées philosophiques.* Paris: L'Aube, 1999.

———. "Le Temps des adieux: Heidegger (lu par) Hegel (lu par) Malabou." *Revue philosophique,* no. 1 (1998): 3–47.

———. " 'This Strange Institution Called Literature': An Interview with Jacques Derrida." In *Acts of Literature,* ed. Derek Attridge, 33–75. New York: Routledge, 1992.

———. *Ulysse gramophone: Deux mots pour Joyce.* Paris: Galilée, 1987. Translated by Geoffrey Bennington under the title "Two Words for Joyce," in *Post-Structuralist Joyce: Essays from the French,* ed. Derek Attridge and Daniel Ferrer, 145–59 (Cambridge: Cambridge University Press, 1984); and by Tina Kendall under the title "Ulysses Gramophone: Hear Say Yes in Joyce," in *Acts of Literature,* ed. Derek Attridge, 256–309 (London: Routledge, 1992).

———. "Une hospitalité à l'infini." In *Manifeste pour l'hospitalité: Autour de Jacques Derrida,* ed. Mohammed Seffahi, 97–106. Paris: Paroles d'aube, 1999.

———. *La Vérité en peinture.* Paris: Flammarion, 1978. Translated by Geoffrey Bennington and Ian McLeod under the title *The Truth in Painting* (Chicago: University of Chicago Press, 1987).

———. "Violence et metaphysique." In *L'Écriture et la différence,* 117–228. Paris: Seuil, 1967. Translated by Alan Bass under the title "Violence and Metaphysics," in *Writing and Difference,* 79–153 (Chicago: University of Chicago Press, 1978).

Derrida, Jacques, and Hélène Cixous. *Voiles.* Paris: Galilée, 1998.

Derrida, Jacques, and Anne Dufourmantelle. *De l'hospitalité.* Paris: Calmann-

Lévy, 1997. Translated by Rachel Bowlby under the title *Of Hospitality* (Stanford: Stanford University Press, 2000).

Derrida, Jacques, and Catherine Malabou. *La Contre-allée.* Paris: La Quinzaine / Louis Vuitton, 1999.

Derrida, Jacques, and Bernard Stiegler. *Échographies: De la télévision.* Paris: Galilée / Institute national de l'audiovisuel, 1996.

Derrida, Jacques, and Gianni Vattimo, eds. *La Religion.* Paris: Seuil, 1996. Translated by Samuel Weber and David Webb under the title *Religion* (Stanford: Stanford University Press, 1998).

Derrida, Jacques, et al., *Marx en jeu.* Paris: Descartes & Cie, 1997.

Deuber-Mankowsky, Astrid. *Der frühe Walter Benjamin und Hermann Cohen: Jüdische Werte, Kritische Philosophie, vergängliche Erfahrung.* Berlin: Verlag Vorwerk 8, 2000.

Dobbels, Daniel, Francis Marmande, and Michel Surya, eds. *Violence et politique (Colloque de Cerisy, 1994),* Lignes, no. 25. Paris: Hazan, 1995.

Dünkelsbühler, Ulrike, *Kritik der Rahmen-Vernunft: Parergon-Versionen nach Kant und Derrida.* Munich: Wilhelm Fink, 1991.

Durkheim, Émile. *Les Formes élémentaires de la vie religieuse: Le Système totémique en Australie.* Paris: Quadrige / Presses Universitaires de France, 1960, 1994.

Emerson, Ralph Waldo. "Self-Reliance." In *Selections from Ralph Waldo Emerson,* ed. Stephen E. Whicher. Boston: Houghton Mifflin, 1957.

Ernst, Wolfgang, and Cornelia Vismann, eds. *Geschichtskörper: Zur Aktualität von Ernst H. Kantorowicz.* Munich: Wilhelm Fink Verlag, 1998.

Eslin, Jean-Claude. *Dieu et le pouvoir: Théologie et politique en Occident.* Paris: Seuil, 1999.

Esposito, Roberto. *Communitas: Origine et destin de la communauté.* Translated from the Italian by Nadine Le Lirzin, preface, "Conloquium," by Jean-Luc Nancy. Paris: Presses Universitaires de France, 2000.

Fenves, Peter. *"Chatter": Language and History in Kierkegaard.* Stanford: Stanford University Press, 1993.

Fichte, Johan Gottlieb. *Grundlage der gesamten Wissenschaftslehre: Als Handschrift für seine Zuhörer.* Intro. Wilhelm G. Jacobs. Hamburg: Felix Meiner, 1997. Translated by Peter Heath and John Lachs under the title *The Science of Knowledge* (Cambridge: Cambridge University Press, 1982).

Fimiani, Mariapaola. *Foucault et Kant: Critique Clinique Éthique.* Trans. Nadine Le Lirzin. Paris: L'Harmattan, 1998.

Foucault, Michel. *L'Archéologie du savoir.* Paris: Gallimard, 1969. Translated by A. M. Sheridan Smith as *The Archeology of Knowledge and The Discourse on Language* (New York: Pantheon Books, 1972).

———. "The Art of Telling the Truth." Trans. A. Sheridan. In *Critique and Power: Recasting the Foucault/Habermas Debate,* ed. Michael Kelly. Cambridge: MIT Press, 1994.

———. *Dits et écrits: 1954–1988.* Ed. Daniel Defert and François Ewald. Paris: Gallimard, 1994.

———. "Mon corps, ce papier, ce feu." In *Folie et déraison: Histoire de la folie à l'âge classique,* 583–603. Paris: Plon, 1972. Translated by Geoff Bennington under the title "My Body, This Paper, This Fire," *Oxford Literary Review* 4, no. 1 (1979): 9–27.

———. "Notice historique." In E. Kant, *Anthropologie du point de vue pragmatique,* trans. M. Foucault. Paris: Vrin, 1964. Republished in Foucault, *Dits et écrits,* vol. 1, ed. Daniel Defert and François Ewald, 288–93 (Paris: Gallimard, 1994).

———. "Qu'est-ce la critique / Critique et Aufklärung." *Bulletin de la Société française de Philosophie* 84 (1990): 35–63. Translated by Kevin Paul Geiman under the title "What Is Critique?," in *What Is Enlightenment?: Eighteenth-Century Answers and Twentieth- Century Questions,* ed. James Schmidt, 382–98 (Berkeley: University of California Press, 1996).

———. "Qu'est-ce que les Lumières?" In *Dits et écrits: 1954–1988,* vol. 4, *1980–1988,* ed. Daniel Defert and François Ewald, 562–78 and 679–88. Paris: Gallimard, 1994. Translated under the title "What Is Enlightenment?" in *The Foucault Reader,* ed. Paul Rabinow, 32–50 (New York: Pantheon Books, 1984).

Frye, Northrop. *The Great Code: The Bible and Literature.* San Diego: Harcourt Brace Jovanovich, 1983.

Fuchs, Gotthard, and Hans Hermann Henrix, eds. *Zeitgewinn: Messianisches Denken nach Franz Rosenzweig.* Frankfurt a. M.: Verlag Josef Knecht, 1987.

Fuld, Werner. *Walter Benjamin, Zwischen den Stuhlen: Eine Biographie.* Munich: Carl Hanser, 1979.

Garber, Marjorie, and Rebecca L. Walkowitz, eds., *One Nation under God?: Religion and American Culture.* Foreword by Cornel West. New York: Routledge, 1999.

Gasché, Rodolphe. "Alongside the Horizon." In *The Sense of Philosophy: On Jean-Luc Nancy,* ed. D. Sheppard et al., 140–56. London: Routledge, 1997.

———. *Inventions of Difference: On Jacques Derrida.* Cambridge: Harvard University Press, 1994.

———. *Of Minimal Things: Studies on the Notion of Relation.* Stanford: Stanford University Press, 1999.

———. "On Critique, Hypercriticism, and Deconstruction: The Case of Benjamin." *Cardozo Law Review* 13, no. 4 (1991): 1115–32.

Gauchet, Marcel. *Le Désenchantement du monde: Une histoire politique de la religion*. Paris: Gallimard, 1985.

Gesenius, Wilhelm. *Hebräisches und Aramäisches Handwörterbuch über das Alte Testament*. Berlin: Springer, 1962.

Giard, Luce. "Biobibliographie." In "Michel de Certeau," *Cahiers pour un temps*, 245 ff. Paris, Centres Georges Pompidou, 1987.

Giard, Luce, et al. *Le Voyage mystique: Michel de Certeau*. Paris: Recherches de science religieuse: Diffusion, Cerf, 1988.

Girard, René. *Des choses cachées depuis la fondation du monde: Recherches avec Jean-Michel Oughourlian et Guy Lefort*. Paris: Bernard Grasset, 1978. Translated by Stephen Bann and Michael Metteer under the title *Things Hidden since the Foundation of the World* (Stanford: Stanford University Press, 1987).

———. *Mensonge romantique et vérité romanesque*. Paris: Bernard Grasset, 1961. Translated by Yvonne Freccero under the title *Deceit, Desire, and the Novel* (Baltimore: Johns Hopkins University Press, 1965).

———. *La Violence et le sacré*. Paris: Éditions Bernhard Grasset, 1972; Hachette/Pluriel, 1999. Translated by Patrick Gregory under the title *Violence and the Sacred* (Baltimore: Johns Hopkins University Press, 1977).

Glendenning, Simon. *On Being with Others: Heidegger, Derrida, Wittgenstein*. London: Routledge, 1998.

Gondek, Hans-Dieter, and Bernhard Waldenfels, eds. *Einsätze des Denkens: Zur Philosophie von Jacques Derrida*. Frankfurt a. M.: Suhrkamp, 1997.

Gray, John. *Enlightenment's Wake: Politics and Culture at the Close of the Modern Age*. London: Routledge, 1995.

Green, Ronald M. *The Hidden Debt: Kierkegaard and Kant*. Albany: State University of New York Press, 1992.

Greisch, Jean. "L'Analyse de l'acte de croire entre histoire et épistémologie." *Recherches de science religieuse* 77, no. 1 (1989): 13–44.

Greisch, Jean, and Jacques Rolland, eds. *Emmanuel Levinas: L'Éthique comme philosophie première*, Colloque de Cerisy-la-Salle. Paris: Cerf, 1993.

Habermas, Jürgen. *Die Einbeziehung des Anderen: Studien zur politischen Theorie*. Frankfurt a. M.: Suhrkamp, 1996.

———. *Faktizität und Geltung: Beiträge zur Diskurstheorie des Rechts und des demokratischen Rechtsstaats*. Frankfurt a. M.: Suhrkamp, 1992.

———. "Kants Idee des ewigen Friedens—aus dem historischen Abstand von 200 Jahren." In *Die Einbeziehung des Anderen: Studien zur politischen Theorie*, 192–236. Frankfurt a. M.: Suhrkamp, 1996. Translated by James Bohman under the title "Kant's Idea of Perpetual Peace, with the Benefit of Two Hundred Years' Hindsight," in *Perpetual Peace: Essays on Kant's Cosmopolitan Ideal*, ed.

James Bohman and Matthias Lutz-Bachmann, 113–53 (Cambridge: MIT Press, 1997).

———. "Die Schrecken der Autonomie: Carl Schmitt auf english." In *Eine Art Schadensabwicklung*, 103–14. Frankfurt a. M.: Suhrkamp, 1987. Translated under the title "Sovereignty and the Führerdemokratie," *Times Literary Supplement*, September 26, 1986.

———. "Taking Aim at the Heart of the Present: On Foucault's Lecture on Kant's 'What Is Enlightenment?'" In *Critique and Power*, ed. Michael Kelly, 149–154. Cambridge, MIT Press, 1994.

———. *Zur Rekonstruktion des historischen Materialismus*. Frankfurt a. M.: Suhrkamp, 1976.

Hadot, Pierre. *Philosophy as a Way of Life*. Ed. and intro. Arnold I. Davidson, trans. Michael Case (Oxford: Blackwell, 1995).

Halbertal, Moshe. *People of the Book: Canon, Meaning, and Authority*. Cambridge: Harvard University Press, 1997.

Hamacher, Werner. "Afformativ, Streik: Entsetzung der Repräsentation in Benjamin's 'Zur Kritik der Gewalt.'" In *Was heisst darstellen?*, ed. C. Hart-Nibbrig. Frankfurt a. M.: Suhrkamp, 1991. Translated by Dana Hollander under the title "Afformative, Strike: Benjamin's "Critique of Violence," in *Walter Benjamin's Philosophy: Destruction and Experience*, ed. Andrew Benjamin and Peter Osborne, 110–38 (London: Routledge, 1994).

———. "Der ausgesetzte Satz: Friedrich Schlegels poetologische Umsetzung von Fichtes absolutem Grundsatz." In *Entferntes Verstehen: Studien zur Philosophie und Literatur von Kant bis Celan*, 195–234. Frankfurt a. M.: Suhrkamp, 1998. Translated by Peter Fenves under the title "Position Exposed: Friedrich Schlegel's Poetological Transposition of Fichte's Absolute Proposition," in *Premises: Essays on Philosophy and Literature from Kant to Celan*, 222–60 (Cambridge: Harvard University Press, 1996).

———. "Ou, séance, touche de Nancy, ici." *Paragraph* 16, no. 2 (1993): 216–31.

———. "Ou, séance, touche de Nancy, ici (II)." *Paragraph* 17, no. 2 (1994): 103–19.

———. "One 2 Many Multiculturalisms." In *Violence, Identity, and Self-Determination*, ed Hent de Vries and Samuel Weber, 284–325 (Stanford: Stanford University Press, 1997).

———. *Pleroma: Zu Genesis und Struktur einer dialektischen Hermeneutik bei Hegel*. In Georg Wilhelm Friedrich Hegel, *"Der Geist des Christentums": Schriften 1796–1800*, 9–333. Frankfurt a. M., 1978. Translated by Nicholas Walker and Simon Jarvis under the title *Pleroma: Reading in Hegel* (Stanford: Stanford University Press, 1998).

Handelman, Susan A. *Fragments of Redemption: Jewish Thought and Literary*

Theory in Benjamin, Scholem, and Levinas. Bloomington: Indiana University Press, 1991.

Hansen, Miriam. *Babel and Babylon: Spectatorship in American Silent Film.* Cambridge: Harvard University Press, 1991.

Hanssen, Beatrice. "'The correct/just point of departure': Deconstruction, Humanism, and the Call to Responsibility." In *Enlightenments: Encounters between Critical Theory and Recent French Thought,* ed. Harry Kunneman and Hent de Vries, 194–210. Kampen: Kok Pharos, 1993.

———. *Critique of Violence: Between Poststructuralism and Critical Theory.* New York: Routledge, 2000.

———. "Philosophy at Its Origin: Walter Benjamin's Prologue to the *Ursprung des deutschen Trauerspiels.*" *Modern Language Notes* 110 (1995): 809–33.

———. *Walter Benjamin's Other History: Of Stones, Animals, Human Beings, and Angels.* Berkeley: University of California Press, 1998.

Haverkamp, Anselm, ed. *Gewalt und Gerechtigkeit: Derrida-Benjamin.* Frankfurt a. M.: Suhrkamp, 1994.

Hegel, Georg Wilhelm Friedrich. *Grundlinien der Philosophie des Rechts.* Ed. J. Hoffmeister. Hamburg: Meiner, 1955. Translated by H. B. Nisbet under the title *Elements of the Philosophy of Right,* ed. Allen W. Wood (Cambridge: Cambridge University Press, 1991).

———. *Vorlesungen über die Philosophie der Religion.* Vols. 3–5 of *Vorlesungen: Ausgewählte Nachschriften und Manuskripte,* ed. Walter Jaeschke. Hamburg: Felix Meiner, 1983, 1984, 1985. Translated by R. F. Brown, P. C. Hodgson, and J. M. Stewart, with the assistance of H. S. Harris, under the title *Lectures on the Philosophy of Religion* (Berkeley: University of California Press, 1984, 1985, 1987).

Heidegger, Martin. *Beiträge zur Philosophie: Vom Ereignis.* Vol. 65 of *Gesamtausgabe* Frankfurt a. M.: Vittorio Klostermann, 1989.

———. *Sein und Zeit.* Tübingen: Max Niemeyer, 1993. Translated by John Macquarrie and Edward Robinson under the title *Being and Time* (New York: Harper & Row, 1962).

———. *Ursprung des Kunstwerks.* In *Holzwege.* Frankfurt a. M.: Vittorio Klostermann, 1972. Translated by Albert Hofstadter under the title *The Origin of the Work of Art,* in *Poetry, Language, Thought* (New York: Harper & Row, 1971).

———. *Wegmarken.* Frankfurt a. M.: Vittorio Klostermann, 1976. Translated by James G. Hart and John C. Maraldo under the title *Pathmarks,* ed. William McNeill (Cambridge: Cambridge University Press, 1998).

Heil, Susanne. *"Gefährliche Beziehungen": Walter Benjamin und Carl Schmitt.* Stuttgart: J. B. Metzler, 1996.

Héritier, Françoise, ed., *De la violence*. Paris: Éditions Odile Jacob, 1996.

———. *De la violence II*. Paris: Éditions Odile Jacob, 1999.

Hersant, Yves, and Fabienne Durand-Bogaert, eds. *Europes: De l'antiquité au XXe siècle* Paris: Robert Lafont, 2000.

Hertz, Neil. "Lurid Figures." In *Reading De Man Reading*, ed. Lindsay Waters and Wlad Godzich, 82–104. Minneapolis: University of Minnesota Press, 1989.

Hervieu-Léger, Danièle. *Le Pèlerin et le converti: La Religion en mouvement*. Paris: Flammarion, 1999.

———. *Religion pour Mémoire*. Paris: Cerf, 1993. Translated by Simon Lee under the title *Religion as a Chain of Memory* (Cambridge: Polity Press, 2000).

Honneth, Axel. *Kampf um Anerkennung: Zur moralischen Grammatik sozialer Konflikte* Frankfurt a. M.: Suhrkamp, 1992.

———. *Die zerrissene Welt des Sozialen: Sozialphilosophische Aufsätze*. 2d ed. Frankfurt a. M.: Suhrkamp, 1999.

Hortian, Ulrich. "Zeit und Geschichte bei Franz Rosenzweig und Walter Benjamin." In *Der Philosoph Franz Rosenzweig (1886–1929)*, ed. Wolfdietrich Schmied-Kowarzik, 2:815- 27. Freiburg: Verlag Karl Alber, 1988.

Humboldt, Wilhelm von. "Über die innere und äussere Organisation der höhere wissenschaftlichen Anstalten in Berlin." *Gesammelte Schriften*, 10:250–60. Berlin, 1903. Translated in *Minerva* 8, no. 2 (1970): 242–50.

Hume, David. *Dialogues Concerning Natural Religion* and *The Natural History of Religion*. Oxford: Oxford University Press, 1993.

Husserl, Edmund. *Ideen zu einer reinen Phänomenologie und phänomenologischen Philosophie*. Vol. 1, ed. Walter Biemel. *Husserliana*, vol. 3. The Hague: Martinus Nijhoff, 1950. Translated under the title *Ideas Pertaining to a Pure Phenomenology and to a Phenomenological Philosophy* (The Hague: Martinus Nijhoff, 1980–82).

———. *L'Origine de la géométrie*, trans. and intro. Jacques Derrida. Paris: Presses Universitaires de France, 1974.

Jauss, Hans Robert. "Literarische Tradition und gegenwärtiges Bewusstsein der Modernität." In *Literaturgeschichte als Provokation*, 11–66. Frankfurt a. M.: Suhrkamp, 1970.

Jay, Martin. "Politics of Translation: Siegfried Kracauer and Walter Benjamin on the Buber-Rosenzweig Bible." In *Permanent Exiles: Essays on the Intellectual Migration from Germany to America*, 198–216. New York: Columbia University Press, 1985.

Jennings, Michael W. *Dialectical Images: Walter Benjamin's Theory of Literary Criticism*. Ithaca: Cornell University Press, 1987.

Joas, Hans. *Die Entstehung der Werte*. Frankfurt a. M.: Suhrkamp, 1997.

———. "The Modernity of War: Modernization Theory and the Problem of Violence." *International Sociology* 14 (1999): 457–72.

Johnson, David. *Hume, Holism, and Miracles.* Ithaca: Cornell University Press, 1999.

Joyce, James. *Finnegans Wake.* Harmondsworth, Middlesex: Penguin Books, 1976.

Kamuf, Peggy. *The Division of Literature; or, The University in Deconstruction.* Chicago: University of Chicago Press, 1997.

Kant, Immanuel. *Anthropologie in pragmatischer Hinsicht.* In *Werke,* ed. Wilhelm Weischedel, 10:395–690. Darmstadt: Wissenschaftliche Buchgesellschaft, 1983. Translated by Victor Lyle Dowdell under the title *Anthropology from a Pragmatic Point of View,* rev. ed. Hans H. Rudnick, intro. Frederick P. Van De Pitte (Carbondale: Southern Illinois University Press, 1978).

———. "Idee zu einer allgemeinen Geschichte in weltbürgerlicher Absicht." In *Werke,* ed. Wilhelm Weischedel, 9:33–50. Darmstadt: Wissenschaftliche Buchgesellschaft, 1983. Translated by H. B. Nisbet under the title "Idea for a Universal History with a Cosmopolitan Purpose," in *Political Writings,* ed. and intro. Hans Reiss, *The Cambridge Edition of the Works of Immanuel Kant,* ed. Paul Guyer and Allen W. Wood, 41–53 (Cambridge: Cambridge University Press, 1991).

———. *Kritik der praktischen Vernunft.* Vol. 6 of *Werke,* ed. Wilhelm Weischedel. Darmstadt: Wissenschaftliche Buchgesellschaft, 1983. Translated by Mary J. Gregor under the title *Critique of Practical Reason,* in *Practical Philosophy,* ed. Mary J. Gregor, *The Cambridge Edition of the Works of Immanuel Kant,* ed. Paul Guyer and Allen W. Wood (Cambridge: Cambridge University Press, 1996).

———. *Kritik der reinen Vernunft.* Vols. 3 and 4 of *Werke,* ed. Wilhelm Weischedel. Darmstadt: Wissenschaftliche Buchgesellschaft, 1983. Translated by Paul Guyer and Allen W. Wood under the title *Critique of Pure Reason, The Cambridge Edition of the Works of Immanuel Kant,* ed. Paul Guyer and Allen W. Wood (Cambridge: Cambridge University Press, 1998).

———. *Kritik der Urteilskraft.* Vol. 8 of *Werke,* ed. Wilhelm Weischedel. Darmstadt: Wissenschaftliche Buchgesellschaft, 1983. Translated by J. H. Bernard under the title *Critique of Judgment* (New York: Hafner, 1951).

———. *Metaphysik der Sitten.* Vol. 7 of *Werke,* ed. Wilhelm Weischedel. Darmstadt: Wissenschaftliche Buchgesellschaft, 1983. Translated by Mary J. Gregor under the title *The Metaphysics of Morals,* in *Practical Philosophy,* ed. Mary J. Gregor, *The Cambridge Edition of the Works of Immanuel Kant,* ed. Paul Guyer and Allen W. Wood (Cambridge: Cambridge University Press, 1996).

———. *Die Religion innerhalb der Grenzen der blossen Vernunft.* Vol. 7 of *Werke,* ed. Wilhelm Weischedel. Darmstadt: Wissenschaftliche Buchgesellschaft,

1983. Translated by George di Giovanni under the title *Religion within the Boundaries of Mere Reason, The Cambridge Edition of the Works of Immanuel Kant*, ed. Paul Guyer and Allen W. Wood (Cambridge: Cambridge University Press, 1996); and by Theodore M. Greene and Hoyt H. Hudson under the title *Religion within the Limits of Reason Alone* (New York: Harper & Row, 1960; orig. pub. 1934).

————. *Der Streit der Fakultäten*. Ed. Klaus Reich. Hamburg: Meiner, 1959. Translated by Mary J. Gregor under the title *The Conflict of the Faculties* (Lincoln: University of Nebraska Press, 1992), and in *The Cambridge Edition of the Works of Immanuel Kant*, ed. Paul Guyer and Allen W. Wood (Cambridge: Cambridge University Press, 1996).

————. "Über den Gemeinspruch: Das mag in der Theorie richtig sein, taugt aber nicht für die Praxis." In *Werke*, ed. Wilhelm Weischedel, 9:127–72. Darmstadt: Wissenschaftliche Buchgesellschaft, 1983. Translated by Mary J. Gregor under the title "On the Common Saying: That May Be Correct in Theory, but It Is of No Use in Practice," in *Practical Philosophy*, ed. Mary J. Gregor, *The Cambridge Edition of the Works of Immanuel Kant*, ed. Paul Guyer and Allen W. Wood, 179–309 (Cambridge: Cambridge University Press, 1996).

————. "Von einem neuerdings erhobenen vornehmen Ton in der Philosophie." In *Werke*, ed. Wilhelm Weischedel, 5:377–97. Darmstadt: Wissenschaftliche Buchgesellschaft, 1983. Translated by Peter Fenves under the title "On a Newly Arisen Superior Tone in Philosophy," in *Raising the Tone of Philosophy: Late Essays by Immanuel Kant, Transformative Critique by Jacques Derrida*, ed. Peter Fenves, 51–72 (Baltimore: Johns Hopkins University Press, 1993).

————. "Was heisst: sich im Denken orientieren?" In *Werke*, ed. Wilhelm Weischedel, 5:267–83. Darmstadt: Wissenschaftliche Buchgesellschaft, 1983. Translated by Allen W. Wood under the title "What Does It Mean to Orient Oneself in Thinking?," in *Religion and Rational Theology, The Cambridge Edition of the Works of Immanuel Kant*, ed. Paul Guyer and Allen W. Wood, 7–18 (Cambridge: Cambridge University Press, 1996).

————. "Zum ewigen Frieden: Ein philosophischer Entwurf." In *Werke*, ed. Wilhelm Weischedel, 9:195–251. Darmstadt: Wissenschaftliche Buchgesellschaft, 1983. Translated by Mary J. Gregor under the title "Toward Perpetual Peace: A Philosophical Project," in *Practical Philosophy*, ed. Mary J. Gregor, *The Cambridge Edition of the Works of Immanuel Kant*, ed. Paul Guyer and Allen W. Wood, 317–51 (Cambridge: Cambridge University Press, 1996).

Kantorowicz, Ernst H. *The King's Two Bodies: A Study in Mediaeval Political Theology*. Preface by William Chester Jordan. Princeton: Princeton University Press, 1997.

Kierkegaard, Søren, *The Concept of Anxiety: A Simple Psychologically Orienting Deliberation on the Dogmatic Issue of Hereditary Sin.* Vol. 8 of *Kierkegaard's Writings,* trans. and ed. Reidar Thomte in collaboration with Albert B. Anderson. Princeton: Princeton University Press, 1980.

———. *The Concept of Irony: With Continual Reference to Socrates.* Vol. 2 of *Kierkegaard's Writings.* Trans. and ed. Howard V. Hong and Edna H. Hong. Princeton: Princeton University Press, 1989.

———. *Fear and Trembling: Dialectical Lyric, by Johannes de Silentio.* In vol. 6 of *Kierkegaard's Writings,* trans. and ed. Howard V. Hong and Edna H. Hong. Princeton: Princeton University Press, 1983.

———. *Papers and Journals: A Selection.* Trans. and intro. Alistair Hannay. Harmondsworth, Middlesex: Penguin, 1989.

———. *Repetition: A Venture in Experimenting Psychology, by Constantin Constantius,* in vol. 6 of *Kierkegaard's Writings,* trans. and ed. Howard V. Hong and Edna H. Hong, 125–231. Princeton: Princeton University Press, 1983.

———. *The Sickness unto Death: A Christian Psychological Exposition for Upbuilding and Awakening.* Vol. 9 of *Kierkegaard's Writings,* trans. and ed. Howard V. Hong and Edna H. Hong. Princeton: Princeton University Press, 1980.

Kirmmse, Bruce H., ed. *Encounters with Kierkegaard: A Life as Seen by His Contemporaries.* Ed. Bruce H. Krimmse, trans. Bruce H. Krimmse and Virginia R. Laursen. Princeton: Princeton University Press, 1996.

Der kleine Pauly: Lexikon der Antike. Munich: Deutscher Taschenbuchverlag, 1979.

Klibansky, Raymond, Erwin Panowsky, and Fritz Saxl. *Saturn und Melancholie: Studien zur Geschichte der Naturphilosophie und Medizin, der Religion und der Kunst.* Trans. Christa Buschendorf. Frankfurt a. M.: Suhrkamp, 1990.

Klossowski, Pierre. *Les Lois de l'hospitalité.* Paris: Gallimard, 1965.

Kodalle, Klaus-M. "Walter Benjamins politischer Dezisionismus im theologischen Kontext: Der 'Kierkegaard' unter den spekulativen Materialisten." In *Spiegel und Gleichnis: Festschrift für Jakob Taubes,* ed. Norbert W. Bolz and Wolfgang Hübener, 301–17. Würzburg, 1983.

Korsgaard, Christine M. *Creating the Kingdom of Ends.* Cambridge: Cambridge University Press, 1996.

———. "Religious Faith, Teleological History, and the Concept of Agency: Comments on Onora O'Neill's Tanner Lectures," manuscript.

Korsgaard, Christine M., with G. A. Cohen, Raymond Geuss, Thomas Nagel, and Bernard Williams. *The Sources of Normativity.* Ed. Onora O'Neill. Cambridge: Cambridge University Press, 1996.

Kripke, Saul. *Naming and Necessity.* Cambridge: Harvard University Press 1980; orig. pub. 1972.

Kymlicka, Will. *Multicultural Citizenship: A Liberal Theory of Minority Rights.*
Oxford: Oxford University Press, 1995.

Lacan, Jacques. *Le Seminaire,* 11. Paris, Seuil, 1973.

Laclau, Ernesto. "Why Do Empty Signifiers Matter to Politics?" In *Emancipa-
tion(s),* 36–46. London: Verso, 1996.

Lacoue-Labarthe, Philippe. *La Fiction du politique: Heidegger, l'art et la politique.*
Paris: Christian Bourgois Éditeur, 1987.

———. "Typographie." In Sylviane Agacinski et al., *Mimises des articulations,*
167–270. Paris: Aubier-Flammarion, 1975. Translated by Christopher Fynsk
under the title "Typography," *Typography: Mimesis, Philosophy, Politics,* intro.
Jacques Derrida, 43–138 (Cambridge: Harvard University Press, 1989).

Lacoue-Labarthe, Philippe, and Jean-Luc Nancy. *The Literary Absolute: The
Theory of Literature in German Romanticism.* Trans. and intro. Philip Barnard
and Cheryl Lester. Albany: State University of New York Press, 1988.

Lacoue-Labarthe, Philippe, and Jean-Luc Nancy, eds. *Le Retrait du politique: Tra-
vaux du centre de recherches philosophiques sur le politique.* Paris: Galilée, 1983.
Translated by Simon Sparks under the title *Retreating the Political* (London:
Routledge, 1997).

Lefort, Claude. *Écrire à l'épreuve du politique.* Paris: Calmann-Lévy, 1992.

———. "Permanence du theólogico-politique?" In *Essais sur le politique: XIXe–
XXe siècles,* 251–300. Paris: Seuil, 1986. Translated by David Macey under the
title "The Permanence of the Theologico-Political?," in *Democracy and Political Theory,* 213–55 (Minneapolis: University of Minnesota Press, 1988).

Lescourret, Marie-Anne. *Emmanuel Levinas.* Paris: Flammarion, 1994.

Levinas, Emmanuel. *À l'heure des nations.* Paris: Minuit, 1988. Translated by Michael B. Smith under the title *In the Time of Nations* (London: Athlone, 1994).

———. *Altérité et transcendance.* Montpellier: Fata Morgana, 1995.

———. *L'au-delà du verset: Lectures et discours talmudiques.* Paris: Minuit, 1982.
Translated by Gary D. Mole under the title *Beyond the Verse: Readings and
Lectures* (Bloomington: Indiana University Press, 1994).

———. *Autrement qu'être ou au-delà de l'essence.* The Hague: Martinus Nijhoff,
1974. Translated by Alphonso Lingis under the title *Otherwise Than Being or
Beyond Essence* (Dordrecht: Kluwer, 1991).

———. *Collected Philosophical Papers.* Trans. A. Lingis. Dordrecht: Martinus
Nijhoff, 1987.

———. *De dieu qui vient à l'idée.* Paris: Vrin, 1982. Translated by Bettina Bergo
under the title *Of God Who Comes to Mind* (Stanford: Stanford University
Press, 1998).

———. "Diachrony and Representation." In *Time and the Other,* trans. Richard A.

Cohen, 97–120. Pittsburgh: Duquesne University Press, 1987. The French text was republished in *Entre nous: Essais sur le penser-à-l'autre*, 177–97 (Paris: Grasset, 1991).

——. *Dieu, la mort et le temps*. Paris: B. Grasset, 1993.

——. *Difficile liberté: Essais sur le judaïsme*. Paris: Albin Michel, 1976. Translated by Seán Hand under the title *Difficult Freedom: Essays on Judaism* (Baltimore: Johns Hopkins University Press, 1990).

——. "Les Dommages causés par le feu." In *Du sacré au saint: Cinq Nouvelles Lectures talmudiques*, 149–80. Paris: Minuit, 1977. Translated by Annette Aronowicz under the title "Damages Due to Fire," in *Nine Talmudic Readings*, 178–97 (Bloomington: Indiana University Press, 1990).

——. *En découvrant l'existence avec Husserl et Heidegger*. Paris: Vrin, 1967.

——. *Entre nous: Essais sur le penser-à-l'autre*. Paris: Grasset, 1991. Translated by Michael B. Smith and Barbara Harshav under the title *Entre nous: Thinking of the Other* (New York: Columbia University Press, 1998).

——. *Éthique et Infini*. Paris: Fayard, 1982.

——. *Humanisme de l'autre homme*. Montpellier: Fata Morgana, 1972.

——. *Les Imprévus de l'histoire*. Montpellier: Fata Morgana, 1994.

——. *La Mort et le temps*. Paris: L'Herne, 1991.

——. *Noms propres*. Montpellier: Fata Morgana, 1975. Translated by Michael B. Smith under the title *Proper Names* (Stanford: Stanford University Press, 1996).

——. *Nouvelles Lectures Talmudiques*. Paris: Minuit, 1996.

——. "La Réalité et son ombre." *Les Temps modernes* 38 (1948): 771–89.

——. *Totalité et Infini*. The Hague: Martinus Nijhoff, 1961. Translated by Alphonso Lingis under the title *Totality and Infinity* (Pittsburgh: Duquesne University Press, 1969).

——. "Transcendance et hauteur." In *Cahier de l'Herne*, ed. Catherine Chalier and Miguel Abensour, 50–74. Paris: L'Herne, 1991.

——. *Transcendance et intelligibilité*. Geneva: Labor et Fides, 1984.

——. *Quelques réflexions sur la philosophie de l'hitlérisme*. Paris: Payot & Rivages, 1997. Translated in *Critical Inquiry* 17, no. 1 (1990): 63–71.

——. *Positivité et transcendance*. Paris: Presses Universitaires de France, 2000.

Leys, Ruth. *Trauma: A Genealogy*. Chicago: University of Chicago Press, 2000.

Libera, Alain de. *La Mystique rhénane: D'Albert le Grand à Maître Eckhart*. Paris: Seuil, 1994.

Lyotard, Jean-François. *La Condition postmoderne: Rapport sur le savoir*. Paris: Minuit, 1979. Translated by Geoffrey Bennington and Brian Massumi under the title *The Postmodern Condition* (Minneapolis: University of Minnesota Press, 1984).

———. *Le Différend.* Paris: Minuit, 1983. Translated by Georges Van Den Abbeele under the title *The Differend: Phrases in Dispute* (Minneapolis: University of Minnesota Press, 1988).

———. *L'Enthousiasme: La Critique kantienne de l'histoire.* Paris: Galilée, 1986.

———. *L'Inhumain: Causeries sur le temps.* Paris: Galilée, 1988. Translated by Geoffrey Bennington and Rachel Bowlby under the title *The Inhuman: Reflections on Time* (Stanford: Stanford University Press, 1991).

———. *Leçons sur l'Analytique du sublime.* Paris: Galilée, 1991. Translated by Elizabeth Rottenberg under the title *Lessons on the Analytic of the Sublime* (Stanford: Stanford University Press, 1994).

Lyotard, Jean-François, et al. *La Faculté de juger.* Paris: Minuit, 1985.

McCarthy, Thomas. *Ideals and Illusions: On Reconstruction and Deconstruction in Contemporary Critical Theory.* Cambridge: MIT Press, 1991.

McCormick, John P. *Carl Schmitt's Critique of Liberalism: Against Politics as Technology.* Cambridge: Cambridge University Press, 1997.

MacIntyre, Alisdair. *After Virtue: A Study in Moral Theory.* London: Duckworth, 1981.

Mackie, J. L. "Evil and Omnipotence." *Mind* 64 (1955): 200–12. Reprinted in *The Philosophy of Religion,* ed. Basil Mitchell, 92–104 (Oxford: Oxford University Press, 1971).

Man, Paul de. *Allegories of Reading: Figural Language in Rousseau, Nietzsche, Rilke, and Proust.* New Haven: Yale University Press, 1979.

Marion, Jean-Luc. *La Croisée du visible.* Paris: Presses Universitaires de France, 1996.

———. *Étant donné: Essai d'une phénoménologie de la donation.* Paris: Presses Universitaires de France, 1997.

———. "Metaphysics and Phenomenology: A Relief for Theology." *Critical Inquiry* 20 (1994): 572–91.

Marrati, Paola. *La Genèse et la trace: Derrida lecteur de Husserl et Heidegger.* Dordrecht: Kluwer, 1998. English translation, by Simon Sparks, forthcoming from Stanford University Press.

Massignon, Louis. *L'Hospitalité sacrée.* Paris: Nouvelle Cité, 1987.

———. *Parole donnée.* Paris: Seuil, 1983.

Medawar, P. B. *Aristotle to Zoos: A Philosophical Dictionary of Biology.* Cambridge: Harvard University Press, 1983.

Mendes-Flohr, Paul. *From Mysticism to Dialogue: Martin Buber's Transformation of German Social Thought.* Detroit: Wayne State University Press, 1989.

Mendes-Flohr, Paul, ed. *The Philosophy of Franz Rosenzweig*. Hanover: Brandeis University Press & University Press of New England, 1988.

Menke, Christoph. *Tragödie im Sittlichen: Gerechtigkeit und Freiheit nach Hegel*. Frankfurt a. M.: Suhrkamp, 1996.

Meier, Heinrich. *Carl Schmitt, Leo Strauss und "Der Begriff des Politischen": Zu einem Dialog unter Abwesenden*. Stuttgart: Metzlerische Verlagsbuchhandlung, 1988. Translated by J. Harvey Lomax under the title *Carl Schmitt and Leo Strauss: The Hidden Dialogue* (Chicago: University of Chicago Press, 1995).

———. *Die Lehre Carl Schmitts: Vier Kapitel zur Unterscheidung politischer Theologie und politischer Philosophie*. Stuttgart: Metzlersche Verlagsbuchhandlung and Carl Ernst Poeschel, 1994). Translated by Marcus Brainard under the title *The Lesson of Carl Schmitt: Four Chapters on the Distinction between Political Theology and Political Philosophy* (Chicago: University of Chicago Press, 1998).

Merkel, Reinhard, and Roland Wittmann, eds. *"Zum ewigen Frieden": Grundlagen, Aktualität und Aussichten einer Idee von Immanuel Kant*. Frankfurt a. M.: Suhrkamp, 1996.

Metzger, Bruce M., and Michael D. Coogan, eds. *The Oxford Companion to the Bible*. New York: Oxford University Press, 1993.

Michaud, Yves. *La Violence*. Paris: Presses Universitaires de France, 1998.

Miller, J. Hillis. "Literary Study in the Transnational University." In J. Hillis Miller and Manuel Asensi, *Black Holes / J. Hillis Miller; or, Boustrophonic Reading*, 3–185. Stanford: Stanford University Press, 1999.

Miller, James. *The Passion of Michel Foucault*. New York: Simon & Schuster, 1993.

Molendijk, Arie L., and Peter Pels, eds. *Religion in the Making: The Emergence of the Sciences of Religion*. Leiden: Brill, 1998.

Mongin, Olivier. "La Parenthèse politique." In *Emmanuel Levinas: L'Éthique comme philosophie première*, ed. Jean Greisch and Jacques Rolland, 315–26. Paris: Cerf, 1993.

Mosès, Stéphane. *L'Ange de l'histoire: Rosenzweig, Benjamin, Scholem*. Paris: Seuil, 1992.

———. *Système et Révélation: La Philosophie de Franz Rosenzweig*. Preface by Emmanuel Levinas. Paris: Seuil, 1982.

———. "Walter Benjamin und Franz Rosenzweig." *Deutsche Vierteljahrschrift für Literaturwissenschaft und Geistesgeschichte* 4 (1982): 622–40.

Naar, M. Introduction, in Emmanuel Kant, *La Religion dans limites de la simple raison*, trans. J. Gibelin, 9–51. Paris: Vrin, 1996.

Nägele, Rainer. "Die Aufmerksamkeit des Lesers: Aufklärung und Moderne." In *Enlightenments: Encounters between Critical Theory and Contemporary French*

Thought, ed. Harry Kunneman and Hent de Vries, 162–79. Kampen: Kok Pharos, 1993.

———. *Theater, Theory, Speculation: Walter Benjamin and the Scenes of Modernity.* Baltimore: Johns Hopkins University Press, 1991.

Nancy, Jean-Luc. *La Communauté désoeuvrée.* Paris: Christian Bourgeois, 1990; orig. pub. 1986. Translated by Peter Connor, Lisa Garbus, Michael Holland, and Simona Sawhney under the title *The Inoperative Community*, ed. Peter Connor (Minneapolis: University of Minnesota Press, 1991).

———. "La Déconstruction du christianisme." *Les Études philosophiques* 4 (1998): 503–19.

———. *Être singulier pluriel.* Paris: Galilée, 1996. Translated by Robert Richardson and Anne O'Byrne under the title *Being Singular Plural* (Stanford: Stanford University Press, 2000).

———. *L'Expérience de la liberté.* Paris: Galilée, 1988. Translated by Bridget McDonald under the title *The Experience of Freedom* (Stanford: Stanford University Press, 1994).

———. *Une pensée finie.* Paris: Galilée, 1990.

Nussbaum, Martha C. *Cultivating Humanity: A Classical Defense of Reform in Liberal Education.* Cambridge: Harvard University Press, 1997.

———. "Kant and Cosmopolitanism." In *Perpetual Peace: Essays on Kant's Cosmopolitan Ideal*, ed. James Bohman and Matthias Lutz-Bachmann, 25–57. Cambridge: MIT Press, 1997.

———. *The Therapy of Desire: Theory and Practice in Hellenistic Ethics.* Princeton: Princeton University Press, 1994.

Nussbaum, Martha C., with respondents. *For Love of Country: Debating the Limits of Patriotism.* Ed. Joshua Cohen. Boston: Beacon, 1996.

O'Neill, Onora. *Constructions of Reason: Explorations of Kant's Practical Philosophy.* Cambridge: Cambridge University Press, 1989.

———. "Kant on Reason, Morality, and Religion." Tanner Lectures, Harvard University, February 1996, manuscript.

Opitz, Michael, and Erdmut Wizisla, eds. *Benjamins Begriffe.* 2 vols. Frankfurt a. M.: Suhrkamp, 2000.

Ott, Hugo. *Martin Heidegger: Unterwegs zu seiner Biographie.* Frankfurt a. M.: Campus, 1988.

Palyi, Melchior, ed. *Hauptprobleme der Soziologie: Erinnerungsgabe für Max Weber.* Munich, 1922.

Pascal, Blaise. *Pensées.* Trans. and intro. A. J. Krailsheimer. Harmondsworth, Middlesex: Penguin, 1966.

Payot, Daniel. *Des Villes-refuges: Témoignage et espacement.* Paris: L'Aube, 1992.

Pelikan, J. *The Idea of the University: A Reexamination.* New Haven: Yale University Press, 1992.

Peperzak, Adriaan, ed. *Ethics as First Philosophy.* London: Routledge, 1995.

———. *To the Other.* West Lafayette, Ind.: Purdue University Press, 1993.

Perkins, Robert L., ed. *Kierkegaard's "Fear and Trembling": Critical Appraisals.* Tuscaloosa: University of Alabama Press, 1981.

Petitdemange, Guy. "Emmanuel Levinas et la politique." In *Emmanuel Levinas: L'Éthique comme philosophie première,* ed. Jean Greisch and Jacques Rolland, 327–54. Paris: Cerf, 1993.

Pranger, Burcht. "Monastic Violence." In *Violence, Identity, and Self-Determination,* ed. de Vries and Weber, 44–57.

———. *Broken Dreams: Bernard of Clairvaux and the Shape of Monastic Thought.* Leiden: E. J. Brill, 1994.

Proust, Françoise. *De la résistance.* Paris: Cerf, 1997.

———. *L'Histoire à contretemps: Le temps historique chez Walter Benjamin.* Paris: Éditions du Cerf, 1994.

Rashdall, Hastings. *The Universities of Europe in the Middle Ages.* 3 vols. Rev. ed. F. M. Powicke and A. B. Emden. Oxford: Oxford University Press, 1997; orig. pub. 1895 and 1934.

Rawls, John. *Collected Papers.* Ed. Samuel Freeman. Cambridge: Harvard University Press, 1999.

———. *The Law of Peoples.* Cambridge: Harvard University Press, 1999.

———. *Political Liberalism.* New York: Columbia University Press, 1993.

———. *A Theory of Justice.* Rev. ed. Oxford: Oxford University Press, 1999.

Readings, Bill. *The University in Ruins.* Cambridge: Harvard University Press, 1996.

Richards, David A. J. *Toleration and the Constitution.* New York: Oxford University Press, 1986.

Ricoeur, Paul. "De l'Absolu à la Sagesse par l'Action." In *Lectures 1: Autour du politique,* 115–30. Paris: Seuil, 1991.

———. *Du texte à l'action: Essais d'herméneutique,* II. Paris: Seuil, 1986.

———. "Kierkegaard et le mal." In *Lectures 2: La contrée des philosophes,* 15–28. Paris: Seuil, 1999.

———. "Le Mal: Un défi à la philosophie et à la théologie." In *Lectures 3: Aux frontières de la philosophie,* 211–33. Paris: Seuil, 1994.

———. "Philosopher après Kierkegaard." In *Lectures 2: La Contrée des philosophes,* 29–45. Paris: Seuil, 1999.

———. "La 'Philosophie politique' d'Éric Weil." In *Lectures 1: Autour du politique,* 95–114. Paris: Seuil, 1991.

426

———. "Pouvoir et violence." In *Lectures 1: Autour du politique*, 20–42. Paris: Seuil, 1991.

———. "Une herméneutique philosophique de la religion: Kant." In *Lectures 3: Aux frontières de la philosophie*, 19–40. Paris: Seuil, 1994. Translated by David Pellauer under the title "A Philosophical Hermeneutics of Religion: Kant," in *Figuring the Sacred: Religion, Narrative, and Imagination*, ed. Mark I. Wallace, 75–92 (Minneapolis: Fortress, 1995).

———. "Violence et langage." *Lectures 1: Autour du politique*, 131–40. Paris: Seuil, 1991.

Riley, Patrick. *The General Will before Rousseau: The Transformation of the Divine into the Civic*. Princeton: Princeton University Press, 1986.

Robbins, Jill. *Altered Reading: Levinas and Literature*. Chicago: University of Chicago Press, 1999.

———. *Prodigal Son / Elder Brother: Interpretation and Alterity in Augustine, Petrarch, Kafka, Levinas*. Chicago: University of Chicago Press, 1991.

———. "Sacrifice" In *Critical Terms for Religious Studies*, ed Mark Taylor, 285–97. Chicago: University of Chicago Press, 1998.

Rogozinski, Jacob. "Ça nous donne tort (Kant et le mal radical)." In *Kanten: Esquisses kantiennes*, 95–111. Paris: Kimé, 1996. Translated under the title "It Makes Us Wrong: Kant and Radical Evil," in *Radical Evil*, ed. Joan Copjec, 30–45 (London: Verso, 1996).

———. *Le Don de la loi: Kant et l'énigme de l'éthique*. Paris: Presses Universitaires de France, 1999.

———. "'Il faut la vérité' (notes sur la vérité de Derrida)." *Rue Descartes* 24 (1999): 13–39.

———. "Vers une éthique du différend." In *Enlightenments: Encounters between Critical Theory and Recent French Thought*, ed. Harry Kunneman and Hent de Vries, 92–120. Kampen: Kok Pharos, 1993.

Rorty, Richard. *Achieving Our Country: Leftist Thought in Twentieth-Century America*. Cambridge: Harvard University Press, 1998.

———. *Philosophy and Social Hope*. Harmondsworth, Middlesex: Penguin, 1999.

———. "Strawson's Objectivity Argument." *Review of Metaphysics* 24 (1970): 207–44.

———. "Transcendental Argument, Self-Reference, and Pragmatism." In *Transcendental Arguments and Science*, ed. Peter Bieri et al., 77–103. Dordrecht: Reidel, 1979.

———. *Truth and Progress: Philosophical Papers*. Cambridge: Cambridge University Press, 1998.

———. "Verificationism and Transcendental Arguments." *Nous* 5 (1971): 3–14.

Rosenzweig, Franz. *Der Stern der Erlösung.* Vol. 2 of *Gesammelte Schriften.* The Hague: Martinus Nijhoff, 1976; orig. pub. 1921. Translated by W. W. Hallo under the title *The Star of Redemption* (New York: Holt, Rinehart &Winston, 1971).

———. *Zweistromland: Kleinere Schriften zu Glauben und Denken.* Vol. 3 of *Gesammelte Schriften.* Ed. Reinhold and Annemarie Mayer. The Hague: Martinus Nijhoff, 1984.

Sandel, Michael J. *Democracy's Discontent: America in Search of a Public Philosophy.* Cambridge: Harvard University Press, 1996.

———. *Liberalism and the Limits of Justice.* 2d ed. Cambridge: Cambridge University Press, 1998.

Schlegel, Friedrich. "Versuch über den Begriff des Republikanismus: Veranlasst durch die Kantische Schrift zum ewigen Frieden." In *Kritische und Theoretische Schriften,* ed. Andreas Huyssen, 3–20. Stuttgart: Reclam, 1978.

Schmied-Kowarzik, Wolfdietrich, ed. *Der Philosoph Franz Rosenzweig (1886–1929).* 2 vols. Freiburg: Karl Alber, 1988.

Schmitt, Carl. *Der Begriff des Politischen.* Berlin: Duncker & Humblot, 1991; orig. pub. 1932. Translated by George Schwab under the title *The Concept of the Political,* foreword by Stracy B. Strong. Chicago: University of Chicago Press, 1996.

———. *Der Leviathan in der Staatslehre des Thomas Hobbes: Sinn und Fehlschlag eines politischen Symbols.* Stuttgart: Klett-Cotta, 1995.

———. *Politische Romantik.* Berlin: Duncker & Humblot, 1991; orig. pub. 1919.

———. *Politische Theologie: Vier Kapitel zur Lehre von der Souveränität.* Berlin: Duncker & Humblot, 1990; orig. pub. 1934. Translated by George Schwab under the title *Political Theology: Four Chapters on the Concept of Sovereignty.* Cambridge: MIT Press, 1985.

———. *Politische Theologie II: Die Legende von der Erledigung jeder Politischen Theologie.* Berlin: Duncker & Humblot, 1990; orig. pub. 1970.

———. *Verfassungslehre.* Berlin: Duncker & Humblot, 1993; orig. pub. 1928.

Scholem, Gershom. *Judaica II.* Frankfurt a. M.: Suhrkamp, 1963.

———. *Major Trends in Jewish Mysticism.* New York: Schocken Books, 1954; orig. pub. 1941.

———. *On Jews and Judaism in Crisis: Selected Essays.* Ed. Werner J. Dannhauser. New York: Schocken, 1976.

———. *Walter Benjamin—Die Geschichte einer Freundschaft.* Frankfurt a. M.: Suhrkamp, 1975.

Shell, Marc. *Children of the Earth: Literature, Politics, and Nationhood.* New York: Oxford University Press, 1993.

Shell, Susan Meld. *The Embodiment of Reason: Kant on Spirit, Generation, and Community.* Chicago: University of Chicago Press, 1996.

Scheuerman, William E. *Carl Schmitt: The End of Law.* Lanham, Md.: Rowman & Littlefield, 1999.

Sorel, Georges. *Réflexions sur la violence.* Ed. Michel Prat, preface by Jacques Julliard. Paris: Seuil, 1990.

Sprinker, Michael, ed. *Ghostly Demarcations: A Symposium on Jacques Derrida's "Specters of Marx."* London: Verso, 1999.

Staal, Frits. *Exploring Mysticism: A Methodological Essay.* Berkeley: University of California Press, 1975.

Steiner, George. *After Babel: Aspects of Language and Translation.* Oxford: Oxford University Press, 1975.

Stewart, Garrett. *Reading Voices: Literature and the Phonotext.* Berkeley: University of California Press, 1990.

Stout, Jeffrey. *Ethics after Babel: The Languages of Morals and Their Discontents.* Boston: Beacon, 1988.

Tamir, Yael. *Liberal Nationalism.* Princeton: Princeton University Press, 1993.

Taubes, Jacob. *Abendländische Eschatologie.* Munich: Mathes & Seitz, 1991.

———. *Ad Carl Schmitt: Gegenstrebige Fügung.* Berlin: Merve, 1987.

———. *Die politische Theologie des Paulus.* Ed. Aleida and Jan Assmann et al. Munich: Wilhelm Fink, 1993.

———. *Vom Kult zur Kultur: Bausteine zu einer Kritik der historischen Vernunft.* Ed. Aleida and Jan Assmann, Wolf-Daniel Hartwich, and Winfried Menninghaus. Munich: Wilhelm Fink, 1996.

Taubes, Jacob, ed. *Der Fürst dieser Welt: Carl Schmitt und die Folgen.* Munich, 1983.

Taylor, Charles. *Philosophical Arguments.* Cambridge: Harvard University Press, 1995.

———. "The Politics of Recognition." In *Multiculturalism and 'The Politics of Recognition,"* ed. Amy Gutmann. Princeton: Princeton University Press, 1992.

———. *Sources of the Self: The Making of the Modern Identity.* Cambridge: Harvard University Press, 1989.

Taylor, Mark C. *Critical Terms for Religious Studies.* Chicago: University of Chicago Press, 1998.

Terpstra, Marin, and Theo de Wit. "'No Spiritual Investment in the World As It Is': Jacob Taubes's Negative Political Theology." In *Flight of the Gods: Philosophical Perspectives on Negative Theology,* ed. Ilse Bulhof and Laurens ten Kate, 319–52. New York: Fordham University Press, 2000.

Theunissen, Michael. *Der Begriff der Verzweiflung: Korrekturen an Kierkegaard.* Frankfurt a. M.: Suhrkamp, 1993.

Thiemann, Ronald F. *Religion in Public Life: A Dilemma for Democracy.* Washington: Georgetown University Press, 1996.

Turk, Horst. "Politische Theologie?: Zur 'Intention auf die Sprache' bei Benjamin und Celan." In *Juden in der deutschen Literatur: Ein deutsch-israelisches Symposium,* ed. Stéphane Mosès and Albrecht Schöne, 330–49. Frankfurt a. M.: Suhrkamp, 1986.

Vattimo, Gianni. *Credere di credere.* Milan: Garzanti, 1996. Translated by Luca d'Isanto and David Webb under the title *Belief* (Stanford: Stanford University Press, 1999).

Veer, Peter van der, and Hartmut Lehmann, eds. *Nation and Religion: Perspectives on Europe and Asia.* Princeton: Princeton University Press, 1999.

Voltaire. *Philosophical Dictionary.* Ed. and trans. Theodore Besterman. London: Routledge, 1972.

Vorländer, Karl. Introduction to Immanuel Kant, *Die Religion innerhalb der Grenzen der blossen Vernunft,* ed. Karl Vorländer. Leipzig: Meiner, 1937.

Vries, Hent de. "Antibabel: The 'mystical postulate' in Benjamin, de Certeau, and Derrida." *Modern Language Notes* 107 (1992): 441–77.

———. "Deconstruction and America." In *Traveling Theory: France and the United States,* ed. Ieme van der Poel, Sophie Berto, and Ton Hoenselaars, 72–98. Cranbury, N.J.: Fairleigh Dickinson University Press, 1999.

———. "De Universiteit als kosmopolis: Martha Nussbaum's 'Cultivating Humanity.'" *Tijdschrift voor Literatuurwetenschap* 3 (1998): 210–22.

———. "Lapsus absolu: Some Remarks on Maurice Blanchot's *L'Instant de ma mort.*" *Yale French Studies* 93 (1998): 30–59.

———. "On Obligation: Lyotard and Levinas." *Graduate Faculty Philosophy Journal* 20, no. 2; 21, no. 1 (1998): 83–112.

———. *Philosophy and the Turn to Religion.* Baltimore: Johns Hopkins University Press, 1999.

———. "Theologie als allegorie: over de status van de joodse gedachtenmotieven in het werk van Walter Benjamin." In *Vier joodse denkers in de twintigste eeuw: Rosenzweig, Benjamin, Fackenheim, Levinas,* ed. H. Heering. Kampen: Kok Pharos, 1987.

———. *Theologie im pianissimo: Die Aktualität der Denkfiguren Adornos und Levinas'.* Kampen: J. H. Kok, 1989. Translated by Geoffrey Hale under the title *Theology in Pianissimo: Theodor W. Adorno and Emmanuel Levinas* (forthcoming from Johns Hopkins University Press).

———. "The Theology of the Sign and the Sign of Theology: The Apophatics of Deconstruction." In *Flight of the Gods: Philosophical Perspectives on Negative*

Theology, ed. Ilse Bulhof and Laurens ten Cate, 165–93. New York: Fordham University Press, 2000.

———. "Theotopographies: Nancy, Hölderlin, Heidegger." *Modern Language Notes* 109 (1994): 445–77.

———. "Winke." In *The Solid Letter: New Readings of Friedrich Hölderlin,* ed. Aris Fioretos, 94–120. Stanford: Stanford University Press, 1999.

———. "Zum Begriff der Allegorie in Schopenhauers Religionsphilosophie." In *Schopenhauer, Nietzsche und die Kunst,* ed. W. Schirmacher, *Schopenhauer-Studien* 4, 187–97. Vienna: Passagen, 1991.

Vries, Hent de, and Harry Kunneman, eds. *Enlightenments: Encounters between Critical Theory and Recent French Thought.* Kampen: Kok Pharos, 1993.

Vries, Hent de, and Samuel Weber *Religion and Media.* Stanford: Stanford University Press, 2001.

———. *Violence, Identity, and Self-Determination.* Stanford: Stanford University Press, 1997.

Wahl, Jean. *Études Kierkegaardiennes.* Paris: Fernand Aubier, 1974.

———. Introduction to Søren Kierkegaard, *Crainte et tremblement, Lyrique-dialectique par Johannes de Silentio,* trans. P. H. Tisseau. Paris: Aubier Montaigne, 1984.

Wanegffelen, Thierry. *L'Édit de Nantes: Une histoire européenne de la tolérance (XVIe–XXe siècle).* Paris: Libraire Générale Française, 1998.

Weber, Samuel. *Institution and Interpretation.* Minneapolis: University of Minnesota Press, 1987.

———. *Mass Mediauras: Form, Technics, Media.* Ed. Alan Cholodenko. Stanford: Stanford University Press, 1996.

———. "Taking Exception to Decision: Walter Benjamin and Carl Schmitt." In *Enlightenments: Encounters between Critical Theory and Contemporary French Thought,* ed. Harry Kunneman and Hent de Vries, 141–61. Kampen: Kok Pharos, 1993.

Weil, Éric. *Logique de la philosophie.* 2d ed. Paris: Vrin, 1967.

———. *Philosophie et réalité: Derniers essays et conférences.* Paris: Beauchesne, 1982.

———. *Problèmes kantiennes.* 2d ed. Paris: Vrin, 1998.

Weithman, Paul J., ed. *Religion and Contemporary Liberalism.* Notre Dame: University of Notre Dame Press, 1997.

Wellbery, David, and John Bender, eds. *The Ends of Rhetoric: History, Theory, Practice.* Stanford: Stanford University Press, 1990.

Wellmer, Albrecht. *Endspiele: Die unversöhnliche Moderne.* Frankfurt a. M.: Suhrkamp, 1993.

————. *Revolution und Interpretation: Demokratie ohne Letztbegründung.* Spinoza Lectures, University of Amsterdam. Assen: Van Gorcum, 1998.

Wheeler, Samuel C., III. *Deconstruction as Analytic Philosophy.* Stanford: Stanford University Press, 2000.

Witte, Bernd. *Walter Benjamin—Der Intellektuelle als Kritiker: Untersuchungen zu seinem Frühwerk.* Stuttgart: J. B. Metzlerische Verlagsbuchhandlung, 1976.

Wittgenstein, Ludwig. *Logisch-philosophische Abhandlung / Tractatus Logico-Philosophicus.* Vol. 1 of *Werkausgabe.* Frankfurt a. M.: Suhrkamp, 1984. Translated by David F. Pears and Brian F. McGuinness under the title *Tractatus Logico-Philosophicus.* London: Routledge, 1995.

Wolterstorff, Nicholas. *Divine Discourse: Philosophical Reflections on the Claim That God Speaks.* Cambridge: Cambridge University Press, 1995.

Index